Langenscheidt
Praxiswörterbücher

# Langenscheidt
LID Editorial

# Praxiswörterbuch
# **Marketing**
# Englisch

**Englisch – Deutsch**
**Deutsch – Englisch**

**Langenscheidt**

Berlin · München · Wien · Zürich · New York

**Bibliografische Information Der Deutschen Nationalbibliothek**
Die Deutsche Nationalbibliothek verzeichnet diese Publikation in der Deutschen Nationalbibliografie; detaillierte bibliografische Daten sind im Internet über http://dnb.ddb.de abrufbar.


Original title: Diccionario LID Inmobiliario

Printed in Spain
ISBN: 978-3-86117-302-1

# Vorwort

Das vorliegende Praxiswörterbuch Marketing Englisch will ein nützliches Werkzeug für Berufstätige im Marketingsektor sowie für Studenten dieser Materie sein. Obwohl wir glauben, dass es sich auch für Übersetzer und Sprachstudenten eignet, sind doch die Hauptadressaten des Wörterbuchs alle diejenigen, die von Berufs wegen im Bereich Marketing tätig sind. Ohne dieses Ziel aus den Augen zu verlieren, haben wir Gebiete mit aufgenommen, die sämtliche Prozesse des Marketing-Sektors abdecken, von der Produktvermarktung bis zur Festigung auf dem Markt sowie auch Vertrieb und Werbung.

Aus diesem Grund haben wir die am häufigsten benutzen Begriffe aus den folgenden Bereichen ausgewählt: Marktforschung, Branding, Werbung, Verkauf, Datenbank-Marketing, Marketing und Online-Verkäufe, Public Relations und Kommunikationsmedien ebenso wie einige allgemeine Grundbegriffe der Unternehmensterminologie und Logistik.

Dieses Wörterbuch soll Studenten die Bedeutung eines bestimmten Begriffs oder einer Abkürzung erklären, soll aber auch für Berufstätige nützlich sein, die die Übersetzung eines Begriffs ins Englische brauchen oder wissen möchten, wie man einen der vielen Anglizismen, die sich in unsere Sprache eingeschlichen haben, auf Deutsch wiedergeben kann. Die Definitionen haben einen eher praktischen als akademischen Schwerpunkt, weshalb viele ein aktuelles Beispiel zur besseren Erläuterung des Begriffs beinhalten. Des Weiteren werden Synonyme bzw. feine Unterschiede für ähnliche Begriffe eines Eintrags geliefert.

Ein umfangreicher Anhang mit häufig benötigten Informationen rundet das Werk ab: Enhalten sind eine Liste der wichtigsten Abkürzungen, eine Liste internationaler Organisationen des Marketing-Sektors, Grafiken zum Marketing-Mix, die BCG Growth-Share Matrix, die Maslow-Pyramide, eine Tabelle mit dem Einheitsgewicht von Papier gemäß Format und Flächengewicht und eine Übersicht der Papiermaße.

Bei der Erstellung dieses Wörterbuchs wurde größter Wert auf Vollständigkeit und Aktualität gelegt. Ohne die engagierte Mitarbeit unserer Übersetzerinnen Kelly Bennett, Anne Fincke und Katja Schloesser wäre dies nicht möglich gewesen. Wertvolle Anregungen kamen außerdem von unserer fachlichen Beraterin Angelika Maier sowie unserer deutschen Lektorin Silke Grauenhorst, denen wir für ihr detailgenaues Lesen danken. Dank gebührt schließlich auch dem Lektorat von LID Editorial, namentlich Beatriz Bernabé und Jeanne Bracken, für die mehrfache Durchsicht des Manuskripts und die Koordination des Projekts.

*Der Verlag*

# Benutzungshinweise

## 1. Beispiele für die alphabetische Ordnung

account
account alignment
account classification
account director
account executive
account planner
account planning
account supervisor
accounting year
accreditation

aktivitätsbasiertes Management *n*
Akzeptanz *f*
allein stehende Werbeanzeige *f*
allgemeine Werbetheorie *f*
allgemeiner Kaufvertrag *m*
Alliteration *f*
Allokation *f*
Alltagsszene *f*
Alphaversion *f*
Alterspyramide *f*

## 2. Abkürzungen

| | |
|---|---|
| *m* | Maskulinum |
| *n* | Neutrum |
| *f* | Femininum |
| *m/pl* | Maskulinum Plural |
| *f/pl* | Femininum Plural |
| *n/pl* | Neutrum Plural |
| *v* | Verb |

# Englisch - Deutsch

# A

**4P's of marketing** - vier Säulen *f/pl*

■ The four variables which combine to make up the marketing mix: Product, Price, Position and Promotion. The longer form "four P's of marketing" is also used.

**AA (average audience) rating** - durchschnittliche Einschaltquote *f*

■ A precise method for measuring an audience as it calculates the number of radio listeners or television viewers for each minute of a programme and then calculates the average. The results are used in negotiation between the media buyer and the media network and for determining which programmes the public likes most.

**A-B split** - A-B-Aufteilung *f*

■ In marketing, the division of a list of names and addresses in two equal parts according to a very simple method: the first name goes on list 1, the second on list 2, the third on list 1, and so on. It is used for mail sales or advertising.

**ABC analysis** - ABC-Analyse *f*

■ The classifying of products, customers, etc. according to sales volume or importance. Under normal circumstances, 20% of products account for 80% of sales (20:80 principle). The system enables identification of products or customers of less interest and checks whether or not prices and conditions, etc. have been correctly applied. A items are of maximum importance and C items are marginal, whereas B items represent a similar percentage of the total number of items and sales.

**above the fold** - über dem Knick

■ The section of a page on a website which is visible without any movement in a vertical direction.

**above-the-line advertising** - Above-the-line-Werbung *f*

■ A term referring to advertising which makes use of media seen as traditional in the advertising world, such as the press, magazines, radio, television, the outside environment or the Internet, which are collectively known as mass media or non-selective media.

**above-the-line media** - Above-the-line-Medien *n/pl*

■ The communications media traditionally used in advertising. The concept includes daily newspapers, supplements, magazines, television, radio, cinema, the outside environment and the Internet. They devote a portion of their time to information, opinion or entertainment, and another portion to advertising.

**absorbed costs** - verrechnete Gemeinkosten *pl*

■ The indirect production costs that are not charged to the customer and are absorbed as general expenses.

**absorption costing** - Kostenabsorption *f*

■ The working out of the cost of a unit including its variable and semi-variable cost and its share in the fixed and indirect or structural costs in line with a range of justifiable criteria. It is said that an activity or the sale of a product absorbs fixed costs when its sale price exceeds the variable cost and uses this difference to cover the fixed costs of the business.

**ACCA** - ACCA

■ An acronym referring to the four steps which make up the DAGMAR advertising model suggested in 1961 by Russell H. Colley - attention, comprehension, conviction and action.

**acceptability** - Akzeptanz *f*

■ In general, the capability for provoking approval. In the case of a new product, its capability for being tested. Before launching a new product, various tests are undertaken to measure its degree of acceptance.

**access budget** - Effizienzschwelle *f*

■ In advertising, the budget needed by a company to introduce itself effectively in a medium. It depends on tariff and the saturation levels of that particular medium.

**accessibility** - Zugänglichkeit *f*
▪ The set of characteristics of a website which facilitate its use by persons with any kind of disability.

**accessory** - Accessoire *n*
▪ In retail selling, an article which when combined with another, attracts the client's attention more powerfully and compels him to buy both. For example, a dress may be shown with a necklace or a bed with sheets in such a way that colours and styles match. It is the same as complementary article.

**accessory service** - Zusatzleistung *f*
▪ A supplementary service offered by a company to complement the main one. It may even be more profitable.

**accordion fold** - Leporello *n*
▪ A zigzag, accordion-like folded advertising brochure that can be extended to its full breadth with a single pull. The effect achieved with this kind of brochure is to arouse the curiosity of the recipient, who has to unfold the brochure in order to see the message.

**account** - Kunde *m*
▪ In advertising, and generally in services, each one of the clients, enterprises or products with which a company works.

**account alignment** - internationale Betreuung *f*
▪ The process by which a brand is handled by the same agency in various or all countries.

**account classification** - Kundenklassifikation *f*
▪ The arrangement of a company's customers' accounts according to the criteria needed for each kind of analysis, for example, ABC sales, by geographical area, by benefits, or by collection problems. The use of connected databases allows for more sophisticated analysis of customers by purchase behaviour and in general, by contrasting all the available data.

**account director** - leitender Kundenbetreuer *m*
▪ The head and coordinator of an accounts or customer service department of an advertising agency. He coordinates the work of his team and directs and promotes client relationships. He also acts as the main spokesperson of the agency in respect of the client and as the representative of the client within the agency.

**account executive** - Kundenbetreuer *m*
▪ The individual responsible for the overall relationship that exist between a company and a client or group of clients.

**account planner** - Werbeplaner *m*
▪ The advertising professional responsible for designing the campaign communication strategy. He defines the communication objectives and suggest the basic lines of communication which will guide all the work of the agency involved in the campaign.

**account planning** - Medienplanung *f*
▪ As part of the advertising work undertaken by an agency, it is the process of defining the communication strategy to be employed in respect of a brand, entity, or product/service.

**account supervisor** - Kundenbetreuer *m*
▪ In the accounts or customer service section of an advertising agency, the person who coordinates the work of an account team.

**accounting year** - Geschäftsjahr *n*
▪ The duration of a company's financial year that, in exceptional circumstances, may be less than 12 months. In Great Britain, it often consists of 13 periods of 4 weeks. It normally coincides with the calendar year, except for agricultural companies (seasonal) and premises open to the public (due to stocktaking and end of season problems).

**accreditation** - Akkreditierung *f*
▪ The process which an organisation undertakes for the purpose of ensuring that a person or institution is capable of undertaking the mission in question. For example, in advertising, it refers to the

document whereby an advertiser certifies that his/her account is being handled by a given agency.

**acculturation** - Akkulturation *f*

■ The adaptation to the culture of a country or company by a new arrival.

**accuracy** - Exaktheit *f*

■ Reliability and conscientiousness in the accomplishment of a task, in the adjustment of financial statements or in the calculation of a value, etc.

**ACORN** - ACORN

■ An acronym meaning 'A classification of residential neighbourhoods' - the classification of residential zones intended to define and predict consumer guidelines in each zone.

**acquisition cost** - Akquisitionskosten *pl*

■ In marketing, the cost necessary for attracting a new customer or subscriber, such as postage expenses or telephone calls.

**acquisition value** - Akquisitionswert *m*

■ The relative value of an item perceived by the purchaser which results from the difference between the price the purchaser was prepared to pay and the actual price of the item.

**across the board** - auf der ganzen Linie

■ A way of planning advertising using a radio or television broadcaster which consists of booking a slot every day at the same time.

**across-the-board broadcast** - globale Verbreitung *f*

■ The broadcast of a programme on radio or television at a fixed hour for five consecutive days a week (usually Monday to Friday). These programmes attract advertisers because they are followed by the same people every day and because advertising is most efficient when it reaches the same individual a minimum amount of times.

**across-the-network** - im gesamten Sendegebiet

■ The simultaneous broadcast of an advertisement or programme on all the transmission points of a radio or television network.

**action device** - Handlungsauslöser *m*

■ A creative resource or device included in a mail offer intended to cause rapid action on the part of the recipient.

**active buyer** - aktiver Käufer *m*

■ A person who has bought a product lately or within a certain period of time.

**active population** - Erwerbsbevölkerung *f*

■ The group of citizens in a country employed in paid work or available to take up paid work even though they may be currently unemployed.

**activity based management** - aktivitätsbasiertes Management *n*

■ A management system based on the control of activities as a means of increasing value for customers.

**Activity-Based Costing (ABC)** - aktivitätsbasierte Kostenermittlung *f*

■ The calculation of costs involved in management based on activities from which it is possible to work out the actual cost incurred for each of the activities carried out by the company.

**ad blocking** - Werbeblocker *m*

■ A programme which eliminates advertising messages from a website. It makes browsing easier, since it eliminates the time needed to download advertising content.

**ad exchange** - Werbungstausch *m*

■ On the Internet, an agreement between two websites whereby each one places on its site an advertising message, banner, button or link which goes directly from one site to the other.

**ad impression** - Werbeaufruf *m*

■ An advertising file or archive sent to an Internet user in response to a request from the user. It is one of the most common procedures for calculating the price of an advertising insert on the Internet (CPT - cost per thousand).

**ad position** - Werbepositionierung *f*

■ The position where an advertisement is placed, whether it be in printed form or within radio or television space. The positioning of the announcement or advertisement depends upon the public or market that is targeted and the budget that is available.

**ad saturation** - Werbungssättigung *f*

■ The level reached by the advertising on a medium with regard to the total content. For the majority of media, setting the optimum saturation level is at their own discretion. Television in Spain is governed by the European Union standards, which limit advertising time to 15% of the total broadcast time, and it may not exceed 12 minutes per hour

**ad server** - Werbeserver *m*

■ On the Internet, a system of controlling advertising messages online. These programmes allow the rotation of various campaigns by placement according to different criteria: defined order, random order, by number of pulses, by market segmentation. For example: shown first are the interactive banners or posters with the greatest number of senders, thus following an order which factors in the effectiveness of the impact of the campaign. Advertising controllers, or ad servers, collect the information from the contacts made and senders generated.

**ad space** - Werbefläche *f*

■ In Internet advertising, the area of a screen set aside for the insertion of advertising statements and messages. Generally speaking, these areas are grouped at the start or side of the screen.

**ad ticker** - Werbeticker *m*

■ An Internet advertising format which, inserted over an advertisement on a site (banner, skyscraper, sponsored box), provides the user with information in real time on subjects in which he is interested, for example, sports news or results, thus increasing his interest in the advertisement.

**ad vehicle** - Werbeträger *m*

■ In a medium, each of the spaces where advertising is inserted. In the print media, every edition, but also every page or part of a page. In the audiovisual media, each day, each hour, each slot. In outdoor advertising, every structure where an advertisement can be placed. On the Internet, each page or each banner.

**adaptation** - Adaptation *f*

■ A change in the size and proportions of an advertisement so that it fits each graphic support. It is also a slight modification so that the same basic idea can be used for different media (for example, magazines and sales outlet material).

**Ad-Booster** - Ad-Booster *m*

■ An innovative and revolutionary advertising format on the Internet achieved by transmitting a video, which allows all advertisers the possibility of broadcasting their television campaigns on the Internet with excellent quality, regardless of whether the user has broadband or dial-up connection. The Ad-Booster format was developed with Flash 5 technology, which means it can be swiftly downloaded with any browser and from any personal computer.

**adbuster** - Adbuster *m*

■ An advertising message which aims to criticise another by destroying or revealing the false strategy hidden behind it. It is a subversive or anti-advertising action in which either the advertisement under criticism is being manipulated or a new advertisement is created using an ironic form of the same language and codes.

**address analysis** - Adressenanalyse *f*

■ A procedure used in direct advertising which consists of checking the data which form part of a given address before proceeding to the corresponding sending procedure.

**adequate sample** - signifikante Stichprobe *f*

■ A sample which limits the risk of error due to chance in answering a poll or in an observation exercise due to its adequate size, manner of selection and the fact that it faithfully represents the universe to be studied. It is equivalent to representative sample.

**ad-free programme** - werbungsfreies Programm *n*

■ A television programme which is transmitted with no advertising breaks. It usually refers to sponsorship by an advertiser. In this case the programme will carry the sponsor's message immediately before and after. Occasionally the sponsorship may be mentioned at some point during the programme.

**ad-hoc study** - Ad-hoc-Studie *f*

■ A study designed for a single interested party for the purpose of obtaining information on a defined topic. It is the opposite of an omnibus survey or study, where a number of interested parties will take part.

**administration to consumer (A2C)** - Administration to Consumer (A2C)

■ Information and initiatives used by a public authority to contact the public. For example, facilities for the payment of taxes and rates via the Internet.

**adshel** - Stadtmöblierung *f* für Werbezwecke

■ An installation which serves both as a bus-shelter and an advertising medium. The idea of this type of street furniture being financed by advertising is attributed to the Frenchman J. C. Decaux in the nineteen-sixties.

**AdVantage** - AdVantage *n*

■ A system marketed by the research company EMER-GFK intended to pre-test television advertising by having the research subjects view a TV programme into which the advertisements under test have been inserted.

**advertainment** - Advertainment *n*

■ A neologism formed by merging the words advertising and entertainment which implies a high level of collaboration between the advertising agencies and the media showing the content. The aim of advertainment is twofold: from the point of view of the advertising agency to contribute its knowledge about public communication objectives and techniques to produce more attractive content thus winning larger audiences for the media; and from the advertiser's point of view, to produce content which supports the image, arguments and motivation for the purchase of their products.

**advertisement** - Werbeanzeige *f*

■ An announcement paid for by an advertiser for the purpose of transmitting a message to a target market using any form of media.

**advertiser** - Werbungstreibender *m*

■ The person or institution who transmits the advertising communication, whether it be for commercial, political or social ends.

**advertising** - Werbung *f*

■ A marketing activity aimed at communicating a message to a specific audience or public. The message is essentially informative and motivating and any means of communication can be used.

**advertising agency** - Werbeagentur *f*

■ A company that provides advisory services relating to publicity, defines communication strategy, creates messages, generally supervising placement and contracting media exposure. It is normally comprised of two main departments, graphic arts - which is responsible for the creative work and accounts - which maintains contacts and supervises projects. It may also include specialists in market research, production, and media planning.

**advertising agent** - Werbeakquisiteur *m*

■ A person who professionally devotes him/herself to acting as an intermediary between an advertiser and an agency. They may plan, manage, work out or execute the advertising action.

**advertising budget** - Werbebudget *n*

■ The amount set aside to cover advertising costs for specific brands and periods. Set in accordance with publicity and communication objectives, the amounts at the company's disposal, historic costs and with estimates of the competitions' expenses.

**advertising consultant** - Werbeberater *m*
■ A freelance professional who advises an advertiser on their advertising actions.

**advertising effectiveness** - Werbewirksamkeit *f*
■ The capacity of a publicity campaign to transmit a particular message, (measured by tests and surveys held before and after dissemination), and to achieve expected behaviour (if the idea is to provoke buying, it can be measured by the number of sales achieved).

**advertising efficiency** - Werbeeffizienz *f*
■ A ratio between the effect of publicity in absolute terms and the amount spent. It is measured by analysing the cost of reaching a thousand potential buyers through each medium, by message recall and by the impact created which is gauged by specific replies to each advertisement.

**advertising expense** - Werbeausgaben *f/pl*
■ The amount spent on media advertising over a specific period. Although it is often referred to, incorrectly, as advertising investment in allusion to the idea of being a useful expense that produces constant value, in reality it is just another expense periodically repeated and which should be justified in relation to the fulfilment of certain communication objectives.

**advertising goal** - Werbeziel *n*
■ In marketing and general communications, a specific end result sought by an advertising campaign resulting in public awareness and actions. It is an essential part of the advertising strategy that serves as a guide for intended messages.

**advertising manager** - Werbemanager *m*
■ The person directly in charge of company advertising and who reports to the Marketing Manager. Although many companies employ product managers to take charge of all matters relating to a particular product, including advertising, large companies such as department stores often have advertising managers that coordinate advertising agency activities, control internal departments and prepare and supervise budgets.

**advertising plan** - Werbeplan *m*
■ A written expression of publicity objectives and means to be used. Although it should form part of an overall communication plan it is usually separate due to its importance. Amongst other matters it looks at strategy, advertising objectives, desired brand recognition, the public to be targeted, message content and the medium to be used.

**advertising showcase agreement** - Schaufenstervereinbarung *f*
■ An agreement between a point of sale and an advertiser to place his products and advertising in a shop-window, display or somewhere similar. In exchange, they get a fixed amount, a discount on purchases, goods on deposit, gifts for drawing amongst customers or something similar. Sometimes the advertiser organises a shop-window competition with important prizes to make sure he receives photographs of the set-ups.

**advertising synergy** - Werbesynergie *f*
■ The condition whereby the combined effect of two or more courses of action is greater than the sum of the individual parts. In marketing, it is a term frequently applied to the strengthening of overall effectiveness of an integrated advertising campaign or marketing effort through the coordinated operation of the several of the elements in the marketing-mix.

**advertising theme** - Werbebotschaft *f*
■ The essence of a message that one wishes to communicate to reinforce a brand position. The theme should not vary, although in the long term, advertisements can be launched with small changes in technique or style.

**advertising threshold** - Reaktionsschwelle *f*
■ The instant in which the first response of a consumer to an advertising campaign is perceived.

**advertising vehicle** - Werbeträger *m*
■ Any object that allows an advertising message to be transmitted, usually distinguished between the medium, which is a homogeneous collection of vehicles such as the radio, and the vehicle itself which could be the radio station in question.

**advertising wearout** - Nachlassen *n* der Werbewirkung
■ The instant in which consumer stops reacting to an advertising campaign because he has been over-exposed to it by the media. This excess may even be negative for the brand.

**advertorial** - Advertorial *n*
■ An advertising message which takes the form of editorial content of the medium into which it is inserted, thus giving "legitimacy" to the information in question, which is supposed to be transmitting or communicating its opinion on social, political or economic matters with a view to influencing some group in power or public opinion. Due to the confusion which the recipient may experience, this should be clearly identified as advertising. A variant of the advertorial is publicity-reporting.

**advocacy advertising** - Lobbywerbung *f*
■ An advertising activity whereby a company or other organisation takes part in a problem or cause of public interest, and shows by means of its messages its agreement or disagreement.

**adware** - Adware *f*
■ On the Internet, programmes which include advertising in return for being free of charge to the users.

**adwords** - Adwords *n/pl*
■ A Google advertising system based on the PPC (pay per click) system consisting of highlighting the searcher's words which carry advertising links inserted into them.

**AE (account executive)** - KB *m* (Kundenbetreuer)
■ The acronym for account executive. It is the person responsible for the global relations of a company with a client or group of clients. It is used particularly in the tertiary sector.

**affiliate** - Partner *m*
■ On the Internet, a person or body which sells on its website the products of a third party in return for a commission agreed by contract. For the sale of products and services, the affiliate publishes interactive banners or the affiliator's buttons which direct the user to his website. Payment may be per sale, per visit or per form. The affiliate may use his website as a promotional instrument or carry out direct marketing campaigns, including advertisements or links to the affiliator's products.

**affiliate forum** - Partnerforum *n*
■ An on-line community where the visitors can comment upon and decide about matters related to affiliate marketing.

**affiliate marketing** - Partnermarketing *n*
■ A commercial agreement between manufacturers or producers and on-line vendors whereby the second undertakes to sell and promote on the Internet the products of the former by directing the visits generated to this website.

**affiliate merchant** - Handelspartner *m*
■ In affiliation programmes, the person responsible for maintaining relationships with the affiliates, monitoring the campaigns and prospecting for and capturing new members.

**affiliate software** - Partner-Software *f*
■ In affiliate marketing, a programme which, as a minimum, provides the affiliate with follow-up and checks on the record of the activity generated by his actions, including details on the number of visits generated, sales and commissions.

**affiliated shop** - Partner-Geschäft *n*
■ An independent establishment belonging to a voluntary chain that supplies the majority of needs and certain marketing services.

**affiliates program** - Partnerprogramm *n*
■ A logical tool which allows a company's website to be used as a platform for

another company's sales. The Internet company which has made most use of this type of programme is Amazon (amazon.com), which achieves a large percentage of its sales through affiliates. Affiliate program contracts must make it very clear that commission will be paid on each and every one of the sales made via the Internet and that sales will be cumulative.

**affinity** - Affinität *f*

■ A similarity between two media, a product and a medium or the audience of a medium and a group of people. Sometimes used as a criterion for selecting a medium, with the objective that an advertisement inserted in a medium will produce a greater possible number of impacts between the people who form the target group.

**affinity coefficient** - Affinitätskoeffizient *m*

■ The number of people in a target group who will be impacted by an insertion in a medium, expressed as a percentage of the total number of people who would be impacted by an insertion in the said medium.

**affinity index** - Affinitätsindex *m*

■ Also referred to as the affinity coefficient, this expresses the degree to which the audience of a medium corresponds to the pre-defined target group. It is the result of dividing the audience of the medium for the target group by the total audience of the said medium. It is usually expressed as a percentage of the total audience of the medium.

**affinity marketing** - Affinitätsmarketing *n*

■ The set of strategies intended to optimise the loyalty of a customer to a brand in order to offer other articles under the same name. It is the transfer of a brand profile to other products and frequently makes use of Internet tools e.g. email or distribution lists.

**afterimage** - bleibender Eindruck *m*

■ The image retained in the consumer's mind after seeing an advertisement, even if it doesn't correspond to the real image seen.

**after-sales service** - Kundendienst *m*

■ The organisation and staff dedicated to looking after the interests or satisfying the needs of clients after a sale has taken place.

**age pyramid** - Alterspyramide *f*

■ A graph showing the number of people as cohorts (age levels) in a population at a given time. The name derives from the physical appearance of the graph which is produced by dividing the population into sexes and arranging the youth, which are normally more numerous, at the bottom. It shows the effects of war, epidemics etc. on the population and allows one to rapidly compare different populations or eras.

**agency** - Agentur *f*

■ An independent company in the services sector which acts as an intermediary. Custom has determined that the companies which act in some specific sectors, such as advertising, travel, transport or customs, and not others, are known as agencies.

**AID analysis** - AID-Analyse *f*

■ In statistics, a multi-variant analysis technique to determine demographic, attitude or socio-economic differences that exist between a buyer and a non-buyer of a product.

**AIDA** - AIDA

■ The acronym for a model designed to effectively send messages to a consumer for the purpose of gaining their Attention, maintaining Interest, stimulating Desire and producing a particular Action.

**AIDCAS** - AIDCAS

■ An advertising model derived from the classical AIDA which includes the components of AIDA plus two more, producing the following sequence: attention, interest, desire, conviction, action and satisfaction.

**aided recall** - gestützte Erinnerung *f*

■ The percentage of the targeted public that name a brand when they are asked to recall the brands of a particular service or category of products. Since the brands are not suggested, sometimes the figures are included within the spontaneous recall bracket when only spontaneous and suggested recall are being measured.

**air date** - Erscheinungstag *m*

▪ The date in which a magazine is distributed to the public or in which an advertising campaign starts.

**aisle** - Gang *m*

▪ In a point of sale, the corridor between shelves where buyers move with their trolleys. Each aisle holds one or various families of related products. In modern hypermarkets, the largest aisles are the one along the tills, another central one and a third in front of the perishable goods or the most appealing ones. There is also an entrance aisle at right angles to these where seasonal and regional products or good on offer are usually placed.

**alliteration** - Alliteration *f*

▪ In the production of advertisements, the repetition of a sound or part of an expression which makes the message easier to remember.

**allocation** - Allokation *f*

▪ The distribution of resources or objectives between different projects, or products or departments within an organisation.

**alpha** - Alphaversion *f*

▪ The test version of a product or service. On the Internet it particularly affects the development of websites which have not emerged from the in-house corporate intranet. The next stage, beta, starts when certain individuals, external to the business or organisation in question, test a product or service before launching it on the market (generally via a group dynamic).

**ambit** - Bereich *m*

▪ The geographical area in which a company's activity is carried out. The company may operate on an international, national, regional or local basis.

**ambush ad** - Werbung *f* aus dem Hinterhalt

▪ An advertisement to be found in an unusual environment or situation, thus benefiting from the surprise effect which its presence causes in the audience. Examples of ambush ads are product placement, environmental advertising or the increasingly common hybrids between advertising and entertainment (advertainment).

**American Academy of Advertising** - Amerikanische Werbeakademie *f*

▪ A USA association of advertising teachers, students and professionals with the aim of promoting training and research into advertising. It publishes the review Journal of Advertising.

**American Advertising Federation (AAF)** - American Advertising Federation (AAF) *f*

▪ A union of USA businesses in the advertising sector consisting of advertising companies, media companies, advertisers and related services. It was set up in 1967 in defence of advertising and its agents, with the specific aim of encouraging and improving the exercise of advertising activities.

**American Association of Advertising Agencies (AAAA)** - Amerikanische Vereinigung *f* der Werbeagenturen (AAAA)

▪ A USA organisation of federal extent which acts as a representative for the professional sector of the advertising business. Set up in 1917, since then it has been offering specialist consultancy information and services to its member advertising agencies.

**American Broadcasting Company (ABC)** - American Broadcasting Company (ABC)

▪ One of the three most important television networks in the United States. It also has seven radio networks with some 1900 stations.

**analysis matrix** - Matrixanalyse *f*

▪ A table normally comprised of two or three rows and columns that represent the alternatives resulting from a combination of two different types of action (for example, business expansion by increasing a product line or entering new markets) or factors (for example, growth-market share).

**analysis of variance (ANOVA)** - Varianzanalyse *f* (ANOVA)

■ A statistical study the purpose of which is to compare the statistical significance of differences obtained from the averages of various samples, when these samples arise from different groups.

**anchor store** - Lokomotive *f*

■ A commercial establishment with a guaranteed public used to attract customers to a shopping centre. It is normally a well known chain store that sells food or clothing. Smaller centres often use cinemas or specific types of restaurants. Given their importance, such stores are often granted ownership of the premises they occupy or an attractive leasing contract.

**Andy awards** - Andy-Preis *m*

■ The awards granted each year by the New York Advertising Club to the best advertisements on television, radio and other media.

**animation** - Belebung *f*

■ In marketing, a set of activities designed to promote the image of a commercial outlet or shopping centre. Its objective is to increase the flow of target buyers as well as increase business. In addition to decoration and music, competitions and sales promotions are also organised.

**announcement** - Kurzwerbespot *m*

■ A very brief television advertisement (approximately ten seconds) which is a reminder of another one broadcast in the same advertising block or which offers general interest information.

**annual report** - Jahresbericht *m*

■ A corporate document published yearly by an organisation and which provides information about the financial situation of the company, and the activities undertaken in past financial years. Although this document is required by the State Authorities of each country, it is designed as a public relations tool for shareholders, possible investors and other interested members of the public.

**anonymity** - Anonymität *f*

■ In research, the condition of a questionnaire whereby the company or organisation promoting the study is kept anonymous. It is fundamental in commercial or political research in order to obtain objective responses. Also, on the part of the participant, it is the guarantee that the informer will not be identified.

**anticipation** - Antizipation *f*

■ In marketing, the capacity to be a step ahead of market trends and demands.

**antizapping commercial** - Anti-Zapping-Werbespot *m*

■ An advertisement with a privileged space in the programming in order to decrease the number of viewers who change channels.

**apathetic shopper** - apathischer Käufer *m*

■ A buyer noted for not minding which supermarket he buys at, not noticing prices or brands and not comparing the quality of different products. In this classification there are three other types of shoppers: economic, ethical and personalised.

**appeal** - Appell *m*

■ An attempt to attract a customer with an offer, an image or an atmosphere answering to his needs or desire.

**appetite appeal** - Appetitanreger *m*

■ A resource frequently used in foodstuff advertising which strives to awaken a desire for the advertised product by making its advertised appearance look delicious, so that it anticipates the taste pleasure which the consumer will enjoy.

**Applebaum model** - Applebaum-Modell *n*

■ A mathematical model used to choose suitable locations for commercial establishments. Through the model it is possible to estimate potential sales at an establishment from a comparative analysis with other points of sale with similar features.

**arch** - Bogen *m*

▪ In a point of sales, a support situated between two stands, over the aisle, where products are placed to attract attention.

**area manager** - Gebietsleiter *m*

▪ The person responsible for the sales of a group of products in a region.

**area sampling** - Gebietsauswahl *f*

▪ Probability cluster sampling in geographical areas determined according to maps (for example, maps of city areas), as a result of a lack of organised lists. After randomly selecting an area, all corresponding elements are surveyed (for example, all houses within the area) either by means of a simple random sample of two clusters or with probability proportional to the size of each group (for example, when the number of houses in each area varies significantly). Its advantage lies in the need to survey only a limited number of groups and elements.

**area-by-area allocation** - Aufteilung *f* nach Gebieten

▪ In marketing, distributing an advertising campaign by geographical zones, for instance, local televisions. It is done according to each zone's objectives, expected sales, need for support of the sales force or network and similar criteria.

**argumentation** - Argumentation *f*

▪ The technique of organising data or facts so that they have a logical order, in such a way that one or two premises reach a conclusion. It is the main process used in persuading consumers in advertising of a rational nature.

**arrangement** - Arrangement *n*

▪ In marketing, order or disposition of furniture, showcases, shelves, desks, displays, windows and other installations in a shop in order to make it more appealing and allow freedom of movement.

**art paper** - Hochglanzpapier *n*

▪ A type of glossy paper used for magazines and photo-engraving.

**article** - Artikel *m*

▪ A group of products that are differentiated by their size or the size of their containers. The same type of product, made by a different manufacturer or in another colour is deemed to be a different article, although they would belong to the same family of products. The size of an article is used as a reference. Groups of articles produced by a manufacturer directly or offered by catalogue are grouped into product lines or product ranges. Articles or selections offered by a distributor are also grouped into product ranges, and these into product families.

**artificial obsolescence** - künstliche Veralterung *f*

▪ The replacement of a product by a new one with only marginal or superficial differences. The real reason for launching the new product is not that it is better than the old one, but that it generates new sales amongst consumers, who are always avid for the latest model.

**as is** - wie gesehen

▪ A product sold to the customer as he sees it with no guarantee that it works and no chance of a refund. It is done in special or clearance sales.

**as it falls concept** - Testkonzept *n*

▪ When a market test has been carried out, this is the system which guarantees that the national media plan following the test will faithfully reproduce the local plan at the large scale.

**ASA (Advertising Standards Authority)** - ASA (Advertising Standards Authority)

▪ An independent British organism which controls the application of its own internal regulations in order to defend public interest. It is linked to other government organisations and it is charged with dealing with the public's claims and complaints. It is financed by advertising companies. Its president is independent and personally elects the members, at least half of which must not come from the advertising world.

**as-it-falls method** - Markt-Testmethode *f*
■ In a test market, a way of calculating an advertising budget simply by considering what corresponds to that geographical area in a national launching campaign.

**asking price** - geforderter Preis *m*
■ The price requested by a person wishing to sell something. In the event that it is not accepted it may subsequently be reduced.

**aspiration level** - Anspruchsniveau *n*
■ The social level a consumer aims to reach by buying a product. Certain goods help in creating an attractive social image and base their message on this.

**assembly line** - Fließband *n*
■ A production system based on the principle of division of labour, in which a certain number of individual components or sub-channels join to form a final unit. A conveyor belt is normally used to transport products from one assembly point to another. Each assembly point is responsible for a particular phase of the production process which determines its position.

**assembly plant** - Montagewerk *n*
■ A factory designed for the purpose of assembling ready made components and thereby producing a finished product.

**assortment** - Sortiment *n*
■ The collection of articles on offer in an establishment or a catalogue. It can include various sections, product families and products, each with their own product range. An assortment is characterised by its variety. The analysis of an assortment is one of the prime functions of a store manager.

**assortment strategy** - Sortimentstrategie *f*
■ A strategy defining a product range with which a wholesaler or retailer decides to compete, based on the extent and variety to be offered.

**assumptive clause** - stille Klausel *f*
■ A condition which is not explicitly specified by the buyer and seller, but which may be deduced from the sector's customs or from the initiative taken by one of the two. For example, if the buyer demands special packaging and shipping it can be assumed that he will cover the costs.

**asymmetric response to price** - asymmetrische Reaktion *f* auf den Preis
■ Consumer behaviour which consists of responding to a loss in a different way to a gain, even when they are the same size. Various studies have shown that a given price increase in a product causes a greater or more intense variation in the response of the consumer than an equivalent reduction in the said price.

**atmosphere** - Stimmung *f*
■ An environment designed to create or reinforce consumers' inclinations towards the purchase or consumption of a product.

**attach-to-merchandise display** - integriertes Display *n*
■ In marketing, a display built with the cardboard case that contains the goods.

**attention** - Aufmerksamkeit *f*
■ The ability of the mind to capture and understand a message. In advertising the attention of consumers is usually scarce and selective.

**attention value** - Aufmerksamkeitswert *m*
■ The capacity a message or advertisement has for attracting and maintaining the attention of people belonging to a sample of the target group. It is measured according to the degree of remembrance of having seen it (mixed among other advertisements) and the degree of correct memorisation.

**attitude** - Einstellung *f*
■ A person's stable state of mind in relation to a product or message. Depends on rational evaluation, emotions and tendency to act accordingly. For example, if a person believes that German cars are manufactured with advanced technology at a fair price, he will be inclined towards German cars. Stable states of mind are therefore difficult to change and therefore

give rise to coherent behaviour in relation to similar stimuli.

**attitude change** - Einstellungsänderung *f*

■ A change in a consumer's disposition or outlook as regards a brand or product. It is a typical objective of an advertising or P.R. campaign.

**attitude scale** - Einstellungsskala *f*

■ A list of opinion statements which imply a positive or negative assessment of the psychological reference object, in the face of which the subject under investigation is required to show his degree of agreement or disagreement. It is used in structured studies with a closed response, normally with five or seven response options.

**attitude study** - Einstellungsstudie *f*

■ Research carried out on consumers designed to detect their attitude towards a product, idea, company or campaign. A prior study is normally conducted to identify the initial situation, followed by an evaluation and a final check carried out to determine whether or not the objectives have been reached.

**attitude toward the product** - Einstellung *f* gegenüber dem Produkt

■ The predisposition, favourable or otherwise, on the part of the consumer regarding a given product or service according to how well it is known, how famous it is, its image and the consumer's previous consumption experiences. The basic objective of advertising is to obtain a favourable attitude on the part of the consumer towards the product or service advertised.

**attitudes** - Einstellungen *f/pl*

■ The disposition of individuals which leads them to react in a given way. One of the objectives of qualitative research is to assess what are the attitudes of a population group, given that they make its members more receptive to given messages or the use of certain products.

**attraction area** - Einzugsgebiet *n*

■ The catchment area of an establishment that depends upon factors such as the type of establishment and product, the average amount purchased, shopping habits, means of transport (on foot, by car etc.), the location of competitors and how the establishment advertises itself. Within the catchment area zones with a higher degree of loyalty, generally corresponding to proximity, can be found. In rural areas it is important to bear in mind market days, festive holidays, and the existence of official centres (health centres, teaching institutes, etc.).

**attraction marketing** - Attraction Marketing *n*

■ Marketing action based on the generation of new customers by a powerful current in favour of the commercial objectives of the company which leads the consumer to lean in that direction.

**attributes** - Attribute *n/pl*

■ The visible or invisible characteristics of products. They may be physical (what the product has), functional (what the product does) or symbolic (what the product connotes or represents). They are the basis of marketing difference, real or fictitious, between products and brands, directly or as a function of the benefits or uses for the consumer deriving from such attributes. In advertising, products and brands are represented either by their attributes or their benefits.

**attrition** - Abgang *m*

■ In relational marketing, the steady loss of customer loyalty towards a brand generally motivated by erosion or disenchantment due to a lack of attention on the part of those responsible for the brand or failure to comply with the commitment associated with it.

**auction** - Versteigerung *f*

■ A system of selling based upon direct and generally public competition between buyers to see who comes up with the best offer, the lot being auctioned going to the highest bidder. The system is also used by public authorities to grant work or service contracts to private companies or for the legal sale of goods in receivership.

Auctions can also take place by means of sealed envelopes, the lot going to the best bid which cannot be improved upon once made public.

**audience** - Publikum *n*

■ The total population exposed to a message in a given advertising medium. The useful audience is the portion of the audience that belongs to the target group. It should not be confused with coverage.

**audience analysis** - Publikumsanalyse *f*

■ Research on the number of individual receivers of different forms of media over a given time, including information on demographic, social-economic factors and lifestyles.

**audience profile** - Publikumsprofil *n*

■ The demographic, socio-professional, socio-economic and psychological characteristics of a programme's audience. It is used to match it with the target group profile and find out if it is worthwhile to buy advertising space in that programme.

**audience share** - Zielgruppenquote *f*

■ Strictly speaking, it should be called cover share or quota. It is the percentage of the target group exposed to a certain advertising campaign. Sometimes it is also applied to the percentage of the target group reached within a certain audience.

**audimeter** - Audimeter *n*

■ An electronic device connected to a television or radio in selected homes to detect when the set is on, and which channel it is tuned to. It does not measure the number of people watching or listening.

**audiovisual advertisement** - audiovisuelle Werbung *f*

■ An advertising message designed with verbal, typographical, composition, sound and image resources in movement, produced using film or video techniques.

**audio-visual display** - audiovisuelles Ausstellungsmaterial *n*

■ A type of point of sales equipment that uses audio-visual means to promote a product. For example in a DIY shop, the use of a tool can be demonstrated on a television set.

**audited circulation** - kontrollierte Verbreitung *f*

■ The distribution of a newspaper subject to the control of an independent organisation such as the ABC.

**augmented product** - erweitertes Produkt *n*

■ The set of benefits a consumer receives with the purchase of a physical product, such as a parts or labour guarantee offered during a period of time after purchasing a car.

**authorized dealer** - autorisierter Händler *m*

■ A trader who receives formal authorisation to sell the products from the manufacturer of the products. Thus the manufacturer publicly recognises the fact that the distributor provides the conditions necessary to perform the said function and provide a correct service to the customer.

**automatic distribution** - automatischer Vertrieb *m*

■ A system of distributing goods by which the wholesaler sends the retailers goods they have not specifically ordered, for example, because they want a sample of all novelties or because they periodically receive fixed amounts of the goods with the highest turnover.

**average cost** - Durchschnittskosten *pl*

■ The cost obtained by dividing the total costs of the company by the number of units produced.

**average cost price** - Durchschnittskostenpreis *m*

■ The total cost divided by the number of units produced. It is the sum of the average fixed cost, which decreases as production increases, and the average variable cost which may be constant but will increase above a certain limit. The average cost diminishes as production increases, reaches a minimum and then increases.

**average mark-on** - Handelsaufschlag *m*

■ The gross average mark-up obtained by dividing the difference between the selling price and the cost price by the cost price, that is to say, it is an average percentage on the cost price not on the selling price.

**average mark-up** - Handelsabschlag *m*

■ The gross average margin obtained by dividing the difference between the sales price and the cost by the sales price, that is to say, it is an average percentage of the sales price. The term margining is used to describe the activity of marking the sales price according to the target margins one wishes to obtain.

**average propensity to consume** - durchschnittliche Konsumquote *f*

■ The quotient of consumption as compared to available income.

**award of contract** - Auftragsvergabe *f*

■ The process of allocating the advertising work required by an advertiser to a given advertising agency.

**awareness-trial-repeat** - Wahrnehmung *f* - Probekauf *m* -Wiederholungskauf *m*

■ The different phases a potential consumer must go through in order to become a regular customer. First he realises that the product or brand exists, then he buys it to try it out and get an opinion and finally, if he is satisfied, he becomes a faithful buyer of that brand.

# B

**B2A (business to administration)** - B2A (Business-to-Administration-Geschäft)

■ Electronic commerce conducted from businesses to public administrations.

**B2B (business to business)** - B2B (Business-to-Business-Geschäft)

■ Electronic commerce conducted between businesses which sell their products or provide their services to other businesses.

**B2C (business to consumer)** - B2C (Business-to-Consumer-Geschäft)

■ Electronic commerce transactions conducted by businesses which sell their products or provide their services to the end consumer.

**B2E (business to employees)** - B2E (Business-to-Employees-Geschäft)

■ A business which sells its products or provides its services to its employees via the Internet.

**B2G (business to government)** - B2G (Business-to-Government-Geschäft)

■ Electronic commerce conducted by businesses who act as intermediaries between the public administration and the people.

**back-door selling** - Verkauf *m* durch die Hintertür

■ The offering of a product or service directly to the decision-maker or the company boss, avoiding the sales or administration departments which could hold up the operation.

**back-office** - innerer Arbeitsbereich *m*

■ The group of human resources and materials that support those activities that are in contact with the public. For instance, in a bank it would be the administration and systems people.

**back-order** - Auftrag *m* im Rückstand

■ An order made to the supplier so as to complete the delivery of goods which it was not able to complete within the stipulated time limit.

**backward integration** - Rückwärtsintegration *f*

■ The acquisition of a supplier, or the signing of a special collaboration contract, with the aim of guaranteeing the supply of a key raw material. It is a vertical type of integration.

**backwardation** - Abschlag *m*

■ A pricing structure in commodities trading whereby commodities delivered in the near future have a higher price than those that will be delivered at a later date.

**baker's dozen** - dreizehn Stück *n/pl*

■ A promotional strategy in which thirteen articles are delivered for the price of twelve. It is common with products with a low margin as the total discount is 7.7%. It is also referred to as a long dozen. In products with a greater margin it is common to see three for two which implies a 33% discount although at times it is shown as being 50%.

**banderole** - Banderole *f*

■ A band of long, thin fabric hung on a wall or between two buildings, with an advertising message.

**bank marketing** - Banken-Marketing *n*

■ The marketing carried out by credit or banking institutions. Also known as financial marketing, although this term is broader in the strict sense as it covers all kinds of institutions and financial businesses, and not just banking institutions.

**banner ad** - Bannerwerbung *f*

■ A style of advertising on the Net in the shape of a rectangle whose size is measured in dots (pixels). It is interactive and links to the location on the advertiser's website where the campaign is located. For example: a banner which advertises product 123 for the company ABC points to the ABC website where product 123 is located, and not to the main page of the company ABC.

**bar chart** - Balkendiagramm *n*

■ Histogram or graphic representation in which data is shown as columns of varying heights, according to value.

**bar code** - Strichcode *m*

■ A symbol whose design alternates black lines of differing thickness with white spaces and which constitutes a coding norm for consumer products, so that each article has its own code. It is foreseen that in the future it will be substituted by RFID chips incorporated into each product.

**bargain** - Schnäppchen *n*

■ A product that is offered for a low price at a sale. When referring to durable goods, the term often means second hand.

**bargain sale** - Ausverkauf *m*

■ The sale of standard items or products with special discounts over a specific period, normally accompanied by intense advertising campaigns. Carried out in certain seasons of the year and at the end of the season, as well as liquidation of stock and store closure. Products are sometimes produced specifically for sales or slightly faulty items are set aside. It is different to a discount sale.

**bartered ad** - wechselseitige Anzeige *f*

■ An advertisement published in a medium in exchange for advertising that medium in another one belonging to the advertiser.

**base line** - Identifikationszeile *f*

■ In an advertisement, indications in a footnote about the company (name, address, telephone, e-mail or website).

**basic assortment** - Grundsortiment *n*

■ A minimum collection of referenced items offered on a permanent basis to satisfy the elementary needs of the clientele. It does not include seasonal products, or unusual products with a low turnover.

**basic benefit** - Hauptnutzen *m*

■ The characteristics which differentiate one product from similar such products. When one relevant aspect is clearly better and does not have big disadvantages, it will be easier to organise a communications strategy based on this advantage. The problem is that there are an abundance of banal and plagiarised goods.

**basic-point pricing system** - Ausgangspunktfakturierung *f*

■ An invoicing system in which the seller designates a given city as a departure point and from there charges all transport costs, even if the factory or warehouse is in a different location.

**Bayes' theorem** - Bayes-Theorem *n*

■ In quantitative research, the procedure used to combine new information with that already known with the aim of revising the probability that certain things occur. It is used most frequently in decision taking in cases of doubt and works by introducing personal or subjective probability expressed in numerical form.

**Bayesian probability** - Bayes'sche Wahrscheinlichkeit *f*

▪ In research techniques, it refers to the degree of probability that a certain thing may happen when that probability is not based on statistical procedures but on the subjective estimations of a person with a lot of experience in the field concerned.

**before-and-after demonstration** - Vorher-Nachher-Vergleich *m*

▪ An advertising method which involves giving an example of the efficiency of the advertised product by visually comparing the before and after results of the use of the product. Said method, which has practically fallen into disuse, required a lot of credibility on the part of the public as to the miraculous effects of certain products (such as hair growth products and weight loss products) and a large amount of permissiveness on the part of the licensing authorities on accepting the advertising.

**behaviour scan** - Verhaltensuntersuchung *f*

▪ An investigative instrument developed by the company IRI (Information Resources Inc.) which reads the bar codes of the purchases of a group of homes and cross references these with the television use of its members, and consequently, with the advertising they have been exposed to.

**behaviouristic segmentation** - verhaltensmäßige Segmentierung *f*

▪ The classification of a population into groups in accordance with one or many variants related to the behaviour patterns of consumers rather than demographic, psychological or socio-economic characteristics. These variables include for example the principal needs that have to be satisfied, the frequency with which they shop and the place they choose, or whether they demonstrate brand loyalty.

**below-the-line advertising** - Below-the-line-Werbung *f*

▪ The advertising actions of a company or institution which are not advertising in the conventional sense of the word. Non-conventional advertising, or "below the line advertising" has experienced an important increase over the last few decades and now exceeds, in terms of investment figures, conventional advertising in the mass media.

**below-the-line media** - nichtklassische Werbeformen *f/pl*

▪ The advertising media which does not form part of the group consisting of newspapers, supplements, magazines, television, radio, cinema and exterior advertising media. The most important examples are direct advertising, and point-of-sale advertising. Despite its short life span, the Internet is considered a conventional medium.

**benefit** - Nutzen *m*

▪ In marketing, the usefulness of consumer goods and services for satisfying one of their needs. It is based on the product attributes, whether these are physical, functional or symbolic. The advantages coincide with the traditional sense of value of use, but also incorporate change and sign values. They are used in the representation, positioning and communication of the goods and can be divided into functional or rational and psychological or emotional advantages, some of which are taken as a starting point to establish the core of the message that the advert will be based upon.

**benefit segmentation** - Nutzensegmentierung *f*

▪ The segmentation of the target public to which a certain advertising action is addressed based on the advantages offered by the product, so as to obtain a higher degree of affinity between the advert and its target audience.

**beta test** - Beta-Test *m*

▪ The test version of a good or service, in its final stages of development, and which is distributed outside the company so that it can be tested (beta-test) to detect possible faults and eliminate these before it is launched on the market. It is used in particular for software programs.

**beta version** - Betaversion *f*
▪ The phase of development of a product before it is marketed in which it is tested by an ample and selected group of users which hold no relation to the manufacturer. It is the same as beta test.

**bias** - Verzerrung *f*
▪ In statistics, the systematic error which appears in the results of a study because the sample taken was not representative of the target group, a biased question was asked, necessary questions were forgotten or similar such errors were made.

**bill insert** - Werbebeilage *f*
▪ The advertising message included in a personalised delivery which refers to a good or service which is different to the main subject of the delivery, the aim being to reduce costs.

**billing** - Fakturierung *f*
▪ The cost of advertising space used by the advertiser in its campaigns. The expenditure or total investment in media on the part of the advertiser or for a brand. It is one of the ways of measuring the advertising strength of advertisers and serves as a basis for determining its position based on its importance. Occasionally used to set the remuneration of the agency, as opposed to the fees system, which are determined based on the number of hours dedicated to the advertiser.

**billing marketing** - Billing-Marketing *n*
▪ A recently developed discipline whose field is the use of invoices, bank account statements and similarly periodic documents which are sent to clients, as a marketing instrument. Until now the main focus was of a legal and administrative nature, however they are now seen as tools for providing information, for creating loyalty and for advertising new goods and services.

**black and white (B&W)** - Schwarz-Weiß-Anzeige *f* (S/W)
▪ A printed advertisement in which only one ink colour is used, normally black on white paper. It is cheaper to produce and publications generally charge less for it. However, it is usually not as attractive as colour advertisements and is less striking.

**black market** - Schwarzmarkt *m*
▪ Clandestine trade, produced when rationing, prohibition or price or consumption controls exist. Prices are determined by the laws of supply and demand, being greater than legally permitted. Typical examples include currency (when restrictions exist) and drugs.

**blanket coverage** - Pauschaldeckung *f*
▪ An advertising campaign which is emitted in a mass medium without previously determining the target group so as to reach as large an audience as possible.

**bleed** - randlos
▪ The presentation of an advertisement or text which occupies the whole page without leaving margins. It is the opposite of case, where the space occupied by the advertisement is smaller than the surface of the page. It is equivalent to bleed off.

**blind advertisement** - anonyme Anzeige *f*
▪ An advertisement in which the advertiser's name doesn't appear. It is frequently used in recruitment advertisements.

**blind test** - Blind-Test *m*
▪ A technique whereby a consumer, without knowing the brand, evaluates different products and makes his comments free of preconceived ideas.

**blink-metre** - Aufmerksamkeitsmessgerät *n*
▪ In advertising, a device which measures the degree of interest a person has in an advertisement by counting the frequency with which his eye blinks.

**blister pack** - Plastikhülle *f*
▪ A pack made of hard pre-shaped plastic in which the product is inserted with an

information or publicity card. It usually has a hook with which to hang it from the display or shelf. It is used for small articles to avoid theft and make it easily identifiable by the consumer. A shrink-pack is different in that it is made of soft plastic which shrinks to adapt to each product's shape.

**block discount** - Blockrabatt *m*

▪ The discount offered when several goods from the same company are consumed. The purpose is to reward the use of lower demand products. An electric company could sell at a certain price per kilowatt/hour to those who use only light and electrical appliances, and reduce this price to those consumers who also pay for electrical heating.

**blog** - Blog *m*

▪ The chronological publication of personal thoughts and webpage links. A blog, or electronic diary is often a combination of what is happening in the author's life and what is happening on the Net: a hybrid between a diary and a guide.

**blurb** - Klappentext *m*

▪ A brief and positive piece of news on a company or its products which is camouflaged in a medium's editorial. Originally, it was only used to describe a summary of a book, printed on its jacket, as promotion by its publishers.

**body language** - Körpersprache *f*

▪ The non-verbal and often unintended form of communication by means of gestures or body movement. When travelling abroad, it is important to be aware of the meaning of different gestures in order to avoid embarrassing situations.

**BOGOF (buy one, get one free)** - zwei zum Preis von einem

▪ A promotional system by which the client receives two identical products for the price of one. Given the usual average margin of goods it is more common, although less striking, to see three for two. The initials B1G1F are also used.

**bonus pack** - Angebotspackung *f*

▪ A container which holds a certain percentage of free product. For example, a cereal pack with 20% more product at the same price or with another smaller cereal pack attached. It is a manner of competing without touching the price as such, which is characteristic of products based on cheap raw materials. It is also a way of introducing new or complementary packaging.

**bottleneck** - Engpass *m*

▪ A stage in a production line or activity, where there is less capacity and which limits the total output of this production line or activity.

**brainstorming** - Ideensammlung *f*

▪ A team process used to find ideas and solutions. The difference with other methods is that here the participants can only give ideas or variations on ideas presented by colleagues, but they cannot criticise or reject them, this being the purpose of a subsequent meeting. In an environment which is free of criticism, and with interaction between participants who know the problem well, it is easier to reach an original solution.

**brand** - Marke *f*

▪ Any sign capable of graphic representation and which serves to distinguish the goods and services of one company from those of other companies in the market.

**brand advertising** - Markenwerbung *f*

▪ The advertising activity aimed at a particular target public in order to create, reinforce or maintain the image and attitudes which that public has of the brand of a product, over and above the product itself.

**brand alliance** - Markenpartnerschaft *f*

▪ The collaboration between complementary brands in which the most well-known brand supports the other by transmitting part of its image and prestige on the market to it.

**brand architecture** - Markenarchitektur *f*

▪ The organisation and hierarchy which governs the portfolio of brands of a company. There are a number of types of brand architecture: monolithic (the same brand is used to offer different goods and services); endorsed (the brands are connected to the main brand by word or visual reference); independent (each brand acts independently). In the major corporations, streamlining its brand portfolio can become crucial to its efficient functioning.

**brand awareness** - Markenbekanntheit *f*

▪ The percentage of the total population or target public that recognises or remembers a particular brand. It is measured by spontaneous response or suggestion.

**brand decisions** - Markenentscheidungen *f/pl*

▪ Aspect of marketing that analyses whether a product should be sold in bulk or with a brand, what type of brand (manufacturers or distributors), what brand in particular and whether small changes should be introduced such as colour, size or the adjectives that accompany it.

**brand development index** - Markenentwicklungsindex *m*

▪ A ratio that compares the percentage sales of a brand in a geographic area with respect to the percentage of the population that area represents. If it is greater than one it signifies that the brand is better positioned in that area than in the market as a whole.

**brand differentiation** - Markendifferenzierung *f*

▪ The capacity that a brand has to give its products a unique and positive image, especially for those attributes which are most important to that brand's target group.

**brand extension** - Markenausdehnung *f*

▪ The utilisation of a brand name to launch products that differ from those in the current product range of a company. The aim is to gain brand recognition and credibility for the product with minimal publicity expenses and to consolidate the value of a brand in the market.

**brand image** - Markenimage *n*

▪ The collection of qualities that a particular brand evokes for the majority of individuals. If the image is a strong one (it does not necessarily have to be positive), the beliefs and feelings produced by the brand will be common and consistent amongst the individuals that make up a certain population. Images can be good or bad depending upon other marketing variables, for example, a traditional image for one watch may be positive whereas it may be a detrimental image for another.

**brand licensing** - Markenlizenzierung *f*

▪ The granting of a licence that the owner of a brand gives to a third person so that they may use the brand in relation to a category of goods. Normally such a licence involves the payment of rights on the part of the person or company to whom the licence is granted.

**brand life cycle** - Markenlebenszyklus *m*

▪ The evolution of a brand, from launch to extinction passing through the growth and maturity stages. A brand is discontinued when the profit margin of a product carrying the brand is less than it costs to promote. Knowing the stage that a brand has reached helps to decide such questions as the incorporation of new products and publicity expenditure.

**brand loyalty** - Markentreue *f*

▪ The loyalty that consumers feel towards a particular brand and which is expressed in the renewed decision to purchase those goods over others. Brand loyalty requires the existence of a good brand image in the mind of the consumer and a good experience on the part of the same with regards to the goods sold under the brand.

**brand management** - Markenmanagement *n*

▪ The systematic and continuous management process aimed at constructing and maintaining over time the competitive advantage of a brand. When it concerns goods, this usually includes the management of the product itself, its price and its advertising. When it concerns services it is particularly focused on client contact. The big brand names have departments specifically dedicated to professionally managing its brand/s.

**brand positioning** - Markenpositionierung *f*

■ The concept or image that a specific brand tries to represent in order to adequately focus on the proper target market or individual consumer. Normally the image is instilled in the consumers mind by specific product campaigns.

**brand preference** - Markenpräferenz *f*

■ The consumer's inclination towards a certain brand instead of its competitors. It is a very important aim in an advertising campaign and a necessary condition for a first purchase to be made, although brand loyalty is also necessary if the purchase is to be repeated.

**brand product** - Markenartikel *m*

■ A product sold under the name of its manufacturer so that the customer can tell it apart from similar goods offered by the competition. A brand product implies a certain image which is trusted by the consumer as opposed to an undifferentiated or commonplace product.

**Brand Profile Analysis** - Markenprofilanalyse *f*

■ A research tool developed by the company Millward Brown which connects the profile of a brand to the category of its goods.

**brand recognition** - Markenwiedererkennung *f*

■ A targeted public's belief that it knows and remembers a make of product, differentiating it from other similar products. It is measured by aided, spontaneous or suggested recollection.

**brand strategy** - Markenstrategie *f*

■ The planning of a group of actions aimed at making the brand contribute towards the goals of a business. The brand strategy should take into account its position on the market so as to be able to maintain its differentiation from its competitors at all times.

**Brand Usage Profile Analysis (BUPA)** - Nutzungsanalyse *f* des Markenprofils

■ A research tool aimed at analysing the relationship which exists between the profile or perception of a brand among a group of consumers and the use that they make of the same, as shown in the purchase of the corresponding goods.

**branding** - Markenpolitik *f*

■ The group of activities relating to the creation, management and appraisal of brands.

**break-even point** - Kostendeckungspunkt *m*

■ The level of production or sales at which income is equal to the costs associated with production and distribution. Given that in any process there are fixed and variable costs, the equilibrium point is obtained by dividing the fixed costs of the company by the average unitary margin.

**bricks and mortar** - traditionelle Geschäfte *n/pl*

■ An expression originating from American-English slang used to refer to companies whose business centre is outside the Net, with the purpose of distinguishing them from those which are based on the Net.

**briefing** - Arbeitsanweisungen *f/pl*

■ The collection of brief, written or spoken instructions which are given to those about to carry out a task. It is usually given in an informative meeting which focuses on the objectives to be fulfilled.

**broadcast** - Übertragung *f*

■ A technique which consists in the simultaneous transmission of the same information to various targets through a communications network, an electronic mail system, radio stations or television or by satellite transmission.

**brochure** - Broschüre *f*

■ A leaflet or pamphlet comprised of a number of printed pages, usually stapled together, containing information on products or the company itself, targeted at a specific public. It can include high quality photographs and printing, but does not generally contain a price list.

**browser registration** - Browserregistrierung *f*
■ The process through which the web address of a site (URL) is included in a database of a certain number of search engines, so that it is made available to users. It is a service normally offered by marketing companies on the Internet.

**bundle pack** - Bündelpackung *f*
■ A package containing two or more units of the same product or different but complementary products; for example, in 2 for 1 promotions or in promotional free gifts.

**burst** - Werbebombardement *n*
■ The act of repeatedly showing an advertisement during a limited period of time to ensure that the audience remembers it. This may well saturate the public, but it is suitable for promoting an event, supporting a launch or opening a point of sale, where the initial atmosphere is very important.

**bus back** - Autobuswerbung *f*
■ An advertisement placed on the rear of a bus and which appeals to advertisers because a large proportion of the public is reached. It is also possible to put the ad on the sides of the bus.

**bus side** - Busseitenwerbung *f*
■ An advertising space placed on the sides of a bus. Occasionally it may join the sides and the roof or take up more space than the usual 90 x 300 cm. An advertisement on the left side is more expensive than on the right side because it is seen more often and it doesn't have to allow for the doors. The advertiser may or may not be the same as the one at the back.

**business plan** - Geschäftsplan *m*
■ A detailed summary of the objectives of a new activity and of the means of achieving those objectives and expected results. Used in large companies to approve new budgets, it is also a basic tool for risk capital investors that supports the creation of a company. It should include: a description of the product or service to be offered, potential market and expected market share, consumer analysis, manufacturing plan with emphasis on new technologies, marketing plan, balances and accounts of provisional results for various years, financial needs and how to cover them, and a plan for a stock floatation if required.

**business unit** - Geschäftsbereich *m*
■ Each part of a business organisation that has its own strategy, management, and budget, although it is not always appropriate from the organisation's point of view to have legal divisions, especially in multinational companies or large groups. Due to this there can be many units within an organisation, or one unit can include various organisations.

**business-to-business marketing** - Investitionsgütermarketing *n*
■ Sale of goods and services in which the end consumer is another company. The importance of each marketing variable, as compared to consumer goods, is different. For example, public relations and direct selling are more complex and advertising is mainly done through trade magazines.

**buyer intention survey** - Kaufabsichtsbefragung *f*
■ A survey conducted to identify the willingness of consumers to purchase a given product, often a new product, as well as the reasons for purchasing or choosing not to purchase the product, and the price at which the product should be sold.

**buyer-readiness stage** - Kaufbereitschaftsphase *f*
■ The period in which a consumer's reaction to a particular product is measured. It may vary from total ignorance to the decision to buy the product.

**buyer's market** - Käufermarkt *m*

■ The market in which the purchasers dominate in exchange relationships because the supply is higher than the demand.

**buying frequency** - Kaufhäufigkeit *f*

■ The average number of purchase operations per period. It is inversely related to the size of the purchase and access difficulty. For example, the frequency of purchases in a corner shop may be daily, whilst in a supermarket or hypermarket it may be two or three times a week or month. The purchasing potential of a site is calculated by combining the buying frequency with the average number of transactions and the number of clients. Also called frequency of purchasing.

**bypass attack** - Umgehungsangriff *m*

■ An attack on a principal competitors' relatively unimportant market so that he will either not be interested or will be unable to properly defend it, thereby consolidating a market position and market share with a view to a more direct attack later on. An example of this would be an attack on an export market prior to a later attack on the national market.

# C

**C2A (citizen to administration)** - C2A (Citizen-to-Administration-Geschäft)

■ A place on the Net whose purpose is to channel and promote the relationship of the citizens with the public administration.

**C2B (consumer to business)** - C2B (Consumer-to-Business-Geschäft)

■ Electronic commerce carried out from consumers to businesses.

**C2C (consumer to consumer)** - C2C (Consumer-to-Consumer-Geschäft)

■ Electronic commerce carried out between consumers.

**call centre** - Call-Center *n*

■ A telesales platform which incorporates the technical and human resources necessary to receive and send telephone contacts. These centres are evolving towards a contact centre, which also incorporates the management of additional channels such as electronic mail, web, fax, SMS and other digital media.

**call rate** - Anzahl *f* der Anrufe

■ In marketing, the number of persons which a tele-salesman contacts over a given period of time.

**calling cycle** - Besuchsrhythmus *m*

■ In marketing, the average time between two phone calls or visits to a client.

**campaign plan** - Kampagnenplan *m*

■ A written description of advertising objectives and the media to be used. In theory, it should be part of a global communication plan but due to its importance and the need for last-minute corrections, it may be an independent plan. Among other subjects it describes strategy, advertising objectives, desired brand personality and recollection, target group, content of the message and the media plan. It is the same as advertising plan.

**cannibalisation** - Kannibalisierung *f*

■ The promoting of a particular brand at the expense of another. When the budget for a brand is too low or the message too similar to an already established brand, consumers only remember the message conveyed by the initial brand advertised.

**canvass** *v* - umwerben *v*

■ To interview a person or group of people with the aim of getting to know their opinions, inducing a certain amount of debate and at the same time selling an idea, product or service.

**capacity** - Kapazität *f*

■ In production, the quantity of work that can be carried out by certain equipment or a factory in normal conditions and with specific technology and organisation. Maximum theoretical capacity does not take breakdowns, maintenance or other problems into account. It is divided into used and idle capacity, according to the actual time in use.

**captive audience** - unfreiwilliges Publikum *n*

■ An audience which due to special circumstances (for example, attending a seminar) can't avoid receiving a certain message.

**captive market** - konkurrenzfreier Markt *m*

■ A monopoly situation in which a buyer cannot refuse the product offered (for example, sale of an intermediate asset to an affiliate).

**captive price** - Monopolpreis *m*

■ A cheap price affixed to a main good whose consumption requires the use of a complementary good. A high price is affixed to the latter which compensates for the reduced margin obtained from the sale of the main good.

**captive product pricing** - Preisbestimmung *f* bei Komplementärprodukten

■ The establishing of an artificial price in order to maximise overall company profits on a particular product and related products, thereby enabling the company to maintain competitive prices for other products whilst making a profit on captive products. For example, a company that produces photographic equipment may keep film prices down and therefore make a profit on developing.

**cartel** - Kartell *n*

■ An agreement between legally independent businesses of the same sector, to reduce the respective rivalry by regulating prices and production.

**case study** - Fallstudie *f*

■ The analysis and discussion of alternative actions of a real or hypothetical situation. This method is the basis of many business studies programmes.

**cash cow** - Geldkuh *f*

■ In a growth-share matrix, the market leader or dominant business in a segment with a low growth rate. It should generate resources in excess of those which it needs to maintain its market share, to invest in other group businesses. It requires a conservative style of management.

**cash discount** - Barzahlungsskonto *m*

■ A discount usually offered by a supplier when the buyer pays in cash or within 10 days of delivery. It is normally 2% to compensate for the lower risk of insolvency and early collection.

**cash flow** - Bargeldfluss *m*

■ The cash input or output in relation to an investment project carried out by a company or branch.

**cash on delivery sale** - Nachnahmeverkauf *m*

■ A sale in which the buyer sends a signed order form and pays the postage costs before receiving the goods. It normally includes a claim and return period, in the event that the buyer is not satisfied with the product. Any sale in which payment is made upon receipt of the goods.

**cast commercial** - Prominenten-Werbespot *m*

■ A television advertisement in which actors staring in the programme appear as models. The advert can be placed in a commercial break of the screening of the actual programme or at any other time. Some laws forbid these so as to avoid confusion between the advertisement and the rest of the programme. Sometimes newsreaders are used who give, apart from notoriety, credibility to adverts screened on other channels.

**catalogue** - Katalog *m*

■ In marketing, a printed list of products offered for sale with a description of features. It normally includes photographs or illustrations and general sales conditions. When sent directly to consumers prices are generally included, whereas in wholesaler or industrial catalogues, prices are normally listed separately.

**catalogue agency** - Abonnement-Agentur *f*

■ An intermediary business acting between periodical publications and possible purchasers, whose main activity consists in gaining subscribers to said magazines. They usually use catalogues listing the periodicals they are offering.

**catalogue buying** - Katalogkauf *m*

■ Purchases in which the desired products are chosen from a catalogue and ordered by telephone, mail or from a representative who visits the customers regularly. The indications which must appear in the order form are the product's reference number, the amount, size (in some cases), the price and the sum due including a possible discount and delivery expenses. The goods are either collected at a distribution point or delivered to the customer's home.

**catalogue sales** - Katalogverkauf *m*

■ Sales in which the buyer chooses the products from a catalogue containing photographs and full details and prices. Catalogues are sent by mail to existing clients or purchased in newsagents. Orders are either made by mail, telephone or in person and goods sent by mail, messenger service or personally collected.

**cause-related promotion** - zweckgebundene Werbung *f*

■ The promotion of a business, following an agreement with a not-for-profit organisation, which aims to increase sales and corporate reputation simultaneously. It can consist, for example, in setting aside part of the sales or the profits for those sales for a particular NGO.

**ceiling price** - Höchstpreis *m*

■ The maximum sales price for certain products that is fixed by a price regulating authority, for example, in the case of fuels.

**celebrity endorsement** - Testimonial *n*

■ A testimonial starring a well-know personality who endorses the benefits of the product which he claims to use regularly.

**census** - Volkszählung *f*

■ The population roll or list compiled by the authorities and which provides a great deal of statistical information (ages, qualifications, professions etc.).

**central aisle** - Mittelgang *m*

■ In modern hypermarkets, the widest corridor along the tills and the perishable goods section along which customers move to reach the corridors that are among the shelves in which products are grouped in families. Gondola ends are especially attractive in the central aisle.

**central warehouse** - Zentrallager *n*

■ The main storehouse of a business which gathers the bulk of manufactured products and from which deliveries to satellite warehouses and points of sale are organised.

**centralised purchasing** - zentraler Einkauf *m*

■ The grouping of purchases by suppliers of a group of business units which operate in a particular geographical area and from one office.

**centre spread** - Anzeige *f* auf der mittleren Doppelseite einer Zeitschrift

■ In printed media, an advertisement which takes up the two centre pages of a publication. It usually stands out because the strength of the fold makes the publication tend to open on that page. It is usually subject to a special rate or the price is calculated by taking the price of an odd page (more expensive) and an even page (cheaper) and adding to both a surcharge for fixed location.

**chain** - Handelskette *f*

■ A company that possesses several similar stores in different areas and maintains a common image, organisation, promotion and distribution system.

**change management** - Management *n* des Wandels

■ A set of procedures designed to ensure that an organisation is constantly capable of adapting to different situations and unexpected problems that continuously arise. Business management experts and consultants are increasingly stressing the need for efficient management of change as a result of the greater speed and international implications of modern day changes.

**check-out product** - Kassenartikel *m*

■ A product placed on display near the check-out desks of a shop. They are articles which are bought on impulse such as batteries, sweets or newspapers. This placement is strategically interesting because the customer can look at the goods and decide to buy while queuing.

**circulation** - Verbreitung *f*

■ The average number of the distributed copies of a magazine (subscriptions, individually sold copies and free copies). When multiplied by the average number of readers per copy it gives the number of readers of the publication, which can also be reached by calculating the print run minus the undistributed copies and the copies returned by the sales outlets.

**city marketing** - Stadtmarketing *n*

■ A branch of marketing which understands the city to be a commercial brand with its own image which needs looking after and forming depending on the aims, developing its potential and combating its negative points. All of this within the framework of a competitive strategy to attract visitors and investors to the city, and providing it with its own sign which distinguishes it from others.

**claim** - Werbeclaim *m*

■ A publicity idea which captures the attention of its target audience, inciting it to adopt an attitude towards the advertised product or service. It is expressed as a sentence in the slogan.

**classified ads** - Kleinanzeige *f*

■ In daily media, advertisements which are grouped together by subject. They are usually small in size and enjoy a special rate. Together they form a separate section of many newspapers. They are also known as classifieds, small ads and free ads.

**CLCM (customer life cycle management)** - Management *n* des Kundenlebenszyklus

■ In relational marketing, the management of the relationship with the client from their first purchase, so as to not lose them and to be able to achieve a return on the investments made in gaining such a client through new offers in cross sales, repeat or renewed purchases, which they will make over the course of the duration of their relationship with them.

**click stream** - Klickstream *m*

■ In Internet advertising, the record of a series of pages which a user has accessed on a particular site during a consultation session. It enables the study of the exact preferences of the user and the optimisation of the presentation and structure of the pages.

**click through rate** - Klickrate *f*

■ The average effectiveness in terms of percentage of an interactive banner. It is obtained by dividing the number of persons who have clicked on the advertisement (click through) by the number of impressions of said advertisement.

**clicks and mortar** - Click-and-Mortar-Unternehmen *n*

■ An expression originating from English-American slang, invented by David Pottruck from the Charles Schwab company. It is used to refer to those companies who have a presence both on the Internet and off it.

**client** - Kunde *m*

■ An individual that regularly uses the services of a professional or company or who regularly shops in the same establishment. By extension a client can be any person who buys or uses the services of an establishment or company or contracts the services of a professional on an occasional basis.

**clientele** - Kundschaft *f*

■ A collective term for all the customers that use or buy the products or services of a company, especially those that do so with a certain regularity.

**clone** - Kopie *f*

■ A product offering the same features as another better-known one. It is usually sold cheaper and may even be more powerful. As long as it doesn't violate a patent, it's legal and is common practice for computers for example.

**closed question** - geschlossene Frage *f*

■ A question in a questionnaire where those being surveyed are forced to choose between some pre-established options. It is the most common type of question although it is less telling and variable, but it does allow for questions to be tabulated easily.

**cluster** - Werbecluster *n*

■ A new method used by some businesses to manage their international marketing activities, which consists in concentrating its resources into countries grouped around a leading market. For example, Coca Cola has assigned Spain as the leader of one its European groups which includes Italy and Portugal.

**cluster analysis** - Cluster-Analyse *f*

■ A research method which consists in gathering the components of a collection of similar characteristics.

**cluster sampling** - Klumpenstichprobe *f*

■ Probability sampling in which the sample is divided into individual and mutually exclusive groups (without omission or repetition). A sample of the groups is randomly chosen (not of all groups as in stratified sampling), and all elements of the group are used (cluster sampling) or a random sample taken of each selected (dual level cluster sampling). Each group must be a scaled reproduction of the sample and therefore be wide ranging, which allows only a few groups to be chosen. Although statistically less efficient, the system is cheaper and easier to control. Cluster sampling may be systematic or carried out in individual areas. Also called conglomerate or group sampling.

**co-branding** - gemeinsame Markenpraxis *f*

■ The use of two or more brands in the sale of a product or provision of a service. For example, associating the sale of a fast-food menu with a brand of soft drinks.

**coded advertisement** - kodierte Anzeige *f*

■ An advertisement or answer coupon with a code which identifies its origin (for example, the newspaper in which a recruitment ad appeared). This is done to value the efficiency of each medium or to classify the answers better.

**cohort analysis** - Kohortenanalyse *f*

■ The systematic study of a group of people with similar basic, social or economic characteristics, by defining and comparing behaviour and events over a given time.

**collar label** - Flaschenhalsetikett *n*

■ Advertising or information placed on bottlenecks.

**collective trademark** - Gemeinschaftsmarke *f*

■ A trademark belonging to an association of producers or specialised organisation that is used by members as a symbol of origin or guarantee of quality, governed by strict controls. Often represented by a simple graphic image (for example, pure new wool).

**commando selling** - Kommandoverkauf *m*

■ The action carried out by an increased or specialised sales force when maintaining or opening a new market. For this, the company increases its number of employees or calls upon a special sales force team. Sometimes the manufacturers' sales team join a wholesalers' in order to motivate and teach them and thus insure a good standing with their customers.

**commercial** - Werbespot *m*

■ An audiovisual publicity message produced using cinematography or video technology, but disseminated in the spaces and at the times established for that purpose by the television medium. This type of message can be of differing lengths, but they are usually 20 or 30 seconds long.

**commercial advertising** - kommerzielle Werbung *f*

■ An advertising activity carried out for commercial purposes, in order to communicate both the existence as well as the benefits of all kinds of goods and services. Currently, this kind of advertising is that which takes up the majority of advertising space and time.

**commercial area** - Gewerbegebiet *n*

■ An area formed by a group of retail outlets where consumers go make their purchases.

**commercial time** - Werbezeit *f*

■ The time available for publicity announcements within a programming framework. The maximum amount of time may be fixed by law, by self-control regulations within the sector or by the internal regulations of the broadcasting station and can vary according to the time of day and the type of programme that is being broadcast.

**commercialisation** - Vermarktung *f*

■ The group of activities intended to encourage sales of pre-designed products or services. Although not as common as the term marketing, it includes many of the same activities, such as market research, promotion, sales, commercial administration and distribution.

**communication advising** - Kommunikationsberatung *f*

■ A business whose task it is to inform and advise other businesses on matters relating to communication plans, helping for example in carrying out and managing the internal and external communications actions, in the choice of suitable communications media, and in sponsorship and patronage task etc. In short, all those communications activities which will reflect in its corporate image.

**communication consultant** - Kommunikationsberater *m*

■ An independent professional or company, expert in communication, whose purpose is to provide information, advice and help in the management of all communication activities which can create or strengthen a positive image of the business that it is advising.

**communication mix** - Kommunikationsmix *m*

■ The set of communication media used by an advertiser to reach the target group during a certain advertising campaign.

**communication objective** - Kommunikationsziel *n*

■ The aim pursued by a message or a campaign, be it advertising, public relations, marketing or the message carried by the actual product. What one wants to put across together with the levels of perception and recollection which one wants to reach.

**communication plan** - Kommunikationsplan *m*

■ A project which brings together all the communications objectives of an organisation, as well as the strategies needed to achieve those objectives and to face all corporate communications problems which may arise within the organisation.

**community support** - soziale Unterstützung *f*

■ The public or private institutions' assistance aimed at individuals or segments of the population with the aim of helping resolve economic or emotional problems.

**comparative advertising** - vergleichende Werbung *f*

■ The type of advertising in which the advertiser contrasts its business, goods or services with those of a competitor or various competitors, with the aim of showing the superiority of its business, goods or services compared to the business, goods or services it is contrasting.

**comparative analysis** - Vergleichsanalyse *f*

■ The evaluation of two or more alternatives or products in order to discover differences and similarities, estimate their relations and measure their cost, efficiency and relative results. Facts and figures are used in order to measure the importance of each attribute to the target group.

**comparison shopper** - Einkäufer *m* von Vergleichsprodukten

■ A person employed by a point-of-sale to investigate periodically its competitors' prices, offers, range, marketing activities and quality and service levels.

**comparison test** - Vergleichstest *m*

■ The evaluation of two or more rival products or services carried out by a company or an independent institution which gives an unbiased opinion. User and consumer magazines tend to carry out and publish this kind of test.

**competition** - Konkurrenz *f*

■ The group of businesses which serves the same market or provides the same service, trying to gain the same potential clients.

**competitive** - wettbewerbsfähig

■ The ability to compete favourably, for example, with a lower price or with a higher quality or a better image.

**competitive advantage** - Wettbewerbsvorteil *m*

■ A situation or circumstance that gives a competitive preference to a country or a company in a concrete economic activity. The advantage may be motivated by superior technology, by the lesser cost of a specific production factor, privileged access to a market, better acknowledgement of a brand, etc.

**competitive analysis** - Konkurrenzanalyse *f*

■ The study of the competitors of a particular company or industry. The study is based on market share, growth rates per sector, strong and weak points, opportunities and threats, negotiating power with suppliers and customers and the possibility of entry and exit of companies.

**competitive claims** - Wettbewerbsvorteile *m/pl*

■ The qualities and advantages of a product over its rivals which the advertiser or manufacturer promotes.

**competitor** - Konkurrent *m*

■ A company, individual or product of similar characteristics, that attempts to fulfil the same needs of a similar or related target public.

**complementary good** - Komplementärprodukt *n*

■ An item which accompanies another when it is used. Distributors will frequently place a complementary product with a high margin next to one that is on offer, for example mayonnaise and asparagus.

**concentrated marketing** - konzentriertes Marketing *n*

■ Marketing focused on a particular segment of the total market, for the purpose of penetrating this market and creating a specialised reputation. Although less flexible and possibly involving greater long term risk, the strategy is recommended when substantial resources are not available, those that are available are specifically suited to that particular sector or competition is limited.

**concentric diversification** - konzentrische Diversifikation *f*

■ A diversification in which a new product, with technological or marketing synergies, is aimed at different clients.

**concept test** - Konzepttest *m*

■ A test used to assess the acceptability that an idea or product might have in the marketplace. In a product development process, concept tests are used for screening potential new product ideas before making a prototype. They are used also to assess the effectiveness of advertising campaigns.

**conditional association** - bedingte Assoziation *f*

■ In research, the degree of association that exists between two variables when other different variables are taken into account. The former are known as control variables.

**confidence level** - Vertrauensniveau *n*

■ The reliability of statistical data obtained from a sample. The degree of certainty that the sample error rate does not exceed the given value. It depends on the size of the sample and the sampling method used. Institutions which carry out surveys are obliged to declare a confidence level of the data and the margin of error of the information they report on.

**consumer** - Verbraucher *m*

■ The person who uses a good or a product, whether or not he is the same person who purchased such a good/product.

**consumer advertising** - Verbraucherwerbung *f*

▪ The direct communication of an advertising message to individuals or families, as opposed to specialist or industrial advertising. Media with large audiences are used, such as television, radio, magazines, billboards, etc.

**consumer association** - Verbraucherorganisation *f*

▪ A group of consumers or service users that have united in order to provide a better defence of their rights. They provide advice, information, organise claims and establish quality controls.

**consumer behaviour** - Konsumentenverhalten *n*

▪ The manner in which consumers evaluate, choose, buy and consume goods and services.

**consumer branding** - Consumer Branding *n*

▪ A brand research specialisation which focuses on the creation and management of brands for consumer goods and articles. The design of packaging and wrapping of such goods and articles is of particular importance in this discipline.

**consumer confidence measure** - Bewertung *f* des Konsumentenvertrauens

▪ A measure of purchase probability of high priced consumer durables. A client will not purchase when his confidence in the future economy is zero, but will purchase more as his confidence rises. This measure takes into account the individuals' economic situation as perceived by him in relation to that of those who surround him.

**consumer good** - Konsumgut *n*

▪ A good or service bought and used directly by the end user and which does not need any productive transformation. It may or may not be durable. Synonym for product.

**consumer price index (CPI)** - Verbraucherpreisindex *m* (KPI)

▪ An index adjusted in accordance with the consumption of the average family unit, which measures the general price levels of this consumption at a particular time in relation to a previous period. The consumer price index is the most commonly used scale for quantifying inflation.

**consumer profile** - Konsumentenprofil *n*

▪ The set of demographic, social and mental characteristics that distinguish the consumers of a brand, clients of an establishment or users of a service. Profiles are obtained through consumer studies and serve to define the sector of the public to be targeted.

**consumer research** - Verbraucherforschung *f*

▪ The compilation and analysis of information regarding consumer characteristics in relation to a need or a product. Purchasing and consumption habits are studied, as are brand recognition and recollection, associated products, seasonal variations, needs that are really satisfied and purchasing intentions. For qualitative studies in-depth interviews and group discussions are used, whereas for quantitative studies consumer interviews and panels are used. Consumer research is complementary to market research.

**consumers' association** - Verbraucherschutzverband *m*

▪ An association of consumers or users of services who join together to defend their rights more effectively. It divulges information, gives advice and organises claims and establishes quality controls.

**content analysis** - Inhaltsanalyse *f*

▪ In marketing, a system for analysing all kinds of documents (such as surveys, graphs or advertisements) in order to study and understand their elements and compare the documents of different advertisers.

**Continuous Replenishment (CRP)** - kontinuierliche Warenversorgung *f*

■ A supply system whereby the supplier of the merchandise delivers the products to the client without interruption nor delay, adapting its production process to the rhythm of orders made by the client. In this way, stock levels and the subsequent costs for maintaining the inventory are effectively reduced.

**continuous research** - fortlaufende Forschung *f*

■ Research carried out over a long period of time which allows comparisons in time and regarding the competition.

**contract manufacturing** - vertragliche Herstellung *f*

■ A contract by which the manufacturing of a product which is designed and marketed by one company is carried out by another, often in a foreign country where production costs are lower.

**control group** - Kontrollgruppe *f*

■ A sample of people, similar to another which will in fact be exposed to a stimulus and which is used as reference in order to evaluate differences and compensate the placebo effect.

**control question** - Kontrollfrage *f*

■ In a questionnaire, a question whose answer allows the validity and sincerity of the remaining answers to be checked.

**controlled test market** - kontrollierter Testmarkt *m*

■ A study which consists in selecting a section of the market (a region, town or point of sale) and carrying out a test aimed at verifying a hypothesis. All the variables which operate in said market are subject to a control to check their respective influence on the final result.

**convenience sampling** - willkürliche Auswahl *f*

■ Non-probability sampling that involves surveys of people that just happen to be in a particular place at a particular time by chance, or that call into a radio programme. It lacks scientific validity, given that samples may often be non-representative.

**convenience store** - 24-Stunden-Laden *m*

■ A store with extended opening hours, including night time and public holidays, that sells its products mainly due to its proximity and convenience. It offers a limited range, concentrating on common items or goods that may be required due to unforeseen circumstances. Margins tend to be relatively large.

**co-op mailing** - Verbundmailing *n*

■ In direct advertising, the collective delivery of a group of messages and promotional actions for different products which are not in competition with each other and which share the same target public.

**coolhunter** - Tendenzberater *m*

■ A consultant who analyses tastes and fashions and is usually employed by market research or advertising agencies. It is their job to spot new tendencies and see what trendsetters are drawn to, as well as identifying changes in lifestyles, especially amongst the young, and new trends in one sector that may affect another.

**cooperative advertising** - kooperative Werbung *f*

■ Advertising which is carried out and financed jointly by two or more organisations, generally a manufacturer of consumer goods and the distributor in a certain geographical area. This cooperative form of advertising usually benefits both parties because it brings the manufacturer closer to a specific target public, whilst increasing the distributor's notoriety by associating him with the image of the manufacturer's brand. In the case of film advertising, this is sometimes financed jointly by the distributor and screener.

**cooperative marketing** - kooperatives Marketing *n*

■ A marketing action carried out jointly by two or more organisations belonging to a single distribution channel. This could be in the form of horizontal cooperation in the case of businesses which belong to the same level or step of the channel, or vertical cooperation if the members of the channel are of a different level.

**co-pack** - gemeinsame Verpackung *f*

■ A promotional technique in which two brands of related products are packaged together in one container.

**copywriter** - Werbetexter *m*

■ The person responsible for writing advertising texts and messages that normally works for an advertising agency teaming up with an art director.

**copywriter adapter** - überarbeitender Werbetexter *m*

■ A copywriter in charge of making the necessary alterations in the text of an advertisement so it is adequate for the target group of each medium or so it can be used in another country.

**copywriting** - Erstellung *f* von Werbetexten

■ The creation of texts and concepts for advertisements and commercials.

**core business** - Hauptgeschäft *n*

■ The basic company activity. Corporations or groups of companies may include several core businesses.

**core product** - Basisprodukt *n*

■ The basic, original product in a product line or family from which the rest of the line is developed.

**corporate advertising** - Unternehmenswerbung *f*

■ Advertising that attempts to promote the image of a company by creating more public awareness or improving the company's reputation rather than advertising a specific product. It can also be called institutional advertising.

**corporate branding** - Corporate Branding *n*

■ The specialisation in brand engineering which focuses on the creation and management of brands for organisations and companies.

**corporate colour** - Unternehmensfarbe *f*

■ The colour or colours that a company, organisation or institution chooses to identify itself, and which it uses to reinforce the visual perception of the basic elements of visual identity (emblems and logos) as well as of all those media necessary (sign boards, signage and architecture).

**corporate communications** - Unternehmenskommunikation *f*

■ The transmission of information about an organisation which any company, organisation or institution carries out for its audience, whether internal or external, using the most suitable methods and channels of information in each case.

**corporate culture** - Unternehmenskultur *f*

■ The group of beliefs and behaviour which reflect the philosophy and idiosyncrasy that define a business, organisation or institution and which determine to a large extent its corporate identity.

**corporate design** - Corporate Design *n*

■ The discipline in charge of the development of the graphic elements forming the visual corporate identity and of their application to all corporate printed matter.

**corporate event** - Unternehmensevent *n*

■ A particularly important and much publicised business occasion, for example the inauguration of a new floor, or the anniversary of its foundation, which has a bearing on the corporate image of the business and requires the participation of professionals in its preparation.

**corporate group** - Unternehmensgruppe *f*

■ A group of companies with common property. There is normally a matrix company that, either directly or through its affiliates, owns 50% of the rest of the companies' capital. It also applies when there exists one or various individual shareholders who own different companies, whenever they are operated in a coordinated way.

**corporate identity** - Corporate Identity *f*

■ The form a business has of presenting itself to the different kinds of public it interacts with. It goes beyond the visual corporate identity and includes all emblems and signs of the business.

**corporate identity manual** - CI-Handbuch *n*

▪ A document which shows a plan to manage and coordinate all the variables which influence the manner in which a business is perceived, such as the choice of its corporate attributes, its communication activities, its behaviour, its goods, its surroundings, its corporate style. It is more and more frequent that these kinds of manuals be produced exclusively in electronic format.

**corporate image** - Unternehmensimage *n*

▪ The opinion, whether positive or negative, that the public has of a business, organisation or institution, as generated by its way of doing things, its actions and communications, its beliefs and values, its company policy and all its other activities and expressions.

**corporate network** - Unternehmensnetzwerk *n*

▪ The extensive network formed by the interconnection of all the networks of a corporation or business, including local, private telephone, voice, data and video transmission. It also includes the permanently assigned communication lines. A classic example of a corporate network is that known as the intranet.

**corporate objective** - Unternehmensziel *n*

▪ The intentions or aims that a business establishes as what it would like to be; for example, that our clients think that we are the leading company in the automobile sector.

**corporate portal** - Unternehmensportal *n*

▪ A company or organisation's official website. Apart from providing information on the company, it usually has some other type of function or reason for attracting visitors. Also known as an enterprise information portal (EIP).

**corporate public responsibility** - öffentliche Verantwortung *f* des Unternehmens

▪ The group of social obligations that a person, group, organisation or institution takes on in relation to its public, both at the time of carrying out its basic or main tasks as well as in its concern for the consequences that those activities have on other social groups outside the organisation. The creation of employment, equal opportunities in the workplace or avoiding contamination are all demonstrations of public responsibility.

**corporate social responsibility** - soziale Verantwortung *f* von Unternehmen

▪ The group of social obligations that a person, group, organisation or institution can take on in relation to the social and environmental surroundings in which it carries out its activity.

**corporate social responsibility plan** - Unternehmensplan *m* für soziale Verantwortung

▪ A project of the investments that an organisation plans to make over a specific period of time in the area of social interest satisfaction. Forecast of the start up of a series of concealed patronage actions which are strategically planned to achieve the objectives defined in the public relations program of the company.

**corrective advertising** - richtigstellende Werbung *f*

▪ An advertisement which has the purpose of correcting an earlier message that was not true or which could lead to confusion. It may be issued on a voluntary basis or as required by a competitor or consumer association.

**co-sponsorship** - Co-Sponsoring *n*

▪ The sponsorship in which two or more sponsors share the costs and limelight proportionately.

**cost price** - Selbstkostenpreis *m*

▪ In the case of a good produced by a company it is the price that includes all quantities consumed in order to achieve that good (raw and auxiliary materials, labour, energy consumption, packaging and the distribution of general expenses, always excluding profit). If the good is purchased, the cost price includes taxes, transportation costs and insurance in addition to the cost of the purchase itself.

**counter** - Ladentisch *m*

■ A stand or table located in stores and used to display products and attend to customers. Although obsolete in supermarkets, etc., counter trading still exists in many traditional sectors.

**coupon ad** - Coupon-Werbung *f*

■ In printed media, an advert in which a voucher or cut-out slip is inserted, which, when sent or delivered to the consumer, serves as a control for the advertiser. It is used by the consumer to request information or to obtain a discount on the price of the product. It is used by the advertiser to verify the effectiveness of the different media used for its advertising.

**coverage** - Werbeabdeckung *f*

■ The percentage of the target public exposed to a particular advertising campaign. At times it is also applied to the absolute number or percentage of the target public within a particular audience that is reached.

**CPC (cost per click)** - CPC *pl* (Klickkosten)

■ In Internet advertising, the cost of each click obtained in a banner campaign. The price of a campaign can be expressed according to a fixed CPC, in which case clicks are contracted instead of impressions.

**CPI** - VPI

■ The initials for consumer price index, a balanced index based upon the consumption of an average family unit that measures the general level of prices of that average consumption at a given moment in relation to a preceding period.

**CPI (cost per inquiry)** - CPI *pl* (Kosten pro Anfrage)

■ In direct marketing, the measurement ratio of the success of a campaign in economic terms which represents the offloaded unit cost per request for information. The result is obtained by dividing the total cost of the commercial campaign by the number of requests for information received.

**CPO (cost per order)** - CPO *pl* (Kosten pro Auftrag)

■ The measurement ratio of the success of a campaign in economic terms which represents the offloaded unit cost per purchase order received. The result is obtained by dividing the total cost of the commercial campaign by the number of purchase orders received.

**creative advertising agency** - Kreativagentur *f*

■ An advertising agency which specialises in offering creative advertising services particularly aimed at conventional advertising methods. These advertising agencies specialising in creativity appeared in the nineteen seventies under the name creative boutiques, the first of these being Saatchi and Saatchi, founded by the brothers Charles and Maurice Saatchi.

**creative department** - Kreativabteilung *f*

■ The department which, within the structure of an advertising agency, is composed of creative personnel, creative directors, editors, art directors and producers of varying media. In terms of functioning it is organised into creative groups formed by an editor and an art director under the supervision of a creative director; who are also included at the same time in the account team, which also includes management and media personnel.

**creative team** - Kreativteam *n*

■ The team of people who are at the heart of the creative task of advertising, and usually consisting of an editor and an art director. Both are in charge of conceiving and developing all advertising and promotional material for the advertiser, both in the form of complete campaigns as in individual advertisements for various media. Each team is in charge of one or a number of accounts.

**credibility** - Glaubwürdigkeit *f*

■ A quality by which something or someone deserves to be believed and what he says is considered true or probable.

**criterion** - Kriterium *n*

■ The scale, opinion or norm used to make a particular selection or choose a course of action.

**CRM (Customer Relationship Management)** - KBM *n* (Kundenbeziehungsmanagement)

■ The philosophy of a company with a complete vision of the client: to know him, to know his needs and to anticipate these to be able to satisfy them even before the client asks for them. The group of activities developed by marketing, sales, after-sales service and promotions departments primarily to create loyalty and improve contact with clients and take better advantage of the opportunities, such as, crossed sales and the launching of new products. All the activities carried out between the business and its actual or potential clients are managed with operative and analytical objectives.

**cross couponing** - Cross-Couponing *n*

■ A sales promotion technique which consists in distributing coupons which allow product A to be obtained for free or at a reduced price when purchasing product B.

**cross merchandising** - kombinierte Absatzförderung *f*

■ A promotional strategy which consists of supporting the sale of a product with others from the same company based on their location in the point of sale, so that the purchaser's attention is drawn towards the product they already know and is displaced towards the new product located in close proximity to the first.

**cross section** - Querschnitt *m*

■ In database marketing, a sample of a randomly generated list using the criteria of a selection of 1 in every n names, until completely crossing the selected list with the number of entries necessary for the sample to be representative.

**cross sell** - Kreuzverkauf *m*

■ A marketing technique used over the phone which consists of selling the caller more than one complementary or additional product to the advertised one which generated the client or potential client's call in the first place.

**cross selling** - Angebot *n* und Verkauf *m* von Zusatzprodukten

■ A type of sale involving offering two or more products, usually complementary, for sale at the same time at an attractive price, with the purpose of sharing the fixed costs and stimulating demand. It is usually used in the service sector, where fixed costs usually make up an important proportion of the total costs.

**cross-cultural differences** - interkulturelle Unterschiede *m/pl*

■ The variations in beliefs, attitudes, customs and behaviour standards from one country, race of people or social class to another.

**cross-sectional study** - Querschnittsuntersuchung *f*

■ Research which focuses on a previously defined group within a town or universe.

**crowding-out** - Verdrängungseffekt *m*

■ The abandonment of a market by the most weak or those for whom the established price makes it not worth it. It is especially applied in the contracting of credit by individuals, when an increase in financing needs of the public administration leads to a rise in the interest rate.

**customer** – Kunde *m*

■ An individual that regularly uses the services of a or company or who regularly shops in the same establishment. The term client is also used.

**customer complaint** - Beschwerde *f* seitens des Kunden

■ The dissatisfaction or disagreement that a client shows towards a commercial action carried out by a business or the features, quality or functioning of a particular product or service marketed by the same. It can lead to a complaint being lodged if the client decides to make its protest known and formalised.

**customer flow** - Kundenstrom *m*
■ The number of people that pass in front of a store (outside), enter (inside) or pass through a particular section, over a given period of time.

**customer loss rate** - Kundenverlustrate *f*
■ The proportion of the number of clients that stop being clients over a given year and the average number of clients that a company has had during a year. Client loss can be inevitable (changes of address, change of business activity, etc.) but in general they should be avoided and the first step is to understand the reason for this loss by putting into action an effective communications system with clients for resolving their problems.

**Customer Profitability Analysis (CPA)** - Kundenprofitabilitätsanalyse *f*
■ The in depth study of the costs and earnings that a consumer has generated and will generate in order to value its profitability in the long term, and to adopt the right actions in each moment.

**Customer Relationship Management (CRM)** - Kundenbeziehungsmanagement *n* (KBM)
■ The philosophy of a company which focuses its business strategy on the relationship with and a complete vision of the client: to know him, to know his needs and to anticipate these in order to satisfy them even before the client asks for them.

**customer service** - Kundendienst *m*
■ A department within a company that deals directly with its clients, answering their questions and resolving their queries. This department should ensure that the client receives a satisfactory response and that their confidence in the company is reinforced, whilst internally transmitting any problems to the relevant department in the company so that they may be resolved.

**customer service centre** - Kundendienstzentrum *n*
■ An office that advises the user or customer, resolves doubts and deals with claims or complaints.

**cyber survey** - Cyberumfrage *f*
■ A survey carried out on a site which allows the study of the market on the Net. On occasion those who reply to the survey receive an incentive in the form of a gift.

**cyclical fluctuation** - Konjunkturschwankung *f*
■ The oscillation in price and sales volume of a product, caused by variations in the economic cycle. Long-term interest rates, for example, fluctuate in a specific manner from boom to recession.

# D

**DAGMAR** - DAGMAR
■ The acronym for Defining Advertising Goals for Measured Advertising Results, an advertising method coined by Russell H. Colley in 1961 which aims to compare the results obtained by advertising with the proposed objectives, something which, as a first step, requires the clear definition of such objectives. It consists of four steps: awareness, comprehension, conviction and action (ACCA).

**dangler** - Banner *m*
■ An element of point of sale advertising designed to be hung from the ceiling of an establishment, normally using a nylon thread or fine wire springs, with the aim of attracting the attention of the consumer as it moves in the air.

**data collection** - Datensammlung *f*
■ The accumulation of facts and information for research or analysis. It is normally kept in computerised files and databases.

**data mining** - Datenschürfung *f*
■ The automatic extraction of predictive data which is hidden in databases. This technique helps to identify and define markets and to increase the company's ability to address its clients, achieving, in that way, a higher profit for its direct advertising campaigns via e-mail (e-marketing).

**data overlays** - Datenbelegung *f*

■ In database marketing, the process of cross referencing two or more lists and annexing to one of these the data contained in the remaining lists about a particular client or entry with the aim of enriching it by introducing more data which increases the information available on a particular entry.

**data warehouse** - Datenspeicher *m*

■ A central and integrated location where information is stored. It requires a software program to know a client's profile better and to respond to his needs. Personalised marketing strategies (one to one) are based on this system.

**database** - Datenbank *f*

■ A method of organising archives, in which a set of related data is stored on a hard disc or some other storage device. By extension, the set of data belonging to a company and used by it in its activities. In some cases it can be marketed for third party use.

**database analysis** - Datenbankanalyse *f*

■ The study of information contained in a database of clients or potential clients with the aim of obtaining a better understanding of these so as to increase the efficiency of marketing actions.

**database manager** - Datenbankverwalter *m*

■ A company or professional who compiles, systematises and markets databases of different origins (public sources, ad hoc surveys) in relation to a particular town and which is then provided to advertisers or direct marketing agencies. Such databases allow the segmentation of the target public in accordance with very specific criteria (sex, occupation, level of income, consumption habits, among others), thus becoming an essential tool in current direct marketing.

**database marketing** - Datenbank-Marketing *n*

■ A direct marketing tool which uses new database management technology to store, analyse and use the information obtained from the affairs between a business and its clients and potential clients, so as to segment and personalise communications to the maximum and offer the most suitable product or service to each client at the appropriate time.

**day-after recall** - 24-Stunden-Erinnerung *f*

■ The study of the opinions of a targeted public concerning a new advertisement (normally on television). This is done by calling the target market by telephone the next day. The spontaneous, aided and suggested recall of a brand is measured, as is the recall of particular scenes, the message that is transmitted, and the overall opinion. It is used to correct any errors that may not have been found in previous trials.

**dealer copy** - Vertriebstext *m*

■ In a joint advert, the advertising slogan that the dealer or retailer places in the space reserved.

**dealer listing** - Händlerliste *f*

■ In printed media, the list of all dealers or retailers, or of those from a particular area, that the manufacturer places in its adverts to facilitate consumer access to the product.

**dealer tag** - Händlerregister *n*

■ In audiovisual media, an additional piece placed at the end of the film or slot with the name and other identifying elements of the dealers or retailers. In national campaigns, the tag can vary locally so as to indicate the retailers of each area.

**decoy** - Scheinadresse *f*

■ The postal details inserted in a file by its owner, corresponding to a real or fictitious person, so that the owner can be informed of the use (authorised or not) of said file or folder. It is a practice used frequently by the owners of lists. Also known as dummy name and salt name.

**defensive marketing** - Defensivmarketing *n*

■ A kind of marketing whereby a business takes on actions with the aim of safeguarding or protecting itself against a negative image that its products or brands have in the market. In general, the business tries to convert the unfavourable perception through intensive advertising campaigns which demonstrate and reinforce the quality of its products and brands.

**degree of exposure** - Wirkgrad *m*

■ The reach of an advert or campaign expressed in terms of the number of persons in the target group who access it and the frequency of this access. It depends on the definition of the target group and the number of placings.

**del credere agent** - Delkredere-Agent *m*

■ An intermediary that sells goods on behalf of a different entity in exchange for a fee that is higher than normal due to the risk involved in being totally responsible for payment.

**Delphi method** - Delphi-Methode *f*

■ A method of predicting demand or market features based on surveys of groups of experts. These consist of several rounds of questions and answers designed in such a way that the previous average response has an affect on opinions (either surveyed or not), in order to gradually reach a consensus in relation to current and especially future situations. It is useful for identifying trends.

**demand forecast** - Nachfrageprognose *f*

■ The estimation of the amount of products that will be ordered by clients in a particular future period. It is a very important concept in marketing as it significantly affects areas such as stock management and pricing policy.

**demarketing** - Demarketing *n*

■ The set of actions aimed at moderating the demand of a product, such as price increases, quality reduction, elimination of marginal clients, reduction of advertising and reduction of sales efforts. This can be due, for example, to temporary scarcity or in order to create a gap in the market for a new product.

**demographic study** - Demografiestudie *f*

■ The data which groups consumers in market segments by statistical characteristics such as age, sex, marital status and environment.

**demonstrator display** - Probiertheke *f*

■ A display, normally in the form of a self-assembly table with a board at its top which serves as a support for the promotion of a product. It is placed temporarily in department stores and supermarkets and is used, with the assistance of a specialised salesperson, to invite consumers to taste the product in the form of a snack. It is used very often in the food and drink sector in general, and is particularly effective for the introduction of new products onto the market.

**denigratory advertising** - verunglimpfende Werbung *f*

■ A type of advertising, which, due to its content, form of presentation or distribution, causes the direct or indirect discredit or defamation of a person, business or its products, services or activities. In the strict sense, denigratory advertising is considered to be the publicity message that discredits the products, services or activities of a business, whether or not it is a competitor.

**department** - Abtellung *f*

■ The part of a business organisation that is dedicated to a particular function within a division, such as production, marketing, or finance.

**depot** - Lager *n*

■ A warehouse of a reduced size in which merchandise, which is to be subsequently transferred to final points of sale, is stored.

**depot location** - Lagerstandort *m*

■ The geographic location of warehouses. Determining the most suitable location for a warehouse or network of these (central, satellite and halfway warehouses) is a very important and complex decision, in which it is necessary to consider multiple elements such as the distance to the origin and destination points of the merchandise, the delivery rhythm of the products, accessibility to the area and its connections to other routes.

**depredatory price** - Dumpingpreis *m*
▪ A product price which is set below its total unit cost, usually with the objective of undercutting competitors.

**deregulation** - Deregulierung *f*
▪ A process which tends to favour the free market and competition between possible service suppliers, eliminating laws, administrative regulations or artificial barriers which favour local monopolies. For example, the deregulation of air traffic.

**descriptive research** - deskriptive Forschung *f*
▪ Research carried out with the purpose of discovering the frequency with which a certain event occurs, or the relationship between two variables. Also known as fundamental or basic research, it contrasts with applied research, whose purpose is to serve as an aid in the decision-taking process.

**design management** - Design-Management *n*
▪ A task which consists of controlling the correct application of the visual corporate identity in all applications in which it is required. It is usually carried out by a specific person in the organisation, generally the communications manager.

**desk research** - Sekundärforschung *f*
▪ Research based upon the study of published information (press, annual reports, etc.) and occasionally with telephone contact, as opposed to practical investigation and field work. It has the advantage of being quick and cheap and it allows subsequent field investigations to be carried out more accurately.

**diagram** - Diagramm *n*
▪ A graphical representation that describes the functional relationship between two or more variable quantities. In statistics, there are different types of diagrams that represent statistical data (for example, histograms and stereograms).

**diary method** - Tagebuchmethode *f*
▪ A research method which consists of the interviewee taking note in a diary of his purchases, product use or exposure to the media.

**dichotomous question** - dichotome Fragestellung *f*
▪ A closed question with only two possible replies, generally yes or no.

**differentiated marketing** - differenziertes Marketing *n*
▪ A type of marketing that uses different combinations of price, products, promotion, advertising and distribution channels for each and every target sector.

**differentiation value** - Differenzierungswert *m*
▪ The value of the difference, whether positive or negative, between a specific offer and its product of reference.

**digisine** - elektronische Zeitschriften *f/pl*
▪ A file or document published and broadcast by electronic means. It may only have text or also contain graphics, images and even audio-visual contents. In the last few years these have become very popular on the Internet, usually in public debate forums or as web pages. Also called e-zine.

**digital branding** - digitales Branding *n*
▪ The creation and management of brands whose life will be focused around a basically digital media (website or interactive presentation).

**digital fingerprint** - digitale Unterschrift *f*
▪ A system which allows the user to verify its identity on the Net.

**digital merchandising** - digitales Marketing *n*
▪ The promotional material on which the corporate image of a company or organisation, or the trademark or sign can be affixed. On the Internet, examples would be screensavers, desktops and e-cards, among others.

**direct advertising agency** - Direktwerbeagentur *f*
▪ A company dedicated to the sending of advertising by post, making sure the adverts and other advertising materials reach the addressees who appear in lists

created for that purpose. Currently facsimiles, e-mails and mobile phone messaging are also used.

**direct channel** - Direktweg *m*
■ A distribution channel in which the products are transferred from the place of manufacture directly to the client, without passing through intermediary storage.

**direct cost** - direkte Produktionskosten *pl*
■ The cost directly associated with production and therefore proportional to the number of fabricated units.

**direct mail advertising** - Briefwerbung *f*
■ A message that goes directly to previously identified consumers, normally by mail. This means of communication permits greater personalisation and a more extensive message.

**direct marketing** - Direktmarketing *n*
■ An interactive marketing system which uses any publicity channel or media to contact the user or potential user of a product or service so as to obtain an individual and measurable response.

**direct marketing agency** - Direktmarketingagentur *f*
■ A company specialising in the management, creation and sending of publicity messages directed at a personalised audience, with the aim of obtaining a measurable response from them.

**direct response** - Direktantwort *f*
■ A commercial communications technique which offers the addressee the possibility of responding to an advert by telephone, post or any other channel proposed in the advert.

**direct response advertising** - Direct-Response-Werbung *f*
■ The advertising which is carried out in the mass media or selected media (personalised delivery, catalogues, door to door delivery) and whose purpose is to encourage a direct response from the addressee, instigated by the advert and through a telephone call, the sending of a coupon or similar such item without the need for the intervention of a salesperson or intermediary.

**direct selling** - Direktverkauf *m*
■ Sales in which a company directly contacts customers without using retail outlets or other intermediaries. Potential customers are contacted through other customers, via telephone, mailings, order forms in specialised magazines or newspaper advertisements and door to door selling. Customer response and sales results are easily measured.

**direct-mail couponing** - Gutscheinversand *m*
■ The mailing of one or more coupons directly to the consumer's home.

**discount** - Diskont *m*
■ An agreed reduction in tariff or public sales price of a specific good or service.

**discount price** - Sonderangebotspreis *m*
■ A reduced price during a period for promotional purposes. It is less aggressive than a liquidation price.

**discount store** - Discounter *m*
■ A store that sells at very low prices on a permanent basis. It has a limited range of products which are frequently second rate brands. It usually operates as a self service shop with cheap installations.

**discussion group** - Diskussionsgruppe *f*
■ On the Internet, a group of users which take part in a common debate forum by sending and receiving electronic messages. Users wishing to take part in one of these groups must add their electronic address to a distribution list which is managed by a list server. Some are co-ordinated by a moderator who selects those messages considered of general interest for transmission to the whole group.

**diseconomies of scale** - abnehmende Skalenerträge *m/pl*
■ The situation whereby the unit cost increases when production capacity increases. In the majority of industrial processes an increase in capacity produces a reduction in unit cost, calculated by dividing the fixed costs by the larger number of units. However, in certain circumstances the reverse occurs.

**disintermediation** - Zwischenhändlerauflösung *f*
■ The removal of intermediaries in a supply chain.

**display** - Aufsteller *m*
■ In marketing, the promotional material that allows goods to be presented at a point of sale in an attractive manner. It is usually made of cardboard and is easily unfolded and assembled. It is set up on the floor, although there are also counter-top versions, and it is usually placed at a gondola end. If it contains products it is known as a display pack.

**display basket** - Schaukorb *m*
■ A large basket within a store used for displaying products on offer.

**display case** - Vitrine *f*
■ An item of furniture protected by a glass front and top in which products are displayed. The consumer can in some cases select a product (as in a freezer cabinet), ask a shop assistant for an item (as in a jewellers), or go to the appropriate establishment (as in a display case on an airport concourse). The term display window is used when it forms part of the front of an establishment.

**display panel** - Schautafel *f*
■ A medium sized sign that displays information on a product, meeting or event.

**dissemination** - Bekanntmachung *f*
■ The spreading of news, product information, knowledge, etc., in order to reach as many people as possible.

**distribution** - Vertrieb *m*
■ The action carried out by the manufacturer to deliver a product through different channels to a retailer for sale to a final consumer. Nowadays, it is more common for large outlets to organise distribution activities. The percentage of value added to high consumption goods by manufacturers is gradually being reduced.

**distribution centre** - Vertriebszentrum *n*
■ An organisation that delivers goods to its own or third party establishments on a regular basis, offering a complete assistance service. It allows for less storage in each establishment and helps the process of receipt of supplies.

**distribution channel** - Vertriebskanal *m*
■ The group of companies that bring the manufactured goods to consumers. It varies in size, depending on the product and manufacturers may use different intermediaries. It normally includes wholesalers and retailers, however it may even refer to direct channels or importers, agents, distributors, loaders, internal branches and wholesale self-service.

**distribution network** - Vertriebsnetz *n*
■ A group of distribution intermediaries which allows the marketing of a product or service. It is usually used in the commercial sense, including exclusivists, wholesalers, retailers and covering both sale and advertising; but it can also refer to the logistical, mailing and personal delivery aspects.

**distribution platform** - Vertriebsplattform *f*
■ A large scale distribution centre, usually belonging to a big chain of hypermarkets or supermarkets, and from which the distribution of products to retail outlets is coordinated.

**distribution support activity** - vertriebsunterstützende Aktivitäten *f/pl*
■ A marketing activity (especially advertising and promotional) aimed at boosting the work of third parties who sell a company's products (for example, an advertisement announcing a prize for those who try a car at the dealer).

**distributor's own brand** - Händlermarke *f*
■ Similar to a white brand, except that it is not clear to consumers that the brand is owned by a chain store and the product may be produced by different manufacturers. Label design and price are similar to manufacturer brands and the objective is therefore not to increase sales or offer cheaper products, rather to improve profit margins given that costs are normally lower. For example, the brand No.7 is a make-up brand owned by Boots. Also known as a private label brand.

**diversified company** - diversifiziertes Unternehmen *n*

■ A company that covers many markets with a wide product range. Some years ago diversified companies were in fashion as the thinking was that cycles in different industries could be compensated for by having different products. However, with the development of the professional raider who would buy up companies and sell them in parts and the theory that shareholders should diversify, not companies, the trend has been to return to a concentration on basic products and a more profitable nucleus, thereby obtaining synergies between similar products and markets more easily.

**dog** - armer Hund *m*

■ In a growth-share matrix, a non-leading business within a low growth sector. It does not generate sufficient resources and the market is not favourable so the business should be restructured or sold or another sector should be sought.

**domestic market** - Hausmarkt *m*

■ The market which is found within national boundaries. Also known as the home market.

**domestic trade** - Binnenhandel *m*

■ Trade carried out between a seller and a purchaser who both reside in the same country. It is the opposite of foreign or international trade.

**donor** - Stifter *m*

■ In direct marketing, the person who takes up the offer to purchase a product or contract a service in order to give a gift to a third person, with the company being responsible for delivering the gift to the addressee on behalf of the purchaser. This kind of a promotion is very common in the subscription sector.

**door-to-door selling** - Haustür-Verkauf *m*

■ Direct selling without a prior selection of appointments, carried out from area to area by means of personal visits. Similar to home selling where a request for information exists and potential buyers are therefore previously known.

**dot-com** - Dotcom *f*

■ The name given to companies created taking advantage of Internet technologies and whose main form of communication and interaction with the target public is web based.

**double pricing** - doppelte Preisauszeichnung *f*

■ The situation where the normal price is crossed out and a promotional price at which a product is being offered is shown alongside. This is only legal if the crossed-out price really corresponds to the price at which the product was previously being sold.

**drive** - Aktion *f*

■ A synonym for advertising campaign which refers in particular to the complementary materials it is comprised of.

**drug advertising** - Arzneimittelwerbung *f*

■ A prospective or enticing offer, informative in nature, aimed at promoting the prescription, dispensing, sale and consumption of pharmaceuticals. The communication or advertising of pharmaceuticals comprises advertising aimed at the public as well as at those qualified to prescribe or dispense drugs, medical visits, the supply of samples, the sponsorship of promotional meetings and the sponsorship of scientific conferences. It is regulated by law.

**dry goods** - Trockengüter *n/pl*

■ All non-liquid goods. In the U.S.A., dry goods largely refer to fabrics, textiles and clothing as articles of trade. In Britain, it also includes dry food products such as coffee, grain, and sugar.

**dumping** - Dumping *n*

■ The flooding of a market, frequently marginal, with merchandise offered at a lower price than that applied on the main or source market.

**duty-free shop** - Duty-Free-Geschäft *n*

■ A store located in the international transit lounge of an airport or seaport that sells products with high margins but without the duty imposed on certain goods, such as alcohol and tobacco, to people leaving the country. By extension it can apply to the commercial activity on board an aeroplane or ship.

**duty-free zone** - zollfreier Bereich *m*

■ The area and premises, which, despite being within the national boundaries, are considered foreign territory for customs purposes. Merchandise which is deposited in these areas is not subject to customs taxes and can be sent on without problem.

**dynamic price** - dynamischer Preis *m*

■ A price which varies in function of supply and demand conditions. It is the contrary of the concept of a fixed price and has developed greatly thanks to sales over the Internet, in which consumers, through auctions or bidding systems, have a considerable influence over the final price established.

# E

**early bird** - Early Bird *m*

■ A creative piece or resource included in a mail shot aimed at encouraging those who respond before the indicated expiry date, with a free gift or discount.

**e-auction** - E-Auktion *f*

■ An auction carried out on a Web site. It can form part of the business to consumer (B2C ), business to business (B2B) or consumer to consumer (C2C) relations.

**e-billing** - E-Billing *n*

■ The process of calculating, configuring and issuing invoices through electronic means.

**e-business** - E-Business *n*

■ A term which, despite its literal definition being used to refer to business carried out using electronic means, is used in general to refer to businesses on the Internet.

**ecological advertising** - Umweltwerbung *f*

■ The social advertising activity aimed specifically at educating, increasing awareness, preventing or acting in favour of protecting and conserving the environment. This expression has been used to refer to advertising messages in which the respectful or advantageous character of the product or service in relation to nature or the environment is used to boast the basic appeals of the message. For example, saying that a washing machine is ecological.

**ecological marketing** - Umweltmarketing *n*

■ The type of marketing which aims at promoting the correct conservation of the environment. To this end it promotes the creation and distribution of easily recyclable products and containers at a reasonable cost, at the same time as spreading different messages with the aim of raising awareness so that citizens do not contaminate their surroundings.

**e-commerce** - E-Commerce *m*

■ Any business transaction where the transfer of information is carried out using digital telecommunications. The primary and most well-known medium used is the Internet, but there are others, such as mobile telephones (WAP technology), or digital television (interactive television).

**economies of scale** - Skalenerträge *m/pl*

■ The reduction in the unit cost of a production process when the annual capacity and production of the same are increased. Economies of scale are produced for various reasons, such as the lower unitary impact on general costs, purchase, distribution and marketing collaboration, the experience curve effect, a higher level of specialisation and a more efficient use of capital assets.

**economies of scope** - Verbundvorteil *m*

■ The reduction in costs or efficiency achieved by a company when different products share a common group of costs in large product portfolios.

**editing** - Bearbeitung *f*

■ In market research, the act of reading, correcting and if necessary, completing the questionnaires of a study until they are fit for digitalisation.

**effective reach** - effektive Reichweite *f*

■ The number of people of a target group who are hit by a campaign a sufficiently high number of times so as to react positively to the advert, but not so high as to react negatively. The effective reach is located within two limits. Both the lower and the higher limits must be previously established. When nothing is indicated to the contrary, it is considered that those people who have received at least three hits have been effectively reached.

**eknowledge** - E-Knowledge *n*

■ Knowledge management, understood as being the creation of value in an organisation from its intangible assets, used for the management and transmission by electronic means.

**elasticity of demand** - Preiselastizität *f* der Nachfrage

■ A measure of the behaviour of demand in relation to price variations. The coefficient between the percentage changes in quantity and price. Demand is inelastic if the percentage change in quantity is inferior to that of price (elasticity is less than one), and is elastic if the percentage change in quantity is greater than that of price (elasticity is greater than one).

**elasticity of supply** - Preiselastizität *f* des Angebots

■ A measure of the behaviour of supply in relation to changes in price. For example, if the price rises by 2% and the quantity supplied rises by more than 2%, supply is elastic. If the rise in supply is less than 2% it is inelastic or rigid.

**electronic storefront** - elektronisches Schaufenster *n*

■ The website on which a business presents a shop in a virtual shopping centre or any other form of association aimed at promoting the electronic commerce of a group of companies.

**electronic wallet** - elektronische Geldbörse *f*

■ A bank card with a microprocessor used as cash payment in shops and services. It is different from charge cards in that the user has previously paid the amount shown on the card and which is reduced in each purchase, instead of having the amount charged to his account. Electronic wallets can be recharged in the banks' cash dispensers.

**email advertising** - E-Mail-Werbung *f*

■ The use of electronic mail to send advertising messages.

**email marketing** - E-Mail-Marketing *n*

■ The permission marketing operations which use electronic mail as a medium and which benefit from the interactive, instantaneous and low cost nature that this provides.

**e-mall** - E-Kaufhaus *n*

■ A collection of electronic shops located in the same virtual space.

**emblem** - Fahne *f*

■ A company standard or brand logo that is placed in stores and factories to facilitate its identification.

**emerging market** - Schwellenmarkt *m*

■ The name which is given to a market which is experiencing high growth.

**e-money** - elektronisches Geld *n*

■ The application of communications systems which allows different financial transactions to be made in real time, such as the electronic transfer of funds, payment by credit card, distance purchases, the purchase of stocks and others.

**emoticon** - Emoticon *n*

■ Group of ASCII characters used to communicate feelings. They are usually used in messages transmitted by e-mail. Some examples are: :-) happy, ;-) wink and :-( sad.

**emotional appeal** - emotionale Ansprache *f*

■ A type of advertising which is designed to appeal to emotions rather than ones' sense of logic or utility. These advertisements are based upon the creation of feelings of love, hate, greed, fear, sexual desire, or humour, and offer the product as a solution to the needs.

**emotional impact** - emotionale Wirkung *f*

■ The creative philosophy provided by William Bernbach, father of the creative revolution, which advocates the concept that advertising messages should have the same emotional effect on consumers as works of art. To this end they turn to emotional appeal (fear, humour, imagination), careful graphic design and an excellent art management team. In this sense pictures are more important than words as they provoke a higher emotional impact.

**employer branding** - Firmen-Branding *n*

■ The part of brand engineering aimed at promoting a solid image of the company among its employees, promoting pride in staying with the company and promoting identification with the actions carried out in favour of its brands.

**end consumer** - Endverbraucher *m*

■ The person that actually uses or consumes a product. May be different from the buyer and influence the decision to purchase to a different degree. For example, a secretary that uses a word processor bought by the head office or a persistent child that wants his mother to buy a particular brand of toys.

**endorsed brand** - Zweitmarke *f*

■ A brand which is supported by another in the form of a guarantee. For example: Corn Flakes, under Kellogg's.

**enhancement list** - Listenerweiterung *f*

■ In database marketing, the process of cross referencing one list against others and in this way adding the information variables corresponding to the same person who appears in more than one list, thus producing an enrichment of the available data in the source database.

**entry barrier** - Zugangsbarriere *f*

■ A difficulty or impediment that a company encounters on trying to enter a new sector, product range or geographic area. For example, large investment in capital, patents, legal requirements, or purchase of lineal space.

**e-procurement** - elektronische Beschaffung *f*

■ A method used by large scale organisations or public administration bodies to request offers for goods and services, via the Internet. It widens the options available and allows better negotiation of conditions as well as facilitating the automation of administrative tasks in the purchase process.

**equal-appearing intervals** - Ankreuzverfahren *n*

■ A research technique in which interviewees are asked to indicate their agreement of disagreement with a preselected list of fixed propositions, without allowing for mid-range or ranking of replies.

**ethical advertising** - Ethik *f* in der Werbung

■ The advertising activity which respects the predominant morals and ethics of a specific context. For example, that which is not sexist, or which respects the rules which ethical codes of advertising establish, such as not associating alcohol consumption with social or sexual success nor encouraging speed in car advertisements.

**ethical price** - moralischer Preis *m*

■ The price which is given to a product according to social, rather than economic criteria. It involves setting an affordable price for consumers, independent of the cost of the product and the price that they would be willing to pay depending on the significance it has for them. For example, the price of a specific pharmaceutical.

**European Advertising Standards Alliance (EASA)** - EASA

■ A not-for-profit organisation which promotes self-regulation of advertising in Europe. Its purpose is to encourage commercial communications to respond to high ethical levels through self-control agencies which exist in each country. Founded in 1992 and with its seat in Brussels, it gathers 28 self-regulation associations of which 4 belong to non-European countries.

**European Association of Communications Agencies (EACA)** - EACA

■ An entity which was founded in 1959 and has its seat in Brussels. It serves as a link between the different associations of advertising agencies in Europe. The different representative organisations of the advertising companies in all the European Union countries, as well as other markets on the continent, are registered here.

**European Society for Opinion and Marketing Research (ESOMAR)** - ESOMAR

■ A professional organisation which groups together the main market research and opinion study specialists in Europe. It has one of the most internationally valued deontological codes, the International Code of Legal Practices in Market and Opinion Research.

**evaluation research** - Evaluationsforschung *f*

■ The motivational research which offers the information necessary to evaluate the results of a programme, a campaign, or a public relations action, checking the fulfilment of objectives. It serves to determine the degree of persuasive efficiency of the public relations, as well as the degree of mutual understanding achieved with the target public.

**event marketing** - Eventmarketing *n*

■ A branch of marketing specialised in designing and managing events for companies and other organisations, which have a special significance for the same and so they have a favourable impact on their corporate image or on that of specific products.

**exclusive distribution** - Exklusivvertrieb *m*

■ A policy that guarantees that certain intermediaries are exclusively granted the right to market a product within a determined geographic area. It allows greater product prestige, control and training of agents.

**executive creative director** - Kreativdirektor *m*

■ The person who runs the creative department of an advertising agency, with responsibilities normally similar to those of the accounts director and in charge of copywriters and art directors.

**exit barrier** - Austrittsbarriere *f*

■ An impediment that a company encounters on trying to leave a sector, a product range or a geographic area . For example, redundancy costs, repercussions for other products, loan covenants, etc.

**expeditionary marketing** - Expeditionsmarketing *n*

■ The type of marketing whose prime objective is to discover new markets and business opportunities in general. It is based on the rigorous analysis of the consumers' needs, technological evolution and competitors' actions.

**expenditure effect** - Kosteneffekt *m*

■ The effect which causes consumers to show a higher sensitivity to the price the higher the proportion of their purchase costs are in relation to their disposable income.

**experience marketing** - Erfahrungsmarketing *n*

■ A marketing method whose main purpose is for consumers to have direct contact with the products of the company. To this end all kinds of activities are organised which allow the consumer to get closer to the brand, such as the participation in games and prize draws, the supply of free samples, or the delivery of company gifts.

**experience survey** - Erfahrungsumfrage *f*

■ A study in which the interviewees are people who are knowledgeable in the subject the survey concerns, generally for professional reasons. These types of studies require much lower samples to those of studies among individuals. A particular type of survey which incorporates repetitions, is the Delphi method.

**exploratory research** - explorative Forschung *f*
▪ A type of research whose purpose is to obtain the necessary information to carry out a subsequent study.

**exposure** - Exposition *f*
▪ The perception of an advert on the part of its receiver. Some psychologists believe that the mere exposure to advertising produces some kind of advertising effect on its own.

**external growth** - externes Wachstum *n*
▪ In strategic analysis, the growth of a company, and by extension an organisation, based on the acquisition, fusion or takeover of other entities which already exist.

**external publication** - externe Zeitschrift *f*
▪ A public relations action which consists of a periodical publication aimed at the external public of a company. It is created with persuasive objectives in mind to maintain the organisation in the public's mind, or to inform of changes and to strengthen the public's attitude towards the same. Its development is usually the responsibility of the external communications section of the department in charge of media relations. Although it includes information about the company, it also covers general interest topics.

**e-zine** - elektronische Zeitschrift *f*
▪ A publication of a daily, weekly, fortnightly, monthly or quarterly nature, produced by one or a number of people, whose subject matter is monographic or general and which is distributed by subscription and via electronic mail. Subscription can be free, only for members, or subject to the payment of a subscription fee. The method of subscription goes from needing only a sign-up message with the subject "subscribe" or to requiring the subscriber to fill out a long questionnaire as well as supplying his credit card number.

# F

**face-to-face action** - Face-to-Face-Marketing *n*
▪ A marketing activity which requires personal contact with the consumer, for example, product tasting in a point of sale.

**facing matter** - gegenüber von Text
▪ The placement of an advertisement in a magazine or newspaper in a page opposite to an editorial text and which, therefore, is read more than if it were opposite another advertisement. In equal size, it is less visible than if it were surrounded by editorial text. Also called against text.

**facing traffic** - verkehrsseitig
▪ In external advertising, the orientation of hoardings towards oncoming traffic.

**facings** - Regalposition *f*
▪ The total number of visible products on a linear shelf in a shop. This number is used to calculate the linear metres that the client will contract for the display of their product on a shelf.

**factorial design** - faktorielles Design *n*
▪ In research, the analysis which entails the study of the effects of the different variables on the final result. Every value of a variable is examined in combination with all the values of the remaining variables.

**family unit** - Familie *f*
▪ The group of people that live in the same home, thereby comprising a single unit of buyers and consumers, normally linked by a family relationship.

**fast moving consumer products (FMCP)** - Schnelldreher *m/pl*
▪ The products belonging to the food and drink, personal hygiene and household cleaning sectors that are usually sold through the same distribution channels, more specifically in large self-service retail stores.

**faulty article** - fehlerhafter Artikel *m*
▪ A product sold at a reduced price due to a slight flaw.

**feasibility study** - Durchführbarkeitsstudie *f*

▪ A study carried out to determine whether or not an idea is profitable, as well as to identify the necessary conditions and means for it to become so.

**fee-basis income** - Einkommen *n* auf Honorarbasis

▪ In advertising, the remuneration paid to an agency. This is usually a previously fixed amount which the advertiser settles in a lump sum or periodically. It is a system which has been consistently replacing the traditional agency commission since Saatchi & Saatchi started to use it in the seventies as a distinctive symbol of the so-called creative agencies or boutiques.

**feedback** - Feedback *n*

▪ A communicated response. The reaction of the receiver to a message. It is only considered as such in bidirectional or reciprocal communication.

**fidelity rate** - Markentreuerate *f*

▪ The percentage of consumers who have bought a brand for the first time and then continue to do so.

**field** - Geschäftsfeld *n*

▪ The functional or product specialisation that a company bases its business around. For example, mass market products, communications technology or financial services.

**field director** - Felddirektor *m*

▪ In a research institute, the person who plans, manages and controls the task of information gathering. This person is sometimes also responsible for the pre-test questionnaire.

**field edit** - Feldarbeitsbearbeitung *f*

▪ The study of information gathered in research in order to check that the planned sources of information have been properly consulted. In survey-based research, it is the verification that all interviews have been performed adequately and were aimed at the people concerned according to the sample design.

**field error** - Feldfehler *m*

▪ In research, the deviation from the initial plan of the number of interviews or characteristics of the interviewees. Field errors must be foreseen from the beginning as well as the correctives which will be used.

**field experiment** - Feldexperiment *n*

▪ A study which entails demarcating a market portion and modifying some of its variables in order to observe their effects in a real situation.

**field force** - Außendienstmannschaft *f*

▪ A group of interviewers who work for a research institute. It can also refer to interviewers who take part exclusively in a field study.

**field marketing** - Feldmarketing *n*

▪ The marketing actions carried out in a given place by a specially-designated team, which covers mass visits, logistical actions and the itinerant display of products.

**field research** - Felduntersuchung *f*

▪ In general, practical investigation as opposed to theoretical or office bound investigation.

**field staff** - Mitarbeiter *m* vor Ort

▪ Employees such as salesmen or market surveyors that work in direct personal contact with clients, as opposed to office or production staff.

**fieldwork** - Feldarbeit *f*

▪ In research, a series of activities aimed at gathering information. Although the term fieldwork applies to any kind of study, it mainly refers to the studies which require interviews with individuals, retailers or professionals of any kind.

**FIFO** - FIFO

▪ A stock valuation and cost allocation system, in which the first product to enter is the first to leave the warehouse and therefore the balance sheet value of inventory is the cost of the last items purchased. The FIFO method, produces much higher profits in inflationary periods than the LIFO system. Initials stand for first in, first out.

**fifty-fifty plan** - Fifty-Fifty-Plan *m*
■ An advertising campaign whose costs are borne equally by the two parties to the contract. It usually happens in campaigns in which a manufacturer and a distributor take part.

**film commercial** - Kinowerbung *f*
■ An audiovisual advertising message conveyed through the cinema by means of cinematographic techniques. Due to the technical quality and narrative of many of these messages they are also know as advertising films.

**filtering** - Filter *m*
■ In Internet advertising, the analysis by a computer program of a request sent by a user with the aim of getting to know their profile and choosing the advertisements which will appear in the requested website.

**final print** - Masterband *n*
■ The final copy of a film or advertisement where sound, special effects, image and overprint has already been synchronised. It is a test copy used to check that other copies or advertisements in the media have been faithfully reproduced. Also called master and answer print.

**final product** - Endprodukt *n*
■ A product that has passed through all the manufacturing and quality control processes and is ready for shipping to the client.

**finished art** - Reinzeichnung *f*
■ A finished advertising piece which an agency creates and which is sent to the media so that they can reproduce it. It is also know as final art.

**firm sale** - Festverkauf *m*
■ A sale that cannot be cancelled or modified unless in the event of force majeure.

**first mover advantage** - First-Mover-Vorteil *m*
■ The lead, often unbeatable, which the first company of considerable size takes when entering a market.

**first time buyer** - Erstkäufer *m*
■ A ranking given to a customer and which classes them as newly acquired. In terms of relational marketing, this ranking is essential, since it is the moment when the creation of customer loyalty begins.

**first-hand** - aus erster Hand
■ Any article offered new for sale by a manufacturer or distributor, as opposed to second hand articles.

**five M's of advertising** - fünf Ms *n/pl* des Anzeigenentwurfs
■ These are the initials which stand for:
- Mission - What are the publicity objectives?
- Money - What amount can be spent?
- Message - What should be said?
- Medium - What medium should be used?
- Measure - How should the results be measured?

**fixed sampling** - feste Stichprobe *f*
■ A type of sampling classified according to the manner of determining sample size, which is predetermined. The most commonly used method, as opposed to sequential sampling.

**fixed-price sale** - Festpreisverkauf *m*
■ A sale in which the consumer or final price, and normally the distributor's margin is previously fixed by the manufacturer or the authorities (price regulation or control). It enables prices to be specified on containers and in advertising and is prohibited in certain sectors and countries.

**flank attack** - Flankenangriff *m*
■ A form of side attack in which the attacker concentrates on increasing a product range or offering smaller or larger variants within a product/market area in which his principal competitor is strong.

**flanker brand** - Flanker Brand *f*
■ A new product within a brand which already markets that product and which launches a new, slightly different version.

**flat fee** - feste Provision *f*
■ An amount charged according to fixed conditions, regardless of the extent of a transaction. Often applied to operations in which the work required does not depend on volume.

**flight** - Welle *f*

■ The period of time during which the advertisements of one campaign are concentrated and is preceded and followed by periods of inactivity. The purpose of a plan of this kind is to concentrate the advertising on the most suitable moments to achieve sales, rather than extending the publicity activity over relatively inactive seasons, something which could be considered a waste of resources.

**flighting** - Werbewellen *f/pl*

■ The method which places advertisements according to a media plan whereby a number of insertions are concentrated in short spaces of time and are separated by periods of inactivity.

**flipping** - Zapping *n*

■ A viewer reaction which consists of switching to another channel with the use of a remote control device to avoid commercials. The aforementioned practice is one of the reasons for the new TV advertising formulas which integrate advertising within audiovisual content. Flipping has reached a new dimension as a result of the launching of new recording devices (TiVo or Replay TV) which allow the user to skip the adverts.

**floor display** - Bodenausstellung *f*

■ A manner of presenting articles for sale by placing them directly on the floor or on a small stand. It is usually used for promotions in which large quantities of products are sold.

**floor-stand** - Bodenverkaufsständer *m*

■ A type of product packaging that also serves as a display stand. It can be placed on gondola ends, on store shelves or directly on the floor.

**flyer** - Werbeflyer *m*

■ A low-cost leaflet which is distributed by hand on the streets, in mailboxes, car parks and underground exits and other similar such places.

**focus group** - Fokusgruppe *f*

■ A group of approximately six to ten people who meet with a co-ordinator to freely exchange opinions about a product. It acts to detect the qualitative advantages and disadvantages of the studied product in relation to the competition (the groups are made up of consumers and non-consumers) which can later be quantified by means of a survey. It is also used for quick, low cost assessment of an advertising campaign.

**folder** - Faltprospekt *n*

■ A printed advertisement of four pages. It consists of a folded sheet and can contain information about conditions of sale and other related topics together with the advertisement.

**follower strategy** - Nachahmerstrategie *f*

■ A strategy based on the developing of new products by quickly and effectively copying the technological advances introduced by the market leader. Success depends on cost structure and production and distribution flexibility.

**follow-up** - Nachfassen *n*

■ An activity that comes after a launch or after carrying out another activity, for example the follow up to a sales visit can take the form of a thank you letter, the sending of an activity plan, or a telephone call that serves as a reminder.

**follow-up advertising campaign** - Nachfassaktion *f*

■ An advertising campaign which follows the previous one. The creativity in the advertisements may be consistent with or different to the first campaign, whilst the advertising investment is usually lower in this second campaign.

**follow-up message** - Follow-Up-Nachricht *f*

■ Message contact made with a client within a follow-up or memo campaign. It is usually used with clients who have not reacted to an initial message and serves to awaken their interest.

**follow-up report** - Follow-Up-Bericht *m*

■ A document periodically-prepared by the accounting department of an advertising agency in order to give a report to the advertiser on the development of a contracted campaign.

**foreign trade** - Außenhandel *m*

■ All the exchanges of goods and services made by one country with the rest of the world.

**forward integration** - Vorwärtsintegration *f*

■ The acquisition of a client or signing of a special collaboration agreement in order to guarantee sales possibilities in a key market segment. It is a vertical type of integration.

**four P's of marketing** - vier Säulen *f/pl*

■ The four variables which combine to make up the marketing mix: Product, Price, Position and Promotion. The shorter form "4 P's of marketing" is also used.

**fragrant ad** - aromatische Anzeige *f*

■ A graphic advertising message which includes some part or element which has been previously pervaded with a given scent or smell. Its a procedure which is commonly used in perfumery advertising in order to announce a new fragrance with a strip of paper or a sachet sample stuck to the advertisement.

**franchise** - Franchising *n*

■ A distribution technique based on the collaboration between a producer or a distributor (franchiser) and another distributor (franchisee). The franchiser grants the franchisee a commercial license and the right to sell their products under the brands, notoriety and image and all associated aspects such as technical, commercial and management assistance.

**franchise chain** - Franchise-Kette *f*

■ A chain of stores that share a common name and image and mutually undertake to supply each other from a buying centre at a national level and a distribution centre at a regional or wholesale level. Each store is owned by an independent person who can cease operating at any time. If the distribution centre belongs to store owners, it operates as a retail cooperative. A voluntary chain is more common in food and drug stores as well as traditional sectors, while franchise chains are used in modern sectors such as textiles, sound and film equipment. Equivalent to a voluntary chain.

**franchising** - Franchising *n*

■ The principle of concession of a trademark and business philosophy , as well as the legal and economic mechanism used to implement the system.

**franking machine** - Frankiermaschine *f*

■ A machine used to print special labels or postage costs on envelopes in order to avoid using stamps. The postal authorities save on printing stamps and companies save time.

**free advertisement** - Gratisanzeige *f*

■ An advertisement which is not charged by the medium where it will appear.

**free issue** - Gratisausgabe *f*

■ A publication which is distributed free of charge to make it known to potential customers or buyers.

**free market** - freier Markt *m*

■ A market structure in which the assigning of resources and establishing of prices is determined by supply and demand. Free markets are open, transparent and no purchaser or seller has a clear advantage

**free trial** - kostenlose Probe *f*

■ A promotional offer which allows customers to try a product or a service over a given period of time without any obligation to purchase.

**frequency** - Frequenz *f*

■ In advertising, the number of times that the people of a target group are "hit" by the insertions of a media plan. The average frequency is the result of dividing the total number of impressions by the number of people concerned. Frequency distribution is the relationship between all the people in a target group grouped according to the number of impressions which they have experienced during a campaign.

**frontal attack** - Frontalangriff *m*

■ A competitive move, whereby a company attacks the main sales outlet of his competitor. This technique should only be applied if the attacker has more resources than the competitor as he will defend himself with everything at his disposal.

**front-end** - Kassenzone *f*

■ The area in a shop where the products which are purchased compulsively and which tend to have high yield are placed.

**full column** - auf Seitenbreite

■ A news item or advertisement that occupies the entire width of a page in a magazine or newspaper, normally in the upper section in the case of a news item and in the lower section if it is an advertisement. In the event that it also occupies the entire length of the columns, it is called "full page".

**full-service agency** - Komplettservice-Werbeagentur *f*

■ An advertising agency specialising in all kinds of communication and which offers a global service including research, media purchase and even simple production, apart from the usual customer service and creation.

**funnel approach** - Funnel-Ansatz *m*

■ In research, a method used in the elaboration of questionnaires which consists of tackling the different topics from a broader and more general approach to a more concrete approach in order to reach the most specific aspect.

# G

**gatefold** - Fensterfalz *m*

■ A magazine advertisement that opens or folds outwards beyond the normal size of the magazine, generally used to promote luxury items where the advertiser is looking to create an impact.

**general advertising theory** - allgemeine Werbetheorie *f*

■ The discipline which tries to offer an objective, thorough, in depth, systematic, or in other words scientific, explanation as to how advertising communication works. Given the complexity and diversity of the elements under study it can be stated that, for the time being, it is a work in progress.

**general sales agreement** - allgemeiner Kaufvertrag *m*

■ An agreement between a supplier and a purchasing centre or individual client which regulates discounts on tariff prices (which the supplier can vary according to the market) during a certain period of time. This avoids the need to negotiate each operation or with each client. It regulates discounts granted in respect of quantity, volume, returns at the end of the year, advertising contributions, gondola ends, payments for broken items, and a system for ordering, reception and payment.

**generic** - generisch

■ A term used to define an article that may be offered by several suppliers without consumers being aware of the difference, either because it is sold in bulk quantities without a particular trademark, or under a white label or private label.

**generic advertising** - Gattungswerbung *f*

■ The advertising of a product or service category (for example, life insurance) without brands appearing. It is paid for by a group or sector of companies that often receive a subsidy.

**geographic segmentation** - geografische Segmentierung *f*

■ The classification of a population or group of individuals taking geographical criteria into account, generally where they live.

**geographical coverage** - geografische Abdeckung *f*

■ An area influenced by a published material or medium because of its distribution in copies (published material) or because it receives the signals sent by a broadcasting station (audiovisual media). The geographical coverage of media can be local, provincial, regional, national or international.

**geographical diversification** - geografische Diversifikation *f*

■ The action of seeking out new markets for the same product, technology or type of client. It is more an extension than a diversification.

**geomarketing** - Geomarketing *n*

■ The discipline or area of knowledge belonging to marketing which studies the commercial decisions related to the spatial aspects of consumption. Geomarketing actions are based on the psychographic resemblances that usually exist among the inhabitants of a common area (neighbourhood, residential district).

**ghost shopper** - Testkäufer *m*

■ A fictitious buyer that tests and compares the quality of services offered by a company and its competitors, acting as if he were a normal client.

**Giffen's paradox** - Giffen-Paradox *n*

■ The observation Robert Giffen made regarding the increase in demand of inferior goods when prices rise. They are essential items such as bread or potatoes, which represent the highest expenditure for poor families. When the prices of these products rise they are able to purchase less goods such as meat and, therefore they have to continue to consume the cheapest products, even though they have become more expensive.

**gift** - Geschenk *n*

■ A good or benefit received freely and voluntarily from another person or that is given to another with the intention of pleasing them.

**gift voucher** - Geschenkgutschein *m*

■ A document in the form of a cheque that is valid for making purchases up to a predetermined value in the establishment that issues it. It is often given as a present allowing the recipient to choose for themselves. Establishments sometimes issue them without receiving payment from a third party as a promotional instrument, as a discount for other purchases or as a refund instead of cash.

**gift-wrap** - Geschenkverpackung *f*

■ The use of special paper to package a purchased product. It sometimes involves a surcharge or the service may only be provided by a particular section which must be visited to receive the service on presentation of the receipt.

**gimmick** - Aufhänger *m*

■ A creative piece or resource included in a mail offer whose aim is to capture the interest of the addressee by attracting them to the offer by means of this novelty feature.

**GIS** - GIS *n*

■ A statistical software package used in geomarketing in order to choose the best location in which to set up a business enterprise.

**global advertising** - weltweite Werbung *f*

■ The advertising action carried out by a company or enterprise, usually a multinational corporation, to spread the same message in different countries.

**global marketing** - globales Marketing *n*

■ The consideration that a product's market is worldwide and that international consumer motivation and features are similar enough to allow proposals that differ only slightly from one country to another. Brand names, types of container and advertising campaigns may vary.

**gold standard brand** - Referenzmarke *f*

■ A brand whose product represents the standard of excellence in its market making other products fall beneath it, for example, Coca-Cola in the coke market and Nescafe in the instant coffee market. It has the best image among its competitors, it enjoys a higher price premium and distributors often sell it with lower profit margins, therefore it holds an insurmountable position over others.

**gondola** - Gondel *f*

■ In product marketing, an item of shop furniture comprised of several shelves used for storing products for display purposes, and which allows consumers to help themselves to the product directly.

**gondola end** - Fußende *n*

■ A privileged area at the end of a line of shelves located at a sales outlet, containing products to be promoted. It may be rented to a particular manufacturer interested in increasing its product sales.

**good** - Gut *n*

■ Any object or service that is perceived as capable of satisfying a need. They may be free goods or economic goods. From a legal point of view, it is everything susceptible to appropriation, and the corresponding rights pertaining to it.

**goodwill** - Firmenwert *m*

■ An intangible asset resulting from the absorption (or fusion) of a company at a higher price than its book value. It represents the value of an up and running business as opposed to a new business and is based on customer portfolio, brand awareness, and experience among other factors.

**gossip** - Klatsch *m*

■ Information or rumour, not necessarily false, that is used with the intention of damaging the image or reputation of a person or brand.

**grade of service** - Servicegrad *m*

■ In general, the percentage of orders fulfilled, with respect to quantity and delivery date. For example, in mobile telephony, the total number of calls that are not blocked within a network, thereby ensuring quality of service and customer satisfaction.

**graph** - Grafik *f*

■ A display of numerical data represented by one or more lines to indicate the relationship.

**graphic design** - Grafik-Design *n*

■ The discipline which consists of the development of original graphic projects and works such as posters, pamphlets, book covers or corporate visual identity elements that transmit audiovisual messages, generally for mass production and printing.

**graphic designer** - Grafikdesigner *m*

■ A professional in charge of designing graphic projects which transmit a message through audiovisual means such as posters, pamphlets, book covers, corporate stationery, packaging or signs on buildings.

**graphic rating scale** - grafische Beurteilungsskala *f*

■ The material used in questionnaires, which consists of giving the interviewees a graph where they can show their personal position regarding each attribute of a concept pointing out the adequate point on a scale.

**green market** - Ökomarkt *m*

■ The market composed of consumers who require eco-friendly products.

**grey market** - grauer Markt *m*

■ The market of original products without quality problems, operated by non-authorised intermediaries to attack an exclusive distribution system. For example, import operations carried out independently to those of an official importer and therefore with no advertising or after sales service expenses. Also referred to as a parallel market. Products are often sold at a lower price without a warranty, however they are not generally considered to be smuggled goods.

**gross audience** - Gesamtaudienz *f*

■ The sum of viewing figures of different media without taking into account duplications.

**gross coverage** - Bruttoabdeckung *f*

■ The number of impressions that a campaign produces in a target group. Many of these impressions are aimed at the same people and therefore, the gross coverage usually goes beyond the target group, sometimes to a great extent.

**gross impressions** - Gesamteindruck *m*

■ The number of impressions that a campaign produces in a target group.

**group product manager** - Gruppenproduktmanager *m*

■ A professional who reports to the marketing manager of a company and who supervises a given group of products and the work of the respective product managers. The organisation of products into groups is an alternative to that of brand groups, but similar in structure.

**growth-share matrix** - BCG-Matrix *f*

▪ A matrix designed by the Boston Consulting Group to classify the business units of a company group, according to expected sector growth (above or below a certain average, for example, 5%) and market share (dominant or not). The terms cow, star, question mark or dog give an initial understanding of the future of each business unit.

**guerrilla attack** - Guerillaangriff *m*

▪ A competitive action consisting of making small intermittent attacks on different opposition territories, with the aim of harassing and demoralising the opponent, and eventually securing permanent footholds. Instead of increasing market share the aim is to bring the price down and thereby reduce the competitors' profits in those markets that are most important to him.

**guerrilla marketing** - Guerilla-Marketing *n*

▪ An unconventional marketing strategy which seeks the best results with the minimum resources.

**guide to the interview** - Umfrageführer *m*

▪ In qualitative research, the list of topics which will be covered in an interview. The order of the topics and the formulation of the questions is left to the discretion of the interviewer.

# H

**half run** - halbe Auflage *f*

▪ The placing of an advertisement in fifty per cent of the copies of a publication. It usually coincides with those that are distributed in a certain geographical area. The price per insertion is higher than half the full price.

**half-page ad** - halbseitige Anzeige *f*

▪ An advertisement that covers half a page of a publication. If horizontally distributed, it is normally placed in the lower section and if vertical, at either end.

**half-page spread** - Halbseitenfüllung *f*

▪ In printed media, an advert whose height is half the page and whose width is double the page. It can be placed in the top part of a publication, in the centre, or at the bottom, which is more usual.

**halo effect** - Halo-Effekt *m*

▪ A phenomenon whereby a characteristic is so strong in an individual that it affects or modifies the impression obtained by other characteristics. It must be avoided, especially in consumer studies and in evaluation of personnel.

**handbill** - Handzettel *m*

▪ A low quality and cheap form of advertising printed on approximately one eighth of a page, used for brief and simple messages, that is manually distributed by hand, car or plane.

**hanger** - Hängeplakat *n*

▪ An advertising poster printed on both sides and often silhouetted which is hung from ceilings so it can move freely.

**hard selling** - Hard-Selling *n*

▪ The intensive promotional activity of a product in which the seller uses all the means available to try to sell the product, regardless of the purchaser's needs. Also known as high-pressure or aggressive selling.

**hard-discount store** - Hard-Discount-Markt *m*

▪ A self-service retail establishment which sells a very limited selection of mass market goods, formed basically by the brands of the distributor. Its prices are very economical, but it has no client oriented services.

**headline** - Titelzeile *f*

▪ The initial phrase of a printed advertisement with a font which stands out, normally of a bigger size than the body of the text, whose aim is to attract the readers' attention and encourage them to read the rest of the advert. In headlines all kinds of rhetorical resources are used in order to facilitate its attention-grabbing purpose.

**head-on location** - Frontalstandort *m*

▪ An advertising signpost or billboard which is placed facing head-on traffic. Its visibility conditions are higher than that of other directions, and so its price is also higher.

**hidden publicity** - versteckte Werbung *f*

▪ A type of publicity which causes confusion among consumers as to the type, origin and value of the advertising statements, despite their content being truthful. The public cannot identify the nature of this kind of publicity statement, because it doesn't recognise it as advertising, and is unaware that the statement comes from an advertiser. For this reason they give it higher credibility, as they do not see its advertising nature.

**high-involvement good** - High-Involvement-Produkt *n*

▪ A product whose purchase requires an important mental activity on the part of the eventual buyer due to its importance: for example, a house or a car. High-involvement goods require an essentially informative, emotion provoking, kind of publicity which corresponds to the relevance of the goods for their target public.

**hire purchase** - Ratenkauf *m*

▪ A type of purchase that allows immediate use of the goods acquired by means of periodical and predetermined partial payment of a principal amount and interest.

**hit** - Hit *m*

▪ On Internet, the measurement which counts all the elements of a page when it is requested by a user. One visit to a site can generate various hits, both for each page which is visited, and for the number of graphic files which each page may contain.

**hitchhike ad** - Sponsorenwerbung *f*

▪ In sponsored programmes, an advert for the product of the sponsor which is broadcast immediately after the programme so as to benefit from the feeling created and the brand association.

**holding power** - Haltekraft *f*

▪ The power of a television or radio programme to keep its audience viewing or listening until the end. It is calculated by comparing the audience at the beginning with the audience at the end of the programme.

**home selling** - Hausverkauf *m*

▪ A type of sales in which the seller personally visits a potential client, after having made previous contact. Different from door to door selling, which covers all potential buyers in a given area, without prior selection.

**hook advertising** - Angelhakenanzeige *f*

▪ An advertisement whose aim is to attract the consumer's attention by distributing a free sample or promising a gift.

**horizontal diversification** - horizontale Diversifikation *f*

▪ A type of diversification in which current clients are offered products that are not related to previous company activities.

**hot prospect** - Interessent *m*

▪ A person with a high probability of purchasing a product or contracting a service and whose intentions are generally declared by himself.

**house agency** - Hausagentur *f*

▪ The advertiser's advertising department , which fulfils the functions of an advertising agency, although sometimes it contracts other companies for special campaigns, especially creative or image based. They appear in only the biggest advertising companies, in particular retailers who have a lot of smaller campaigns.

**household** - Haushalt *m*

▪ A person or group of people that usually live together. It tends to coincides with a family nucleus (parents and children). As a unit, they have rights and obligations and they serve as the basis for certain marketing studies.

**households using television (HUT)** - Haushalte *m/pl* mit Fernseher

■ The number of homes in a panel which have their television turned on and are, therefore, supplying facts on the average audience. The panel is made up of a sample representative of the total national households. These homes have had audiometers installed which, in a semi-automatic manner, register details on the television's status (on or off), the use that is made of it and the number of persons who are in front of it. By extension, the total number of households with the television on.

**housewife time** - Hausfrauenzeit *f*

■ The hours during which a large part of a radio or television audience is made up of housewives, such as after lunch when soap operas are transmitted. It is the ideal time for advertising products such as detergents or high consumption cosmetics.

**hub transport system** - zentrales Transportsystem *n*

■ A process of transporting merchandise which consists of establishing a reference base from where products are transported to their destination points, with the transport vehicle returning each time to the base location once the merchandise has been delivered.

**Huff model** - HUFF-Modell *n*

■ The mathematic model for measuring the capacity of attraction that a commercial premises has over a consumer, based on the surface area of the premises and the time it takes the consumer to walk around the same.

**humorous style** - Humorstil *m*

■ An advertising form which appeals to the sense of humour of the receiver and so achieves an effect in favour of the advertised brand. Care must be taken that the humour reverts back to the product rather than the humorous situation itself.

**hypermarket** - Hypermarkt *m*

■ A store open to the general public with a large range of products, mainly food, household goods and textiles, normally organised on one floor with surface areas ranging from 2,500 to 10,000 m² and located on the outskirts of large cities. It sales are normally related directly to price.

**hypothesis** - Hypothese *f*

■ A guess or assumption that further research or events will either prove to be true or false.

# I

**IAA (International Advertising Association)** - IAA (International Advertising Association)

■ A worldwide association founded in 1938 and currently established in 96 countries which works in defence of the interests of advertising agencies and other marketing disciplines and the media in their role as advertising supports. It is a professional association and not sectorial and so it associates professionals of differing sectors. Its objectives are to promote the exchange of ideas among its associates and promote the exercise of commercial freedom before the international authorities.

**illegal advertising** - illegale Werbung *f*

■ A poster or other type of advertisement which has been published or placed without due authorisation.

**illuminated billboard** - Leuchtreklame *f*

■ An exterior advertising message, characteristic of urban areas, which has a lighting system incorporated into it so that it may be seen at night. This lighting system can be internal, such as on some specific street furniture features, or external such as on certain hoardings which receive illumination from a number of spotlights aimed at its surface.

**image advertising** - Imagewerbung *f*

■ An advertising activity whose aim is to create, maintain, reinforce or modify the attitudes and beliefs that a specific target public, or a section of society, have of the item concerned, whether that be a business, a product or a service, a cause or even an activity or sector.

**image audit** - Image-Audit *n*

■ The revision of the status of the corporate image of a company, organisation or institution, carried out by professionals outside the entity, and which consists of examining each of the variables that have an effect on the overall image (for example, the communications plan) so as to determine the necessary actions in each case.

**image campaign** - Image-Kampagne *f*

■ A programme which plans and coordinates the advertising actions carried out by a business, whose aim is to create, maintain, reinforce or modify the image that a specific public may have of it.

**image consultancy** - Imageberatung *f*

■ The business whose task it is to inform and advise other businesses on the actions which need to be taken to achieve, reinforce or maintain a positive image.

**image consultant** - Imageberater *m*

■ An independent professional or company whose function is to inform and advise a business on the actions which need to be taken to achieve, reinforce or maintain a positive image.

**image crisis** - Imagekrise *f*

■ The situation which is produced within a business when it has a negative or straying image: for example, when its target public knows the products but not the company behind them. This is generally preceded by an identity crisis.

**imitation** - Imitation *f*

■ The illegal use of a brand, product or design that differs from the original but is so similar that the consumer associates it with the original. It is not the same as a forgery in the strict sense because it doesn't try to convince the purchaser that it is an original, but it is still illegal because it takes over another's value. In general, the voluntary reproduction of a thing made to look like another.

**impact** - Wirkung *f*

■ The effect produced on public opinion by a publicity event or message.

**imperfect competition** - unvollkommener Wettbewerb *m*

■ A market situation in which some or all of the conditions necessary for the existence of perfect competition are not met.

**implementation** - Implantation *f*

■ The establishment or putting into effect of a plan or activity, including the direct actions involved and the studies that precede the carrying out of said actions. When used with relation to commercial premises, it encompasses the finding of those premises, space distribution studies, start up operations, etc.

**impression** - Eindruck *m*

■ A signal or mark that one thing leaves on another. In psychology, the "first impression" is an instant judgement or non-reflexive opinion that someone forms of a person or thing without having paused to reflect on goodwill or miscalculation.

**impulse** - Impuls *m*

■ A momentary and rapid excitement or feeling that impels one to do something or to cease doing something. An impulse purchase is one that is made without previously having made a decision to purchase, generally small value items bought on whim or staple items with a known brand.

**impulse buying** - Impulskauf *m*

■ A purchase which is not planned before entering the point of sale and which is made on seeing the product and its sale conditions (price, promotion, limited availability, form of payment or other).

**in bound** - Inbound *m*

■ In the area of telemarketing, the initial steps taken by a client or prospective client in order to contact the customer service department of a brand via telephone or electronic mail.

**in-and-out promotion** - Blitzwerbung *f*

■ The short duration advertising in a point of sale designed to provoke a rapid turnover of the product.

**incentives agency** - Motivationsagentur *f*

▪ A professional organisation which is in charge of the custom design and management of activities which stimulate the team spirit of a company or organisation through trips, prizes, conventions and special events.

**incidence** - Inzidenz *f*

▪ In market research, the frequency with which an event occurs in a group. The percentage of the population which is included in the group when specific selection criteria are used. A more selective criteria gives way to smaller and homogenous groups, whilst less selective criteria gives way to bigger and heterogeneous groups.

**inclination** - Zuneigung *f*

▪ Propensity, affection or love towards a thing. It is a natural psychological and more or less irresistible tendency.

**income effect** - Einkommenseffekt *m*

▪ The variation in the demand of a product as a result of changes in the level of disposable income. A good is said to be inferior when rises in income produce a reduction in demand (for example, chicory). If the opposite is true then it is a normal or superior product.

**income segmentation** - Segmentation *f* nach Einkommen

▪ The grouping of consumers according to their personal or family income.

**Incorporated Society of British Advertisers (ISBA)** - Incorporated Society of British Advertisers (ISBA)

▪ A British association of advertisers whose purpose is to defend the interests of its associates in the commercial communication field in Europe. Founded in the year 1900, it currently has 300 associated companies.

**incremental analysis** - Inkrementalanalyse *f*

▪ A study of the increase in the amount of public reached by a campaign as advertising investment is increased.

**independent trader** - unabhängiger Handelsbetrieb *m*

▪ An establishment whose owner is not a member of an association. They made trade alone without the support of a particular supplier, or join a voluntary franchise group.

**in-depth interview** - freies Vorstellungsgespräch *n*

▪ An interview in which the interviewer allows interviewees to speak freely without asking them questions and only prompting. Also referred to as a free interview, and the opposite of a guided interview, in which interviewers ask specific questions. Useful for preliminary research phases.

**indirect advertising** - indirekte Werbung *f*

▪ The advertising of a brand which notoriously characterises a product subject to restricted advertising, for example, alcohol or tobacco, but applied to a completely different product, such as nuts and dried fruit or sports goods. Its purpose is to increase brand recognition on the product which is subject to restricted advertising, rather than to sell the other product.

**industrial goods** - Industriegut *n*

▪ Goods used in the production of other goods. For example, machinery, tools, and raw materials. Not designed for individual consumption, they require specific marketing techniques.

**industrial marketing** - Industriemarketing *n*

▪ Marketing that specialises in company to company sale of industrial products where importance is placed on technical specifications, reliability and guarantee of supply, as well as quality control, in addition to good business relations at different levels.

**industrial partner** - tätiger Teilhaber *m* ohne Kapitaleinlage

▪ A person that contributes services and professional or technical know-how to a company, instead of capital, in exchange for a share of future profits.

**industrial property** - gewerbliches Eigentum *n*

■ Special property rights acquired personally by either the inventor or discoverer of a product or machine that give the right to exclusive exploitation of the product for industrial or commercial purposes, either directly or by cession to third parties. The scope of these rights includes other signs of personal rights such as a name or trade mark.

**inelastic demand** - inelastische Nachfrage *f*

■ Demand that does not respond to price changes. The consumer is indifferent to changes in the price of the product and will consume the same quantity.

**inertia selling** - Zusendung *f* unverlangter Ware

■ A sale which is carried out automatically, unless the client specifically indicates that it doesn't want to purchase. This is the classic sales method used by book clubs.

**inferior good** - inferiores Gut *n*

■ An essential good whose demand grows with the increase in price because consumers do not have the income necessary to buy superior goods of greater value and, and thus, have to consume more of what continues to be cheaper, as the Giffen paradox explains. Also called Giffen goods.

**in-flight publication** - Flugwerbung *f*

■ The advertising which is designed to be freely distributed among the passengers of an air line. Its capacity for discrimination is high, and such a situation is taken advantage of by advertisers in order to insert campaigns aimed at the reader, such as relating to hotels, trips, restaurants or products for companies.

**infomercial** - Infomercial *n*

■ A graphic advert which takes the form of a report or documentary. It can take up more than one page of a newspaper or magazine and uses as a basic element, verbal argumentation styles, whether accompanied by images or not.

**informal communication** - informelle Kommunikation *f*

■ The social interaction through messages transmitted through un-official channels. It mainly concerns interpersonal, spontaneous communication known as word of mouth.

**information power** - Informationsmacht *f*

■ The power sustained by the capacity of an organisation to provide useful information to another. If the latter wants access to said information, it must allow itself to be influenced to a certain extent by the former. It is currently one of the most important sources of power, due to the high need for information that companies have if they want to make effective marketing decisions.

**informative advertising** - informative Werbung *f*

■ Advertising that transmits basic information about the product. It is often used in the launching phase, in order to build initial demand. This advertising promotes awareness of a new product available in the market.

**inherent drama** - Drama *n*

■ A creative philosophy, emotional in nature, developed by Leo Burnett, which maintains that the best form of achieving efficiency in advertising messages is to invent dramas (or representations of dramas) that interest and move consumers, whether they are based on the very history of the brand or emerge directly from the product. To this end, brand personalities should be created wherever possible, who embody the stories, such as the Marlboro cowboy or the Kellogg's mascots.

**inherited audience** - mitgeschlepptes Publikum *n*

■ The part of an audience of a radio or television programme that remains listening or watching the screen as a follow on from the previous programme. If the new programme is not to their liking, they will turn it off and eventually be partially or totally substituted by those interested in the new programme. The start of any programme which follows on from another with a high audience can count on a high percentage of inherited audience.

**in-home audience** - Zuhausepublikum *n*

▪ The group of persons who expose themselves to the media of the home. This can be audiovisual or printed media. Occasionally a higher qualitative significance is given to in-home audiences than to audiences in other locations.

**in-house magazine** - Hauszeitschrift *f*

▪ A form of public relations action consisting of a periodical publication aimed at the internal public of the organisation. It is a reciprocal communication instrument between the company and its employees and has a double function being both informative and integrating. It aims to inform the personnel of the organisation about social, economic and technical themes which affect them, as well as creating and strengthening a sense of purpose in the company which tend to make them more favourable towards it.

**in-line display** - Inline-Display *n*

▪ A display designed to be placed on the shelves of the gondola ends in points of sale.

**innovation** - Innovation *f*

▪ In marketing, the development of a product, process or service in a different form to that already in existence.

**inputs and outputs table** - Eingangs- und Ausgangs-Tabelle *f*

▪ A matrix for each industrial sector that indicates the percentage of sales directed at other sectors, such as raw materials or semi-finished products and products that go to the final consumer. Purchases from other sectors and the additional value that they create are also included in the table. It is used to study the sectorial interrelations and to see the effects produced by a variation in demand in a sector or field of activity. It was invented by Leontieff.

**inquiry** - Anfrage *f*

▪ In direct marketing, the reply to a commercial offer consisting of requesting more information on the advertised product or service, without any obligation to buy.

**instalment sale** - Ratenverkauf *m*

▪ A credit sale in which part payments are established at regular intervals, normally monthly or quarterly. Amounts are often constant and include interest charges as well as principal amortisation (French method).

**institutional advertising** - Institutionelle Werbung *f*

▪ A persuasive communications action in public relations, with an advertising style and manner, which refers to a company, institution, association or group and which aims to achieve acceptance and support from its public for the individual or legal entity to which it refers. Although, in general, it is used as a synonym for corporate advertising, some authors differentiate it from that term, relating it instead to the persuasive communication aimed at the public, transmitted by the institutions and government agencies.

**in-store merchandising** - Werbung *f* im Geschäft

▪ The design, organisation and activities carried out in the interior of a commercial establishment with the purpose of making it more attractive to the consumer and thus increasing its sales, especially with regards to cheaper goods.

**integrated commercial** - integrierte Werbung *f*

▪ An advertisement in which two or more products or services, or two or more brands, of the same or different manufacturers are included. It is also used to refer to an advertisement which is inserted within a programme instead of in a commercial break, in which case it usually concerns products which the very actors of the programme wear, use or consume and for which the name of the brand is clearly shown. The price for this kind of advertising is not listed and is the result of an agreement between the producer of the programme and the advertiser before performance.

**integrated marketing communications (IMC)** - integrierte Marketingkommunikation *f*

■ An increasingly more creative discipline whose purpose is to integrate the different communication activities carried out by a company or institution, from the same perspective, whether they are designed to promote the sale of the goods or services (marketing communication) or to manage the corporate image (corporate communication). It covers, among others, advertising, sales promotion, marketing and public relations. Said perspective has been taken on to a large extent by communications groups which have appeared as a result of their transformation from the old service agencies. Occasionally referred to as global communications.

**intensive distribution** - Intensivvertrieb *m*

■ A policy that endeavours to place a determined product in as many outlets as possible. Used for mass market goods and normally by means of wholesalers.

**interactive** - interaktiv

■ A term used to describe those advertising media which require the receiver of the advert to do something more than just merely read or listen to the communication for it to take place. The ultimate interactive media, although not the only one, is the Internet.

**interactive agency** - interaktive Agentur *f*

■ An advertising company specialised in offering advertising services for interactive media, such as the Internet.

**interactive display** - interaktives Display *n*

■ A display which requires the participation of the consumer in the sales process by providing information on his needs and preferences through the use of a computer keyboard or touch screen. The computer processes the information and offers a purchase recommendation.

**internal marketing** - internes Marketing *n*

■ The application of marketing principles within a company. The workers are considered to be consumers and so the company must know their needs and adopt the measures necessary to motivate them and improve their production. This way, the complete organisation will be focused on the market and the results will be optimum.

**internal reference price** - interner Referenzpreis *m*

■ The price that the consumer hopes a product will have and against which he compares the sales price. It is the price the consumer stores in his memory and considers to be just and right to pay for such a product.

**internal validity** - interne Validierung *f*

■ In commercial research, the process to which obtained information is subjected in order to verify that it is related to already existing data considered to be true by the company. In the case of a discrepancy, it is necessary to find the origin of the error and which data should be modified.

**international advertising** - internationale Werbung *f*

■ The advertising activity carried out by a company or entity to be spread throughout the media of more than one country, thus reaching new markets.

**international advertising agency** - internationale Werbeagentur *f*

■ An advertising company which carries out its activity in a number of countries. The internationalisation process of the agencies began in the 1920s in the United States and has been expanding progressively until its current status which covers all the world, in response to the growth of its multinational clients.

**International Association of Advertising (IAA)** - International Association of Advertising (IAA)

■ The only international organisation which covers agencies, advertisers, communications media and related services.

It acts as an international forum with the aim of promoting the beneficial paper of advertising in society, as well as the development of commercial communications media. It has its seat in New York and currently carries out its activities in 95 countries.

**International Association of Business Communicators (IABC)** - Internationaler Verband *m* für Geschäftskommunikation (IABC)

▪ An International Association of public relations professionals created in 1970 and with its seat in San Francisco, which aims to be a network for professionals who encourage their members to improve the efficiency of the strategic management of communications within their organisations.

**international brand valuation** - globale Markenbeurteilung *f*

▪ A study which measures the global value of the primary brands of the main countries in accordance with different parameters: sales, profitability, seniority, and continuity in the market, communications policy, growth potential, perceived quality, presence in consumers' minds and other similar such parameters. The most well-known studies are those carried out by Interbrand and Landor.

**International Congress and Conventions Association (ICCA)** - Internationaler Kongress- und Tagungsverband *m* (ICCA)

▪ The international association which unites national groups of organisations specialised in conferences and conventions, whether public or private in nature.

**International ECHO Awards** - internationaler ECHO-Award *m*

▪ The prizes which are awarded each year by the North American Direct Marketing Association (DMA) to the best international direct marketing campaigns.

**international marketing** - internationales Marketing *n*

▪ A type of marketing which is applied when different transnational exchanges take place, i.e. between two or more nations. The intense development of transport systems and new information technologies have caused an increase in international marketing. The ways to enter foreign markets, the current regulations in transactions and sociocultural values are important aspects to be considered by the companies which are looking for or have overseas clients.

**International Public Relations Association (IPRA)** - International Public Relations Association (IPRA)

▪ An international association of public relations professionals and researchers founded in London in 1955 with the aim of creating a channel of international exchange of ideas and experiences between public relations professionals as well as developing and publishing research and holding meetings and conferences to promote the knowledge of public relations practices at an international level.

**Internet advertising** - Internetwerbung *f*

▪ The advertising activity which uses the Net for its transmission, whether through advertising spaces specifically created for that purpose, for example banners, or through the creation of its own website.

**interruption marketing** - Interruption-Marketing *n*

▪ A traditional method for attracting consumers' attention through advertisements which interrupt the person's activity so as to redirect his attention to the advertised goods or services (adverts which cut into television programmes or films, adverts which interrupt the reading of an article in a magazine or newspaper, or advertising which floods mailboxes, among others). This traditional method of advertising contrasts with the current consent marketing.

**interstitial ad** - Zwischenanzeige *f*

▪ In Internet advertising, an advert which appears between two pages of content. If a user clicks on a link to go to another page, the interstitial ad will appear before connecting to the next page. The optional advertisement appears during idle time and when its icon is clicked.

**introduction town** - Einführungsstandort *m*

■ The town in which the opening of a business unit of a chain takes place.

**introductory offer** - Einführungsangebot *n*

■ A marketing tactic in which part of the product or service margin is sacrificed in order to take the form of a gift or an additional discount so as to make the offer more attractive, converting it into a hook for capturing new clients.

**introductory price** - Einführungspreis *m*

■ A price fixed for a new market in which a company wishes to launch a product previously launched in other areas. It is usually slightly lower in order to favour initial sales, although a skimming strategy may also be adopted.

**intrusive advertising** - aufdringliche Werbung *f*

■ The advertising messages which are introduced into an already established space (a radio or television programme, or newspaper or magazine page, or mailbox) with the aim of benefiting from the attention the receiver was already giving to such space. In contrast to this intrusive method of traditional advertising is the rise of the current advertising method which requests the receivers permission before sending them messages, within the framework of the new consent marketing whose main medium is electronic mail. In contrast to the unrequested sending of direct advertising are the Robinson lists.

**involuntary attention** - unbeabsichtigte Aufmerksamkeit *f*

■ The type of attention given to the majority of adverts. Despite a lack of interest, the advertisement produces an effect, even if this is over time and after repeated hits.

**island display** - Inselanzeige *f*

■ An individual display, usually large in size, which can be accessed and viewed from all directions (360º).

**isolated advertisement** - isolierte Anzeige *f*

■ An advertisement with a higher fee which assures the advertiser that no other publicity will be placed next to his.

**itemized rating scale** - Antwortskala *f*

■ In a questionnaire, the kind of question in which the interviewees are asked to express their reply by indicating on a previously prepared scale which position better reflects their opinion on the subject matter of the question.

**itinerant display** - Wanderanzeige *f*

■ An advertising poster placed on a mobile stand which changes place using a predefined route. It generally contains advertisements on both sides.

**itinerant sale** - Wandergewerbe *n*

■ A sale made outside a commercial establishment, normally from a truck or van, in rural areas. Often carried out without the required permit.

**itinerary** - Befragungsweg *m*

■ A randomly established route to be followed by an market research interviewer in order to guarantee a randomly selected group of interviewees, departing from one or more points in a neighbourhood and establishing streets, houses and apartments blocks to be visited. In the case of sales people the term route tends to be used.

# J

**jingle** - Erkennungsmelodie *f*

■ A brief and light musical interlude that is heard repeatedly during an advertising message that helps to identify and remember the advertisement in question as well as giving it some meaning.

**Johnson box** - Johnson-Box *f*

■ The head of text positioned within a box at the beginning of a letter to highlight the main message and call the reader's attention to the contents of the same. It is named after the creator of this concept in direct marketing.

**judgement sampling** - Selektivauswahl *f*

■ A type of non-probability sampling in which subjects are subjectively chosen (for example, experts or people that previously responded in a particular way). It is suitable for detailed studies and those that mainly require qualitative conclusions.

**junk mail** - unerwünschte Werbung *f*

■ A derogatory term for promotional mail, especially when poorly designed or inappropriately addressed. Often thrown away without being opened. The rate of response to this kind of mail can be less than one in a thousand.

**just in time** - just-in-time

■ A production and stock management system that minimises stock levels as needs are planned exactly and an exceptional level of service is obtained from suppliers. Suppliers, using the same system, may make several deliveries a day as serving a client from a large central warehouse may not result in significant financial savings. The merchandise arrives at the place where it is to be used at precisely the right moment.

# K

**Key Performance Indicator (KPI)** - Key Performance Indicator *m* (KPI)

■ The criteria in relation to which the quality of a service provided by a company is evaluated. In logistics, it is usually used as an indicator of the compliance with delivery deadlines and breakage of the merchandise.

**keyword** - Schlagwort *n*

■ On the Internet, the group of characters which a user introduces in a search engine or a site to look for information. A common advertising technique is that the advertiser's banner appears when the user searches using a particular keyword.

**keyword marketing** - Schlagwort-Marketing *n*

■ On the Internet, the marketing activity whose purpose is to sell keywords in search engines.

**kicker** - Anreiz *m*

■ A quality or condition that makes a product particularly attractive and enables the quick closure of an agreement. It is used, above all, on the financial products market and may consists of an interest rate ceiling or floor, an exchange opportunity, conversion, special depreciation or greater liquidity in certain circumstances.

**KITI (Keyword integrated text insertion)** - KITI (kennwortintegrierte Texteingabe)

■ The patented technology which allows the client to appear at the top of the list of search results. The client's slogan appears in blue with a direct link to its URL. Due to its more informative than advertising appearance it is very profitable.

**knock-out price** - Räumungsverkaufspreis *m*

■ A very reduced sale price in order to sell off a product, either to finish with a certain product line due to the launch of another or because of a change in or closure of the business.

**know-how** - Fachkenntnis *f*

■ The collection of specialised knowledge and practical techniques which allow the efficient development of a process, differentiating it from the market average. As it implies an added value it can be marketed and the object of a know-how transfer contract, which is more global and practical than a technology or technical assistance transfer contract.

# L

**label** - Etikett *n*

■ A piece of paper or fabric attached to a product for identification purposes. It normally includes the brand, the name and address of the manufacturer, health or industrial certifications, a list of ingredients and additives, sell-by date or use-by date, packaging date and batch number, recommendations on use, weight or volume, size, colour, etc. Original designs and drawings are normally used to help identify the product category and in recollecting the brand.

**latitude of price acceptance** - Spielraum *m* der Preisannahme

■ The range of prices which are found between the maximum price a consumer is willing to pay for a product and the minimum price below which the consumer loses trust in the quality levels of a product.

**launch** - Einführung *f*

■ The process of introducing a new product or service on the market, usually accompanied by an advertising campaign. The elements of the marketing mix (product, pricing, place, and promotion) must be carefully planned and prepared before the launch starts. Internal marketing of the product, including training and motivation of the sales force, is also very important.

**launch price** - Produkteinführungspreis *m*

■ The price that is fixed for a new product. If it is launched in a new market it is called the introduction price. If it is accompanied with a new package design, label, product formula or communication strategy then it is referred to as the re-launch price.

**law of demand** - Nachfragegesetz *n*

■ A law of economics which states that the demand for a good is inversely proportional to its price. The higher the price, the lower the demand and vice versa.

**law of large numbers** - Gesetz *n* der großen Zahlen

■ A statistical law that enables forecasts based on observed behaviour of large groups, according to which the overall movements of large groups tend to be the same.

**law of supply** - Angebotsgesetz *n*

■ A law of economics which sates that the supply of a good is directly proportional to its price. The higher the price, the higher the supply and vice versa. In certain cases there can be a regressive supply, for example, if a farmer panic sells in fear of a substantial price drop, or a worker who decides to work less upon reaching a certain level in his career.

**law of supply and demand** - Gesetz *n* von Angebot und Nachfrage

■ A law of economics which states that the price of a particular good is obtained from the interaction between supply and demand, and it is that which makes the amount supplied equal the amount demanded on the market.

**leading brand** - Führermarke *f*

■ A brand which controls the market of a certain category of products and achieves the highest market share.

**leading product** - führender Artikel *m*

■ A product with a relatively high market share that is easily recognised by consumers and is used by the manufacturer to stimulate sales of other products in the same product family. Sales forces and publicity concentrate on these products which, to a large degree, determine the manufacturer's image and profit.

**leading question** - Suggestivfrage *f*

■ A question which contains an implicit answer. It should be avoided so that a bias does not appear in the information collected.

**leaflet** - Diptychon *n*

■ An advertising brochure usually folded in half or in three.

**letterpress ad** - typografische Anzeige *f*

■ An advertisement whose text is composed by the same newspaper in which it appears. It is not usually used in large scale advertisements, which are composed in their entirety by the agency, but it is very common in classified ads.

**lettershop** - Agentur *f* für Direktmailing

■ In direct marketing, the company dedicated to the manipulation, classification and sending of large amounts of commercial packages, taking charge of folding the pieces and putting them in envelopes as well as stamping them in a generally automated process.

**lexicalization** - Lexikalisierung *f*

▪ A language phenomenon whereby the name of a specific brand becomes generic in relation to the particular category of goods the brand belongs to. It occurs when the brand is the inaugurator of the category or the market leader. Classical examples are Hoover, for vacuum cleaners; Sellotape, for adhesive tape; or Tipp-Ex, for correction fluid.

**license** *v* - lizenzieren *v*

▪ To grant an official permission to use a determined manufacturing or marketing process that is normally patented, within a geographical area in exchange for a license fee or royalty. This is a rapid method that avoids international red tape, but may involve a substantial investment in transferring and controlling know-how, given that licensees' interests often collide with those of the licenser.

**license agency** - Lizenzagentur *f*

▪ A company which specialises in managing the assignment of licenses for the use of patented characters from cartoon strips or animated films for promotional or advertising purposes. It acts as an intermediary between the owner of the license and the interested advertiser. The price for the license is directly proportional to the character's popularity and the intended use of the same.

**life-span** - Lebensdauer *f*

▪ The display life of a promotional advertising element. The life-span will determine the type and quality of the materials used in the manufacturing process.

**lifestyle** - Lebensstil *m*

▪ The set of characteristics (social relationships, culture, consumption habits) that define a group of people (social classes, urban or rural environment). In advertising, a term used to describe advertisements for brands that are based on the lifestyles pursued by a target audience.

**lifestyle targeting** - Lebensstil-Aufteilung *f*

▪ The manner of defining target groups in accordance with lifestyles, such as activities, preferences or use of leisure time, as opposed to the traditional manner of using sociodemographic variables such as sex, age, social class or population density of the area where the people live.

**LIFO** - LIFO

▪ This initials for Last In First Out - a stock valuation system in which the last product to enter is the first to leave the warehouse. In inflationary periods, the LIFO process results in undervalued stock, thereby producing lower operating profits than the system First In First Out (FIFO), though higher than under the Next In First Out (NIFO) method.

**Likert scale** - Likert-Skala *f*

▪ A scale that facilitates response to questionnaires, by previously defining levels, normally from 1 to 5, although also from 1 to 3 and 1 to 7. 1 normally means to disagree completely and 5 to totally agree. The scale is sometimes based on even numbers in order to promote a specific response.

**line-filling** - Ergänzung *f* der Produktlinie

▪ An activity designed to extend a company's product line within the same range by including different sizes or features. For example, a company that sells 5 kg packets of biscuits and decides to offer packets of 1kg and 2kg.

**line-stretching** - Erweiterung *f* der Produktlinie

▪ An activity designed to increase a company product line to include ranges either above or below their current line in the market, for example a company producing small computers extending their range to include lap-top computers.

**liquidation sale** - Räumungsverkauf *m*

▪ A type of discount sale in which final stock of a certain season or range of products is reduced in order to sell everything. It could coincide with the closure or sale of a business.

**list** - Liste *f*

■ In direct marketing, the list of entries corresponding to clients or potential clients of a good or service. The list is one of the main elements of all direct marketing actions.

**list broker** - Listenverteiler *m*

■ A person or entity in charge of marketing client and potential client lists, whether independently or on behalf of a third person, acting in this last case as an intermediary.

**list building** - Listenerstellung *f*

■ A term used in direct sales for the selection and development of a list of names and addresses that may provide a more appropriate response to certain products or services.

**list maintenance** - Listenwartung *f*

■ The continuous cleaning and updating process of the data contained in a list so as to avoid duplication and obsolescence.

**list price** - Listenpreis *m*

■ A publicly fixed price by a supplier and from which agreed discounts may be deducted.

**list renting** - Miete *f* von Adressenlisten

■ In direct sales, the payment for the use of a list of names and addresses that are considered of value in a particular operation. It may or may not include the right to specific details of the list and later use.

**local advertising** - Lokalwerbung *f*

■ The advertising carried out by a company for distribution on media supports throughout the city or region where its activity is located or where it wishes to strengthen a national campaign.

**local advertising agency** - lokale Werbeagentur *f*

■ An advertising company which carries out its activity in a local area or region.

**location strategy** - Standortstrategie *f*

■ The criteria, parameters and procedures used by a company to situate outlets such as stores, bank branches or fast food restaurants. When analysing potential sales, a study is carried out on the target public, purchasing power, location of nearby company and competitor outlets, as well as available premises, size, prices and the advantages of leasing or buying.

**logo** - Logo *n*

■ An abbreviation commonly used to refer to logotype.

**logotype** - Logotyp *m*

■ The visual identifier of a brand. It is frequently confused with the term brand, which covers more intangible aspects. In specialised media, it is used to name the typographical elements of a brand, whilst symbol is used to designate the graphic elements, and the fusion of the two is known as the combination logo.

**London International Advertising Awards** - London International Advertising Awards

■ The advertising design and creativity awards founded in 1985 to foster creative advertising. Prizes are awarded to television, radio, cinema, graphic media, package design and interactive advertising.

**loss leader** - Lockangebot *n*

■ An object or good sold at a very low price, possibly below purchase price, in order to bring clients in. Also known as a crowd puller or customer puller, although these terms can be used for products that attract for reasons other than price, such as exclusivity, better quality etc.

**loss of purchasing power** - Kaufkraftverlust *m*

■ The reduction in one's capacity to acquire goods due to inflation or fluctuations in the rate of exchange, when one speaks of a currency comparing it to the same currency or to another currency in another time period.

**lot** - Posten *m*

■ A quantity of materials purchased, produced or sold as a unit at any given time. A lot may include items that are the same (hourly production of a machine), similar (books) or different (promotional items for different products).

**lovemark** - Lovemark *f*
■ The philosophy created by the agency Saatchi & Saatchi which aims to introduce a brand into the heart of culture, creating feelings of love and respect for the same in people. Some examples are: Lladro porcelain, Ferrari cars and Harley Davidson motorbikes.

**loyalty** - Treue *f*
■ Faithfulness towards a particular brand, product or idea, even if it is not locally available or more expensive than other substitutes. Identifying loyal consumers helps to define target markets.

**loyalty marketing** - Kundenbindung *f*
■ A characteristic of a marketing strategy which is conceived and put into place with the aim of gaining consumer confidence in a product, a service, a brand or a point of sale and promoting their loyalty to the same.

**loyalty scheme** - Bonuspunkte *m/pl*
■ A promotional technique aimed at achieving repeat purchases and through which the client obtains points which can be accumulated and redeemed against some sort of incentive or gift. A typical example are airline company promotions which award points for each trip taken, which later take the form of a free ticket to the destination the accumulated points allow.

**LTF (life time value)** - Customer Lifetime Value *m*
■ In database marketing, the measurement ratio of the investment made in one client by a company, not in the short term but rather over the course of his life or duration as a client. It is a commonly used ratio in the insurance sector.

**lucrative advertisement** - kommerzielle Werbung *f*
■ A publicity message whose aim is to satisfy a lucrative purpose. The broadcasters are businesses or entities who try to promote their goods or services or their image.

**luminous ad** - Leuchtanzeige *f*
■ An external advertising message characteristic of urban areas, built with fluorescent tubes (usually neon) for positioning on the upper part of buildings or commercial premises. The light can be fixed or flashing and may use a variety of colours to set a simpler message, in the form of a sign, composed of just the brand, or a more complex message including an advertising slogan or an illustration of the product.

**luxury good** - Luxusgut *n*
■ A product whose demand increases at a higher rate than the increase in buying power of the purchaser and which is an indicator of belonging to a privileged social minority.

# M

**M2B (mobile to business)** - Mobil *n* für Geschäft
■ A business model which consists of electronic commerce conducted by mobile phone.

**mail bombing** - Mail-Bombing *n*
■ The indiscriminate and mass sending of messages with the aim of flooding an electronic mail box.

**mail questionnaire** - Briefumfrage *f*
■ In research, a self-administered questionnaire which is sent by mail. In many studies a mixed communication system is used, in which the interviewer personally delivers the questionnaire to the interviewee and gives him instructions on how to complete it and return it by mail.

**mail research** - Briefforschung *f*
■ In research, the study which uses the postal system for communication between the interviewer and interviewee. It is not used very often due to the low number of results it produces.

**mailing** - Direktwerbung *f*
■ In direct sales, communication by mail to a selected list of addresses without prior request by the addressee. The organisation can send it to their own clients, or contract a specialist company

with classified files corresponding to different criteria (geography, occupation etc.), and with automatic envelope stuffing and addressing systems, as well as reduced postage rate agreements.

**mailing pack** - Postsendung *f*

■ The term used to describe a package or complete piece created to advertise a service or a product to be sold by mail. It generally consists of an envelope, leaflet, order card and return envelope.

**mail-order advertising** - Versandwerbung *f*

■ Advertisements whose purpose is the promotion of goods which are marketed by any kind of distance selling. They usually contain a coupon for placing orders or a telephone number or e-mail address. The delivery of the product is done by mail or any other courier system.

**mail-order selling** - Versandhandel *m*

■ Sales in which a potential buyer receives promotional information on a product either in a magazine or sent directly to his home. Customer selection is based on random choice, previous purchase, membership to a particular club or association or credit card lists. Orders are normally sent and received by mail and paid cash on delivery.

**main advertisement** - Hauptanzeige *f*

■ The most important of a series of advertisements or entire publicity campaign. Although not necessarily the first that appears, it normally absorbs the most resources.

**maintenance campaign** - Aufrechterhaltung *f*

■ A media plan which consists of a low but constant investment with the aim of achieving hits on the target public which create a synergy with previous hits. It can be programmed in an isolated manner, but it usually precedes a high intensity campaign.

**major retail outlets** - Großverkaufsflächen *f/pl*

■ A generic term used to describe hypermarkets, large department stores and specialist shopping centres with surface areas exceeding 4,000 m2. Features include a wide range of products and periodical loss leader sales.

**makegood** - Ersatzanzeige *f*

■ The free insertion of an advertisement which occurs when the originally planned insertion did not take place or was produced with errors. In audiovisual media, this substituted advert should be transmitted at a time when the audience is similar in size and composition to that of the failed advert. Many stations opt for immediately repeating the advertisement if they find errors in its transmission.

**manufacturer store** - Fabrikverkauf *m*

■ A commercial establishment lacking in decorative and advertising elements, which belongs to the manufacturer of a product and from which he sells directly to the end consumer at reasonable prices.

**manufacturing to order** - Auftragsproduktion *f*

■ The manufacturing that begins when there is a definite commitment with a buyer. It is common with high value products or those that have characteristics that have to be adjusted to the specific needs of each buyer.

**margin** - Handelsspanne *f*

■ The difference between sales price and cost price. If only accumulated variable costs are considered, the term absorption margin is used. If depreciation is deducted, it is referred to as net margin (although taxes would also have to be deducted) and if not, gross margin. If only production costs are considered, the term industrial margin is used and if all costs are accounted for, it is called commercial margin which is equivalent to net margin. It may be expressed as a percentage (normally of sales price) or the difference in total amounts.

**marginal cost price** - Grenzkostenpreis *m*

■ The increase in total cost when production increases by one unit. The marginal cost curve can decrease at the beginning, but ends up increasing due to the law of diminishing returns. In a situation of perfect competition, maximum profit occurs when the market price and the marginal cost of a company are equal.

**mark up** *v* - den Preis heraufsetzen *v*

■ To fix margins per reference, group, section, etc., in order to obtain a suitable average gross margin as well as the necessary competitiveness. Sales price is established by applying mark-ups to cost prices, with the exception of loss leaders or rounding off in price points.

**markdown** *v* - Preis herabsetzen *v*

■ The reduction of public sale price of a good due to a special offer, end of a season or in order to liquidate stocks.

**marked price** - ausgewiesener Preis *m*

■ The price shown on merchandise in an establishment. In certain cases it is sufficient to show the price on a shelf.

**market** - Markt *m*

■ A place at which products are offered for sale, normally at regular intervals. Negotiations are regulated often by established custom. Communications technology developments have enabled markets in which goods are not required to be physically displayed. Market size depends on the number of people that need the product, possess the necessary resources to buy it and are willing to offer such resources in exchange, at a given price.

**market area** - Marktgebiet *n*

■ The geographic area in which a product or service is sold, ranging from a neighbourhood to the whole world. Some companies divide their market area into regions or zones, headed in descending order of size by a director, manager, area supervisor and sales representative.

**market area potential** - Marktgebietspotential *n*

■ An evaluation of sales possibilities in a specific area that can be defined geographically or by buyer segments.

**market control** - Marktbeherrschung *f*

■ A situation whereby a company can control the market of a product, and thereby determine its price and availability.

**market coverage** - Marktdeckung *f*

■ The percentage of clients visited by a sales force out of the total of potential clients. The percentage that buy the product is the numerical distribution.

**market development** - Marktentwicklung *f*

■ A marketing strategy which consists of directing a specific product developed by the company at new markets with the aim of increasing demand for the same. In order to do this the company looks for new uses for the product and new groups of consumers who could be interested in purchasing it.

**market gap** - Marktlücke *f*

■ A market need that is not satisfactorily covered, allowing a company with a competitive or original product, price or form of distribution to enter the market. It is a niche in a market that has not been fully exploited.

**market leader** - Marktführer *m*

■ A company or brand that has the largest market share of a determined product or service. It normally has the largest brand acknowledgement and in many cases, a high level of quality and price.

**market maturity** - Reifephase *f* des Marktes

■ The third phase of a product or market's life cycle, featuring stable sales and profits. Most products are in this phase. The most common marketing activities include: re-sectoring, brand repositioning, attempts to increase consumption per client, quality or presentation upgrading, distribution channels with greater reach and attack or defence in price wars.

**market niche** - Marktnische *f*

■ A market sector that is significantly different to others, due to a product's value for money, features, customers, distribution channels, parallel services or geographical area. The niche must be large enough and with sufficient potential growth to make the specialisation profitable without attracting, or at least limiting, the entry of competitors.

**market penetration** - Marktdurchdringungsstrategie *f*

▪ A strategy designed to increase product sales in current markets by means of a more aggressive marketing policy, for example, lower prices and greater publicity. Other strategies include new markets, new products or a combination of both, as part of a diversification plan.

**market permeability** - Marktdurchdringbarkeit *f*

▪ The possibilities that certain factors, such as publicity or promotions, might have of influencing a particular market. A market is considered to be more permeable if it is more easily influenced.

**market power** - Marktmacht *f*

▪ The capacity of an individual or a group of sellers or buyers to influence the price of a good or service on the market. The absolute absence of market power constitutes a necessary condition for the existence of perfect competition.

**market price** - Marktpreis *m*

▪ The price at which supply and demand are equalled. By extension it is the going market price, presuming a sale or purchase can take place at that price.

**market research** - Marktforschung *f*

▪ The compilation and analysis of information regarding the characteristics of a real or potential market with special emphasis on the following data: total volume; evolution; competitors' shares of market purchases and sales; numerical and adjusted distribution and the net participation of each brand; distribution channels and their methods of service, payment, tariffs and condition scales; competitors' strong points and weaknesses; input and output barriers; and sector divisions. Market research is complementary to consumer research.

**market segmentation** - Marktsegmentierung *f*

▪ The division of consumers into categories according to their buying habits in order to improve business strategy. Usually the different market segments have different ways of behaving, and it is necessary to develope different marketing tactics based on these differences in order to efficiently cover the entire market.

**market share** - Marktanteil *m*

▪ The percentage sales of a brand compared to the total sales in a market. It can refer to brand share or manufacturers share. Normally it is calculated by knowing the sales of a brand and estimating the total market. Market share is the equivalent of multiplying the balanced distribution by the net participation which in a certain measure shows the efficiency of the sales force and the respective marketing.

**market sharing** - Marktaufteilung *f*

▪ An agreement between many companies offering the same product that under normal conditions would be competing in the same market, whereby they divide a particular market geographically or according to distribution channels. In some cases the price is fixed and quotas are agreed.

**market sluggishness** - Marktagonie *f*

▪ A market situation featuring a lack of activity and reduction in prices.

**market study** - Marktstudie *f*

▪ The study and analysis of current or potential market information on a particular product, based on general features such as size, trends, sectors, competitors, distribution channels and consumer needs.

**market test** - Markttest *m*

▪ An action organised scientifically with the aim of estimating the success of a product and its marketing plan, including samples, store simulations, market surveys, etc. The investment in market tests depends upon the research budget, calendar pressures, launch risks, and expenses or investment in the product itself.

**market weighting campaign** - regional gestärkte Kampagne *f*

■ A campaign in which advertising pressure is increased in a particular region to a higher level than would correspond to it due to its population or sales. It responds to varying necessities, among which the fact that in such a region there is a higher sales potential, there are more efficient media supports or a temporary weakness has been detected in a key competitor. Local media are usually used to support the weight that the national media has in that area.

**marketing** - Marketing *n*

■ A science that studies consumers, identifies needs and searches for ways of satisfying such needs by creating business opportunities. The objective is to increase consumer satisfaction as well as company equity and not the consumption of a particular product. It covers a series of techniques grouped into different areas: market and consumer research, product and process innovation, market position studies, advertising, public relations, sales promotion, distribution, planning and control. More than just a company division, marketing is seen as a system of organising different company departments in relation to consumption.

**marketing audit** - Marketing-Prüfung *f*

■ The checking and evaluation of the actions carried out in a marketing plan. The market components, business objectives and commercial strategies are analysed in detail, systematically and periodically together with the study of the asset performance so as to check their correct functioning or detect deficiencies in their use. In this way, measures necessary to correct possible inefficiencies can be adopted.

**marketing flop** - Flop *m*

■ A product which does not achieve commercial success. It is estimated that 80% of all new products are marketing flops.

**marketing information system** - Marketinginformationssystem *n*

■ The set of people, equipment and procedures designed to collect, classify, analyse, value and distribute information required by marketing technicians. It consists of four sub-systems: internal data, marketing intelligence; marketing investigation; and marketing analysis.

**marketing management** - Marketing-Management *n*

■ One of the main management functions of a company, whose responsibility is to market the goods and services of the same, through market studies and forecasts, developing new products, brand management, price policies, delivery, sales and advertising.

**marketing mix** - Marketing-Mix *m*

■ The collection of marketing tools made available to the professionals who operate in the market. They have been grouped in four big sections: product, pricing, place and promotion. Advertising is contained within the promotion section and both its activity as well as its results are considered to fall within the general framework of marketing, without the need to separate it from the rest of the tools.

**marketing myopia** - Marketingmyopie *f*

■ The type of marketing management with a limited view over a short period of time, without taking into account the future evolution of events which can have a harmful effect on the business activity. It usually occurs when a company defines its business in terms of production instead of market orientation.

**marketing plan** - Marketingplan *m*

■ The planned activity of the marketing department of a company or group of products including sales and profit objectives and fixing of budgets required for the launch or withdrawal of products, publicity, promotions, pricing and distribution, etc.

**marketing public relations** - Marketing *n* für Public Relations

■ The use of public relations strategies and techniques to support marketing actions. The holding of a press conference or an event to present the new product for example. This does not imply that these are marketing or commercial actions. They are public relations techniques because they affect the image of the company and serve as a support to commercial actions such as advertising and promotion.

**marketing strategy** - Marketingstrategie *f*

▪ A document which gathers the basic principles that inspire the marketing plan, and the reasons for choosing these and not others, including among others: objectives to be reached, target public, product characteristics, position, price and distribution channels, communication plan and marketing budget. Deciding the best strategy for a product or service is the main task handled by the marketing department.

**marketing synergy** - Marketing-Synergie *f*

▪ An activity which consists of supporting a recently launched product or a product which is having difficulties on the market, with a more well known or successful product. It is also used to jointly support products which require each other for consumption, for example, when a brand of tonic is marketed together with a brand of gin.

**marketing to children** - Marketing *n* für Kinder

▪ A special kind of marketing which has emerged as a result of the reduction in the population of children in the majority of developed countries, which is a threat to those companies whose main activity is focused on that market segment, and which is aimed at satisfying children's needs and persuading those people who take part in the purchase decision making process of children's goods.

**marketing to the older consumers** - Marketing *n* für Senioren

▪ The result of demographic evolution which has lead the population segment corresponding to the elderly to grow considerably, with its corresponding business opportunities. For this reason, a specific area within marketing has been developed which is aimed at applying the general principles to this market segment.

**market-orientation** - Verbraucherorientierung *f*

▪ The philosophy that governs the activities of companies with advanced marketing systems, designed to constantly identify and even anticipate consumer needs, as opposed to companies that design and sell their own products or those produced by technological progress.

**MARKOR** - MARKOR

▪ A measurement scale which is used to respond to a series of questions from which it is possible to evaluate the degree of market orientation of a company. An acronym for market orientation.

**masked advertising** - Schleichwerbung *f*

▪ A type of deceptive advertising that hides commercial messages under an informative appearance.

**Maslow's hierarchy** - Maslow'sche Bedürfnispyramide *f*

▪ The scale of necessities according to Maslow, covering primary needs such as food and drink right up to complex needs such as social acceptance.

**mass communication** - Massenkommunikation *f*

▪ Social interaction through messages, which uses mass communication methods for the transmission of the same. It shouldn't be considered a communication aimed at the masses: this incorrect interpretation originates from the hypodermic needle theory whereby the audience is believed to be formed of individuals who act passively and irrationally to the messages they receive.

**mass media** - Massenmedien *n/pl*

▪ The communication channels that reach large audiences such as television, radio and magazines. In general, messages are not well segmented, however large coverage and efficiency is available for simple messages or important consumer goods.

**mass production** - Massenproduktion *f*

■ The production of large quantities of a product, normally carried out with specialised machinery and a large degree of job division. The product is uniform or has minor variations (colour, packaging, accessories, etc.). This type of production may or may not be carried out in a continuous series and is used for low cost products that do not have major design or personalisation requirements. It is the opposite of limited production.

**masterbrand** - Hauptmarke *f*

■ A brand which refers to all the products and services offered by a company. For example any car brand in relation to each model, together with its corresponding sub-brand.

**m-commerce** - M-Commerce *m*

■ Electronic commerce conducted via mobile phone.

**media** - Medien *n/pl*

■ The collection of material and human resources responsible for the distribution of news and information (such as the press, radio or television).

**media administration** - Medienverwaltung *f*

■ The service which some advertising agencies and all media agencies provide to advertisers which consists in investigating, contacting, negotiating, purchasing, invoicing and managing advertising space in the media and on behalf of the advertiser.

**media agency** - Medienzentrale *f*

■ An advertising agency specialised in offering research, planning and procurement of advertising space and time in the media. The media agencies have absorbed to a great extent these services which were previously carried out by full service advertising agencies.

**media analysis** - Medienanalyse *f*

■ The study of the different media in order to select those which are going to be most useful, efficient and cheap respectively for an advertising campaign. The choice lies mainly between mass and selective media.

**media broker** - Medien-Broker *m*

■ In Internet advertising, the agency which offers its advertisers up to date information on the frequency of consultation, number of hits and the users' profiles of the different sites where their advertising pages can be inserted, with the guarantee of achieving the desired impression. It acts on behalf of the advertiser, whereas the broker responsible for sales of advertising markets the space that the providers of the content create.

**media budget** - Medienbudget *n*

■ The part of an advertising budget used fro media inserts. Some years ago this made up 90% of the budget for conventional advertising with the remaining 10% used for production expenses, for example the production of films, but nowadays the proportion is 75/25.

**media buyer** - Medieneinkäufer *m*

■ In an advertising agency or media agency, the person in charge of the implementation of a media plan by contracting advertising space with the media or media supports.

**media buying** - Medienkauf *m*

■ The planning, reservation and purchase of the spots most appropriate for a specific advertising campaign in selected media. Normally carried out by an advertising agency or a specialised agency, under the supervision of the advertiser.

**media buying agency** - Medieneinkaufsagentur *f*

■ An advertising agency which specialises in the procurement of advertising space in the media for the insertion of adverts on behalf of another agency or advertiser. The commission paid is lower than that of full service agencies as its activity is limited to media. The media buying agencies appeared as a consequence of the necessity of advertising agencies to become associated so as to achieve better economic conditions from the media. Currently, almost all media buying agencies have become media agencies as they offer additional planning and research services. They sometimes offer advertising creation, and to this end they subcontract creative agencies.

**media buying club** - Medieneinkaufsgruppe *f*

■ A group of advertising companies which offers procurement of advertising spaces and time in the media in order to achieve better conditions through bulk buying.

**media buying service** - Medieneinkaufsdienst *m*

■ The service which media agencies provide to their clients and which consists in contracting, on behalf of the advertiser, advertising space in the media. This service includes all aspects of management, including payment.

**media consumption** - Medienkonsum *m*

■ The percentage of a population or target group which is exposed to the media for a limited amount of time. It is generally expressed in terms of exposure to the media over the last period: yesterday for daily media, television and radio; last week for supplements, weekly magazines and the cinema; the last fortnight for fortnightly magazines; and the last month for monthly magazines and the Internet.

**media plan** - Medienplan *m*

■ The organisation of publicity measures and vehicles to be used during a specific campaign, taking into account appearance dates, frequency, coverage and expense budget, etc.

**media planner** - Medienplaner *m*

■ In the media department of an advertising agency, the professional who arranges the media plans and who supervises their appearance.

**media planning** - Planung *f* der Werbemittel

■ The process of organising publicity measures and vehicles to be used during a specific campaign. The most important factors are: characteristics of the targeted public, coverage requirements and frequency in accordance with the message, available expense budget, and media being used by the competition. The planning stage is the intermediate stage between investigation and purchase of advertising means.

**media research** - Medienuntersuchung *f*

■ The compilation and analysis of information regarding the characteristics and costs of communications media with the aim of better planning and purchasing of media space.

**media support** - Medienunterstützung *f*

■ The use of advertising in conventional media as part of a marketing campaign.

**media translation** - Medienäquivalenz *f*

■ In a market trial, the process of identifying the media which would correspond to a geographic location immersed in a wider market, with the purpose of using them in the trial. In contrast, it is also the identification of media at a national level on extrapolating the data from a market trial.

**megamarketing** - Megamarketing *n*

■ The strategic coordination of economic, psychological, political and public relations factors for the purpose of achieving cooperation between a large number of allies and entering or operating in a particular market. It may be a necessary approach before entering a controlled market, in which the four P's of McCarthy would have to include two more: politicians and public opinion.

**memory test** - Erinnerungstest *m*

■ A test to which a corporate symbol is subjected to see if it is remembered or not. It consists in showing the symbol a number of times to a group of people together with other corporate symbols. At the end of the session those persons are asked to describe the symbols they recall.

**merchandise** - Ware *f*

■ Any consumer product that may be individually or collectively owned, therefore satisfying a human need and capable of being bought or sold. It is equivalent to consumer goods.

**merchandising** - Merchandising *n*

■ Any activity directed towards increasing the sales of goods through retail outlets. It is designed to show a product or service in a favourable light so that it will be purchased by the consumers, and includes advertising, point-of-purchase displays, guarantee seals, special sales and in-store promotion.

**me-too product** - Nachahmungsprodukt *n*

■ A product which covers the same needs as another product that already exists in the market and is launched in order to complete a range of products without a substantial effort to modify or improve it. It is not an imitation, and is correctly identified by the manufacturer.

**MGM (member get member)** - MGM (member get member)

■ The marketing technique through which a person belonging to a club or association or a client of a company promotes the introduction of a new member in exchange for some sort of an incentive. Chain recruitment is directly related to membership marketing.

**micromarketing** - Mikromarketing *n*

■ The method of marketing aimed at small size market segments or niches. It involves taking the segmentation process to the extreme thus achieving small groups of consumers to whom marketing actions are directed. It is usually carried out with the help of a client database and the use of direct telecommunications media such as the telephone, mail or personal visits.

**misleading advertising** - irreführende Werbung *f*

■ Any advertising which creates confusion on the part of the consumer, and which may affect his economic behaviour. In order for this kind of advertising to take place, it is not necessary for the consumers to actually be deceived, it is sufficient simply for such deception or confusion is to be considered possible or potential.

**mission statement** - Mission *f* des Unternehmens

■ A brief description of corporate purpose used to inform employees and external agents of a company's objectives and priorities. It is a practice that became popular at the end of the 80's, although of little value if not well defined. The main advantage lies in the internal preparation process, given that it helps to focus attention on what the company expects to achieve and therefore highlight its priorities.

**mobile advertising** - mobile Werbung *f*

■ A type of advertising which is shown on a vehicle or towed by one. It usually goes with music or messages said over a loudspeaker in order to attract attention. It is used for intensive promotion of a venue over a period of time such as a circus show or a political rally.

**mobile marketing** - mobiles Marketing *n*

■ A branch of marketing which uses mobile phones in the sending and receipt of SMS messages, whether as an instrument of relational marketing, or as an advertising resource for sales, or a public relations action. Marketing via mobile has increased the possibilities of interactivity significantly given that it allows a direct and immediate relationship with the addressee wherever he may be.

**mobile outdoor advertising** - Verkehrsmittelwerbung *f*

■ The collection of advertising media placed on the outside of public or private transport vehicles.

**monolithic brand** - monolithische Marke *f*

■ The use of the same name and visual style for the complete corporate structure and all product ranges and services of a company. This is the case for Renault, BMW or IBM.

**monopolistic competition** - monopolistischer Wettbewerb *m*

■ An intermediate form of competition between monopoly and perfect competition, described by Chamberlin and Robinson. It deals with a multi-competitor market that offers a product (as in perfect competition), but demand preferences exist. Because of this, the products offered are not equal in the opinion of consumers, therefore each producer has a monopoly on his specific version of the product (as in a monopoly). Preferences can be the consequence of the differentiation of products, advertising or other factors. Monopolistic competition is in fact quite frequent.

**monopoly** - Monopol *n*

▪ A market in which only one supplier determines the prices and amounts offered. It can be stable in the case of a natural or legally imposed monopoly (for example, a fiscal monopoly to facilitate tax collection). Or it may be produced in the case of new or very sophisticated products, especially when they are protected by patents or when there are strong import barriers.

**motivation research** - Motivationsstudie *f*

▪ The study and analysis of reasons, desires and needs of consumers, as well as positive and negative motivation. It is used to identify and structure motives and subsequently predict behaviour.

**multibrand strategy** - Multimarkenstrategie *f*

▪ A commercial strategy which consists of the sale of similar goods and services by the same company under different brands.

**multinational marketing** - multinationales Marketing *n*

▪ The part of international marketing which segments the market into countries, thus adopting a different strategy for each of them in accordance with the specific and differentiating qualities.

**multiple-answer question** - Frage mit Mehrfachantwort *f*

▪ In quantitative research, a question to which all interviewees can give more than one valid answer. The total number of replies obtained can be higher than the number of people interviewed.

**mystery shopper** - Testkäufer *m*

▪ A fictitious purchaser who checks and compares the quality of the service offered by a company and its competitors, presenting himself as a normal client.

# N

**name gathering** - Namenssammlung *f*

▪ A promotional technique similar to recommending a friend whereby the client or supporter of the brand is asked to send by mail the names and contact details of friends and acquaintances, who might be interested in the brand, so that the company can contact them personally to offer them a product or service.

**naming** - Benennung *f*

▪ A brand engineering discipline focused on the invention of the name itself. It has to be capable of being registered and of reflecting the values and qualities on which it bases its position, as well as fulfilling certain formal criteria.

**national advertising agency** - nationale Werbeagentur *f*

▪ A domestic-owned advertising agency which carries out its activities in the area of a particular country. The national advertising agencies have experienced a significant downturn recently and, in many cases, have gone on to form part of international advertising networks.

**national launch** - nationale Einführung *f*

▪ A new product launching technique which consists of introducing the product onto the entire national market from the very beginning, instead of distributing it progressively by area.

**near-pack** - Gratisprodukt *n*

▪ A product, normally complementary, placed in a point of sale next to another product and which is sometimes given free with the purchase of the latter. It is often used to get recognition for the new product on the market or to promote the purchase of an already existing product.

**need** - Bedürfnis *n*

▪ Something required for individual well-being that motivates its acquisition. Marketing activities are designed to identify unsatisfied needs in order to determine the best way of fulfilling demand.

**net participation** - Nettomarktanteil *m*

▪ The percentage of sales of a particular brand, in relation to total sales of the product through retail stores, used as an indication of selling ability according to reputation and price. May diminish as a result of increased distribution to new outlets at which the brand is not as well known.

**net price** - Nettopreis *m*

▪ The price at which no further discounts are accepted. In practice it is often the final price, after deducting all discounts from the tariff or catalogue price.

**neutral price** - Neutralpreis *m*

▪ A price which is fixed to a product so that its market quota is not affected.

**new business department** - Abteilung *f* für Neukunden

▪ The department in charge of gaining possible new clients, who are compatible with the other clients the company handles, by carrying out the appropriate research.

**new product development** - Entwicklung *f* neuer Produkte

▪ The set of activities that lead to the renewal of a product portfolio using technological innovations, client suggestions or the appearance of new requirements. This requires close cooperation from the outset between the research and development department, production department and marketing department, and which must continue throughout all the phases: idea selection, technical evaluation, product development, manufacturing process, market tests and launching.

**niche marketing** - Nischen-Marketing *n*

▪ A company strategy which selectively looks for sectors of the market (segments or niches) in which to operate, so as to be able to offer its products or services there. On many occasions the objective of the positioning strategy is to occupy a market niche.

**niche media** - Nischen-Medien *n/pl*

▪ The advertising media which reaches small and very homogenous groups of the population.

**Nielsen** - Nielsen

▪ The informal name by which A.C. Nielsen Co. Limited is known. A research and marketing service firm specializing in sales audits to provide data on distribution in points of sale It also monitors investments in media advertising.

**NIFO** - NIFO *n*

▪ The initials for Next In First Out, a stock valuation system that assigns outgoing goods with a replacement value. If inflation exists, this system increases cost price and decreases accounting profit, even more than the LIFO system.

**non bleed** - ohne Beschnitt

▪ A manner of printing advertisements in periodical publications, whereby the surface of the advert respects the normal margins of the publication. It is the opposite of bleed off or bleed.

**no-name product** - Gattungsmarke *f*

▪ A product traded under a name which is not a recognised brand and which is usually sold in discount stores due to its favourable price. Its market quota increases in accordance with its bearing on the purchase decisions of the purchasers for certain products. It is the equivalent of generic.

**non-profit marketing** - Non-Profit-Marketing *n*

▪ A marketing activity carried out on behalf of a public institution or entity without the intention of making a profit (for example, museums or symphonic orchestras). It contrasts with the marketing activities developed on behalf of a company and aimed as making a profit.

**numerical distribution** - Distributionsdichte *f*
■ The percentage of stores offering a particular brand, divided by the total number of stores. It is an index that measures market penetration in relation to the number of outlets, without taking into account their size, which is measured by the distribution quality index.

# O

**observational study** - Beobachtungsstudie *f*
■ A research method which shows how users act when faced with a particular product. In this way, specific problems that the use of such a product can incur are discovered and the adjustments needed to eliminate these faults can been decided upon.

**odd article** - herabgesetzter Artikel *m*
■ A product which is sold with a reduction because it lacks an accessory or complement. It can also be referred to as a remainder or broken lot.

**odd page** - ungerade Seite *f*
■ The right-hand side page of a publication. Advertisements appearing on odd pages have a greater chance of being read and therefore are more expensive.

**office error** - Abschlussfehler *m*
■ In quantitative investigation, an error made in the design, coding, correction or computerisation of a questionnaire. It may also refer to an error made in keying in or presenting the results.

**official ad** - offizielle Anzeige *f*
■ An advertisement which a public organisation, such as a town hall, county or court is obliged to place, and which gives general interest information such as decrees, work contracts or auctions. It is charged at a different rate to general advertising.

**off-price system** - Off-Price-System *n*
■ An offer system which consists of regularly reducing (i.e. each week) the profit margin by a specific percentage which varies in accordance with the rhythm of sales, until most of the stock is sold. It involves selling as much as possible at the highest price possible. It is used for perishable goods such as fashion textiles or aircraft seats.

**oligopolistic competition** - oligopolistische Konkurrenz *f*
■ Equivalent to oligopoly. A market situation in which the few producers that exist attempt to make agreements that improve their financial situation at the expense of consumers. If there are only two suppliers, it is a duopoly and if there is one, a monopoly.

**oligopoly** - Oligopol *n*
■ A market situation in which the few producers that exist attempt to make agreements that improve their financial situation at the expense of consumers. If there are only two suppliers, it is a duopoly and if there is one, a monopoly.

**oligopsony** - Oligopson *n*
■ A market situation in which there are very few purchasers, who normally act in agreement so as to fix the purchase conditions of the products. If there are only two purchasers, it is a duopsony and if there is only one, a monopsony.

**omnibus survey** - Sammelumfrage *f*
■ A survey carried out by a specialist company on behalf of various clients where they each include a small number of questions that are of special interest to them. By not repeating the identifying variables, (demographic and socio-economic questions) a saving can be made and the survey can be more objective.

**one-shot mail** - One-Shot-Versand *m*
■ In mail-order selling, the commercial letter in which the addressee is presented with one product. All offer and creativity efforts are concentrated on motivating the purchase of the presented product. It is not used for low cost goods, unless they are mass consumption goods, as the cost per reply is not compensatory.

**one-to-one communication** Eins-zu-eins-Kommunikation *f*

■ The face-to-face transfer of information between two or more persons.

**one-to-one marketing** - One-to-One-Marketing *n*

■ A type of marketing which during a given sales period makes use of databases and interactive communications in order to sell to a specific client, who is addressed personally. It implies a knowledge of the consumer's tastes and preferences, in order to be able to adapt the products or services offered.

**one-way communication** - unidirektionale Kommunikation *f*

■ The transfer of messages in one direction, from the sender to the receiver, without the possibility of response. It appears in cases where there is a lack of motivational research of the public and of the effects that messages have on their audience.

**online editing** - Spitzenmontage *f*

■ A type of digital editing which is used to produce the final image which will form part of the ad or audiovisual material. The pictures are reassembled at full resolution, a process which is carried out in special studios using the content from the offline edit. At this point the special effects, if any, are added as well the signs or overlying text which form part of the final product.

**online marketing-mix** - Online-Marketingmix *m*

■ The collection of marketing tools and strategies which have developed through the convergence of the Net, mobile telephones and television.

**online service** - Onlinedienst *m*

■ Any service that is delivered via Internet. This can be simple, such as the provision of information by online newspapers or more complicated such as online banking services where the customer can carry out banking operations. It can also cover educational and entertainment needs. In recent years offering an online service has become an important part of the marketing strategy for a company's products or services.

**on-pack premium** - Geschenk *n*

■ A gift included in the packaging of the product. It sometimes also refers to a coupon or other type of offer.

**open question** - offene Frage *f*

■ A question in a questionnaire where those being surveyed are allowed to freely express their opinion, without being forced to choose between a series of options. The questioner must record the answer in the truest manner possible.

**open-ended question** - offene Frage *f*

■ A question which the interviewee may reply to freely using his own words. This reply should then be recorded word for word by the interviewer and, in a subsequent stage of the study, should be coded by grouping together replies with a similar meaning, even if the same words are not used.

**opening** - Eröffnungswerbung *f*

■ The group of correctly planned promotional and publicity events surrounding the inauguration of an establishment. Suppliers may often be required to sponsor activities.

**operational marketing** - operatives Marketing *n*

■ The part of marketing which is in charge of developing, in the short term, the actions which relate to the four fundamental tools: product, price, place and promotion. It is also known as tactical marketing.

**opinion leaders** - Meinungsbildner *m*

■ The people who, due to their economic class, social position or profession, set the trends of the public opinion of a country. The advertising can be aimed at those leaders in campaigns which require the diffusion or extension of a message of social or public character, or they can even be used in a prescriptive manner for the commercial advertising of a product or service.

**opportunity to see (OTS)** - Durchschnittskontakt *m*

▪ The likelihood that a person from the target group has entered into contact with the campaign advertisement. It is produced in printed media when the person has read or seen the copy the advertisement is in; in television and radio, when the person is tuned in to the channel or station that is transmitting the advertisement at the time of its broadcast; in the cinema when the person is in the room where the advertisement is screened and outside, when the person passes in front of the location where the advert is placed. It is also used as a synonym for frequency, to indicate the number of times that each person has been able to enter into contact with the campaign advertisements.

**optimistic strivers** - optimistische Streber *m/pl*

▪ A type of consumer in a pan-European classification of lifestyles. This type can only be found in the south of Europe. They are youngsters with talent, who are ambitious and who are in transit between the country and the suburbs with the possibility of becoming opulent.

**optimum capacity** - optimale Kapazität *f*

▪ A level of production that results in the lowest production cost per unit. It tends to be lower than maximum capacity as despite the fact that the effects of fixed costs are diminished, there may be additional consumption of energy, more expensive labour costs, supply problems, or maintenance problems that mean that working at maximum capacity is not worthwhile.

**optimum price** - Optimalpreis *m*

▪ The ideal price for achieving the business objectives.

**optimum quantity ordered** - optimale Bestellmenge *f*

▪ The quantity of a product ordered by a client which allows him to minimize his overall costs of stock management.

**opt-in** - Anmeldung *f*

▪ In the dynamics of permission marketing, the option which is included on a site for inclusion on a distribution list.

**opt-in email** - E-Mail-Abonnement *n*

▪ The electronic mail which is received from a company or organisation which has been previously informed by the receiver that they want to receive information on that company's activities, products or latest news.

**orange good** - orange Waren *f/pl*

▪ A consumer good which is replaced at a moderate rhythm, for example, clothing which is worn out over time or goes out of fashion.

**order cycle** - Bestellzyklus *m*

▪ The process of successive logistical activities which take place over the period of time between two orders, and which is repeated in an identical or similar manner over time.

**order discount** - Mengenrabatt *m*

▪ The reduction given on a price due to the volume of an order, not taking into account the accumulated purchase volume of that client, but bearing in mind the reduced costs involved in handling a bulk order (for example a full truck). Together with volume discounts and promotional allowances it constitutes one of the three basic commercial discounts.

**order fill rate** - Bestell-Erfüllungsrate *f*

▪ The proportion of purchase orders which have been completely delivered in a specific period of time.

**order number** - Auftragsnummer *f*

▪ A reference number that identifies an order for services or products and used to facilitate communications between buyers and sellers with regards to invoicing and general administrative control.

**order point** - Bestellpunkt *m*

▪ In stock management it is the level of stock that advises when a normal order should be carried out. It is calculated by formulas that take into account the demand for the product and the time that it takes to be received from the supplier. The costs of ordering, storage and stock-out are included.

**ordinary advertising** - Normalwerbung *f*

▪ In television, the advertising which is screened on pre-set days and times. In contrast, extraordinary advertising is that which takes place when times are changed due to the repeat broadcasting of a special programme.

**outbound telemarketing** - ausgehendes Telemarketing *n*

▪ A type of telemarketing which consists of making phone calls from a call centre to a previously selected public.

**outdated** - veraltet

▪ The need to adjust or adapt to determined circumstances at a particular moment, for example to keep abreast of new technology.

**outdoor advertising** - Outdoor-Werbung *f*

▪ An advertising activity which uses various media which are likely to attract the attention of people in open spaces or on streets and which can in general be seen by the public due to their location in public areas, for the transmission of its message.

**outdoor advertising agency** - Outdoor-Werbeagentur *f*

▪ An advertising agency which is focused on the running and management of certain outdoor advertising media.

**outlet store** - Fabrikverkauf *m*

▪ A commercial establishment located in the outskirts of cities which sells, at very low prices, surplus articles from the biggest brands or those which were not sold during the season in the normal retail outlets. When it is the manufacturers themselves who sell their surplus directly to the consumer, they are known as factory outlets.

**outsourcing** - Outsourcing *n*

▪ The obtaining of a non-vital service or component from an external supplier. It provides greater flexibility, saves time and money and normally results in higher quality and specialisation.

**overproduction** - Überproduktion *f*

▪ Manufacturing in excess of the level of production that the market can absorb at current prices. If it is a temporary situation, goods can be stockpiled with the financial costs that this involves, but in the long term the rhythm of production must slow down or new markets must be sought out.

**over-promise** - leeres Versprechen *n*

▪ In advertising, an exaggeration which does not correspond to the reality of the advertised product, thus provoking a negative reaction on the part of the audience. It constitutes a procedure to be avoided at all costs, unless it is done in a humoristic context.

**overvalued** - überbewertet

▪ Any good that has a price that exceeds its real price.

# P

**pack shot** - Sortimentspräsentation *f* einer Marke

▪ The closing scene of an advertising film in which the products appear clearly identified with the brand name. They can be accompanied by raw materials or finished products and the manufacturer's logo usually appears.

**package** - Verpackung *f*

▪ A container used to encase a product. There are different types of promotional packaging. Gift packaging enables the container to be used after its contents have been consumed while bulk packaging involves larger than usual containers. Grouped packaging offers products with other complementary items and multiple packages contain various items of the same product that are sold together. Returnable packaging may be re-cycled.

**package insert** - Packungswerbung *f*

■ The advertising included in the packaging of a product which refers to other products of the company, or even different companies, and which are complementary to the first (spare parts, refills, or others).

**packaging** - Verpackung *f*

■ The design of the boxes, packets, wrappers, stickers, and other external elements of the products to be marketed, including the selection of materials, and taking into consideration legal, aesthetic and economical factors which are required for the distribution of the product.

**packaging** - Verpacken *n*

■ The preparation of goods prior to storage or transportation by placing them in adequate boxes or bundles. The term can also be used with reference to the preparation of attractive packages used at point of sale for marketing products.

**packaging studio** - Verpackungsfirma *f*

■ A company specialised in the design of containers and the display and packaging of products.

**painted wall** - Wandwerbung *f*

■ An advertisement which takes advantage of walls without windows, usually being the sides of buildings. The advertisements are painted directly on the walls which are contracted for long periods of time.

**paired comparison** - Paarvergleich *m*

■ In quantitative investigation, the manner of drafting some questions whereby the interviewees are asked to indicate which of the two contrasting statements they are more in agreement with.

**palletise** *v* - palettieren *v*

■ To place on a pallet, in an organised manner, the boxes or merchandise which is to be transported. The levels are placed in alternate facing directions, so as to provide a sounder structure. Sometimes the joints are secured with glue, with a metal strip on the top, or by wrapping the entire pallet and its contents with a plastic covering. Placing the pallets in columns reduces stability, but increases the weight that can be supported as all the walls of the boxes coincide.

**palletised shipment** - Palettenversand *m*

■ The transport of returnable or non-returnable goods on pallets designed to facilitate loading and unloading.

**panel** - Panel *n*

■ A stable sample representative of a universe, used for continuous statistical analysis, normally relating to market research.

**pantry check** - Vorratskammertest *m*

■ Brand checking by visual examination, often carried out in surveys and consumer panels.

**parent advertising agency** - Mutteragentur *f*

■ The central office of a transnational agency, from where all internationalisation processes are carried out before reaching the national market.

**pass-along audience** - Sekundärpublikum *n*

■ The readers of a periodical publication who have not purchased the copy nor are family members of its purchaser. They read it on occasion, for a short period of time and probably with less attention, and they are therefore considered to be of less advertising value. They are taken into account at the time of calculating the medium's audience and for some media they can be numerous, for example, real-life magazines which are read in hairdresser's. Also known as occasional audience.

**pass-along rate** - Pass-along-Rate *f*

■ On the Internet, the percentage of people who pass on a message or file to others.

**passer-by** - Passant *m*

■ In external advertising, the person who can be considered a part of the audience of an advert because he has passed in front of the same.

**patronage** - Mäzenat *n*

■ The philanthropic act of sponsorship which is not communicated publicly and so cannot be considered a public relations action nor a marketing action.

**pay per click (PPC)** - Bezahlung *f* per Klick

■ In Internet advertising, the agreement between the advertiser and search engine or other type of site, whereby the former will pay for all the downloads from its site generated by the search engine.

**pay per lead (PPL)** - Bezahlung *f* per Aktion

■ On the Internet, the form of advertising payment which consists in paying for each visitor recommended to the site.

**pay per sale (PPS)** - Bezahlung *f* per Kauf

■ A form of advertising payment on the Internet which consists in paying for the sales generated by the media concerned.

**peak demand** - Spitzennachfrage *f*

■ A high intensity level of demand and by extension a period in which a high level of demand occurs.

**peak hours** - Hauptbelastungszeit *f*

■ A period of maximum demand, for example when telephone calls or electrical consumption are at their highest. The term can also be applied to the time of day when traffic is heaviest.

**peak time** - Stoßzeit *f*

■ In marketing, the hours of maximum consumption (e.g. The audience of a means of communication or clients of a commercial establishment).

**peak-load pricing** - Spitzenlasttarif *m*

■ A price strategy in which demand for the product is stimulated in phases parallel to another price promotion, financing it with the higher prices charged during peak demand phases. In the telephone sector is it normal to see this strategy used.

**penetration** - Marktdurchdringung *f*

■ The quality of having considerable presence or influence in a particular market, measured by market share and brand awareness.

**penetration price** - Durchdringungspreis *m*

■ A price which is fixed to a new product and which is below the level of prices of competing products in order to reduce the perceived purchase risk and stimulate consumers' demand. It is usually used on those products which are not particularly innovative, and once a sufficient market quota is achieved, the price is progressively increased until its foreseen normal level is reached.

**penetration rate** - Durchdringungsrate *f*

■ The percentage of individuals of a target population out of the whole population who purchase or recognise a particular product, brand or publicity message.

**perfect competition** - vollständiger Wettbewerb *m*

■ The ideal form of competition where a large number of purchasers and sellers exist, as well as the complete freedom to set up in the market. Information flows quickly and in equal quantities to all participants and the transaction or transport costs are insignificant in comparison to the price of the product.

**performance advertising** - Performance-Werbung *f*

■ A new kind of external advertising which is staged in the street and which consists of a surprise showing creating a great impact on a very crowded area of the city. For example, MINI's "It's a MINI adventure" campaign saw cars parked on the sides of buildings in London.

**perimeter advertising** - statische Werbung *f*

■ A collection of media for advertising located in a sports precinct or circuit, such as those which are located on the perimeter of a football pitch. Quite often the audience of these media are increased due to the possibility of them being captured by television cameras, which allows for television transmission at a low cost. In certain circumstances, despite forming a part of outdoor advertising, these media are counted as a sports sponsorship investment.

**perishable good** - verderbliche Güter *n/pl*
▪ Goods destined for use or consumption within a limited period of time on the assumption that beyond that time period they will deteriorate or become worthless.

**permanent display** - Daueraufsteller *m*
▪ An advertising element whose duration is estimated to be prolonged or has the characteristics of extreme exposure. In these cases, the materials used in their design are no longer cardboard and its derivatives but wood, metal and other such materials. Evidently, its costs, as well as its production process, are higher.

**permission marketing** - Erlaubnismarketing *n*
▪ Marketing which is based on having obtained the previous authorisation from the client to send them information on the business offer. These marketing actions are directed exclusively at consumers who have given their prior consent, something which is an absolutely necessity for deliveries by e-mail or mobile given the increase of junk mail (undesired advertising messages). It can also be called authorised marketing and is the opposite of intrusive marketing.

**personal interview** - persönliches Interview *n*
▪ In research, the conversation which takes place between two people, interviewer and interviewee, who are present in the same place and in which the former interviews the latter on the subjects included in a guide, or reads the questions of a survey.

**personal selling** - Direktverkauf *m* durch Vertreter
▪ A type of selling in which the seller directly contacts a client, normally used in industrial sales or when the product is expensive or difficult to understand or use.

**personalisation** - Personalisierung *f*
▪ In direct advertising, the adaptation of a message to the person that will receive it by means of mentioning names with frequency, taking personal circumstances into account, considering previous responses etc.

**personalised copy** - persönliches Exemplar *n*
▪ An issue of a publication that features the name of the recipient in order to give an impression of exclusivity or special attention.

**persuasion** - Überzeugung *f*
▪ The process of inducing a change in attitude, or behaviour through arguments and reasoning.

**persuasive communication** - überzeugende Kommunikation *f*
▪ Social interaction through messages, planned by the source or broadcaster, with the conscious aim of provoking changes in image, attitude, intention, behaviour or habit in the receiver in relation to a specific psychological object, whether real or ideal.

**persuasive objective** - überzeugendes Ziel *n*
▪ The objective or aimed purpose of the broadcaster of persuasive communication and which is differentiated from other types of communication. It focuses on the search for notoriety, creation, modification or reinforcement of the image, attitude, intention, behaviour or habits that the public has towards the object of reference.

**phone selling** - Telefonverkauf *m*
▪ Sales carried out by calling the potential purchaser directly by telephone.

**photo agency** - Bildagentur *f*
▪ An agency which commissions photos or keeps the work of associated photographers in order to sell it to publishers and press and advertising agencies. Some photo agencies are specialised in fields such as sport, music or the sea.

**physical distribution** - physischer Vertrieb *m*
▪ The part of logistics science that deals with the flow of final products from the factory to the client. Depending on the integration with other marketing activities,

it may include: sales forecasts, production planning, transport, storage and distribution, order processing and customer service.

**pie chart** - Tortendiagramm *n*

■ A graphic representation of the results of a survey which takes the form of a circle divided into segments, each of which represents the values of a variable and in which the corresponding angle (and therefore the area) is proportional to the frequency it represents.

**piggyback** - Packungsbeilage *f*

■ An extra advertising element which is placed inside the packaging of a product, usually a commercial pamphlet, another product of the same brand or any other type of incentive. In mail-order sales it is often used to send another commercial offer in the package of a previously ordered product.

**piggyback commercials** - Mehrfachwerbung *f*

■ Television advertisements which correspond to products of the same advertiser and which are broadcast in the same advertising block, one after the other, with the aim of paying the best insertion rates, to support one product with the other or to obtain a higher presence of the advertiser in the viewer's mind. On occasion it is one commercial used for two different products belonging to the same advertiser in order to reduce costs.

**piggyback promotion** - Huckepack-Werbung *f*

■ An advertising method which consists in offering the purchase of a specific product with interesting conditions providing that another is purchased. It occasionally involves receiving a free sample of the offered product on purchasing the other.

**pilot programme** - Pilotprogramm *n*

■ A programme which is normally of short duration and limited scope that precedes the definitive programme by way of a test to detect possible design flaws and indicate the probable results and effectiveness of the definitive programme.

**pilot store** - Testgeschäft *n*

■ The prototype of a commercial establishment used as a model for other owned or franchised stores, to train personnel or to try out a new concept in the market, product range, price or any other variable.

**pilot survey** - Pilotumfrage *f*

■ A survey carried out with a reduced universe in order to detect and correct possible design faults before proceeding with the definitive survey.

**piracy** - Raubkopie *f*

■ The illegal copying of computer programs or of reputed brands of products.

**plan** *v* - planen *v*

■ To prepare a programme of activities in which economic variables and objectives are fixed, the required financial resources and their source are established and the specific objectives during a given period are determined.

**planned obsolescence** - geplante Obsoleszenz *f*

■ A marketing technique which consists in artificially programming the duration of a product so that it needs to be replaced before its use has finished. Planned obsolescence can be material (for example, including an important part of the product which deteriorates before the rest), through the launching of new models which leave previous models outdated, through new designs or through new versions of the product becoming more popular. Planned obsolescence is one of the practices most criticised in marketing by consumer groups. It is also known as artificial obsolescence.

**planned psychological obsolescence** - Veralterung *f*

■ A technique aimed at substituting one product for another new product based on the perception of the former by the user, who will tend to consider it old even if it is perfectly usable. For example, the introduction of a new style of clothing, the introduction of a new car design which only affects its external image, or a book which changes its cover. On occasion, planned psychological obsolescence is achieved by changing the packaging or the brand of a product. It forms part of planned or artificial obsolescence.

**planning** - Planung *f*

■ An organised activity that fixes objectives, determines strategies, and puts into effect the material and personal means that are required to achieve those objectives.

**plan-o-gram** - Planogramm *n*

■ A diagram which shows the layout of the products on a shelf in a point of sale.

**point of sale** - Verkaufsstelle *f*

■ An establishment, or each division within an establishment, that sells a particular category of products.

**point of sale material** - Werbematerial *n* für die Verkaufsstelle

■ A manufacturer message to a consumer that is maintained at the time of purchase. It may be achieved by different methods such as posters, stickers, display items or music.

**point of sale terminal** - Kassenterminal *n*

■ A specialised terminal in a computer system where financial transactions are carried out. For example, checkout points in shops and cash dispensers.

**pole topper** - Anzeiger *m*

■ An advertising element which fulfils the function of highlighting a point, area or product. It is located in high-up areas, or areas which stand out, so as to catch the consumer's attention. By extension, the poster located at the top of a pole to obtain maximum visibility in the establishment.

**policy on returned goods** - Rückgabepolitik *f*

■ The agreement reached between supplier and receiver of the merchandise which determines the measure to which each of the parties will bear the costs of the return of the product should the client wish to do so for whatever reason.

**political advertisement** - politische Werbung *f*

■ An advertising message whose aim is to satisfy the image or electoral objectives of the parties or public entities.

**political marketing** - Politmarketing *n*

■ The extrapolation of marketing ideas into the political area, in accordance with which, the parties tend to see their electorate as the manufacturers of the mass consumption products see their consumers. Therefore, political marketing covers all those activities developed by a political group for a political meeting aimed at asserting the party's image over that of its competitors and to organise a consistent and notorious presence of the same in the electoral conflict, in accordance with the image they plan to give off.

**political price** - politischer Preis *m*

■ An artificially-established price, normally by the Government, to favour a particular sector of producers or consumers. It takes political interests into account more than market circumstances. It can be a minimum or guaranteed price to protect the producers, a maximum price to protect the consumers or to reduce inflation or a fixed price. The Government should be able to buy or sell stocks in order to guarantee market fluidity.

**polybag** - Plastikumschlag *m*

■ The packaging of plastic material which acts as an envelope in the commercial delivery to the client. It is often used to send magazines and catalogues.

**popularise** *v* - bekannt machen *v*

■ To convert a minor product into something known and appreciated by the majority of people through an advertising campaign or public relations.

**population** - Bevölkerung *f*

■ In research, the group of people whose characteristics are to be studied. The analysis of all the elements of the population give way to a census. If the analysis is limited to a number of randomly selected elements, the study is by sample.

**population pyramid** - Bevölkerungspyramide *f*
■ A graphic representation, normally triangular or spindle shaped, that reflects the sex and age composition of a population.

**pop-under ad** - Pop-Under *n*
■ On the Internet, an advertising format which consists of a window which opens on the screen after exiting the page that was visited.

**pop-up** - Aufklappwerbung *f*
■ A catalogue or container which contains a section which pops out when opened and whose aim is to surprise and attract the consumers' attention.

**pop-up ad** - Pop-Up *n*
■ On the Internet, an advertising format which consists of a floating window which opens on the screen on top of the page being visited when the user clicks on part of this page.

**pop-up window** - Pop-Up-Fenster *n*
■ An advertising technique which consists of presenting the advertising message in a new browser window which opens automatically on the Internet user's screen.

**position** - Position *f*
■ In advertising, the place an advert occupies in a medium. According to its position it has a higher or lower possibility of being seen, something which gives rise to different rates or surcharges on the price. For example, odd numbered pages are more expensive, as also the first position in a television advertising block. Some positions appear in the rates with a specific price, other rates have to be requested from the media planner in exchange for a charge.

**positioning map** - Positionsgrafik *f*
■ The graphic representation on a map with two axes showing the position of various competing brands in accordance with specific attributes which are important to the target public or market. It aids in determining the ideal position by looking for gaps in the market.

**positive option** - ausdrückliche Zustimmung *f*
■ A reply model which requires the express consent of the receiver for the commercial offer to be considered accepted.

**postage and handling** - Versandkosten *pl*
■ The costs involved in shipping goods from the point of manufacture (or purchase) to the point of use (or sale). For instance, freight costs, customs or insurance costs.

**postage paid** - portofrei
■ A letter or reply card included in the direct mailing and whose postage is paid by the sender/advertiser with the agreement of the postal services (the authorisation number will appear on the letter). It encourages a positive reply to the offer on the part of the consumer. Postage paid is a universal practice in direct mail advertising.

**poster billboard** - Werbeplakat *n*
■ An external advertising medium which consists of a framework in the form of a flat surface onto which the printed pages of the advertisement are stuck. This is the most usual type of billboard .

**posting period** - Kampagnenlaufzeit *f*
■ The time during which the advertisements of an outdoor advertising campaign should be exhibited. The previously strict system, which imposed high penalties on measuring by complete months the duration of the campaigns, has been replaced by a much more flexible system whereby it is possible to sign up for weeks and even days.

**postmark advertising** - Druckwerbung *f*
■ The advertising which is printed on letters of correspondence at the same time as cancelling the stamp or franking the letter.

**postponed delivery** - Lieferverzögerung *f*
■ The delayed delivery of the product with respect to the agreed delivery date. It can cause serious damage to the client as there is the possibility that he will find himself in stock-out.

**post-test** - Werbewirksamkeitsstudie *f*
■ A quantitative study, using a sample of the targeted public, to determine the impact of an advertising message. In a 24 hour test, recall and first reactions can be measured and when a campaign is completed a more detailed study can be conducted.

**potential** - Potential *n*
■ Something that is possible although not yet real. In marketing, it is a noun which refers collectively to the resources and capabilities of an individual, brand or company. When used as an adjective referring to a market, client, production capability, etc. it indicates that it is considered attainable although it has still not been achieved.

**potential audience** - potentielles Publikum *n*
■ The maximum number of persons who can enter into contact with a medium in a specific period of time. The length of time considered is fundamental for the calculation of the potential audience as the number of people exposed to said medium may increase, sometimes considerably, simply by prolonging the period in question.

**potential market** - potentieller Markt *m*
■ A possible demand for a good or service, in other words, people with a particular need that can be satisfied by a good or service (a theoretical market) with the necessary resources to acquire it, including current markets of a particular company or its competitors, as well as possible increases due to greater product knowledge, purchasing power, number of consumers or consumption per capita.

**PPC (pay per click)** - PPC (Pay per Click)
■ An Internet advertising system based on results.

**pre-coded questionnaire** - vorcodierter Fragebogen *m*
■ A questionnaire to which, prior to its use, a numerical code has been assigned to each possible answer so as to facilitate its computerisation and key-in.

**preference** - Präferenz *f*
■ A priority or advantage that a person or thing has over another when put into an order using determined criteria or values.

**premium price** - Aufpreis *m*
■ The difference in price that a consumer is willing to pay for a particular product due to its higher brand image over that of its competitors. The premium price tends to measure the value of a particular brand and the loyalty of its consumers towards it.

**premium rate** - Prämiensatz *m*
■ In advertising, the cost for inserting an advertisement with special position conditions. These conditions can cover anything from the specific date or time requirements on the radio, to a specific page in printed media. This price is sometimes reflected in a higher than normal rate in the medium, whilst at other times it takes the form of a surcharge on the base rate.

**pre-pack** - vorverpackt
■ A system which incorporates the display and the unit to be delivered (i.e., the product) which acts both as the external packaging, and which, once open, fulfils the function of a display including graphics on its interior. It is a generic name used to define a floor or worktop display, designed to be packaged together with the product and sent to the point of sale in one unit. This type of display is often used for high rotation products, as it hugely simplifies replacement. A typical example are product dispensers.

**presentation** - Präsentation *f*
■ A ceremony in which a new product is exhibited and, in general, an idea or report expressed for the first time before an audience using audio-visual means.

**press** - Presse *f*
■ A collective term for newspaper publications, especially those that appear on a daily basis.

**press agent** - Presseagent *m*
■ A person specialised in the distribution of information to the mass media

regarding a person or organisation with the aim that they disseminate it. This meaning is generally limited to the entertainment and sporting fields. In a pejorative sense, it is also used to refer to the information twister who misinforms the public, with the aim of promoting the interests of the organisation he is employed by.

**press conference** - Pressekonferenz *f*

■ A public relations event aimed at the mass media which consists in a meeting with journalists organised by an organisation or a person, so that the spokesperson informs the press of a relevant piece of news, and replies to the questions that the journalists may have.

**press kit** - Pressemappe *f*

■ A public relations tool aimed at the mass media which consists of a document with information about an organisation, written in a journalistic style, and which serves to present the company to the media. It usually also includes press releases. Also known as a media kit.

**press office** - Pressestelle *f*

■ The area of a public relations department which is in charge of the relations with the media through press releases, regular meetings with journalists, press conferences, the preparation of reports and press kits, and collaboration in the drafting of magazines, bulletins and reports. Its database of media professionals must be kept up to date and information should be kept on the interests of each media.

**press relations** - Pressebeziehungen *f/pl*

■ The professional and periodic communications with the press and other media kept by a company in order to achieve and maintain a positive image for itself and its products. Apart from issuing press releases, factory visits are arranged, as are interviews with company directors, reports on new products, information regarding company results, etc. Press relations are particularly important when answering questions from communications media during periods of crisis or in unfavourable situations.

**press release** - Pressemitteilung *f*

■ A brief news story issued by an organisation for publication in selected media outlets. Sometimes referred to as a press statement, although this is usually distributed to all the media. It is a common form of public relations designed to communicate annual data, appointments and product launches.

**prestige** - Prestige *n*

■ Good reputation and credit, esteem and renown that inspire respect and admiration for a product or service. Prestigious articles have a price above their value or practical utility and are bought to demonstrate the purchasers' wealth or importance.

**prestige price** - Prestigepreis *m*

■ The high price fixed to usually luxurious products which aim to transmit an image of quality and distinction.

**pre-survey** - Voruntersuchung *f*

■ A study carried out prior to emitting an advertising message in order to determine the possible reaction. It can be done using a mock-up, which is cheaper, although it is better to use a finished film. It is usually a qualitative study using group discussion techniques with people representing the targeted public. It is also used to try out a questionnaire before carrying out a massive survey, allowing errors to be corrected.

**pre-test** - Vortest *m*

■ A trial carried out before taking a final decision (for example, the production of an original advertisement, new packaging or the contracting of personnel). It is usual to use mock-ups in order to avoid large investment.

**price** - Preis *m*

■ The value or quantity of money that is associated with an item of goods. The price is always linked with the idea of an exchange based upon that which the market can offer for it.

**price cut** - Preisnachlass *m*

■ A higher discount reduction in the price of a product or service with the aim of achieving a specific objective such as increasing the market quota, fighting against a new competitor or making room for a superior product.

**price cutting** - Preissenkung *f*

■ A marketing tactic which consists of reducing the price of a product over a period of time or indefinitely, in order to counteract unfavourable circumstances in the market (for example, the launch of a new product or price cut by a competitor) or to promote a favourable circumstance (such as increasing the market quota because the elasticity of the price has increased).

**price differentiation** - Preisdifferenzierung *f*

■ A technique used to adapt product features (quality, warranty, minimum delivery, term of payment, etc.) to each individual customer's requirements, and especially to fix prices that optimise company profits. The difference may be beneficial to consumers (for example, the price differentiation in air fares).

**price discount** - Rabatt *m*

■ A reduction made to the price of goods or services, without any special reason.

**price discrimination** - Preisdiskriminierung *f*

■ The establishing of different prices for a similar or exact product that does not reflect a proportional difference in cost and attempts to adapt to the intensity of demand in different sectors in order to maximise profits. It may be based on different types of clients, locations, period of the day or year, or type of product finishing or packaging.

**price effect** - Preiseffekt *m*

■ The variation in the demand of a product as a result of changes in its price. Normally consumption drops as the price rises and vice-versa.

**price escalation clause** - Preisanpassungsklausel *f*

■ A contract clause referring to price variations caused by changes in labour and raw material cost indexes, used in purchase or service contracts with extended delivery periods, for example, construction or engineering services.

**price fall** - Preisverfall *m*

■ A rapid drop in sales price due to a reduction in demand or increase in supply. Usually the result of a change in tastes or style although it may be widespread if the cause affects an entire regional economy.

**price fixing** - Preisabsprache *f*

■ An agreement between competitors to sell their products at a certain price. This is an illegal activity, though relatively common during short periods of time. In addition to price, other conditions may be established, such as form of payment and advertising costs.

**price indication** - Preisangabe *f*

■ The indication of the price of a product. European regulations state that products on offer to consumers must show their sales price and their unit measurement price.

**price list** - Preisverzeichnis *n*

■ A document in which the seller indicates the price of his products (even recommending the retail price), the discounts applicable and the payment and delivery terms. Large clients that often have a joint buying centre, may set a meeting at the beginning of the year to agree the fixed discounts on the prices that may be in force at any one time.

**price range** - Preisspanne *f*

■ The difference between the minimum and maximum price of a good during a given period.

**price regulation** - Preisregulierung *f*

■ The regulation of the prices at which products are sold. In some cases it is the Government which fixes or established the price regulation of certain products by establishing what are known as authorised prices.

**price sensitive** - preisabhängig

■ A product or service whose sales are higher or lower depending on their price. They are very elastic in terms of price.

**price war** - Preiskrieg *m*

■ A market situation in which competition between companies is carried out largely by reducing sales price. Usually, the price covers the variable and fixed cost, and provides a normal profit but, in certain circumstances (for example, with a drop in demand, the entrance of a new competitor on the market, or a competitor trying to increase market share, etc.), the group of competitors in the market are forced to sell at a loss, or without even covering all their fixed costs.

**pricing strategy** - Preispolitik *f*

■ The part of a marketing strategy which refers to the price of the product or service. It depends on the positioning and the situation in the lifecycle of the product (skimming at the beginning and milking at the end) and has to be coherent with the rest of the strategy, for example, if it is a selected public the price will be high and the media used in advertising will be exclusive with extra weight given to public relations acts or events. A low price will be accompanied by less advertising or mass media and frequent promotion. The price is fixed in relation to that which the target public is willing to pay, and not calculated according to the cost plus a profit margin.

**pricing tactic** - Preistaktik *f*

■ An action within the pricing strategy to adjust it to a specific objective, such as stopping a competitors launch, facilitating the introduction of the product in a geographic location, or the selling off of stock for a version which is about to become artificially obsolete.

**primary audience** - Hauptpublikum *n*

■ In printed media, the peoples who purchase a publication or live in the home of the person who purchases it. These people are considered to form a qualified group within the group of readers of said publication.

**primary source** - Hauptquelle *f*

■ In research techniques, the source which gathers different information and subsequently supplies it to those interested as secondary data.

**primary wholesaler** - erster Großhändler *m*

■ A wholesaler whose main purpose is to gather products of different sources into groups of origin and channel them to their destinations.

**prime time** - Hauptsendezeit *f*

■ In radio or television, those transmission hours that attract the largest listening or viewing audiences, generally late afternoon or early evening, when news programmes, films or general interest programmes are transmitted. As they are the peak hours, publicity time and tariffs are also at their highest.

**print advertisement** - Druckwerbung *f*

■ An advertising message designed with verbal, typographical, composition and fixed image resources (photographs or illustrations), and produced using printing techniques.

**private brand** - Gattungsmarke *f*

■ A name which designates the products which are sold in a commercial establishment under its name and not that of its manufacturer. Also known as own-label brand.

**private consumption** - Verbrauch *m* des Privatsektors

■ The total consumption of goods and services at a microeconomic level of the private sector of the economy (companies, consumers, etc.). Also called consumer spending.

**probability** - Wahrscheinlichkeit *f*

■ The measure of expectation, certainty or possibility that an event will take place. Statistical probability is, according to the law of large numbers, the value at which the relative frequency is closest when a number of random experiments are carried out, expressed as a number between 0 (impossible occurrence) and 1 (certain occurrence), or often shown as a percentage.

**probability sampling** - Wahrscheinlichkeitsauswahl *f*

▪ A type of sampling in which all elements have a known probability (different to zero) of being included in the sample. It is almost always more representative than non-probability sampling and also enables estimates of error factors. There are three main methods: simple random, stratified and cluster sampling or consecutive combinations of the three.

**product** - Produkt *n*

▪ Any object or service that is perceived as capable of satisfying a requirement. It is the result of a creative effort, and is offered to the consumer under certain characteristics. It is equivalent to the term good. There are products or goods that are free and economical that in turn are divided into consumption and investment. Consumer products are classified by families, articles and references.

**product advertising** - Produktwerbung *f*

▪ The advertising activity which aims to make a specific product known to its target public or to persuade them of the advantages and benefits that its use and acquisition will generate.

**product brand** - Produktmarke *f*

▪ A brand which is associated to a single product, distinguishing it from the remaining products of the company.

**product class** - Produktkategorie *f*

▪ A group of substitutive products which maintain a certain level of cohesion or homogeneity as they satisfy the same specific need. The best way to see if two products belong to the same category is to adopt the consumer's point of view and analyse from their perspective whether they are interchangeable or respond to the same purchase needs.

**product complaints report** - Beschwerdebericht *m*

▪ A report in which the complaints received in relation to a particular product or reference are listed. It can also gather the observations of the franchisee in relation to the defective supply made to its business unit or the complaints by clients as to faults in the product sold.

**product development** - Produktentwicklung *f*

▪ A marketing strategy which consists of introducing improvements to the product so as to increase consumer demand.

**product differentiation** - Produktdifferenzierung *f*

▪ The implementing of complementary features, quality improvements, styles or brand image that distinguish one product from others and enables greater profitability. Consumers appreciate the added value while direct price competition is reduced.

**product elimination** - Produktbeseitigung *f*

▪ The ordered withdrawal of a product from the market once it stops making profits or serving its purpose.

**product family** - Produktfamilie *f*

▪ A group of similar products due to the fact that they cover similar needs or have common production processes or distribution channels. The main differences are based on quality, raw materials and manufacturer. It is a classification that is used mainly by distributors to facilitate profitability calculations, store placement, inventory substitution and comparison and is not the same as a product range.

**product image** - Produktimage *n*

▪ The intrinsic image of a product, although at times it may be heavily influenced by the image of a brand.

**product life cycle (PLC)** - Produktlebenszyklus *m* (PLC)

▪ In simple terms the life of a product can be split into four phases namely introduction, growth, maturity and decline. Sales grow in the first three phases and fall in the last, as do profits, although it must be noted that in the introductory stage there may be losses.

**product line** - Produktlinie *f*

▪ A set of uniform products that satisfy similar needs and are offered to the public under the same brand. If the line is complete, it is called a product range. Each product may include several items and references.

**product market** - Produkt-Markt-Verhältnis *n*

▪ A concept based on the characteristics of the product offered on the market, the technology used in its creation, the group of consumers to whom it is directed and the function that it fulfils, or the needs that it satisfies as concerns those consumers. It is also known as the business strategy unit, although at times this term encompasses more than the product-market and is therefore a broader term.

**product mix** - Produktreihe *f*

▪ A group of products manufactured by the same company grouped together with the purpose of strengthening each other. The combination of products constitutes one of the most usual marketing tactics, so that products already on the market support newer products or those which have a lower profit margin support those which have a high profit margin. On occasion they are grouped together under one brand or they may have their own specific brand.

**product orientation** - Produktionsorientierung *f*

▪ A marketing focus whereby the business centres its activity around product policies, using its productive resources and without investigating the market needs. This orientation is successful in sectors where products are limited and levels of demand are higher than production capacity, and so there are no problems at the time of placing the product on the market. However, in competitive sectors where supply levels are high a market orientation strategy is more suitable than a product orientation strategy.

**product placement** - Produktbeistellung *f*

▪ An advertising technique which consists of placing a product with its corresponding brand, or making reference to its brand, in a television series or a film. It can be active (when the product forms part of the action or its brand is mentioned by the characters) or passive (when it is simply present in the scene). It is a technique which is on the rise due to the loss of efficiency of the conventional forms of television advertising. It is also now used in other entertainment products such as books and computer games.

**product range** - Produktpalette *f*

▪ In a strict sense, the set of different items of the same product differentiated by colour or additional complements. Differentiation by size or fit, provides various references for the same product. In the wider sense, it is used as a synonym for product line or range of sections.

**product range analysis** - Sortimentsanalyse *f*

▪ The study and quantifying of the items offered at any given time. Variables include the type of outlet, competitor and supplier activities, consumer suggestions, actual storage facilities and sales outlet display, as well as gross margin and rotation per item, group and section.

**product range balancing** - Produktlinienharmonisierung *f*

▪ Action of co-ordinating the different characteristics of a range of products (such as appearance, size, price and security regulations) so that it meets the needs and desires of consumers more effectively.

**product range breadth** - Sortimentsbreite *f*

▪ The average number of products offered by a specific unit. The range may vary a great deal from one unit to another. A large range and limited stock of each product is intended to cover the greatest possible number of needs and ensure a high level of rotation at the expense of losing a certain number of sales and customers.

**product range depth** - Sortimentstiefe *f*

■ The average number of articles or references offered by each product. There is a lot of depth when the client can choose between many options such as size, colour and accessories. It reduces the rotation of each reference but attracts a select clientele and can increase the average gross margin.

**product training** - Probenutzung *f*

■ An event marketing activity which consists of putting a product at the disposal of a group of specialists for a specific period of time (for example, a new make of car) so that they can try it out for themselves and at a later stage give their opinion to the media (for example, in motoring magazines).

**product trial** - Produkttest *m*

■ A trial done during the market research on a panel of consumers who experiment with the product for a period of time and then give their opinion.

**production good** - Produktionsgut *n*

■ Any good aimed at producing other consumer or investment goods. It is absorbed into the manufacturing process, for example, a machine. Equivalent to investment goods.

**production-oriented** - produktionsorientiert

■ A company policy focused on launching products developed by its own experts, given that they are easier to produce or more suited to production installations, instead of being based on consumer needs.

**productive capacity** - Produktionskapazität *f*

■ The volume of production that a company can reach by using all available resources, or a production line or equipment at full capacity, taking maintenance and possible breakdowns into account.

**professional magazine** - Berufsmagazin *n*

■ A magazine whose readers belong to a profession, similar to specialist and sectorial magazines, but different to general interest magazines. It is the optimum channel for getting corporate and technical messages across to a specific target public and although its spread can be reduced, its power of discrimination is very large, and the percentage of wasted impacts is therefore reduced.

**promotion** - Vertriebspolitik *f*

■ In its broadest sense, a promotion is one of the elements of the marketing mix, which consists of the group of activities aimed at achieving the sales of a product of service. Advertising is the most visible of these activities, but not the only one. Special offers and sponsorship also form a part of promotion.

**promotion shelf** - Werberegal *n*

■ A shelf which due to its large size or special placement attracts customers' attention more easily and is therefore used for visibly displaying articles on promotion.

**promotion validity period** - Werbezeitraum *m*

■ The period during which an advertising campaign takes place. It could be a general campaign defined by the franchiser for application to all areas of the network and which will be conveniently planned in the advertising programme for the whole chain. It can also be a local campaign applied to a specific unit of the network with the purpose of increasing sales figures.

**promotional allowance** - Rabatt *m* zur Absatzförderung

■ The reduction of tariff prices for relevant reasons, such as product introduction, reinforcement in a geographic zone or to support a particular client. It can take the form of an allowance per product unit purchased or an agreed price for a lump sum (for example, the cost of a gondola end or an advertisement in a magazine etc.).

**promotional marketing** - Verkaufsmarketing *n*

■ The term used to describe advertising actions considered from a strategic point of view and in contrast to the advertising tactics efficiently performed in each case.

**promotional pack** - Aktionspackung *f*
■ A pack which gives the consumer information on a promotion such as a prize draw, a self-liquidating premium or collectable or a competition. This term is sometimes used for a bonus pack.

**promotional sale** - Sonderverkauf *m*
■ Similar to discount selling, but focused on very few products and sections and designed to present new items and increase customer turnover. Temporary discounts attract buyers and accelerate purchasing decisions.

**prompted reply** - vorgegebene Antwort *f*
■ In market research, the reply of the interviewee based on providing him with a range of possible answers from which he should chose the one which most corresponds to his point of view.

**propensity to consume** - Konsumtendenz *f*
■ The disposition of an economy to channel the majority of its available income towards consumption, rather than savings. The purpose of advertising is to encourage the propensity to consume towards this goal.

**prospect** - möglicher Kunde *m*
■ An individual or an activity which is the object of a commercial or communications action, which due to its characteristics is likely to purchase certain products, even if for different reasons it doesn't do so in the end. It is closer to purchasing than a purely potential client and for that reason it is contacted directly.

**prototype** - Prototyp *m*
■ An original model on which final tests are carried out before proceeding with the manufacture of the final product.

**prototype market** - Prototyp-Markt *m*
■ A marketing environment in which the activity subject of a franchise has been tried and developed successfully, whether through pilot units, or through conventional business units, whether privately owned or franchised. Its parameters and variables are verified and defined in detail for observation in other market segments for the granting of new franchises. The peculiarities of the reference market constitute a key factor in any planning process of the business expansion into a franchise.

**provision market** - Versorgungsmarkt *m*
■ A central market or place where wholesalers provide normally perishable goods to retailers. Wholesalers are grouped by type of product and prices may be easily compared. Term often used to describe the place at which specialised retailers sell their products at stands.

**psychographic analysis** - psychografische Analyse *f*
■ In research, the study of a population as to its points of interest, opinions and attitudes.

**psychological price** - psychologischer Preis *m*
■ A price which ends in an odd number, normally 5 or 9,to make it lower than the higher round number, and thanks to which a sensation of saving is transmitted to the consumer. For example, setting a price at £995 or £999 instead of £1000.

**public** - Publikum *n*
■ A group of people that are distinguished by a common characteristic. In general, it is the group of people to whom a product, artistic representation, service or message is aimed.

**public affairs** - öffentliche Angelegenheiten *f/pl*
■ The public relations of an organisation with institutions, public bodies, political parties, corporations and pressure groups to promote its participation in public policy, and to adapt to public expectations. Public affairs is also the name given to the public relations with a public institution or body in relation to its external public.

**public marketing** - öffentliches Marketing *n*
■ The marketing carried out by entities or other bodies belonging to the Public Administration who provide services to the citizens. Profit-based government owned businesses are not included.

**public orientation campaign** - Kampagne *f* zur öffentlichen Orientierung

■ The persuasive communication, using advertising forms and styles, transmitted primarily by Public Administration bodies through mass media, containing instructions and guidelines for the public on matters of general interest (such as public, health or safety topics).

**public relations** - Public Relations *pl* (PR)

■ A management strategy which governs the way an individual, company or collective behaves in order to create a particular public image itself. It is also used to promote the favourable attitude, intention or behaviour of its public towards it. In order to achieve these aims, and using strategies based on scientific research, persuasive communication techniques are used which, however, are usually presented with a different appearance.

**public relations agency** - Public Relations-Agentur *f*

■ A company in charge of developing a client's positive image within its target group and the media.

**public relations plan** - Public Relations-Strategieplan *m*

■ A project detailing the steps to be taken by an organisation in its relationship with its public in order to reach its persuasive objectives (their acceptance and support) or mutual understanding. It consists of four phases: investigation, planning, implementation and assessment.

**Public Relations Society of America (PRSA)** - Public Relations Society of America (PRSA)

■ A United States association of public relations professionals founded in 1947 with the aim of promoting the development of this sector of activity, as well as that of its professionals, via training programmes, information exchange forums and local and national research projects.

**public service advertising** - Benefizwerbung *f*

■ A social advertising activity which is carried out and broadcast for charity. The cost of this kind of action is not paid by the advertiser, as he is socially responsible and does not have an advertising budget, but rather it is taken on by the advertising agency, which provides its creative services free of charge, and through the communications media which also grants the advertising space and time in the same manner.

**public service announcement** - Werbung *f* für die Öffentlichkeit

■ An advertisement which is carried out and broadcast for free, as its purpose is to promote social welfare. It is made by public or private not-for-profit organisations who either aim to promote their services, programmes or activities or educate and raise the awareness of its receivers.

**public service campaign** - Öffentlichkeitskampagne *f*

■ An advertising campaign whose purpose is not to sell goods and services for economic reasons, but to spread an idea or a custom which is accepted as desirable in the community. The inherent costs of such a campaign can be taken on by the promoting organisation, but it is also possible that the process is carried out for free by the professionals in the sector and the media.

**publicity** - Publicity *f*

■ An impersonal form of stimulating demand or of influencing the opinion or behaviour of a group towards a company by means of a mass media communication that is not paid for by the company or organisation benefiting from the communication. Sometimes this information cannot be controlled, especially in terms of when it appears.

**publimetry** - Werbewirkungsforschung *f*

■ An area of marketing whose function is to measure the results of an advertising campaign through consumer analysis.

**pull** - Nachfragegrad *m*

■ In the area of direct marketing, the rate of measurement of the success of a commercial action which results in finding the percentage of replies to the total number of letters sent, whether gross or net.

**purchase intention** - Kaufabsicht *f*

■ The phase that comes before a purchase decision when all the factors that influence the final decision have not been weighed up, but when an impulse is felt to satisfy a need in a particular way. The measure of the percentage of the population that finds itself in this phase, and the strength of their intentions, helps to adopt certain marketing measures. In the case of consumer products with a short shelf life, the purchase intention and repeat purchase intention are taken into account.

**purchase order** - Kaufauftrag *m*

■ A formal offer made by a potential buyer of certain goods at a given price and quantity, as specified on the order. The operation is completed upon acceptance by the seller. In practice, it is often the purchaser that accepts general conditions offered by a seller, subsequently sending a purchase order to facilitate replacement orders.

**purchase price** - Kaufpreis *m*

■ The amount paid to the seller when something is purchased.

**purchasing power** - Kaufkraft *f*

■ The capacity to buy goods and services in physical units with an amount of money. Purchasing power diminishes when inflation and the cost of living increases.

**purge** - Säuberung *f*

■ In database marketing, the act of cleaning this list by deleting those entries not considered useful.

**pyramid selling** - Verkauf *m* im Pyramidensystem

■ Also referred to as a chain sale or a snowballing sale. Although it has many forms, the operation mainly consists of obliging a purchase with the prospect of selling a far greater amount in the future (for example, cosmetics or toiletries). It often involves underlying deceit.

# Q

**qualitative** - qualitativ

■ That which cannot be expressed in a numerical or measurable form, but takes into account the characteristics or qualities of something.

**qualitative analysis** - qualitative Analyse *f*

■ The examination of relevant factors that are unable to be quantified, in order to reach a specific decision.

**quality certificate** - Qualitätszertifikat *n*

■ A document issued by a company selling a product guaranteeing that it meets the specifications that are characteristic of said product. It is normally accompanied by a guarantee whereby the company commits itself to replacing or repairing the product, free of charge, should it prove to be defective before a set period of time has elapsed. The quality certificate indicates the existence of quality control procedures in the company.

**quality control** - Qualitätskontrolle *f*

■ The regulations and operations used to ensure that the results of a particular process satisfy predetermined criteria. It is mainly performed by operators and teams, but may be subject to a further quality inspection.

**quality control plan** - Qualitätskontrollplan *m*

■ A programme specifying the objectives, methods, sampling systems and decisions to be taken with relation to monitoring and controlling the quality of a product or service.

**quality of life** - Lebensqualität *f*

■ The extent to which a person or society is able to enjoy goods and services in general.

**quality of service** - Servicequalität *f*

■ A subjective evaluation by the user of a system. It is calculated by objective measurement of key customer satisfaction criteria.

**quantitative** - quantitativ

■ That which takes into account the amount of something.

**questionnaire** - Fragebogen *m*

■ A printed form containing answers and instructions to be followed by a pollster, providing spaces for the responses given by the person being polled. Sometimes the person questioned will fill the form in directly. It should be clearly organised as different parts of the questionnaire may be used depending upon replies given to early questions. It should also be set up in such a way as to help with subsequent tabulation of the results.

**quick response** - Quick Response *f*

■ A management system based on predictive consumption models which converts the market into the engine of the production and stock maintenance processes. The model allows stock management costs to be minimised and for the products to be delivered in the space and time agreed with the client.

**quota sampling** - Quotenauswahl *f*

■ Non-probability sampling which is similar to convenience sampling, given that sample elements are not defined, however somewhat corrected by applying sample quotas that are similar to real situations (for example, a sample that must include 51% of women). There is no guarantee that relevant features have been taken into account, nor that the sample is representative, due to the fact that it was not randomly selected. Quotas are also difficult to establish. It should not be confused with stratified sampling.

# R

**R&D** - FuE

■ The initials which correspond to research and development. The group of activities aimed at improving and innovating the products and processes of a company from a technological, rather than a commercial, point of view. It is more applied research than basic research.

**rack jobber** - Regalgroßhändler *m*

■ A supplier in exclusive charge of selecting different product references, supplying and generally managing a section in a large sales outlet without it being apparent to the consumer. Used for products with a great variety of references such as books or music, it normally guarantees the store owner a certain sales volume or margin. The owner often charges a commission, although sometimes the section is rented at a fixed price and the supplier takes the marginal profit or loss. It is different to a concessionaire or licensed dealer, such as a perfume counter in a shop, because there it is apparent to the consumer that space has been ceded.

**radio advertising** - Radiowerbung *f*

■ The advertising activity which is broadcast in the spaces and times agreed with the radio stations for that purpose.

**radio commercial** - Radiowerbung *f*

■ An advertising message designed with verbal and sonorous resources (voice, silence, special effects, music) and produced using audio technology.

**random sampling** - stichprobenartige Auswahl *f*

■ The election of a group or item in such a way that any similar group or item would have the same probability of being selected, without any particular method being followed to predetermine or stratify the selection.

**range advertising** - Serienwerbung *f*

■ An advertising activity carried out by a company in order to make the public aware of the different varieties of a product that the company manufactures.

**rate of forgetfulness** - Vergessensrate *f*

■ An indicator of how rapidly a consumer forgets a brand or advertising message.

**rationale** - Begründung *f*

■ The logical argument that supports a strategy or advertising campaign.

**rationing** - Rationierung *f*

■ The effect of directly distributing scarce merchandise between consumers at prices, quantities and conditions set by the authorities. As the laws of supply and demand do not apply the appearance of a black market is probable.

**reach** - Reichweite *f*

■ The total number of people in the target group which are hit by a medium or a campaign, independently of the number of times each person is hit, as it is a net concept from which duplicates have been subtracted. Sometimes the expression net reach is used. It is the equivalent of coverage.

**reach** - Reichweite *f*

■ In Internet advertising, the number of persons who view an advertisement or banner.

**reader confidence** - Lesertreue *f*

■ The regularity with which readers of a publication open themselves up to subsequent editions. The loyal reader of a newspaper or magazine is that which reads all or almost all issues, whilst the disloyal or occasional reader is a person who frequently changes publications or doesn't usually read that kind of media.

**readers per copy** - Leser *m* pro Ausgabe

■ The average number of people who read each issue of a regular publication. It is calculated by dividing the audience or readers of said publication by the number of copies distributed (circulation).

**real market** - realer Markt *m*

■ The actual demand for goods and services from different competitors at a given time.

**reason why** - Warum *n*

■ The justification, especially used in printed advertisements, of the aspects of a product which offer benefits to its consumer, providing them with a reason why they should buy it. By extension, this term is also used to describe rational advertising which uses reasons or arguments as a mechanism for the main persuasion.

**rebranding** - Markenwechsel *m*

■ The process of revising a brand which, on occasion, leads to its substitution for another, and which is usually produced when the brand has not withstood the passage of time or when the market or company circumstances change (e.g. due to a fusion or acquisition).

**receiver** - Empfänger *m*

■ In communications, the person or group of people who receive a message via a communications channel. The message can be distorted by problems in understanding the language used, or by the prior beliefs or understandings of the person receiving the message and their psychological state.

**reception environment** - Empfangskontext *m*

■ In advertising communications, the specific environment which surrounds the reception and interpretation of adverts on the part of the receiver. Despite being decisive for the understanding and efficiency of the advertising message, it is the context which is least controlled by the broadcaster.

**recognition** - Wiedererkennung *f*

■ The system used in audience studies of printed media which consists of presenting a list of publications with their respective logos so that the interviewee can identify those which it recalls having read in the period stipulated in the study. This system is also used to measure the suggested recall of adverts.

**recyclable** - wiederverwertbar

■ A product made with materials that can be used again for a similar or a different purpose.

**recyclable container** - wiederverwertbare Verpackung *f*

■ A container made of a material that may be re-used to produce other containers or products, for example, aluminium cans. It is different to a returnable container, given that it cannot be used directly as another container as the material has to be re-processed.

**red good** - rote Ware *f*

■ Goods which are consumed and replaced at high speed, for example, foodstuffs.

**redemption** - Einlösung *f*

■ In marketing, the provision of a coupon to buy a product or to obtain a gift. These coupons are found in products previously purchased or can be obtained by mail or through newspapers. The manufacturer reimburses the wholesaler the discount plus a premium for their collaboration as an incentive because generally this system is rejected by distribution channels. There are firms that specialise in controlling the whole exchange process. The percentage of redemption can be used to measure the success of a promotion.

**re-engineering** - Umstrukturierung *f*

■ An organisational analysis of procedures and resources employed in a process or company carried out in order to increase quality, reduce costs, achieve faster replacement times and improve client and employee satisfaction. The objective is to eliminate all processes that do not add value from the client's point of view.

**reference group** - Bezugsgruppe *f*

■ The group of people which an individual attempts to imitate or whose values, lifestyle or social and economic class he aspires to have. In order to achieve the implication of the target public, the advertisement usually uses a representation of the reference group in its messages rather than that to which the target actually belongs, reflecting, in that way, his aspirations and desires rather than his real situation.

**reference price** - Referenzpreis *m*

■ The price in relation to which consumers assess that of a specific product. Its importance derives from the fact that consumers assess prices in comparative terms rather than in absolute terms. In order to assess whether a price is expensive or cheap, the consumer compares it to other prices, which are reference prices for that particular decision.

**reference value** - Bezugswert *m*

■ The price of a product which the offer in question competes with and which the consumer considers to be a better purchase alternative.

**referral premium** - Werbeprämie *f*

■ An advertising incentive that the advertiser offers his client for recommending and selling one of his products or services to a family member or friend.

**refill** - Nachfüllpackung *f*

■ A product that is used to fill another. Normally it refers to a product which is similar or complementary to the one that has been emptied.

**refund** - Rückzahlung *f*

■ In general, the return of the amount paid for a particular good. It can be partial or total, and can be the result of an incentive by the seller (for example, for not providing a service) or at the request of the purchaser.

**refusal to answer** - Antwortverweigerung *f*

■ One of the possible causes of error in a survey. It is produced when a person who is to be interviewed refuses to take part in the study. It can also occur with reference to particular questions in a questionnaire. If such a refusal is more frequent in a homogenous group of the interviewees an error in the conclusions will occur, for example, if the voters of a particular party hide their vote more than those of others.

**regional distribution centre** - regionaler Vertrieb *m*

■ A warehouse with a pre-established geographical range in which the merchandise of a company is located for its subsequent delivery to the final points of sale located in the corresponding area.

**registered design** - registriertes Design *n*

■ The design of the corporate identity of a company (including colours, form and any other specific attribute) which have been duly registered in the Public Register, so that its use is exclusively reserved for that company.

**registered trademark** - registrierte Marke *f*

■ A trademark which has been duly registered in the Public Register, guaranteeing its owner the right of exclusive use and the right to oppose the subsequent registration of similar trademarks. The register is divided into classes corresponding to different segments of activity and covers the jurisdiction of one country, although its extension or registration in other countries can be requested. In certain nations (such as the United States), in order to register a trademark real use has to have been made of the product under such trademark.

**Reilly model** - Reilly-Modell *n*

■ A mathematical model according to which the relative commercial attraction of two cities over a third is directly proportional to the population of those and inversely proportional to the square of their distance to the third.

**Reinforce** *v* - verstärken *v*

■ Enlarging the frequency and weight of an advertising campaign by means of greater investment.

**relationship marketing** - Beziehungsmarketing *n*

■ A marketing activity aimed at establishing an individual, personalised and continuous relationship between a company or a brand and the user or potential user of its products or services with the aim of creating a bond which lasts over time. It currently constitutes one of the most important focuses of marketing, especially in mature and competitive markets in which it is more profitable to keep a client than to gain a new one.

**relative market share** - relativer Marktanteil *m*

■ The result reached by dividing market share by the dominant competitor's share (the largest share of the market) or the following competitor's share (if the company concerned is the dominant competitor). This index of market position serves to select the objectives in a selective price war and above all to indicate the freedom of movement and relative costs that each competitor has.

**re-launching** - Wiedereinführung *f*

■ A campaign to give a new impulse to an activity (e.g. to a product or to a brand). It is not appropriate to talk of a new launch as the changes involved are changes in image or are superficial.

**release** - Version *f*

■ Each of the versions or publications of a system or computer program, or an instruction manual, etc. They are adaptations with small improvements on a basic version and are numbered consecutively or by version date.

**reorganisation** - Reorganisation *f*

■ The adaptation of an existing organisation to new circumstances.

**repertoire** - Repertoire *n*

■ Within the same type of product, the brands which a consumer purchases occasionally or which it is willing to purchase if it can't find its usual brand.

**repetition** - Wiederholung *f*

■ The number of times that an advert is placed in a medium during an advertising campaign. It is sometimes used to indicate the number of times a person of the target group enters into contact with the advert of the campaign. In this last case it is a synonym of frequency.

**replenishment** - kontinuierliche Lagerauffüllung *f*

■ The process by which an organisation receives supplies over time. If it's accompanied by the term efficient, it refers to the reduction or elimination of the costs of a supply chain which do not give value to the product.

**replenishment time** - Bestellintervall *m*

■ The time which passes between two orders being made.

**resale** - Wiederverkauf *m*

■ The sale of a product a short time after its original purchase, generally at a higher price.

**research and development (R&D)** - Forschung *f* & Entwicklung *f* (FuE)
■ The group of activities aimed at improving and innovating the products and processes of a company from a technological point of view, rather than a commercial point of view. It is more applied research than basic research.

**research department** - Forschungsabteilung *f*
■ In the organigramme of an advertising agency, the section dedicated to the documentation, analysis and control of data in relation to communications plans and the carrying out of campaigns.

**resizing** - Redimensionierung *f*
■ The process of adaptation of an organisation to market circumstances, normally with a tendency to reduce cost budgets and workforce, in which case the terms simplification or downsizing can also apply.

**respondent** - Befragter *m*
■ A person who answers a questionnaire or a survey whether conscious of the fact or not. Anonymity is normally guaranteed.

**response function** - Antwortfunktion *f*
■ The reaction of consumers to different levels of advertising pressure. It is generally measured in terms of the number of people who respond positively to an advertising message based on the number of hits received. The response studied can be knowledge of the brand, knowledge of the characteristics of the advertised products, or sales.

**response per thousand circulation** - Antwort pro Tausend *f*
■ In a direct response advertising campaign, the number of replies received for every one thousand copies of the publication or publications in which the advertisement is inserted.

**response rate** - Antwortrate *f*
■ The percentage of interviewees who respond to a questionnaire compared to the total number of people contacted. In mail surveys, the percentage of the replies received compared to the total number of surveys sent.

**response rate per thousand circulation** - Antwort pro Tausend *f*
■ The number of people who respond positively to the message contained in a press advertisement, expressed as a percentage of the number of copies (in thousands) which make up the circulation of the newspaper the advertisement is published in. It is usually used to measure the success of the medium as a promotional vehicle.

**retail buying group** - Einzelhandelsgruppe *f*
■ The group formed by a generally high number of retailers with the aim of making group purchases from suppliers thus obtaining greater negotiating power.

**retail price** - Einzelhandelspreis *m*
■ The sales price to the consumer. It is usually the final net price since discounts are hardly ever applied.

**retail sales** - Einzelhandelsverkauf *m*
■ The sales made to the final consumer in small quantities. It is the practice of the retailer, who purchases in bulk from the wholesaler.

**retailer** - Einzelhändler *m*
■ Merchant who sells goods directly to the final consumer. A retailer normally purchases goods from one or various wholesalers, although some major manufacturers may supply him directly or through distributors.

**retailer panel** - Einzelhandelspanel *n*
■ A group of stores that are periodically analysed by a company that specialises in gathering data on purchases, sales, stock and prices of different products and brands. The panel is constantly updated in order to ensure that the data obtained is representative of all stores and to register those that close down. Used to complement consumer panels as a source of information on distribution channel purchases and stock.

**retention marketing** - Retention Marketing *n*
■ The marketing action which focuses all its energy in conserving clients and

fostering long-term relationships with them. It constitutes one of the statements of the CRM (Customer Relationship Management) business philosophy.

**return** - Rückgabe *f*

■ Delivery to the seller by the buyer of goods previously bought, within the trial period or due to important defects in the merchandise. It also implies the seller returning the purchase price to the buyer.

**returnable container** - Pfandverpackung *f*

■ A container that can be returned to its original place of purchase and cleaned for re-use.

**reverse marketing** - Beschaffungsmarketing *n*

■ The type of marketing used when it is the client or purchaser who takes the exchange initiative and establishes the main conditions of the transaction. It usually occurs with organisational clients who have a strong negotiating power, or in certain Internet market places in which it is the purchaser himself who is subject to the purchase conditions he chooses and the suppliers who bid for the client.

**RFM (recency, frequency and money)** - RFM-Methode *f*

■ In the area of database marketing, the trio of variables to be taken into account in order to value a client and which correspond to the assessment of the time that has passed since his last purchase, the frequency of purchase in a specific period of time and the amount of money spent in that same period of time.

**rich ad** - reiche Anzeige *f*

■ An advertisement on the Internet which is rich in expression due to the instruments it uses, including animation, sound, video and interactivity, currently through technologies such as Flash (interactive animation) or Streaming (the continuous transmission of audio and video), and of program languages such as Java or JavaScript.

**road show** - Informationsveranstaltung *f*

■ A commercial technique for presenting products or services through mobile exhibitions which move from one place to the next according to a predefined route. This model of presentation is often used in political campaigns, in which the candidate travels with his delegation in special vehicles equipped with the necessary materials and which often include telecommunications networks.

**roll-in** - Einschub *m*

■ A television advertisement whose advertising message is integrated into the programme into which it is inserted, without any breaks or indications of the existence of such an advertisement.

**rollout marketing** - progressives Marketing *n*

■ A technique for launching a new product, used above all in the U.S.A., that consists of launching the product in one part of the market with the idea of subsequently covering demand elsewhere. It is used in large complex markets when the competition would similarly not be in a position to jump ahead and launch a product on the whole market.

**rotation** - Durchlauf *m*

■ The estimation of the amount of time needed to exhaust the stock of a product. In POSA, rotation is a determining factor as it conditions the manufacture: if the element should have a long display life and the rotation of the product is expected to be high, this should affect the resistance of the material used in its manufacture in order to ensure that the element can fulfil its function during the entire established period. The use of more or higher quality material will have a bearing on the final cost of the display.

**royalty** - Lizenzgebühr *f*

■ The amount that has to be paid for the use of, for example, an industrial property right, a patent or a registered trademark in the name of another. It is usually a proportional amount, defined in terms of a percentage or by unit produced or sold. In some cases an initial fixed amount is paid.

**run-of-network** - Run-Of-Network *n*

■ In Internet advertising, the purchase option according to which the impressions of the advertisement can appear on any page of the site which comprise the advertising network.

**run-of-press** - Run-Of-Press *f*

■ A press advertisement which is inserted in a publication without the need to specify a particular placement. The publication is free to place it at its discretion, even though certain unwritten guidelines are used according to which said advertisements are inserted in the informative part of the newspaper. The fixed placement requirement is usually subject to a special fee or charge.

# S

**sale by auction** - Versteigerungsverkauf *m*

■ A sale in which several buyers compete for a good or service, that is awarded to the highest bidder, provided that the price offered exceeds the starting price. Bids may be spoken aloud or made in closed envelopes. In Dutch auctions, the price is gradually reduced until accepted.

**sale by sample** - Verkauf *m* nach Muster *n*

■ A sale in which a buyer acquires a product based on the characteristics of a sample provided by a seller and the right to refuse the final product delivered if it is not the same as the sample.

**sale by subscription** - Subskriptionsverkauf *m*

■ A sale in which a buyer subscribes and makes a commitment to purchase and the seller reserves the right to not complete the sale in the event of insufficient subscriptions. The advantage for the buyer lies in a reduced launching price. It is common practice in the real estate and publishing sectors.

**sales appeal** - Verkaufsanreiz *m*

■ The capacity of a point of sale to gain a particular number of potential clients, due to its geographical location and, within a particular shopping centre, due to its exterior and interior design. For this reason, the Spanish chain Zara has given more importance to the commercial attraction of its establishments, situated in privileged areas of big cities despite the high rents, than to advertising expenses.

**sales catalogue** - Verkaufskatalog *m*

■ The printed matter used by an agent or commercial representative of a company to inform the retailers of the range of products that it makes and with the aim of inciting sales. It is usually used in the process of gaining new clients, with the aim of providing a good company image.

**sales chart** - Verkaufskurve *f*

■ Graphic and chronological representation of sales that serves to compare products, salesmen, variations over historical sales or budget deviations.

**sales contract** - Kaufvertrag *m*

■ Contract by virtue of which one party (seller) undertakes to deliver an object to another (buyer), who subsequently undertakes to pay a certain amount of money or its equivalent. Also called a purchase contract.

**sales exclusivity** - Exklusivvertrieb *m*

■ The distribution of products by a company by means of certain intermediaries but excluding others within the same sector. A company can, for example, exclusively represent a particular product within a specific geographic area.

**sales expenses** - Verkaufskosten *pl*

■ All expenses related to the commercialization activity such as discounts, commissions, advertising and promotions, etc.

**sales folder** - Verkaufsprospekt *m*

■ A leaflet, usually illustrated and printed with high quality materials, that the sales representative of a company uses to promote a new product among retailers. It is informative in nature and aims to create a good impression on the part of the trader who can subsequently pass this impression on to its clientele.

**sales force** - Verkaufspersonal *n*

▪ The group of employees in charge of selling company products through direct contact with the clients, as well as planning and organising the suitability of products and clients within the territory. This second aspect implies marketing knowledge and the establishment of qualitative long-term objectives. The sales force usually consists of salesmen, supervisors, branch or area managers and to this end are different from commission agents or distribution representatives, although it is common practise that a large part of their earnings depends upon the sales that they make.

**sales force support activity** - verkaufsunterstützende Aktivitäten *f/pl*

▪ A marketing activity (especially advertising and promotional), aimed at boosting the work of the sales force (e.g. by means of a competition for direct customers, or a prize for shop windows, for example).

**sales forecast** - Verkaufsprognose *f*

▪ An estimate of the sales that a company thinks it can achieve during a given period, based upon the sales results for previous periods and also taking into account foreseen market conditions and planned marketing activities.

**sales letter** - Werbebrief *m*

▪ A letter sent to potential customers to encourage and persuade them to buy a product or attend a sales presentation.

**sales manager** - Verkaufschef *m*

▪ The person that supervises the salespeople and commissioned representatives that a company has in a particular region, and who is ultimately responsible for preparing and reaching sales budget figures.

**sales method** - Verkaufsmethode *f*

▪ The method of fixing the advertising and communications budget based on relating it to the sales: either by assigning a fixed amount according to each unit sold or to be sold, or by a percentage of the sales made or foreseen. Other methods are by objectives, dependent on competition, availability and the arbitrary method.

**sales network** - Vertriebsnetz *n*

▪ The group of people and means used by a company to sell their products. Apart from the sales force made up by sales people, it can also include people who work on a commission basis and distributors.

**sales orientation** - Verkaufsorientierung *f*

▪ The marketing focus whereby the company carries out an intense and aggressive promotional activity with the aim of persuading the consumer to buy the product using all means available.

**sales pitch** - Verkaufsmasche *f*

▪ The speech that a sales representative uses in his professional activity to try to convince the possible buyer to purchase a particular product. Other than rational arguments it includes appeals to the emotions and affective arguments which the salesperson knows how to combine with the first according to his experience and professional skills.

**sales plan** - Verkaufsplan *m*

▪ A fundamental part of a company's planning that looks at the amount of products to sell per area or zone, client and period of time. It includes expected prices and margins and the cost of commercial activities that are to be adopted, such as promotions and publicity. It takes into account variations in the sales force, launching and withdrawal of products, and seasonal variations, as well as the competition's activities, overall market evolution and evolution by segments.

**sales price** - Schlussverkaufspreis *m*

▪ A very reduced price in order to clear products off the shelves, normally due to the end of a season.

**sales promotion** - Verkaufsförderung *f*

▪ A part of marketing that includes the commercial measures (gondola ends, displays, discounts, etc.) that push the introduction and sales of a product. It is sporadic and has immediate objectives, as opposed to advertising measures.

**sales quota** - Verkaufsquote *f*
■ The sales objectives assigned to a sales representative, company, or to a line of products. Completion is accompanied by incentives or prizes. It is normally somewhat higher than the sales budget used to make investment and production decisions.

**sales region** - Verkaufsgebiet *n*
■ The territory covered by a salesperson or group of salespeople based in a subsidiary office or regional distribution centre. Different routes are established within each zone. The division of a country into zones is made for geographical reasons, or due to the history of the company, type of client and distribution, and sometimes so that they coincide with criteria established by market research companies.

**sales representative** - Handelsvertreter *m*
■ A person who sells the products or services of a company and generally covers a specific geographic area. In some cases they may be employees of the company or they may work for themselves, charging a commission to the company that they represent. The shortened term "sales rep" is commonly used.

**sales route** - Verkaufsroute *f*
■ The itinerary that a sales representative should follow to visit his clients in an optimum manner. Each route is repeated every 7, 14 or 28 days, depending upon the importance of each client. To optimise a route sometimes marginal clients are maintained to help reduce fixed costs. The distribution route may or may not coincide with the sales route depending upon the orders obtained.

**sales-arguments book** - Vertriebshandbuch *n*
■ A publication that sets out the strong points of a product or service that should be emphasised when selling the item to a potential customer. It also includes the best responses to possible objections.

**salient attribute** - Hauptattribut *n*
■ The fundamental characteristic of a product which defines it for the consumer. It is possible that different target audiences are defined precisely because they give more importance to different attributes. For example, the fundamental attribute of a raincoat for some people is that it provides warmth, but for others it could be the style, the material, the weight, or that it isn't bulky and doesn't crease.

**sample** - Muster *n*
■ In marketing, an example or small quantity of a product offered to the consumer, in general for free, so that he can test its quality.

**sample** - Umfragebasis *f*
■ A group of selected statistics used to represent a population. The number and sampling procedure should be chosen scientifically to enable valid conclusions.

**sample book** - Musterbuch *n*
■ A catalogue with photographs and descriptions of products offered by a seller, designed to facilitate sales. In some sectors, actual articles are used as samples.

**sample mortality** - Ausfallquote *f*
■ In any kind of research, the number of elements of the sample which begin the study and do not end it. In research of more than one stage, the number of elements of the prime sample which do not complete all stages of the study. In panel research, the number of panellists who leave the study for whichever reason.

**sample product** - Musterpackung *f*
■ A commercial technique which consists in including smaller packages than the original containing a selection of the product with the aim of promoting it, freely or at a reduced price, among consumers or distributors.

**sample survey** - Repräsentativerhebung *f*
■ A study consisting in the analysis of a universe through a sample representative of the total.

**sampler** - Ausstellungsstück *n*
■ A counter or floor display which allows the consumer to try the product before

purchasing. It is frequently used in the cosmetics sector.

**sampling** - Stichprobenentnahme *f*

■ The action of selecting a sample after a process of selection. Sampling may or may not be based on probability, and either fixed or sequential.

**sampling control** - Musterprüfung *f*

■ The part of the fieldwork of a study which involves checking that the interviews have been carried out with the corresponding people, in accordance with the design of the sample.

**sampling error** - Stichprobenfehler *m*

■ In research, the error fallen into due to the mere fact of studying a universe through a sample. It is the difference between the values observed and the average of those values in repeated measurements.

**sampling method** - Auswahlverfahren *n*

■ A form of selecting a sample. The most common methods are: random sampling with or without displacement, stratified and systematic sampling.

**sandwich-board man** - Plakatträger *m*

■ A person that communicates an advertising message by means of posters suspended from his back and chest. He may also be in a costume, following a set route and handing out flyers.

**saturation** - Sättigung *f*

■ The maximum level in the use of a factor or in the coverage of a market. To exceed this level implies getting negative results (for example, too much advertising can lead to rejection, or excess distribution of a product which makes storekeepers' interest decline if too many of them carry that product).

**saturation point** - Sättigungsschwelle *f*

■ The level at which the demand for a good or service is fully satisfied so that growth in sales is limited to replacements or to cover the possible growth of the population.

**scanner bar-code reader** - Strichcodelesegerät *n*

■ A device used at supermarket check-outs to read bar codes and automatically print tickets and adjust stock. It reduces work and the possibility of error when marking products and prices and enables greater rotation of merchandise.

**scarcity** - Not *f*

■ The general absence of goods, fundamentally foodstuffs or essential goods, over an extended period of time.

**schedule** - Ablaufplan *m*

■ An organised plan of activities in which each activity is assigned a time indicating when it should take place.

**scientific persuasion model** - wissenschaftliches Überzeugungsmodell *n*

■ The symmetrical bidirectional model of public relations. The simplified representation of managerial public relations, strategically planned, based on the scientific research of the attitude of the public, for which persuasive objectives are set in terms of creation, reinforcement or improvement of the public image of the organisation, its acceptance and the behaviour of the public towards it.

**scoring** - Einschätzung *f*

■ The assessment technique of a potential or probable client in accordance with set variables, for example, to determine whether to contact such a client in a sales plan or whether to give him a certain credit level.

**seal of guarantee** - Garantiemarke *f*

■ A symbol which can be represented graphically, used by a group of companies under the control and authorization of its holder, which certifies that the products or services marked with this symbol fulfil common requirements such as quality, components, geographical origin, technical conditions, the production process of the product or the provision of services. The owner is usually a region, a country, a guarantee of origin of a product or a sectorial trade association.

**search-related banner** - Suchbanner *n*

■ The possibility offered by search engines whereby a specific advertisement appears when a user searches for a particular key word. Also known as word-buying.

**season** - Saison *f*

■ With regard to a particular activity, a period of time that is considered separately as it has certain characteristics. It may consist of various days, months or even years and, during which time the sale of seasonal articles multiplies (for example the sale of sun tan lotions during summer months). At the end of a season, products are normally sold at a discount.

**seasonal business** - Saisongeschäft *n*

■ Purchases and sales made exclusively in one particular period of the year. Normally related to agricultural harvests, weather conditions or customs. The periods do not normally coincide with calendar years, but rather finish just before the beginning of the next season.

**seasonal fluctuation** - saisonbedingte Fluktuation *f*

■ The oscillation in price or sales volume of a product in a specific season of the year. Seasonal fluctuations in price are superimposed on cyclical fluctuations and sector trends.

**seasonal sale** - Saisonverkauf *m*

■ A sale that takes place at a particular time of year (e.g. umbrellas in winter). Companies either complete their product range with others, try to promote sales of their product throughout the entire year or only offer it in certain months.

**seasonality** - Saisonabhängigkeit *f*

■ The variation in sales that is repeated in the same season of the year, due to climate, customs and holidays. An example of a seasonal product is a bathing suit.

**second source** - Zweitlieferant *m*

■ The manufacturer of a product who is authorised to produce it by the company who originally designed it, and holds its patents and rights.

**secondary advertiser** - sekundärer Werbetreibender *m*

■ An advertiser which uses the advertising time or space of a main advertiser with the latter's agreement.

**sectorial marketing** - sektorales Marketing *n*

■ The marketing which is applied to each of the different areas of economic or social activity. Reference can therefore be made to financial marketing, service marketing, social causes marketing, tourism marketing, and senior citizen marketing, among others.

**segment** - Segment *n*

■ A part of a general market formed by a collection of consumers of a product or service that have been sufficiently characterised and identified and are interested in a specific variant of that product or service. A company, in so far as its objectives and possibilities allow, specialises in one or more segments that can be extensive or niche markets.

**segment** *v* - segmentieren *v*

■ To divide a group in different parts according to their common characteristics.

**segmentation** - Segmentierung *f*

■ An activity that aims to identify comparable sets of buyers in order to specialise the production, distribution or communication of a particular variant of a product or service. Upon carrying out a segmentation study, a company finds new opportunities for more adequately satisfying requirements and starts changing its production, publicity, etc.

**segmentation fence** - Segmentierungsbarriere *f*

■ In marketing, the requirement that consumers have to fulfil to have access to advantageous purchase options such as a price reduction. It is normal to offer, for example, discounts to younger people, or people older than a certain age.

**selection bias** - Auswahlverzerrung *f*

■ The source of errors in a survey which originates from inaccuracies always in the same direction on selecting the elements of a sample. It can lead to the invalidation of the results of the survey.

**selective advertising** - selektive Werbung *f*

■ Advertising addressed to a very restricted group of people.

**selective distortion** - selektive Verzerrung *f*

■ The process by which a consumer interprets an advertising message in a different way to another consumer, due to personal knowledge and previous experience. Understanding is the intermediate phase between receiving and retaining a message.

**selective distribution** - selektiver Vertrieb *m*

■ An intermediate policy between exclusive and intensive distribution. More than one outlet exists per area, however manufacturers directly control and support the stores that stock their brand.

**selective price war** - selektiver Preiskrieg *m*

■ A market situation in which the attacking competitor chooses the areas where his relative market quota is lowest, as objectives in its price war. It selects the type of product, packaging, client or geographic area where it is relatively weak, and as such, has less to lose if a full-scale price war breaks out.

**selective recall** - selektive Erinnerung *f*

■ The process by which an audience only remembers a fraction of a transmitted message, normally that part that has been emphasised, although sometimes the novelty element is remembered or some other element that clashes with created expectations.

**self-liquidating premium** - selbstdeckende Werbeprämie *f*

■ A sales promotion where a complementary product is offered at a reduced price that covers costs but is still, nevertheless, very attractive to the consumer. The reduced cost is achieved through bulk buying or by ordering a special production.

**self-mailer** - Self-Mailer *m*

■ A piece of direct advertising which can be sent by mail to its addressee without the need to place it in an envelope because it is self-closing.

**self-promotion** - Eigenwerbung *f*

■ The advertising that some media carry out on their own behalf using their own spaces to promote a programme or special edition. It is frequent in television and is considered part of the advertising content at the time of calculating the time that this media dedicates to advertising.

**self-regulation** - Selbstregulierung *f*

■ The rules that a company or a group (for example, advertising agencies) imposes upon itself so that its products and services meet minimum requirements of quality, security, impartiality, objectivity or restrictions on attacks on the competition or celebrities.

**self-selling sale** - Selbstverkaufssystem *n*

■ A sale in which the distributor is also the seller, in that they restock shelves, attempt to sell new products, deliver the goods, invoice and collect (for example, dairy products, soft drinks and frozen goods). Different from itinerant sales in that self-selling sales are carried out by deliverers employed by a company with a large factory or distribution warehouse.

**self-serve advertising** - Selbstbedienungswerbung *f*

■ On the Internet, the advertising acquired directly on the advertisers site without the intervention of an intermediary, representative or seller.

**self-service** - Selbstbedienung *f*

■ A type of establishment in which the public is able to directly choose the majority of items available on shelves. It is the opposite to traditional counter sales and normally employed by supermarkets and hypermarkets.

**sellers' market** - Verkäufermarkt *m*

■ A market in which suppliers have a clear advantage, given that demand exceeds supply.

**sellers' shortages** - Angebotsengpass *m*
■ A situation created when goods or services are not in sufficient demand to cover available supply at current market prices.

**sell-in** - Einzelhändlerpräsentation *f*
■ The commercial activity during which the representative for a manufacturer presents the retailer with a new product and motivates him to promote its sale to the end consumers. This activity is usually supported by a sales folder.

**selling cost** - Verkaufskosten *pl*
■ The cost encompassing all activities necessary to offer the product to the client.

**selling off** - Verkaufslawine *f*
■ The hasty selling of goods or stocks whose price is dropping in order to sell them before the price drops even further.

**selling point** - Verkaufsargument *n*
■ Each of the strong points of a product or service that are used when making a sale.

**selling price** - Verkaufspreis *m*
■ The price at which a product is sold, which may coincide with the tariff price.

**selling unit** - Verkaufseinheit *f*
■ The smallest unit of a product sold in a retail shop.

**sequence bias** - Abfolgeverzerrung *f*
■ In surveys, the influence that previous questions have on subsequent questions.

**sequential sampling** - sequentielles Stichprobenverfahren *n*
■ A type of sampling in which the size of the sample (obviously variable, as opposed to fixed sampling), depends on the information that is gradually compiled. Each phase includes a decision based on whether or not the data obtained allows a conclusion, or if more information is required. Used to control production series.

**serialized sales** - Verkauf *m* als Sammelwerk
■ A type of sale in which buyers gradually complete a collection (though with no commitment to buy), by buying individual issues on a weekly, fortnightly or monthly basis. The number of people that actually complete a collection is substantially lower than those that begin. It is a traditional way of selling for publishers via newsagents and newsstands.

**services marketing** - Dienstleistungsmarketing *n*
■ A discipline corresponding to the branch of marketing which studies the specific and differential characteristics of the marketing of non-tangible products.

**set-up** - Montage *f*
■ In marketing, the final organising of a store before it opens to the public.

**seven R's** - sieben Rs *n/pl*
■ A teamwork analysis system. The initials correspond to reason for being, regulations, roles, relations rituals, recompenses and results.

**seven S's** - 7-S-Modell *n/pl*
■ A scheme for analysing an organisation and its strategy developed by Tom Peters and McKinsey. The seven "S's are: Shared values; Structure; Style; Systems; Staff; Strategy; and Skills.

**sex segmentation** - Segmentierung nach Geschlecht *f*
■ A marketing strategy that consists of differentiating products according to the sex of the buyer or potential user, for example, disposable nappies for boys and girls.

**sexist advertising** - sexistische Werbung *f*
■ The advertising which, through its messages, accentuates the differences between men and women favouring a stereotypical view of both social groups and feeding the prejudices between them.

**shelf life** - Haltbarkeit *f* im Lager
■ A term used to define the active life of specific products and devices stored in warehouses waiting to be substituted for others that are installed in operating systems and equipment. Some products, such as batteries or film rolls, have a

limited life span, whereas others become obsolete because of the evolution of the equipment or the technology.

**shelf-space** - Regalfläche *f*
▪ The number of fronts that a product or item has in the display unit of a store. The size is usually assigned in proportion to its profitability or its sales, giving priority to the distributor brands.

**shock advertising** - Schockwerbung *f*
▪ An advertising campaign, generally social in nature, whose contents are expressed in a verbal or visual language which, whether due to its harshness or due to the surprise it causes, is a "blow" to the receiver. The aim of this kind of message is to achieve a high notoriety with regards to the subject or problem it expresses. For example, the British advertisement in which a baby is injecting itself.

**shopping centre** - Einkaufszentrum *n*
▪ A collection of retail shops concentrated in a purpose-built area where clients can buy all manner of goods. They tend to include one or two shops that are the driving force and ensure a certain flow of people, such as a well-known food or clothing store.

**shopping channel** - Teleshop *m*
▪ A television space with offers direct to the public which, in exchange for payment, promotes the sales of a product or service. There are cable television channels exclusively dedicated to telesales and they are focused on times with very little audience.

**shop-window** - Schaufenster *n*
▪ The area of a store that is visible from the outside, in which products and messages are presented to the general public.

**short ad** - Kurzanzeige *f*
▪ A term used in newspaper circles to describe a characteristically brief publicity announcement.

**show room** - Ausstellungsraum *m*
▪ A shop or exposition which presents a representative array or the totality of proposed products for sale. It offers the possibility of making orders directly on location and, sometimes, tasting the samples.

**shutter** - Pulldown-Fenster *n*
▪ A non-clickable publicity advert which opens in a shutter in the centre of the opening page of an Internet site. It appears on downloading the page and closes itself after around 10 seconds, leaving a small clickable icon on the screen which allows the user to open it again.

**skimming** - Abschöpfen *n*
▪ A practice that consists of fixing a price higher than that which will later become the normal price when launching a product, or introducing minor improvements or differences to attract clients with higher purchasing power, in order to make an extra profit. Not to be confused with milking.

**skimming price** - Abschöpfungspreis *m*
▪ A high price which is fixed to a new product to aim it at a market segment with high buying power and high interest for technological innovation. Once this top segment is reached, the price is gradually dropped, thus reaching market segments which are more price sensitive. It is normally applied to products which involve technological innovation, and is also known as the strategy which makes the most of the market because consumers pay the highest price they are willing to pay.

**slice-of-life style** - Alltagsszene *f*
▪ A type of commercial or advertisement in which people use a particular product brand in their everyday lives.

**slogan** - Slogan *m*
▪ A brief phrase which finalises an advertisement in the form of a conclusion. It serves to fix, synthetically, the positioning of the brand or product and to also give continuity to a multimedia advertising campaign, made up of numerous originals in the different media.

**social advertising** - soziale Werbung *f*
▪ The commercial advertising activity in which the product or service and its

advantages are sacrificed in favour of a social theme that the advertiser tries to demonstrate or "report". A commercial advertising space becomes the showcase of the "reported" cause, and so the controversy on the ethics of these actions is almost guaranteed, with the brand emitting the message becoming the main beneficiary. The Italian fashion company Benetton successfully carried out these kinds of advertising actions during the 1990's.

**social and cultural codes** - soziokultureller Code *m*

■ The group of social and cultural elements that advertising reproduces and uses in its messages. For example, rules of behaviour, topics, stereotypes or fashions.

**social class** - Gesellschaftsklasse *f*

■ Each of the strata, hierarchically placed, in which society is divided. Society is usually classified as high, middle (also middle-high, middle-middle, and middle-low) and low. The difference between classes is fundamentally due to economic reasons, although other factors such as education or culture are influential. It constitutes one of the criteria for the segmentation of a population in marketing terms.

**social marketing** - soziales Marketing *n*

■ Marketing designed to develop activities that affect society as a whole. It is different to commercial marketing in that competing organisations fight for the same cause. Such competitors may assist social marketers in many ways, however they can also create fragmented markets and other problems.

**social mobility** - soziale Mobilität *f*

■ The willingness to change social environments. It is broken down horizontally (change of residence) and vertically (social class).

**socio-economic segmentation** - sozioökonomische Segmentierung *f*

■ The classification of a population into groups in accordance with one or many socio-economic variants, fundamentally life style and personality such as, for example, education, job type, income, or religion. It is generally combined with demographic criteria to obtain more precision when dividing into homogeneous groups that differ from other groups in the above mentioned variables and in their behaviour towards a particular product or brand.

**soft selling** - Soft-Selling *n*

■ A sales technique based on indirect evocative messages so that the purchase decision comes from the client and not from the strength of the arguments put forward by the seller. By extension, the type of advertising used in these terms.

**solus position** - allein stehende Werbeanzeige *f*

■ The location of an advertisement in any media, whether printed or audiovisual, so that it appears on its own without any adjacent advertisement. The tariff is higher to that of advertisements which appear in blocks or together. The tariff sometimes takes the form of a surcharge on the price.

**space allocation** - Standortzuweisung *f*

■ The optimum use of space for displaying products in a shop in order to maximise sales. Generally, only sales figures of a particular item are taken into consideration and a proportional amount of space is allocated, whereas space management takes into account potential sales of the product and of associated products, plus gross margins and direct costs which may vary from one product to another.

**spatial association** - räumlicher Zusammenschluss *m*

■ A collaboration between retailers which consists of being located in the same place or geographical location with the aim of attracting a higher number of consumers to the area.

**spatial competition** - räumlicher Wettbewerb *m*

■ The inter-company rivalry which is centred around a specific geographical area.

**special conditions** - Sonderkonditionen *f/pl*

■ The special purchase conditions which a seller grants a client, thanks to which the latter benefits from a lower sale price. In commercial distribution it is common for the distributor to take advantage of the discounts given to him by the supplier or manufacturer for different reasons (such as prompt payment, seasonal markdowns, discounts for placing products in special locations).

**speciality store** - Fachgeschäft *n*

■ A store that concentrates on a particular type of article, within which it has a fairly broad product range with a variety of brands and accessories and staff on hand to give advice and other specialist services.

**speciality trade** - Fachhandel *m*

■ Generally a retail establishment with a selected range of products and large supply, with a greater capacity to inform its clients and handle specific orders.

**spending unit** - Konsumeinheit *f*

■ A statistical term used for a household, individual or other group of people that pool their income and take the whole community into account when deciding upon their spending.

**sponsorship** - Sponsoring *n*

■ On the Internet, the economic contribution agreed between the company owning the website and the sponsoring company, usually in exchange for corporate presence and preferential advertising space on the site.

**sponsorship** - Sponsoring *n*

■ In general, an advertiser who pays for part or all of the expenses of a sports exhibition, concert or other show in return for advertising rights.

**spontaneous recall** - spontane Erinnerung *f*

■ The percentage of the targeted public that name a brand when asked to recall brands that have been advertised in a given period, or some other general stimulus.

**sports marketing** - Sportmarketing *n*

■ The branch of marketing which considers sports personalities and clubs to be brands whose image has to be promoted and popularised, and obtaining the corresponding return for leasing this image to interested companies or entities. An example is the company Real Madrid Marketing Japan which the Spanish club created at the beginning of 2004 with various Japanese entities with the aim of channelling the advertising exploitation of the brand in that country.

**standard error estimate** - mittlerer Schätzfehler *m*

■ A statistical term which reflects the average error made in the prediction of any variable. In marketing it is commonly used to refer to sales predictions. As to its concrete application in logistics, the concept is used to determine the level of safety stock needed to face an unforeseen increase in demand.

**standard of living** - Lebensstandard *m*

■ The level of satisfaction of a person or group of people's needs, measured by a quantity of goods and services that may be purchased with real income. A low standard of living only enables basic needs to be satisfied and is common in underdeveloped countries and marginal groups.

**standard price** - Zielpreise *m/pl*

■ The purchase, sale or cost price that is the objective of a company, and that is set at the planning stage. They are also called budgeted or normal prices. Actions are planned at production and marketing levels to determine these prices in accordance with previous history, strategies and means. They are compared with real prices in the long-term in order to calculate deviations.

**standardisation** - Normierung *f*

■ The classification adjustment to a type, model or norm, and by extension the adaptation of a product or system to that which is considered normal.

**standardised product** - Standardprodukt *n*

■ A type of product in which the brand is of little importance as the consumer perceives the differences to be trivial or insubstantial. This situation arises because of the intrinsic characteristics of the product, due to the lack of adequate advertising pressure, and due to the pricing policy of large stores which favours the consumer selecting a product on the basis of price.

**staple good** - Basisartikel *m*

■ A high turnover product that forms part of a basic selection of goods that, almost by necessity, should be on offer to the public. Consumers remember the price of these products and they are the most indicative of the pricing policy of a particular store.

**star** - Star *m*

■ In a growth-share matrix, the market leader or dominating company in a high growth industry. Although the leader may be consuming the same level of financial resources as it is generating, it is an ideal situation that requires an innovative style of management.

**starter product** - Hauptprodukt *n*

■ A product marketed with the aim of generating one or a number of subsequent complementary purchases of other products, whether replacement parts, refills or accessories, for example, Pandora bracelets and charms.

**static advertising** - Bandenwerbung *f*

■ Any advertising which lacks movement. Although advertising in printed media also possesses this characteristic, the term is applied in general to outdoor advertising located in public roads and sports stadiums and which appears on television during the broadcasting of an event.

**static firm** - statisches Franchisesymbol *n*

■ A franchise company which has achieved sufficient market development and consequently, stops or limits the incorporation of new franchises. Also that which, despite having vacant markets, does not proceed to new openings and keeps its dimensions constant.

**status symbol** - Statussymbol *n*

■ A product that transmits an image of prestige to the user and which is purchased to a large extent to be used as a sign of social importance within the sector of population to which it is directed. If a product manages to gain that image it can be sold at a higher price which in turn reinforces its exclusivity and prestige. It can also lead to rejection by people who do not wish to convey that type of image.

**stereotype** - Stereotyp *n*

■ A fixed and oversimplified image or idea of something or somebody that usually does not respond to reality.

**stickiness** - Stickiness *f*

■ The effectiveness of a website as to its capacity to attract and retain users, and to promote their active participation. From a marketing point of view, the success of a site cannot be measured in the number of visits but rather the quality of the same, as well as the time that the visitors stay connected to the site and the manner in which they enter into contact with those responsible for the site.

**stimulational marketing** - Stimulationsmarketing *n*

■ The type of marketing employed to reactivate a stagnant or inexistent demand. The main purpose of stimulational marketing actions is to create a market through the analysis of consumers' needs and the offer of products with useful and valued attributes.

**stimulus** - Anreiz *m*

■ That which provokes or causes action to satisfy a need.

**stock** - Bestand *m*

■ The material kept in storage at the point of sale, of distribution or production.

**stock availability** - Bestandsverfügbarkeit *f*

■ The stock which can be used at any moment to fulfil an order. If there is not enough stock available to fill an order a stock-out would occur.

**stock centralisation** - Bestandszentralisierung *f*
■ The act of storing stock in a single point to facilitate its management and to avoid scattering which would be prejudicial from the point of view of cost efficiency.

**stock depreciation** - Bestandswertminderung *f*
■ The process of loss in value that stock undergoes during its time in storage. It can be due to different reasons, such as physical deterioration or technical obsolescence.

**stock-out** - fehlende Lagerbestände *m/pl*
■ A shortage of a product that should normally be in a warehouse when an order is received. The acceptable percentage depends upon the sector and client, however it should not be excessively high and therefore damage the company's reputation of good service, nor excessively low which would mean the warehouse is overstocked.

**stockpiling** - Horten *n*
■ The process by which the number of products in the warehouse exceeds the stock level established as normal. It can be due to an overestimation of demand or due to a preventive action against a foreseen increase in sales.

**store island** - Verkaufsinsel *f*
■ A large and solitary display of a product, either in a special item of furniture or simply piled up, in order to draw the public's attention to the product in a store. It differs from a gondola end in that it is isolated in the middle of a passage.

**strategic alliance** - strategische Allianz *f*
■ The strategic association between companies with the aim of achieving a long term objective. It usually occurs between companies which work in close markets but which do not compete against each other.

**strategic marketing** - strategisches Marketing *n*
■ The part of marketing which analyses threats and opportunities in the area in which it works, as well as the resources and internal capabilities of the company itself, with the aim of planning medium and long term action measures to attain the organisational objectives.

**strategic research** - strategische Forschung *f*
■ Market research which offers the necessary information for preparing a public relations programme.

**stratified sampling** - geschichtete Stichprobe *f*
■ A type of probability sampling in which the sample is divided into individual and mutually exclusive levels, in which a sole independent sample is randomly taken. If the levels are well defined, the system is extremely accurate and enables smaller confidence intervals. Stratified sampling may be proportional or non-proportional. The former uses successive samples that are proportional to the relative importance of each sample level. In non-proportional sampling, variability is incorporated in such a way that the sample size increases according to variability. The system enables substantial cost reduction and the difference between quota sampling is that sample elements are chosen randomly. Non-proportional sampling is also referred to as compensated sampling.

**structured questionnaire** - strukturierter Fragebogen *m*
■ In quantitative investigation, the type of questionnaire in which the questions and the possible answers to each question are predetermined. The interviewer should ask the questions in the order in which they appear in the questionnaire, repeating the text word for word in each case. He will not be able to note down more answers than those which appear as possible alternatives to each question. The structure of a questionnaire allows for adjustment depending on whether or not it contains open questions.

**stuffer** - Werbeeinlage *f*
■ A promotional piece which is inserted as a filler in an already existing

communication by mail between a client and the company. For example, the leaflets with special offers which are put in envelopes together with the phone or electricity bill or with bank statements.

**sub-brand** - Submarke *f*

▪ A brand that has its own visual identity and personality, and which can be distinguished from the main brand or masterbrand that covers all the goods of the same manufacturer.

**subliminal advertising** - unterschwellige Werbung *f*

▪ A type of advertising which, through production techniques, can act on the target public without being consciously perceived. In other words, subliminal advertising tries to act on the subconscious of the consumers via imperceptible stimuli, inciting the consumption of the advertised products. However, despite the myths surrounding it, its efficiency has not been demonstrated.

**substitute goods** - Substitutionsgüter *n/pl*

▪ Economic goods that satisfy a similar need. A rise in price of one of them will give rise to an increase in the demand of the other. It is the opposite of complementary goods.

**substitution effect** - Substitutionseffekt *m*

▪ A variation in the quantity demanded of a particular product as a result of a change in the price of another substitute product, the level of income remaining constant.

**subvertising** - subversive Werbung *f*

▪ An activity carried out by individuals or anti-system sectors with the aim of criticising the previously broadcast advert or campaign, or also brand or company, but using the same advertising tool for this purpose: whether due to the existence of a social controversy surrounding the product (for example alcohol or tobacco), due to the language or strategy used in the message (such as some of the advertisements for fashion or Calvin Klein perfumes) or even to condemn socially criticisable policies or actions carried out by certain multinationals (such as McDonald's or Nike).

**successful idealists** - erfolgreiche Idealisten *m/pl*

▪ A type of consumer in a pan European classification of lifestyles. They represent 5-15% of the population, are rich and enjoy art, healthy eating and ecology.

**suggested recall** - suggerierte Erinnerung *f*

▪ The percentage of the targeted public that recognise a brand when it is named. The total level of awareness of the brand is measured.

**suggestions box** - Vorschlagsbriefkasten *m*

▪ A box placed at a sales outlet or in a company in which customers or employees deposit their opinions, recommendations or even complaints.

**supply** - Angebot *n*

▪ In economics, the quantity of a good offered in a particular market at a given time and at a given price or set of prices. In theory, supply and demand coincide at equilibrium price. If prices go up, supply increases and demand decreases.

**supply chain** - Lieferkette *f*

▪ The group of interdependent organisations which participate in the reception and delivery of goods, from their origin or place where the raw materials are produced, to the final destination where the product is purchased, used or consumed by the purchaser.

**surround session** - Surround-Session *f*

▪ An advertising format on the Internet site of The New York Times newspaper which allows the same advertisement to follow the visitor through all the pages he visits in the digital newspaper.

**survey** - Umfrage *f*

▪ A procedure used to obtain information by asking or observing a collective in a systematic and structured fashion. When the universe being studied is vast, a sample group is chosen.

**survey by contact** - Kontaktbefragung *f*

■ A survey in which the surveyor has direct contact with a representative of the collective being studied, who replies to questions contained in a questionnaire. Contact is normally by means of a personal interview, either prearranged or random, although postal or telephone contact is also possible.

**survey by observation** - Beobachtungsbefragung *f*

■ A survey in which the surveyor observes the behaviour of the chosen universe in accordance with observation instructions but without establishing direct contact. Used to check that certain actions take place (for example, displaying of point of sale material, use of crash helmets by motorcyclists, etc.).

**survey by subscription** - Umfrage *f* durch Subskription

■ A fixed unique survey organised by a specialised company that sells it, either before or after carrying it out, to various clients with similar needs, all of whom receive the same results. Not to be confused with an omnibus survey.

**switcher consumer** - untreuer Verbraucher *m*

■ A consumer who is not loyal to one brand in the same category of goods, but rather alternates his consumption between two or more brands.

**switching cost** - Wechselkosten *pl*

■ The costs which a purchaser incurs when he stops buying from his normal supplier and goes on to purchase from a new supplier. It includes all costs related to the process of searching for a new supplier, the start up of a new agreement and the adaptation of certain standards to the characteristics of the seller.

**SWOT analysis** - SWOT-Analyse *f*

■ A framework, used in marketing analysis to assess the situation of a company and which is centred around the Strengths, Weaknesses, Opportunities and Threats which it has.

**systematic sampling** - systematische Stichprobenentnahme *f*

■ A type of probability cluster sampling in which samples are comprised of n number of elements after random selection using an ordered list. It is cluster sampling of a level, given that the sample includes the entire group selected by an arithmetic progression. It may be made more representative by ensuring elements at both ends of the sample (for example, stores with maximum and minimum surface areas). Precaution should be taken to avoid natural intervals.

# T

**tachistoscope** - Tachistoskop *n*

■ An instrument used in research which indicates the time that the interviewees gaze has been focused on each of the parts of an image or graphic. It is usually used in the pre-test of advertisements so as to know which elements have awoken most interest.

**tactile ad** - Werbung *f* zum Anfassen

■ A graphic advertising message which includes elements of paper, material or plastic designed to be touched, giving the receiver the possibility of directly appreciating some of the characteristics of the product.

**take or pay** - take or pay

■ A clause by virtue of which a buyer undertakes to buy and pay for merchandise in specified quantities and periods or, upon failing to do so, compensate the seller for an amount up to the total value of the goods. Often used in long term supply contracts to protect the seller.

**tangible** - greifbar

■ An adjective for goods and assets that indicates they have a material form and can therefore be handled physically.

**tangible product** - greifbares Produkt *n*

■ A product that can be felt and touched, as opposed to a service, which is intangible.

**target group** - Zielgruppe *f*

■ The specific sector of the population to whom a product or advertising message is aimed, whether they be the buyers or consumers of the product. The target public is defined by demographic, geographic, and socio-economic characteristics and by life style.

**target group behaviour** - Zielgruppenverhalten *n*

■ A characteristic of Internet advertising which allows the response to the advertisement to be known in real time, and consequently also the profile of the users.

**target reach** - Zielgruppenabdeckung *f*

■ In an advertising campaign, the audience of a medium that belong to the target group or the people of the target group exposed to a medium.

**targeting** - gezielte Werbung *f*

■ An activity which involves purchasing publicity space on sites which respond to the characteristics of the target group at whom the campaign is aimed.

**taste** - Geschmack *m*

■ The way in which each person appreciates things. Consumer tastes are one of the factors studied by marketing.

**tasting** - Kostprobe *f*

■ A promotional activity where foods or beverages can be sampled. It can be carried out at a gondola end or at a factory or warehouse.

**tear-off coupon** - Coupon *m* zum Ausschneiden

■ In printed media, the part of the advertisement which is cut out and sent to request information, make an order or gain a discount. It is frequently used to identify the orderer or the medium from which the response has originated.

**teaser advertising** - Lockwerbung *f*

■ A form of advertising communication consisting of a series of incomplete messages that begin to make sense in successive waves in order to draw attention and awaken curiosity. Although more interest may be generated, heavier investment is required as repetition is needed for the brand to penetrate.

**teaser campaign** - Lockkampagne *f*

■ A campaign prior to the definitive campaign which tries to awaken public interest by concealing elements as important as the product itself or the advertised brand.

**technical sales** - technischer Verkauf *m*

■ The selling of complex mechanical, electrical etc. products to the customer. Since this requires expert knowledge about the product, technical salespersons are usually engineers or with related education. Technical selling typically requires long customer-seller relations, and reliable after-sales technical support.

**telemarketing** - Telemarketing *n*

■ A communications technique which uses the telephone as a transmission channel or as a reply medium to promote and sell products or services, or to carry out opinion polls and research surveys of the market.

**telephone interview** - telefonische Befragung *f*

■ In market studies, the interview which uses the telephone as a means of communication. Many telephone interviews are carried out with the aid of a computer, either to select the numbers to dial, or to instantly register the replies.

**telepromotion** - Telepromotion *f*

■ The communication of the benefits of a product using the programmes and presenters of a television station. They are spaces approximately 60 seconds long in which, using a script, the presenters or television personalities or actors represent a situation surrounding the product which allows it to be shown and prescribed.

**telesales** - Televerkauf *m*

■ A method of selling whereby the purchaser does not enter into physical contact with the product, but rather purchases through a different medium, such as a catalogue, the telephone, the television, a web page or by e-mail.

**television advertising** - Fernsehwerbung *f*

■ The audiovisual advertising activity which is spread through spaces and times established in a television station for that purpose. The most normal spaces are 20 or 30 seconds long grouped into blocks and broadcast between programmes or interrupting the broadcast of the same.

**test area** - Gebietstest *m*

■ The geographical area in which a given market test will be carried out.

**test market** - Testmarkt *m*

■ The geographical area in which a product is launched in order to estimate its success. Several representative cities are normally chosen and different marketing plans implemented (for example, advertising, handouts, introductory offers and vouchers for other products. An evaluation is made of brand awareness, product testing and repeated purchases. Although the process is effective, it may cause a delay in product launching, alert competitors and results difficult to interpret.

**testimonial** - Testimonial-Werbung *f*

■ An advertising format in which a personality gives an account of his direct experience with the product. He normally offers a positive testimonial which acts as a reference or recommendation for the generic consumers to whom the message is directed. It can take many different forms, from a famous personality to a customer who is satisfied and who acts as a model for the target group.

**text link** - Textlink *m*

■ The advertising or promotional links which appear on a web page, electronic message, Internet portal or any other medium used on the Internet in the form of text. They can appear as part of a news item, promoting a section, in a directory list, in an index, as a recommended link, or other form.

**text link exchange** - Textlinkaustausch *m*

■ The agreement between two sites whereby each one places advertising text on its site with a hyperlink to the other site.

**theoretical market** - theoretischer Markt *m*

■ A theoretical demand for a good or service, in other words, people with a particular need that can be satisfied by a good or service regardless of whether or not they possess the necessary resources (potential market) or are real consumers (natural market).

**three for the price of two** - nimm drei, zahl zwei

■ A promotion in which three items are given for the price of two. This type of promotion is used in products with a relatively high margin as it implies a discount of 33% although at times it is presented as being a 50% discount. In the United States the offer tends to be two for one. In general they are used as loss leader products, seeking the profits that can be obtained from other products that the consumer buys having been attracted to the point of sale by the offer.

**tie-in** - Verbundaktion *f*

■ The marketing action in which diverse entities (manufacturers, distributors, sellers etc.) participate in a coordinated manner, each putting in their part. In the case of advertising, it particularly refers to the advertisements carried out jointly by manufacturers and distributors.

**tie-in advertisement** - Verbundwerbung *f*

■ An advertisement which covers more than one product or service, whether or not they belong to the same advertiser. In special cases it is joint advertising, generally carried out by the manufacturer of the product and its distributor.

**tie-in agreement** - Verbundvereinbarung *f*

■ The agreement between two companies to give an offer on products or an advertising communication joining or linking their brands.

**tie-in sales** - Verbundverkauf *m*

■ The sale of a product with the condition or requirement that the purchaser simultaneously or subsequently purchases another product from the company. It is a practice persecuted by authorities in defence of competition.

**tiered statements** - gestaffelte Sendungen *f*

▪ A marketing technique based on segmenting a client base into sections or blocks in accordance with certain criteria so as to communicate offers, incentives or other messages.

**time preference** - zeitliche Präferenz *f*

▪ A consumer preference that manifests itself by choosing either present consumption or future consumption (or present saving).

**top-of-mind brand** - Top-of-mind-Marke *f*

▪ A brand (or advertising campaign) which the studied target public designates in first place when answering the corresponding question, thus showing its leadership. Advertising aims to make a brand improve in terms of recollection in the minds of the customers and improve the image that it wishes to transmit.

**total audience** - Gesamtpublikum *n*

▪ The number of persons who have seen, read, watched or listened to one or various advertisements in a campaign.

**total cost** - Gesamtkosten *pl*

▪ The sum of fixed and variable costs that a company or product has.

**tourism advertising** - Tourismuswerbung *f*

▪ An advertising activity which is carried out in order to make the characteristics and attractiveness of a particular place, city, community, county or country known, with the aim of increasing the choice of that place as a tourist or holiday destination on the part of the target public at which it is aimed.

**tourism marketing** - Tourismusmarketing *n*

▪ A type of marketing which is applied specifically to the tourist sector due its distinctive qualities in that area of activity.

**trade advertising** - Handelswerbung *f*

▪ Advertising which is aimed at wholesalers and retailers of a type of product to provide those intermediaries with the arguments and relevant details such as the support given for advertising expenses, rotation indexes or new products under the brand. It is also useful for motivating the strength of sales.

**trade directory** - Firmenverzeichnis *n*

▪ A guide containing names and details of businesses in a sector or geographical area, classified in a convenient way. They are usually listed according to activity.

**trade fair marketing** - Messemarketing *n*

▪ A branch of marketing whose purpose is the design and management of fairs and specialised functions recognised as being of great public importance which affect not only the companies, products and services which form part of them, but also the cities in which they are held, and contributing to their public projection within the area of city marketing.

**trade magazine** - Fachzeitschrift *f*

▪ A magazine with a readership that belongs to a sector or that share a specific interest, as opposed to a general interest or consumer magazine. It is the optimum channel for reaching a particular public with technical messages and to carry out sales from company to company or industrial sales.

**trade marketing** - Handelsmarketing *n*

▪ The strategic alliance between members of a distribution channel situated on different levels through which they develop cooperation agreements so as to achieve mutual gains and to satisfy consumers' demands more efficiently.

**trade name** - Handelsname *m*

▪ The name by which an establishment or company wishes to be known to the general public, which does not necessarily coincide with its official name.

**trade sale** - Verkauf *m* an Wiederverkäufer

▪ A restricted type of sale made only to intermediaries in a specific sector and usually involving special discounts.

**trade-in sale** - Verkauf *m* mit Inzahlungnahme

▪ A sale in which the price of a new product is reduced by that of a similar used product given in exchange, that may or may not be of the same brand or in working condition.

**trademark** - Handelsmarke *f*

■ The name chosen by a manufacturer to designate his products. As with the logotype, it is formed of a graphic representation, a typeface and specific colours to insure its differentiation from other trademarks.

**traffic** - Verkehr *m*

■ In market studies, the collection of vehicles, goods or people that pass by a certain point whether it be inside or outside an establishment.

**train station advertising** - Bahnhofswerbung *f*

■ An outdoor medium which consists of placing posters of different sizes in train stations or in the interior of trains.

**transaction marketing** - Transaktionsmarketing *n*

■ A type of marketing centred around boosting sporadic exchanges between the vendor and the client, aimed at closing transactions in the short term independently of the consequences on the relationship in the long term.

**transnational advertising agency** - transnationale Werbeagentur *f*

■ An advertising agency which, having its main office in a specific country (the United States, the United Kingdom, France, Japan), installs branches or purchases advertising agencies in other countries in order to be able to operate at an international level.

**transport advertising** - Transportmittelwerbung *f*

■ An advertisement placed on a means of transport or in relation to it, such as posters on buses.

**trendsetter** – Trendsetter *m*

■ A person who starts a new fashion or trend. In market research, trendsetters are an important factor to take into account when marketing to the under 30s and in particular to teenagers.

**trial** - Versuch *m*

■ The action and effect of trying something before its final use.

**turnover** - Umsatz *m*

■ The total number of units sold over a period of time and their total value. It is also referred to as volume of sales.

**turnover** - Nettoumsatz *m*

■ Total company sales over a given period, less sales tax (for example, VAT).

**two way public relations** - bidirektionale Öffentlichkeitsarbeit *f*

■ A type of public relations based on the mutual communication between the organisation and its public. They base the design of their strategic programme on the scientific research of the public.

**two-part price** - Zweikomponentenpreis *m*

■ The price applied in the service sector whereby a fixed amount of money is set for contracting a service or other variable according to the use made of the same. It is used in the telephone, electricity and water supplies industries.

**two-step programme** - Zwei-Stufen-Programm *n*

■ A direct marketing action set in two steps. In general the first step consists of a communication via an 0800 number so that the target public can call and identify itself showing its interest in the advertised product or service. In general the second step consists of the emission, via a telephone call, mail or visit from a specialised agent so that the company can sell the stated product directly to the person or persons who identified themselves in the first step of the action.

# U

**umbrella brand** - Dachmarke *f*

■ A common brand under which other brands of products or different companies are protected so as to economise on the marketing and promotion of the entire group.

**unbiased** - erwartungstreu
■ In research, it is the statistical value whose value is equal to the population parameter which is being measured. It is produced when the average of all the measurements equals the population value.

**uncertainty** - Ungewissheit *f*
■ Doubt, perplexity or lack of security about a future result. Company activities imply the assumption of risk and uncertainty.

**undifferentiated marketing** - undifferenziertes Marketing *n*
■ A type of marketing that applies the same price, product, promotion, advertising and distribution channels to all clients, with the belief that the relative sectors are not different enough to warrant a different marketing approach.

**unfair competition** - unfairer Wettbewerb *m*
■ A style or form of acting in a market which contravenes the legal norms or customs which govern competition between companies, for example, in the quality of the products or the information provided about them.

**unique selling proposition (USP)** - einzigartiges Verkaufsargument *n* (EVA)
■ The advertising term for an argument that forms the core of communication strategy when selling a product or service. The word unique refers to the product being exclusive and excellent. This type of sales argument is based on the product attributes or on the fact that only this brand has these attributes.

**unit** - Einheit *f*
■ A lower level in a business organisation, headed by a manager, that has a defined purpose and a certain amount of autonomy. There are normally a number of such units as in the case of branches of a supermarket or a bank.

**unit cost** - Stückkosten *pl*
■ The cost obtained by dividing the total costs of the company by the number of units produced. Equivalent to average cost.

**universe** - Grundgesamtheit *f*
■ All the elements of a specific category that exist in reality. They are the individuals that cover certain criteria and those upon which a market study is carried out, although for practical purposes a limited study of a representative sample may be required.

**unsaleable** - unverkäuflich
■ A product that cannot be sold, generally due to poor quality or new legal regulations.

**unsold** - unverkauft
■ A product that has not been sold at the end of a period of time. The term is generally applied to products affected by changes in fashion, the end of a season, technological obsolescence or the launch of a better product.

**unstructured interview** - unstrukturiertes Interview *n*
■ An open or in-depth interview without a defined questionnaire. Normally used in preliminary phases to identify all possible factors and obtain new ideas.

**up-market** - hochpreisig
■ An adjective used to describe brands or products with a higher price than others with similar purposes, due to their better quality or brand image. The consumer doesn't choose among them because of the price, as with lower range articles.

**upper class** - Oberschicht *f*
■ The group of people who occupy the highest posts in the social scale according to social-economic variables. By extension, it is used to qualify advertising media (primarily magazines) whose audience predominantly belong to said social class.

**upsell** - Zusatzverkauf *m*
■ A marketing technique used in telephone marketing which consists in selling the caller more than one unit of the advertised product which has generated the client or potential client's call. It is generally presented as the purchase of an additional unit, whether to give as a gift or to store, at a lower price.

**upselling** - Upselling *n*

■ The sale of more or better services than those originally requested by the client.

**urban tribes** - Jugendbanden *f*

■ Groups of young people that are united by external symbols (for example the way in which they style their hair, their clothing, vehicles etc,) or by vague ideological concepts.

**useful audience** - Zielpublikum *n*

■ The part of the audience which belongs to the target group. They are those persons most likely to purchase the product under promotion i.e. those who due to their characteristics were the basis for the creation of the campaign.

**utility** - Nutzen *m*

■ The satisfaction of needs obtained by the use of a good. It determines the value of a good in terms of interest in its use and benefit.

# V

**validity** - Validität *f*

■ In research techniques, the capacity of a measuring instrument to ensure the observed differences correspond to real differences, and not constant or random errors.

**VALS (values, attitudes and lifestyles)** - VALS (values, attitudes and lifestyles)

■ A classical psychographical method which classifies consumers according to their vital values and lifestyles as divided into four categories: directed by necessity, directed by external factors, directed by internal factors and directed by integrated factors, this last category combines the best of the first two.

**valuation** - Wertermittlung *f*

■ An expert estimation of the market value of an asset.

**value** - Wert *m*

■ The usefulness of a good that permits the exchange of an equivalent amount of money. It is something subjective, that can only be quantified at the precise moment of sale and purchase.

**value** *v* - bewerten *v*

■ To evaluate and put a price upon a good.

**value added** - Wertschöpfung *f*

■ The increase in price produced at each phase of a production process. The added value is obtained by deducting the cost of all the necessary materials or services acquired externally from the price of the finished product.

**value analysis** - Wertanalyse *f*

■ A systematic market analysis procedure used to evaluate all cost factors involved in producing a particular product, according to its value or use to consumers. It enables features and functions to be added or subtracted, based on the benefits derived by the consumer, and not only on technical grounds.

**value-based pricing** - wertbezogene Preisfestlegung *f*

■ The procedure for determining a price based on market orientation. The important factor is not to launch a product which will incur a specific cost and try to make it profitable by adding a margin on this cost, but rather the origin of the process is the consumer to whom an value is offered at an certain price, whilst trying to be cost efficient in the launch of the product in order to achieve a return on the offer.

**vending-machine sales** - Verkauf *m* aus Verkaufsautomaten

■ Sales made via dispensing machines in which buyers insert coins or a card before receiving a particular product (cigarettes, soft drinks, etc.). These machines are normally located in public places, often by specialised companies that rent space from shop owners.

**verbal code** - verbaler Code *m*

■ The group of verbal elements which can be used in advertising, which include the headline, slogan, text body and closing statement.

**vertical agreement** - vertikales Abkommen *n*

■ An agreement between companies operating at different levels of the production and marketing processes.

**vertical diversification** - vertikale Diversifikation *f*

■ The diversification of company activities designed to absorb past or future activities to those currently being carried out. Also referred to as vertical integration.

**viability** - Durchführbarkeit *f*

■ The capacity or possibility of a company or project progressing in such a way that long term profitability is assured. Also called feasibility.

**video game advertising** - In-Game-Werbung *f*

■ An advertising method which uses videogames as a medium, through the presence of the brand or the product in the development of the action. It constitutes a new way of product placement. Whilst originally it was the manufacturers of videogames who asked for the presence of brands to give credibility to the scenes, it is now the brands themselves who have discovered videogames as a new advertising medium particularly aimed at the younger population.

**viewers' panel** - Zuschauerpanel *n*

■ A stable and representative sample of television viewers in a particular area, used to estimate the ratings of a television channel or programme.

**viewers share** - Zuschaueranteil *m*

■ The proportion of the group of viewers which corresponds to each channel at a specific moment. It is expressed in terms of percentage and varies constantly as a consequence of viewers joining and leaving a programme and of the changes from one station to another.

**viral marketing** - Virales Marketing *n*

■ A special kind of marketing which tries to get the consumers to act as prescribers and to recommend the purchase of the product to other potential consumers. On many occasions it is necessary to use compensation and incentive programmes which boost the creation of an attractive network of clients.

**visual corporate identity** - visuelle Corporate Identity *f*

■ The group of graphical elements which represent a company, organisation or institution, identifying it and differentiating it from all the others: logotypes, symbols and corporate colours.

**visual key** - optisches Leitmotiv *n*

■ The graphical element which dominates an advertising campaign and which is used in all media that the same comprises, helping to unite the different insertions.

**volume discount** - Mengenrabatt *m*

■ A reduction in tariff prices given due to the accumulated volume over a period by a client, not taking into account the size of orders that they have been placing, but bearing in mind the lower costs involved in serving a principal client.

**voluntary chain** - freiwillige Handelskette *f*

■ A chain of stores that share a common name and image and mutually undertake to supply each other from a buying centre at a national level and a distribution centre at a regional or wholesale level. Each store is owned by an independent person who can cease operating at any time. If the distribution centre belongs to store owners, it operates as a retail cooperative. A voluntary chain is more common in food and drug stores as well as traditional sectors, while franchise chains are used in modern sectors such as textiles, sound and film equipment.

# W

**warehouse** - Lager *n*

■ The place where stock is stored. It is possible that the establishment is used for wholesale purposes, whether in the traditional sense with a counter or in the form of a wholesale self-service or as a distribution centre for delivery to the retailer. In the past it was used as an establishment with retail facilities.

**warfare marketing** - kriegerisches Marketing *n*

■ The application of the principles of strategy and military tactics to marketing.

**warm point** - warmer Punkt *m*

■ An area in a sales establishment where sales are positive. Naturally there is a greater display of products in the entrance and exit of an establishment and close to high consumption articles. Warm points can be created artificially through decoration, especially illumination. Cold points are those areas that are not between two warm points and therefore have hardly any traffic.

**waste circulation** - vergeudete Rundsendungen *f*

■ The issues of a publication which are considered wasted for the purposes of a specific advertising campaign due to having been addressed to people who do not belong to the target group.

**watchdog** - Prüfer *m*

■ The person in charge of supervising compliance with statutes, regulations and agreements.

**weighted distribution** - gewichtete Distributionsdichte *f*

■ The percentage of total sales by outlets offering a particular brand, divided by the total market for such product. It indicates actual market penetration, given that it accounts for the number of outlets as well as size.

**weighting** - Gewichtung *f*

■ On developing a target group, the act of giving more or less relative importance to different segments of the population, and giving them a specific weight different to that of the whole.

**wet test** - Produkteinführungstest *m*

■ The sale of a limited edition of a product, moving on to the mass manufacturing of the same on the basis of the success achieved in the marketing of the sample.

**white goods** - weiße Ware *f*

■ Name derived from a reference to early household appliances that came only in a white colour. White goods are household appliances, such as refrigerators, washers, dryers and freezers.

**wholesale price** - Großhandelspreis *m*

■ The sales price to retailers or large consumers, normally involving discounts on the tariff price.

**wholesale sale** - Großhandelsverkauf *m*

■ A sale to retailers or consumers of large quantities, by wholesalers that buy from manufacturers or importers.

**wholesale trade** - Großhandel *m*

■ A type of trading in which clients are intermediaries and do not consume the products they purchase.

**wholesaler** - Großhändler *m*

■ A company that sells goods to retailers and consumers of large quantities, purchasing from many different manufacturers. Depending on the sector, the number of references may range from 2,000 to 100,000. It is not normally an exclusive distributor for the majority of goods sold and may sell at any price, although often in compliance with manufacturer trade policies.

**window dressing** - Schaufenstergestaltung *f*

■ The group of techniques designed to convey a message more clearly and with greater appeal by designing window space. Window dressers must be aware of a product's features and its target public, and able to attract interest, provide information on the product and convince potential buyers to enter the store.

**word association** - Wortassoziation *f*

■ A research technique which consists of suggesting some key words to the interviewee so that he can reply with other words which are triggered by the first. It is used to discover suitable or unsuitable connotations which certain subjects awaken.

**word of mouth** - Mund-zu-Mund-Propaganda *f*
■ Information or rumour that is transmitted in an oral and disorganised fashion. It contributes decisively to brand and product image.

**word-of-mouth advertising** - Mundpropaganda *f*
■ A type of advertising which is carried out spontaneously by the users of a product when they are satisfied with the products and services. It does not require a medium for its transmission.

# Deutsch - Englisch

# A

**24-Stunden-Erinnerung** *f* - day-after recall

■ Studie, die die Meinung des Zielpublikums über eine neue Werbung (i.d.R. im Fernsehen) erfasst. Wird am folgenden Tag telefonisch durchgeführt. Gemessen werden die spontane, gestützte und suggerierte Erinnerung, die Szenen, an die sich die Personen erinnern, die übermittelte Botschaft und die Gesamtmeinung. Dient dazu, sehr schwerwiegende Fehler, die im Prätest nicht entdeckt wurden, zu berichtigen.

**24-Stunden-Laden** *m* - convenience store

■ Laden mit stark ausgedehnten Öffnungszeiten, einschließlich nachts und an Sonn- und Feiertagen, der aufgrund seiner Nähe und Annehmlichkeit verkauft. Das Angebotssortiment ist beschränkt, mit dem Schwerpunkt auf den gebräuchlichsten Artikeln und möglichen unvorhergesehenen Käufen. Die Angebotsschwerpunkte sind sehr unterschiedlich.

**7-S-Modell** *n/pl* - seven S's

■ Schema für die Analyse einer Organisation und ihrer Strategie, das von Tom Peters und McKinsey entwickelt wurde. Entspricht den Anfangsbuchstaben der englischen Begriffe shared values (gemeinsame Werte), structure (Struktur), style (Stil), systems (Systeme), staff (Personal), strategy (Strategie) und skills (Fähigkeiten).

**A-B-Aufteilung** *f* - A-B split

■ Im Marketing, Unterteilung einer Namen- und Adressliste in zwei gleiche Teile nach einer sehr einfachen Methode: der erste Name ist Teil der Liste 1, der zweite Teil der Liste 2, der dritte Name wiederum Teil der Liste 1 und so weiter. Wird bei Verkauf und Werbung auf dem Postweg verwendet, um den durchschnittlichen Rücklauf vor Übernahme der Gesamtkosten zu bestimmen.

**ABC-Analyse** *f* - ABC analysis

■ Klassifizierung von Produkten, Kunden usw. gemäß ihrem Umsatz oder ihrer Bedeutung. Normalerweise erzielen 20% der Produkte 80% des Umsatzes (20/80-Regel). Durch die Analyse können weniger interessante Produkte oder Kunden identifiziert werden. Gleichzeitig kann überprüft werden, ob die Preise, Konditionen usw. korrekt festgelegt wurden. Die A-Artikel werden als äußerst wichtig eingestuft, während C-Artikeln als unwichtig gelten. Die B-Artikel nehmen einen ähnlichen Anteil an der Gesamtzahl der Artikel wie am Gesamtumsatz ein.

**Abfolgeverzerrung** *f* - sequence bias

■ In der Statistik der Einfluss von vorherigen Fragen auf die Antworten auf nachfolgende Fragen.

**Abgang** *m* - attrition

■ Im Bereich des Beziehungsmarketings versteht man hierunter den langsamen Verlust der Kundenbindung zugunsten einer anderen Marke. Er entsteht durch Ermüdung oder Enttäuschung, die auf eine mangelnde Aufmerksamkeit der für die Marke verantwortlichen Stellen oder auf ein nicht eingehaltenes Produktversprechen zurückzuführen sind.

**Ablaufplan** *m* - schedule

■ Geordneter Plan von Tätigkeiten, in dem auch aufgeführt wird, zu welchem Zeitpunkt diese voraussichtlich stattfinden.

**abnehmende Skalenerträge** *m/pl* - diseconomies of scale

■ Situation, wenn die Stückkosten bei steigender Produktionskapazität zunehmen. Bei der Mehrzahl der Industrieprodukte führt eine Ausweitung der Produktionsmenge zu einer Senkung der Stückkosten, da sich die Fixkosten auf eine größere Stückzahl umlegen lassen. Es gibt jedoch auch Prozesse, in denen sich dies anders herum verhält.

**Abonnement-Agentur** *f* - catalogue agency

■ Unternehmen, das zwischen regelmäßig erscheinender Werbung und möglichen Käufern agiert und dessen wichtigste Aktivität darin besteht,

Abonnenten für Zeitschriften zu werben. Die Publikationen werden in der Regel in Katalogen angeboten.

**Above-the-line-Medien** *n/pl* - above-the-line media

■ Traditionell in der Werbung verwendete Medien. Hierzu gehören Tageszeitungen, Beilagen, Zeitschriften, Fernsehen, Radio, Kino, externe Medien und das Internet.

**Above-the-line-Werbung** *f* - above-the-line advertising

■ Bezeichnet Werbung in Massenmedien, d. h. in Medien, die der klassischen Kommunikation zugeordnet werden können: Presse, Zeitschriften, Radio, Fernsehen, Großanzeigen oder auch das Internet. Ein Teil der verfügbaren Zeit bzw. des verfügbaren Platzes dient Informations-, Meinungs- oder Unterhaltungsinhalten, der andere Teil wird für Werbung verwendet.

**Abschlag** *m* - backwardation

■ Preisstruktur beim Handel von Verbrauchsgütern, bei der Lieferungen in naher Zukunft einen höheren Preis haben als Lieferungen zu einem späteren Datum.

**Abschlussfehler** *m* - office error

■ Bei der Mengenforschung, Fehler beim Entwurf des Fragebogens, bei der Codierung, Korrektur oder Umsetzung in der Informatik. Tabellenfehler oder Ergebnisdarstellungsfehler.

**Abschöpfen** *n* - skimming

■ Praxis, im Moment der Produkteinführung einen Preis festzusetzen, der später nach unten korrigiert wird. Dies wird gemacht, um diesen hohen Preis beim zahlungswilligen Publikum abzuschöpfen und somit einen Extragewinn zu erzielen. In speziellen Fällen bemüht man sich auch, durch geringfügige Verbesserungen oder Veränderungen, Kunden mit einer größeren Kaufkraft anzuziehen.

**Abschöpfungspreis** *m* - skimming price

■ Preis für ein Produkt, der für ein Marktsegment mit großer Kaufkraft und Interesse für technologische Innovation zunächst hoch angesetzt und mit zunehmender Markterschließung nach unten korrigiert wird. Wird normalerweise auf Produkte angewendet, die eine große technologische Innovation beinhalten. Wird auch Strategie der maximalen Marktnutzung genannt, da die Verbraucher den höchsten Preis zahlen, den sie zu zahlen bereit sind.

**Abteilung** *f* - department

■ Teil einer Unternehmung, der für die Durchführung eines bestimmten Funktionsbereichs innerhalb eines Geschäftsbereichs verantwortlich ist. Dabei kann es sich um die Produktion, den Verkauf oder die Finanzabteilung handeln. Der Hauptabteilung steht ein Direktor vor, sie besteht aus mehreren Abteilungen.

**Abteilung** *f* **für Neukunden** - new business department

■ Abteilung, die potentielle Kunden anwirbt, diese müssen in das Kundenprofil passen. Die Abteilung erstellt die dafür nötigen Prognosen und Pläne.

**ACCA** - ACCA

■ Abkürzung für die vier Schritte des Werbemodells DAGMAR, das im Jahr 1961 von Russell H. Colley vorgestellt wurde: Attention, Comprehensiveness, Conviction and Action (Aufmerksamkeit, Verständnis, Überzeugung und Handlung).

**Accessoire** *n* - accessory

■ Im Einzelhandel, Artikel, der zusammen mit einem anderen an Attraktivität gewinnt und daher mehr Aufmerksamkeit erregt und so zum Kauf beider Produkte anregt. Ein Kleid kann z. B. zusammen mit einer passenden Halskette oder ein Bett mit passender Decke und Bezug ausgestellt werden. Andere Bezeichnung: Komplementärartikel.

**ACORN** - ACORN

■ Englische Abkürzung für „A classification of residential neighbourhoods". Klassifizierung von Wohngegenden zur jeweiligen Bestimmung und Vorhersage des Konsumverhaltens.

**Adaptation** *f* - adaptation

■ Im Layout, Verändern von Größe und Proportionen einer Anzeige, damit diese in die verschiedenen grafischen Medien passt. Auch versteht man hierunter jede kleine Veränderung, damit eine Basiswerbeidee in mehreren unterschiedlichen Medien verwendet werden kann (zum Beispiel, in Zeitschriften und als Werbematerial in den Verkaufsstellen).

**Ad-Booster** *m* - Ad-Booster

■ Video-Werbeformat im Internet. Hierdurch kann Fernsehwerbung im Internet mit hoher Qualität und unabhängig von Breitband- oder Einwahlverbindungen verbreitet werden. Das Ad-Booster-Format wurde zusammen mit der Flash 5-Technologie entwickelt, wodurch ein schneller Download mit allen Browsern und von jedem PC aus gewährleistet wird.

**Adbuster** *m* - adbuster

■ Werbetext, mit dem Werbung hinterfragt werden soll. Die Werbung wird so verfremdet, dass die eigentliche Werbestrategie offen gelegt wird. Bei diesen subversiven Aktionen werden Werbungen so kritisiert oder manipuliert, dass eine neue, allerdings ironische Werbung entsteht, die sich der ursprünglichen Werbesprache und -codes bedient.

**Ad-hoc-Studie** *f* - ad-hoc study

■ Studie für einen einzigen Interessenten mit dem Ziel, Informationen über ein bestimmtes Thema zu erhalten. Gegenteil: Umfragen und Rahmenstudien, an denen mehrere Interessenten teilnehmen.

**Administration to Consumer (A2C)** - administration to consumer (A2C)

■ Informationen und Initiativen einer öffentlichen Behörde zur Kontaktaufnahme mit den Bürgern. Beispiel: Online-Zahlung von Steuern und Gebühren.

**Adressenanalyse** *f* - address analysis

■ Verfahren der direkten Werbung, bei dem die Angaben einer bestimmten Adresse vor dem Versand überprüft werden.

**AdVantage** *n* - AdVantage

■ System, das vom Forschungsunternehmen EMER-GFK vermarktet wird und bei dem Werbespots vorher getestet werden. Hierbei sieht die untersuchte Zielgruppe ein Fernsehprogramm, das die zu testenden Spots beinhaltet.

**Advertainment** *n* - advertainment

■ Kunstwort aus Advertising (Werbung) und Entertainment (Unterhaltung). Es bezeichnet eine intensive Zusammenarbeit zwischen Werbeagentur und Medien, bei der zwei Ziele verfolgt werden: die Werbeagentur stellt ihre Kenntnisse über Ziele und Strategien für öffentliche Kommunikation zur Verfügung, um attraktivere Inhalte zu gestalten, das werbende Unternehmen möchte sein Image lancieren und zum Kauf seiner Produkte motivieren.

**Advertorial** *n* - advertorial

■ Kunstwort aus Advertising und Editorial. Die Werbebotschaft übernimmt die Inhaltsform des Mediums, in das sie eingefügt wird. Dadurch wird die angebliche soziale, politische oder wirtschaftliche Information „legitimiert". Aufgrund der möglichen Verwechslung seitens des Empfängers muss das Advertorial klar als Werbung gekennzeichnet sein. Eine Variante des Advertorial ist die Werbereportage.

**Adware** *f* - adware

■ Im Internet, Programme, die für den Benutzer gratis sind, weil sie Werbung beinhalten.

**Adwords** *n/pl* - adwords

■ Werbesystem von Google basierend auf der PPC-Formel (pay per click - Zahlung per Klick), die darin besteht, Suchwörter in Werbeverknüpfungen hervorzuheben.

**Affinität** *f* - affinity

■ Im Marketing, Ähnlichkeit zwischen zwei Medien, einem Produkt und einem Medium oder der Zielgruppe eines Mediums und einer bestimmten Personengruppe. Wird zuweilen als

Kriterium zur Medienwahl benutzt, damit eine Anzeige die größtmögliche Wirkung in der Zielgruppe erreicht.

**Affinitätsindex** *m* - affinity index

▪ Anzahl der Personen aus einer Zielgruppe, die über eine Werbung in einem Medium erreicht wird. Ausgedrückt wird sie als Prozentsatz der Gesamtanzahl an Personen, die potenziell von dieser Werbung erreicht würde. Auch Affinitätskoeffizient.

**Affinitätskoeffizient** *m* - affinity coefficient

▪ Anzahl der Personen aus einer Zielgruppe, die über eine Werbung in einem Medium erreicht wird. Ausgedrückt wird sie als Prozentsatz der Gesamtanzahl an Personen, die potenziell von dieser Werbung erreicht würde. Auch Affinitätsindex.

**Affinitätsmarketing** *n* - affinity marketing

▪ Zusammenschluss von Strategien, die die Kundenbindung an eine Marke optimieren sollen, um weitere Artikel unter dem gleichen Namen anzubieten. Es handelt sich um die Profilübertragung einer Marke auf andere Produkte. Häufig werden hierzu Internet-Tools (E-Mail, Newsletter-Gruppen usw.) verwendet.

**Agentur** *f* - agency

▪ Selbstständiges Unternehmen im Dienstleistungsbereich, das als Vermittler fungiert. Die Verwendung dieses Begriffs hat dazu geführt, dass man Unternehmen, die einem bestimmten Sektor (Werbung, Versicherungen, Tourismus) angehören, als Agenturen bezeichnet.

**Agentur** *f* **für Direktmailing** - lettershop

▪ Beim Direktmarketing ein Unternehmen, das die Handhabung, Klassifizierung und den Versand von großen Mengen an Werbung übernimmt, insbesondere das Falten und Verpacken der einzelnen Teile und die Frankierung, meist in einem automatisierten Ablauf.

**AIDA** - AIDA

▪ Modell zur Entwicklung wirksamer an die Verbraucher gerichteter Werbebotschaften. Das Wort AIDA ist aus den Anfangsbuchstaben der englischen Begriffe Attention, Interest, Desire, Action gebildet, die für die einzelnen Phasen der gewünschten Werbewirkung stehen: Die Werbebotschaft soll die Aufmerksamkeit des Verbrauchers erlangen (attention), sein Interesse für das Produkt wecken (interest), ein Kaufverlangen erwecken (desire) und schließlich zur Handlung (action), also in der Regel zum Kauf, führen.

**AID-Analyse** *f* - AID analysis

▪ In der Statistik Technik der multivarianten Analyse, mit deren Hilfe die Unterschiede bezüglich der Einstellung, der demografischen und der sozioökonomischen Faktoren bestimmt werden, die zwischen einem Käufer und einem Nicht-Käufer eines Produkts bestehen. Die Abkürzung steht für „automatic interaction detector". Im Deutschen spricht man auch von Kontrastgruppenanalyse.

**AIDCAS** - AIDCAS

▪ Aus dem AIDA-Modell abgeleitetes Werbemodell, das zwei weitere Phasen hinzufügt und somit die Sequenz wie folgt vervollständigt: Aufmerksamkeit (attention), Interesse (interest), Wunsch (desire), Überzeugung (conviction), Handlung (action) und Zufriedenheit (satisfaction).

**Akkreditierung** *f* - accreditation

▪ Verfahren einer Organisation, mit dem gewährleistet wird, dass eine Person oder eine Institution zur Durchführung ihres Auftrages berechtigt ist. In der Werbebranche ist die Akkreditierung das Dokument, mit dem der Inserent bestätigt, dass sein Konto von einer bestimmten Agentur gehandhabt wird.

**Akkulturation** *f* - acculturation

▪ Anpassung eines Einwanderers oder eines neuen Mitarbeiters an die Kultur eines Landes oder eines Unternehmens.

**Akquisitionskosten** *pl* - acquisition cost

▪ Im Marketing, Ausgaben, die zur Gewinnung eines neuen Kunden oder

Abonnenten erforderlich sind (z. B. Briefporto oder Telefonkosten).

**Akquisitionswert** *m* - acquisition value

■ Relativer Wert der von einem Käufer erhaltenen Ware, der sich aus dem Unterschied zwischen dem vom Kunden gezahlten Preis und dem tatsächlichen Warenwert ergibt.

**Aktion** *f* - drive

■ Im Marketing, Synonym zu Werbekampagne, insbesondere bezüglich der Materialien, die diese hinzufügt.

**Aktionspackung** *f* - promotional pack

■ Verpackung, die den Verbraucher über eine Promotionsaktion informiert, zum Beispiel durch ein Preisausschreiben, einen Wettbewerb oder die Beilegung von Aufklebern oder Sammlungsstücken.

**aktiver Käufer** *m* - active buyer

■ Person, die ein Produkt vor kurzem oder in einem bestimmten zurückliegenden Zeitraum erworben hat.

**aktivitätsbasierte Kostenermittlung** *f* - Activity-Based Costing (ABC)

■ Berechnung von Kosten nach Aktivität. Hierdurch können die wirklichen Kosten der einzelnen Aktivitäten eines Unternehmens erstellt werden.

**aktivitätsbasiertes Management** *n* - activity based management

■ Managementsystem, bei dem vor allem mit Aktivitäten Wertsteigerungen für die Kunden erzielt werden.

**Akzeptanz** *f* - acceptability

■ Die Fähigkeit eines neuen Produkts, zu Probekäufen zu animieren. Bevor ein neues Produkt auf den Markt kommt, werden verschiedene Tests durchgeführt, um dessen Akzeptanzgrad zu messen.

**allein stehende Werbeanzeige** *f* - solus position

■ Anordnung einer Anzeige in einem audiovisuellen Medium oder Printmedium, so dass sie allein stehend ohne benachbarte Anzeigen erscheint. Der Tarif für diese Art Werbeanzeige ist höher als für Block- oder Gruppenanzeigen.

**allgemeine Werbetheorie** *f* - general advertising theory

■ Theorie, die eine objektive, rigorose, ausreichende und systematische, d. h. wissenschaftliche Erklärung über die Wirkung der Werbekommunikation geben will. Aufgrund der Komplexität und Diversität ihres Gegenstands ist anzumerken, dass es sich um eine noch ausbaufähige Werbetheorie handelt.

**allgemeiner Kaufvertrag** *m* - general sales agreement

■ Rahmenabkommen zwischen einem Lieferanten und einer Einkaufszentrale oder einem Einzelkunden, in dem Preisnachlässe auf die Listenpreise (diese kann der Lieferant dem Markt folgend verändern) während eines bestimmten Zeitraums festgelegt werden. Verhindert die Aushandlung für jedes Geschäft oder jeden Kunden einzeln. Bestimmt die Nachlässe auf das Volumen der Gesamtbestellmenge und von Einzelbestellungen, Rückerstattungen zum Jahresende, werbemäßige Unterstützung und Regalpflege, Gutschriften für Bruch, und die Bestellungsabwicklung und Bezahlung.

**Alliteration** *f* - alliteration

■ In der Werbung Wiederholung eines Tons oder eines Teils eines Ausdrucks. Hierdurch steigt die Erinnerung an die Werbebotschaft.

**Allokation** *f* - allocation

■ Im Marketing, Verteilung von Mitteln und Zielen auf die verschiedenen Projekte, Produkte oder Abteilungen einer Organisation.

**Alltagsszene** *f* - slice-of-life style

■ Plot eines Films, ohne besondere Geschichte. Bei einem Werbefilm verwenden eine oder mehrere Personen die Marke in ihrem normalen Alltag.

**Alphaversion** *f* - alpha

■ Probeversion eines Produkts oder einer Dienstleistung. Die darauf folgende Betaphase beginnt, wenn bestimmte externe Personen oder Organisationen darum gebeten werden, ein Produkt oder eine Dienstleistung vor der Markteinführung zu testen, (im Allgemeinen über eine Gruppendynamik). Im Internet betrifft dies insbesondere die Entwicklung von Seiten, die nicht aus dem firmeninternen Netz stammen.

**Alterspyramide** *f* - age pyramid
■ Graphische Darstellung einer Bevölkerung in einem bestimmten Moment, entsprechend der Verteilung auf verschiedene Altersklassen. Der Name geht auf die Darstellung zurück, bei der nach Geschlechtern unterteilt wird, und bei der die gewöhnlich zahlreicheren Jüngeren unten dargestellt werden. Ermöglicht die Darstellung von Kriegs- und Epidemiefolgen usw. und den schnellen Vergleich zwischen verschiedenen Bevölkerungen und Epochen.

**American Advertising Federation (AAF)** *f* - American Advertising Federation (AAF)
■ Zusammenschluss von nordamerikanischen Firmen der Werbebranche. Sie wurde im Jahre 1967 zur Verteidigung der Werbung und ihrer Mitwirkenden mit dem einzigen Ziel der Förderung und Verbesserung der Werbeaktivität ins Leben gerufen.

**American Broadcasting Company (ABC)** - American Broadcasting Company (ABC)
■ Einer der drei wichtigsten landesweiten Fernsehsehsender in den Vereinigten Staaten. Besitzt auch sieben Radiostationen mit rund 1900 lokalen Frequenzen.

**Amerikanische Vereinigung** *f* **der Werbeagenturen (AAAA)** - American Association of Advertising Agencies (AAAA)
■ US-amerikanische Organisation auf Staatsebene, die die Werbebranche vertritt. Sie wurde im Jahr 1917 gegründet und bietet seitdem spezifische Informationen und Dienstleistungen zur Beratung der ihr angeschlossenen Werbeagenturen.

**Amerikanische Werbeakademie** *f* - American Academy of Advertising
■ Nordamerikanischer Verband von Lehrern, Studenten und Berufstätigen aus dem Bereich Werbung. Ziele sind die Förderung der Ausbildung und der Forschung. Veröffentlicht die Zeitschrift Journal of Advertising.

**Andy-Preis** *m* - Andy awards
■ Preis, der jedes Jahr vom Werbeclub New York für die besten Werbespots des Jahres in Fernsehen, Radio und anderen Medien verliehen wird.

**Anfrage** *f* - inquiry
■ Im Direktmarketing die Reaktion auf ein Angebot bestehend aus der Frage nach mehr Information über das Produkt oder die angebotene Dienstleistung ohne jegliche Kaufverpflichtung.

**Angebot** *n* - supply
■ Menge eines Gutes, die auf dem Markt, zu einem bestimmten Zeitpunkt zu einem Preis angeboten wird. In der Theorie besteht zwischen Angebot und Nachfrage ein Gleichgewichtspreis. Wäre der Preis höher, würde sich das Angebot vergrößern und die Nachfrage würde sinken, und da zwischen den Mengen kein Gleichgewicht mehr bestünde, würde sich der Gleichgewichtspreis wieder einstellen.

**Angebot** *n* **und Verkauf** *m* **von Zusatzprodukten** - cross selling
■ Verkaufsmodalität, bei der zwei oder mehr Produkte, meist Zusatzprodukte, gleichzeitig zu einem attraktiven Preis angeboten werden, um auf diese Weise Fixkosten zu teilen und die Nachfrage anzukurbeln. Wird hauptsächlich im Dienstleistungsbereich angewendet, in dem die Fixkosten üblicherweise einen wesentlichen Anteil der Gesamtkosten darstellen.

**Angebotsengpass** *m* - sellers' shortages
■ Güter oder Dienstleistungen, die nicht in ausreichender Menge angeboten werden, um die zum aktuellen Marktpreis bestehende Nachfrage zu decken.

**Angebotsgesetz** *n* - law of supply
■ Wirtschaftsgesetz das besagt, dass das Angebot eines Gutes direkt proportional zu seinem Preis ist. Je höher der Preis, desto höher das Angebot und umgekehrt.

In bestimmten Fällen kann es zu einem atypischen Verlauf der Angebotskurve kommen, z. B. durch einen Landwirt, der aus Angst vor weiteren starken Preissenkungen verkauft oder durch einen Arbeiter, der sich bei Erreichung eines bestimmten Lohnniveaus dazu entschließt, weniger zu arbeiten.

**Angebotspackung** *f* - bonus pack

■ Verpackung, die einen Teil des Produkts gratis enthält, so z. B. eine Cornflakes- bzw. Müslipackung, die 20% Prozent mehr zum gleichen Preis enthält oder die mit einer kleineren kostenlosen Zusatzpackung verkauft wird. Es ist eine Art, in die Wettbewerbsoffensive zu gehen, ohne unmittelbar am Preis zu drehen, was häufig bei niedrigpreisigen Basisprodukten angewandt wird. Dient auch dazu, neue oder zusätzliche Packungsgrößen einzuführen.

**Angelhakenanzeige** *f* - hook advertising

■ Anzeige, die zum Ziel hat, die Aufmerksamkeit des Verbrauchers zu wecken, indem ein Muster verteilt oder ein Werbegeschenk versprochen wird.

**Ankreuzverfahren** *n* - equal-appearing intervals

■ Forschungstechnik, in der die Befragten aus vorher festgelegten Antworten bestimmen müssen, welchen sie zustimmen und welchen nicht, wobei keine Zwischengrade oder Nuancierungen der Antworten möglich sind.

**Anmeldung** *f* - opt-in

■ In der Dynamik des Marketing auf Anfrage die Option, sich in eine Verteilerliste einzutragen.

**anonyme Anzeige** *f* - blind advertisement

■ Anzeige, die nicht den Namen oder die Identität des Werbetreibenden enthält. Wird häufig bei Stellenausschreibungen verwendet.

**Anonymität** *f* - anonymity

■ In der Forschung Fragebogenbedingung, bei der das Unternehmen oder die Organisation der Studie anonym bleibt. In der Markt- und politischen Forschung für die Objektivität der Antworten unabdinglich. Vom Standpunkt des Befragten aus die Garantie, dass er als informierende Person nicht veröffentlicht wird.

**Anreiz** *m* - kicker

■ Merkmal oder Bedingung, die ein Produkt besonders attraktiv machen oder den schnellen Abschluss eines Vertrags ermöglichen. Anreize werden besonders in den Märkten für Finanzprodukte eingesetzt und können beispielsweise in einer Zinsober- oder -untergrenze bestehen, einer Möglichkeit zur Kündigung, Umwandlung oder Sondertilgung oder einer höheren Liquidität unter bestimmten Umständen.

**Anreiz** *m* - stimulus

■ Anlass oder Beweggrund für etwas. Ziel eines Anreizes ist es, zu erreichen, dass ein Bedürfnis befriedigt wird.

**Anspruchsniveau** *n* - aspiration level

■ Im Marketing, soziales Niveau, das der Verbraucher durch den Kauf eines Produkts erreichen möchte. Bestimmte Artikel tragen zur Schaffung eines sozial attraktiven Images bei und heben dies in ihren Werbebotschaften besonders hervor.

**Anti-Zapping-Werbespot** *m* - antizapping commercial

■ Werbespot, der einen bevorzugten Platz innerhalb des Programms einnimmt, um die Anzahl der Zuschauer zu senken, die den Kanal wechseln.

**Antizipation** *f* - anticipation

■ Im Marketing, Fähigkeit, den neuen Forderungen und Geschmacksrichtungen des Marktes zuvorzukommen.

**Antwort pro Tausend** *f* - response rate per thousand circulation

■ Bei einer Werbekampagne für Direktantworten, die Anzahl der Antworten, die pro Tausend Exemplaren der Werbung oder Werbungen mit der Anzeige eingehen.

**Antwortfunktion** *f* - response function

■ Reaktion der Verbraucher auf den unterschiedlichen Druck, der von der

Werbung ausgeübt wird. Im Allgemeinen wird diese nach Anzahl der Personen gemessen, die die Werbung je nach Kontaktzahl positiv aufnehmen. Die erforschte Antwort kann die Markenkenntnis, Markenbild, Kenntnis über die Eigenschaften des Produkts oder Verkauf sein.

**Antwortrate** *f* - response rate

■ Anteil der Befragten, die einen Fragebogen ausfüllen in Bezug auf die Gesamtzahl der kontaktierten Personen.

**Antwortskala** *f* - itemized rating scale

■ In einem Fragebogen der Frageentwurf, bei dem die Befragten ihre Antwort als Positionen auf einer vorher vorbereiteten Skala angeben müssen, die ihre Meinung über den Fragengegenstand am besten wiedergibt.

**Antwortverweigerung** *f* - refusal to answer

■ Mögliche Fehlerquelle in Fragebögen. Tritt ein, wenn eine zu befragende Person sich weigert, an der Umfrage teilzunehmen. Kann auch bei bestimmten Fragen vorkommen. Sollte die Verweigerung häufiger in einem homogenen Teil der Befragten vorkommen, kann es zu einem Fehler bei der Schlussfolgerung kommen, z. B. wenn die Wähler einer bestimmten Partei eher ihre öffentliche Zusage verweigern als andere.

**Anzahl** *f* **der Anrufe** - call rate

■ Im Marketing Anzahl der Personen, mit denen ein Telefonverkäufer innerhalb einer bestimmten Zeit in Kontakt tritt.

**Anzeige** *f* **auf der mittleren Doppelseite einer Zeitschrift** - centre spread

■ In den Druckmedien versteht man hierunter eine Anzeige, die die beiden mittleren Seiten einer Ausgabe belegt. Fällt meist direkt ins Auge, da eine Zeitung oder Zeitschrift in der Regel spontan in der Mitte aufgeschlagen wird. Hat einen besonderen Tarif, der am Preis einer ungeraden (teureren) Seite und dem einer geraden (günstigeren) Seite errechnet wird, wobei dem Endpreis ein Zuschlag für den festen Anzeigenplatz zugefügt wird.

**Anzeiger** *m* - pole topper

■ Werbeelement, das auf einen Punkt, einen Bereich oder ein Produkt hinweist. Wird an hohen Stellen oder aus dem Regal herausragend angebracht, um die Aufmerksamkeit des Verbrauchers zu erregen.

**apathischer Käufer** *m* - apathetic shopper

■ Käufer, dem es egal ist, in welchem Supermarkt er einkauft und der weder Preise und Marken beachtet noch Qualitätsvergleiche anstellt. Innerhalb dieser Klassifikation gibt es 3 weitere Käufertypen: ökonomische, ethische und personalisierte Käufer.

**Appell** *m* - appeal

■ In der Werbung, Versuch, einen Kunden mit einem Angebot, einem Bild oder einem Ambiente anzulocken, das seinen Bedürfnissen oder seinen Wünschen entspricht.

**Appetitanreger** *m* - appetite appeal

■ Häufig in der Nahrungsmittelwerbung benutzte Ressource, die auf Grund der Darstellung den Appetit des potenziellen Käufers anregen soll.

**Applebaum-Modell** *n* - Applebaum model

■ Mathematisches Modell, das zur richtigen Auswahl von Geschäften benutzt wird. Mit seiner Hilfe können die potentiellen Verkäufe eines Geschäfts ausgehend von einer Vergleichsanalyse mit anderen, ähnlichen Verkaufsstellen ermittelt werden.

**Arbeitsanweisungen** *f/pl* - briefing

■ Gesamtheit von kurzen mündlichen oder schriftlichen Anweisungen, die denjenigen erteilt werden, die eine Arbeit durchführen werden. Erfolgt in der Regel in einer Informationsversammlung, bei der die zu erfüllenden Ziele im Mittelpunkt stehen. Meist wird der englische Ausdruck verwendet.

**Argumentation** *f* - argumentation

■ Logische Anordnung von Daten oder Fakten, so dass sich aus einer oder zwei Prämissen eine Schlussfolgerung ergibt. In der Werbung sollen hiermit Verbraucher überzeugt werden. Diese

Methode wird vor allem in rational begründeter Werbung verwendet.

**armer Hund** *m* - dog

■ In einer Matrix aus Marktwachstum und Marktanteil ein Geschäftsfeld ohne Marktführerschaft und mit niedrigem Wachstum. Erzeugt nicht ausreichende Gewinne und der Markt ist nicht attraktiv, weshalb das Geschäft restrukturiert werden sollte, man nach anderen Segmenten suchen oder das Geschäft verkauft werden sollte.

**aromatische Anzeige** *f* - fragrant ad

■ Grafische Werbemitteilung, die ein Element oder Teil enthält, das zuvor mit einem bestimmten Duft oder Aroma imprägniert wurde. Es handelt sich hierbei um ein sehr geläufiges Verfahren bei der Werbung für Parfüme zur Verbreitung eines neuen Dufts über einen Papierstreifen oder in Form eines Probenumschlags, der auf die Werbeanzeige aufgebracht ist.

**Arrangement** *n* - arrangement

■ Im Marketing, Aufbau oder Anordnung der Möbel, Vitrinen, Regale, Ladentische, Displays, Schaufenster und anderer Einrichtungsgegenstände eines Geschäfts. Hierdurch soll die Attraktivität gesteigert und die Produkte besser zugänglich gemacht werden.

**Artikel** *m* - article

■ Gesamtheit an Produkten, die sich untereinander nur durch ihre Verpackungsgröße unterscheiden. Das gleiche Produkt, das von einem anderen Unternehmen oder in einer anderen Farbe hergestellt wird, wäre ein anderer Artikel, obwohl beide eigentlich zur selben Produktfamilie gehören. Alle Größen eines Artikels werden mit einer bestimmten Referenznummer ausgestattet.

**Arzneimittelwerbung** *f* - drug advertising

■ Informationswerbung, die zum Konsum von Medikamenten anregt. Diese Kommunikation oder Werbung umfasst die Publikumswerbung, die Werbung bei Personen, die diese verschreiben oder vertreiben, Arztbesuche, Probenverteilung, Sponsoring von wissenschaftlichen Kongressen. Vom Gesetz genau reguliert.

**ASA (Advertising Standards Authority) -** ASA (Advertising Standards Authority)

■ Unabhängige britische Organisation, die die Anwendung eigener Normen zur Verteidigung öffentlicher Interessen überwacht. Sie ist mit verschiedenen staatlichen Organisationen verbunden und zur Weiterleitung von Klagen und Reklamationen der Öffentlichkeit verpflichtet. Finanziert wird diese Organisation von der Werbebranche. Der Präsident ist unabhängig und wählt die Mitglieder persönlich aus, von denen mindestens die Hälfte nicht der Werbewirtschaft angehören darf.

**asymmetrische Reaktion** *f* **auf den Preis** - asymmetric response to price

■ Verbraucherverhalten, das auf einen Verlust anders als auf einen Gewinn reagiert, selbst wenn dieser das gleiche Ausmaß besitzt. Verschiedene Studien haben belegt, dass eine bestimmte Preissteigerung eines Produkts eine höhere und intensivere Reaktionsvarianz des Verbrauchers hervorruft als eine äquivalente Preisreduzierung.

**Attraction Marketing** *n* - attraction marketing

■ Marketing, das auf der Anwerbung neuer Kunden über eine große Aktion für die Produkte der Firma basiert, durch die die Kunden in die gewünschte Richtung gelenkt werden.

**Attribute** *n/pl* - attributes

■ Sichtbare oder unsichtbare Produktmerkmale. Sie können physischer (was das Produkt aufweist), funktionaler (was das Produkt macht) oder symbolischer (was das Produkt darstellt) Natur sein. Sie bilden die Grundlage der reell vorhandenen oder fiktiven Unterscheidungen im Marketing zwischen Produkten und Marken. Diese Unterscheidung erfolgt direkt oder in Bezug auf den Gewinn oder den Nutzen für den Verbraucher, der sich aus den Attributen ergibt. In der Werbung werden entweder die Attribute oder die Vorteile von Produkten herausgestellt.

**Audimeter** *n* - audimeter

■ Gerät, das in ausgewählten Haushalten an den Fernsehapparat (oder das Radio) angeschlossen wird und mit dem festgestellt wird, wann der Fernseher eingeschaltet ist und welchen Sender die Familie sieht.

**audiovisuelle Werbung** *f* - audiovisual advertisement

■ Werbebotschaft, die auf Sprache, Typographie, einen bestimmten Aufbau, Tonelemente und Bewegtbilder zurückgreift und Film- und Videotechniken einsetzt.

**audiovisuelles Ausstellungsmaterial** *n* - audio-visual display

■ Ausstattung in Geschäften, mit denen ein Produkt unter Zuhilfenahme audiovisueller Mittel beworben wird, so z. B. ein Fernseher in einem Baumarkt, über den ein Werbeprogramm für Werkzeuge läuft.

**auf der ganzen Linie** - across the board

■ Planung von Werbung für einen Radio- oder TV-Sender. Hierbei wird ein Werbeplatz täglich für die gleiche Uhrzeit gebucht.

**auf Seitenbreite** - full column

■ Redaktioneller Beitrag oder Werbeanzeige, der oder die die gesamte Breite einer Zeitungs- oder Zeitschriftenseite einnimmt und hervorgehoben ist. Handelt es sich um eine Nachricht, ist diese meist im oberen Bereich platziert, im Fall einer Werbeanzeige im unteren Bereich der Seite. Nimmt die Werbeanzeige darüber hinaus noch die gesamte Seitenhöhe in Anspruch, spricht man von einer ganzseitigen Anzeige.

**aufdringliche Werbung** *f* - intrusive advertising

■ Werbung, die sich in einem anderen Bereich einführt (Radio- oder Fernsehprogramm, Zeitungs- oder Zeitschriftseite oder ein Postkasten) und Nachrichten aussendet, die die Aufmerksamkeit des Empfängers dieses Bereichs ausnutzen. Dieser aufdringlichen Art der Werbung steht die Werbung gegenüber, bei der der Empfänger vorher seine Zustimmung gibt, dessen Hauptzielgruppe die Empfänger von E-Mails sind. Dem gegenüber stehen die Robinsonlisten oder Schwarzen Listen (Schutzlisten) mit Kontaktdaten von Personen, die keine unaufgeforderte Werbung erhalten wollen.

**Aufhänger** *m* - gimmick

■ Teil oder kreative Ressource in einer Werbebotschaft, deren Ziel die Erregung der Aufmerksamkeit des Empfängers ist, wobei das Angebot in einem Spielelement verpackt ist.

**Aufklappwerbung** *f* - pop-up

■ Katalog oder Packung mit einer herausragenden Werbesektion, deren Zweck die Überraschung und Erregung der Aufmerksamkeit des Verbrauchers ist. Es wird auch oft der englische Ausdruck verwendet.

**Aufmerksamkeit** *f* - attention

■ Die Fähigkeit, eine Botschaft aufzunehmen und zu verstehen. In der Werbung ist die Aufmerksamkeit gewöhnlich selten und selektiv.

**Aufmerksamkeitsmessgerät** *n* - blink-metre

■ In der Werbung, Gerät, das eingesetzt wird, um den Grad des Interesses einer Person für eine Anzeige zu messen, indem man die Häufigkeit der Augenzuckungen misst.

**Aufmerksamkeitswert** *m* - attention value

■ Fähigkeit einer Werbebotschaft oder Anzeige, die Aufmerksamkeit einer Stichprobe der Zielgruppe zu wecken und zu erhalten. Wird anhand eines Erinnerungswertes gemessen (Anzeige in einem Block sehen und sich erinnern).

**Aufpreis** *m* - premium price

■ Mehrpreis, den der Käufer für ein bestimmtes Produkt aufgrund seines besseren Markenbildes gegenüber der Konkurrenz zu zahlen bereit ist. Der Aufpreis misst den Wert einer bestimmten Marke und die Kundentreue.

**Aufrechterhaltung** *f* - maintenance campaign

■ In der Werbung, Medienplan bestehend aus der geringen aber durchgehenden Investition zur Kontaktaufnahme mit dem Zielpublikum, um die Synergie mit vorherigen Kontakten aufrechtzuerhalten. Kann isoliert programmiert werden oder von einer Kampagne oder Welle mit starker Intensität eingeleitet werden.

**Aufsteller** *m* - display

■ Werbematerial, das eine ansprechende Präsentation der Ware am Verkaufspunkt ermöglicht. In der Regel aus Karton und leicht auseinanderzufalten und aufzubauen. Steht auf dem Boden und wird am Kopfende eines Regals aufgestellt. Es gibt auch auf der Ladentheke stehende Verkaufsständer. Es wird auch oft der englische Ausdruck verwendet.

**Aufteilung** *f* **nach Gebieten** - area-by-area allocation

■ Im Marketing die Aufteilung des Budgets für eine Werbekampagne nach geographischen Gebieten, zum Beispiel nach regionalen Fernsehsen-dern. Sie wird je nach Zielen im jeweiligen Gebiet - der erwarteten Verkäufe, der erforderlichen Unterstützung der Außendienstmitarbeiter und der Verkaufsorganisation oder ähnlichen Kriterien - vorgenommen.

**Auftrag** *m* **im Rückstand** - back-order

■ Bestellung, die direkt an den Zulieferer aufgegeben wird, um die Warenlieferung zu vervollständigen, die im Zeitraum der vorangegangenen Bestellung nicht realisiert werden konnte.

**Auftragsnummer** *f* - order number

■ Referenznummer, die eine Bestellung eines Kunden identifiziert und die Kommunikation bei möglichen Problemen, die Rechnungsstellung und die Verwaltung im Allgemeinen erleichtert.

**Auftragsproduktion** *f* - manufacturing to order

■ Herstellung eines Gegenstandes, mit der erst dann begonnen wird, wenn mit dem Käufer eine definitive Vereinbarung getroffen wurde. Dies ist normalerweise bei sehr teueren Produkten der Fall oder bei Produkten, die über Charakteristika verfügen, die den individuellen Bedürfnissen jedes Kunden angepasst werden müssen.

**Auftragsvergabe** *f* - award of contract

■ Im Marketing, Vergabe des Werbeauftrags eines Anzeigekunden an eine Agentur.

**aus erster Hand** - first-hand

■ Neuprodukt. Ware, die vom Hersteller oder Händler als neu angeboten wird. Gegenteil von Waren aus zweiter Hand oder Gebrauchtwaren.

**ausdrückliche Zustimmung** *f* - positive option

■ Antwortmodell, bei dem zur Annahme eines Verkaufsangebots ein ausdrückliches „JA" durch den Empfänger der Mitteilung gefordert wird.

**Ausfallquote** *f* - sample mortality

■ In jeder Forschung, Anzahl der Teilnehmer, die eine Studie beginnen, diese aber nicht beenden. In einer mehrstufigen Forschung, Anzahl der Elemente der Erstauswahl, bei denen nicht alle Studienetappen abgeschlossen werden. In der Panelforschung Anzahl der Panelelemente, die die Studie aus irgendeinem Grund abbrechen.

**Ausgangspunktfakturierung** *f* - basic-point pricing system

■ Rechnungsstellungssystem, bei dem der Verkäufer eine Stadt als Ursprungspunkt festlegt und die Beförderungskosten von dort ab berechnet, auch wenn er in manchen Fällen die Ware von einer anderen Fabrik oder einem anderen Lager aus sendet.

**ausgehendes Telemarketing** *n* - outbound telemarketing

■ Art des Telemarketing, bei dem von einem Büro aus Anrufe an vorher ausgewählte Leute erfolgen.

**ausgewiesener Preis** *m* - marked price

■ Auf den Waren eines Geschäftes angegebener Preis. In bestimmten Fällen genügt es, den Preis am Regal anzugeben.

**Außendienstmannschaft** *f* - field force

■ Im Marketing, Mitarbeiter, die für ein Forschungsinstitut arbeiten. Kann auch zur Gestaltung der Außendienstmannschaft für eine Studie verwendet werden.

**Außenhandel** *m* - foreign trade

■ Beziehungen im Waren- und Dienstleistungsaustausch zwischen einem Land und dem Rest der Welt

**Ausstellungsraum** *m* - show room

■ Geschäft oder Raum, in dem eine repräsentative Auswahl von zu verkaufenden Produkten steht. Es ist möglich, vor Ort zu bestellen, manchmal auch Produkte zu probieren.

**Ausstellungsstück** *n* - sampler

■ Muster oder offene Packung, die es dem Verbraucher ermöglicht, das Produkt vor dem Kauf zu probieren. Wird oft zum Verkauf von Kosmetika benutzt.

**Austrittsbarriere** *f* - exit barrier

■ Bestehende Schwierigkeit oder Verbot, der oder dem sich ein Unternehmen gegenübersieht, wenn es seine Tätigkeit in einem Sektor, einem Produktbereich oder einem geographischen Gebiet beenden möchte. Z. B. Kosten für Abfindungen, Rückwirkungen auf andere Produkte, Kreditvorbehalte usw.

**Ausverkauf** *m* - bargain sale

■ Verkauf normaler Waren mit einem besonderen und zeitlich befristeten Nachlass, normalerweise begleitet von intensiven Werbekampagnen. Wird zu bestimmten Zeiten des Jahres durchgeführt, zum Saisonende sowie zur Lagerräumung und wegen Geschäftsaufgabe. Gelegentlich werden Artikel speziell für diese Sonderverkäufe hergestellt, oder es werden leicht beschädigte Artikel verkauft. Ist vom Discount- oder Rabattverkauf zu unterscheiden.

**Auswahlverfahren** *n* - sampling method

■ Methode zur Auswahl einer Stichprobe. Die wichtigsten Auswahlverfahren sind die Zufallsauswahl mit und ohne Zurücklegen, die geschichtete und die systematische Stichprobe.

**Auswahlverzerrung** *f* - selection bias

■ Durch experimentelle Mess- und Beurteilungsfehler oder durch nicht zufälliges Stichprobensammeln verursachter Effekt, der statistische Ergebnisse systematisch verfälscht. Kann die Ergebnisse einer Umfrage ungültig machen.

**Autobuswerbung** *f* - bus back

■ Anzeige, die auf der Rückseite eines Linienbusses angebracht ist. Wird von Werbetreibenden geschätzt, da die erreichte Zielgruppe wichtig ist. Es gibt auch die Möglichkeit, auf den Seitenflächen Werbebotschaften anzubringen.

**automatischer Vertrieb** *m* - automatic distribution

■ System des Vertriebs von Waren, bei dem der Großhändler die Einzelhändler mit Produkten beliefert, die diese nicht ausdrücklich bestellt haben. Dies geschieht z. B., wenn Muster aller neuen Produkte bestellt oder wenn regelmäßig Produkte mit dem höchsten Umsatz geliefert werden.

**autorisierter Händler** *m* - authorized dealer

■ Händler, der eine formelle Verkaufsgenehmigung des Herstellers zum Verkauf von dessen Produkten erhält. Der Hersteller erkennt somit an, dass der Händler alle notwendigen Voraussetzungen zum Verkauf seiner Produkte erfüllt und einen entsprechenden Kundendienst leisten kann.

# B

**B2A (Business-to-Administration-Geschäft)** - B2A (business to administration)

■ Elektronischer Handel, der von und auf Antrieb von privaten Unternehmen (business) mit der öffentlichen Verwaltung (administration) abgewickelt wird. Es wird auch oft der englische Begriff benutzt.

**B2B (Business-to-Business-Geschäft)** - B2B (business to business)

■ Elektronischer Handel, der zwischen Unternehmen (business) abgewickelt wird, die ihre Produkte oder Dienstleistungen an andere Unternehmen (business) verkaufen. Es wird auch oft der englische Begriff benutzt.

**B2C (Business-to-Consumer-Geschäft)** - B2C (business to consumer)

■ Elektronische Handelsgeschäfte, die von Unternehmen (business) abgewickelt werden, die ihre Produkte oder Dienstleistungen an den Endverbraucher (consumer) verkaufen. Es wird auch oft der englische Begriff benutzt.

**B2E (Business-to-Employees-Geschäft)** - B2E (business to employees)

■ Elektronische Handelsgeschäfte, bei denen ein Unternehmen (business) seine Produkte oder Dienstleistungen an seine Angestellten (employees) verkauft. Es wird auch oft der englische Begriff benutzt.

**B2G (Business-to-Government-Geschäft)** - B2G (business to government)

■ E-Mail, die von Unternehmen entwickelt wurde, die als Verbindung zwischen der öffentlichen Regierung und den Bürgern agiert. Wird auch Geschäft-zu-Regierung genannt. Es wird auch oft der englische Begriff benutzt.

**Bahnhofswerbung** *f* - train station advertising

■ Außenwerbung, die aus Plakaten unterschiedlicher Größe besteht und an Bahnhöfen oder in den Zügen angebracht ist.

**Balkendiagramm** *n* - bar chart

■ Histogramm oder grafische Darstellung, in der die Daten durch Balken dargestellt werden, deren Länge proportional zu den jeweiligen Werten liegt.

**Bandenwerbung** *f* - static advertising

■ Gesamtheit aller Werbeträger, die in einem Bereich oder Sportplatz aufgestellt sind. Oft wird die Audienz der Werbung erhöht, weil Fernsehkameras diese ggf. einblenden und so die Verbreitung über das Fernsehen zu niedrigem Preis geschieht. In bestimmten Fällen und trotz des Ersatzes der Außenwerbung werden diese Träger für Sportsponsoren verbucht.

**Banderole** *f* - banderole

■ Schmale, längliche Fahne, die an einer Wand hängt (Wimpel) oder zwischen zwei Gebäuden angebracht ist und eine Werbebotschaft enthält.

**Banken-Marketing** *n* - bank marketing

■ Von Kredit- oder Bankinstituten betriebene Werbung. Wird auch als Finanzwerbung bezeichnet, obwohl dieser Begriff im strengen Sinn weitgreifender ist, da er sämtliche Finanzinstitute und -geschäfte und nicht nur den Bankensektor umfasst.

**Banner** *m* - dangler

■ Element an der Verkaufsstelle, das von der Decke hängt und im Allgemeinen mit Nylonfäden oder dünnen Drahtfedern angebracht wird und die Aufmerksamkeit des Verbrauchers beim Durchlaufen der Verkaufsstelle wecken soll.

**Bannerwerbung** *f* - banner ad

■ Im Internet, rechteckiges Werbeformat, dessen Größe in Punkten (Pixel) angegeben wird. Ist interaktiv und mit der Website des Inserenten, in der die Werbekampagne gestellt wurde, verlinkt. So ist z. B. ein Banner, in dem das Produkt 123 der Firma ABC annonciert wird, mit der genauen Stelle in der Website von ABC verbunden, in dem das Produkt 123 angeboten wird, und nicht mit der Startseite der Firma ABC.

**Bargeldfluss** *m* - cash flow

■ Bargeldzu- und -abflüsse, die mit einem Investitionsprojekt der Gesellschaft oder Filiale verbunden sind. Man benutzt auch den Begriff Cash-Flow.

**Barzahlungsskonto** *m* - cash discount

■ Preisnachlass, den der Lieferant dem Kunden gewährt, wenn dieser bar oder innerhalb von 10 Tagen nach Erhalt der Ware bezahlt. In der Regel beträgt der Preisabzug 2% und wird für das geringere Risiko des Zahlungsausfalls und die beschleunigte Zahlung gewährt.

**Basisartikel** *m* - staple good

■ Produkt, das viel verkauft wird, im Basissortiment enthalten ist und dessen Bereitstellung sozusagen obligatorisch ist. Die Preise dieser Artikel werden von den Hausfrauen am stärksten beachtet und tragen entscheidend zum Preis-Image des Geschäftes bei, d. h. der Wahrnehmung bezüglich der Preisgestaltung aller angebotenen Produkte.

**Basisprodukt** *n* - core product

■ Ursprüngliches Produkt einer Produktlinie oder -familie, das die Basis für den Rest der späteren Entwicklung der Produktpalette bildet.

**Bayes'sche Wahrscheinlichkeit** *f* - Bayesian probability

■ Im untersuchungstechnischen Bereich versteht man hierunter den Wahrscheinlichkeitsgrad, dass ein Umstand oder ein Ereignis eintritt. Wobei die Wahrscheinlichkeit nicht auf statistischen Vorgängen beruht, sondern auf der subjektiven Einschätzung eines Experten.

**Bayes-Theorem** *n* - Bayes' theorem

■ Vorgehen der quantitativen Untersuchung, bei dem neue Information mit bereits bestehender kombiniert wird, um die Wahrscheinlichkeit des Eintretens bestimmter Umstände oder Ereignisse vorherzusagen. Wird oft bei der Abwägung von Entscheidungen eingesetzt, die unter ungewissen Umständen getroffen werden müssen. Hierzu werden persönliche oder subjektive Wahrscheinlichkeiten in numerischer Form verwendet.

**BCG-Matrix** *f* - growth-share matrix

■ Von der Boston Consulting Group entworfene Matrix zur Bewertung von Geschäftsfeldern einer Unternehmensgruppe als Funktion aus erwartetem Wachstums des Segments (mehr oder weniger 5-10% reales Wachstum) und dem relativen Marktanteil des eigenen Geschäftsbereichs in diesem Segment (beherrschend oder nicht). Die daraufhin erfolgende Einstufung als Cash Cow, Star, Fragezeichen oder Dogs ermöglicht eine oberflächliche Einschätzung des Geschäftsbereichs.

**Bearbeitung** *f* - editing

■ In der Marktforschung das Lesen, Korrigieren, Vervollständigen von Fragebögen einer Forschung, bis diese digitalisiert werden können.

**bedingte Assoziation** *f* - conditional association

■ In der Untersuchung versteht man hierunter den Verbindungsgrad, der zwischen zwei Variablen besteht, wenn gleichzeitig anderweitige unterschiedliche Variablen (Kontrollvariablen) berücksichtigt werden.

**Bedürfnis** *n* - need

■ Etwas, das von einem Individuum für sein eigenes Wohlbefinden notwendig ist. Das Individuum verspürt einen Anreiz, einen verspürten Mangel auszugleichen. Die Marketingforschung sucht nach nicht oder nur mangelhaft befriedigten Bedürfnissen, um neue Produkte anzubieten, die diese Bedürfnisse abdecken.

**Befragter** *m* - respondent

■ Person, die einen Fragebogen beantwortet oder die einer Befragung entweder bewusst oder unbewusst ausgesetzt ist. Ihre Anonymität wird dabei gewährleistet.

**Befragungsweg** *m* - itinerary

■ Zufällig festgelegter Ablauf, den der Befrager verfolgen muss, um die zufällige Auswahl der Befragten zu gewährleisten. Man beginnt an einem oder an mehreren Punkten (dabei geht man nach Wohnvierteln vor) und es werden die Straßen, Häuser und Wohnungen bestimmt, die besucht werden sollen. Im Fall von Verkäufern spricht man von der Reiseroute.

**Begründung** *f* - rationale

■ Logisches Argument, das eine Strategie oder Werbekampagne stützt.

**bekannt machen** *v* - popularise *v*
■ Ein Minderheitenprodukt durch eine Werbekampagne und/oder Öffentlichkeitsarbeit bei vielen Menschen bekannt und beliebt machen.

**Bekanntmachung** *f* - dissemination
■ Verbreitung von Nachrichten, Produkten oder Kenntnissen usw. auf eine Art und Weise, die sie der größtmöglichen Anzahl von Personen zur Kenntnis bringt.

**Belebung** *f* - animation
■ Im Marketing, Maßnahmen zur Förderung des Images einer Verkaufseinrichtung oder eines Einkaufszentrums. Ziel ist es, den Publikumsverkehr der Zielgruppe zu erhöhen und gleichzeitig die Kauftätigkeit anzuregen. Um dies zu erreichen, setzt man Dekoration und Musik ein und veranstaltet Wettbewerbe, fördert den Absatz usw.

**Below-the-line-Werbung** *f* - below-the-line advertising
■ Fachbegriff aus dem Englischen, der alle seitens eines Unternehmens oder einer Institution betriebenen Werbeaktionen umfasst, die nicht unter die konventionelle Werbung fallen. Die unkonventionelle oder „Below-the-line"-Werbung hat in den letzten Jahrzehnten verstärkt an Bedeutung gewonnen und hat in Bezug auf Investitionssummen selbst die in Massenmedien erscheinende konventionelle Werbung übertroffen.

**Benefizwerbung** *f* - public service advertising
■ Karitative Werbung mit sozialer Funktion. Die Kosten dieser Werbeaktion werden nicht vom Werbenden getragen, da es sich um ein soziales Werk ohne öffentlichen Kostenvoranschlag handelt, sie werden zum Teil von der Werbeagentur getragen, die ihre kreativen Dienste kostenfrei zur Verfügung stellt, bzw. vom Kommunikationsmedium, das seinen Werberaum zur Verfügung stellt.

**Benennung** *f* - naming
■ Disziplin der Markeneinführer, die sich auf die Erfindung eines Namens für neue Produkte konzentriert. Dieser muss eingetragen werden können, die Werte und Attribute widerspiegeln, die die Grundlage für die Positionierung der neuen Produkte bilden und außerdem bestimmten formellen Anforderungen genügen.

**Beobachtungsbefragung** *f* - survey by observation
■ Befragung, bei welcher der Befragende das Verhalten der Bevölkerung in Bezug auf bestimmte Beobachtungsregeln feststellt, aber mit niemandem direkt in Kontakt tritt. Die Beobachtungsbefragung wird auch verwendet, um bestimmte Sachverhalte nachzuweisen (z. B. verpflichtende Benutzung des Sturzhelms, Bereitstellung des Materials am Verkaufspunkt usw.).

**Beobachtungsstudie** *f* - observational study
■ Forschungsverfahren, das die Beurteilung eines Benutzerverhaltens für ein bestimmtes Produkt gestattet. Auf diese Weise können die speziellen Probleme dieses Verhaltens entdeckt und Anpassungen mit dem Ziel der Beseitigung von Konfliktpunkten vorgenommen werden.

**Bereich** *m* - ambit
■ Geographischer Raum, in dem ein Unternehmen tätig ist. Dies kann international, landesweit, regional oder im Ort sein.

**Berufsmagazin** *n* - professional magazine
■ Zeitschrift, deren Leser Mitglied einer Berufsgruppe sind, ähnlich wie bei Fachzeitschriften und anders als bei allgemeinen Zeitschriften. Idealer Kanal, um einem bestimmten Publikum technische und korporative Nachrichten zukommen zu lassen, denn trotz geringerer Verbreitung ist die Wirkung sehr hoch und es werden unnütze Werbekontakte vermieden.

**Beschaffungsmarketing** *n* - reverse marketing
■ Marketingart, die angewandt wird, wenn die Initiative zur Kontaktaufnahme vom

Kunden oder Käufer ausgeht und dieser die Grundbedingungen der Transaktion festlegt. Normalerweise bei Organisationskunden mit starker Verhandlungsmacht oder auf bestimmten Internetmärkten, in denen der Käufer selbst die Verkaufsbedingungen stellt, und bei denen die Bietenden versuchen, den Auftrag zu ersteigern.

**Beschwerde** *f* **seitens des Kunden** - customer complaint

■ Unzufriedenheit oder Diskrepanz, die der Kunde gegenüber der Werbeaktion eines Unternehmens oder gegenüber des Nutzens, der Qualität oder Funktionalität eines bestimmten Produkts oder einer Dienstleistung äußert. Kann zu einer Reklamation führen, falls der Kunde sich dazu entscheidet, seine Beschwerde schriftlich zu vermerken und zu formalisieren.

**Beschwerdebericht** *m* - product complaints report

■ Bericht, in dem Zwischenfälle mit dem Produkt oder seinem Bezug aufgeführt sind. Kann z. B. Bemerkungen des Franchise-Nehmers in Bezug auf fehlerhafte Lieferungen an sein Geschäft oder Kundenbeschwerden über ein defektes Verkaufsprodukt beinhalten.

**Bestand** *m* - stock

■ Gesamtheit der an einem Verkaufs-, Vertriebs- oder Herstellungsort gelagerten Güter.

**Bestandsverfügbarkeit** *f* - stock availability

■ Lagerbestände, die zu einem bestimmten Zeitpunkt zur Bearbeitung einer Bestellung genutzt werden können.

**Bestandswertminderung** *f* - stock depreciation

■ Wertminderung der Bestände während ihrer Lagerdauer, zum Beispiel aufgrund physikalischen Verfalls oder technischer Veralterung.

**Bestandszentralisierung** *f* - stock centralisation

■ Vereinigung der Bestände zur Vereinfachung ihrer Verwaltung und Vermeidung einer Zerstreuung, die vom Standpunkt der Kosteneffizienz schädlich wäre.

**Bestell-Erfüllungsrate** *f* - order fill rate

■ Anteil der Bestellungen von Ware, die vollständig in einem bestimmten Zeitraum geliefert werden.

**Bestellintervall** *m* - replenishment time

■ Zeit, die zwischen zwei Bestellungen vergeht.

**Bestellpunkt** *m* - order point

■ In der Lagerbestandsverwaltung, Bestandsschwelle, bei der eine normale Bestellung empfohlen wird. Wird mit Hilfe von Formeln berechnet, die die Produktnachfrage und die Lieferzeit berücksichtigen. Ebenso werden die Kosten der Bestellung, der Lagerhaltung und die Opportunitätskosten durch entgangenen Gewinn aufgrund fehlenden Lagerbestandes eingeschlossen.

**Bestellzyklus** *m* - order cycle

■ Prozess von logistischen Folgeaktivitäten, der in einem Zeitraum zwischen zwei Bestellungen verläuft und sich auf die gleiche oder ähnliche Weise mit der Zeit wiederholt.

**Besuchsrhythmus** *m* - calling cycle

■ Im Marketing versteht man hierunter die durchschnittliche Zeitdauer zwischen zwei Besuchen oder Anrufen bei einem Kunden.

**Beta-Test** *m* - beta test

■ Testversion von Produkten oder Dienstleistungen, die praktisch fertig sind. Sie werden außerhalb des Unternehmens zu Testzwecken (Beta-Tests) verteilt, um so mögliche Fehler zu finden und diese vor der Markteinführung zu beseitigen. Wird insbesondere bei Informatikprogrammen verwendet.

**Betaversion** *f* - beta version

■ Entwicklungszustand eines Produkts vor seiner Marktreife, in dem es der Probe einer breiten und ausgewählten Gruppe unternehmensfremder Nutzer unterworfen wird. Wird auch als Beta-Test bezeichnet.

**Bevölkerung** *f* - population

▪ In der Forschung die Gesamtheit der Personen, deren Merkmale untersucht werden sollen. Die Analyse sämtlicher Bevölkerungselemente gibt den Zensus. Wenn sich die Untersuchung auf eine eingeschränkte Zahl zufällig ausgewählter Personen beschränkt, handelt es sich um eine Stichprobe.

**Bevölkerungspyramide** *f* - population pyramid

▪ Graphische Darstellung der Zusammensetzung einer Bevölkerung nach Geschlecht und Altersgruppen, die im idealtypischen Fall die Form eines Dreiecks hat.

**bewerten** *v* - value *v*

▪ Auswerten, einem Gut einen Preis zuordnen.

**Bewertung** *f* **des Konsumentenvertrauens** - consumer confidence measure

▪ Instrument zur Messung der Kaufwahrscheinlichkeit eines langlebigen und hochpreisigen Artikels. Der Kunde wird nicht kaufen, wenn sein Vertrauen in die Zukunft gleich null ist, und er wird mehr kaufen, wenn seine Zuversicht größer ist. Dieses Instrument berücksichtigt zusätzlich die wirtschaftliche Lage der Person, wie sie von ihr selbst und im Vergleich zum Umfeld empfunden wird.

**Bezahlung** *f* **per Aktion** - pay per lead (PPL)

▪ Im Internet Abrechnungsmodalität, bei der pro interessiertem Besucher bezahlt wird.

**Bezahlung** *f* **per Kauf** - pay per sale (PPS)

▪ Abrechnungsmodalität für Werbung im Internet, bei der abhängig von den erzielten Verkäufen bezahlt wird.

**Bezahlung** *f* **per Klick** - pay per click (PPC)

▪ Im Internet, Abkommen zwischen dem Veröffentlicher der Anzeige und dem Betreiber einer Suchmaschine oder einer anderen Site, wobei ersterer alle Downloads seiner Site, die von der Suchmaschine erzeugt werden, bezahlt.

**Beziehungsmarketing** *n* - relationship marketing

▪ Das Beziehungsmarketing oder englisch Relationship Marketing widmet sich dem Auf- und Ausbau langfristiger Kundenbeziehungen. Es verfolgt das Ziel, mehr Kunden, zufriedene Kunden und profitable Kunden für das Unternehmen oder eine Marke zu gewinnen. Anders als im bisherigen Marketing wird der Fokus also nicht auf zum Beispiel den Preis oder das Produkt gelegt, sondern auf die Beziehung von Unternehmen beziehungsweise Marke und Kunde.

**Bezugsgruppe** *f* - reference group

▪ Personengruppe, die ein Individuum nachahmen möchte, bzw. deren Werte, Lebensstil oder Sozialschicht und wirtschaftliche Lage. Werbung muss hier in ihren Werbemitteilungen die Wünsche und Motivation der Zielperson aufgreifen, nicht die reale Situation. Gruppe, mit der eine andere Gruppe verglichen wird.

**Bezugswert** *m* - reference value

▪ Produktpreis, mit dem das Angebot in Wettbewerb tritt und von dem der Verbraucher annimmt, eine gute Kaufalternative zu sein.

**bidirektionale Öffentlichkeitsarbeit** *f* - two way public relations

▪ Wissenschaftliche, auf gegenseitiger Kommunikation begründete Öffentlichkeitsarbeit zwischen der Organisation und ihrem Publikum. Ausgehend von der wissenschaftlichen Meinungsforschung werden strategische Programme für die Zielgruppe entworfen.

**Bildagentur** *f* - photo agency

▪ Agentur, die auf eigene Rechnung Fotos in Auftrag gibt, oder die Arbeiten angeschlossener Fotografen verfügbar hält, um sie an Verlage, Presse- oder Werbeagenturen zu verkaufen. Einige Bildagenturen spezialisieren sich auf bestimmte Themen wie Sport, Musik oder Wasseraufnahmen.

**Billing-Marketing** *n* - billing marketing

▪ Junge Werbedisziplin, bei der Rechnungen, Kontoauszüge und ähnliche

Dokumente regelmäßig als Werbeinstrumente genutzt und an die Kunden verschickt werden. Bisher konzentrierte sich diese Form der Werbung größtenteils auf den juristischen- und Verwaltungssektor. In jüngster Zeit jedoch treten auch Instrumente zur Information, Kundenbindung sowie zur Verkaufsförderung von neuen Produkten und Dienstleistungen auf.

**Binnenhandel** *m* - domestic trade

■ Handel zwischen einem Käufer und Verkäufer, die im selben Land ansässig sind. Gegenteil zum Außenhandel oder internationalen Handel.

**bleibender Eindruck** *m* - afterimage

■ Eindruck, der im Gedächtnis des Verbrauchers zurückbleibt, nachdem er eine Anzeige gesehen hat, auch wenn dieser Eindruck vielleicht nicht mit dem wirklich Gesehenen übereinstimmt.

**Blind-Test** *m* - blind test

■ Technik, bei welcher der Verbraucher unterschiedliche Produkte bewertet ohne deren Marke zu kennen, und so frei von vorgefassten Konzepten

**Blitzwerbung** *f* - in-and-out promotion

■ Kurze Werbung am Verkaufspunkt, um den schnellen Verkauf eines Produkts zu fördern.

**Blockrabatt** *m* - block discount

■ Rabatt, der für den Verbrauch verschiedener Produkte eines Unternehmens gewährt wird. Zweck ist, die Nutzung der nachfrageärmeren Produkte zu belohnen. So kann ein Stromversorgungsunternehmen denjenigen Verbrauchern, die Strom nur zur Beleuchtung und zum Betrieb von Haushaltsgeräten nutzen, eine Kilowattstunde zu einem bestimmten Preis anbieten. Zugleich kann es diesen Preis für diejenigen Verbraucher senken, die zusätzlich Strom für den Betrieb einer Elektroheizung nutzen.

**Blog** *m* - blog

■ Veröffentlichung von persönlichen Gedanken und Weblinks in chronologischer Abfolge. Ein Blog oder elektronisches Tagebuch ist oft ein Mix von Ereignissen aus dem Leben einer Person und Neuheiten im Internet, sozusagen eine Mischung aus Tagebuch und Leitfaden.

**Bodenausstellung** *f* - floor display

■ Präsentation zum Verkauf bestimmter Artikel direkt auf dem Boden oder auf einem kleinen Podest. Wird gewöhnlich bei Verkaufsaktionen eingesetzt, bei denen Produkte in großen Mengen verkauft werden.

**Bodenverkaufsständer** *m* - floor-stand

■ Spezieller Einrichtungsgegenstand zur Präsentation eines bestimmten Produkts. Nimmt Funktionen der Anordnung des Produkts wahr und stimuliert den Kauf. Wird an den Endseiten der Verkaufsregale, auf Theken und Regalen oder direkt auf dem Boden aufgestellt.

**Bogen** *m* - arch

■ Vorrichtung in einem Geschäft, die zwischen zwei Ständen über einem Gang angebracht ist und auf der Produkte stehen, die eine höhere Aufmerksamkeit erreichen sollen.

**Bonuspunkte** *m/pl* - loyalty scheme

■ Werbetechnik, um den wiederholten Kauf von Produkten zu fördern, wobei der Kunde bei jedem Kauf Bonuspunkte erhält, die er bei Erreichen einer bestimmten Punktzahl gegen eine Vergünstigung oder ein Geschenk eintauschen kann. Typisches Beispiel sind Fluggesellschaften, die bei jedem Flug Bonuspunkte oder Meilen vergeben, die bei einer bestimmten Anzahl gegen einen Freiflug eingetauscht werden können.

**Briefforschung** *f* - mail research

■ In der Meinungsforschung, Studie, die den Postweg zwischen Fragesteller und Beantworter nutzt. Wird aufgrund der geringen Antwortrate nur sehr wenig eingesetzt.

**Briefumfrage** *f* - mail questionnaire

■ In der Meinungsforschung, per Post zugesendeter Fragebogen. In vielen Studien wird ein Mischkommunikationssystem verwendet, bei dem der

Fragesteller den Fragebogen persönlich überreicht und Anweisungen zum Ausfüllen und zur Rücksendung per Post gibt.

**Briefwerbung** *f* - direct mail advertising

▪ Botschaft, die direkt an vorher identifizierte Personen geht, normalerweise per Post. Dieses Medium erlaubt eine stärkere Personalisierung und eine umfangreichere Botschaft.

**Broschüre** *f* - brochure

▪ Werbeschrift, die aus mehreren gedruckten Blättern besteht und Information über ein Produkt oder über das Unternehmen selbst enthält. Sie ist an ein Publikum gerichtet, von dem man annimmt, dass es an der Information interessiert ist. In der Regel enthält sie viele Fotografien und Abbildungen, jedoch meist keine Preisliste.

**Browserregistrierung** *f* - browser registration

▪ Vorgang, bei dem eine Internetadresse (URL) in die Datenbanken verschiedener Suchmaschinen registriert und somit den Usern zugänglich gemacht wird. Diese Dienstleistung wird in der Regel von Unternehmen für Internet-Marketing angeboten.

**Bruttoabdeckung** *f* - gross coverage

▪ Anzahl der Kontakte, die eine Kampagne auf ein objektives Publikum hat. Viele dieser Kontakte richten sich an die gleichen Personen, wodurch die Bruttoabdeckung im Allgemeinen und manchmal im besonderen Maße die objektive Gruppe übertrifft.

**Bündelpackung** *f* - bundle pack

▪ Verpackung, die zwei oder mehr Einheiten eines gleichen Produkts oder verschiedener, sich ergänzender Produkte enthält, z. B. eine 2x1-Verkaufskampagne oder Gratispackungen.

**Busseitenwerbung** *f* - bus side

▪ Werbung auf den Seitenflächen eines Autobusses. Gelegentlich reicht diese bis an das Dach des Busses oder kann die Fläche von gewöhnlich 90x300 cm überschreiten. Der Preis einer Werbefläche auf der linken Seite ist höher, weil die Werbung hier stärker wahrgenommen wird und keine Fläche für die Türen freigehalten werden muss. Der Werbetreibende kann zugleich Werbung auf der Rückseite anbringen.

# C

**C2A (Citizen-to-Administration-Geschäft)** - C2A (citizen to administration)

▪ Webseite im Internet, die sich damit befasst, die Beziehungen zwischen den Bürgern und der öffentlichen Verwaltung zu kanalisieren und zu fördern. Es wird auch oft der englische Begriff benutzt.

**C2B (Consumer-to-Business-Geschäft)** - C2B (consumer to business)

▪ Elektronischer Handel, der von und auf Antrieb von den Verbrauchern mit Unternehmen abgewickelt wird. Es wird auch oft der englische Begriff benutzt.

**C2C (Consumer-to-Consumer Geschäft)** - C2C (consumer to consumer)

▪ Elektronischer Handel, der zwischen den Verbrauchern untereinander abgewickelt wird. Es wird auch oft der englische Begriff benutzt.

**Call-Center** *n* - call centre

▪ Telemarketing-Plattform, die die notwendigen technologischen und personellen Mittel umfasst, um Aktivitäten betreffend dem Erhalt und der Vergabe von telefonischen Kontakten durchzuführen. Diese Plattformen haben sich zu Kontaktzentren, oder Contact Centers, entwickelt, die auch die Verwaltung von zusätzlichen Kanälen wie E-Mail, Web, Fax, SMS und andere digitale Medien umfassen.

**Cash Cow** - cash cow

▪ In einer Marktwachstums-Marktanteils-Matrix bezeichnet der Begriff einen Geschäftsbereich, der in einem Segment mit geringem Wachstum Marktführer ist oder eine dominierende Stellung hat. Dieser muss mehr Mittelzuflüsse erzeugen als zur Beibehaltung seiner Marktquote nötig sind, um diese in andere Geschäftsbereiche der Gruppe zu investieren. Erfordert eine konservative Führung. Wird auch Goldesel genannt.

**CI-Handbuch** *n* - corporate identity manual
■ Dokument, das einen Plan zur Bearbeitung, Handhabung und Koordinierung aller Variablen enthält, die das Image und die Identität eines Unternehmens nach außen beeinflussen, z. B. die Wahl der Firmenattribute, kommunikative Aktivitäten, Verhalten, Produkte, Umfeld, Unternehmensstil. Diese Handbücher werden immer mehr ausschließlich in digitalen Formaten geschaffen.

**Click-and-Mortar-Unternehmen** *n* - clicks and mortar
■ Ausdruck aus dem englisch-amerikanischen Sprachgebrauch, der von David Pottruck von der Firma Charles Schwab für diejenigen Unternehmen erfunden wurde, die sowohl im Internet als auch in anderen Medien präsent sind.

**Cluster-Analyse** *f* - cluster analysis
■ Untersuchungsmethode, die darin besteht, die Komponenten bzw. Teilnehmer einer Gruppe mit ähnlichen Eigenschaften zusammenzufassen.

**Consumer Branding** *n* - consumer branding
■ Spezialisierung der Markenpolitik, die sich auf die Schaffung und Führung von Marken für Produkte und Konsumartikel konzentriert. In dieser Disziplin ist das Design der Verpackungen dieser Produkte und Artikel von besonderer Erheblichkeit.

**Corporate Branding** *n* - corporate branding
■ Spezialisierung der Markenpolitik, die sich auf die Schaffung und Führung von Marken für Organisationen und Unternehmen konzentriert.

**Corporate Design** *n* - corporate design
■ Disziplin, die sich mit der Entwicklung und Schaffung grafischer Elemente für die visuelle Identität von Unternehmen sowie mit der Anwendung dieser Elemente auf Vordrucke, Briefpapier und Werbematerial des Unternehmens befasst.

**Corporate Identity** *f* - corporate identity
■ Art und Weise, in der sich ein Unternehmen jeweils unterschiedlichem Publikum vorstellt, mit dem es Beziehungen aufnimmt. Es wird auch der englische Begriff verwendet.

**Co-Sponsoring** *n* - co-sponsorship
■ Sponsoring, bei dem sich zwei oder mehr Sponsoren die Kosten und den Protagonismus im Verhältnis zu ihrer Investition teilen.

**Coupon** *m* **zum Ausschneiden** - tear-off coupon
■ In den Printmedien Teil einer Werbeanzeige, den man ausschneiden und für den Erhalt von Information, Bestellungen oder den Erhalt von Preisnachlässen zurücksenden kann. Wird oft zur Datenerfassung verwendet.

**Coupon-Werbung** *f* - coupon ad
■ In den Druckmedien versteht man hierunter eine Anzeige, die einen Gutschein oder Coupon zum Herausschneiden enthält, den der Verbraucher einsenden oder vorlegen kann, was dem Aufgeber der Anzeige wiederum als Kontrolle dient. Der Verbraucher kann mithilfe von Coupons Information oder einen Rabatt auf den Produktpreis erlangen. Der Werbetreibende kann hierdurch die Wirksamkeit der verschiedenen Werbeträger, in denen er seine Anzeige gesetzt hat, überprüfen.

**CPC** *pl* **(Klickkosten)** - CPC (cost per click)
■ In der Internetwerbung versteht man hierunter die Kosten pro angefallenem Klick auf eine Bannerwerbung. Der Preis für eine solche Werbekampagne kann auch anhand fixer Klickkosten festgesetzt werden, wobei sich der Preis nach einer Mindestklickrate richtet.

**CPI** *pl* **(Kosten pro Anfrage)** - CPI (cost per inquiry)
■ In der Direktwerbung versteht man hierunter die Erfolgsmessung einer

Werbekampagne unter wirtschaftlichen Gesichtspunkten aufgrund des Verhältnisses von Stückpreis zu Informationsanfragen. Wird errechnet, indem man die Gesamtkosten der Werbekampagne durch die Anzahl der erhaltenen Informationsanfragen teilt. Ist auch unter der englischen Abkürzung CPI bekannt

**CPO** *pl* **(Kosten pro Auftrag)** - CPO (cost per order)

■ Erfolgsmessung einer Werbekampagne unter wirtschaftlichen Gesichtspunkten aufgrund des Verhältnisses von Stückpreis zu Bestellungseingang. Wird errechnet, indem man die Gesamtkosten der Werbekampagne durch die Anzahl der eingegangenen Bestellungen teilt. Ist auch unter der englischen Abkürzung CPO bekannt.

**Cross-Couponing** *n* - cross couponing

■ Technik der Verkaufsförderung, bei der Coupons verteilt werden, mittels derer man beim Kauf eines Produktes B ein Produkt A entweder kostenlos oder zu einem reduzierten Preis erhält.

**Customer Lifetime Value** *m* - LTF (life time value)

■ Deckungsbeitrag, den ein Kunde während seines gesamten „Kundenlebens" realisiert, diskontiert auf den heutigen Tag.

**Cyberumfrage** *f* - cyber survey

■ Umfrage, die von einer Webseite gestartet wird und die ermöglicht, eine Untersuchung der Marktlage im Internet anzustellen. Personen, die an der Umfrage teilnehmen, erhalten manchmal einen Anreiz oder eine Belohnung in Form eines Geschenks.

# D

**Dachmarke** *f* - umbrella brand

■ Bezeichnet innerhalb des Marketings die übergeordnete Marke einer Markenfamilie von unterschiedlichen Produkten oder Unternehmen, um ihre gemeinsame Kommerzialisierung und Potenzierung wirtschaftlich zu gestalten.

**DAGMAR** - DAGMAR

■ Akronym für „Defining Advertising Goals for Measured Advertising Results", einer Werbemethode von Russell H. Colley aus dem Jahre 1961, die die Ergebnisse aus der Werbung mit den vorgenommenen Zielen vergleicht, was als ersten Schritt eine klare Definition der Ziele erfordert. Die Methode umfasst vier Stufen: Awareness (Bewusstsein), Comprehension (Verständnis), Conviction (Überzeugung) und Action (Aktion), ACCA.

**Datenbank** *f* - database

■ Organisationsmethode für Dateien, in denen eine Menge von Daten, die sich aufeinander beziehen, auf einer Festplatte oder einer anderen Speichervorrichtung untergebracht sind. Die Menge an Unternehmensdaten, die von der Unternehmung für ihre Betriebszwecke verwendet wird. In einigen Fällen werden sie auch veröffentlicht, damit sie von Dritten verwendet werden können.

**Datenbankanalyse** *f* - database analysis

■ Studie über den Informationsinhalt in einer Datenbank von Kunden oder möglichen Kunden zur Steigerung der Wirksamkeit der Marketingaktionen.

**Datenbank-Marketing** *n* - database marketing

■ Werkzeug des direkten Marketings, das die neuen Technologien der Datenbankverwaltung zum Speichern, Analysieren und Nutzen der vom Unternehmen erreichten Beziehung mit seinen Kunden benutzt, um die Kommunikation so weit wie möglich zu personalisieren und das beste Produkt bzw. die beste Dienstleistung für jeden Kunden anzubieten.

**Datenbankverwalter** *m* - database manager

■ Unternehmen oder Einzelpersonen, die Datenbanken verschiedener Herkunft (öffentliche Quellen, Adhoc-Umfragen) neu zusammenstellen, systematisieren und zu Gewerbezwecken nutzen, wobei sich diese auf eine bestimmte Bevölkerung beziehen und sie den Werbeträgern oder den Werbeagenturen zur Verfügung stellen. Datenbanken ermöglichen die Einteilung des Zielpublikums nach ganz spezifischen Kriterien (Geschlecht, Beruf, Gehaltsgruppe, Konsumgewohnheiten u. a.), an die sich die Werbeaktion richtet und stellt ein nicht wegdenkbares Werkzeug des derzeitigen Direktmarketing dar.

**Datenbelegung** *f* - data overlays

■ Im Marketing der Datenbanken, die Überlappung von zwei oder mehr Listen, wobei eine die restlichen Daten eines Kunden enthält und die Datenbank weiter ausfüllen soll, um die größtmögliche Zahl an Daten zu erhalten und die Information über die Eingabe so weit wie möglich zu belegen.

**Datensammlung** *f* - data collection

■ Beschaffung von Informationen und Daten, die in einer Untersuchung oder Analyse verwendet werden sollen. Diese werden in Archiven und Datenbanken gespeichert.

**Datenschürfung** *f* - data mining

■ Automatische Extraktion von vorhersehbarer Information, die in Datenbanken versteckt ist. Diese Technik hilft bei der Identifizierung von Märkten und bei der Potenzierung des Unternehmens bei der Kundenansprache, sodass das Direktmarketing per E-Mail (e-Marketing) rentabler wird.

**Datenspeicher** *m* - data warehouse

■ Zentraler Speicherort für die Information. Erfordert ein Informatikprogramm zur Erkennung des Kundenprofils und Reaktion auf seine Anforderungen. Auf diesem System basieren die personalisierten Marketingstrategien (One-to-One).

**Daueraufsteller** *m* - permanent display

■ Werbeelement, das lange genutzt wird oder dessen Ausstellungsbedingungen extrem sind. Deshalb sind die Designmaterialien nicht mehr aus Pappe o. Ä., sondern aus Metall, Holz usw. Die Produktionskosten für diesen Werbeträger sind vergleichsweise hoch.

**Defensivmarketing** *n* - defensive marketing

■ Marketingart, bei der das Unternehmen Aktionen zur Veränderung eines negativen Bildes seiner Marken auf dem Markt unternimmt. Im Allgemeinen versucht das Unternehmen dieses negative Bild durch intensive Werbekampagnen zu löschen, welche die Produkt- und Markenqualität beweisen und bestärken.

**Delkredere-Agent** *m* - del credere agent

■ Kommissionär, der Waren im Auftrag eines Unternehmens verkauft und dafür eine höhere als die übliche Provision erhält, weil er das gesamte Zahlungsausfallrisiko trägt.

**Delphi-Methode** *f* - Delphi method

■ Methode zur Vorhersage der Nachfrage oder der Charakteristika eines Marktes, die auf Befragungen von Expertengruppen basiert. Sie besteht aus mehreren Frage- und Antwortrunden. Mit jeder neuen Fragerunde werden jedem Fachmann sämtliche Antworten der Vorrunde vorgelegt. Man geht davon aus, dass die Antworten der anderen Experten seine Meinung beeinflussen, so dass letztlich ein Konsens über die aktuelle Situation und insbesondere die Zukunft entsteht. Diese Methode kann nützlich sein, um Tendenzen zu erkennen.

**Demarketing** *n* - demarketing

■ Maßnahmen zur Mäßigung der Nachfrage nach einem Produkt, wie Erhöhung der Preise, Verschlechterung der Produktqualität, Herausnahme von wenig rentablen Kunden, Verringerung der Werbung und Reduzierung der Verkaufanstrengungen. Grund kann zum Beispiel eine vorübergehende Knappheit sein, oder die Absicht, ein neues Produkt herauszubringen.

**Demografiestudie** *f* - demographic study

■ Information, die Verbrauchergruppen in Marktsegmente aufgliedert und sich dabei auf Statistikdaten wie Alter,

Geschlecht, Familienstand und Wohngegend bezieht.

**den Preis heraufsetzen** *v* - mark up *v*

■ Berechnung der Margen nach Produkten, Produktfamilien, Abteilungen usw., um eine angemessene durchschnittliche Gewinnspanne zu erreichen, bei gleichzeitiger Wettbewerbsfähigkeit in jedem Bereich. Die Verkaufspreise werden durch Aufschlag dieser Margen auf die Einkaufs- oder Herstellkosten bestimmt, mit Ausnahme von Lockvogelprodukten und gerundeten Preisen bei Packgrößenänderungen.

**Deregulierung** *f* - deregulation

■ Prozess, der darauf zielt, den freien Wettbewerb zwischen den möglichen Anbietern einer Dienstleistung zu fördern, indem Bestimmungen oder künstliche Schranken abgeschafft werden, die Positionen eines örtlichen Monopols begünstigen. Ein Beispiel ist die Deregulierung im Flugverkehr.

**Design-Management** *n* - design management

■ Der Begriff Designmanagement bietet einer Organisation einen Ansatz, designrelevante Entscheidungen markt- und kundengerecht zu treffen sowie designrelevante (Unternehmens-) Prozesse zu optimieren. Es ist eine langandauernde umfassende Aktivität auf allen Ebenen unternehmerischen Handelns. Designmanagement agiert in der Schnittmenge von Management und Design und fungiert als Bindeglied zwischen den Plattformen Technologie, Design, Management und Marketing an internen und externen Schnittstellen des Unternehmens.

**deskriptive Forschung** *f* - descriptive research

■ Forschungsdesign, das die zu beschaffenden Informationen von vornherein genau festlegt und diese lediglich beschreibt. Gegenteil ist angewandte Forschung, deren Ziel die Hilfe bei der Entscheidungsfindung ist.

**Diagramm** *n* - diagram

■ Grafische Darstellung der funktionalen Beziehung zwischen zwei oder mehreren Variablengruppen. In der Statistik existieren unterschiedliche Diagrammtypen, die statistische Daten widerspiegeln (z. B. Histogramme und Stereogramme).

**dichotome Fragestellung** *f* - dichotomous question

■ Geschlossene Frage mit nur zwei Antwortmöglichkeiten.

**Dienstleistungsmarketing** *n* - services marketing

■ Teil des Marketings, der die spezifischen und unterschiedlichen Aspekte der Vermarktung von immateriellen Produkten untersucht.

**differenziertes Marketing** *n* - differentiated marketing

■ Marketing, bei dem je nach Zielsegment verschiedene Kombinationen aus Preis, Produkt, Werbung und Vertriebskanal eingesetzt werden.

**Differenzierungswert** *m* - differentiation value

■ Eine im Rahmen der Wirtschaftlichkeitsanalyse durchgeführte Berechnung der Kostenvorteile bzw. -nachteile, die durch die Verwendung und den Kauf eines alternativen Produkts im Vergleich zum bisherigen entstehen.

**digitale Unterschrift** *f* - digital fingerprint

■ System, das einem Benutzer seine Identität im Netz bestätigt.

**digitales Branding** *n* - digital branding

■ Erzeugung und Leitung von Marken, die hauptsächlich in einem digitalen Medium (Site oder interaktive Vorführung) entwickelt werden.

**digitales Marketing** *n* - digital merchandising

■ Werbematerial, auf dem das Unternehmenslogo einer Firma oder Organisation oder das Warenzeichen abgebildet ist. Im Internet gehören dazu Bildschirmschoner, Desktop-Bilder, E-Cards u. a.

**Diptychon** *n* - leaflet

■ Werbeprospekt der einmal, normalerweise in der Mitte, gefaltet ist.

**Direct-Response-Werbung** *f* - direct response advertising

■ Als Direct-Response-Werbung wird innerhalb der Marktkommunikation des Marketing jede Werbemaßnahme bezeichnet, die eine direkte Ansprache des möglichen Kunden mit der Aufforderung zur Antwort enthält. Die nachfolgende Stufe im Marketing ist der Direktverkauf.

**Direktantwort** *f* - direct response

■ Kommunikationstechnik, die dem Empfänger die Möglichkeit zur Antwort auf die Werbung per Telefon, Post oder über andere in der Werbung aufgezeigte Kanäle gibt.

**direkte Produktionskosten** *pl* - direct cost

■ Kosten, die in direktem Zusammenhang mit der Produktion stehen und sich deshalb proportional zur Produktionszahl verhalten.

**Direktmarketing** *n* - direct marketing

■ Als Direktmarketing (auch Direct-Response-Werbung) oder Dialogmarketing wird innerhalb der Marktkommunikation des Marketing jede Werbemaßnahme bezeichnet, die eine direkte Ansprache des möglichen Kunden mit der Aufforderung zur Antwort enthält. Die nachfolgende Stufe im Marketing ist der Direktverkauf.

**Direktmarketingagentur** *f* - direct marketing agency

■ Agentur, die sich mit dem Direktmarketing beschäftigt.

**Direktverkauf** *m* - direct selling

■ Verkauf, bei dem das Unternehmen direkt mit dem Kunden in Kontakt tritt, ohne Verkaufsstellen oder Zwischenhändler einzusetzen. Die potentiellen Kunden werden aufgrund von Empfehlungen anderer Kunden, durch Werbeverkaufssendungen, Briefkampagnen, Bestellcoupons in Fachzeitschriften oder Zeitungen und durch Haustürverkauf angesprochen. Hierbei ist es relativ leicht möglich, den Einfluss jeder Kampagne und jeden Verkäufers zu messen.

**Direktverkauf** *m* **durch Vertreter** - personal selling

■ Verkauf, bei dem der Verkäufer in direkten Kontakt mit dem Kunden tritt. Diese Methode wird in der Regel im industriellen Verkauf eingesetzt, oder wenn das Produkt teuer oder schwer zu verstehen oder benutzen ist.

**Direktweg** *m* - direct channel

■ Vertriebskanal, in dem die Produkte vom Herstellungsort ohne Zwischenlagerung direkt an den Kunden geliefert werden.

**Direktwerbeagentur** *f* - direct advertising agency

■ Firma, die sich mit dem Versand von Werbung per Post beschäftigt und die Anzeigen und andere Werbegegenstände an Empfänger einer dazu erstellten Liste verschickt. In der Regel verfügt eine Direktwerbeagentur über eine Möglichkeit der automatischen Einkuvertierung und Adressierung, sowie über ein Abkommen für reduzierte Postgebühren. Heutzutage werden auch Fax, E-Mail und SMS verwendet.

**Direktwerbung** *f* - mailing

■ Mitteilung, die durch die Post an eine Reihe von Adressen geschickt wird, ohne dass diese zuvor vom Empfänger angefordert wurde. Die Organisation kann diese an ihre eigenen Kunden schicken oder ein darauf spezialisiertes Unternehmen damit beauftragen, dass dieses die Mitteilung aufgrund einer Datei verschickt, die nach bestimmten Gesichtspunkten strukturiert ist (geographisch, nach der Beschäftigung usw.).

**Discounter** *m* - discount store

■ Geschäft, das zu dauerhaft sehr niedrigen Preisen verkauft. Hat ein beschränktes Produktsortiment, häufig mit zweitrangigen Marken. Arbeitet im Selbstbedienungssystem und mit einer billigen Einrichtung.

**Diskont** *m* - discount

■ Vereinbarte Reduzierung des Listenpreises oder Verkaufspreises einer bestimmten Ware gegenüber einem Kunden.

**Diskussionsgruppe** *f* - discussion group

▪ Im Internet, Menge von Benutzern, die an einem Debattenforum mittels der Versendung und des Empfangs elektronischer Botschaften teilnehmen. Die Benutzer, die einer solchen Gruppe beitreten möchten, müssen ihre E-Mail-Adresse einer Distributionsliste beifügen, die von einem Listen-Server verwaltet wird. Manche Diskussionsgruppen werden von einem Moderator koordiniert, der sich um die Filtrierung der Botschaften und um die Verbreitung der Nachrichten kümmert, die er für von allgemeinem Interesse hält.

**Distributionsdichte** *f* - numerical distribution

▪ Prozentualer Anteil der Läden, in denen eine Marke vertreten ist, an der Gesamtheit der bestehenden Läden. Es handelt sich hierbei um eine Kennzahl, die die Verbreitung einer Marke in Abhängigkeit der Läden, in denen die Marke vertreten ist, misst. Dabei wird die Bedeutung der einzelnen Verkaufsstellen nicht berücksichtigt, diese würde durch eine andere Kennzahl, den Qualitätsgrad der Distribution, gemessen.

**diversifiziertes Unternehmen** *n* - diversified company

▪ Unternehmen, das viele Märkte mit verschiedenen Produktpaletten bedient. Dies war vor einigen Jahren in Mode, da man davon ausging, dass die Zyklen der verschiedenen Branchen sich gegenseitig kompensieren. Mit dem Aufkommen von „Aktienhaien", die sich darauf spezialisieren, Unternehmen aufzukaufen und in Einzelteilen zu verkaufen, und der Theorie, dass der Aktionär und nicht das Unternehmen diversifizieren sollte, kehrt man mittlerweile zur Konzentration auf die Basisprodukte und den rentabelsten Kernbereich der Aktivitäten zurück, um so leichter Synergieeffekte zwischen ähnlichen Produkten und Märkten zu erreichen.

**doppelte Preisauszeichnung** *f* - double pricing

▪ Den normalen Preis durchgestrichen und darunter groß den herabgesetzten Preis zeigen, zu dem der Artikel verkauft wird. Ist nur dann gesetzlich zulässig, wenn der höhere Preis tatsächlich der ist, zu dem der gleiche Artikel zuvor verkauft wurde.

**Dotcom** *f* – dot-com

▪ Bezeichnung für im Internet entstandene Firmen, deren Webplattform als Hauptmedium für Kommunikation und Kontakt mit dem Zielpublikum dient.

**Drama** *n* - inherent drama

▪ In der Werbung, kreative Emotionsphilosophie, die von Leo Burnett ins Leben gerufen wurde und besagt, dass eine der besten Wirkungen der Werbenachrichten die Erfindung von Dramen ist (oder Darstellungen), die den Verbraucher interessieren und bewegen, egal ob sie auf der Vergangenheit der Marke oder direkt vom Produkt ausgehend entstehen. Dazu müssen fiktive Menschen geschaffen werden, die die Marke verkörpern, z. B. der Cowboy von Marlboro oder der Hahn von Kellogg's.

**dreizehn Stück** *n/pl* - baker's dozen

▪ Verkaufsförderungsstrategie, bei der dreizehn Artikel zum Preis von zwölf abgegeben werden. Ist gebräuchlich bei Artikeln mit einer niedrigen Spanne, da der Gesamtnachlass 7,7% beträgt. Bei Produkten mit einer größeren Spanne wird in der Regel das System drei zum Preis von zwei angewandt, was einem Nachlass von 33% entspricht, wenngleich dieser manchmal als 50% dargestellt wird.

**Druckwerbung** *f* - print advertisement

▪ Gedruckte Werbenachricht aus Text und festen Bildern (Foto oder Illustration).

**Dumping** *n* - dumping

▪ Überschwemmung des Marktes mit Waren zu einem Preis, der niedriger ist, als der eigentliche Marktpreis oder der unterhalb der Herstellungskosten liegt.

**Dumpingpreis** *m* - depredatory price

▪ Preis eines Produktes, der unterhalb des Einzelproduktpreises liegt, und die Verbraucher anlocken soll.

**Durchdringungspreis** *m* - penetration price

■ Preis, der für ein neues Produkt unterhalb dem der Konkurrenzprodukt angelegt wird, um das Risiko beim Kauf zu senken und die Nachfrage der Verbraucher zu stärken. Wird oftmals bei Produkten verwendet, die keinen hohen Neuigkeitswert haben. Wird nach Erreichen eines ausreichenden Marktanteils der Preis progressiv gesteigert, bis er den vorgesehenen Preis erreicht.

**Durchdringungsrate** *f* - penetration rate

■ Anteil der Personen einer Zielbevölkerung, die Käufer, Kenner o. Ä. in Zusammenhang mit einer Marke oder Werbenachricht sind.

**Durchführbarkeit** *f* - viability

■ Fähigkeit oder Möglichkeit zu Fortschritten in einem Unternehmen oder Projekt, so dass die langfristige Rentabilität gesichert ist.

**Durchführbarkeitsstudie** *f* - feasibility study

■ Studie, mit der man feststellt, ob eine Idee durchführbar ist und ob es sich lohnt, diese Idee zu verwirklichen. Die Studie beinhaltet ebenfalls die Voraussetzungen und Mittel, die zur Verwirklichung der Idee notwendig sind.

**Durchlauf** *m* - rotation

■ Zeitintervall, das bis zum Auslauf eines Produktes vergeht. In der Produktion bestimmt die Rotation, denn sie gibt die Produktion vor: wenn das Element eine lange Ausstellungsdauer hat und die Rotation des Produkts hoch eingeschätzt wird, muss das Material zur Herstellung entsprechend bereitgestellt werden, damit das Element seine Funktion im festgelegten Zeitraum erfüllen kann. Der Verbrauch von mehr Material oder Material höherer Qualität schlägt sich auf den Endpreis nieder.

**durchschnittliche Einschaltquote** *f* - AA (average audience) rating

■ Präzises Verfahren zur Bestimmung des Gesamtpublikums, mit dem jede Minute die Anzahl der Radiohörer oder Fernsehzuschauer berechnet und anschließend der Mittelwert ermittelt wird. Die Ergebnisse werden für die Verhandlung zwischen Medieneinkäufer und Medienbetreiber und zur Ermittlung der beliebtesten Programme verwendet.

**durchschnittliche Konsumquote** *f* - average propensity to consume

■ Quotient aus Konsum und verfügbarem Einkommen.

**Durchschnittskontakt** *m* - opportunity to see (OTS)

■ Die Kontaktwahrscheinlichkeit mit einem Werbeträger. Bei Druckmedien, wenn eine Person das Exemplar mit der Anzeige gelesen oder durchblättert hat; im Fernsehen und Radio, wenn die Person den Kanal oder die Frequenz zu dem Zeitpunkt benutzt, zu dem die Werbung ausgestrahlt wird; im Kino wenn eine Person in dem Saal war, in dem die Anzeige ausgestrahlt wird und im Freien, wenn die Person an der Stelle vorbeigeht, an der die Anzeige platziert ist. Wird auch als Synonym für Frequenz benutzt, um die Zahl der Kontakte pro Person mit den Anzeigen der Kampagne anzugeben.

**Durchschnittskosten** *pl* - average cost

■ Die Durchschnittskosten werden berechnet, indem die Gesamtkosten, die ein bestimmtes Produkt oder eine bestimmte Produktgruppe verursacht, durch die produzierte Stückzahl dividiert werden.

**Durchschnittskostenpreis** *m* - average cost price

■ Gesamtkosten geteilt durch die Anzahl der hergestellten Einheiten. Die Summe der durchschnittlichen Fixkosten, die mit Erhöhung der Produktion abnehmen und der durchschnittlichen variablen Kosten, die konstant sein können, aber ab einer bestimmten Grenze in der Regel zunehmen. Die Durchschnittskosten sinken bei Erhöhung der Produktion, erreichen ein Minimum und steigen anschließend.

**Duty-Free-Geschäft** *n* - duty-free shop

■ Geschäft, das sich im internationalen Transitbereich eines Flughafens oder

Hafens befindet und Waren mit größeren Handelsspannen, aber ohne die Steuern, die in jedem Land auf bestimmte Produkte wie Tabak und Alkohol erhoben werden, verkauft. Im weiteren Sinne bezeichnet man damit auch den Verkauf im Flugzeug oder Schiff selbst.

**dynamischer Preis** *m* - dynamic price

■ Preis, der je nach Angebot und Nachfrage schwankt. Gegensatz zum Festpreis. Wurde dank Internet immer mehr entwickelt, wobei der Verbraucher über Auktionshäuser oder durch Bieten einen wichtigen Einfluss auf die Festlegung des Endpreises ausübt.

# E

**EACA** - European Association of Communications Agencies (EACA)

■ Non-profit Organisation mit Sitz in Brüssel, die sich als Lobbying- und Serviceorganisation der europäischen Kommunikationsagenturen versteht. Sie arbeitet eng mit allen bedeutenden nationalen und internationalen Organisationen der Werbe- und Kommunikationsbranche zusammen.

**Early Bird** *m* - early bird

■ Der Early Bird ist ein Anreiz für den Empfänger einer Direktwerbesendung, seine Antwort möglichst schnell zurückzuschicken. Early Birds können zum Beispiel Geschenke sein, die nur in begrenzter Anzahl vorhanden sind und an alle Reagierenden in der Reihenfolge der Antworteingänge verteilt werden. Oder Angebote zu einem besonders günstigen Preis, der aber nur bis zu einem bestimmten Datum gilt. Oder eine befristete Zusatzverlosung von Geld- oder Sachpreisen an alle, die bis zu einem festgelegten Termin antworten. Durch viele Tests wurde bewiesen, dass der Einsatz eines Early Bird die Reaktionsfristen verkürzt und die Zahl der Reaktionen erhöht.

**EASA** - European Advertising Standards Alliance (EASA)

■ Die EASA (Europäische Allianz der Werbeselbstkontrolle) ist das gemeinsame Sprachrohr der Werbewirtschaft in Europa für alle Fragen der Werbeselbstkontrolle, deren Förderung und Durchsetzung. Ursprünglich als Zusammenschluss der nationalen selbstdisziplinären Einrichtungen gegründet, konnte die EASA durch den Beitritt auch anderer Organisationen aller Stufen der Werbebranche die Strukturen ihrer Verantwortung erweitern und vertiefen.

**E-Auktion** *f* - e-auction

■ Auktion einer Webseite. Kann in den Beziehungen der Firma mit dem Verbraucher (B2C), Firma zu Firma (B2B) oder Verbraucher zu Verbraucher (C2C) integriert sein.

**E-Billing** *n* - e-billing

■ Aufstellung und Sendung von Rechnungen über elektronische Medien.

**E-Business** *n* - e-business

■ Obwohl per wörtlicher Definition auf die Durchführung von Geschäften über elektronische Medien gerichtet, wird E-Business allgemein zur Bezeichnung von Geschäften über das Internet benutzt.

**E-Commerce** *m* - e-commerce

■ Elektronischer Handel. Fernhandel über digitale Telekommunikationswege. Das bekannteste Medium ist Internet, allerdings gibt es auch Möglichkeiten über Telefone (WAP) oder das Fernsehen (interaktives Fernsehen), eCommerce zu treiben.

**effektive Reichweite** *f* - effective reach

■ Anzahl der Personen einer Zielgruppe, die von einer Werbekampagne aufgrund der ausreichenden Zahl der Kontakte positiv auf eine Werbung reagieren, wobei die Zahl der Kontakte nicht so hoch sein darf, dass die Empfänger negativ reagieren. Der Wirksamkeitsbereich wird von zwei Grenzwerten festgelegt, die vorher zu bestimmen sind. Im Allgemeinen werden mindestens drei Kontakte mit einer Person als ausreichend angesehen.

**Effizienzschwelle** *f* - access budget
▪ In der Werbung, Mittel, die zur effizienten Werbung in einem Medium benötigt werden. Die Höhe der Mittel hängt von den Preisstufen und der Sättigung des Mediums ab.

**Eigenwerbung** *f* - self-promotion
▪ Werbung, die einige Medien (vor allem Fernsehen) für sich selbst machen, wobei sie ihre eigenen Werbeflächen benutzen, um für eine Sendung oder eine Sonderausgabe zu werben. Wird eingerechnet in die Zeit, die dieses Medium der Werbung widmen kann.

**Eindruck** *m* - impression
▪ Zeichen oder Merkmal, das eine Sache auf einer anderen Sache hinterlässt. In der Psychologie versteht man unter dem „ersten Eindruck" eine spontane Beurteilung einer Person oder eine unüberlegt gefasste Meinung über eine Person oder eine Sache, ohne über den eventuellen eigenen Irrtum länger nachzudenken.

**Einführung** *f* - launch
▪ Im Marketing, Zeitpunkt, an dem ein neues Produkt den direkten Kunden und den Endverbrauchern vorgestellt wird. Grundlage ist in der Regel eine Werbekampagne, nachdem der Vertriebsweg feststeht. Wichtig ist das interne Marketing im Unternehmen, um Anfangsprobleme zu überwinden und die volle Unterstützung des gesamten Personals zu erreichen.

**Einführungsangebot** *n* - introductory offer
▪ Preis zur Einführung eines Produktes, das vorher bereits woanders eingeführt wurde, auf einem neuen Markt. Liegt in der Regel etwas niedriger, um die Erstkäufe anzuregen, es kann jedoch auch eine Abschöpfungsstrategie verfolgt werden.

**Einführungspreis** *m* - introductory price
▪ Preis zur Einführung eines Produktes, das vorher bereits woanders eingeführt wurde, auf einem neuen Markt. Liegt in der Regel etwas niedriger, um die Erstkäufe anzuregen, es kann jedoch auch eine Abschöpfungsstrategie verfolgt werden.

**Einführungsstandort** *m* - introduction town
▪ Stadt, in der die Eröffnung einer Geschäftseinheit der Kette durchgeführt wird.

**Eingangs- und Ausgangs-Tabelle** *f* - inputs and outputs table
▪ Matrix, die für jeden Industriesektor den Anteil seiner Verkäufe angibt, der an andere Sektoren geht (wie Rohstoffe oder Halbfertigerzeugnisse), und die Produkte, die an den Endverbraucher gehen. Ebenso erscheinen in ihr die Käufe von anderen Sektoren und die erzeugte Wertschöpfung. Wird eingesetzt, um die wechselseitigen Beziehungen zwischen den Sektoren zu untersuchen und um die Auswirkungen einer Veränderung der Nachfrage in einem Sektor oder Tätigkeitsfeld zu sehen. Wurde von W. Leontief entwickelt. Auch Input-Output-Tabelle genannt.

**Einheit** *f* - unit
▪ Unterste Ebene in einer Unternehmensorganisation, an deren Spitze ein Gruppenleiter steht. Normalerweise bestehen mehrere untereinander vergleichbare Gruppen, wie es bei Supermärkten, Bankgeschäftsstellen usw. der Fall ist.

**Einkäufer** *m* **von Vergleichsprodukten** - comparison shopper
▪ Person, die von einer Verkaufsstelle eingestellt ist, um regelmäßig Preise, Angebote, Sortiment, Werbeaktivitäten und das Qualitäts- und Serviceniveau der Wettbewerber zu untersuchen.

**Einkaufszentrum** *n* - shopping centre
▪ Menge von Einzelhandelsgeschäften, die an einer Stelle konzentriert sind, wo die Verbraucher deshalb jede Art von Gütern kaufen können. Haben gewöhnlich ein oder zwei bekannte Geschäfte, die als Magnet dienen und den Zufluss der Kundschaft sichern sollen, z. B. einen großer Supermarkt oder ein bekanntes Bekleidungsgeschäft.

**Einkommen** *n* **auf Honorarbasis** - fee-basis income

■ In der Werbung, Vergütung der Agentur über einen zuvor festgesetzten Betrag, den der Auftraggeber einmalig oder in regelmäßigen Abständen bezahlt. Es handelt sich hierbei um eine Formel, die die traditionelle Agenturenprovision ersetzen soll, und die in den 70er-Jahren von Saatchi & Saatchi als Unterscheidungssymbol zu den sogenannten Agenturen oder Kreativboutiquen eingeführt wurde.

**Einkommenseffekt** *m* - income effect

■ Veränderung der Nachfrage nach einem bestimmten Gut aufgrund von Veränderungen des verfügbaren Einkommens. Man spricht von inferioren Wirtschaftsgütern, wenn die Erhöhung des Einkommens zu einem Rückgang der Nachfrage nach diesem Gut führt (z. B. bei einigen billigen Grundnahrungsmitteln). Der gegenteilige Fall ist bei einem normalen Gut gegeben.

**Einlösung** *f* - redemption

■ Abgabe von Rabattgutscheinen oder Coupons, um ein Produkt zu kaufen oder ein Geschenk zu erhalten. Die Coupons erhält der Verbraucher mit anderen Produkten oder durch Wurfsendungen, in den USA allerdings häufiger durch die Zeitung. Der Hersteller erstattet dem Einzelhändler den Rabatt plus eine Prämie für seine Mitarbeit, da der Vertriebskanal dieses System im Allgemeinen ablehnt. Es gibt spezialisierte Unternehmen, die den gesamten Einlöseprozess kontrollieren. Der Prozentsatz der Einlösung erlaubt die Messung der Wirksamkeit dieser Verkaufsförderungsmaßnahme.

**Einschätzung** *f* - scoring

■ Bewertung eines potentiellen Kunden aufgrund bestimmter Variablen zur Risikoeinschätzung, z. B. zur Bestimmung, ob er in einem Verkaufsplan kontaktiert wird oder um zu entscheiden, ob er ein bestimmtes Kreditniveau bekommt.

**Einschub** *m* - roll-in

■ Fernsehwerbung, bei der die Werbemitteilung im Programm integriert ist und der Zuschauer keinen Schnitt für das Vorhandensein der Werbung feststellen kann.

**Einstellung** *f* - attitude

■ Im Marketing, dauerhafte Haltung oder Gemütsverfassung einer Person gegenüber einem Produkt oder einer Botschaft. Sie wird von der rationalen Bewertung seitens der Person, ihren Gefühlen und ihrem Willen, entsprechend tätig zu werden, bestimmt. Wenn jemand zum Beispiel denkt, dass deutsche Autos hochwertige Technologie zu einem angemessenen Preis bieten, wird er zum Kauf von deutschen Autos neigen.

**Einstellung** *f* **gegenüber dem Produkt** - attitude toward the product

■ Eine positive oder negative Prädisposition des Verbrauchers im Hinblick auf ein bestimmtes Produkt oder eine Dienstleistung. Faktoren sind die Bekanntheit, das Image und vorhergehende Erfahrungen mit dem Produkt. Das Hauptziel von Werbung ist das Erzielen einer positiven Einstellung des Verbrauchers gegenüber dem beworbenen Produkt oder der beworbenen Dienstleistung.

**Einstellungen** *f/pl* - attitudes

■ Im Marketing, Veranlagung, auf eine bestimmte Art zu reagieren. Eines der Ziele der qualitativen Forschung besteht in der Erfassung der Einstellungen einer Zielgruppe, da diese die Offenheit gegenüber einer Botschaft oder für den Gebrauch von Produkten bestimmen.

**Einstellungsänderung** *f* - attitude change

■ Veränderung der Haltung des Verbrauchers gegenüber einer Marke oder einem Produkt. Sie ist ein typisches Ziel einer Werbe- oder PR-Kampagne.

**Einstellungsskala** *f* - attitude scale

■ Liste mit Meinungsäußerungen, die eine positive oder negative Bewertung des psychologischen Referenzobjekts implizieren. Die untersuchte Person soll die Intensität ihrer Zustimmung oder Ablehnung zum Ausdruck bringen. Wird in strukturierten Untersuchungen mit geschlossener Antwort und im Allgemeinen mit fünf oder sieben Antwortmöglichkeiten benutzt.

**Einstellungsstudie** *f* - attitude study

▪ Untersuchung, bei der die Einstellung der Verbraucher zu einem Produkt, einer Idee, einem Unternehmen oder einer Kampagne gemessen wird. Zunächst wird die Ausgangssituation untersucht, danach erfolgt eine Bewertung und schließlich eine Abschlussuntersuchung, um zu überprüfen, ob die geplanten Ziele erreicht worden sind.

**Eins-zu-eins-Kommunikation** *f* - one-to-one communication

▪ Individuelle Zuschneiden einer oder mehrerer Marketing-Maßnahmen auf jeden Kunden mit Hilfe statistischer Verfahren. Das Ziel lässt sich mit „Individualisieren statt Personalisieren" auf den Punkt bringen. Statt einzelner Kundenmerkmale (wie Einkommen oder Alter etc.) werden Kundenprofile generiert. Auch 1:1 Marketing.

**Einzelhandelsgruppe** *f* - retail buying group

▪ Gruppierung, die von einer im Allgemeinen hohen Anzahl an Einzelhändlern gebildet wird, um die Käufe an die Lieferanten gemeinsam durchzuführen und so eine höhere Verhandlungsstärke zu erlangen.

**Einzelhandelspanel** *n* - retailer panel

▪ Menge von Letztverkaufsstellen, die regelmäßig von einer Spezialfirma erfasst wird, um Daten über Einkaufs- und Verkaufsverhalten, Lagerbestände und Preise der verschiedenen Produkte und Marken zu erhalten. Das Panel wird aktualisiert, um die Repräsentativität über die Gesamtheit des Einzelhandels zu gewährleisten und um schließende Geschäfte durch andere zu ersetzen. Es ergänzt das Verbraucherpanel, indem es Daten über das Einkaufsverhalten und die Lagerhaltung im Vertriebskanal liefert.

**Einzelhandelspreis** *m* - retail price

▪ Verkaufspreis an den Verbraucher. Üblicherweise der Endpreis, da es kaum Preisnachlässe gibt.

**Einzelhandelsverkauf** *m* - retail sales

▪ Verkauf an den Endverbraucher in kleinen Mengen. Wird von Einzelhändlern durchgeführt, die vom Großhändler in größeren Einheiten kaufen.

**Einzelhändler** *m* - retailer

▪ Händler, der die Waren direkt und in kleinen Mengen an den Endverbraucher verkauft. Der Einzelhändler kauft normalerweise bei einem oder zwei Großhändlern ein, obwohl einige große Fabrikanten ihn direkt oder durch Transporteure beliefern.

**Einzelhändlerpräsentation** *f* - sell-in

▪ Tätigkeit, bei der ein Produktvertreter einem Einzelhändler ein neues Produkt vorstellt und ihm, meist unter Vorführung eines Verkaufsprospekts, eine Vergünstigung anbietet, damit dieser den Verkauf an die Endkäufer fördert.

**einzigartiges Verkaufsargument** *n* **(EVA)** - unique selling proposition (USP)

▪ Werbeargument, auf dem eine Werbekampagne basiert. Der Begriff „einzigartig" bedeutet nur eines, exklusiv, ausgezeichnet. Exklusive, vorteilhafte Eigenschaft eines bestimmten Produktes, die kein anderes Konkurrenzprodukt aufweist.

**Einzugsgebiet** *n* - attraction area

▪ Gebiet, in dem das Zielpublikum eines Geschäftes lebt. Abhängig von der Art des Geschäftes, des Produkts, den durchschnittlichen Ausgaben, den Kaufgewohnheiten und der Fortbewegung (zu Fuß, im Auto usw.), der Konkurrenzsituation und der Werbung des Geschäfts. Innerhalb des Einzugsgebietes werden Zonen größerer Kundenbindung unterschieden, die in der Regel durch die Nähe zum Geschäft bestimmt werden. In ländlichen Gebieten müssen Markttage, Feiertage und das Vorhandensein von öffentlichen Einrichtungen (Krankenhäuser, Bildungseinrichtungen usw.) berücksichtigt werden.

**E-Kaufhaus** *n* - e-mall

■ Elektronischer Zusammenschluss mehrerer Geschäfte im gleichen virtuellen Raum.

**E-Knowledge** *n* - eknowledge

■ Effizientes Knowledge-Management, ermöglicht den Mitarbeitern schnell und unkompliziert an eine Vielzahl hochaktueller Informationen und Know-how zu gelangen. Knowledge-Management umfasst zahlreiche Wissensquellen wie z. B. Datenbanken, Websites oder individuelles Wissen und gelangt erst durch die regelmäßige Pflege und die Erfassung der Zusammenhänge zu seiner wahren Bedeutung. Die Vernetzung von vorhandenen und neuen Informationen, Erfahrungen, Ideen und Werten ist es, die das Wissen eines Unternehmens immer wieder aktualisiert und erweitert.

**elektronische Beschaffung** *f* - e-procurement

■ Unter elektronischer Beschaffung (auch eProcurement genannt) versteht man die Beschaffung von Gütern und Dienstleistungen über das Internet. Sie wird vor allem im Bereich des betrieblichen, also des professionellen Einkaufs genutzt.

**elektronische Geldbörse** *f* - electronic wallet

■ Intelligente Bankkarte, die mit einem Mikroprozessor versehen ist, und als Barzahlungsmittel in Geschäften verwendet wird. Im Unterschied zu Kreditkarten belastet sie den Betrag dem Girokonto nicht bei jeder Zahlung, sondern der Benutzer hat zuvor den als verfügbar angezeigten Betrag auf die Karte geladen und braucht ihn nun bei jeder Operation stückweise auf. Diese Karten können an den Geldautomaten der Banken und Sparkassen aufgeladen werden.

**elektronische Zeitschriften** *f/pl* - digisine

■ Archiv oder Dokument, das über elektronische Medien veröffentlicht und verbreitet wird. Kann nur Text oder auch Grafiken und Bilder oder audiovisuelle Inhalte enthalten. In den letzten Jahren haben die im Internet verbreiteten elektronischen Zeitschriften an Popularität gewonnen, sowohl in den öffentlichen Diskussionsforen als auch auf Webseiten.

**elektronisches Geld** *n* - e-money

■ Anwendung der Kommunikationssysteme zur Durchführung verschiedener wirtschaftlicher Transaktionen in Echtzeit, wie z. B. Fondsüberweisungen online, Kreditkartenzahlungen, Ferneinkäufe, Verkauf von Wertpapieren, usw.

**elektronisches Schaufenster** *n* - electronic storefront

■ Ort, an dem das Unternehmen ein Geschäft in einem virtuellen Einkaufszentrum oder in einer anderen Form zur Förderung des eCommerce einer Firmengruppe zur Schau stellt.

**E-Mail-Abonnement** *n* - opt-in email

■ E-Mail, die man auf eigenen Wunsch von einer Firma oder Organisation über ihre Aktivitäten, Produkte usw. erhält.

**E-Mail-Marketing** *n* - email marketing

■ Genehmigte Marketingaktionen, die E-Mails als Träger benutzen und sich die Interaktivität, Unmittelbarkeit und niedrigen Kosten davon zunutze machen.

**E-Mail-Werbung** *f* - email advertising

■ Verwendung von E-Mails zum Versand von Werbenachrichten.

**Emoticon** *n* - emoticon

■ Gruppierung von ASCII-Zeichen, deren Bestimmung es ist, einen Gefühlszustand mitzuteilen. Werden häufig in E-Mails verwendet. Einige Beispiele sind: :-) Lächeln, ,-) Zwinkern und :-( Traurigkeit.

**emotionale Ansprache** *f* - emotional appeal

■ Grundlage einer Werbebotschaft, die nicht an logische Argumente oder den rationalen Nutzen appelliert, sondern darauf basiert, Gefühle wie Liebe, Hass, Stolz, Furcht, sexuelles Verlangen oder Humor zu erzeugen, um ein bestimmtes Verhalten zu erreichen.

**emotionale Wirkung** *f* - emotional impact

■ Kreative Philosophie von William Bernbach, dem Vater der kreativen

Revolution, die besagt, dass die Werbenachrichten die Verbraucher auf die gleiche emotionale Weise ansprechen müssen, wie Kunstwerke. Dazu beruft man sich auf die emotionalen Ansprüche (Angst, Humor, Fantasie), ein gut durchdachtes Grafikdesign und eine ausgezeichnete kreative Leitung, da in diesem Fall die Bilder sehr viel wichtiger als die Worte sind, da sie einen höhere Wirkung auf Emotionsebene haben.

**Empfänger** *m* - receiver

▪ Person oder Gruppe von Personen, die eine Botschaft durch einen Kommunikationskanal erhält. Die Nachricht kann verzerrt ankommen, aufgrund von Verständnisproblemen mit der verwendeten Sprache, der vorhandenen Kenntnisse und Überzeugungen des Empfängers oder seines psychischen Zustandes.

**Empfangskontext** *m* - reception environment

▪ In der Werbung, spezifische Umgebung für Empfang und Auslegung der Werbung durch den Empfänger. Obwohl für das Verständnis und die Wirkung der Werbemitteilung entscheidend ist, ist dieser Kontext vom Sender weniger steuerbar.

**Endprodukt** *n* - final product

▪ Erzeugnis, das alle Herstellungsphasen und Qualitätskontrollen durchlaufen hat und zum Versand an den Kunden bereit ist.

**Endverbraucher** *m* - end consumer

▪ Person, die das Produkt tatsächlich nutzt oder verbraucht. Der Endverbraucher kann vom Käufer verschieden sein und mehr oder weniger dessen Entscheidung beeinflussen. Beispiele hierfür sind die Sekretärin, die ein Textverarbeitungssystem verwendet, das von der Firma gekauft wurde, oder das Kind, das darauf besteht, dass seine Mutter die Marke kauft, bei der es Sammelbilder gibt, usw.

**Engpass** *m* - bottleneck

▪ Produktionsprozess oder einem Handlungsvorgang, die den gesamten Vorgang beschränkt, weil in diesem Bereich geringere Kapazitäten zur Verfügung stehen.

**Entwicklung** *f* **neuer Produkte** - new product development

▪ Alle Aktivitäten, die es ermöglichen, die Produktpalette eines Unternehmens zu erneuern, ausgehend von technologischen Innovationen, Anregungen der Kunden oder dem Auftauchen neuer Bedürfnisse. Dies erfordert eine enge Zusammenarbeit der Abteilungen für Forschung und Entwicklung, Produktion und Marketing von Anfang an und über alle Phasen: Ideenauswahl, technische und kommerzielle Bewertung, Entwicklung des Produkts und des Fertigungsprozesses, Marktproben und Markteinführung.

**Erfahrungsmarketing** *n* - experience marketing

▪ Empfehlungsmarketing. Bedeutet praktisch nichts anderes als die wiederholte Weitergabe von Erfahrungen. Es wird berichtet, was der Verbraucher und andere bei der Verwendung des Produktes erlebt haben. Erfahrungsberichte Dritter sind immer die beste Werbung für das Produkt.

**Erfahrungsumfrage** *f* - experience survey

▪ Studie, in der die Befragten die Materie, um die es sich bei der Befragung handelt, im Allgemeinen aus beruflichen Gründen kennen. Diese Art von Studie erfordert weit weniger Proben als bei Umfragen mit Einzelpersonen. Eine Sonderform ist die Delphi-Methode.

**erfolgreiche Idealisten** *m/pl* - successful idealists

▪ Verbrauchertyp in einer paneuropäischen Typenbezeichnung von Lebensstilen. Sie vertreten 5-15% der Bevölkerung, sind reich und mögen Kunst, gesundes Essen und Ökologie.

**Ergänzung** *f* **der Produktlinie** - line-filling

▪ Tätigkeit, die darauf gerichtet ist, die Produktlinie eines Unternehmens innerhalb des gleichen Produktbereiches zu erweitern, indem unterschiedliche

Packgrößen oder gleiche Basisprodukte mit unterschiedlichen Merkmalen aufgenommen werden. Z. B. ein Unternehmen, das Kekse in 5 kg Schachteln verkauft und neue Schachteln mit 1 kg und 2 kg auf den Markt bringt.

**Erinnerungstest** *m* - memory test

■ Bei diesem Test wird ein bestimmtes Firmensymbol zusammen mit anderen Firmensymbolen einer Personengruppe mehrere Male gezeigt. Nach dem Test sollen die Personen die Symbole beschreiben, an die sie sich erinnern.

**Erkennungsmelodie** *f* - jingle

■ Kurzes und leichtes musikalisches Element, das mehrmals während einer Werbebotschaft auftaucht, eventuell mit dem Slogan zusammen, und das die Erinnerung an die Botschaft und ihre Wiedererkennung erleichtert, sowie zur Aussage beiträgt. Auch Werbejingle genannt.

**Erlaubnismarketing** *n* - permission marketing

■ Marketing basierend auf der vorherigen Genehmigung durch den Kunden zum Erhalt von Informationen bezüglich des Geschäftsangebots. Die Marketing-Aktionen richten sich nur an die Verbraucher, die zuvor ihre Zustimmung gegeben haben, was beim Versand von E-Mails oder Handynachrichten wichtig ist (wegen des Spam-Filters).

**Eröffnungswerbung** *f* - opening

■ Summe aller Aktivitäten, die bezüglich Verkaufsförderung und Werbung anlässlich der Eröffnung einer Einrichtung unternommen werden. Um eine erfolgreiche Geschäftseröffnung sicherzustellen, ist eine genaue Planung der unterschiedlichen Aktivitäten von grundlegender Bedeutung. Normalerweise bittet man die Lieferanten darum, sich in irgendeiner Form an den Anstrengungen zu beteiligen.

**Ersatzanzeige** *f* - makegood

■ Kostenlose Einfügung einer Anzeige, für eine ausgefallene oder fehlerhafte Anzeige. Bei den audiovisuellen Medien muss diese Ersatzanzeige dann gesendet werden, wenn die Zuschauer gleich viele oder gleich zusammengesetzt sind, wie das Publikum der nicht gesendeten Anzeige. Viele Stationen wählen die Wiederholung der Anzeige, wenn Probleme bei der Sendung aufgetreten sind.

**Erscheinungstag** *m* - air date

■ Tag, an dem eine Zeitschrift auf den Markt kommt oder an dem eine Werbekampagne beginnt.

**Erstellung** *f* **von Werbetexten** - copywriting

■ Schaffung von Texten und Konzepten für Anzeigen und Werbespots.

**erster Großhändler** *m* - primary wholesaler

■ Großhändler, dessen Hauptfunktion die Sammlung von Produkten verschiedener Quellen und deren Kanalisierung zu den jeweiligen Zielorten ist.

**Erstkäufer** *m* - first time buyer

■ Klassifizierung eines Kunden als Neuzugang. Im Beziehungsmarketing ist diese Klassifizierung von äußerster Wichtigkeit, um mit den Aktivitäten zur Gewinnung von Kundentreue zu beginnen.

**erwartungstreu** - unbiased

■ In der statistischen Forschung der statistische Wert, der dem zu messenden Parameter der Grundgesamtheit entspricht. Liegt vor, wenn der Mittelwert aller ausgeführten Messungen dem Wert der Grundgesamtheit entspricht.

**erweitertes Produkt** *n* - augmented product

■ Summe aller Vorteile oder Nutzen, die der Verbraucher durch den Kauf eines physischen Produktes erhält. Dies kann zum Beispiel bei einem Auto die Garantie auf Teile während eines bestimmten Zeitraums nach dem Kauf einschließen.

**Erweiterung** *f* **der Produktlinie** - line-stretching

■ Tätigkeit, die darauf gerichtet ist, die Produktlinie eines Unternehmens auf obere oder untere Marktbereiche zu erweitern, z. B. wenn ein Anbieter von Kleinrechnern Personalcomputer mit in sein Programm aufnimmt.

**Erwerbsbevölkerung** *f* - active population

▪ Gesamtheit der Bürger eines Staates, die in bezahlter Arbeit stehen oder zur Annahme einer entlohnten Tätigkeit zur Verfügung stehen, auch wenn sie zur Zeit arbeitslos sind.

**ESOMAR** - European Society for Opinion and Marketing Research (ESOMAR)

▪ Abkürzung für European Society for Opinion and Marketing Research. Die ESOMAR ist die Weltvereinigung der professionellen Markt- und Meinungsforscher. Ursprünglich als europäischer Verband gegründet, zählen heute mehr als 4.000 Mitglieder in weltweit 100 Ländern - sowohl Anbieter als auch Nachfrager von Marktforschung - dazu. Die Mission der ESOMAR ist eine weltweite Förderung der Markt- und Meinungsforschung, um die Entscheidungsfindung in Unternehmen und der Gesellschaft zu verbessern.

**Ethik *f* in der Werbung** - ethical advertising

▪ Werbeaktivität, welche die Moral und die vorherrschende Ethik in einem bestimmten Kontext einhält, z. B. nicht chauvinistisch ist und die ethischen Prinzipien der Werbung selbst einhält (Alkohol nicht mit gesellschaftlichem/ sexuellem Erfolg gleichstellt oder die Geschwindigkeit von Autos propagiert).

**Etikett** *n* - label

▪ Ein Stück Papier oder Stoff, das an einem Produkt angebracht ist, um dessen Unterscheidung von anderen Produkten zu ermöglichen. Es enthält in der Regel die Marke, den Namen und den Herstellungsort, Kontrollvermerk durch das Gesundheitsamt und durch die Industrie, Bestandteile und Zusatzstoffe, Verfallsdatum oder Haltbarkeitsdatum, das Datum der Abfüllung und die Chargennummer, Gebrauchsempfehlungen oder -anweisungen, Gewicht oder Volumen, Größe, Farbe, usw. Um die Identifizierung des Produkts zu vereinfachen und um einen höheren Wiedererkennungsgrad der Marke zu erreichen, werden originelle und der Unterscheidung dienende Designs und Bilder entwickelt.

**European Association of Communications Agencies (EACA)** - European Association of Communications Agencies (EACA)

▪ Non-profit Organisation mit Sitz in Brüssel, die sich als Lobbying- und Serviceorganisation der europäischen Kommunikationsagenturen versteht. Sie arbeitet eng mit allen bedeutenden nationalen und internationalen Organisationen der Werbe- und Kommunikationsbranche zusammen.

**Evaluationsforschung** *f* - evaluation research

▪ Planung, Durchführung und Nutzen der PR-Maßnahmen werden systematisch mit sozialwissenschaftlichen Methoden bewertet. Bestimmt den Wirksamkeitsgrad von Public Relations und das gegenseitige Verständnis zwischen Unternehmen und Publikum.

**Eventmarketing** *n* - event marketing

▪ Eventmarketing (auch Event-Marketing, Live-Kommunikation, Live-Marketing) bezeichnet die zielgerichtete und systematische Planung von Veranstaltungen (Messen, Außendienstkonferenzen, Verkaufspräsentationen, Sport- und Kulturveranstaltungen) als absatzpolitisches Instrument oder image- und meinungsbildungsfördernde Maßnahmen zur Durchsetzung der Unternehmensziele im Rahmen der Marketing-Kommunikation.

**Exaktheit** *f* - accuracy

▪ Zuverlässigkeit und Pünktlichkeit bei der Erfüllung einer Aufgabe, beim Ausgleich von Finanzpositionen, bei der Berechnung eines Wertes, usw.

**Exklusivvertrieb** *m* - exclusive distribution

▪ Geschäftspolitik, durch die man bestimmten Handelsunternehmen den exklusiven Vertrieb eines Produktes in einem bestimmten geographischen

Gebiet garantiert. Diese Politik stärkt das Image und erlaubt es, den Händler zu kontrollieren und zu dirigieren.

**Expeditionsmarketing** *n* - expeditionary marketing

■ Marketing, dessen Hauptziel die Entdeckung neuer Märkte und Geschäftsmöglichkeiten ist. Basiert auf der gründlichen Analyse der Verbraucherbedürfnisse, der technischen Entwicklung und der Aktivitäten der Konkurrenz.

**explorative Forschung** *f* - exploratory research

■ Untersuchungsdesign der Marktforschung, das bei geringem Kenntnisstand zur Gewinnung zusätzlicher Erkenntnisse herangezogen wird. Es dient der Konkretisierung von Marketing-Entscheidungsproblemen, der Präzisierung der durch weitere Marktforschung zu beschaffenden Informationen.

**Exposition** *f* - exposure

■ Im Marketing, Wahrnehmung einer Werbung durch einen Empfänger. Einige Psychologen glauben, dass die Exposition an sich schon eine Werbewirkung hat.

**externe Zeitschrift** *f* - external publication

■ Regelmäßige Veröffentlichung des Unternehmens an unternehmensexternes Publikum. Ziele sind die Überzeugung von der Wichtigkeit der Organisation und die Änderung oder Erweiterung des Publikums zur Akzeptanz und Stützung des Unternehmens. Meist wird die externe Zeitschrift in der Abteilung für externe Kommunikation in Zusammenarbeit mit den Medien ausgearbeitet. Obwohl sie Informationen über die Firma enthält, nimmt sie doch hauptsächlich Themen des öffentlichen Interesses auf.

**externes Wachstum** *n* - external growth

■ In der strategischen Analyse, Wachstum einer Firma durch Erweiterung einer Organisation, basierend auf der Akquisition, Fusion oder Übernahme von anderen bereits bestehenden Firmen.

# F

**Fabrikverkauf** *m* - outlet store, manufacturer store

■ Verkaufsstellen, die meist außerhalb des Stadtzentrums liegen und Artikel bekannter Marken oder Restposten zu sehr viel günstigeren Preisen verkaufen. Wenn es sich um die Hersteller selbst handelt, verkaufen diese die Restposten direkt an den Käufer in einem sogenannten Outlet-Store.

**Face-to-Face-Marketing** *n* - face-to-face action

■ Marketingaktivität mit direktem und persönlichem Kontakt zum Verbraucher, z. B. Verkostung an einem Verkaufspunkt.

**Fachgeschäft** *n* - speciality store

■ Geschäft, das sich auf eine Sparte von Artikeln konzentriert. Besitzt ein recht tiefes Produktsortiment mit einer großen Vielfalt an Marken und Zubehörartikeln. Das Personal kann beraten und besondere Dienstleistungen anbieten.

**Fachhandel** *m* - speciality trade

■ Geschäft, in der Regel im Einzelhandel, mit einem ausgewählten und spezialisierten Angebot an Produkten. Es zeichnet sich durch eine größere Sortimentstiefe, bessere Beratung und Information und eine erhöhte Anpassungsfähigkeit an die individuellen Kundenwünsche aus.

**Fachkenntnis** *f* - know-how

■ Gesamtheit der spezialisierten Kenntnisse und praktischen Techniken, die es erlauben, einen Prozess effektiv und in gegenüber dem Marktdurchschnitt differenzierter Form durchzuführen. Da die Fachkenntnisse einen zusätzlichen Mehrwert mit sich bringen, können sie vermarktbar und Gegenstand eines Know-how-Transfervertrages sein, der globaler und praxisbezogener als ein Vertrag über Technologietransfer oder technische Unterstützung ist. Neben der Bezeichnung Fachkenntnisse wird häufig auch der englische Begriff Know-how verwendet.

**Fachzeitschrift** *f* - trade magazine

■ Zeitschrift, deren Zielpublikum einem Sektor angehört oder speziellen Interessengebiet, im Gegensatz zu den allgemeinen Zeitschriften. Optimaler Kanal, um dieses Publikum mit technischen Botschaften zu erreichen und den Verkauf von Unternehmen an Unternehmen oder Industrieverkauf durchzuführen.

**Fahne** *f* - emblem

■ Firmenflagge oder Flagge, die eine Marke symbolisiert, und die man in den Verkaufspunkten und den Fabriken anbringt, um die Identifikation zu fördern. Sie hat ihren Ursprung im Logo des Unternehmens oder der Marke.

**faktorielles Design** *n* - factorial design

■ In der Forschung, Analyse der Wirkung verschiedener Faktoren auf ein Endergebnis; jeder einzelne Wert einer Variable wird in Kombination mit den einzelnen Werten der anderen Variablen analysiert.

**Fakturierung** *f* - billing

■ In der Werbung, Kosten der Werbefläche in den vom Werbetreibenden in seinen Kampagnen benutzten Medien. Gesamtheit von Ausgaben oder Geldaufwand in Werbemedien seitens eines Inserenten oder einer Marke. Eine der Werbebemühungen der Inserenten und Basis, um den einzelnen Werbeeinsatz nach Wichtigkeit einzustufen. Wird manchmal auch zur Festsetzung der Bezahlung an die Werbeagentur verwendet, im Gegensatz zum Berechnungssystem der Honorare, die anhand einer Stundenabrechnung kalkuliert werden.

**Fallstudie** *f* - case study

■ Analyse und Diskussion der Handlungsalternativen einer realen oder hypothetischen Situation. Diese Methode ist die Basis zahlreicher Elemente der betriebswirtschaftlichen Ausbildung.

**Faltprospekt** *n* - folder

■ Auf vier Seiten eines gefalteten Blattes gedruckte Anzeige. Kann neben der Werbung auch Informationen zu den Verkaufsbedingungen oder anderen Themen von Interesse enthalten.

**Familie** *f* - family unit

■ In der Werbung, Personengemeinschaft mit einem gemeinsamen Wohnsitz, die einen Haushalt im volkswirtschaftlichen Sinn darstellt. Normalerweise sind die Personen miteinander verwandt.

**Feedback** *n* - feedback

■ Kommunikationsprozess, der dem ursprünglichen Empfänger einer Botschaft die Möglichkeit zur Reaktion an den Sender einräumt. Wird nur in der bidirektionalen oder reziproken Kommunikation verwendet.

**fehlende Lagerbestände** *m/pl* - stock-out

■ Fehlen eines Produkts, in dem Moment, in dem die Bestellung eintrifft, obwohl es sich normalerweise auf Lager befindet. Der Prozentsatz der akzeptablen Fehlbestände ist in jedem Sektor unterschiedlich und hängt auch vom Kunden ab. Der Fehlbestand darf jedoch nie so hoch sein, dass er dem Image der Lieferbereitschaft des Unternehmens schadet. Er darf jedoch auch nicht so gering sein, dass es zu überhöhten Lagerbeständen führt. Der Begriff ist gleichbedeutend mit der Nichtlieferbarkeit eines Produkts.

**fehlerhafter Artikel** *m* - faulty article

■ Produkt, das verbilligt verkauft wird, weil es einen kleinen Fehler aufweist.

**Feldarbeit** *f* - fieldwork

■ In der Forschung, Aktivitäten zur Sammlung von Information. Auch wenn in jeder Studie von Feldarbeit gesprochen werden kann, wird der Begriff hauptsächlich für Studien verwendet, in denen Umfragen stattfinden, egal welchen Typs (Privatumfragen, Detailumfragen, Berufsumfragen usw.).

**Feldarbeitsbearbeitung** *f* - field edit

■ Prüfung der Informationen, die in einer Untersuchung gesammelt wurden, zur Kontrolle, ob sämtliche vorgesehenen Informationsquellen richtig ausgewertet wurden. In Umfragenstudien Prüfung, dass alle Umfragen auf die vorgesehene Weise und mit allen vorgesehenen Personen durchgeführt wurden.

**Felddirektor** *m* - field director

■ In einer Forschungseinrichtung, Person die die Arbeit der Informationssammlung plant, leitet und steuert. In einigen Fällen ist der Felddirektor ebenfalls für den Vortest (auch Prätest) des Fragebogens zuständig.

**Feldexperiment** *n* - field experiment

■ Studie bestehend aus der Eingrenzung eines Marktteils und der Modifikation einiger Variablen zur Beobachtung ihrer Wirkung in einer echten Situation.

**Feldfehler** *m* - field error

■ In der Forschung, Abweichung von der Anfangsplanung, der Anzahl der Umfragen oder der Merkmale der umfragenden Mitarbeiter. Der Feldfehler ist von Anfang an in Betracht zu ziehen, genauso wie die Abhilfemaßnahmen, die dagegen unternommen werden können.

**Feldmarketing** *n* - field marketing

■ Marketinghandlungen, die in einem bestimmten Gebiet und durch ein eigens dazu zusammengestelltes Team durchgeführt werden, einschließlich Massenbesuchen, Logistikaktionen und Produktausstellungen.

**Felduntersuchung** *f* - field research

■ Praktische Forschung, im Gegensatz zu einer theoretischen- oder Schreibtischuntersuchung.

**Fensterfalz** *m* - gatefold

■ Anzeige in einer Zeitschrift, die sich öffnen oder aufklappen lässt und somit über das eigentliche Format der Zeitschrifthinausgeht. Es kann sich dabei um eine Anzeige handeln, die eine halbe vertikale Seite in Anspruch nimmt, oder aber um eine ganz- oder halbseitige Anzeige. Die einseitige Anzeige befindet sich in der Regel auf einer der inneren Umschlagsseiten. Die doppelseitige Anzeige ist normalerweise in der Mitte. Diese Art der Werbeanzeigen wird bei Luxusprodukten verwendet, mit denen man eine große Bekanntheit erreichen will.

**Fernsehwerbung** *f* - television advertising

■ Audiovisuelle Werbung, die durch Werberäume und Werbezeiten eines Fernsehsenders verbreitet wird. Die Werbespots dauern in der Regel 20 oder 30 Sekunden. Neben der Unterbrecherwerbung innerhalb einer Sendung gibt es auch die Blockwerbung zwischen Fernsehsendungen.

**feste Provision** *f* - flat fee

■ Provision in Form eines Fixbetrags, der unabhängig von der Höhe der Transaktion ist. Die feste Provision ist gebräuchlich bei Geschäften, bei denen die durchzuführende Arbeit unabhängig ist von ihrem Auftragswert.

**feste Stichprobe** *f* - fixed sampling

■ Klassifizierung der Stichprobe gemäß der Form der Bestimmung des Stichprobenumfangs, der a priori festgelegt wird. Dies ist die gebräuchlichste Methode und steht im Gegensatz zur sequentiellen Stichprobe (freie, veränderliche Stichprobe in Zeitreihenuntersuchungen).

**Festpreisverkauf** *m* - fixed-price sale

■ Verkauf, bei dem der Preis für den Verbraucher und normalerweise auch Händlerpreis und -spanne vom Hersteller oder der öffentlichen Verwaltung (regulierte oder amtlich festgelegte Preise) festgesetzt werden. Ermöglicht es, den Preis auf der Verpackung und in der Werbung anzugeben. Ist in einigen Sektoren und Ländern verboten.

**Festverkauf** *m* - firm sale

■ Verkauf, der nicht annulliert oder geändert werden kann, außer in Fällen von höherer Gewalt.

**FIFO** - FIFO

■ Methode zur Inventarbewertung und zur Kostenverteilung. FIFO bedeutet, dass die Ware, die zuerst in das Lager eingegangen ist, das Lager auch zuerst wieder verlässt. Somit beläuft sich der Bilanzwert der Lagerbestände auf den Wert der Ware, die zum Schluss erworben wurde. In Zeiten verstärkter Inflation führt die FIFO-Methode zu höheren Gewinnen als andere Methoden, wie z. B. LIFO. FIFO ist die Abkürzung des englischen Begriffs first in, first out.

**Fifty-Fifty-Plan** *m* - fifty-fifty plan

■ Werbekampagne, deren Kosten zu fünfzig Prozent von beiden Teilnehmern getragen werden. Wird im Allgemeinen für Kampagnen verwendet, bei denen ein Hersteller und ein Vertreiber aufgeführt sind.

**Filter** *m* - filtering

■ Bei der Netzwerbung die Analyse der abgeschickten Anfrage eines Anwenders durch ein Informatikprogramm, um das Profil des Anwenders zu erfassen und die einzusetzenden Anzeigen der aufgerufenen Seite auszuwählen.

**Firmen-Branding** *n* - employer branding

■ Bestandteil des Markenengineerings, das sich auf die Potenzierung eines soliden Firmenimages bei den Mitarbeitern stützt, sodass diese stolz sind, Teil der Firma zu sein und dort zu bleiben, wobei die Identifizierung mit den Handlungen zugunsten der Firmenmarken gefördert wird.

**Firmenverzeichnis** *n* - trade directory

■ Aufstellung, die in einer bestimmten Reihenfolge die Namen und weiteren Angaben zu den Unternehmen eines Wirtschaftssektors oder einer Region enthält. Die Anordnung und Unterteilung erfolgt meist nach dem Tätigkeitsfeld der Unternehmen.

**Firmenwert** *m* - goodwill

■ Nicht greifbarer Wert, der im Preis zum Ausdruck kommt, der bei der Übernahme (oder Fusion) eines Unternehmens zu bezahlen ist und über dessen eigentlichem Buchwert liegt. Der Firmenwert stellt den Wert der Unternehmung als Wirtschaftseinheit dar, und sich aus dem Kundenstamm, der Marke, der Erfahrungswerte usw. zusammen.

**First-Mover-Vorteil** *m* - first mover advantage

■ Ein First-Mover-Vorteil bezeichnet die Vorteile, die dem Unternehmen entstehen, das in einem Markt zuerst seine Leistungen anbietet.

**Flankenangriff** *m* - flank attack

■ Art des Umgehungsangriffs, bei der man sich auf Erweiterungen der Produktpalette oder auf besonders kleine und große Größen innerhalb des gleichen Produkt- oder Marktbereichs, in dem der Hauptkonkurrent stark ist, konzentriert.

**Flanker Brand** *f* - flanker brand

■ Eine Marke, die auf einem Markt lanciert wird, auf dem dasselbe Unternehmen bereits andere ähnliche Marken platziert hat.

**Flaschenhalsetikett** *n* - collar label

■ Am Flaschenhals angebrachtes Werbeetikett oder Information.

**Fließband** *n* - assembly line

■ Produktionssystem, das auf dem Prinzip der Arbeitsteilung beruht und in dem Einzelteile oder Teile verschiedener Fertigungsstraßen am Ende zu einem Ganzen zusammengefügt werden. Normalerweise werden dabei Transportbänder verwendet, die das Produkt, das sich gerade in der Fertigung befindet, zu den Monteuren der verschiedenen Arbeitsstufen befördern. Dabei hat jeder Mitarbeiter für einen bestimmten Arbeitsschritt die Verantwortung, wodurch sein Platz am Band bestimmt wird. Die Personen, die in der Endmontage arbeiten, stehen demnach am Ende des Bandes.

**Flop** *m* - marketing flop

■ Produkt ohne Erfolg im Handel. Schätzungsweise sind 80% aller neuen Produkte Flops.

**Flugwerbung** *f* - in-flight publication

■ Werbung, die einzig und allein an Passagiere einer Fluggesellschaft verteilt wird. Ihre Diskriminierungskapazität ist sehr hoch, weshalb die werbenden Firmen die entsprechenden Kampagnen für das Leserpublikum nutzen, wie z. B. Hotelwerbung, Reisen, Restaurant oder Firmenprodukte.

**Fokusgruppe** *f* - focus group

■ Gruppe von sechs bis zehn Personen, die sich mit einem Moderator oder Animateur trifft, um frei ihre Meinungen über ein Produkt auszutauschen. Dies dient dazu, auf qualitativer Ebene die Vorteile und Nachteile des untersuchten Produkts gegenüber der Konkurrenz zu finden (es werden Gruppen von Käufern und Nichtkäufern gebildet), die später durch eine Umfrage quantifiziert werden können. Diese Untersuchungstechnik wird auch für eine schnelle und kostengünstige Bewertung des Verständnisses einer Werbekampagne verwendet.

**Follow-Up-Bericht** *m* - follow-up report

■ Ein regelmäßig von der Buchhaltungsabteilung eines Werbeunternehmens erarbeitetes Dokument zur Information über die Entwicklung der unter Vertrag gegebenen Kampagne an einen Kunden.

**Follow-Up-Nachricht** *f* - follow-up message

■ Kontaktaufnahme mit einem Kunden per Post in einer durchgehenden Werbekampagne. Im Allgemeinen wird diese nicht an Kunden verschickt, die auf ein anfängliches Schreiben keine Reaktion gezeigt haben.

**Forschung** *f* **& Entwicklung** *f* **(FuE) -** research and development (R&D)

■ Gesamtheit der Handlungen die darauf gerichtet sind, die Produkte und Prozesse eines Unternehmens aus technologischer und nicht aus handelspolitischer Sicht zu verbessern und zu erneuern. Es handelt sich dabei eher um angewandte Forschung als um Grundlagenforschung.

**Forschungsabteilung** *f* - research department

■ Im Organigramm einer Werbefirma die Abteilung zur Dokumentation, Analyse und Steuerung der Daten in Bezug auf die Kommunikationsplanung und Durchführung von Kampagnen.

**fortlaufende Forschung** *f* - continuous research

■ Forschung, die über sehr lange Zeitdauer fortgesetzt wird und Vergleiche im Zeitablauf und gegenüber Wettbewerbern erlaubt.

**Frage mit Mehrfachantwort** *f* - multiple-answer question

■ Bei Umfragen eine Frage, auf die der Befragte mehr als eine gültige Antwort geben kann. Die Gesamtanzahl der erhaltenen Antworten kann die Zahl der Befragten überschreiten.

**Fragebogen** *m* - questionnaire

■ Druckerzeugnis, das Fragen und Anweisungen enthält, denen der Befragende zu folgen hat. Gleichzeitig enthält der Fragebogen Platz für die Antworten, die gegeben werden und die von ihm in den dafür vorgesehenen Platz eingetragen werden müssen. Manchmal antwortet der Befragte auch direkt. Ein Fragebogen muss eindeutig strukturiert sein, da der Befragende je nach Antwort unterschiedliche Teile des Fragebogens verwendet. Außerdem sollte er eine anschließende Darstellung der Ergebnisse in einer Tabelle leicht ermöglichen.

**Franchise-Kette** *f* - franchise chain

■ Ladenkette mit gleichem Namen und Aussehen. Sie verpflichtet sich dazu, sich landesweit gemeinsam durch eine Einkaufszentrale zu versorgen und durch eine Vertriebsstelle oder einen Großhändler auf regionaler Ebene. Jede Geschäftsstelle ist Eigentum einer selbständigen Person, welche die Kette jederzeit verlassen kann. Wenn die Vertriebsstelle den Eigentümern der Läden gehört, handelt es sich um eine Einzelhandelsgenossenschaft. Freiwillige Handelsgesellschaften sind eher im Lebensmittel- und Drogeriebereich üblich, d. h. in den traditionellen Sektoren, im Gegensatz zu Franchiseunternehmen, die in weniger traditionellen Sektoren vorzufinden sind, wie im Textil- oder audiovisuellen Sektor oder bei Schnellrestaurants.

**Franchising** *n* - franchise

■ Verteilungsstrategie basierend auf der Zusammenarbeit zwischen einem Produzenten und dem Vertreiber (Franchisegeber) und einem anderem Vertrieb (Franchisenehmer). Der Produzent erlässt dem Vertreiber eine Handelslizenz zum Verkauf seiner Produkte mit Ausnutzung seiner Marke oder Marken, seines Images und mithilfe seiner technischen und gewerblichen Abteilung, sowie Leitungshandlungen.

**Frankiermaschine** *f* - franking machine

■ Maschine, die besondere Aufkleber oder den Portobetrag auf zu versendende Umschläge druckt, so dass man auf herkömmliche Briefmarken verzichten kann. Dadurch erspart sich der Postdienst den Druck von Briefmarken, und die Unternehmen gewinnen Zeit und Kontrolle.

**freier Markt** *m* - free market

■ Marktstruktur, bei der die Ressourcenallokation (Mittelverwendung) und Preissetzung dem Wechselspiel von Angebot und Nachfrage überlassen bleiben. Ein freier Markt ist homogen, transparent, und kein Käufer oder Verkäufer verfügt über eine Machtposition.

**freies Vorstellungsgespräch** *n* - in-depth interview

■ Vorstellungsgespräch, bei dem der Interviewer den Befragten frei reden lässt, ohne ihm Fragen zu stellen, und ihm Brücken baut, wenn er ins Stocken oder aus dem Konzept gerät. Es handelt sich dabei um das Gegenteil zu einem Vorstellungsgespräch, dessen Ablauf fest vorgeschrieben ist, und in welchem der Interviewer konkrete Fragen stellt. Erfolgversprechend in der Anfangsphase eines Gesprächs.

**freiwillige Handelskette** *f* - voluntary chain

■ Ladenkette, die einen gemeinsamen Namen hat und über das gleiche Aussehen verfügt. Sie verpflichten sich dazu, sich landesweit gemeinsam durch eine Einkaufszentrale zu versorgen und durch eine Vertriebsstelle oder einen Großhändler auf regionaler Ebene. Jede Geschäftsstelle ist Eigentum einer selbständigen Person, welche die Kette jederzeit verlassen kann. Wenn die Vertriebsstelle den Eigentümern der Läden gehört, handelt es sich um eine Einzelhandelsgenossenschaft. Freiwillige Handelsgesellschaften sind eher im Lebensmittel- und Drogeriebereich üblich, in den traditionellen Sektoren, im Gegensatz zu Franchiseunternehmen, die in weniger traditionellen Sektoren vorzufinden sind, wie im Textil- oder audiovisuellen Sektor oder bei Schnellrestaurants.

**Frequenz** *f* - frequency

■ Medienauswahl umfasst die Suche nach jenem Medium, mit dem die gewünschte Anzahl an Kontakten mit dem Zielpublikum am kosteneffizientesten erreicht werden kann. Die Durchschnittsfrequenz ist das Ergebnis nach Division der Gesamtkontakte durch kontaktierte Personen. Die Frequenzverteilung ist die Beziehung zwischen allen Personen der Zielgruppe, die nach Anzahl der Kontakte, die sie während der Kampagne empfangen haben, gruppiert wird.

**Frontalangriff** *m* - frontal attack

■ Direkter Angriff auf die Haupteinnahme- und -gewinnquelle des Konkurrenzunternehmens. Diese Technik wird nur angewandt, wenn der Angreifer über mehr Ressourcen verfügt als der Wettbewerber, weil dieser sich unter Einsatz aller Kräfte verteidigen wird.

**Frontalstandort** *m* - head-on location

■ In der Außenwerbung, Ausrichtung eines Plakats oder einer Tafel in Richtung des Verkehrsstroms. Die Sichtbarkeitsvoraussetzungen sind höher las bei anderen Ausrichtungen, daher ist der Kostenpunkt höher.

**FuE** - R&D

■ Abkürzung für Forschung und Entwicklung.

**führender Artikel** *m* - leading product

■ Artikel, der einen hohen Marktanteil hat und der bei Hausfrauen einen hohen Erinnerungswert besitzt. Der Produzent nutzt diesen Artikel zur Verkaufsförderung anderer Artikel, die derselben Produktfamilie angehören. Auf ihn konzentrieren sich die Verkaufsanstrengungen und die Werbemaßnahmen. Geschäftsergebnis und Image des Herstellers hängen in großem Umfang von diesem Artikel ab.

**Führermarke** *f* - leading brand

▪ Marke, die den Markt einer bestimmten Produktkategorie anführt und die höchste Marktbeteiligung erreicht.

**fünf Ms** *n/pl* **des Anzeigenentwurfs** - five M's of advertising

▪ Die Initialen kommen von den englischen Begriffen Mission, Money, Message, Media und Measurement. Mission: was sind die Ziele der Werbung?; Money: welcher Betrag kann ausgegeben werden?; Message: was soll ausgesagt werden?; Media: welche Medien sollen eingesetzt werden?; Measurement: wie sollen die Ergebnisse gemessen werden?

**Funnel-Ansatz** *m* - funnel approach

▪ In der Forschung, Methode der Zusammenstellung von Fragebögen vom breiten, allgemeinen Ansatz hin zum konkreten, spezifischen Aspekt.

**Fußende** *n* - gondola end

▪ Privilegierter Bereich am Anfang und Ende eines Regals in einem Geschäft. Der Händler platziert an diesen Stellen die Produkte, deren Absatz er fördern möchte oder er vermietet sie an einen Hersteller, der daran interessiert ist, durch diese Positionierung die Verkaufszahlen seiner Produkte zu steigern.

# G

**Gang** *m* - aisle

▪ An einem Verkaufsort der Weg zwischen den Regalen, auf dem sich die Käufer mit ihren Einkaufswagen bewegen. In jedem Gang werden eine oder mehrere Produktfamilien untereinander artverwandter Produkte angeboten. In modernen Großsupermärkten sind folgende Gänge am größten: ein quer verlaufender Gang vor den Kassen, ein weiterer zentral gelegener Gang und ein dritter vor dem Abschnitt mit den verderblichen Frischwaren oder den Waren mit dem größten Absatz, zuletzt ein rechtwinklig hierzu verlaufender Eingangsbereich, in dem gewöhnlich Sonderangebote, regionale Spezialitäten oder der Jahreszeit angepasste Produkte angeboten werden.

**Garantiemarke** *f* - seal of guarantee

▪ Die Garantiemarke ist ein Zeichen, das unter der Kontrolle des Markeninhabers von verschiedenen Unternehmen gebraucht wird und dazu dient, die Beschaffenheit, die geographische Herkunft, die Art der Herstellung oder andere gemeinsame Merkmale von Waren oder Dienstleistungen dieser Unternehmen zu gewährleisten. Der Markeninhaber ist im Allgemeinen eine Region, ein Land, eine Herkunftsbezeichnung oder ein Sektorverbund.

**Gattungsmarke** *f* - private brand

▪ Gattungsmarke, auch Weiße Ware oder No-Name-Produkt (von englisch no name, „namenlos") ist ein Verbrauchserzeugnis, das sich nicht zuvorderst durch ein unterscheidbares Zeichen – wie Name, Abbildungen, Buchstaben, Zahlen, Hörzeichen, dreidimensionale Gestaltung wie Form der Ware und der Verpackung –, unter dem die Ware vertrieben wird, auszeichnet, sondern sich vor allem durch die Zugehörigkeit zu einer Gattung von anderen Erzeugnissen unterscheidet. Gattungsmarken sind neutral, meist betont schlicht verpackt und liegen preislich im unteren Bereich. Das Gegenstück zu Gattungsmarken sind Markenartikel.

**Gattungsmarke** *f* - no-name product

▪ Produkt, das ohne bekannte Marke vorgestellt und im Allgemeinen in Discountern verkauft wird, zu einem vorteilhaften Preis. Die Marktquote steigt, wenn die Kaufentscheidung der Verbraucher immer öfter auf bestimmte Produkte der No-Name-Marke fällt.

**Gattungswerbung** *f* - generic advertising

▪ Werbung für eine Klasse von Produkten oder Dienstleistungen (z. B. Lebensversicherungen), ohne Erwähnung von Marken. Wird von den Unternehmen eines Sektors bezahlt, die häufig öffentliche Subventionen erhalten.

**Gebietsauswahl** *f* - area sampling

■ Gebündelte Zufallsauswahl in geografischen Zonen auf der Basis von Plänen. Nach der Zufallsauswahl eines Gebiets werden alle Mitglieder der entsprechenden Gruppen (zum Beispiel alle Haushalte) entweder mit einer einfachen Zufallsstichprobe zweier Cluster oder proportional zur Wahrscheinlichkeit der Größe jeder Gruppe untersucht (wenn z. B. die Anzahl der Haushalte in jeder Gegend stark variiert). Dies bietet den Vorteil, dass nur eine reduzierte Anzahl an Gruppen und Elementen untersucht werden muss.

**Gebietsleiter** *m* - area manager

■ Person, die für den Verkauf einer Produktgruppe in einem Gebiet verantwortlich ist.

**Gebietstest** *m* - test area

■ Geografischer Bereich, in dem eine bestimmte Marktprobe durchgeführt wird.

**geforderter Preis** *m* - asking price

■ Vom Verkäufer geforderter Preis. Falls dieser Preis nicht akzeptiert wird, kann er schrittweise gesenkt werden.

**gegenüber von Text** - facing matter

■ Lage einer Werbeanzeige in einer Zeitschrift oder einer Zeitung auf einer einem redaktionellen Beitrag gegenüberliegenden Seite. Sie wird stärker wahrgenommen als wenn sie gegenüber einer anderen Werbeanzeige liegen würde. Bei gleicher Größe wird sie jedoch weniger stark wahrgenommen als wenn sie innerhalb des Textes platziert wäre (von redaktionellem Teil umgeben).

**Geldkuh** *f* - cash cow

■ In einer Marktwachstums-Marktanteils-Matrix bezeichnet der Begriff einen Geschäftsbereich, der in einem Segment mit geringem Wachstum Marktführer ist oder eine dominierende Stellung hat. Dieser muss mehr Mittelzuflüsse erzeugen als zur Beibehaltung seiner Marktquote nötig sind, um diese in andere Geschäftsbereiche der Gruppe zu investieren. Erfordert eine konservative Führung. Wird auch Cash-Cow genannt.

**gemeinsame Markenpraxis** *f* - co-branding

■ Verwendung von zwei oder mehr Marken beim Verkauf eines Produkts oder einer Dienstleistung, z. B. Verkauf eines Fastfood-Menüs mit einer Marke von Erfrischungsgetränken um die Marken zu assoziieren.

**gemeinsame Verpackung** *f* - co-pack

■ Technik der Verkaufsförderung, bei der zwei Marken von miteinander in Beziehung stehenden Produkten in derselben Verpackung erscheinen.

**Gemeinschaftsmarke** *f* - collective trademark

■ Marke einer Herstellervereinigung oder einer spezialisierten Einrichtung, die von ihren Mitgliedern als Symbol für den Herkunftsnachweis oder als Qualitätsgarantie verwendet wird und strengen Kontrollen unterworfen ist. Sie ist häufig mit einer einfachen Zeichnung verbunden (z. B. reine Schurwolle).

**generisch** - generic

■ Kennzeichnung die verwendet wird, um zu zeigen, dass der Artikel durch mehrere Lieferanten geliefert werden kann, ohne dass der Konsument diese leicht unterscheiden kann. Das wird entweder dadurch erreicht, dass die Ware unverpackt ohne Markennamen verkauft wird oder indem sie als No-Name-Produkt oder unter dem Namen des Vertreibers verkauft wird.

**geografische Abdeckung** *f* - geographical coverage

■ Bereich unter dem Einfluss eines Mediums oder Trägers, in dem Exemplare desselben vertrieben werden sollen (Druckmedien) oder in dem von der Sendestation ausgegebene Signale empfangen werden (audiovisuelle Medien). Die geografische Abdeckung eines Mediums kann lokal, landesweit, regional, national oder international sein.

**geografische Diversifikation** *f* - geographical diversification

■ Suche nach neuen Absatzmärkten für das gleiche Produkt, die gleiche

Technologie und den gleichen Kundentyp. Es handelt sich dabei eher um eine Ausweitung als um eine Diversifizierung.

**geografische Segmentierung** *f* - geographic segmentation

■ Einteilung der Bevölkerung oder einer Personengruppe nach geographischen Kriterien, normalerweise nach dem Wohnort oder der Region.

**Geomarketing** *n* - geomarketing

■ Geomarketing bezeichnet die Planung, Koordination und Kontrolle kundenorientierter Marktaktivitäten von Unternehmen mittels geographischer Informationssysteme. Oftmals wird hier die ähnliche Psychografie ausgenutzt, die bei Einwohnern des gleichen Gebiets (Siedlung, Stadtteil) auftritt.

**geplante Obsoleszenz** *f* - planned obsolescence

■ Marketingtechnik bestehend aus der künstlichen Programmierung eines Produkts, so dass es aufgrund seiner begrenzten Lebensdauer ersetzt werden muss. Diese kann im Material begründet sein, über die Vermarktung von neuen Modellen die das Vormodell alt erscheinen lassen, , über neues Design oder In-Mode-Kommen neuerer Versionen des Produkts stattfinden. Eine der vom Verbraucherstandpunkt aus am meisten kritisierten Praktiken im Marketing . Auch künstliche Obsoleszenz genannt.

**Gesamtaudienz** *f* - gross audience

■ Summe der Audienz von verschiedenen Trägern ohne Einbeziehung von Duplikationen.

**Gesamteindruck** *m* - gross impressions

■ Im Marketing, Anzahl der Kontakte, die eine Kampagne in einem objektiven Publikum erzeugt.

**Gesamtkosten** *pl* - total cost

■ Summe aus Fixkosten und variablen Kosten für ein Unternehmen oder ein Produkt.

**Gesamtpublikum** *n* - total audience

■ Anzahl aller Personen, die eine oder mehrere Anzeigen oder Spots einer Werbekampagne gesehen, gelesen oder gehört haben.

**Geschäftsbereich** *m* - business unit

■ Jeder Teil einer betrieblichen Organisation mit eigener Strategie, Führung und eigenem Haushalt. Die rechtliche Trennung ist unter organisatorischen Gesichtspunkten nicht immer angemessen, besonders bei multinationalen Unternehmen oder großen Unternehmensgruppen. Deshalb können innerhalb einer Gesellschaft mehrere Geschäftsbereiche existieren, ein Geschäftsbereich kann aber auch mehrere Gesellschaften einer Gruppe umfassen.

**Geschäftsfeld** *n* - field

■ Spezialisierung der Aktivität eines Unternehmens in Bezug auf Funktionen oder Produkte. Zum Beispiel können dies Massenkonsumartikel, Kommunikationstechnologie oder Finanzdienstleistungen sein.

**Geschäftsjahr** *n* - accounting year

■ Dauer der Geschäftstätigkeit einer Gesellschaft, die in Ausnahmefällen weniger als 12 Monate betragen kann. In Großbritannien besteht es gelegentlich aus 13 Perioden von jeweils 4 Wochen. Es fällt normalerweise mit dem Kalenderjahr zusammen, nur bei landwirtschaftlichen Unternehmen (durch die Ernte) und im Einzelhandel (durch das Problem der Inventarerstellung und das Saisonende) ist dies nicht der Fall.

**Geschäftsplan** *m* - business plan

■ Genaue Zusammenfassung der Ziele einer neuen Aktivität und dem vorhergesehenen Mitteleinsatz und der Ergebnisse. Wird in Großunternehmen für die Billigung neuer Budgets angewandt und ist wesentlich für die Investoren von Risikokapital, die Unternehmensgründungen begünstigen. Der Plan sollte folgendes beinhalten: Beschreibung der anzubietenden Ware oder Dienstleistung, Zielmarkt und angestrebter Marktanteil, Verbraucheranalyse, Produktionsplanung mit besonderem

Gewicht auf neuen Technologien, Marketingplan, voraussichtliche Bilanzen und Gewinn- und Verlustrechnungen für mehrere Jahre, Finanzbedarf und wie dieser gedeckt werden soll, und eventuell Plan zur Börseneinführung.

**Geschenk** *n* - gift

▪ Gut oder Nutzen, das man gratis und freiwillig von einer anderen Person erhält, oder das man einem anderen mit der Absicht macht, ihn zu erfreuen.

**Geschenk** *n* - on-pack premium

▪ Gabe in der Verpackung des Produkts. Oftmals ein Coupon oder ein anderes Angebot.

**Geschenkgutschein** *m* - gift voucher

▪ Dokument in Form eines Schecks, ausgestellt von einem bestimmten Geschäft, das seinem Inhaber erlaubt, dort für einen bestimmten Betrag einzukaufen. Durch den Geschenkgutschein kann die Person, die das Geschenk erhält, sich dieses selbst aussuchen. Das Geschäft kann den Gutschein als Werbeinstrument einsetzen, indem es nicht auf eine Vorausbezahlung durch einen Dritten besteht. Der Gutschein kann aber auch als Abzug beim Kauf eines anderen Gegenstandes verwendet werden oder, im Fall eines Umtauschs, wenn das Geschäft das Geld nicht zurückerstatten möchte.

**Geschenkverpackung** *f* - gift-wrap

▪ Verwendung eines besonderen Geschenkpapiers, um eine im Geschäft gekaufte Ware einzupacken. Dies ist in der Regel ein kostenloser Service; manchmal muss der Kunde jedoch eine Gebühr zahlen oder einen speziellen Verpackungsstand aufsuchen.

**geschichtete Stichprobe** *f* - stratified sampling

▪ Wahrscheinlichkeitsauswahl, bei der die Grundgesamtheit in erschöpfende und sich nicht überschneidende Schichten eingeteilt wird und in jeder Schicht eine unabhängige Zufallsstichprobe vorgenommen wird. Sofern die Schichten geeignet gewählt worden und intern sehr homogen sind, führt dieses Verfahren zu einer höheren Genauigkeit und erlaubt ein engeres Konfidenzintervall. Eine geschichtete Stichprobe kann proportional oder nichtproportional sein. In ersterem Fall ist der Umfang jeder Teilstichprobe proportional zum relativen Gewicht jeder Schicht in der Grundgesamtheit.

**geschlossene Frage** *f* - closed question

▪ Frage in einem Fragebogen, bei der der Befragte gezwungen ist, unter mehreren vorgegebenen Antworten zu wählen. Ist die häufigste Frageform und ermöglicht eine leichte Erfassung der Antworten, ist jedoch weniger aufschlussreich und bietet weniger Variantenreichtum.

**Geschmack** *m* - taste

▪ Art und Weise, nach der jede Person gewisse Sachen oder Situationen beurteilt. Der Geschmack oder die Vorlieben der Konsumenten ist einer der Teilbereiche, mit dem sich die Marktforschung beschäftigt.

**Gesellschaftsklasse** *f* - social class

▪ Jede der hierarchisch angeordneten Ebenen, in die eine Gesellschaft unterteilt werden kann. Die Schichten lassen sich in obere, mittlere und untere Klasse unterscheiden. Die Unterscheidung der Klassen erfolgt heute hauptsächlich auf Grund wirtschaftlicher Gesichtspunkte, obwohl auch andere Faktoren, wie Ausbildung oder Kultur eine Rolle spielen.

**Gesetz** *n* **der großen Zahlen** - law of large numbers

▪ Statistisches Gesetz, das die Verallgemeinerung von Vorhersagen für Verhalten ermöglicht, das bei großen Gruppen beobachtet wurde. Das Gesetz besagt, dass sich zufällige Bewegungen bei einer großen Zahl von Individuen tendenziell ausgleichen.

**Gesetz** *n* **von Angebot und Nachfrage** - law of supply and demand

▪ Wirtschaftgesetz das besagt, dass sich der Preis für ein bestimmtes Gut aus der Wechselwirkung zwischen Angebot und Nachfrage ergibt. Durch den Preis werden die angebotene und die nachgefragte Menge am Markt einander angeglichen.

**gestaffelte Sendungen** *f* - tiered statements

■ Marketingtechnik, die auf der Segmentierung einer Kundendatenbank nach einem bestimmten Kriterium in Abschnitte oder Blöcke basiert, um Offerten, Vergünstigungen und andere Mitteilungen gezielt versenden zu können.

**gestützte Erinnerung** *f* - aided recall

■ Prozentsatz des Publikums, das eine Marke nennt, wenn man es bittet, sich an die Marken einer bestimmten Dienstleistung oder Produktklasse zu erinnern. Da hierbei die Marke nicht suggeriert wird, wird die gestützte Erinnerung manchmal in das Konzept der spontanen Erinnerung mit eingeschlossen, wenn nur zwischen spontan und suggeriert unterschieden wird.

**Gewerbegebiet** *n* - commercial area

■ Räumliches Gebiet, das aus mehreren Niederlassungen bzw. Betriebsstätten des Einzelhandels zusammengesetzt ist, die Waren direkt an den Verbraucher verkaufen.

**gewerbliches Eigentum** *n* - industrial property

■ Sonderform des Eigentums, die der Erfinder oder Entdecker eines Produktes oder einer Maschine von sich aus erwirbt; gibt das Recht zur exklusiven Verwertung dieses Werks für industrielle oder kommerzielle Zwecke, direkt oder durch Überlassung an Dritte. Umfasst weitere Formen, die ein persönliches Recht darstellen, wie den Namen oder die Handelsmarke.

**gewichtete Distributionsdichte** *f* - weighted distribution

■ Prozentualer Anteil an den Gesamtverkäufen, den die Läden, in denen die Marke vertreten ist, am Gesamtmarkt dieses Produktes halten. Diese Kennziffer gibt die tatsächliche Marktdurchdringung der Marke an, da sie sowohl die Anzahl der Verkaufsstellen, als auch deren Bedeutung berücksichtigt.

**Gewichtung** *f* - weighting

■ Bei der Erstellung einer Zielgruppe, die Bewertung einzelner Bevölkerungssektoren je nach ihrer Wichtigkeit.

**gezielte Werbung** *f* - targeting

■ Erwerb von Werbeflächen an Orten, die den Eigenschaften der Zielgruppe entsprechen.

**Giffen-Paradox** *n* - Giffen's paradox

■ Zuerst von Robert Giffen im 19. Jahrhundert beobachtetes Phänomen, bei dem die Nachfrage nach einem Gut bei Erhöhung seines Preises steigt. Dies tritt bei bestimmten absolut inferioren Gütern des Grundbedarfs auf, wie Brot oder Kartoffeln, die den Hauptanteil der Ausgaben von armen Haushalten ausmachen. Wenn deren Preis steigt, sinkt die Möglichkeit der Haushalte, Güter wie Fleisch zu kaufen, so dass sie mehr von den (trotz Preiserhöhung) billigeren Gütern konsumieren müssen.

**GIS** *n* - GIS

■ Ein Geoinformationssystem (Kurzform GIS) oder Geografisches Informationssystem ist ein rechnergestütztes Informationssystem, das aus Hardware, Software, Daten und den Anwendungen besteht. Mit ihm können raumbezogene Daten digital erfasst und redigiert, gespeichert und reorganisiert, modelliert und analysiert sowie alphanumerisch und grafisch präsentiert werden.

**Glaubwürdigkeit** *f* - credibility

■ Werturteil, wonach eine Sache oder eine Person es verdient, dass man ihr glaubt, und wodurch man etwas als wahr oder wahrscheinlich bewertet.

**globale Markenbeurteilung** *f* - international brand valuation

■ Studie über den globalen Wert der Hauptmarken der wichtigsten Länder, die u. a. folgende Parameter beurteilt: Verkauf, Rentabilität, Alter und Marktkontinuität, Kommunikationspolitik, Wachstumspotential, wahrgenommene Qualität, Bewusstsein beim Verbraucher.

Die bekanntesten Studien sind die von Interbrand und Landor durchgeführten.

**globale Verbreitung** *f* - across-the-board broadcast

■ In den Medien, Verbreitung eines Programms im Fernsehen oder im Radio zu einer bestimmten Uhrzeit während 5 aufeinanderfolgenden Wochentagen (gewöhnlich von Montag bis Freitag). Diese Programme sind für die Werbebranche sehr interessant, da täglich das gleiche Publikum erreicht wird und hierdurch die Werbewirksamkeit steigt.

**globales Marketing** *n* - global marketing

■ Konzept, das davon ausgeht, dass der Markt für ein Produkt die gesamte Welt ist, und dass die Motivationen und Charakteristika der Verbraucher weltweit ähnlich genug sind, um ein wenig differenziertes Angebot für die einzelnen Länder machen zu können. Vor Ort können leicht abweichende Marken, Verpackungen oder Werbekampagnen eingesetzt werden, aber der Ansatz ist identisch.

**Gondel** *f* - gondola

■ Im Marketing, Möbelstück, das aus mehreren Regalen besteht und in dem die Produkte eines Ladens einsortiert werden, damit der Kunde das Produkt leichter wahrnimmt und sich selbst bedienen kann.

**Grafik** *f* - graph

■ Darstellung numerischer Daten durch eine oder mehrere Linien oder geometrische Formen, welche die Beziehung darstellen, durch die diese Daten untereinander verbunden sind.

**Grafik-Design** *n* - graphic design

■ Disziplin bestehend aus der Erarbeitung von originellen grafischen Werken und Projekten zur Vermittlung visueller Nachrichten, wie z. B. Werbeplakate, Prospekte, Bucheinbände, Elemente für die unternehmerische Identität, im Allgemeinen serienmäßig oder auf Papier oder Ähnlichem wiedergegeben.

**Grafikdesigner** *m* - graphic designer

■ Designer, der sich mit der Durchführung von technischen Projekten beschäftigt, die visuell eine Nachricht vermitteln, wie z. B. Werbeplakate, Prospekte, Bucheinbände, Unternehmensunterlagen, Einbände oder Wandbeschriftungen.

**grafische Beurteilungsskala** *f* - graphic rating scale

■ In einem Fragebogen verwendetes Material bestehend aus einer Grafik, in der er der Teilnehmer seine persönliche Position in Bezug auf die einzelnen Attribute des angezeigten Konzepts markieren kann.

**Gratisanzeige** *f* - free advertisement

■ Anzeige, deren Veröffentlichung vom Medium, in dem sie erscheint, geschenkt wurde.

**Gratisausgabe** *f* - free issue

■ Exemplar einer Werbung, das zur Steigerung des Kenntnisgrads bei möglichen Kunden oder Käufern führen soll.

**Gratisprodukt** *n* - near-pack

■ Produkt, das an einem Verkaufspunkt zusammen mit einem anderen Produkt aufgeführt ist und beim Kauf dieses Produkts zugegeben wird. Dies wird häufig zur Einführung eines Produkts auf dem Markt oder zur Ankurbelung des Verkaufs eines bereits bestehenden Produkts durchgeführt.

**grauer Markt** *m* - grey market

■ Markt für Originalprodukte ohne Qualitätsprobleme, der von nicht autorisierten Händlern betrieben wird, um ein Exklusivvertriebssystem anzugreifen. Ein Beispiel sind Einfuhren am offiziellen Importeur vorbei, der Kosten für Werbung und technischen Kundendienst trägt. Wird auch als Parallelmarkt bezeichnet. Häufig wird zu niedrigeren Preisen und ohne Servicegarantie verkauft. Im Allgemeinen handelt es sich aber nicht um Schmuggelware.

**greifbar** - tangible

■ Eigenschaft von Gütern oder Vermögensgegenständen, die körperliche Form haben und daher stofflich gehandhabt werden können.

**greifbares Produkt** *n* - tangible product

■ Produkt, das man berühren kann, im Gegensatz zu Dienstleistungen, die nicht greifbar sind.

**Grenzkostenpreis** *m* - marginal cost price

■ Zunahme der Gesamtkosten bei Erhöhung der Produktion um eine Einheit. Die Grenzkostenkurve kann anfangs abnehmenden Verlauf haben, steigt aber am Ende aufgrund des Gesetzes der abnehmenden Grenzerträge an. Bei vollständiger Konkurrenz ist die gewinnmaximierende Angebotsmenge diejenige, bei der Marktpreis und Grenzkosten der Unternehmung gleich sind.

**Großhandel** *m* - wholesale trade

■ Tätigkeit des Großhändlers, dessen Kunde ein Händler ist, der zum Weiterverkauf und nicht für den Konsum einkauft.

**Großhandelspreis** *m* - wholesale price

■ Verkaufspreis an Großhändler oder Großverbraucher. Vom Listenpreis werden die Nachlässe abgezogen (Einführungspromotion usw.).

**Großhandelsverkauf** *m* - wholesale sale

■ Verkauf an Einzelhändler oder Großverbraucher in größeren Einheiten. Wird vom Großhändler durchgeführt, der beim Hersteller oder Importeur in großen Mengen einkauft.

**Großhändler** *m* - wholesaler

■ Unternehmen, das sich dem Verkauf en gros von Waren an Einzelhändler und Großverbraucher widmet. Kauft von vielen Herstellern, und obwohl nach Sektoren unterschiedlich, kann es zwischen 2000 und 10 000 Produkte führen. Gewöhnlich besucht der Groß- den Einzelhändler einmal wöchentlich und hat für die Mehrheit der angebotenen Waren keine Exklusivabnahmeklausel. Hat die Möglichkeit zu dem von ihm gewünschten Preis zu verkaufen, obwohl er gewöhnlich mit dem Hersteller in dessen Vermarktungspolitik zusammenarbeitet.

**Großverkaufsflächen** *f/pl* - major retail outlets

■ Allgemeine Gattungsbezeichnung für große Supermärkte („Hypermärkte"), Kaufhäuser, Einkaufszentren und Fachmärkte mit einer Verkaufsfläche von mehr als 4000 qm. Dies umfasst also alle Gruppen von großflächigen Läden oder Abteilungen, die eine große Sortimentsvielfalt anbieten und regelmäßig Sonderangebote für Lockvogel- oder Werbeartikel machen.

**Grundgesamtheit** *f* - universe

■ Alle Elemente einer bestimmten Klasse, die in der Wirklichkeit existieren. Es handelt sich um die Individuen, die bestimmte Merkmale aufweisen und über die eine Untersuchung (z. B. eine Marktstudie) durchgeführt werden soll, wenngleich man sich aus praktischen Gründen oft auf eine repräsentative Stichprobe beschränken muss.

**Grundsortiment** *n* - basic assortment

■ Mindestmenge von Artikeln, die ständig angeboten werden, um die Befriedigung der Grundbedürfnisse der Kunden zu ermöglichen. Umfasst keine Saisonartikel oder ungewöhnliche Produkte mit geringem Umsatz.

**Gruppenproduktmanager** *m* - group product manager

■ Zuständiger für den Marktdirektor eines Herstellers, der mit der Leitung einer bestimmten Produktgruppe betraut ist und die Arbeit der zugehörigen Produktleiter überwacht. Die Organisation in Produktgruppen stellt eine Alternative zur Markengruppe dar, ist aber in ihrer Struktur ähnlich.

**Guerillaangriff** *m* - guerrilla attack

■ Im Marketing, Besteht in der wiederholten Durchführung kleiner Angriffe auf verschiedenen Gebieten des Gegners, mit der Absicht, ihn zu bedrängen und zu demoralisieren. Ziel ist weniger, den eigenen Marktanteil zu steigern, als vielmehr die Verkaufspreise und Gewinne des Wettbewerbers auf seinen wichtigsten Märkten zu senken.

**Guerilla-Marketing** *n* - guerrilla marketing
■ Guerilla-Vermarktung; bezeichnet die Wahl ungewöhnlicher Aktionen im so genannten Marketing, die mit untypisch geringem Mitteleinsatz eine große Wirkung erzielen sollen.

**Gut** *n* - good
■ Jeder Gegenstand oder jede Dienstleistung, die in der Lage dazu sind, ein Bedürfnis zu befriedigen. Es kann sich dabei um frei verfügbare oder um wirtschaftlich zu erwerbende Güter handeln. Aus juristischer Sicht versteht man darunter alles, was Gegenstand eines Richterspruchs sein kann, ebenso wie die Rechte darüber.

**Gutscheinversand** *m* - direct-mail couponing
■ Briefversand von einem oder mehreren Gutscheinen an die Postanschrift des Verbrauchers.

# H

**halbe Auflage** *f* - half run
■ Einsatz von Werbung in der Hälfte der Exemplare einer Veröffentlichung. Vor allem in bestimmten geografischen Gebieten auftretend. Der Preis des Einsatzes ist höher als die Hälfte des Gesamttarifs.

**Halbseitenfüllung** *f* - half-page spread
■ Anzeige, die die halbe Seite eines Werbeträgers ausfüllt, der die doppelte Breite einer normalen Seite hat. Kann im oberen oder unteren Teil (gewöhnlich) oder in der Seitenmitte angeordnet sein.

**halbseitige Anzeige** *f* - half-page ad
■ Anzeige, die die halbe Seite eines Werbeträgers ausfüllt. Gewöhnlich auf dem unteren Teil bei horizontaler Aufteilung und auf den Rändern bei vertikaler Aufteilung. Man spricht von Seitenraub, wenn sie eine halbe Seite ausfüllt, aber im unteren rechten Quadranten einer ungeraden (rechts liegenden) Seite oder dem unteren linken Quadranten einer geraden (links liegenden) Seite zentriert ist.

**Halo-Effekt** *m* - halo effect
■ Phänomen, durch das ein Charaktermerkmal bei einer Person so stark ausgeprägt ist, dass der Eindruck, den man von den anderen Wesensmerkmalen erhält, davon betroffen oder dadurch verändert wird. Dies muss vor allem bei Untersuchungen des Käuferverhaltens und bei Personalbeurteilungen vermieden werden.

**Haltbarkeit** *f* **im Lager** - shelf life
■ Begriff zur Definition der aktiven Lebensdauer von bestimmten Produkten und Geräten, die gelagert werden, um andere, in Betrieb befindliche Systeme und Geräte zu ersetzen. Zu unterscheiden ist zwischen der Nutzungsdauer wie bei Batterien oder Fotofilmen und der Veralterung aufgrund der Weiterentwicklung des Geräts oder der Technologie.

**Haltekraft** *f* - holding power
■ Fähigkeit eines Radio- oder TV-Programms zur Aufrechterhaltung der Zuhörer- bzw. Zuschauerzahl bis zu seinem Ende. Wird durch Vergleich der Audienz zu Anfang und zum Ende des Programms errechnet.

**Handelsabschlag** *m* - average mark-up
■ Im Handel, Differenz zwischen Netto-Verkaufspreis und Einstandspreis (Wareneinsatz). Wird auf den Einstandspreis oder die Selbstkosten aufgeschlagen. Stellt das Entgelt für die vom Handel erbrachte Leistung dar. Setzt sich aus den Handlungskosten und dem Gewinn zusammen. Kann als absoluter Betrag oder als relative Prozentzahl angegeben werden. Auch Kalkulationszuschlag; bei umgekehrter Rechnung spricht man von Handelsaufschlag, beides sind Ausdrücke für die Handelsspanne.

**Handelsaufschlag** *m* - average mark-on
■ Im Handel, Differenz zwischen Netto-Verkaufspreis und Einstandspreis (Wareneinsatz). Wird vom Verkaufspreis abgezogen. Stellt das Entgelt für die vom

Handel erbrachte Leistung dar. Setzt sich aus den Handlungskosten und dem Gewinn zusammen. Kann als absoluter Betrag oder als relative Prozentzahl angegeben werden. Bei umgekehrter Rechnung spricht man von Handelsabschlag, beides sind Ausdrücke für die Handelsspanne.

**Handelskette** *f* - chain

▪ Vertriebsunternehmen, das über mehrere ähnliche Einrichtungen in verschiedenen Gebieten verfügt. Sie haben alle das selbe Aussehen, die selbe Organisationsform sowie gemeinsame Werbestrategien und Vertriebssysteme.

**Handelsmarke** *f* - trademark

▪ Name, der von einem Hersteller zur Bezeichnung seiner Produkte verwendet wird. Liegt oft in Form eines Logos mit spezifischen Farben und Schriftarten vor, um es von anderen Marken zu unterscheiden.

**Handelsmarketing** *n* - trade marketing

▪ Strategische Allianz zwischen Mitgliedern des Vertriebskanals, die sich auf unterschiedlichem Niveau befinden, wobei Kooperationsvereinbarungen erarbeitet werden, um beiderseitig Vorteile zu erzielen und die Nachfragen der Konsumenten effizient zu erfüllen.

**Handelsname** *m* - trade name

▪ Bezeichnung, unter der die Öffentlichkeit eine bestimmte Einrichtung oder Unternehmung kennt, und durch die diese sich von allen anderen unterscheidet. Muss nicht mit dem Gesellschaftszweck oder dem rechtlichen Namen der Gesellschaft übereinstimmen.

**Handelspartner** *m* - affiliate merchant

▪ Bei Partnerprogrammen die Person, die die Beziehungen zu den Partnern pflegt, die Kampagnen kontrolliert und Neukunden wirbt.

**Handelsspanne** *f* - margin

▪ Differenz zwischen Verkaufspreis und den Kosten eines Produktes. Wenn nur die akkumulierten variablen Kosten berücksichtigt werden, spricht man von Deckungsbeitrag. Falls Abschreibungen abgezogen werden, erhält man die Nettogewinnspanne (obwohl tatsächlich noch die Steuern abgezogen werden müssten), sonst die Bruttogewinnspanne. Falls nur die Produktionskosten berücksichtigt werden, spricht man von der Herstellerspanne, und falls alle Kosten in die Berechnung eingehen, von der Handelsspanne, die der Nettogewinnspanne entspricht. Kann ein Prozentsatz (gewöhnlich Gewinn gemessen am Verkaufspreis) oder eine Differenz in Absolutbeträgen sein.

**Handelsvertreter** *m* - sales representative

▪ Verkäufer oder Verkaufsrepräsentant, der ein geographisches Gebiet abdeckt. In den USA bringt man den Begriff meist in Verbindung mit dem Verkauf an die Industrie oder Einzelhändler, während er in Deutschland eher für einen Kommissionär verwendet wird, der nicht bei der Firma beschäftigt ist, deren Produkte er verkauft.

**Handelswerbung** *f* - trade advertising

▪ Vom Hersteller an den Groß- und Einzelhandel gerichtete Bewerbung von Produkten, um den Zwischenhändlern Argumente und relevante Daten wie Werbeausgaben, Rotationsindizes oder neue Produkte unter dieser Marke zu liefern. Dient auch der Motivation der eigenen Verkaufskraft.

**Händlerliste** *f* - dealer listing

▪ In Druckmedien die Liste aller Händler oder Einzelhändler, bzw. derer eines Gebiets, denen der Hersteller seine Anzeigen für den Zugang durch den Verbraucher zur Verfügung stellt.

**Händlermarke** *f* - distributor's own brand

▪ Der weißen Marke ähnliche Marke, mit dem Unterschied, dass es für den Verbraucher nicht offensichtlich ist, dass es sich um eine Marke des Handelsunternehmens handelt, die einen von diesem verschiedenen Hersteller haben kann. Gestaltung der Etikette und Verkaufspreis des Produkts sind ähnlich dem der Herstellermarken. Ziel des Händlers ist nicht die Absatzzunahme oder das Erreichen eines preisgünstigen Images, sondern die Erhöhung der Gewinnspanne, da der Einkaufspreis gewöhnlich niedriger ist. Zum Beispiel die Marken Universum und Privileg von Quelle oder Bullkraft von Neckermann.

**Händlerregister** *n* - dealer tag
■ In audiovisuellen Medien die Anzeige des Namens oder eines anderen Elements zur Identifizierung der Vertriebe und Händler am Ende des Films oder Spots. In nationalen Kampagnen kann das Register je nach Gebiet unterschiedlich sein.

**Handlungsauslöser** *m* - action device
■ Kreativer Bestandteil einer Postwerbesendung, mit dem eine schnelle Handlung des Empfängers bezweckt wird.

**Handzettel** *m* - handbill
■ Bedrucktes Papier von geringer Qualität und niedrigen Kosten, gewöhnlich von etwa DIN-A5 bis DIN-A6 Größe, das als Unterstützung einer kurzen und einfachen Werbebotschaft gedacht ist. Es wird entweder per Hand verteilt oder von einem Auto oder Kleinflugzeug abgeworfen.

**Hängeplakat** *n* - hanger
■ Auf beiden Seiten bedrucktes Werbeplakat, häufig shilouettenförmig, das frei von der Decke hängt und sich in der Luft dreht.

**Hard-Discount-Markt** *m* - hard-discount store
■ Einzelhandelsgeschäft mit Selbstbedienung, das eine sehr eingeschränkte Zahl von Produkten hohen Verbrauchs verkauft, die hauptsächlich Eigenmarken sind. Der Preis ist im Allgemeinen sehr niedrig, allerdings werden dem Verbraucher im Gegenzug kaum Dienstleistungen angeboten.

**Hard-Selling** *n* - hard selling
■ Hard-Selling ist die Bezeichnung für besonders aggressive Verkaufsmethoden. Die zu erreichenden kurzfristigen Umsatzziele stehen an oberster Stelle. Wird auch als Druckverkauf oder aggressiver Verkauf bezeichnet.

**Hauptanzeige** *f* - main advertisement
■ Wichtigste Anzeige in einer Serie von Anzeigen oder in der gesamten Werbekampagne. Dies ist nicht unbedingt die erste; in der Regel fällt sie mit dem Werbeträger oder dem Originalentwurf zusammen, für den am meisten Mittel eingesetzt werden.

**Hauptattribut** *n* - salient attribute
■ Hauptmerkmal eines Produkts, das dieses für einen Verbraucher definiert. Es ist möglich, dass verschiedene Zielgruppen von verschiedenen Attributen angesprochen werden. Für manche spielt z. B. hauptsächlich die Funktion eine Rolle, während andere Wert auf Design, Material, Gewicht usw. legen.

**Hauptbelastungszeit** *f* - peak hours
■ Tageszeitraum, in dem die Nachfrage (zum Beispiel beim Stromverbrauch oder Telefon) am höchsten ist.

**Hauptgeschäft** *n* - core business
■ Grundlegende Geschäftstätigkeit eines Unternehmens. In größeren Unternehmen oder Gruppen von Unternehmen kann es mehrere Hauptgeschäftsbereiche geben.

**Hauptmarke** *f* - masterbrand
■ Die Hauptmarke ist meist die erste und profitstärkste Marke eines Unternehmens. Durch so genannte Schutzmarken und Kampfmarken kann die Hauptmarke vor Angriffen des Wettbewerbs abgeschirmt werden.

**Hauptnutzen** *m* - basic benefit
■ Eigenschaft, die ein bestimmtes Produkt von ähnlichen Produkten unterscheidet. Soweit sich das Produkt in einem Punkt deutlich von den anderen abhebt und keine größeren Gegenposten vorliegen, gestaltet sich die Strukturierung einer auf dieser besonderen Eigenschaft basierenden Kommunikationsstrategie einfach. Probleme entstehen bei einer Vielzahl von Plagiaten und unerheblichen Konkurrenzprodukten.

**Hauptprodukt** *n* - starter product
■ Produkt, das mit dem Ziel vermarktet wird, den späteren Kauf von ergänzenden

Produkten wie Ersatzteilen, Auffüllteilen und Zubehör zu fördern.

**Hauptpublikum** *n* - primary audience
■ Bei den Druckmedien, Personen, die eine Veröffentlichung kaufen oder mit Personen zusammenleben, die diese kaufen. Diese Personen bilden eine der Lesergruppen der Veröffentlichung.

**Hauptquelle** *f* - primary source
■ In der Forschung eine Quelle, die verschiedene Informationen sammelt und diese später an Interessenten als Sekundärdaten weitergibt.

**Hauptsendezeit** *f* - prime time
■ Zeitraum im Programmschema, der das größte Publikum anzieht. Aufgrund der Gewohnheiten der Verbraucher ist dies in der Regel der frühe Abend. Die Sender bringen Nachrichten, Spielfilme oder Spielshows, die ein möglichst breites Publikum ansprechen. Da dies die attraktivste Werbezeit ist, sind die Tarife höher und die Gesamtwerbezeit länger.

**Hausagentur** *f* - house agency
■ Eigene Werbeabteilung des Werbeträgers, die die Funktionen der Werbeagentur übernimmt, auch wenn diese einstweilen andere Unternehmen für besonders kreative oder Image-Kampagnen unter Vertrag nimmt.

**Hausfrauenzeit** *f* - housewife time
■ Zeit, in der die meisten Fernsehzuschauer Hausfrauen sind, zum Beispiel nach dem Mittagessen oder bei bestimmten Seifenopern. Dies ist das ideale Werbeumfeld für Produkte wie Waschmittel oder Kosmetikprodukte für den Massenmarkt.

**Haushalt** *m* - household
■ Personen oder Gruppe von Personen, die gewöhnlich zusammenleben. In der Regel handelt es sich dabei um die Kernfamilie (Eltern und Kinder). Als Einheit hat die Familie Rechte und Pflichten und dient als Basis für bestimmte Marktuntersuchungen.

**Haushalte** *m/pl* **mit Fernseher** - households using television (HUT)
■ Anzahl der Haushalte mit eingeschaltetem Fernseher und Aufzeichnung der Daten der Durchschnittsaudienz. Der HUT besteht aus einem repräsentativen Muster der nationalen Gesamtzahl an Haushalten mit Audiometer, bei der halbmechanisch die Daten über den Apparatzustand registriert werden (an oder aus), die Verwendung des Apparats und die Personen, die sich vor dem Gerät aufhalten. Erweitert die Anzahl aller Haushalte mit Fernseher.

**Hausmarkt** *m* - domestic market
■ Markt innerhalb der nationalen Gebietsgrenzen. Auch interner Markt.

**Haustür-Verkauf** *m* - door-to-door selling
■ Verkauf im Haus oder Geschäft des Kunden, ohne den Besuchten zu kennen oder eine Vorauswahl zu treffen. Wird gebietsweise durchgeführt, wobei an jeder Haustür geklingelt wird. Ähnelt dem Hausverkauf, bei diesem liegt jedoch eine Anfrage vor, so dass der Kaufinteressent in gewisser Weise bekannt ist.

**Hausverkauf** *m* - home selling
■ Verkauf, bei dem der Verkäufer die möglichen Käufer nach einer vorherigen Auswahl persönlich in ihrem Haus aufsucht. Unterscheidet sich vom Haustürverkauf dadurch, dass dieser alle Haushalte eines Gebietes ohne vorherige Auswahl abdeckt.

**Hauszeitschrift** *f* - in-house magazine
■ Kommunikationsinstrument für die Kommunikation zwischen der Firma und ihren Mitarbeitern. Erfüllt eine Doppelfunktion: Information und Integration. Möchte die Mitarbeiter der Organisation über die aktuellen sozialen, wirtschaftlichen und technischen Themen informieren und ein für das Unternehmen günstiges Zugehörigkeitsgefühl der Mitarbeiter erzeugen.

**herabgesetzter Artikel** *m* - odd article
■ Produkt, das mit Ermäßigung verkauft wird, weil ihm ein Zubehörteil oder Accessoire fehlt.

**High-Involvement-Produkt** *n* - high-involvement good
■ Produkt mit hohem Kaufwert oder hoher Verbrauchsdauer (z. B. ein Auto oder ein

Haus), für dessen Erwerb sich der Kunde mit dem Produkt sehr gründlich auseinandersetzen muss. Da sich der Kunde für die Entscheidungsfindung stark engagiert, entwickelt er eine höhere Markentreue als bei niedrigem Einbezug. Hier greift das Egoprinzip, da der Kunde seine eigene Kaufentscheidung in der Regel als richtig ansieht.

**Hit** *m* - hit

▪ Im Internet das Maß, mit dem sämtliche Elemente einer Seite gezählt werden, wenn diese von einem Benutzer aufgerufen wurde. Ein Seitenbesuch kann daher mehrere Hits haben, sowohl für die einzelnen Seiten der Site, als auch für die Anzahl der grafischen Elemente, die auf dieser Seite angesehen werden können.

**Hochglanzpapier** *n* - art paper

▪ Glänzendes und sehr satiniertes Papier, das in Büchern und Zeitschriften zum Druck von Fotos verwendet wird.

**hochpreisig** - up-market

▪ Gesamtheit der Marken oder Produkte mit einem höheren Preis als andere, die ähnliche Funktionen erfüllen, aufgrund ihrer besseren Qualität oder des Images der Marke. Der Verbraucher wählt zwischen ihnen nicht in Funktion des Preises wie bei den Artikeln am unteren Preisbereich.

**Höchstpreis** *m* - ceiling price

▪ Maximal erlaubter Verkaufspreis für bestimmte Güter, der von einer Preisaufsichtsbehörde festgesetzt wird, z. B. für Brennstoffe.

**horizontale Diversifikation** *f* - horizontal diversification

▪ Diversifizierung, durch die man den aktuellen Kunden Produkte anbietet, die nicht mit den bisher schon angebotenen Produkten in Verbindung stehen.

**Horten** *n* - stockpiling

▪ Anhäufung von Gütern über der normalen Bestandsmenge. Kann entstehen, wenn eine größere Nachfrage erwartet wird, oder auch durch eine Überschätzung der Nachfrage.

**Huckepack-Werbung** *f* - piggyback promotion

▪ Der Begriff Huckepack-Werbung bezeichnet ein Angebot oder eine Werbung, die bei einer anderen Kampagne mitläuft und keine Kosten verursacht. Kann auch als Gratisprobe dem Produkt beigelegt werden.

**HUFF-Modell** *n* - Huff model

▪ Das HUFF-Modell ist ein ökonometrisches Prognosemodell für die Berechnung des Einzugsbereichs eines Einkaufszentrums. Es wurde 1963 von Darrel Huff entwickelt. Es berechnet in Abhängigkeit von Distanzen und Attraktivitäten die Wahrscheinlichkeit, mit der Kunden einen bestimmten Angebotsstandort aufsuchen. Damit ist es möglich, die Größe von Einzugsgebieten einzelner Einzelhandelsstandorte abzubilden. Es ist ein in der Einzelhandelsforschung anerkanntes und oft eingesetztes Verfahren, welches insbesondere auf lokaler Ebene für Prognosen über die Auswirkungen bestimmter Baumaßnahmen, wie bspw. die Errichtung eines neuen Einkaufszentrums, verwendet wird.

**Humorstil** *m* - humorous style

▪ Werbeformat, das den Sinn für Humor des Empfängers zum Erreichen einer positiven Wirkung der angepriesenen Marke sucht. Hier ist vorsichtig vorzugehen, damit der Humor zugunsten des Produkts gerichtet ist und dieses nicht lächerlich erscheinen lässt.

**Hypermarkt** *m* - hypermarket

▪ Verkaufseinrichtung für das breite Publikum, die über ein großes Sortiment, hauptsächlich im Bereich Lebensmittel, Textilien und Haushaltswaren verfügt. Der Großmarkt befindet sich normalerweise auf einem Stockwerk, mit einer Verkaufsfläche von 2.500 - 10.000 m² und ist in den Außenbezirken einer Großstadt angesiedelt. Der Verbrauchergroßmarkt verkauft im Wesentlichen über den Preis mit beachtlichen Sonderangeboten.

**Hypothese** *f* - hypothesis

■ Annahme, auf Grund der man zu einer Schlussfolgerung kommt. Die Arbeitshypothese dient als Grundlage für eine Untersuchung, die ihre Gültigkeit definitiv bestätigen oder verwerfen soll. Die Hypothese findet Anwendung in der Forschung und in der Statistik.

# I

**IAA (International Advertising Association)** - IAA (International Advertising Association)

■ Die IAA ist eine einzigartige, weltweite und führende Vereinigung von anerkannten Persönlichkeiten aus allen Bereichen der Marketing-Kommunikation. Die Organisation vereinigt die Repräsentanten von Werbeauftraggebern, Medienunternehmen sowie Kommunikations- und Werbeagenturen. Sie wurde 1938 gegründet und hat sich in der Zwischenzeit zur führenden, weltweiten Organisation entwickelt, die sich zu Gunsten der Konsumenten und der werbetreibenden Wirtschaft für die freie Meinungsäußerung im Bereich der kommerziellen Kommunikation einsetzt. Ihr Hauptsitz ist New York, sie ist in 95 verschiedenen Ländern aktiv.

**Ideensammlung** *f* - brainstorming

■ Vorgehensweise in der Gruppenarbeit zur Suche nach Ideen oder Lösungen. Der Unterschied zu anderen Verfahren beruht darauf, dass hier die Teilnehmer nur Ideen oder Abänderungen zu Ideen, die von anderen Kollegen vorgestellt wurden, einbringen können, aber nicht diese kritisieren oder verwerfen können, was erst das Ziel eines späteren Treffens ist. In einer kritikfreien Atmosphäre und mit der Interaktion zwischen Teilnehmern, die das Problem genau kennen, ist es leichter, zu einer originellen Lösung zu gelangen. Wird auch Brainstorming genannt.

**Identifikationszeile** *f* - base line

■ In einer Anzeige sind dies Hinweise in einer Fußnote auf die Gesellschaft (Name, Adresse, Telefonnummer, e-Mail oder Website).

**illegale Werbung** *f* - illegal advertising

■ Anschlag oder anderer Anzeigentyp, der ohne Erlaubnis erschienen ist oder angebracht wurde.

**im gesamten Sendegebiet** - across-the-network

■ Gleichzeitige Verbreitung eines Werbespots oder eines Fernsehprogramms in allen Ausstrahlungsgebieten eines Radio- oder Fernsehsenders.

**Image-Audit** *n* - image audit

■ Zustandsprüfung des Unternehmensimages, das im Auftrag einer Firma, Organisation oder Institution von Mitarbeitern eines Drittunternehmens durchgeführt wird und die in der Untersuchung alle Variablen zum Aufbau des genannten Images besteht (z. B. Kommunikationsplan), um die für jeden Fall notwendigen Aktionen zu bestimmen.

**Imageberater** *m* - image consultant

■ Unabhängiger Berater oder Mitarbeiter eines Unternehmens zur Information und Beratung einer Firma über die durchzuführenden Handlung zum Erreichen, Stärken oder Aufrechterhalten eines positiven Images.

**Imageberatung** *f* - image consultancy

■ Firma, deren Ziel die Information und Beratung anderer Firmen über die durchzuführenden Handlungen zum Erreichen, Stärken oder Aufrechterhalten eines positiven Images ist.

**Image-Kampagne** *f* - image campaign

■ Geplantes und koordiniertes Programm für Werbeaktionen, das von einer Agentur durchgeführt wird, deren Ziel die Erzeugung, Aufrechterhaltung, Stärkung oder Änderung des Images ist, das ein bestimmtes Publikum von der Marke hat.

**Imagekrise** *f* - image crisis

■ Situation eines Unternehmens mit einem negativen oder geteilten

Image: z. B. wenn das objektive Publikum die Produkte kennt, aber die Firma dahinter nicht. Im Allgemeinen folgt eine Identitätskrise.

**Imagewerbung** *f* - image advertising

■ Werbeaktivität, deren Zweck die Erzeugung, Aufrechterhaltung, Stärkung oder Änderung des Ansehens und Glaubens einer bestimmten objektiven Öffentlichkeit oder der Gesellschaft insgesamt ist und zu deren Gunsten eine Einrichtung, Kategorie, Produkt oder Dienstleistung, eine Ursache oder gegebenenfalls sogar eine Aktivität oder ein Sektor entsteht.

**Imitation** *f* - imitation

■ Ungesetzliche Benutzung eines Markennamens, eines Produkts oder einer Gestaltungsform, die sich zwar vom Original unterscheidet, diesem aber so ähnlich ist, dass der Kunde sie mit dem Original verwechseln kann. Unterscheidet sich von der Fälschung, bei der das Produkt als Original angeboten wird. Im Allgemeinen versteht man darunter eine bewusst herbeigeführte Nachbildung einer Sache, die einem anderen Gegenstand sehr ähnlich ist.

**Implantation** *f* - implementation

■ Beginn oder Ingangsetzung eines Planes, einer Einrichtung oder einer Aktivität. Sie umfasst sowohl die vorherigen Studien, als auch die direkten Maßnahmen für die Verwirklichung. Benutzt man den Begriff im Zusammenhang mit Handelseinrichtungen, versteht man darunter ebenfalls die Platzverteilung innerhalb eines Ladens und seine Eröffnung. Manchmal findet auch eine vorherige Standortauswahl statt.

**Impuls** *m* - impulse

■ Innerer Beweggrund, schneller und momentaner Anreiz, der uns dazu bewegt oder veranlasst, etwas zu tun oder zu unterlassen. Man spricht von Impulskauf, wenn man über den Kauf vorher nicht nachgedacht hat. In der Regel handelt es sich dabei um Käufe, die aus einer Laune heraus erfolgen, bei denen kleine Mengen erworben werden oder Markenartikel, die zur Befriedigung von Grundbedürfnissen dienen.

**Impulskauf** *m* - impulse buying

■ Der Impulskauf (Spontankauf, Reizkauf) ist eine spontane Kaufentscheidung, die aufgrund eines Reizes (Sehreiz, Preis, Promotion, limitierte Auflage u. Ä.) an der Einkaufsstätte ausgelöst wird.

**Inbound** *m* - in bound

■ Im Sektor Telemarketing der eingehende Anruf eines Kunden oder Interessenten zur telefonischen oder schriftlichen Kontaktaufnahme mit der Kundenbetreuung einer Marke.

**Incorporated Society of British Advertisers (ISBA)** - Incorporated Society of British Advertisers (ISBA)

■ Britische Vereinigung von Werbeanbietern zur Verteidigung der Interessen der Mitglieder auf dem Gebiet der kommerziellen Kommunikation in Europa. Gegründet im Jahr 1900 und derzeit mit über 300 Mitgliedunternehmen.

**indirekte Werbung** *f* - indirect advertising

■ Werbung für eine Marke, die durchgehend an die Werbung einer untersagten Werbung erinnert (Tabak oder Alkohol), aber für ein vollkommen anderes Produkt wirbt, z.B. Studentenfutter oder Sportartikel. Ziel ist mehr die Erinnerung an das untersagte Produkt als der Verkauf des beworbenen Produkts.

**Industriegut** *n* - industrial goods

■ Produkte, die in der Herstellung anderer Güter verwendet werden und nicht für den privaten Konsum bestimmt sind, wie zum Beispiel Maschinen, schwere Werkzeuge oder Rohstoffe. Zu ihrer Vermarktung sind spezielle Marketingtechniken erforderlich.

**Industriemarketing** *n* - industrial marketing

■ Marketing, das auf den Verkauf von Industrieprodukten an Unternehmen spezialisiert ist. Dabei gewinnen die technischen Daten, die Zuverlässigkeit, die

Sicherheit der zeitgerechten Lieferung, die Qualitätskontrolle und gute persönliche Beziehungen mit den verschiedenen Unternehmensebenen, die am Kaufprozess beteiligt sind, an Bedeutung.

**inelastische Nachfrage** *f* - inelastic demand

■ Nachfrage, die nicht auf Preisänderungen reagiert: der Konsument ist indifferent bei Änderungen des Produktpreises und konsumiert die gleiche Menge.

**inferiores Gut** *n* - inferior good

■ Gut des Grundbedarfs, das bei steigendem Einkommen weniger nachgefragt wird. Gelegentlich wird der Begriff auch enger gefasst für Giffen-Güter verwendet; dies sind solche Güter, die bei steigendem Preis stärker nachgefragt werden; die Preiserhöhung entspricht einem sinkenden Realeinkommen, so dass die Verbraucher kein Geld zum Kauf superiorer Güter übrig haben und diese durch das trotz Preiserhöhung immer noch billigere Giffen-Gut ersetzen (Giffen'sches Paradox).

**Infomercial** *n* - infomercial

■ Grafische Werbung in Form einer Reportage oder Doku-Sendung. Kann mehr als eine Seite in der Zeitung oder Zeitschrift einnehmen und wird als Grundelement der mündlichen Argumentation benutzt, egal ob durch Bilder unterlegt oder nicht.

**Informationsmacht** *f* - information power

■ Macht einer Organisation aufgrund ihrer Fähigkeit zur Weitergabe von Informationen an eine andere. Wenn letztere Zugang zu der Information wünscht, muss sie sich in gewissem Maße durch erstere beeinflussen lassen. Hierbei handelt es sich um eine der derzeit wichtigsten Machtquellen, da viele Unternehmen Informationen zur erfolgreichen Entscheidungsfindung z. B. im Bereich Marketing benötigen.

**Informationsveranstaltung** *f* - road show

■ Werbetechnik zur Vorstellung von Produkten und Dienstleistungen durch mobile Ausstellungen, die von einem Ort zum anderen wandern und einer vorbestimmten Route folgen. Wird vor allem bei den politischen Kampagnen benutzt, in denen der Kandidat mit sondergefertigten Fahrzeugen, die das gesamte Material transportieren, reist. Oft wird der englische Begriff verwendet.

**informative Werbung** *f* - informative advertising

■ Werbung, die grundlegende Informationen über ein Produkt vermittelt. Sie wird in der Regel in der Produkteinführungsphase eingesetzt, um aufzuklären und die Anfangsnachfrage aufzubauen, zum Beispiel um den digitalen Mobilfunk vom analogen zu differenzieren.

**informelle Kommunikation** *f* - informal communication

■ Soziale Interaktion, die über nicht offizielle Nachrichtenkanäle übertragen wird. Es handelt sich im Grunde um eine spontane Kommunikation zwischen Einzelpersonen (auch Mund-zu-Mund-Kommunikation).

**In-Game-Werbung** *f* - video game advertising

■ Werbeart, bei der Videospiele als Träger benutzt werden, indem eine Marke oder ein Produkt in den Handlungsablauf eingefügt wird. Markenhersteller haben in jüngerer Zeit ein immer größeres Interesse an der Werbung in Videospielen gezeigt, deren Zielgruppe besonders die jugendliche Bevölkerung ist.

**Inhaltsanalyse** *f* - content analysis

■ Im Marketing, System zur Analyse sämtlicher Art von Schriftstücken (z. B. Umfragen, Grafiken oder Anzeigen) mit dem Ziel, ihre Bestandteile aufzuschlüsseln und zu verstehen, um sie zwischen den Werbetreibenden zu vergleichen.

**Inkrementalanalyse** *f* - incremental analysis

■ Studien bezüglich der Zunahme des kontaktierten Publikums durch eine Kampagne, die in dem Maß der Werbeaufwendung ansteigt.

**Inline-Display** *n* - in-line display

■ Anzeigeschirm, der in den gleichen Regalen oder Gondeln angebracht wird, in denen sich das Verkaufsprodukt befindet.

**innerer Arbeitsbereich** *m* - back-office

■ Gesamtheit der personellen und materiellen Mittel, die die unmittelbar in Kontakt mit der Öffentlichkeit stehenden Aktivitäten des Unternehmens unterstützen. In einer Bank z. B. das Verwaltungspersonal und die EDV-Abteilung.

**Innovation** *f* - innovation

■ Entwicklung eines Produktes, Prozesses oder einer Dienstleistung in einer anderen, noch nicht existierenden Form.

**Inselanzeige** *f* - island display

■ Einzelanzeige, die normalerweise so groß ist, dass sie aus jeder Richtung (360°) ersichtlich bzw. zugänglich ist.

**Institutionelle Werbung** *f* - institutional advertising

■ Überzeugende Kommunikationshandlung des öffentlichen Dienstes, mit Werbeformen und -stilen, die sich auf ein Unternehmen, eine Institution, einen Verband oder eine Gruppe beziehen und die Annahme und Unterstützung dieser natürlichen oder juristischen Person durch das Publikum fördert. Im Allgemeinen wird institutionelle Werbung als Synonym zu Körperschaftswerbung verwendet, manche Autoren unterscheiden sie jedoch und identifizieren sie als überzeugende Kommunikation mit Ausrichtung auf die Öffentlichkeit, die von Öffentlichen Behörden ausgegeben wird.

**integrierte Marketingkommunikation** *f* - integrated marketing communications (IMC)

■ Integrierte Marketing- bzw. Markenkommunikation oder verkürzt Integrierte Kommunikation, im Englischen auch als Integrated Marketing Communication (IMC) bezeichnet, beschreibt die inhaltliche und/oder formale Abstimmung aller Maßnahmen der Markenkommunikation, um die durch die Kommunikation erzeugten Eindrücke zu vereinheitlichen und zu verstärken.

**integrierte Werbung** *f* - integrated commercial

■ Anzeige, die zwei oder mehr Produkte oder Dienstleistungen oder zwei oder mehr Marken des gleichen Herstellers oder verschiedener Hersteller einschließt. Ebenfalls Werbung, die in ein Programm eingeschlossen ist. Im Allgemeinen handelt es sich um Produkte, die die Darsteller des Programms tragen, benutzen oder verbrauchen und deren Markenname offensichtlich ist. Der Preis für die integrierte Werbung ist nicht im Tarif enthalten sondern wird zwischen dem Produzenten und dem Werbenden vor der Ausstrahlung ausgehandelt.

**integriertes Display** *n* - attach-to-merchandise display

■ Im Marketing, Display aus der Verpackung des angebotenen Produkts.

**Intensivvertrieb** *m* - intensive distribution

■ Vertriebspolitik durch die erreicht werden soll, dass ein bestimmtes Produkt in allen Einrichtungen verfügbar ist. Diese Politik wird bei Produkten mit hohen Konsumraten praktiziert. Häufig werden Großhändler eingesetzt, um die kleinen Läden zu erreichen.

**interaktiv** - interactive

■ Jene Werbemedien, die dem Empfänger der Werbung für die Kommunikation etwas mehr abverlangen als die Lektüre oder Anhörung. Das wohl beste aber nicht einzige interaktive Medium ist das Internet.

**interaktive Agentur** *f* - interactive agency

■ Werbeagentur, die sich auf das Angebot von Werbedienstleistungen für interaktive Medien, wie z. B. Internet, spezialisiert hat.

**interaktives Display** *n* - interactive display

■ Bildschirm, der die Teilnahme des Verbrauchers im Kaufprozess erfordert, indem dieser über eine Tastatur oder Touchscreen seine Anforderungen und Vorzüge angibt. Der Computer verarbeitet die Einträge und gibt eine Kaufempfehlung.

**Interessent** *m* - hot prospect

■ Person mit hoher Kaufwahrscheinlichkeit eines Produkts oder einer Dienstleistung, da das Interesse daran von ihm selbst erklärt wurde.

**interkulturelle Unterschiede** *m/pl* - cross-cultural differences

■ Abweichungen in den Überzeugungen, Einstellungen, Gebräuchen und Verhaltensnormen, die Bürger verschiedener Länder oder Angehörige unterschiedlicher Volksgruppen oder Gesellschaftsschichten haben.

**International Association of Advertising (IAA)** - International Association of Advertising (IAA)

■ Die IAA ist eine einzigartige, weltweite und führende Vereinigung von anerkannten Persönlichkeiten aus allen Bereichen der Marketing-Kommunikation. Die Organisation vereinigt die Repräsentanten von Werbeauftraggebern, Medienunternehmen sowie Kommunikations- und Werbeagenturen. Sie wurde 1938 gegründet und hat sich in der Zwischenzeit zur führenden, weltweiten Organisation entwickelt, die sich zu Gunsten der Konsumenten und der werbetreibenden Wirtschaft für die freie Meinungsäußerung im Bereich der kommerziellen Kommunikation einsetzt. Ihr Hauptsitz ist New York, sie ist in 95 verschiedenen Ländern aktiv.

**International Public Relations Association (IPRA)** - International Public Relations Association (IPRA)

■ Eine 1955 gegründete Organisation international tätiger PR-Fachleute mit über 650 Mitgliedern in 71 Ländern. beim Wirtschafts- und Sozialrat der Vereinten Nationen mit beratendem Status anerkannt: Generalsekretariat in London; Mitgliedersekretariat in Genf; Anschrift über die DPRG.

**internationale Betreuung** *f* - account alignment

■ Betreuung einer Marke durch ein und dieselbe Agentur in mehreren oder allen Ländern.

**internationale Werbeagentur** *f* - international advertising agency

■ Werbeagentur, die in mehreren Ländern aktiv ist. Die Internationalisierung der Agenturen begann in den 20er Jahren des vergangenen Jahrhunderts in den USA und hat sich bis heute progressiv weiterentwickelt. Baut multinationale Kunden auf.

**internationale Werbung** *f* - international advertising

■ Als internationale Werbung bezeichnet man Werbemittel (Anzeigen, Werbespots, Plakate, Funkspots), die in mehreren Ländern eingesetzt werden, wobei sie auf die Eigenarten der Empfänger mehr oder weniger zugeschnitten sind.

**internationaler ECHO-Award** *m* - International ECHO Awards

■ Auszeichnung, die jährlich von der Direct Marketing Association (DMA) an die besten Werbekampagnen verliehen wird.

**Internationaler Kongress- und Tagungsverband** *m* **(ICCA)** - International Congress and Conventions Association (ICCA)

■ Internationaler Branchenverband für die Kongress- und Meeting-Industrie, 1963 gegründet. Der ICCA ist der einzige Verband, dessen Mitglieder aus den wichtigsten Leistungsträgern der Bereiche Veranstaltungsplanung und -durchführung, Transport und Beherbergung kommen. Die Internationalität der Organisation zeigt sich vor allem darin, dass die rund 850 Mitglieder aus über 80 Ländern kommen. Der Hauptsitz des ICCA ist Amsterdam, Niederlande, regionale Vertretungen gibt es in Asien, Nord- und Südamerika.

**Internationaler Verband** *m* **für Geschäftskommunikation (IABC)** - International Association of Business Communicators (IABC)

■ Globales Netz von Kommunikationsexperten, die sich dafür engagieren, Unternehmenseffizienz durch strategische Kommunikation zu verbessern. Der

IABC wurde 1970 gegründet und bedient über 13.500 Mitglieder in 67 Ländern, 100 regionale Verbände und 10.000 Unternehmen.

**internationales Marketing** *n* - international marketing

■ Beinhaltet die Planung, Koordination und Kontrolle aller auf ausländische Märkte ausgerichteten Marketing-Aktivitäten insbesondere im Hinblick auf unterschiedliche Anforderungen, Bedürfnisse und Gepflogenheiten der Kunden. Spielt bei der heutigen Globalisierung eine immer größere Rolle.

**interne Validierung** *f* - internal validity

■ In der Industrieforschung, Vergleich der erhaltenen Information mit vorher angenommenen Daten zur Plausibilitätsprüfung. Bei einer Diskrepanz muss der Fehler gesucht werden, um zu sehen, welche Informationen geändert werden müssen.

**interner Referenzpreis** *m* - internal reference price

■ Preis, der aufgrund von Erfahrungen oder Erwartungen im Gedächtnis des Kunden gespeichert ist und bei Kaufentscheidungen mit dem vorliegenden Preis verglichen wird.

**internes Marketing** *n* - internal marketing

■ Umfasst die Anwendung von Marketingaktivitäten auf interne Zielgruppen zur gezielten Bedürfnisbefriedigung von Mitarbeitern und die innerbetriebliche Umsetzung von extern ausgerichteten Marketingkonzepten. Internes Marketing will also einerseits eine stärkere Mitarbeiterorientierung im Unternehmen erreichen und andererseits eine gezielte Verhaltensbeeinflussung bei den Mitarbeitern zur effizienten und effektiven Umsetzung von absatzmarktbezogenen Marketingkonzepten vornehmen. Damit handelt es sich um eine Schnittstelle zwischen Personal-, Organisations- und Marketingmanagement.

**Internetwerbung** *f* - Internet advertising

■ Unter Internetwerbung wird Werbung verstanden, die in unterschiedlichen Formen über das Medium Internet verbreitet wird.

**Interruption-Marketing** *n* - interruption marketing

■ Traditionelles Verfahren, bei dem die ausgesandte Werbebotschaft den Empfänger bei einer anderen Tätigkeit unterbricht und seine Aufmerksamkeit auf die angebotenen Produkte oder Dienstleistungen richtet (z. B. TV-Werbung, Anzeigen in einer Zeitschrift oder einer Tageszeitung, Werbung im Posteingang). Diese traditionelle Methode ist im Gegensatz zum Permission-Marketing zu verstehen, das derzeit häufigeren Einsatz findet.

**Investitionsgütermarketing** *n* - business-to-business marketing

■ Verkauf von Waren und Dienstleistungen, bei dem der Endkunde ein anderes Unternehmen oder die öffentliche Hand ist. Der Anteil der verschiedenen Marketingwerkzeuge ist anders als beim Verkauf von Konsumgütern. So sind z. B. die persönlichen Beziehungen und der direkte Verkauf selbst komplexer und die Werbung basiert mehr auf Fachzeitschriften.

**Inzidenz** *f* - incidence

■ In der Marktforschung, Häufigkeit, mit der ein Ereignis in einem Kollektiv auftritt. Anteil einer Bevölkerung, die in eine Gruppe einbezogen wird, wenn bestimmte Auswahlkriterien benutzt werden. Stark beschränkten Auswahlkriterien führen zu kleinen und homogenen Gruppen, während breit gefasste zu großen heterogenen Gruppen führen.

**irreführende Werbung** *f* - misleading advertising

■ Jede Werbung muss klar und wahr sein, da nach dem Gesetz gegen den unlauteren Wettbewerb (UWG) irreführende Werbung verboten ist. Allgemein unzulässig sind danach unwahre Aussagen bzw. bildliche Darstellungen, wahre Aussagen bzw. bildliche Darstellungen, sofern sie von den Angesprochenen falsch verstanden werden sowie unvollständige Angaben, wenn es sich um Angaben handelt, die für den Kaufentschluss erforderlich sind (z. B. das Verschweigen, dass es sich um ein Auslaufmodell oder eine Ware zweiter Wahl handelt). Maßgebend ist dabei jeweils der Eindruck, den die Werbung beim Publikum erweckt.

**isolierte Anzeige** *f* - isolated advertisement

■ Anzeige, zu einem höheren Tarif, die dem Inserenten garantiert, dass sich neben seiner Anzeige keine weitere befinden wird.

# J

**Jahresbericht** *m* - annual report

■ Firmendokument, das jährlich veröffentlicht wird und in dem über die Finanzlage des Unternehmens sowie über die Projekte in den letzten Geschäftsjahren informiert wird.

**Johnson-Box** *f* - Johnson box

■ Hierbei handelt es sich um eine spezielle Darstellungstechnik auf Werbebriefen. Dabei wird in knappen Worten und durch ein Kästchen (Box) eingerahmt auf den wesentlichen Punkt des Briefes hingewiesen. Die Box ist dabei so platziert, dass sie beim Öffnen des Mailings ins Auge springt. Name nach dem Erfinder des Konzepts.

**Jugendbanden** *f* - urban tribes

■ Gruppen von Jugendlichen, die sich um äußerliche Symbole (zum Beispiel Haarschnitt und Kleidung, Fahrzeuge, Musik) oder verschwommene ideologische Konzepte sammeln.

**just-in-time** - just in time

■ Produktions- und Lagerhaltungssystem, das immer an der unteren Bedarfsgrenze operiert, in dem es den Bedarf genau plant und eine zielgenaue Belieferung durch die Lieferanten anstrebt. Diese können mehrere Male am gleichen Tag anliefern, da sie ihrerseits nach dem gleichen System arbeiten, denn falls sie von einem Zentrallager aus liefern würden, würden keine großen finanziellen Einsparungen erzielt. Die Ware trifft genau in dem Moment und genau an dem Ort ein, an dem sie anschließend verarbeitet wird.

# K

**Kampagne** *f* **zur öffentlichen Orientierung** - public orientation campaign

■ Überzeugende Kommunikation mit Werbeformen und -stil, die hauptsächlich von öffentlichen Behörden über die Massenmedien ausgegeben werden und Anweisungen und Vorgaben für die Öffentlichkeit in Bezug auf Probleme des allgemeinen Interesses geben (z. B. Gesundheitsfragen usw.).

**Kampagnenlaufzeit** *f* - posting period

■ Zeit, in der die Anzeigen einer Werbekampagne publiziert werden sollten. Flexible Kampagnendauer und Buchung von Wochen und sogar Tagen ist möglich.

**Kampagnenplan** *m* - campaign plan

■ Schriftliche Darlegung der Werbeziele und der einzusetzenden Medien. Obwohl er theoretisch Teil eines globalen Kommunikationsplans sein sollte, kann er wegen seiner Bedeutung und der notwendigen kurzfristigen Anpassungen ein unabhängiger Plan sein. Unter anderem befasst er sich mit der Strategie, den Werbezielen, der Personalität und dem gewünschten Erinnerungswert der Marke, der Zielgruppe, dem Inhalt der Botschaft und dem Mediaplan. Entspricht dem Werbeplan.

**Kannibalisierung** *f* - cannibalisation

■ Entwicklung einer Marke auf Kosten der Werbung einer anderen. Wenn das Budget für eine Marke zu gering ist oder die Werbebotschaft der einer bereits etablierten Marke sehr ähnlich ist, dann entsteht beim Verbraucher die Erinnerung oder der Eindruck, die Werbung der etablierten Marke gesehen zu haben.

**Kapazität** *f* - capacity

▪ In der Produktion versteht man hierunter das Arbeitsvolumen, das von einer bestimmten Anlage oder einem Werk unter normalen Bedingungen und mit spezifischer Technologie und Organisation geleistet werden kann. Die maximale theoretische Kapazität kalkuliert keine Ausfälle, Wartungen oder andere Probleme ein. Je nach der tatsächlich Einsatzzeit, unterscheidet man zwischen genutzter und ungenutzter Kapazität.

**Kartell** *n* - cartel

▪ Abkommen zwischen juristisch selbständigen Unternehmen desselben Sektors, mit dem Ziel, durch Preis- und Produktionsregulierungen den gegenseitigen Wettbewerb zu reduzieren.

**Kassenartikel** *m* - check-out product

▪ Produkt, das in einem Regal nahe der Kasse in einem Geschäft ausliegt. Artikel, die durch Impulskäufe erworben werden, z. B. Batterien, Süßigkeiten oder Zeitungen. Diese Platzierung erscheint strategisch interessant, weil der Kunde während er in der Schlange steht die ausgestellten Artikel betrachten und sich zum Kauf entscheiden kann.

**Kassenterminal** *n* - point of sale terminal

▪ Spezialisiertes Terminal eines Informatiksystems von dem aus Finanztransaktionen ausgeführt werden. Zum Beispiel die Kassenterminals der Ladengeschäfte und die Bargeldautomaten der Banken.

**Kassenzone** *f* - front-end

▪ Ort, an dem die Produkte des Impulskaufs positioniert werden, die meist eine hohe Rentabilität bringen.

**Katalog** *m* - catalogue

▪ Gedruckte Liste der zum Verkauf angebotenen Produkte und ihrer Eigenschaften. Die Liste enthält in aller Regel Fotografien oder Abbildungen und die allgemeinen Verkaufsbedingungen. Wenn sie direkt für den Endverbraucher bestimmt ist, enthält sie Preise, während beim Verkauf an den Großhändler oder an die Industrie meist eine getrennte Preisliste vorliegt.

**Katalogkauf** *m* - catalogue buying

▪ Kauf, bei dem die gewünschten Waren in einem Katalog ausgewählt werden und per Telefon, Post oder bei einem Vertreter, welcher die Kunden regelmäßig besucht, bestellt werden. Die Hinweise, die auf dem Bestellschein enthalten sein müssen, sind die Referenznummer des Produkts, die Menge, die Größe (in bestimmten Fällen), der Preis und der Gesamtbetrag einschließlich eines möglichen Rabatts und der Versandkosten. Die Waren können an speziellen Auslieferungsstellen abgeholt werden oder werden direkt nach hause geliefert.

**Katalogverkauf** *m* - catalogue sales

▪ Verkauf, bei dem der Käufer seine Auswahl anhand eines Kataloges trifft, in dem Fotos, vollständige Beschreibungen und Preise der Produkte erscheinen. Der Katalog wird per Post an die Altkunden versandt oder kann an Kiosken erworben werden. Die Bestellung kann per Post, Telefon oder persönlich vorgenommen werden. Der Kunde erhält die Ware in der Regel per Post, Transportunternehmen, oder er holt sie selbst ab.

**Kaufabsicht** *f* - purchase intention

▪ Der Kaufentscheidung vorangehende Phase, in der die unterschiedlichen Faktoren, die in die endgültige Kaufentscheidung mit eingehen, noch nicht abgewogen wurden. Jedoch ist bereits die Bereitschaft dazu vorhanden, ein Bedürfnis in einer bestimmten Form zu befriedigen. Die Messung des prozentualen Anteils in der Bevölkerung, der sich in dieser Phase befindet und der Stärke seiner Kaufabsicht, ermöglicht den sinnvollen, zielgerichteten Einsatz von Marketingmaßnahmen. Bei Verbrauchsgütern unterscheidet man zusätzlich zwischen der Bereitschaft zum Probekauf und zum Wiederkauf.

**Kaufabsichtsbefragung** *f* - buyer intention survey

▪ Umfrage zur Untersuchung der Annahme seitens der Verbraucher eines für gewöhnlich neuen, Produktes sowie der Motive für Kauf oder Ablehnung und des Preises, zu dem das Produkt angeboten werden sollte.

**Kaufauftrag** *m* - purchase order

■ Formeller Auftrag des möglichen Käufers eine bestimmte Ware zu erwerben, in einer Menge und zu einem Preis und unter Bedingungen, die in einem Dokument näher bestimmt sind. Mit der Annahme durch den Verkäufer wird der Vertrag rechtlich wirksam. In der Praxis ist es häufig so, dass der Käufer die allgemeinen Geschäftsbedingungen (AGB) des Verkäufers akzeptiert und ein Bestellformular einschickt, um so Auffüllbestellungen zu erleichtern.

**Kaufbereitschaftsphase** *f* - buyer-readiness stage

■ Zeitabschnitt, der die Entwicklung der Reaktion des Verbrauchers auf die Existenz eines Produkts misst. Die Phase kann von der völligen Unkenntnis der Existenz des Produkts bis zur endgültigen Kaufentscheidung reichen.

**Käufermarkt** *m* - buyer's market

■ Markt, in dem die Wechselbeziehungen von der Käuferseite beherrscht sind, da das Angebot größer als die Nachfrage ist.

**Kaufhäufigkeit** *f* - buying frequency

■ Durchschnittliche Anzahl der innerhalb einer Periode erfolgten Käufe. Diese Zahl verhält sich invers zum Kaufumfang und den notwendigen Kaufanstrengungen, z. B. kann man in einem Laden um die Ecke täglich einkaufen, während man in einem Supermarkt oder Großmarkt nur zwei oder drei Mal in der Woche bzw. im Monat kaufen würde.

**Kaufkraft** *f* - purchasing power

■ Fähigkeit zum Erwerb einer bestimmten Menge an Waren und Dienstleitungen mit einer bestimmten Geldmenge. Die Kaufkraft nimmt mit Steigen der Inflation und der Lebenshaltungskosten ab.

**Kaufkraftverlust** *m* - loss of purchasing power

■ Bei einer Währung, Verringerung der realen Kapazität zum Erwerb von Gütern, hervorgerufen durch Inflation oder Wechselkursänderungen. Wert zu einem Zeitpunkt verglichen mit dem Wert der selben oder einer anderen Währung zu einem anderen Zeitpunkt.

**Kaufpreis** *m* - purchase price

■ Preis, den der Käufer an den Verkäufer zahlt. Abzuziehen sind die Rechnungsnachlässe, aber nicht die variable Rückvergütung. Obwohl es in der Praxis üblich ist, darf bei der Berechnung des Selbstkostenpreises der Rabatt für frühzeitige Zahlung (Skonto) nicht abgezogen werden, da dies eine Finanzierungs- und keine kommerzielle Entscheidung ist.

**Kaufvertrag** *m* - sales contract

■ Vertrag, durch den sich eine Person (Verkäufer) verpflichtet, eine Sache an eine andere Person (Käufer) zu übergeben, die sich wiederum dazu verpflichtet, einen festgelegten Preis in Form von Geld oder einer anderen Form, die diesen Wert darstellt, zu bezahlen.

**KB** *m* **(Kundenbetreuer)** - AE (account executive)

■ Person, die für die gesamten Beziehungen eines Unternehmens mit einem bestimmten Kunden oder einer Gruppe von Kunden verantwortlich ist. Wird speziell in der Dienstleistungsbranche verwendet.

**KBM** *n* **(Kundenbeziehungsmanagement)** - CRM (Customer Relationship Management)

■ Firmenphilosophie mit einer integralen Vision des Kunden, um diesen kennenzulernen, seine Bedürfnisse zu erkennen und diese vorausgreifend zu decken, noch bevor der Kunde selbst sich über seinen Bedarf bewusst ist. Gesamtheit von Aktivitäten, die von den Abteilungen für Werbung, Verkauf, Kundendienst und Verkaufsförderung hauptsächlich dazu entwickelt werden, um Kunden zu binden, den Kontakt mit den Kunden zu verbessern und Gelegenheiten effizienter nutzen zu können, z. B. im Fall von Kreuzverkäufen und Markteinführungen neuer Produkte. Es werden alle zwischen dem Unternehmen und seinen bestehenden oder potentiellen Kunden betriebene Aktivitäten mit operativen und analytischen Zielsetzungen behandelt.

**Key Performance Indicator** *m* **(KPI) -** Key Performance Indicator (KPI)

■ Key Performance Indicator (KPI) bezeichnet in der Betriebswirtschaftslehre Kennzahlen, anhand derer der Fortschritt oder der Erfüllungsgrad hinsichtlich wichtiger Zielsetzungen oder kritischer Erfolgsfaktoren innerhalb einer Organisation gemessen werden kann.

**Kinowerbung** *f* **-** film commercial

■ Audiovisuelle Werbemitteilung, die über das Medium Kino verbreitet wird. Aufgrund der technischen und erzählerischen Qualität vieler dieser Mitteilungen werden dies auch Werbefilme genannt.

**KITI (kennwortintegrierte Texteingabe) -** KITI (Keyword integrated text insertion)

■ Patentierte Technologie, mit der erreicht werden soll, dass der Kunde an erster Stelle in den Suchmaschinen steht. Das Kundenmotto wird blau angezeigt und ist direkt mit seiner Webseite verknüpft. Da die Anzeige eher als Information denn als Werbung angesehen wird, zeigt sie einen starken Erfolg.

**Klappentext** *m* **-** blurb

■ Kurze positive Nachricht über ein Unternehmen oder seine Produkte, die im redaktionellen Teil eines Kommunikationsmediums erscheint. Wurde ursprünglich nur für die Kurzbeschreibung eines Buches zu Werbezwecken seitens des Verlags verwendet, wobei der Text gewöhnlich auf der Umschlagsklappe abgedruckt ist.

**Klatsch** *m* **-** gossip

■ Nachricht oder Gerücht, das nicht unbedingt falsch ist, das man aber dazu benutzt, dem Ansehen einer Person oder einer Marke zu schaden.

**Kleinanzeige** *f* **-** classified ads

■ In den täglich erscheinenden Medien versteht man hierunter die Anzeigen, die nach Themen in Gruppen eingeteilt sind. Sie sind meist klein im Format und haben Sonderpreise. Zusammengefasst bilden sie in vielen Tageszeitungen einen separaten Bereich. Werden auch als Kurzanzeigen und Billiganzeigen bezeichnet.

**Klickrate** *f* **-** click through rate

■ Durchschnittliche Effektivität eines interaktiven Werbeplakats oder Banners, die in Prozent angegeben wird. Der Wert wird errechnet, indem man die Anzahl der Personen, die die Seite, auf der das Banner steht, aufgerufen haben durch die Anzahl der tatsächlichen Klicks auf die Anzeige teilt.

**Klickstream** *m* **-** click stream

■ In der Internetwerbung versteht man hierunter das Erfassen der in chronologischer Reihenfolge besuchten Internetseiten, die der Nutzer einer Website während eines Besuchs aufgerufen hat. Dies ermöglicht eine äußerst genaue Untersuchung der Vorlieben des Nutzers und eine Optimierung der Darstellung und Strukturen der besuchten Seite.

**Klumpenstichprobe** *f* **-** cluster sampling

■ Zufälliges Auswahlverfahren, bei dem die Bevölkerung in vollständige und sich gegenseitig ausschließende Gruppen (ohne Auslassungen oder Überschneidungen) unterteilt wird. Man wählt zufällig eine Stichprobe aus diesen Gruppen aus (es ist keine Stichprobe aus allen Gruppen) oder man benützt alle Elemente einer Gruppe (einstufiges Bündel) oder man entnimmt ein Zufallsmuster aus allen ausgewählten Gruppen (zweistufiges Bündel). Jede Gruppe muss eine reduzierte Reproduktion der Gesamtbevölkerung darstellen und deshalb möglichst umfangreich sein, was die Auswahl nur einiger weniger Gruppen erlaubt. Obwohl statistisch gesehen weniger effizient, hat diese Methode geringere Erhebungskosten und ist besser zu kontrollieren. Die Klumpenstichprobe kann systematisch oder gruppiert sein und wird auch als Mischprobenentnahme oder Gruppenstichprobe bezeichnet.

**kodierte Anzeige** *f* - coded advertisement

■ Anzeige oder Antwortcoupon, mit einem Code, der es ermöglicht, seine Herkunft festzustellen (z. B. die Zeitung, in der eine Stellenanzeige erschien), um die Effektivität jedes Mediums zu messen oder Reaktionen bessern einstufen zu können.

**Kohortenanalyse** *f* - cohort analysis

■ Systematische Untersuchung einer bestimmten Personengruppe, die sich durch Ähnlichkeit in demographischen, sozialen oder wirtschaftlichen Merkmalen auszeichnet. Dabei werden die Verhaltensweise der Gruppe und Ereignisse in der Gruppe während eines begrenzten Zeitraums definiert und verglichen.

**kombinierte Absatzförderung** *f* - cross merchandising

■ Werbestrategie, die darin besteht, den Verkauf eines Produkts auf andere Produkte derselben Firma zu stützen, die in derselben Verkaufsstelle ausliegen. Auf diese Weise soll erreicht werden, dass sich die Aufmerksamkeit des Käufers nicht nur auf das bereits bekannt Produkt, sondern auch auf das nebenliegende neue Produkt richtet.

**Kommandoverkauf** *m* - commando selling

■ Aktion einer verstärkten oder spezialisierten Außendienstabteilung zu Zwecken der Marktpflege und Erschließung neuer Märkte. Für diese Aufgabe erweitert das Unternehmen die Abteilung oder stellt eine spezielle Verkaufsmannschaft ein. Manchmal begleiten die Verkäufer des Herstellerunternehmens diejenigen des Großhändlers, um diese zu motivieren, im Produktverkauf zu unterweisen und um sich einer guten Einführung des Produkts bei den Kunden zu versichern.

**kommerzielle Werbung** *f* - commercial advertising

■ Werbeaktivität, die auf kommerzielle Zwecke ausgerichtet ist, um sowohl das Vorhandensein als auch den Nutzen verschiedener Produktklassen oder Dienstleistungstypen mitzuteilen. Nimmt derzeit die größte Werbefläche bzw. die meiste Werbezeit in Anspruch.

**kommerzielle Werbung** *f* - lucrative advertisement

■ Werbenachricht, deren Ziel die Zufriedenstellung eines kommerziellen Zwecks ist. Sender sind meist Firmen oder Unternehmen, die ihre Produkte oder Dienstleistung oder ihr Image fördern möchten.

**Kommunikationsberater** *m* - communication consultant

■ Selbständiger Fachmann oder Unternehmen im Kommunikationsbereich, dessen Aufgabe darin besteht, seinen Kunden zu informieren, zu beraten und ihm bei der Bearbeitung von kommunikationstechnischen Aktivitäten zu helfen, die zur Schaffung oder Festigung eines positiven Image beitragen können.

**Kommunikationsberatung** *f* - communication advising

■ Unternehmen, das andere Unternehmen in Bezug auf Fragen des Kommunikationsplans informiert und berät und hierbei beispielsweise bei der Umsetzung und Bearbeitung der internen und externen Kommunikation, der Wahl der angemessenen Kommunikationsmedien, beim Sponsoring, usw. Hilfestellung bietet. Kurz gesagt, bei all den kommunikativen Aktivitäten, von denen das Unternehmensimage beeinflusst wird.

**Kommunikationsmix** *m* - communication mix

■ Gesamtmenge der Kommunikationsmedien, die von einem Werbetreibenden eingesetzt werden, um eine Zielgruppe mit einer bestimmten Werbekampagne zu erreichen.

**Kommunikationsplan** *m* - communication plan

■ Projekt, das die Kommunikationsziele eines Unternehmens sowie die Strategien zur Erlangung dieser Ziele und zur Lösung von eventuell intern auftretenden kommunikationstechnischen Problemen enthält.

**Kommunikationsziel** *n* - communication objective
■ Zweck, der mit einer Botschaft oder Kampagne verfolgt wird, sei es im Bereich der Werbung, der Öffentlichkeitsarbeit, der Verkaufsförderung oder der Packungsbeschriftung. Das was man zusammen mit den Wahrnehmungswerten und Erinnerungswerten erreichen will.

**Komplementärprodukt** *n* - complementary good
■ Ein Artikel, der zur Benutzung eines anderen Artikels benötigt wird. Im Handel wird oft ein Artikel mit einer größeren Spanne einem Artikel, der zu einem Aktionspreis angeboten wird, zugeordnet (z. B. Mayonnaise und Spargel).

**Komplettservice-Werbeagentur** *f* - full-service agency
■ Werbeagentur, die auf alle Arten von Kommunikationsmaßnahmen spezialsiert ist und die komplette Dienstleistungspalette anbietet, die Marktforschung, Mediabuchung und auch einfache Produktionen einschließt; außer den gewöhnlicheren Leistungen wie Gestaltung und Kundenbetreuung.

**Konjunkturschwankung** *f* - cyclical fluctuation
■ Preisschwankungen und Schwankungen in den Verkaufszahlen eines Produktes, die durch Veränderungen im Wirtschaftskreislauf begründet sind. Zum Beispiel schwanken die langfristigen Zinsen auf eine bestimmte Art und Weise beim Übergang von der Hochkonjunktur zur Rezession.

**Konkurrent** *m* - competitor
■ Unternehmen, Einzelperson oder Produkt mit ähnlichen Merkmalen, dessen Ziel die Bedürfnisbefriedigung derselben oder in Verbindung stehender Zielgruppen ist.

**Konkurrenz** *f* - competition
■ Gesamtheit von Unternehmen, die denselben Markt bedienen oder dieselbe Dienstleistung zur Verfügung stellen, und dieselben potentiellen Kunden erreichen wollen.

**Konkurrenzanalyse** *f* - competitive analysis
■ Untersuchung der Mitbewerber eines Unternehmens oder der Konkurrenzsituation in einem Sektor. Dabei werden unter anderem Marktanteile und Wachstumsraten nach Segmenten, Stärken, Schwächen, Chancen und Bedrohungen der Konkurrenten, Verhandlungsmacht gegenüber Zulieferern und Kunden sowie Markteintritte und -abgänge untersucht.

**konkurrenzfreier Markt** *m* - captive market
■ Monopolistische Situation des Marktes, in welcher der Käufer das ihm angebotene Produkt nicht ablehnen kann (z. B. Verkauf eines Zwischenprodukts an eine Tochtergesellschaft).

**Konsumeinheit** *f* - spending unit
■ Bezeichnung in der Statistik für einen Haushalt, eine Einzelperson oder Gruppe von Personen, die gemeinsam über die Verwendung ihrer Einnahmen für den Konsum entscheiden.

**Konsumentenprofil** *n* - consumer profile
■ Menge demografischer, sozialer und persönlichkeitsbezogener Merkmale, welche die Käufer einer Marke, die Kunden eines Geschäfts oder die Nutzer einer Dienstleistung kennzeichnet. Das Profil erhält man mittels der Verbraucherforschung, es dient zur Zielgruppenbestimmung.

**Konsumentenverhalten** *n* - consumer behaviour
■ Art, wie die Verbraucher Waren und Dienstleistungen bewerten, auswählen, kaufen und konsumieren.

**Konsumgut** *n* - consumer good
■ Gut oder Dienstleistung, die direkt vom Endverbraucher gekauft und benutzt werden und keines Umwandlungs- oder Bearbeitungsprozesses bedürfen. Es kann sich hierbei um Gebrauchsgüter und Verbrauchsgüter handeln. Synonym von Produkt.

**Konsumtendenz** *f* - propensity to consume
■ Bereitschaft, in einer Volkswirtschaft, den Hauptteil des verfügbaren

Einkommens für Konsum auszugeben, statt zu sparen. Werbeziel ist die Erhöhung der Konsumtendenz für eine bestimmte Marke.

**Kontaktbefragung** *f* - survey by contact

▪ Form der Befragung, bei der der Befragende in direkten Kontakt mit einer Person tritt, die der zu untersuchen Gruppe angehört und sie Fragen eines Fragenbogens beantworten lässt. Der Kontakt findet normalerweise in einer direkten Unterredung statt, entweder durch systematische Stichprobenauswahl mit genau festgelegter Vorgehensweise und bei der Person zu Hause, oder aber mit Personen, die zufällig an einem bestimmten Punkt vorbeilaufen. Der Kontakt kann auch per Post oder Telefon zustande kommen.

**kontinuierliche Lagerauffüllung** *f* - replenishment

▪ Bestellsystem, bei dem eine Organisation Langzeitlieferungen erhält. Durch die verkaufsgesteuerte Lagerauffüllung werden Kosten der Lieferkette eingespart, die dem Produkt keinen Wert bringen. Auch kontinuierliche Warenversorgung oder Dauernachschub.

**kontinuierliche Warenversorgung** *f* - Continuous Replenishment (CRP)

▪ System der Warenversorgung, bei dem der Zulieferer die Produkte ohne Störungen oder Verzögerungen an den Kunden liefert und den Herstellungsprozess an den Rhythmus der vom Kunden aufgegebenen Bestellungen angleicht. Auf diese Weise können die Lagerbestände und somit auch die Instandhaltungskosten des Bestands reduziert werden.

**Kontrollfrage** *f* - control question

▪ Frage in einem Fragebogen, deren Beantwortung die Überprüfung der Gültigkeit und ernsthaften Beanwortung der übrigen Antworten ermöglicht.

**Kontrollgruppe** *f* - control group

▪ Gruppe von Personen, die einer anderen Gruppe ähnlich ist, die tatsächlich einem bestimmten Stimulus ausgesetzt wird, sie dient als Referenzelement dient, um die Unterschiede zu bewerten und den Placeboeffekt zu kompensieren.

**kontrollierte Verbreitung** *f* - audited circulation

▪ Verbreitung einer Zeitung, die der Kontrolle einer unabhängigen Organisation unterliegt.

**kontrollierter Testmarkt** *m* - controlled test market

▪ Marktforschung, die darin besteht, einen Teil des Marktes abzugrenzen (eine Region, eine Stadt, eine Verkaufsstelle), um in diesem Segment einen Test zur Überprüfung einer Hypothese durchzuführen. Alle in diesem Segment existierenden Variablen werden einer Kontrolle unterzogen, um den Einfluss der einzelnen Variablen auf das Endergebnis zu überprüfen.

**konzentriertes Marketing** *n* - concentrated marketing

▪ Marketing, das sich auf ein Segment innerhalb des Gesamtmarkts konzentriert und versucht, in diesem einen hohen Marktanteil und Expertenruf zu erreichen. Diese Strategie ist zwar weniger flexibel und auf lange Sicht riskanter, kann jedoch dann empfehlenswert sein, wenn das Unternehmen nur über geringe Mittel verfügt und die vorhandenen Ressourcen für das gewählte Segment am besten geeignet sind oder es dort weniger Konkurrenz gibt.

**konzentrische Diversifikation** *f* - concentric diversification

▪ Diversifizierung, wobei ein neues Produkt, das über Synergieeffekte im technologischen Bereich oder im Bereich der Absatzwirtschaft verfügt, auf neue Zielgruppen ausgerichtet wird.

**Konzepttest** *m* - concept test

▪ Test, der untersuchen soll, wie ein neues Produkt oder eine Idee im Markt angenommen wird. In Produktentwicklungsverfahren werden Konzepttests eingesetzt, um potentielle neue Produktideen vor Herstellung eines

Prototyps zu überprüfen. Ebenso dienen diese Tests dazu, den Wirkungsgrad von Werbekampagnen einschätzen zu können.

**kooperative Werbung** *f* - cooperative advertising

■ Werbung, die gemeinsam von zwei oder mehr Firmen betrieben und finanziert wird, in der Regel von einem Konsumartikelhersteller und seinem Verteiler innerhalb eines bestimmten geografischen Gebiets. Von dieser kooperativen Werbeform profitieren in aller Regel beide Teilnehmer, da hierbei das Angebot des Herstellers einem bestimmten Zielpublikum präsentiert wird, während der Bekanntheitsgrad des Verteilers in Verbindung mit dem Markenimage wächst. Im Fall von Filmwerbung wird diese Werbeform gemeinschaftlich vom Verteiler und vom Aussteller finanziert.

**kooperatives Marketing** *n* - cooperative marketing

■ Werbeaktion, die von zwei oder mehr, einem Distributionskanal zugehörigen Organisationen betrieben wird. Man spricht von horizontaler Zusammenarbeit, wenn die kooperierenden Unternehmen demselben Niveau oder derselben Stufe des Kanals angehören. Bei der vertikalen Zusammenarbeit gehören die Mitglieder des Distributionskanals verschiedenen Ebenen an.

**Kopie** *f* - clone

■ Produkt, das die gleichen Leistungen wie ein anderes bekannteres bietet. Es wird gewöhnlich billiger verkauft und kann sogar noch leistungsfähiger sein. Es ist legal, solange nicht gegen ein Patent verstoßen wird. Tritt häufig in der Computerbranche auf.

**Körpersprache** *f* - body language

■ Form der nonverbalen Kommunikation, die zum Teil unbewusst erfolgt und auf Gesten oder Körperhaltung beruht. Gerade bei Auslandsreisen ist es wichtig, die Bedeutung verschiedener Gesten richtig deuten zu können, um eventuell peinlichen Situationen vorzubeugen.

**Kostenabsorption** *f* - absorption costing

■ Bestimmung der Stückkosten eines Produkts einschließlich der variablen und semivariablen Kosten und Ermittlung des Anteils an den Gesamtkosten (Struktur- oder Fixkosten und sonstige indirekte Kosten) auf Grund geeigneter Kriterien. Eine Tätigkeit oder der Verkauf eines Produkts absorbiert Fixkosten, wenn der Verkaufspreis über den variablen Kosten liegt. Diese Differenz wird als Deckungsbeitrag bezeichnet, da sie zur Deckung der Fixkosten des Unternehmens beiträgt.

**Kostendeckungspunkt** *m* - break-even point

■ Produktions- oder Verkaufsmenge, bei der die Einnahmen gleich den gesamten mit Herstellung und Vertrieb verbundenen Kosten sind. Da in jedem Prozess fixe und variable Kosten auftreten, erhält man die Gewinnschwelle, indem man die Fixkosten des Unternehmens durch den durchschnittlichen Stückdeckungsbeitrag teilt.

**Kosteneffekt** *m* - expenditure effect

■ Effekt, nach dem die Verbraucher eine höhere Preisempfindlichkeit zeigen, wenn der Kostenanteil im Vergleich zum monatlich verfügbaren Betrag hoch ist.

**kostenlose Probe** *f* - free trial

■ Werbeangebot, in dem ein Kunde das Produkt oder den Dienst ohne Verkaufszusage seinerseits für einen bestimmten Zeitraum ausprobieren kann.

**Kostprobe** *f* - tasting

■ Werbeaktivität, bei der man Lebensmittel oder Getränke zum Probieren anbietet. Dies kann zwischen den Verkaufsregalen oder direkt in der Fabrik oder Weinkellerei stattfinden.

**Kreativabteilung** *f* - creative department

■ Abteilung einer Werbeagentur, in der das Kreativpersonal arbeitet, das sich aus den Kreativdirektoren, Redakteuren, Art-Direktoren und Produzenten verschiedener Medien zusammensetzt. Organisatorisch ist sie in Kreativteams mit je einem Redakteur und einem

Art-Direktor aufgeteilt, die einem Kreativdirektor unterstehen. Die Teams sind in die Kontenabteilung integriert, dem das Führungspersonal und das Medienpersonal zugeordnet sind.

**Kreativagentur** *f* - creative advertising agency

■ Werbeunternehmen, das sich auf Kreativdienstleistungen im Marketingbereich insbesondere für herkömmliche Medien spezialisiert. Kreative Werbeagenturen gab es bereits in den siebziger Jahren des 20. Jahrhunderts. Vorreiter der so genannten Kreativboutiquen war die von den Brüdern Charles und Maurice Saatchi gegründete Saatchi & Saatchi.

**Kreativdirektor** *m* - executive creative director

■ Person, die die Kreativabteilung leitet, die zusammen mit Kundenbetreuung (Accounts), Produktion, Medienkauf und Verwaltung eine Werbeagentur bildet. Je nach der Agentur kann er einen ähnlichen Verantwortungsbereich wie der Art-Director haben und die Texter und Designer führen.

**Kreativteam** *n* - creative team

■ Struktur oder Basiszelle des Kreativprozesses in der Werbung, die aus dem Redakteur und dem Art-Direktor besteht. Beide befassen sich mit dem Konzept und der Ausarbeitung aller Werbe- und Verkaufsförderungsmaterialien für den Inserenten, und zwar sowohl in Form von vollständigen Kampagnen als auch individuellen Anzeigen für verschiedene Medien. Jedes Team führt eine oder mehrere Kundenkonten.

**Kreuzverkauf** *m* - cross sell

■ Telefonisch eingesetzte Marketingtechnik, die darin besteht, dem anrufenden Interessenten ein Produkt zu verkaufen, zusätzlich zu einem angebotenen Artikel, der das ursprüngliche Interesse des Kunden oder potentiellen Käufers geweckt hat.

**kriegerisches Marketing** *n* - warfare marketing

■ Anwendung der Prinzipien von Militärstrategien und -taktiken auf das Marketing.

**Kriterium** *n* - criterion

■ Aspekt, Meinung oder Regel das man verwendet, um sich für eine bestimmte Vorgehensweise zu entscheiden.

**Kunde** *m* - account

■ In der Werbung und im Dienstleistungssektor, Gesamtheit aller Kunden, Unternehmen oder Produkte, mit denen man arbeitet.

**Kunde** *m* - client

■ Person, die regelmäßig die Dienste eines Freiberuflers oder Unternehmens in Anspruch nimmt oder gewöhnlich in demselben Geschäft einkauft. Im weiteren Sinne versteht man darunter jede Person, die eine Dienstleistung einer Unternehmung oder einer Einrichtung kauft oder in Anspruch nimmt oder einen Vertrag mit einem Freiberufler abschließt, auch wenn dies nur gelegentlich und nicht regelmäßig geschieht.

**Kundenbetreuer** *m* - account executive, account supervisor

■ Person, die in einer Werbeagentur für sämtliche Kundenbeziehungen zuständig ist.

**Kundenbeziehungsmanagement** *n* **(KBM)** - Customer Relationship Management (CRM)

■ Unternehmensphilosophie, die ihre Geschäftsstrategie auf die Beziehung und die integrale Vision des Kunden konzentriert, um diesen kennenzulernen, seine Bedürfnisse zu erkennen und diese vorausgreifend zu decken, noch bevor der Kunde selbst sich über seinen Bedarf bewusst ist.

**Kundenbindung** *f* - loyalty marketing

■ Merkmal einer Marktstrategie zur Förderung des Vertrauens der Verbraucher in das Produkt, die Dienstleistung, Marke oder Verkaufsstelle und Förderung der Markenloyalität.

**Kundendienst** *m* - customer service

■ Abteilung innerhalb eines Unternehmens, die den direkten Kontakt mit den Kunden pflegt, indem sie auf deren Anfragen und Reklamationen antwortet. Sie muss sicherstellen, dass der Kunde eine zufriedenstellende Antwort erhält, die seine Firmentreue stärkt, und gleichzeitig das entdeckte Problem zur entsprechenden Abteilung zur Lösungsfindung weiterleiten.

**Kundendienst** *m* - after-sales service
■ Organisation und Personal, das nach der Abwicklung des Kaufs die Interessen der Kunden wahrnehmen und ihre Bedürfnisse befriedigen soll.

**Kundendienstzentrum** *n* - customer service centre
■ Stelle, die die Nutzer informiert, ihre Fragen beantwortet und Beschwerden entgegennimmt.

**Kundenklassifikation** *f* - account classification
■ Anordnung der Kundenkonten eines Unternehmens nach Kriterien, die für die jeweilige Analyse von Interesse sind, zum Beispiel nach Rentabilität, Absatzgebieten oder Problemen der Zahlungseintreibung. Durch die Nutzung verknüpfter Datenbanken kann eine genauere Kundenanalyse bzgl. des Kaufverhaltens und allgemein durch den Vergleich sämtlicher Daten angestellt werden.

**Kundenprofitabilitätsanalyse** *f* - Customer Profitability Analysis (CPA)
■ Tiefgreifende Untersuchung der vom Verbraucher bisher und zukünftig erzeugten Kosten und Einnahmen, anhand derer die Rentabilität im zeitlichen Verlauf bewertet wird, um in jeder Situation entsprechende Maßnahmen treffen zu können.

**Kundenstrom** *m* - customer flow
■ Anzahl der Personen, die innerhalb eines bestimmten Zeitraums vor einem Geschäft (extern) vorbeilaufen, es betreten (intern) oder durch eine Abteilung laufen.

**Kundenverlustrate** *f* - customer loss rate
■ Quotient aus der Zahl der innerhalb eines Jahres verlorenen Kunden und der durchschnittlichen Kundenanzahl eines Unternehmens während des Jahres. Der Verlust von Kunden kann zum Teil unvermeidbar sein (Wechsel des Wohn- oder Firmensitzes, der Geschäftstätigkeit, usw.), sollte jedoch größtenteils vermieden werden; dazu ist es wichtig, seine Gründe zu kennen und ein wirksames System zur Kommunikation und zur Problemlösung einzurichten.

**Kundschaft** *f* - clientele
■ Gesamtheit der Nutzer oder Käufer der Waren oder Dienstleistungen eines Unternehmens, besonders diejenigen, die eine gewisse Kundentreue und regelmäßige Verwendung zeigen.

**künstliche Veralterung** *f* - artificial obsolescence
■ Ersetzung eines Produkts durch ein neues, das nur geringfügig oder rein äußerlich verändert wurde. Mit dem neuen Produkt sollen Verbraucher, die immer das neueste Modell besitzen möchten, zum Kauf angeregt werden.

**Kurzanzeige** *f* - short ad
■ Werbeanzeige, die sich durch Knappheit auszeichnet.

**Kurzwerbespot** *m* - announcement
■ Sehr kurze Anzeige im Fernsehen von ungefähr 10 Sekunden Länge, die zur Erinnerung an einen anderen längeren Spot dient, der im gleichen Werbeblock ausgestrahlt wurde oder der allgemeine Informationen enthält.

# L

**Ladentisch** *m* - counter
■ Präsentationsvorrichtung, in der Regel in Form einer verlängerten Tischplatte in den Verkaufsstellen, um das Produkt auszustellen und Kunden zu bedienen. Obwohl der Ladentisch in Supermärkten und anderen Verkaufsstellen längst überholt ist, erhält er sich in zahlreichen traditionellen Sektoren.

**Lager** *n* – warehouse, depot
■ Ort, an dem Bestände aufbewahrt werden. Es besteht die Möglichkeit, dass dieser Raum auch dazu dient, um an Großhändler zu verkaufen, entweder auf

traditionelle Art und Weise über den Ladentisch, in Form der Selbstbedienung (siehe auch Cash and Carry) oder als Vertriebszentrum für die Belieferung des Einzelhandels. Das Lager kann auch einer der Öffentlichkeit zugänglichen Verkaufseinrichtung beigeordnet sein und umfasst dann diejenigen Warenbestände, die sich nicht in den unmittelbaren Verkaufsräumen befinden sondern auf Vorrat gehalten werden.

**Lagerstandort** *m* - depot location

▪ Geografische Lage der Lager. Die Auswahl der besten Lage für ein Lager oder ein Lagernetz (Zentrale, Satellit und Transit) ist eine wichtige und komplexe Entscheidung, in der mehrere Faktoren wie Distanz zum Herstellungsort, Zielort der Waren, Lieferrhythmus zur Übergabe der Produkte und Anschlüsse zu wichtigen Verkehrsverbindungen in Betracht gezogen werden müssen.

**Lebensdauer** *f* - life-span

▪ Ausstellungszeit eines Werbeelements in der Öffentlichkeit. Die Dauer bestimmt den Typ und die Qualität der Materialien, die für den Herstellungsprozess verwendet werden.

**Lebensqualität** *f* - quality of life

▪ Ausmaß, in dem eine Person oder Gesellschaft Zugang zum Genuss der verfügbaren Güter und Dienstleistungen im physischen, sozialen und kulturellen Bereich hat.

**Lebensstandard** *m* - standard of living

▪ Grad der Bedürfnisbefriedigung einer Person oder einer Gruppe von Personen. Wird in der Kaufkraft gemessen, der Menge an Gütern und Dienstleistungen, die eine Person mit seinem tatsächlichen Einkommen kaufen kann. Ein niederer Lebensstandard erlaubt nur die Befriedigung der Grundbedürfnisse und ist unterentwickelten Ländern und Randgruppen zugehörigen Personen eigen.

**Lebensstil** *m* - lifestyle

▪ Gesamtheit an Eigenschaften (soziale Beziehungen, Kultur, Verbrauchsgewohnheiten), die eine Gruppe von Personen kennzeichnet (soziale Schicht, städtische oder ländliche Umgebung). Wird im Bereich der Werbung dazu benutzt, Anzeigen zu entwerfen, die einen bestimmten vom Zielpublikum erstrebten Lebensstil widerspiegeln und das beworbene Produkt mit diesem in Verbindung bringen (kann ein echt gelebter Lebensstil sein oder auch nicht).

**Lebensstil-Aufteilung** *f* - lifestyle targeting

▪ Art der Definition der Zielgruppe, die auf die Kriterien des Lebensstils anspricht, wie z. B. Aktivitäten, Vorzüge oder Freizeitgestaltung, gegenüber der traditionellen Form der Verwendung von soziodemografischen Variablen der Geschlechter, des Alters der sozialen Schicht oder Bevölkerungszahl.

**leeres Versprechen** *n* - over-promise

▪ Werbeübertreibung, die das beworbene Produkt nicht einlöst, und die eine negative Reaktion beim Empfänger auslöst. Muss unbedingt vermieden werden, es sei denn sie wird mit Humor angegangen.

**leitender Kundenbetreuer** *m* - account director

▪ Verantwortlicher und Koordinator für die Buchhaltung oder den Kundendienst einer Werbeagentur. Er koordiniert die Arbeit seines Teams und leitet und fördert die Kundenbeziehungen. Er vertritt die Agentur gegenüber den Kunden und die Kunden innerhalb der Agentur.

**Leporello** *n* - accordion fold

▪ In der Werbung, Werbefaltblatt, das in Zick-Zack-Form bzw. in Form eines Akkordeons gefaltet ist und sich in einem Zug auffalten lässt. Durch dieses Format soll die Aufmerksamkeit des Empfängers geweckt werden, der das Faltblatt aufklappen muss, um die darin enthaltende Nachricht zu entdecken.

**Leser** *m* **pro Ausgabe** - readers per copy

▪ Durchschnittszahl der Personen, die eine Ausgabe einer regelmäßigen Veröffentlichung lesen. Wird durch Teilen der Leserschaft der genannten

Veröffentlichung (Leserzahl) durch die Anzahl der verkauften Exemplare (Umlauf) errechnet.

**Lesertreue** *f* - reader confidence

■ Quote, mit der sich die Leser eine Veröffentlichung den Folgeausgaben verpflichten. Ein treuer Leser einer Zeitung oder Zeitschrift ist ein Leser, der alle oder fast alle Nummern liest, während ein untreuer oder Gelegenheitsleser ein Leser ist, der die Veröffentlichungen oftmals wechselt oder diese Art von Träger gar nicht konsumiert.

**Leuchtanzeige** *f* - luminous ad

■ Eine Leuchtanzeige ist eine elektrisch beleuchtete Sichtwerbung, die mit einem Beleuchtungssystem zur Bereitstellung der Sicht bei Nacht dient. Besteht meist aus Neonlicht und wird oben weithin sichtbar angebracht. Das Licht kann durchgehend, blinkend oder in verschiedenen Farben zur Konfiguration einer einfachen Nachricht sein, z. B. eine Marke oder ein ganzer Schriftzug.

**Leuchtreklame** *f* - illuminated billboard

■ Eine Leuchtreklame ist eine elektrisch beleuchtete Sichtwerbung, die mit einem Beleuchtungssystem zur Bereitstellung der Sicht bei Nacht dient. Leuchtreklame kann intern oder extern auf städtischen Einrichtungen angebracht sein, wie z. B. auf Zäunen.

**Lexikalisierung** *f* - lexicalization

■ Phänomen aus der gesprochenen Sprache, in der eine bestimmte Marke als generischer Begriff für eine Produktkategorie benutzt wird. Dies geschieht, wenn eine Marke sich zu einem Marktführer entwickelt. Klassische Beispiele sind: Tempo für Taschentücher, Tesa für Klebefilm, Labello für Lippenpflegestift, Pampers für Windeln, usw.

**Lieferkette** *f* - supply chain

■ Gesamtheit der voneinander abhängigen Organisationen, die beteiligt sind am Empfangs- und Lieferprozess der Produkte von ihrem Herkunfts- oder Herstellungsort bis zu ihrem endgültigen Zielort, an dem das Produkt vom Käufer erworben, benutzt oder konsumiert wird.

**Lieferverzögerung** *f* - postponed delivery

■ Verspätete Lieferung eines Produkts in Bezug auf einen vorher festgelegten Zeitpunkt. Kann für den Kunden ein ernstes Problem darstellen, da seine Bestände möglicherweise aufgebraucht sind.

**LIFO** - LIFO

■ Vorgang bei der Bestandsbewertung, wobei man davon ausgeht, dass die Ware die zuletzt eingelagert wurde, die Ware ist, die das Lager zuerst wieder verlässt, weshalb dieser Wert im Betriebsrechnungskonto verwendet wird. In Zeiten hoher Inflationsraten hat dieser Bewertungsvorgang eine Unterbewertung des Lagerbestandes zur Folge, was zu geringeren Betriebsgewinnen führt als andere Bewertungsverfahren, wie z. B. das FIFO, obgleich zu höheren als das NIFO. Die Abkürzung stammt aus dem Englischen und steht für: Last in, first out und würde im Deutschen wörtlich zuletzt rein, zuerst raus lauten.

**Likert-Skala** *f* - Likert scale

■ Skala, die die Beantwortung von Fragebögen, sowie die Erfassung und Weiterbearbeitung der Antworten erleichtert. Dabei sind die Antwortmöglichkeiten in Form einer Skala vorgegeben, die meist von 1 bis 5 reicht (auch 1 bis 3 und 1 bis 7 sind gebräuchlich). 1 bedeutet normalerweise völlige Ablehnung der vorgelegten Aussage, 5 völlige Zustimmung. Gelegentlich wird eine Skala von 1 bis zu einer geraden Zahl verwendet, um eine neutrale Aussage zu verhindern und zu einer positiven oder negativen Stellungnahme zu zwingen.

**Liste** *f* - list

■ Im Direktmarketing, die Beziehung von Einträgen in Zusammenhang mit Kunden oder möglichen Kunden eines Produkt oder einer Dienstleistung. Die Liste ist eines der Hauptelemente sämtlicher Handlungen des Direktmarketings.

**Listenerstellung** *f* - list building

■ Im Direktverkauf, Auswahl und Erstellung vom Listen mit Namen und Adressen, die für den Verkauf bestimmter Waren und Dienstleistungen besonders geeignet erscheinen.

**Listenerweiterung** *f* - enhancement list

■ Im Marketing der Datenbanken die Überlappung von zwei oder mehr Listen, wobei eine die restlichen Daten eines Kunden enthält und die Datenbank weiter erweitern soll, um die größtmögliche Zahl an Daten zu erhalten und die Information über die Eingabe so weit wie möglich zu erweitern.

**Listenpreis** *m* - list price

■ In der Preisliste eines Zulieferers öffentlich festgelegter Preis; von diesem werden die vereinbarten Nachlässe abgezogen.

**Listenverteiler** *m* - list broker

■ Person oder Firma, die sich mit der Vermarktung von Kunden- und möglichen Kundenlisten beschäftigt, egal ob er eigennützig oder nach Auftrag durch einen Dritten und in diesem Fall als Zwischenmann agiert.

**Listenwartung** *f* - list maintenance

■ Durchgehender Reinigungs- und Aktualisierungsvorgang von Daten aus einer Liste, um Doppeleinträge und Veralterung zu vermeiden.

**Lizenzagentur** *f* - license agency

■ Auf Leitung der Lizenzvergabe zur Veröffentlichung oder Verwendung zu Werbezwecken von patentierten Persönlichkeiten aus der Geschichte, Zeichentrick usw. spezialisiertes Unternehmen, das die Inhaberfirma der Lizenz mit der Werbefirma in Verbindung bringt. Der Lizenzpreis steht in direkter Beziehung zu dem Bekanntheitsgrad der Persönlichkeit und der Verwendung, die dieser zugeteilt werden soll.

**Lizenzgebühr** *f* - royalty

■ Betrag, der zu zahlen ist für die Nutzung eines gewerblichen Schutzrechtes, Patentes, einer Marke usw., die auf den Namen eines anderen registriert sind. In der Regel ein anteilsmäßiger Betrag, der als Prozentsatz oder pro hergestellte oder verkaufte Einheit definiert ist. In einigen Fällen wird ein fester Anfangsbetrag gezahlt.

**lizenzieren** *v* - license *v*

■ Das Recht zur Benutzung eines Herstellungs- oder Vermarktungsverfahrens, das normalerweise patentiert ist, in einem geographischen Gebiet gegen Zahlung von Lizenzgebühren einräumen. Diese Methode wird im internationalen Marketing eingesetzt, weil sie ermöglicht, schnell und ohne große Investitionen in neue Märkte einzutreten. Allerdings kann sie große Anstrengungen für die Übertragung und Kontrolle der nötigen Kenntnisse erfordern, da die Interessen des Lizenzgebers und des Lizenznehmers nicht immer übereinstimmen.

**Lobbywerbung** *f* - advocacy advertising

■ Werbetätigkeit, durch die sich ein Unternehmen oder eine andere gesellschaftliche Gruppe in einer Angelegenheit öffentlich engagiert und über Mitteilungen Zustimmung oder Ablehnung signalisiert.

**Lockangebot** *n* - loss leader

■ Artikel, der zu einem sehr niedrigen Preis, oft unterhalb des Einkaufspreises, verkauft wird, um das Publikum ins Geschäft zu locken. Die Anziehungskraft des Artikels kann auch in anderen Gründen als dem Preis bestehen (Exklusivverfügbarkeit, bessere Qualität usw.).

**Lockkampagne** *f* - teaser campaign

■ Vorbereitende Kampagne, bei der versucht wird, das Interesse des Publikums mittels der Geheimhaltung von wichtigen Elementen zu wecken, wie dem Produkt oder der Marke. Es wird auch oft der englische Ausdruck verwendet.

**Lockwerbung** *f* - teaser advertising

■ Kommunikationsform, in der unvollständige Botschaften übermittelt werden, die erst in Verbindung mit weiteren Aussendungen vollen Sinn erlangen, um die Aufmerksamkeit anzuziehen und die Neugierde zu wecken. Erzeugt ein größeres Interesse, erfordert aber eine hohe Investition, da die Werbung wiederholt werden muss, damit die Marke im Gedächtnis haften bleibt. Es wird auch oft der englische Ausdruck verwendet.

**Logo** *n* - logo

■ Abkürzung, die allgemein für Logotyp (Firmenzeichen) benutzt wird.

**Logotyp** *m* - logotype

■ Das Firmenlogo (Logotyp) ist Teil des visuellen Erscheinungsbildes (Corporate Design) eines Unternehmens. Ein Firmenlogo kann aus einem oder mehreren Buchstaben, einem Bild oder auch aus einer Kombination dieser Elemente bestehen. Nach anderer Meinung besteht ein Logo zwingend aus Wort- und Bildmarke, da es sich andernfalls lediglich um ein Signet oder aber um die reine Wortmarke handeln würde. Gerade aus der Kombination der beiden entsteht erst das Logo. Ein gutes Firmenlogo sollte prägnant und wiedererkennbar sein und als Identifikationsmerkmal für das gesamte Unternehmen stehen.

**lokale Werbeagentur** *f* - local advertising agency

■ Werbeagentur, die ihre Aktivitäten auf Lokal- oder Regionalebene ausübt.

**Lokalwerbung** *f* - local advertising

■ Von einer Firma durchgeführte Werbung, die auf den Werbeträgern einer Stadt oder Region verbreitet wird, in der sie ihre Aktivitäten ausführt oder zur Stärkung einer landesweiten Kampagne.

**Lokomotive** *f* - anchor store

■ Verkaufseinrichtung, die viele Kunden anzieht und dazu dient, den Kundenverkehr in einem Einkaufszentrum sicherzustellen. In der Regel sind dies Großmärkte für Lebensmittel und/oder Bekleidung. In kleineren Zentren, die mehr auf Freizeit als auf Einkauf ausgerichtet sind, können sie durch Kinos oder bestimmte Restaurants ersetzt werden. Angesichts ihrer Bedeutung für den Erfolg des Einkaufszentrums erhalten sie in manchen Fällen die Geschäftsräume als Eigentum oder einen sehr vorteilhaften Mietvertrag.

**London International Advertising Awards** - London International Advertising Awards

■ Preis für die besten Arbeiten in Werbung, Design und digitalen Medien, seit 1985.

**Lovemark** *f* - lovemark

■ Von Saatchi & Saatchi erzeugte Philosophie, die eine Marke als Ursprung einer Kultur einführen möchte und bei den Menschen Liebe und Emotionen für diese wecken soll, z. B. Ferrari für Autos, Harley Davidson für Motorräder und Apple für Computer.

**Luxusgut** *n* - luxury good

■ Produkt, dessen Nachfrage mit der höheren Kaufkapazität des Käufers steigt und das Zeichen der Zugehörigkeit zu einer sozialen Minderheit ist.

# M

**Mail-Bombing** *n* - mail bombing

■ Wahlloses und massives Versenden von Werbebotschaften mit dem Ziel, die Mailbox einer E-Mail-Adresse zu sättigen.

**Management** *n* **des Kundenlebenszyklus** - CLCM (customer life cycle management)

■ In der relationalen Werbung versteht man hierunter die Bearbeitung der Beziehung mit dem Kunden vom ersten Moment des Kaufs eines Produkts, und zwar um den Kunden nicht zu verlieren und somit die früheren gemachten Investitionen zu rentabilisieren, die mithilfe von neuen Angeboten aus Kreuzverkäufen, Wiederholung oder Erneuerung von Käufen zu Zwecken der Kundenwerbung gemacht wurden, und die während der Dauer der Beziehung mit dem Kunden realisiert werden. Ist auch unter der englischen Abkürzung CLCM bekannt.

**Management** *n* **des Wandels** - change management

■ Verfahren, die gewährleisten sollen, dass eine Organisation sich ständig an die verschiedenen Situationen und unerwartet auftretende Probleme anpasst. Experten in Unternehmensführung und Unternehmensberater betonen zunehmend die Notwendigkeit effizienten Managements des Wandels, da die Veränderungen heute schneller ablaufen und weitreichende internationale Folgen haben.

**Marke** *f* - brand

■ Repräsentatives grafisches Zeichen oder Symbol, das dazu dient, die Produkte oder Dienstleistungen eines Unternehmens gegenüber denen anderer Unternehmen zu unterscheiden.

**Markenarchitektur** *f* - brand architecture

■ Organisation und Hierarchie innerhalb des Markenportfolios eines Unternehmens. Es gibt unterschiedliche Typen der Markenarchitektur: monolithische (verschiedene Produkte und Dienstleistungen werden mit derselben Marke angeboten); indossierte (die Untermarken sind mit der Hauptmarke durch eine namentliche oder visuelle Referenz verbunden); unabhängige (jede Marke tritt in unabhängiger Form auf). In Großunternehmen kann sich die Rationalisierung des Markenportfolios kritisch auf eine effiziente Führung des Unternehmens auswirken.

**Markenartikel** *m* - brand product

■ Produkt, das unter dem Namen seines Herstellers verkauft wird, damit der Verbraucher es von ähnlichen Artikeln unterscheiden kann, die von Konkurrenzunternehmen angeboten werden. Ein Markenartikel bringt ein bestimmtes Image mit sich, auf das sich der Konsument verlässt, und das es von einem undifferenzierten oder banalen Produkt unterscheidet.

**Markenausdehnung** *f* - brand extension

■ Verwendung einer Marke für die Markteinführung von Produkten, die sich von den bisher von der Marke abgedeckten Produkten unterscheiden. Ziel ist es, Markenwiedererkennung und Glaubwürdigkeit für das Produkt mit geringeren Werbeausgaben zu erreichen und den Markenwert zu festigen.

**Markenbekanntheit** *f* - brand awareness

■ Prozentsatz der Gesamtbevölkerung oder des Zielpublikums, das eine Marke kennt oder sich an sie erinnert. Der Bekanntheitsgrad wird durch spontane Reaktion oder suggerierte Wiedererkennung gemessen.

**Markendifferenzierung** *f* - brand differentiation

■ Fähigkeit einer Marke, den Produkten derselben ein einzigartiges und positives Image zu vermitteln, insbesondere bezüglich der Merkmale des Produkts, die für die Zielgruppe dieser Marke am wichtigsten sind.

**Markenentscheidungen** *f/pl* - brand decisions

■ Teil des Marketing, der untersucht, ob ein Produkt mit einer Marke oder als No-Name-Artikel verkauft wird, welche Art von Marke (Hersteller- oder Händlermarke) und welche konkrete Marke verwendet wird, und ob kleine Änderungen in der Anwendung der Marke in Bezug auf Farben, Größe und begleitende Adjektive vorgenommen werden.

**Markenentwicklungsindex** *m* - brand development index

■ Verhältniszahl, die den Prozentsatz der Verkäufe einer Marke in einem geographischen Gebiet mit dem Prozentsatz der Bevölkerung, die dieses Gebiet repräsentiert, vergleicht. Wenn dieser Wert größer als 1 ist, besagt dies, dass die Marke in diesem Gebiet besser als im Marktdurchschnitt positioniert ist.

**Markenimage** *n* - brand image

■ Gruppe von Merkmalen, die einer bestimmten Marke von den meisten Personen zugeschrieben werden. Wenn das Image stark ist (was nicht unbedingt positiv sein muss), ruft die Marke bei den Personen einer bestimmten

Bevölkerungsgruppe gemeinsame und untereinander konsistente Überzeugungen und Gefühle hervor. Das Image kann in Abhängigkeit von den übrigen verwendeten Marketingvariablen gut oder schlecht sein; z. B. kann ein eher traditionelles Image für eine Uhr positiv, für eine andere dagegen negativ sein.

**Markenlebenszyklus** *m* - brand life cycle
■ Entwicklung einer Marke von ihrer „Geburt" bis zu ihrem „Tod", wobei dazwischen die Phasen des Wachstums und der Reife liegen. Eine Marke stirbt, wenn die Gewinnspanne eines Markenprodukts unter den Kosten für die Aufrechterhaltung der Marke liegt. Wenn man weiß, in welcher Phase sich eine Marke befindet, hilft dies, die richtigen Entscheidungen über die Aufnahme von Produkten und die Werbeausgaben zu treffen.

**Markenlizenzierung** *f* - brand licensing
■ Genehmigung, die der Eigentümer einer Marke an einen Dritten erteilt, damit dieser die Marke in Zusammenhang mit einer Produktkategorie verwenden kann. In aller Regel bringt eine solche Genehmigung die Zahlung von Gebühren mit sich, die seitens des Lizenzempfängers zu leisten sind.

**Markenmanagement** *n* - brand management
■ Systematischer und fortlaufender Ablauf, mit dem Ziel, den Wettbewerbsvorteil einer Marke aufzubauen und aufrecht zu erhalten. In Bezug auf Produkte umfasst er die eigentliche Produktführung, den Preis und die Werbung. In Bezug auf Dienstleistungen konzentriert sich der Ablauf auf den Umgang mit dem Kunden. Großunternehmen verfügen über besondere Abteilungen, die sich ausschließlich mit der Führung ihrer Marke bzw. Marken befassen.

**Markenpartnerschaft** *f* - brand alliance
■ Zusammenarbeit zwischen Komplementärmarken, bei der die Marke mit dem größten Bekanntheitsgrade die andere Marke unterstützt, indem sie einen Teil ihres Marktimages und Ansehens auf die nicht so bekannte Marke überträgt.

**Markenpolitik** *f* - branding
■ Gesamtheit von Aktivitäten im Zusammenhang mit der Schaffung, der Führung und Bewertung von Marken. Wird auch als Branding bezeichnet.

**Markenpositionierung** *f* - brand positioning
■ Konzept oder Image, das die Marke, die ein bestimmtes Produkt repräsentiert, zu vermitteln sucht, um sich der Nachfrage der Verbraucher und des Marktes anzupassen. Normalerweise werden bestimmte Marketingkampagnen durchgeführt, durch die das Image des Produktes im Geist der Verbraucher geprägt wird.

**Markenpräferenz** *f* - brand preference
■ Tendenz eines Verbrauchers zu einer bestimmten Marke anstatt zu den Konkurrenzmarken. Ist ein sehr wichtiges Ziel einer Werbekampagne und ist unabdingbare Bedingung für den Erstkauf eines Produkts, wogegen die Markentreue unverzichtbar für den Wiederholungskauf ist.

**Markenprofilanalyse** *f* - Brand Profile Analysis
■ Untersuchungswerkzeug, das von der Firma Millward Brown entwickelt wurde, mit dem das Profil einer Marke mit der Kategorie seiner Produkte verglichen wird.

**Markenstrategie** *f* - brand strategy
■ Planung einer Reihe von Aktionen, mit denen erreicht werden soll, dass die Marke zur Erlangung der Geschäftsziele beiträgt. Die Strategie muss dabei die Positionierung der Marke berücksichtigen, um in jeder Situation ihre Differenzierung vom Wettbewerber beizubehalten.

**Markentreue** *f* - brand loyalty
■ Treue der Verbraucher zu einer Marke, die folglich durch den wiederholten Kauf der Produkte dieser Marke anstatt anderer Produkte zum Ausdruck kommt. Die Markentreue erfordert ein positives Image der Marke im Auge des Verbrauchers und eine positive Erfahrung

des Kunden mit den Produkten dieser Marke.

**Markentreuerate** *f* - fidelity rate

▪ Prozentsatz der Verbraucher, die eine Marke zum ersten Mal gekauft haben und dies weiterhin wiederholt tun.

**Markenwechsel** *m* - rebranding

▪ Vorgang, bei dem eine Marke in einigen Fällen durch eine andere ersetzt wird, nachdem eine Markenprüfung ergeben hat, dass die Marke im Lauf der Zeit untergegangen ist oder sich die Markt- oder Unternehmensumstände (Fusion, Übernahme) verändert haben.

**Markenwerbung** *f* - brand advertising

▪ Werbeaktivität, die sich an ein bestimmtes objektives Publikum richtet, mit dem Zweck, das Image und die Einstellungen, die dieses Publikum gegenüber der Marke eines bestimmten Produkts hat, zu schaffen, beizubehalten, zu verstärken oder zu ändern.

**Markenwiedererkennung** *f* - brand recognition

▪ Die Tatsache, dass das Zielpublikum eine Marke erkennt und sich an sie erinnert und sie von anderen ähnlichen unterscheidet. Wird durch die gestützte, die spontane und die suggerierte Wiedererkennung gemessen.

**Marketing** *n* - marketing

▪ Wissenschaft, die den Verbraucher untersucht, seine Bedürfnisse identifiziert und durch die Schaffung von Geschäftsmöglichkeiten zu befriedigen sucht. Ihr Ziel ist es, die Zufriedenheit der Verbraucher und gleichzeitig den Unternehmenswert zu erhöhen, und nicht lediglich den Verbrauch eines bestimmten Produktes zu steigern. Das Marketing umfasst eine Reihe von Techniken, die in verschiedenen Bereichen zusammengefasst werden: Markt- und Verbraucherforschung, Markt- und Prozessinnovation, Positionsuntersuchung, Werbung, Public Relations, Verkaufsförderung, Vertrieb sowie Planung und Kontrolle. Das Marketing ist weniger als eine weitere Abteilung des Unternehmens zu betrachten, sondern vielmehr als Ansatz zur Organisation der Beziehungen zwischen den Abteilungen und des Unternehmens mit dem Verbraucher. Als deutscher Begriff wird Absatzwirtschaft verwendet, der allerdings enger gefasst ist.

**Marketing** *n* **für Kinder** - marketing to children

▪ Als Folge der demografischen Veränderung in den Entwicklungsländern und der abnehmenden Geburtszahlen ist dieser spezielle Marketing-Typ entstanden, dessen Zielgruppe Kinder sind und der darauf abzielt, die Bedürfnisse von Kindern zu erfüllen und diejenigen Personen zum Kauf zu überzeugen, die an dem Entscheidungsprozess zum Kauf von Kinderprodukten beteiligt sind.

**Marketing** *n* **für Public Relations** - marketing public relations

▪ Benutzung von Strategien und Techniken für die Öffentlichkeitsarbeit (Public Relations) zur Unterstützung von Marketing-Aktionen. Die einfache Abhaltung einer Pressekonferenz zur Präsentation eines neuen Produkts beinhaltet zum Beispiel nicht, dass es sich um Handels- oder Marketing-Aktionen handelt. Vielmehr geht es um PR-Techniken, da sie das Image des Unternehmens betreffen und als Unterstützung für kommerzielle Aktionen wie Werbung oder Promotion dienen.

**Marketing** *n* **für Senioren** - marketing to the older consumers

▪ Als Folge der demografischen Veränderung in den Entwicklungsländern und der bedeutenden Zunahme dieses Bevölkerungssegments sind wichtige Geschäftsmöglichkeiten entstanden. Aus diesem Grund wurde innerhalb des Marketings ein spezifischer Bereich entwickelt, der auf die Anwendung allgemeiner Marketingprinzipien auf dieses Marktsegment ausgerichtet ist.

**Marketinginformationssystem** *n* - marketing information system

▪ Personen, Geräte und Verfahren, die zur Sammlung, Klassifizierung, Analyse,

Bewertung und rechtzeitigen Bereitstellung der Informationen dienen, die von den Marketingverantwortlichen benötigt werden. Das System besteht aus vier Subsystemen: internes Datensystem, Marketingaufklärungssystem, Marktforschungssystem und Marketing-Kostenrechungssystem.

**Marketing-Management** *n* - marketing management

■ Eine der leitenden Abteilungen eines Unternehmens, dessen Aufgabe die Vermarktung der Produkte und Dienstleistungen ist, und die über Studien und Marktprognosen die Entwicklung von neuen Produkten, Markenleitung, Preispolitik, Vertrieb, Verkauf und Werbung verwaltet.

**Marketing-Mix** *m* - marketing mix

■ Im Marketing-Mix werden Marketing-Strategien in konkrete Aktionen umgesetzt: absatzpolitische Fragen „wie und wo machen wir Werbung", „welche Vertriebskanäle nutzen wir" werden hier für einen bestimmten Zeitraum (in der Regel ein Jahr) durchgeplant. Der Marketing-Mix unterteilt sich in die Elemente (auf Englisch) „4 Ps": Product, Price, Place, Promotion.

**Marketingmyopie** *f* - marketing myopia

■ Die Marketingmyopie wurde von Levitt entwickelt bzw. erkannt. Die Marketingmyopie besagt, dass die Mitarbeiter eines Unternehmens vom eigenen Produkt so überzeugt sind, dass Sie die Erfordernisse des Marktes nicht richtig einschätzen können.

**Marketingplan** *m* - marketing plan

■ Plan, der die Tätigkeit der Marketingabteilung eines Unternehmens oder einer Produktgruppe zusammenfasst und Ziele für Absatz, Gewinne und Kommunikation enthält. Er konkretisiert die Maßnahmen und das Budget für die Markteinführung oder Rückziehung von Produkten, Werbung, Promotion, Preise und Vertrieb. Der Plan wird in der Regel jährlich erstellt und ist Bestandteil des Jahresgeschäftsplanes.

**Marketing-Prüfung** *f* - marketing audit

■ Kontrolle und Beurteilung der Marketingplanaktionen. Analysiert detailliert, systematisch und regelmäßig die Marktkomponenten, die Unternehmensziele und Werbestrategien, sowie die Leistung der Aktiva zur Bestätigung des fehlerfreien Funktionierens oder Erkennung von Fehlern bei der Verwendung. Auf diese Weise können Maßnahmen zur Korrektur möglicher Marketingfehler ergriffen werden.

**Marketingstrategie** *f* - marketing strategy

■ Umfasst langfristige, globale Verhaltenspläne zur Erreichung der Marketing- und Unternehmensziele eines Unternehmens und ist Teil des strategischen Managements. Der Teilbereich der Marketingstrategie sollte ganzheitlich, unter Berücksichtigung der Ziel-, Strategie- und Instrumentebene geführt werden. Strategien lassen sich als Konzepte zur Erreichung eines Soll-Zustandes bezeichnen. Ausgegangen wird vom Ist-Zustand. Marketinginstrumente sollten dabei in geordneter Art und Weise angewendet werden.

**Marketing-Synergie** *f* - marketing synergy

■ Die Unterstützung eines neuen Produkts oder eines Produkts, das auf dem Markt keinen Erfolg hat, mit einem anderen, bekannteren oder erfolgreicheren Produkt. Die Marketing-Synergie wird auch zur Unterstützung von Produkten benutzt, deren Konsum sich ergänzt: zum Beispiel wenn für eine Tonic-Marke zusammen mit einer Gin-Marke geworben wird.

**MARKOR** - MARKOR

■ Englische Abkürzung für „market orientation". Die Marktorientierung eines Unternehmens bezeichnet die Fähigkeit, Märkte mit ihren Kunden und Wettbewerbern richtig zu verstehen und das Wissen über den Markt in innovative Produkte umzusetzen.

**Markt** *m* - market

■ Ort, an dem Produkte zu ihrem Verkauf angeboten werden, gewöhnlich während einem genau festgelegten Zeitplan. Auf ihm bestehen Regeln, die vor allem auf Brauchtum zurückgehen, um die Geschäftsabwicklung zu regulieren. Die Entwicklung der Kommunikationsmittel erlaubt das Bestehen von Märkten ohne notwendigen physischen Kontakt. Das Marktvolumen hängt von der Anzahl der Personen ab, die ein Bedürfnis nach dem Produkt haben, von den ausreichenden finanziellen Mitteln und von der Bereitschaft, diese Mittel für dieses Gut zu einem bestimmten Preisen einzutauschen.

**Marktagonie** *f* - market sluggishness
■ Marktsituation mit wenig Aktivitäten und einem allgemeinem Preisverfall.

**Marktanteil** *m* - market share
■ Anteil der Verkäufe einer Marke an den Gesamtverkäufen, die am Markt durchgeführt wurden. Man kann von einem Marktanteil einer Marke oder von einem Marktanteil eines Fabrikanten sprechen. Normalerweise kann der Marktanteil dadurch bestimmt werden, dass der Gesamtmarkt geschätzt wird und die Verkaufszahlen der Marke bekannt sind. Der Marktanteil entspricht dem Produkt aus dem gewichteten Vertriebswert und dem Nettomarktanteil, die in gewisser Weise die Effizienz der Verkaufskräfte und des Marketing veranschaulichen.

**Marktaufteilung** *f* - market sharing
■ Übereinkunft zwischen mehreren Unternehmen, die das gleiche Produkt anbieten und unter normalen Bedingungen auf dem gleichen Markt miteinander in Wettbewerb stehen würden, um sich einen bestimmten Markt geographisch oder nach Vertriebskanälen aufzuteilen. Manchmal wird der Preis festgesetzt und Mengenquoten vereinbart. Diese Vereinbarungen sind in der Regel ungesetzlich, da sie die Gesetze gegen Wettbewerbsbeschränkungen verletzen.

**Marktbeherrschung** *f* - market control
■ Möglichkeit eines Unternehmens, den Markt eines Produktes vollständig zu kontrollieren und über dessen Preis und Verfügbarkeit zu entscheiden.

**Marktdeckung** *f* - market coverage
■ Prozentsatz, der von einer Verkaufsmannschaft besuchten Kunden im Verhältnis zu allen potentiellen (möglichen) Kunden. Der Anteil der besuchten Kunden, der tatsächlich kauft, gibt die Distributionsdichte an.

**Marktdurchdringbarkeit** *f* - market permeability
■ Einflussmöglichkeiten von Faktoren wie Werbung und Verkaufsförderung auf einen bestimmten Markt. Ein Markt ist umso leichter durchdringbar, je stärker er zu beeinflussen ist.

**Marktdurchdringung** *f* - penetration
■ Die Marktmacht eines Produkts, das am Markt eingeführt ist und Marktmacht besitzt, wird im Marktanteil oder im Erinnerungswert einer Marke gemessen. Zum Beispiel ist die Marktdurchdringung einer Tageszeitung ihr Prozentanteil an den gesamten Zeitungslesern einer Region.

**Marktdurchdringungsstrategie** *f* - market penetration
■ Wachstumsstrategie mit den bestehenden Produkten auf den aktuellen Märkten, mittels einer aggressiveren Marketingpolitik (zum Beispiel durch Senken der Preise oder Erhöhung der Werbung). Andere Strategien sind die der Neuerschließung von Märkten (bestehende Produkte auf neuen Märkten), der Produktinnovation (neues Produkt auf bestehendem Markt) oder beide kombiniert in einer Diversifikationsstrategie.

**Marktentwicklung** *f* - market development
■ Marktstrategie bestehend aus der Vermarktung eines bestimmten Produkts, das die Firma für neue Märkte herstellt, um die Nachfrage zu stärken. Dafür sucht die Firma neue Anwendungen für das Produkt und neue Verbrauchergruppen, die am Kauf interessiert sein könnten.

**Marktforschung** *f* - market research
■ Sammlung und Analyse von Information über die typischen Merkmale eines bestehenden oder potentiellen Marktes, wobei besonderer Wert auf folgende Daten

gelegt wird: gesamtes Marktvolumen; Marktentwicklung; Marktanteile der Wettbewerber bei Käufen und Verkäufen; Umschlagshäufigkeit; numerischer und gewichteter Vertrieb; Nettobeteiligung jeder Marke; Vertriebskanäle, mit ihrer Art der Dienstleistungserbringung, der Zahlung, der Gebühren und der Konditionentabellen; Stärken und Schwächen der Wettbewerber; Eintritts- und Austrittsbarrieren sowie den Möglichkeiten zur Unterteilung in Segmente. Die Marktforschung wird durch die Verbraucherforschung vervollständigt.

**Marktführer** *m* - market leader

▪ Unternehmen oder Marke, die bei einer bestimmten Ware oder einer bestimmten Dienstleistung den größten Marktanteil haben. Normalerweise handelt es sich dabei um die Marke mit dem höchsten Bekanntheitsgrad und in vielen Fällen um diejenige mit dem höchsten Preis und der besten Qualität.

**Marktgebiet** *n* - market area

▪ Geographische Zone, in der ein Produkt verkauft wird. Sie kann von einem Stadtviertel bis zur gesamten Welt reichen. Manche Unternehmen teilen das Gebiet in Regionen oder Zonen ein, während bei anderen die Reihenfolge der Größen umgekehrt ist. Der Verantwortliche führt in der Regel in absteigender Reihenfolge den Titel Direktor, Leiter, Chef und Beauftragter.

**Marktgebietspotential** *n* - market area potential

▪ Bewertung der Verkaufsmöglichkeiten in einem speziellen Bereich, der als räumliches Gebiet oder nach Käufersegmenten abgegrenzt werden kann.

**Marktlücke** *f* - market gap

▪ Bedürfnis des Marktes, das nicht in ausreichender Form befriedigt wird. Die Marktlücke erlaubt einem Unternehmen mit wettbewerbsfähigen und neuen Produkten, Vertriebsformen oder Preisen den Zutritt in einen bisher nicht bedienten Markt. Es handelt sich um eine Marktnische, die nicht maximal ausgeschöpft wird.

**Marktmacht** *f* - market power

▪ Fähigkeit eines Einzelnen oder einer Gruppe von Käufern oder Verkäufern, den Preis eines auf dem Markt angebotenen Gutes oder einer Dienstleistung zu beeinflussen. Das völlige Fehlen von Marktmacht ist notwendige Voraussetzung dafür, dass vollständige Konkurrenz herrscht.

**Marktnische** *f* - market niche

▪ Teil eines Marktes, der sich vom übrigen Markt hinreichend unterscheidet. Die Differenzierung kann hervorgerufen sein durch das Preis-Leistungsverhältnis, Merkmale des Produktes, der Kundschaft, des Vertriebskanals, der verbundenen Service-Leistungen oder des Marktgebietes. Die Nische muss hinreichend groß sein und ausreichend Wachstumspotential haben, um eine rentable Spezialisierung zu ermöglichen, ohne dass sie zum Eintritt neuer, größerer Wettbewerber führt oder diesen zumindest erschwert. Wenn die Nische nicht hinreichend bedient wird, liegt eine Marktlücke vor.

**Marktorienterung** *f*- MARKOR

▪ Englische Abkürzung für „market orientation". Die Marktorientierung eines Unternehmens bezeichnet die Fähigkeit, Märkte mit ihren Kunden und Wettbewerbern richtig zu verstehen und das Wissen über den Markt in innovative Produkte umzusetzen.

**Marktpreis** *m* - market price

▪ Preis, zu dem sich Angebot und Nachfrage ausgleichen. Letztlich angewandter Preis, wenn wir zu diesem Preis kaufen oder verkaufen können.

**Marktsegmentierung** *f* - market segmentation

▪ Unterteilung der Verbraucher in Kategorien nach Kaufgewohnheiten zur Verbesserung der unternehmerischen Handlung. Oft fordern verschiedene Segmente eines Marktes verschiedene Verhaltensmodelle. Daher ist die Entwicklung unterschiedlicher Marketingtaktiken basierend auf den Unterschieden bei den möglichen Verbrauchern wichtig, um den gesamten Markt effektiv abzudecken.

**Marktstudie** *f* - market study

■ Untersuchung und Analyse der Information über einen aktuellen oder potentiellen Markt eines Produkts. Konzentriert sich auf allgemeine Aspekte, wie Marktvolumen, Marktentwicklung, Segmente, Wettbewerber, Vertriebskanäle und Konsumentenbedürfnisse.

**Markttest** *m* - market test

■ Wissenschaftlich organisierte Tätigkeit mit dem Ziel, den Erfolg eines Produkts und seines Marketingplans abzuschätzen. Umfasst Mengen von Stichproben, unechter Geschäfte, Panels von Geschäften, Versuchsmärkte und Umfragen. Die Investition in den Versuch hängt vom Marktforschungsbudget ab, vom Termindruck, vom Risiko der Markteinführung und den Ausgaben oder der Investition in das eigentliche Produkt und dessen Markteinführung.

**Markt-Testmethode** *f* - as-it-falls method

■ In einem Probemarkt, Form, das Werbebudget zu kalkulieren, indem man berücksichtigt, welcher Betrag in diesem Gebiet innerhalb einer nationalen Kampagne der Produktlancierung hätte aufgewendet werden müssen.

**Maslow'sche Bedürfnispyramide** *f* - Maslow's hierarchy

■ Bedürfnishierarchie; beruht auf einem vom US-amerikanischen Psychologen Abraham Maslow 1943 veröffentlichten Modell, um Motivationen von Menschen zu beschreiben.

**Massenkommunikation** *f* - mass communication

■ Kommunikationsprozess, bei dem Aussagen öffentlich (das heißt allgemein zugänglich) über technische Übertragungs- und Verbreitungsmittel an ein weit verstreutes, anonymes Publikum verbreitet werden. Die technischen Mittel, die Massenkommunikation durch Bild, Schrift und/oder Ton ermöglichen, werden Massenmedien genannt.

**Massenmedien** *n/pl* - mass media

■ Kommunikationsmittel, die ein großes Publikum erreichen, wie Fernsehen, Radio und Zeitschriften. Werbung in den Massenmedien ermöglicht im Allgemeinen keine gute Segmentierung der Botschaften, gewährleistet jedoch eine große Reichweite und Wirksamkeit für einfache Botschaften oder Massenkonsumartikel.

**Massenproduktion** *f* - mass production

■ Herstellung großer Mengen eines Erzeugnisses, normalerweise mit Spezialmaschinen und starker Arbeitsteilung. Das Produkt ist undifferenziert oder mit sehr kleinen Veränderungen (Farbe, Verpackung, Zubehör usw.). Gegenteil von begrenzter Produktion und kann in Fließfertigung erfolgen oder nicht. Wird benutzt für Artikel mit niedrigen Kosten und ohne große Anforderungen an Design oder Personalisierung.

**Masterband** *n* - final print

■ Endgültige Kopie eines Spielfilms oder eines Werbespots, wo der Ton, die Spezialeffekte, das Bild und die Einblendungen schon synchronisiert worden sind. Dient als Zeugnis dafür, dass weitere Kopien oder Anzeigen in Medien originalgetreu vorgenommen worden.

**Matrixanalyse** *f* - analysis matrix

■ Tabelle, die gewöhnlich aus zwei oder drei Zeilen und Spalten besteht, in denen schematisch die Alternativen aus der Kombination zweier Handlungsmöglichkeiten dargestellt werden (zum Beispiel Geschäftsausweitung durch Erweiterung der Produktlinie oder die Bedienung neuer Märkte). Sie kann auch aus zwei Variablen bestehen, z. B. Marktwachstum und relativer Marktanteil.

**Mäzenat** *n* - patronage

■ Das Mäzanat ist philanthropisch. Wird nicht öffentlich mitgeteilt. Kann nicht als Public Relations-Aktion oder Marketing-Aktion angesehen werden.

**M-Commerce** *m* - m-commerce

■ Elektronischer Handel über das Mobiltelefon.

**Medien** *n/pl* - media
■ Gesamtheit an materiellen und menschlichen Mitteln, die zur Verbreitung von Nachrichten und Information dienen (Presse, Fernsehen, Radio usw.).

**Medienanalyse** *f* - media analysis
■ Studie der verschiedenen bestehenden Kommunikationsmedien mit dem Ziel diejenigen auszuwählen, welche die nützlichsten, wirksamsten und billigsten im jeweiligen Fall einer Werbekampagne sein werden. Grundsätzlich kann man zwischen den Massenmedien und den selektiven Medien wählen.

**Medienäquivalenz** *f* - media translation
■ In einer Marktprüfung der Prozess zur Identifizierung der Medien und Werbeträger, die einem geografischen Gebiet in einem größeren Markt entsprechen würden. Andersherum die Identifizierung der entsprechenden Medien auf nationaler Ebene durch Extrapolieren der Daten einer Marktprüfung.

**Medien-Broker** *m* - media broker
■ In der Internetwerbung eine Agentur, die Informationen über die Häufigkeit der Benutzung einer Site und das Benutzerprofil der verschiedenen Sites bereitstellt, in welche die Werbeseiten mit Garantie zum Erhalt der gewünschten Wirkung eingefügt werden können.

**Medienbudget** *n* - media budget
■ Teil des Werbebudgets, das für die Einfügung von Werbespots in den Kommunikationsmedien verwendet wird. Bis vor einigen Jahren machte es 90 % des Budgets aus, das für herkömmliche Werbung verwendet wurde, wobei die restlichen 10 % für Produktionskosten, zum Beispiel zur Produktion von Filmen zur Verfügung standen; derzeit ist die Proportion jedoch 75/25.

**Medieneinkäufer** *m* - media buyer
■ In einer Werbe- oder Medienagentur die Person, die mit der Planung, Reservierung, Verhandlung und dem Kauf von Werbeflächen bzw. Werbezeiten beauftragt ist.

**Medieneinkaufsagentur** *f* - media buying agency
■ Werbeagentur, die auf den Kauf von Werbeflächen in den Medien zur Einfügung von Werbespots im Auftrag einer anderen Agentur oder eines Inserenten spezialisiert ist. Die Provision für diese Agenturen ist geringer als die für Agenturen mit vollem Service, da sich ihre Tätigkeit beschränkt.

**Medieneinkaufsdienst** *m* - media buying service
■ Dienstleistung von Medienzentralen, bestehend aus dem Kauf von Werbeflächen in den Medien im Namen und auf Rechnung des Inserenten. Diese Dienstleistung umfasst alle Verwaltungselemente, einschließlich der Zahlung.

**Medieneinkaufsgruppe** *f* - media buying club
■ Werbeunternehmensgruppe, die Dienstleistungen zum Kauf von Werbeflächen in den Medien bereitstellt, um durch den Kauf in großen Mengen vorteilhafte Konditionen zu erhalten.

**Medienkauf** *m* - media buying
■ Planung, Reservierung und Kauf von Werbefläche bzw. Werbezeit, die für eine bestimmte Werbekampagne in den dafür ausgewählten Medien am besten geeignet sind. Normalerweise wird diese Tätigkeit von der Werbeagentur oder einer speziellen Agentur unter Aufsicht des Inserenten durchgeführt.

**Medienkonsum** *m* - media consumption
■ Prozentanteil der Bevölkerung oder Zielgruppe, die sich den Medien für eine bestimmte Zeit aussetzt. Im Allgemeinen wird er im Hinblick auf die Aussetzung der Medien während des letzten Zeitraums gemessen: der gestrige Tag für Tageszeitungen, Fernsehen und Radio; die letzte Woche für Beilagen, Wochenzeitschriften und Kino; der letzte Monat für monatlich erscheinende Zeitschriften und Internet.

**Medienplan** *m* - media plan
■ Ergebnis der Planung der für eine bestimmte Kampagne zu nutzenden

Werbemedien. Bestimmt die Werbeträger und den genauen Kalender der einzelnen Schaltungen, die erwartete Reichweite und Häufigkeit, sowie das Werbebudget.

**Medienplaner** *m* - media planner

▪ In der Medienabteilung einer Werbeagentur die Person, die die Medienpläne umsetzt und ihre Umsetzung überwacht.

**Medienplanung** *f* - account planning

▪ Der von einer Werbeagentur durchgeführte Ablauf zur Definition der Kommunikationsstrategie für eine Marke, Institution, ein Produkt oder eine Dienstleistung.

**Medienunterstützung** *f* - media support

▪ Verwendung von Werbung in herkömmlichen Medien als Teil einer Marketingkampagne.

**Medienuntersuchung** *f* - media research

▪ Sammlung und Analyse von Informationen über die Charakteristika und die Kosten der Kommunikationsmedien, um eine effektive und kostengünstige Planung und Buchung von Werbezeit und -fläche zu ermöglichen.

**Medienverwaltung** *f* - media administration

▪ Dienstleistungen, die von einigen Werbeagenturen und allen Medienzentralen geleistet werden, bestehend aus der Untersuchung, Kontaktaufnahme, Verhandlung, Kauf, Abrechnung und Verwaltung von Werbeflächen in den Medien im Namen und auf Rechnung des Inserenten.

**Medienzentrale** *f* - media agency

▪ Eine neuere Bezeichnung für diese Unternehmensart ist die Medienagentur, die auf die Untersuchung, Planung und den Kauf von Werbeflächen und -zeiten in den Kommunikationsmedien spezialisiert ist. Die Medienzentralen haben einen Großteil der Dienstleistungen der Werbeagenturen absorbiert.

**Megamarketing** *n* - megamarketing

▪ Strategische Koordinierung von wirtschaftlichen, psychologischen, politischen und PR-Aspekten, mit der Absicht, die Zusammenarbeit von möglichst vielen Verbündeten zu erreichen, um in einen bestimmten Markt einzudringen oder dort tätig zu sein. Dieser Ansatz kann erforderlich sein, wenn man in einen stark vom Staat beeinflussten und reglementierten Markt eintreten will; in diesem Fall kommen zu den klassischen vier P des Marketing (Product, Price, Place, Promotion) nach McCarthy noch zwei hinzu: Politicians (Politiker) und Public Opinion (öffentliche Meinung).

**Mehrfachwerbung** *f* - piggyback commercials

▪ Fernsehwerbung für Produkte eines Herstellers, die im gleichen Werbeblock ausgestrahlt werden, meist hintereinander, um bessere Werbepreise zu erhalten und ein Produkt auf das andere zu stützen, damit der Werbeträger länger im Kopf des Empfängers präsent bleibt. In manchen Fällen handelt es sich um zwei verschiedene Produkte des gleichen Anbieters, um Kosten zu sparen.

**Meinungsbildner** *m* - opinion leaders

▪ Personen, die aufgrund ihres Status, ihrer sozialen Position oder ihres Berufs die Tendenzen der Öffentlichkeit in einem Land vorgeben. Die Werbung kann sich in Kampagnen an diese Menschen richten, um eine soziale oder öffentliche Nachricht zu verbreiten oder sie sogar dazu benutzen, die Werbung für ein Produkt oder eine Dienstleistung zu fördern.

**Mengenrabatt** *m* - volume discount, order discount

▪ Abzug vom Listenpreis auf Grund der Gesamtbestellmenge durch einen Kunden in einem bestimmten Zeitraum, unabhängig der Größe der einzelnen Bestellungen, die er gemacht hat. Dabei werden die geringeren Kosten berücksichtigt, die die größeren Kunden verursachen. Synonym für Rückvergütung.

**Merchandising** *n* - merchandising

▪ Bezieht sich innerhalb der Kommunikationspolitik des Marketing von Konsumgütern auf die Produktion, den

Vertrieb und die Werbung für Markenartikel, die das gleiche Logo oder die gleiche Botschaft transportieren wie ein bekanntes Markenprodukt, ohne dabei jedoch den gleichen Nutzen zu bieten. Insbesondere wird auf diese Weise ein positives ideelles Markenimage planmäßig auf eine Vielzahl von Gebrauchsgütern transferiert.

**Messemarketing** *n* - trade fair marketing

▪ Marketingzweig, der sich mit der Organisation und Durchführung von Fachmessen beschäftigt, die nicht nur die beteiligten Unternehmen, Produkte und Dienstleistungen betreffen, sondern auch die Städte, in denen die Messe stattfindet, womit zum so genannten Stadtmarketing beigetragen wird.

**MGM (member get member)** - MGM (member get member)

▪ Freundschaftswerbung, d. h. Kunden werben Kunden an und werden dafür belohnt.

**Miete** *f* **von Adressenlisten** - list renting

▪ Im Direktverkauf, die Benutzung gekaufter Listen mit Namen und Adressen, die man für den Erfolg einer bestimmten Aktion für besonders geeignet hält. Kann das Recht einschließen, die genaue Zusammensetzung der Liste zu kennen und diese für spätere Aktionen einzusetzen.

**Mikromarketing** *n* - micromarketing

▪ Marketing, das sich an Einzelpersonen oder kleine Gruppen richtet. Mikromarketing bildet den Gegensatz zur Massenabsatzstrategie und zielt auf die besonderen Interessen und Bedürfnisse von Einzelpersonen ab, indem es kundenspezifische Produkte oder Dienstleistungen anbietet. Es ähnelt dem Nischenmarketing, widmet sich aber nicht einer großen Nische, sondern einer großen Zahl kleiner Nischen.

**Mission** *f* **des Unternehmens** - mission statement

▪ Kurze Beschreibung der Aufgabe eines Unternehmens, die dazu dient, den Mitarbeitern und interessierten Außenstehenden die Ziele der Firma und die Faktoren, denen sie am meisten Bedeutung beimisst, zu erläutern. Dies kam Ende der 1980er Jahre in Mode und ist von geringem Wert, wenn die Aussagen sehr allgemein sind. Am interessantesten ist dabei der Prozess der internen Erarbeitung, der dazu dient, die Erwartungen zu konzentrieren und zu identifizieren, was das Unternehmen hervorheben und verstärken will.

**Mitarbeiter** *m* **vor Ort** - field staff

▪ Beschäftigte, die in direktem Kontakt mit den Kunden arbeiten, im Gegensatz zum Verwaltungs- oder Produktionspersonal. Ein Beispiel sind die Verkäufer, oder die Interviewer einer Marktforschungsgesellschaft.

**mitgeschlepptes Publikum** *n* - inherited audience

▪ Teil des Programmpublikums von Radio oder Fernsehen, das am Gerät bleibt, weil es das vorherige Programm gesehen/gehört hat. Wenn das neue Programm nicht seinen Anforderungen genügt, verlässt er dies und wird teilweise oder ganz von Interessenten an dem neuen Programm ersetzt. Der Start eines Programms, das auf ein anderes mit hohem Publikum folgend gesendet wird, kann von einer hohen Anzahl an mitgeschlepptem Publikum ausgehen.

**Mittelgang** *m* - central aisle

▪ Hierunter versteht man den Gang, der in großen Kaufhäusern parallel zu den Kassen und den verderblichen Waren verläuft. Der Mittelgang ist breiter als die anderen Gänge und man gelangt somit besser zu den Artikeln, die nach Gruppen sortiert in den Regalen ausliegen. Die Endpunkte des Mittelgangs sind besonders attraktive Stellen zur Warenauslage.

**mittlerer Schätzfehler** *m* - standard error estimate

▪ Ausdruck in der Statistik, der den durchschnittlichen Fehler bei der Vorhersage einer Variabel widerspiegelt. Im Marketing wird er gewöhnlich für

Verkaufsprognosen verwendet. In der Logistik wird dieses Konzept zur Bestimmung des Sicherheitsbestands benutzt, der zur Befriedigung einer nicht vorhergesehenen Nachfrage vorhanden sein muss.

**Mobil** *n* **für Geschäft** - M2B (mobile to business)

▪ Geschäftsmodell, in dem der elektronische Handel über das Handy stattfindet.

**mobile Werbung** *f* - mobile advertising

▪ Werbungstyp, die an einem Fahrzeug oder einem Anhänger angebracht ist. Wird gewöhnlich von über Lautsprecher ausgestrahlter Musik oder Slogans begleitet, um mehr Aufmerksamkeit zu erwecken. Wird vor allem verwendet, um intensiv ein Ereignis oder eine Veranstaltung zu bewerben, zum Beispiel eine Zirkusaufführung oder eine Wahlkampfveranstaltung.

**mobiles Marketing** *n* - mobile marketing

▪ Die Umschreibung von Marketingmaßnahmen unter Verwendung drahtloser Telekommunikation und mobiler Endgeräte mit dem Ziel, Konsumenten möglichst direkt zu erreichen und zu einem bestimmten Verhalten zu führen. Bezeichnet jede Art von kommunikativ geschäftlichen Aktivitäten, bei der die Anbieter Leistungen auf der Basis mobiler Endgeräte wie digitale Inhalte (Spiele, Songs, Videos usw.), Informationen (News, Alerts, Produktinformationen) und/oder Transaktionen wie Shopping, Videostreaming, Zahlungen usw. aufbaut und damit bei potentiellen Konsumenten Aufmerksamkeit erregt und im Idealfall zu Verkaufsabschlüssen führt.

**möglicher Kunde** *m* - prospect

▪ Individuum oder Zielobjekt einer Werbeaktion und/oder Werbekommunikation, dessen Merkmale darauf hinweisen, dass er bestimmte Produkte kaufen könnte, obwohl er diese aus verschiedenen Gründen noch nicht kauft. Er ist dem Kauf einen Schritt näher als ein reiner möglicher Kunde und wird aus diesem Grund direkt kontaktiert.

**monolithische Marke** *f* - monolithic brand

▪ Benutzung des gleichen Namens und der gleichen optischen Erscheinung für die gesamte Unternehmensstruktur und die gesamte Produkt- und Dienstleistungspalette eines Unternehmens. Zum Beispiel Renault, BMW oder IBM.

**Monopol** *n* - monopoly

▪ Markt, in dem ein einziger Anbieter den Preis und die angebotenen Mengen bestimmt. Es kann stabil sein in Fällen des natürlichen Monopols oder der Besteuerung (zum Beispiel fiskalisches Monopol, um die Steuererhebung zu erleichtern). Es tritt auch in Fällen neuer oder hochentwickelter Produkte auf, besonders wenn diese durch Patente geschützt sind oder hohe Markteintrittsbarrieren bestehen.

**monopolistischer Wettbewerb** *m* - monopolistic competition

▪ Unter einer monopolistischen Konkurrenz (auch: monopolistischer Wettbewerb oder heterogenes Polypol) versteht man einen Markt, auf dem zwar ähnlich wie im Polypol sehr viele Anbieter auftreten, der aber unvollkommen ist. Die Unvollkommenheit kann dadurch hervorgerufen sein, dass z. B. die Nachfrager räumliche, zeitliche oder sachliche Präferenzen haben, oder weil die gehandelten Güter nicht homogen sind, sich also in gewissen Merkmalen unterscheiden (Produktdifferenzierung). In der Realität ist diese Marktform recht häufig anzutreffen. Beispiele für solche Märkte sind Märkte für zahlreiche Güter und Dienstleistungen des täglichen Bedarfs (z. B. Brot, Fleisch, Obst und Gemüse, Friseure, Reinigungen).

**Monopolpreis** *m* - captive price

▪ Günstiger Preis, der für ein Hauptprodukt festgesetzt wurde, für dessen Verbrauch ein Zusatzprodukt notwendig ist. Um die durch den Verkauf des Hauptproduktes erzielte reduzierte Gewinnspanne auszugleichen, wird für das Zusatzprodukt ein erhöhter Preis festgesetzt.

**Montage** *f* - set-up
■ Abschließende Arbeiten an einer Einrichtung oder Anlage vor ihrer Eröffnung.

**Montagewerk** *n* - assembly plant
■ Fabrik für den Zusammenbau von vorbereiteten Einzelteilen und die Erstellung des Endprodukts, normalerweise mit einer Fertigungsstraße unter Einsatz von Robotern.

**moralischer Preis** *m* - ethical price
■ Preis für ein Produkt nach moralischen eher als nach wirtschaftlichen Gesichtspunkten. Ziel ist ein zumutbarer Preis für die Verbraucher, unabhängig von dem Preis, den diese aufgrund des Produktwertes zu zahlen bereit wären.

**Motivationsagentur** *f* - incentives agency
■ Professionelle Einrichtung, die sich auf den Entwurf und die Leitung nach Auftrag durch Dritte für Handlungen spezialisiert hat, die den Teamgeist einer Firma oder Organisation durch Reisen, Prämien, Konventionen und Sonderveranstaltungen stimulieren.

**Motivationsstudie** *f* - motivation research
■ Untersuchung und Analyse der Beweggründe, Wünsche und Bedürfnisse der Konsumenten sowie der Anreize oder Störvariablen in ihrem Verhalten. Sie dient dazu, die Motive der Konsumenten zu kennen und in eine Hierarchie zu bringen, um ihr Verhalten vorhersagen zu können.

**Multimarkenstrategie** *f* - multibrand strategy
■ Absicherung bzw. Beherrschung eines Marktsegments durch mehrere Marken.

**multinationales Marketing** *n* - multinational marketing
■ Marktstrategie eines Unternehmens, damit die Marktbearbeitung für mehrere Länder oder soziokulturell selbständige Marktgebiete angepasst wird.

**Mundpropaganda** *f* - word-of-mouth advertising
■ Werbung, die Benutzer der Produkte spontan ausführen, wenn sie mit den Produkten oder Dienstleistungen zufrieden gewesen sind. Bedarf keines anderen Mediums zur Vermittlung.

**Mund-zu-Mund-Propaganda** *f* - word of mouth
■ Information oder Gerücht, das sich mündlich und unkontrolliert verbreitet. Die Mund-zu-Mund Propaganda trägt entscheidend zum Image eines Produkts oder einer Marke bei.

**Muster** *n* - sample
■ Im Markt ein Exemplar oder eine geringe Menge eines Produkts, die dem Verbraucher gegeben wird, im Allgemeinen kostenfrei, damit er die Qualität des Produkts kennen lernen kann.

**Musterbuch** *n* - sample book
■ Katalog mit Fotografien und Beschreibung der Produkte, den der Verkäufer mit sich führt, um deren Verkauf zu fördern. In manchen Wirtschaftszweigen haben die Verkäufer die angebotenen Produkte körperlich bei sich, zumindest in Form eines Musters.

**Musterpackung** *f* - sample product
■ Werbetechnik, bei der kleinere Verpackungen als im Original ausgegeben werden, entweder gratis oder zu einem reduzierten Preis für den Verbraucher oder den Lieferanten. Sie beinhalten eine Auswahl des Produkts und sollen dieses fördern.

**Musterprüfung** *f* - sampling control
■ Feldarbeit einer Studie, bei der geprüft wird, ob die durchgeführten Umfragen mit den Personen wirklich der Ausarbeitung für die Auswahl entsprechen.

**Mutteragentur** *f* - parent advertising agency
■ Hauptsitz einer multinationalen Agentur, von der aus Internationalisierungsvorgänge gestartet werden, bis der nationale Markt erreicht wird.

# N

**Nachahmerstrategie** *f* - follower strategy
■ Strategie der Entwicklung neuer Produkte, bei der möglichst schnell und

effektiv die Fortschritte kopiert werden, die vom führenden Unternehmen im Bereich der Technologie oder des Marketing eingeführt worden sind. Um damit Erfolg zu haben, muss man Kostenführer und sehr flexibel im Bereich der Produktion und des Vertriebs sein, weil das erste Produkt in diesen Bereichen geschlagen werden muss.

**Nachahmungsprodukt** *n* - me-too product

▪ Produkt, das die gleichen Bedürfnisse wie ein anderes bereits im Markt vorhandenes deckt und zur Ergänzung der Produktpalette ohne große Verbesserungs- oder Differenzierungsbemühungen in den Markt eingeführt wird. Ist keine Imitation im Sinne einer Fälschung, sondern wird von seinem Hersteller korrekt identifiziert.

**Nachfassaktion** *f* - follow-up advertising campaign

▪ Direkte Fortsetzung einer Werbekampagne oder eines Direktmailings. Hierbei soll der Erinnerungswert verstärkt werden. Positive Eindrücke der ersten Aktion werden ausgenutzt. Die Follow-Ups orientieren sich danach an dieser ersten Anzeige, so dass ein einheitliches Gesamtbild feststellbar wird. Es wird auch oft der englische Ausdruck benutzt.

**Nachfassen** *n* - follow-up

▪ Tätigkeit im Anschluss an die erstmalige Durchführung einer neuen Handlung. Im Falle eines Verkaufsbesuches kann dieses Nachfassen z. B. in einem Dankesbrief, der Zusendung eines Aktionsplanes oder einem Erinnerungsanruf bestehen. Es wird auch oft der englische Begriff benutzt.

**Nachfragegesetz** *n* - law of demand

▪ Wirtschaftsgesetz das besagt, dass die nachgefragte Menge eines Gutes sich umgekehrt proportional zu seinem Preis verhält. Je höher der Preis, desto geringer die Nachfrage und umgekehrt.

**Nachfragegrad** *m* - pull

▪ Beim Direktmarketing die gemessene Erfolgsstufe einer Werbehandlung, die sich aus dem Reaktionsanteil bezogen auf die Gesamtversandzahl ergibt, brutto oder netto.

**Nachfrageprognose** *f* - demand forecast

▪ Die Nachfrageprognose ist ein wichtiger Bestandteil der betrieblichen Abläufe. Sie hilft dabei, unter anderem folgende Fragen zu beantworten: Sollen neue Kapazitäten aufgebaut oder eventuell alte abgebaut werden? Zu welcher Zeit sollten Betriebsferien stattfinden? Wann wird die Nachfrage nach einem Gut so gering sein, dass sich eine weitere Produktion nicht lohnt (im PC-Bereich oft anzutreffen)? Wie gehe ich mit sporadischer Nachfrage um?

**Nachfüllpackung** *f* - refill

▪ Produkt, das wieder aufgefüllt wird. Normalerweise handelt es sich um das selbe Produkt oder ein Produkt, das dem leeren ähnlich ist oder es ergänzt.

**Nachlassen** *n* **der Werbewirkung** - advertising wearout

▪ Moment, in dem der Verbraucher beginnt, nicht mehr auf eine Werbekampagne zu reagieren, weil er die Werbebotschaft zu oft in den Medien wahrgenommen hat. Ein solches Übermaß kann sogar schädliche Folgen für die Marke haben.

**Nachnahmeverkauf** *m* - cash on delivery sale

▪ Verkauf, bei dem der Käufer eine unterschriebene Bestellkarte einschickt und bei Erhalt der Ware an den Postdienst zahlt. Er verfügt in vielen Fällen über eine Reklame- und Rückgabefrist, wenn er nicht zufrieden ist. Schließt jeden Verkauf ein, bei dem die Ware bei Erhalt bezahlt wird.

**Namenssammlung** *f* - name gathering

▪ Werbetechnik, die der der Weiterempfehlung an Freunde ähnelt, in der der Kunde oder an der Marke Interessierte gebeten wird, Namen und Kontaktdaten von Freunden und Bekannten zu senden, an die sich die Marke wenden kann, um ihnen ihr Produkt oder Dienstleistung zu verkaufen.

**nationale Einführung** *f* - national launch

■ Einführung des Produkts auf dem gesamten nationalen Markt, statt es nach Gebieten und progressiv einzuführen.

**nationale Werbeagentur** *f* - national advertising agency

■ Werbeagentur mit nationalem Vermögen, die ihre Aktivität in einem bestimmten Land tätigt. Die nationalen Werbeagenturen sind in letzter Zeit weltweit stark zurückgegangen und sind oftmals Teil von internationalen Werbenetzwerken geworden.

**Nettomarktanteil** *m* - net participation

■ Prozentsatz der Verkäufe einer Marke an den Gesamtverkäufen dieses Produktes in den Geschäften, wo dieses Produkt angeboten wird. Zeigt an, wie leicht ein Artikel abgesetzt werden kann, wenn er einmal in ein Geschäft eingeführt worden ist. Dieser Wert hängt vom Image und Preis des Produktes ab. In Zeiten starker Erhöhung der Distributionsquote kann der Wert abnehmen, da das Produkt in vielen neuen Verkaufsstellen angeboten wird, wo die Marke weniger bekannt ist, und von Seiten des Konsumenten noch keine Kaufgewohnheit besteht.

**Nettopreis** *m* - net price

■ Preis, auf den keine Nachlässe akzeptiert werden. In der Praxis benutzt man diese Bezeichnung für den Endpreis nach Abzug aller Nachlässe auf den Listen- oder Katalogpreis.

**Nettoumsatz** *m* - turnover

■ Gesamtumsatz eines Unternehmens in einer bestimmten Periode, abzüglich der im Verkaufspreis enthaltenen Steuern (z. B. Mehrwertsteuer).

**Neutralpreis** *m* - neutral price

■ Preis, der für ein Produkt festgelegt wird, um den Marktanteil nicht zu beeinträchtigen.

**nichtklassische Werbeformen** *f/pl* - below-the-line media

■ Werbemedien, die sich von den üblichen wie Tageszeitungen, Beilagen, Zeitschriften, Fernsehen, Radio, Kino und Werbeflächen unterscheiden. Die wichtigsten Medien sind die Direktwerbung und Werbung an Verkaufsstellen. Das relativ junge Medium Internet fällt unter die Gruppe der konventionellen Medien.

**Nielsen** - Nielsen

■ Kurzbezeichnung für das Unternehmen A. C. Nielsen Co. Limited, das größte Marktforschungsunternehmen, spezialisiert auf die Verkaufsprüfung zur Bereitstellung von Vertriebsdaten für die einzelnen Verkaufsstellen. Kontrolliert ebenfalls die Werbeinvestitionen in den Medien.

**NIFO** *n* - NIFO

■ Bewertungssystem von Lagerbeständen, das ausgehende Einheiten zum Wiederbeschaffungswert (Preis der nächsten zu erwerbenden Einheit) ansetzt. Dies führt zu einem Kostenanstieg der Güter und vermindert den buchhalterischen Gewinn, im Fall von Inflation noch stärker als nach dem LIFO-Prinzip.

**nimm drei, zahl zwei** - three for the price of two

■ Werbeaktion, bei der drei gleiche Artikel zum Preis von zweien abgegeben werden. Dies wird bei Produkten mit einer relativ hohen Handelsspanne eingesetzt, da es einen Nachlass von 33% bedeutet, der allerdings manchmal als 50% dargestellt wird. In den USA ist das Angebot von zwei für den Preis von einem üblich. Im Allgemeinen wird diese Methode als Lockvogel oder Reklameartikel verwendet, wobei Gewinn durch den Absatz anderer Produkte gesucht wird, die der Verbraucher kauft, nachdem er durch das Sonderangebot ins Geschäft gelockt worden ist.

**Nischen-Marketing** *n* - niche marketing

■ Unternehmensstrategie, die selektiv Marktsektoren (Nischen) sucht, um dort ihre Produkte bzw. Dienstleistungen anzubieten. Die Belegung einer Marktnische ist eines der Ziele der Maketingstrategie, d.h. der Positionierung auf dem Markt.

**Nischen-Medien** *n/pl* - niche media
■ Werbeträger, der kleine, sehr homogene Gruppen der Bevölkerung erreicht.

**Non-Profit-Marketing** *n* - non-profit marketing
■ Marketingaktivität, die zugunsten einer öffentlichen Einrichtung ohne lukrative Vorteile durchgeführt wird (Museen, Orchester). Gegenteil zu den Marketingaktivitäten von Firmen, die auf einen wirtschaftlichen Nutzen abzielen.

**Normalwerbung** *f* - ordinary advertising
■ Im Fernsehen die Werbung, die an vorher festgelegten Tagen zu festgelegten Uhrzeiten ausgestrahlt wird. Das Gegenteil ist die Extrawerbung, deren Ausstrahlung aufgrund einer erneuten Ausstrahlung eines Sonderbeitrags oder -programms erfolgt.

**Normierung** *f* - standardisation
■ Typifikation, Angleichung oder Anpassung an einen Typ, ein Modell oder eine Norm. Anpassung eines Produkts oder eines Systems an das, was als normal eingestuft wird.

**Not** *f* - scarcity
■ Allgemeines Fehlen von Gütern, hauptsächlich Nahrungsmitteln und Gütern des Grundbedarfs, während eines langen Zeitraums.

**Nutzen** *m* - utility
■ Bedürfnisbefriedigung, die man durch die Nutzung eines Gutes erlangt. Bestimmt den Wert eines Gutes und das Interesse an seiner Nutzung.

**Nutzen** *m* - benefit
■ In der Werbung versteht man hierunter die Brauchbarkeit von Produkten oder Dienstleistungen für den Verbraucher, wenn diese seinen Bedarf decken. Beruht auf den physischen, funktionalen oder symbolischen Attributen der Produkte. Der Nutzen stimmt mit dem traditionellen Gebrauchswert überein und beinhaltet zusätzlich die Wechsel- und Zeichenwerte. Der Nutzen wird in der Darstellung, Positionierung und Kommunikation von Produkten verwendet. Er wird einerseits in den funktionalen oder rationalen Nutzen und andererseits in den psychologischen oder emotionalen Nutzen unterteilt, wobei eine der beiden Typologien als Referenz für die Kommunikationsachse dient, auf der die Werbeanzeige basiert.

**Nutzensegmentierung** *f* - benefit segmentation
■ Segmentierung der Zielgruppe, an die eine bestimmte Werbeaktion gerichtet ist. Sie basiert auf dem Nutzen, der aus dem angebotenen Produkt gezogen wird. Auf diese Weise erhält man einen höheren Affinitätsgrad zwischen der Werbeanzeige und den möglichen Produktinteressenten.

**Nutzungsanalyse** *f* **des Markenprofils** - Brand Usage Profile Analysis (BUPA)
■ Untersuchungswerkzeug für die Beziehung zwischen dem Profil oder dem Wahrnehmungsgrad der Marke hinsichtlich einer Verbrauchergruppe und dem Gebrauch, den diese Gruppe von der Marke macht und der sich im Kauf der einzelnen Produkte äußert.

# O

**Oberschicht** *f* - upper class
■ Gesamtheit von Personen, die auf der sozialen Skala gemäß sozioökonomischen Variablen die höchste Position einnehmen. Bezieht sich auch auf Werbeträger (hauptsächlich Zeitschriften), zu deren Publikum vornehmlich Personen aus dieser Klasse gehören.

**offene Frage** *f* - open question, open-ended question
■ Frage in einem Fragebogen, bei der der Befragte frei seine Meinung ausdrücken kann, ohne dass er gezwungen ist, zwischen einer Reihe von Vorgaben zu wählen. Der Befrager muss die Antwort so wort- und sinngetreu wie möglich festhalten. In manchen Fällen ist es ausreichend, die ähnlichste Antwort unter den vorher ausgewählten zu markieren, so dass die Datenerfassung erleichtert wird.

**öffentliche Angelegenheiten** *f/pl* - public affairs

■ Öffentliche Beziehungen einer Organisation mit Institutionen, öffentlichen Organen, politischen Parteien, Unternehmen und Interessengruppen, um diese zu Teilnahme in der Öffentlichkeitspolitik anzutreiben und sich an die öffentlichen Anforderungen anzupassen.

**öffentliche Verantwortung** *f* **des Unternehmens** - corporate public responsibility

■ Gesamtheit der sozialen Verpflichtungen, die eine Person, Gruppe, Organisation oder Institution im Bezug auf ihre öffentliche Verantwortung eingeht, und zwar sowohl hinsichtlich der Umsetzung ihrer grundlegenden oder fundamentalen Aktivitäten als auch hinsichtlich der Sorge um die Folgen, die diese Aktivitäten für firmenfremde Gesellschaftsgruppen haben können. Die Schaffung von Arbeitsplätzen, Chancengleichheit am Arbeitsplatz oder die Vorbeugung vor Umweltbelastung sind Beispiele für öffentliche Verantwortung.

**öffentliches Marketing** *n* - public marketing

■ Von Einheiten oder Organismen der öffentlichen Behörden durchgeführtes Marketing, die Dienstleistungen an die Bürger weitergeben. Betrifft keine Firmen mit staatlichem Anteil, die einen Gewinn bezwecken.

**Öffentlichkeitskampagne** *f* - public service campaign

■ Werbekampagne, die Waren oder Dienstleistungen ohne wirtschaftliches Interesse sondern zur Verbreitung eines Verhaltens, das von der Gesellschaft als wünschenswert angesehen wird, bewirbt. Die inhärenten Kosten können von der Werbeorganisation übernommen werden, es ist allerdings auch möglich, dass der Vorgang kostenlos von Fachleuten des Sektors und der Medien durchgeführt wird.

**offizielle Anzeige** *f* - official ad

■ Anzeigen, die obligatorisch einen öffentlichen Organismus enthalten, wie z. B. die Stadtverwaltung, Bezirk oder Gericht und Daten von öffentlichem Interesse ausgeben, wie z. B. Edikte, Untervertragnahmen oder Auktionen. Hat einen anderen Tarif als normale Werbung.

**Off-Price-System** *n* - off-price system

■ Im Off Price-System werden Artikel, oft Auslauf- und Überschussware sowie Produkte zweiter Wahl, deutlich unter dem Verkaufspreis anderer Handelsbetriebe angeboten, ähnlich wie bei Outlet-Stores. Im Gegensatz zu diesen geht die Initiative jedoch nicht vom Hersteller, sondern vom Einzelhändler aus, der somit auch bei verschiedenen Herstellern einkaufen kann. Oft in der Textilindustrie oder bei Flughäfen.

**ohne Beschnitt** - non bleed

■ Art des Anzeigendrucks bei regelmäßigen Veröffentlichungen, wobei die Anzeige im Rahmen der allgemeinen Veröffentlichung bleibt.

**Ökomarkt** *m* - green market

■ Von Verbrauchern, die ökologische Produkte fordern, zusammengestellter Markt.

**Oligopol** *n* - oligopoly

■ Marktsituation, in der nur wenige Anbieter existieren, die gewöhnlich untereinander Abkommen anstreben, durch die sie ihre eigene wirtschaftliche Situation auf Kosten der Konsumenten verbessern. Im Falle von zwei Anbietern spricht man von einem Duopol, bei nur einem einzigen Anbieter vom Monopol.

**oligopolistische Konkurrenz** *f* - oligopolistic competition

■ Gleichbedeutend mit Oligopol. Marktsituation, in der nur wenige Anbieter existieren, die gewöhnlich untereinander Abkommen anstreben, die ihre eigene wirtschaftliche Situation auf Kosten der Konsumenten verbessern. Im Falle von zwei Anbietern spricht man von einem Duopol, bei nur einem einzigen Anbieter vom Monopol.

**Oligopson** *n* - oligopsony

■ Marktsituation, in der nur wenige Käufer existieren, die in vielen Fällen geschlossen auftreten, um die Kaufbedingungen des Produktes in ihrem Sinn zu beeinflussen. Falls es nur zwei Nachfrager gibt, spricht man von einem Duopson, im Falle eines einzigen Nachfragers von einem Monopson.

**One-Shot-Versand** *m* - one-shot mail

▪ Beim Fernversand, einmaliger Versand einer Produktwerbung, wobei das gesamte Angebot und alle Kreativität sich auf den Verkauf des angepriesenen Produkts konzentrieren. Wird nicht bei Produkten mit niedrigem Preis verwendet, es sei denn, man möchte den massiven Kauf anregen, da die Antwortkosten sonst nicht kompensiert würden.

**One-to-One-Marketing** *n* - one-to-one marketing

▪ Unter One-to-One-Marketing (alternativ 1:1-Marketing) versteht man das individuelle Zuschneiden einer oder mehrerer Marketing-Maßnahmen auf jeden einzelnen Kunden mithilfe statistischer Verfahren. Das Ziel lässt sich mit "Individualisieren statt Personalisieren" auf den Punkt bringen. Statt einzelner Kundenmerkmale (wie Einkommen oder Alter etc.) werden Kundenprofile generiert.

**Online-Marketingmix** *m* - online marketing-mix

▪ Marketing, im Zusammenspiel zwischen Mobiltelefon, Internet und Fernsehen.

**Onlinedienst** *m* - online service

▪ Jeder über das Internet gelieferte Dienst. Dieser Dienst kann sehr einfach sein, z.B. die Bereitstellung von Informationen durch Online-Zeitungen oder komplexer wie z.B. das Online-Banking, bei dem der Kunde Bankaktivitäten online durchführen kann. Er kann ferner Ausbildungs- oder Unterhaltungsanforderungen erfüllen. In den letzten Jahren ist der Online-Dienst ein wichtiger Bestandteil der Marketingstrategie für Produkte und Dienstleistungen eines Unternehmens geworden.

**operatives Marketing** *n* - operational marketing

▪ Marketingbereich, in dem die kurzfristige Entwicklung von Aktionen stattfindet mit Einsatz der vier wichtigsten Instrumente: Produkt, Preis, Vertrieb und Kommunikation. Auch taktisches Marketing.

**optimale Bestellmenge** *f* - optimum quantity ordered

▪ Durch einen Kunden bestellte Produktmenge, die zur Reduzierung der Gesamtkosten der Bestandsverwaltung ausgelegt ist.

**optimale Kapazität** *f* - optimum capacity

▪ Produktionsniveau, das zu den niedrigsten Stückkosten führt. Es liegt in der Regel etwas unterhalb der Maximal-kapazität, denn bei maximaler Auslastung ist zwar der Einfluss der Fixkosten geringer, aber es können ein höherer Energieverbrauch, teurere Arbeitskräfte mit Überstunden und Probleme mit Lieferung oder Wartung auftreten, die es nicht empfehlenswert machen, an der Kapazitätsgrenze zu arbeiten.

**Optimalpreis** *m* - optimum price

▪ Idealer Preis im Hinblick auf die Erreichung der Unternehmensziele.

**optimistische Streber** *m/pl* - optimistic strivers

▪ Verbrauchertyp einer paneuropäischen Klassifizierung von Lebensstilen. Diese Art Verbraucher gibt es nur in Südeuropa. Meist handelt es sich um talentierte, ehrgeizige junge Menschen, die im Übergang zwischen den Vorstädten und dem Land leben und die Möglichkeit sehen, reich zu werden.

**optisches Leitmotiv** *n* - visual key

▪ Grafisches Element, das in einer Werbekampagne dominiert und in allen Medien verwendet wird, die für eine Kampagne benutzt werden.

**orange Waren** *f/pl* - orange good

▪ Verbrauchsgut, dass einen mäßigen Verlauf aufweist, z. B. Kleidungsartikel, die mit der Zeit abnutzen oder aus der Mode kommen.

**Outdoor-Werbeagentur** *f* - outdoor advertising agency
■ Werbeagentur, die sich auf die Nutzung und Verwaltung bestimmter Träger für die Außen-Werbung spezialisiert hat.

**Outdoor-Werbung** *f* - outdoor advertising
■ Werbeaktivität, die als Werbeträger Medien unterschiedlichster Art verwendet, um die Aufmerksamkeit der Menschen in offenen Räumen, Straßen, Plätzen auf sich zu ziehen, die im Allgemeinen gut eingesehen werden können, weil sie entsprechend positioniert sind.

**Outsourcing** *n* - outsourcing
■ Bezug einer Dienstleistung oder eines Teils von einem Dritten, außerhalb des Unternehmens. Dies bringt mehr Flexibilität, einen geringeren Zeitaufwand für die Führung und geringere Investitionen, sowie normalerweise eine stärkere Spezialisierung, geringere Kosten und höhere Qualität.

# P

**Paarvergleich** *m* - paired comparison
■ Bei der quantitativen Forschung, Art der Formulierung von Fragen, bei der die Befragten darum gebeten werden, anzugeben, welcher der beiden gegenteiligen Behauptungen sie eher zustimmen.

**Packungsbeilage** *f* - piggyback
■ Werbeelement, das im Allgemeinen in einer Produktverpackung mit eingeschlossen wird, z. B. ein Werbeprospekt, ein anderes Produkt der gleichen Marke oder irgendein anderes Produkt. Beim Postverkauf ist dieses sehr beliebt, denn es kann einem zuvor bestellten Produkt beigefügt werden.

**Packungswerbung** *f* - package insert
■ Werbung in einer Produktverpackung mit Werbung für andere Produkte aus dem gleichen Haus, oder sogar von anderen komplementären Unternehmen (Ersatzteile o. Ä.).

**Palettenversand** *m* - palletised shipment
■ Transport von Waren auf Paletten. Dabei kann es sich um Einweg- oder Mehrwegpaletten handeln. Erleichtert das Auf- und Abladen.

**palettieren** *v* - palletise *v*
■ Anbringen der zu transportierenden Waren oder Kisten in geordneter Form auf einer Palette. Die Waren werden versetzt aufeinander gestapelt, um eine gute Stabilität zu gewährleisten. Manchmal mit einer Verspundung verstärkt, mit einem Metallband im oberen Teil oder die gesamte Palette mit einer Plastikfolie verpackt. Die Verladung übereinander vermindert die Stabilität, begünstigt aber die Beständigkeit der Waren.

**Panel** *n* - panel
■ Im Zeitablauf gleich bleibende Stichprobe aus einer Grundgesamtheit, die für fortlaufende statistische Analysen, wie Marktstudien verwendet wird.

**Partner** *m* - affiliate
■ Im Internet, Person oder Institution, die auf ihrer Webseite Produkte eines Dritten gegen eine vertraglich festgelegte Provision anbietet. Zum Verkauf der Produkte oder Dienstleistungen schaltet der Partner z. B. interaktive Banner, die den Benutzer direkt auf die Seite des Partners leiten. Die Vergütung kann pro Verkauf, pro Besuch oder pro Formular berechnet werden. Der Partner kann seine Seite als Promotionsinstrument oder zur Durchführung von Direktmarketingkampagnen verwenden (einschließlich Anzeigen oder Verknüpfungen zu eigenen Produkten).

**Partnerforum** *n* - affiliate forum
■ Online-Gemeinschaft, in der Besucher das Partnermarketing kommentieren und diskutieren können.

**Partner-Geschäft** *n* - affiliated shop
■ Unabhängiges Geschäft, das an eine freiwillige Händlerkette angeschlossen ist, die ihm den größten Bedarf stellt und bestimmte Marketing-Dienstleistungen liefert.

**Partnermarketing** *n* - affiliate marketing

■ Handelsvertrag zwischen Herstellern oder Produzenten und Online-Verkäufern. Letztere verkaufen und bewerben die Produkte der Hersteller im Internet, indem sie ihre Besucher auf dessen Webseite weiterleiten.

**Partnerprogramm** *n* - affilliates program

■ Logisches Tool, das die Nutzung der Webseite einer Firma als Verkaufsplattform einer anderen Firma ermöglicht. Im Internet führt Amazon (amazon.com) die Entwicklung solcher Programme an, wobei das Unternehmen einen wesentlichen Verkaufsanteil dank seiner Partnerunternehmen erwirtschaftet. Die Programmverträge der Partnerunternehmen müssen deutlich hervorheben, dass für jeden einzelnen Verkauf, der über das Internet stattfindet, eine Provision angerechnet wird und dass die Verkäufe kumulativ betrachtet werden.

**Partner-Software** *f* - affiliate software

■ Beim Partnermarketing ein Programm, das zumindest dem Partner eine Kontrolle der von ihm generierten Aktivitäten einschließlich Einzelheiten über die Anzahl der Besuche, Verkäufe und Provisionen ermöglicht.

**Pass-along-Rate** *f* - pass-along rate

■ Im Internet, der Anteil an Personen, der sich Nachrichten oder Dateianhänge schickt.

**Passant** *m* - passer-by

■ In der Außenwerbung, Person, an der Werbung vorbeigekommen ist.

**Pauschaldeckung** *f* - blanket coverage

■ Werbekampagne, die über ein Massenmedium ohne vorherige Festlegung der Zielgruppe verbreitet wird, um auf diese Weise das größtmögliche Publikum zu erreichen.

**Performance-Werbung** *f* - performance advertising

■ Neue Form der Außenwerbung, durch eine überraschende Darstellung mit großer Auswirkung. Ein Beispiel dafür ist die Schmückung des Brandenburger Tors zur Werbung für die Fußball WM 2006.

**Personalisierung** *f* - personalisation

■ Im persönlichen Verkauf, Anpassung eines Gesprächs an die jeweilige Person, mit mehrmaliger namentlicher Ansprache, unter Berücksichtigung der Persönlichkeitsmerkmale, mit Eingehen auf die Antworten usw. Etwas Allgemeines auf eine persönliche Ebene bringen, indem man qualifizierende oder kennzeichnende Aspekte einbringt.

**persönliches Exemplar** *n* - personalised copy

■ Exemplar, das den Namen des Besitzers trägt, um ihm mehr Exklusivität und damit mehr Aufmerksamkeit zu verleihen.

**persönliches Interview** *n* - personal interview

■ In der Forschung, Gespräch zwischen zwei Personen, Befrager und Befragter, die sich am gleichen Ort aufhalten und bei dem ersterer letzteren über die Themen befragt, die in einem Fragebogen aufgeführt sind.

**Pfandverpackung** *f* - returnable container

■ Verpackung, die am selben Ort zurückgegeben werden kann, an dem sie gekauft wurde, damit sie gereinigt und anschließend erneut verwendet werden kann. Im Gegensatz dazu kann bei einer wieder verwertbaren Verpackung das Material dem Recycling und einer neuen Verwendung zugeführt werden, aber die Verpackung kann nicht unmittelbar erneut verwendet werden.

**physischer Vertrieb** *m* - physical distribution

■ Der Teil der Logistik, der den physikalischen Güterfluss von Fertigprodukten betrifft, und zwar vom Fabrikanten bis zum Kunden. Je nach dem wie die Eingliederung der übrigen Bereiche der Absatzwirtschaft gestaltet ist, kann die Logistik folgende Bereiche umfassen: Vorausberechnung der Verkaufszahlen, Produktionsplanung, Transport, Lagerhaltung und Aufteilung, Bestellwesen und Kundendienst.

**Pilotprogramm** *n* - pilot programme

■ Programm von begrenzter Dauer und mit freiwillig reduzierter Reichweite, das als Versuch dem endgültigen Programm vorhergeht und mögliche Fehler im Programmentwurf sowie Anhaltspunkte für dessen wahrscheinliche Ergebnisse und Effektivität liefert.

**Pilotumfrage** *f* - pilot survey

■ Untersuchung einer stark reduzierten Stichprobe, um mögliche Mängel im Design der Studie zu entdecken und diese vor Durchführung der endgültigen Umfrage beheben zu können.

**Plakatträger** *m* - sandwich-board man

■ Person, die eine Werbenachricht dadurch verbreitet, dass sie Plakate auf Brust und Rücken trägt. Die Person kann verkleidet sein, Reklamezettel verteilen und dabei eine gewisse Strecke zurücklegen.

**planen** *v* - plan *v*

■ Vorgang der Ausarbeitung eines Handlungsprogramms, in dem wirtschaftliche Variablen und Ziele festgesetzt, die nötigen finanziellen Mittel und deren Herkunft festgelegt sowie die konkreten Ziele für das Bezugsjahr bestimmt werden.

**Planogramm** *n* - plan-o-gram

■ Schema, das die Anordnung von Produkten in den Regalen einer Verkaufsstelle anzeigt.

**Planung** *f* - planning

■ Organisierte Aktivität zur Festlegung von Zielen, Bestimmung von Strategien, und Ingangsetzung der notwendigen materiellen und personellen Mittel zur Zielerreichung.

**Planung** *f* **der Werbemittel** - media planning

■ Auswahl der Werbemittel, mit denen eine bestimmte Werbebotschaft verbreitet werden soll. Die wichtigsten Kriterien sind: Merkmale des Zielpublikums, angestrebte Reichweite und Kontakthäufigkeit der Werbebotschaft, verfügbares Werbebudget und Nutzung der Werbeträger durch die Konkurrenz. Die Planung ist die Phase zwischen Untersuchung und Kauf von Werbeplatz oder -zeit und hat den Mediaplan (Plan der Werbemittel) zum Ergebnis.

**Plastikhülle** *f* - blister pack

■ Verpackung, die aus hart geformtem Plastik besteht, in der das Produkt und ein Informations- oder Werbebeiblatt enthalten ist. Hat gewöhnlich eine Lasche mit der man sie an einem Haken oder Regal befestigen kann. Wird gewöhnlich bei kleinen Artikeln verwendet, um Diebstahl zu verhindern und die Identifikation durch den Verbraucher zu erhöhen. Unterscheidet sich von der Folie, die aus weichem Kunststoff besteht und sich der immer Form des Produktes anpasst.

**Plastikumschlag** *m* - polybag

■ Hülle aus Plastikmaterial, als Umschlag einer Werbesendung. Sehr beliebt beim Senden von Zeitschriften und Katalogen.

**politische Werbung** *f* - political advertisement

■ Werbenachricht, deren Zweck die Befriedigung der Wahlziele oder des Images der Parteien oder politischen Einrichtungen ist.

**politischer Preis** *m* - political price

■ Preis, der künstlich - in der Regel von der Verwaltung - festgelegt wird, um einen bestimmten Sektor oder die Verbraucher zu begünstigen. Berücksichtigt mehr die politischen Interessen als die Marktumstände. Kann ein Mindest- oder Garantiepreis sein, um die Hersteller zu schützen, ein Höchstpreis, um die Verbraucher zu schützen, oder ein Festpreis. Die Verwaltung muss die Möglichkeit haben, Lagerbestände zu kaufen oder zu verkaufen, um einen flüssigen Marktablauf zu gewährleisten.

**Politmarketing** *n* - political marketing

■ Marketingansatz in dem Parteien die Wähler wie Firmen den Verbraucher betrachten. Politisches Marketing oder Politmarketing spielt gerade heute im Medienzeitalter und bei der wachsenden Bedeutung der Wechselwähler eine immer wichtigere Rolle. Zielgruppenorientierung geht mit Professionalisierung der Politik einher.

**Pop-Under** *n* - pop-under ad

■ Beim Pop-under wird zusätzlich zur betrachteten Seite ein weiteres Browserfenster geöffnet, das ausschließlich die Werbung enthält. Das Pop-under wird im Hintergrund geöffnet und der Nutzer bemerkt es erst, wenn er das Hauptfenster des Browsers schließt.

**Pop-Up** *n* - pop-up ad

■ Werbeformat im Internet bestehend aus der auftauchenden Anzeige in einem Bildschirmfenster auf der besuchten Seite, wenn eine Stelle auf dieser angeklickt wird.

**Pop-Up-Fenster** *n* - pop-up window

■ Werbetechnik, bei der die Werbung in einem neuen Browserfenster automatisch geöffnet wird und das gewünschte Hauptfenster überlagert.

**portofrei** - postage paid

■ Brief oder Antwortkarte in einem Direktversand, dessen Porto der Absender zahlt. Fördert die positive Antwort auf das Angebot seitens der Verbraucher. Portofrei ist eine gängige Praxis bei der Direktwerbung.

**Position** *f* - position

■ In der Werbung, Ort der Werbung auf einem Träger. Je nach Position wird der Anzeige eine größere oder kleinere Aufmerksamkeit zuteil, weshalb auch die Tarife unterschiedlich angesetzt sind. Ungerade Seiten sind teuerer als gerade, und der erste Werbespot ist teuerer als die folgenden.

**Positionsgrafik** *f* - positioning map

■ Grafische Darstellung auf einem zweiachsigen Plan zur Anzeige der verschiedenen Konkurrenzmarken und spezifischen Attributen folgend, die für das Zielpublikum oder den Zielmarkt wichtig sind. Hilft bei der idealen Positionierung in Marktlücken.

**Posten** *m* - lot

■ Menge, die auf einmal gekauft, produziert oder verkauft wird. Ein Posten kann aus gleichen Elementen bestehen (Produktion einer Maschine in einer Stunde), aus ähnlichen Elementen (Posten zum Verkauf angebotener Bücher) oder aus unterschiedlichen Elementen (Paketverkauf zweier unterschiedlicher Produkte zur Verkaufsförderung). Auch Los.

**Postsendung** *f* - mailing pack

■ Einzelsendung zur Werbung für eine Dienstleistung oder ein Produkt, das per Post vertrieben wird. Im Allgemeinen besteht es aus einem Umschlag, Schreiben, Bestellformular und einem frankierten Rückumschlag.

**Potential** *n* - potential

■ Möglich, aber noch nicht wirklich. Als Substantiv wird es auf die Menge der Ressourcen und Fähigkeiten einer Person, einer Marke oder eines Unternehmens angewandt. Dient zur Qualifikation von Märkten, Kunden, der Produktionskapazität usw., bedeutet einen Wert, den wir als erreichbar ansehen, der aber noch nicht erreicht worden ist.

**potentieller Markt** *m* - potential market

■ Mögliche Nachfrage nach einem Gut oder einer Dienstleistung, d. h. Personen mit einem Bedürfnis, das durch dieses Gut oder Dienstleistung befriedigt werden kann (theoretischer Markt), und die über ausreichende Mittel verfügen, um es in dieser Form zu befriedigen. Umfasst den gegenwärtigen Markt (des eigenen Unternehmens und der Konkurrenz) und die mögliche Erhöhung durch eine bessere Kenntnis des Produktes oder des Bedürfnisses, oder durch die Zunahme der Kaufkraft, der Zahl der Verbraucher oder des Pro-Kopf-Verbrauches.

**potentielles Publikum** *n* - potential audience

■ Höchstzahl der Menschen, die mit dem Medium oder Träger in einer festgelegten Zeit in Kontakt treten können. Die Zeitdauer ist bei der Berechnung des potentiellen Publikums ein Hauptfaktor, da die Anzahl der von diesem Medium erreichten Personen steigen kann, sogar erheblich, wenn die Dauer verlängert wird.

**PPC (Pay per Click)** - PPC (pay per click)

▪ Ergebnisbasiertes Werbesystem im Internet.

**Präferenz** *f* - preference

▪ Vorrang oder Vorteil, den eine Person oder Sache gegenüber einer anderen besitzt, wenn nach einem bestimmten Beurteilungskriterium eine Rangordnung gebildet wird.

**Prämiensatz** *m* - premium rate

▪ In der Werbung, die Kosten zum Einsatz einer Werbung zu besonderen Bedingungen oder an einer bestimmten Position. Diese Bedingungen reichen von einem festen Datum oder einer festen Stunde im Radio zu einer konkreten Seite in den Druckmedien. Oft ist ein höherer Tarif der Prämiensatz, manchmal auch ein Aufpreis auf den Grundpreis.

**Präsentation** *f* - presentation

▪ Veranstaltung, bei der ein neues Produkt vorgestellt wird, und, allgemein, erstmalige Darlegung einer Idee oder eines Berichts vor Zuhörern mit audiovisuellen Hilfsmitteln.

**Preis** *m* - price

▪ Wert oder Geldmenge, die mit einem Gut verbunden ist. Der Preis ist immer an die Idee des Güteraustauschs gebunden, sprich daran was der Markt für den Erwerb eines Gutes zu zahlen bereit ist.

**Preis herabsetzen** *v* - markdown *v*

▪ Mindern des Endverkaufspreises einer Ware mit dem Ziel diese als Sonderangebot, in einem Saisonschlussverkauf oder Räumungsverkauf zu veräußern.

**preisabhängig** - price sensitive

▪ Produkt oder Dienstleistung mit höheren oder geringeren Verkäufen in Abhängigkeit zum Preis.

**Preisabsprache** *f* - price fixing

▪ Absprache zwischen Firmen, die Konkurrenten zu sein scheinen, um ihre Waren zu bestimmten Preisen zu verkaufen. Diese Art von Abkommen ist gesetzlich verboten, wird jedoch relativ häufig praktiziert, wenn auch nicht in beständiger Form. Zusätzlich zu den Preisen kann das Abkommen auch andere Konditionen mit einschließen z. B. bezüglich Zahlungserleichterungen und Werbekosten.

**Preisangabe** *f* - price indication

▪ Anzeige eines Produktpreises. Die europäische Richtlinie legt fest, dass die angebotenen Produkte den Verbrauchern den Kaufpreis anzeigen müssen, sowie den Kaupreis pro Maßeinheit.

**Preisanpassungsklausel** *f* - price escalation clause

▪ Bedingung des Kaufvertrags, die es dem Verkäufer gestattet, den Verkaufspreis z. B. aufgrund gestiegener Materialkosten anzupassen.

**Preisbestimmung** *f* **bei Komplementärprodukten** - captive product pricing

▪ Festsetzung eines künstlichen Preises für ein bestimmtes Produkt, um aus diesem und den mit ihm in Beziehung stehenden Produkten den maximalen Gesamtgewinn zu ziehen und zugleich den Preis der anderen Produkte wettbewerbsfähig zu halten, denn der Gewinn wird mit dem Komplementärprodukt gemacht. So kann etwa der Hersteller von fotografischen Geräten den Preis von Filmen niedrig halten und somit einen Gewinn aus der Filmentwicklung erzielen.

**Preisdifferenzierung** *f* - price differentiation

▪ Technik, um die Eigenschaften der Ware oder Dienstleistung (Qualität, Garantie, Mindestlieferung, Zahlungsfrist usw.) an die Anforderungen und Möglichkeiten jedes Kunden anzupassen, und insbesondere um die Preise festzulegen, die den Gewinn der Unternehmung maximieren. Die dadurch bedingte Diskriminierung kann für den Verbraucher vorteilhaft sein, da sie ihm ein Paket aus Preis und Bedingungen bietet, das besser auf ihn zugeschnitten ist (z.B. Flugtarife).

**Preisdiskriminierung** *f* - price discrimination

▪ Festsetzung unterschiedlicher Preise für ein und dasselbe Produkt oder ein ähnliches Produkt, das keinen wesentlichen Unterschied bei den Kosten verursacht. Mit diesem System der Preisfestsetzung versucht man, die unterschiedlichen Nachfrageintensitäten innerhalb der einzelnen Segmente auszunutzen, um den maximalen Gewinn zu erzielen. Die Segmentation kann nach Kunden, Ort, Tageszeit oder Jahreszeit, Veredelungsart oder Verpackungsart vorgenommen werden.

**Preiseffekt** *m* - price effect

▪ Änderung der nachgefragten Menge eines Gutes infolge von Änderungen seines Preises. Normalerweise sinkt der Verbrauch, wenn der Preis steigt, und umgekehrt.

**Preiselastizität** *f* **der Nachfrage** - elasticity of demand

▪ Misst das Nachfrageverhalten in Bezug auf Preisveränderungen. Bestimmt wird sie aus dem Quotienten der prozentualen Mengenveränderung und der prozentualen Preisveränderung. Die Nachfrage ist unelastisch, wenn die prozentuale Veränderung der Nachfrage kleiner ist als die prozentuale Veränderung des Preises (E<1). Die Nachfrage ist elastisch, wenn die prozentuale Veränderung in der Nachfrage größer ist als die prozentuale Veränderung des Preises (E>1). Auch Nachfrageelastizität.

**Preiselastizität** *f* **des Angebots** - elasticity of supply

▪ Misst das Verhalten der Angebotsmenge im Verhältnis zu Preisänderungen. Steigt der Preis z. B. um 2% , und die angebotene Menge steigt um mehr als 2% , dann ist die Angebotsfunktion elastisch. Steigt das Angebot um weniger als 2% , ist das Angebot unelastisch oder starr. Auch Angebotselastizität.

**Preiskrieg** *m* - price war

▪ Situation auf einem Markt, auf dem der Wettbewerb zwischen den Firmen hauptsächlich über das Absenken der Verkaufspreise ausgetragen wird. In der Regel deckt der Verkaufspreis die variablen und fixen Kosten ab und erlaubt noch die Erzielung eines Gewinns. Unter bestimmten Umständen (z. B. bei einem Nachfragerückgang, Eintritt von neuen Marktteilnehmern, Absicht eines etablierten Marktteilnehmers seinen Marktanteil zu erhöhen usw.) können die gesamten Wettbewerber dazu gezwungen sein, den Preis so weit zu senken, dass dieser Gewinn nicht mehr erwirtschaftet wird oder sogar so weit, dass nicht einmal mehr die gesamten Fixkosten abgedeckt werden.

**Preisnachlass** *m* - price cut

▪ Sonderpreis oder Rabatt auf den Preis eines Produkts oder einer Dienstleistung zum Erreichen eines bestimmten Ziels, wie z. B. Marktanteilserhöhung, Kampf gegen einen neuen Konkurrenten oder Nischenschaffung für ein hochwertigeres Produkt.

**Preispolitik** *f* - pricing strategy

▪ Die Preispolitik verfolgt hauptsächlich das Ziel, mit Hilfe der Preisgestaltung Kaufanreize zu setzen. Ein wichtiges Entscheidungsproblem ist die Preisuntergrenze. Die Preisobergrenze dagegen wird durch die Nachfrage festgelegt. Sie liegt grundsätzlich dort, wo der vom Kunden wahrgenommene Preis mit seiner Wertschätzung des Produktes übereinstimmt.

**Preisregulierung** *f* - price regulation

▪ Regelung der Preise, zu denen Produkte verkauft werden. In manchen Fällen gibt der Staat die Preise für bestimmte Produkte über die so genannten genehmigten Preise vor.

**Preissenkung** *f* - price cutting

▪ Marketingtaktik, die aus dem Heruntersetzen des Produktpreis für einen vorher festgelegten Zeitraum besteht, um einer negativen Marktentwicklung entgegenzuwirken (z. B. Markteinführung oder Preisnachlass bei einer Konkurrenzmarke) oder eine positive Entwicklung zu starten (Marktanteilsteigerung aufgrund der erhöhten Preisflexibilität).

**Preisspanne** *f* - price range

■ Bei Aktien, Bereich vom niedrigsten zum höchsten Kurs einer Aktie. Im Lauf eines bestimmten Zeitraums, zum Beispiel einer Börsensitzung.

**Preistaktik** *f* - pricing tactic

■ In der Preispolitik die Handlung zur Anpassung auf ein bestimmtes Ziel, z. B. Bremsen der Markteinführung eines Konkurrenten, Einführung des Produkts in einem bestimmten geografischen Gebiet oder Ausverkauf einer Version, die eine künstliche Obsoleszenz erleiden soll.

**Preisverfall** *m* - price fall

■ Schnelle Verminderung der Verkaufspreise, verursacht durch einen Nachfragerückgang oder eine starke Angebotszunahme. Sie hängt gewöhnlich mit dem Wandel des Geschmacks oder der Gewohnheiten der Verbraucher zusammen, kann aber auch allgemein sein, wenn die Ursache die gesamte Wirtschaft einer Region betrifft.

**Preisverzeichnis** *n* - price list

■ Dokument, in dem der Verkäufer die Preise seiner Produkte (teilweise auch Preisempfehlungen für den Einzelhandel) und die Rabatte und Lieferungs- und Zahlungsbedingungen angibt. Die Großkunden, die oft in Einkaufszentralen zusammengeschlossen sind, handeln zu Jahresanfang feste Nachlässe auf den Listenpreis aus, der zum jeweiligen Zeitpunkt in Abhängigkeit von der Entwicklung der Kosten und der Gesamtnachfrage gilt. Listenpreis ist gleichbedeutend mit Katalogpreis.

**Presse** *f* - press

■ Sammelbegriff für periodische Druckschriften, insbesondere Tageszeitungen.

**Presseagent** *m* - press agent

■ Fachmann für die Verteilung von Information an die Kommunikationsmassenmedien durch eine Person oder Organisation, damit diese die Medien weiterleiten. Im Allgemeinen ist dieser Beruf dem Schauspiel und Sport vorbehalten.

**Pressebeziehungen** *f/pl* - press relations

■ Berufsmäßige und regelmäßige Kommunikation mit der Presse und anderen Massenmedien, um ein positives Image des Unternehmens und seiner Produkte zu erreichen und zu wahren. Dazu werden Pressemitteilungen, Fabrikbesuche, Interviews mit der Unternehmensführung und Berichte über neue Produkte vorbereitet, für Medienpräsenz bei den Hauptversammlungen der Aktionären oder anderen Versammlungen gesorgt, um über die Ergebnisse des Unternehmens zu berichten, und insbesondere werden die Fragen der Medienvertreter in ungünstigen Situationen oder Krisen beantwortet.

**Pressekonferenz** *f* - press conference

■ Public Relations-Aktion, die sich an die Massenmedien richtet und Journalisten versammelt, denen eine wichtige Mitteilung gemacht wird und auf deren Fragen geantwortet wird.

**Pressemappe** *f* - press kit

■ Public-Relations-Aktion, die sich an die Massenmedien richtet und aus einem Dokument mit Informationen über die Organisation besteht, das journalistisch geschrieben ist und das Unternehmen vorstellen soll. Enthält normalerweise Pressemitteilungen. Auch Pressedossier genannt.

**Pressemitteilung** *f* - press release

■ Kurze Mitteilung, die eine Organisation an die daran interessierten Kommunikationsmedien verschickt, damit diese sie kostenlos verbreiten. Diese Art von Mitteilung kann man auch als Pressenotiz oder Presseverlautbarung bezeichnen, obwohl sie nicht nur auf die Presse beschränkt ist. Es ist eine gebräuchliche Form im Bereich der Öffentlichkeitsarbeit, um Jahresraten, Ernennungen, Eröffnungen und Neueinführungen von Produkten bekannt zu geben.

**Pressestelle** *f* - press office

▪ Informationsdienst einer Unternehmung oder Institution für die Medien, der als Sprecher der Organisation auftritt, Pressemitteilungen verbreitet und auf die Fragen der Medienvertreter antwortet.

**Prestige** *n* - prestige

▪ Guter Ruf, Wertschätzung und Ansehen, die Respekt und Bewunderung hervorrufen. Prestigeartikel haben einen Preis, der deutlich höher ist als ihr Wert oder praktischer Nutzen, und werden gekauft, um den Wohlstand oder die Bedeutung des Erwerbers zu zeigen.

**Prestigepreis** *m* - prestige price

▪ Erhöhter Preis, der im Allgemeinen für Luxusartikel festgelegt wird, die Qualität und Besonderheit ausdrücken sollen.

**Probenutzung** *f* - product training

▪ Marketingaktivität, die die Benutzung des Produkts während einer bestimmten Zeit von Fachleuten zulässt (z. B. ein neues Automodell), damit sie selbst das neue Produkt erfahren und so danach ihre Meinung darüber an die öffentlichen Medien weitergeben können (z. B. in den Autozeitschriften).

**Probiertheke** *f* - demonstrator display

▪ Ausstellungsmöbel, meist Klapptisch mit einem Plakat darüber zur Unterstützung einer Produktpromotion. Wird zeitweise in großen Verkaufsflächen, wie Supermärkten, aufgestellt. Hier lädt eine Verkaufsperson den Verbraucher zum “Probieren” ein. Wird häufig im Lebensmittelbereich eingesetzt und ist besonders zur Einführung von neuen Produkten auf dem Markt wirksam.

**Produkt** *n* - product

▪ Jeglicher Gegenstand oder Dienstleistung, die gemäß der Wahrnehmung der Verbraucher in der Lage sind, ein Bedürfnis zu befriedigen. Ergebnis eines schöpferischen Bemühens und wird dem Verbraucher unter bestimmten Eigenschaften angeboten. Gleichbedeutend mit dem Begriff Gut. Es gibt freie und knappe Produkte oder Güter, wobei letztere wiederum in Konsum- und Investitionsgüter unterteilt werden. Die Konsumprodukte werden nach Familien, Artikeln und Varianten eingeteilt.

**Produktbeistellung** *f* - product placement

▪ Werbetechnik bestehend aus der Einbringung des Produkts mit seiner entsprechenden Marke in einer Fernsehserie oder in einem Kinofilm. Kann aktiv (Produkt ist an der Interaktion beteiligt oder die Marke wird von den Darstellern angesprochen) oder passiv (lediglich in der Szene vorhanden) sein. Die Technik befindet sich aufgrund des Rückgangs der Wirkung der herkömmlichen Werbung im Aufschwung und wird auch für andere Unterhaltungsmedien wie z. B. Bücher und Videogames benutzt. Es wird auch oft der englische Begriff benutzt.

**Produktbeseitigung** *f* - product elimination

▪ Geordnete Rücknahme eines Produkts ohne Gewinnvorteile oder Funktionen.

**Produktdifferenzierung** *f* - product differentiation

▪ Einführung von Merkmalen, Zusätzen, Eigenschaften, Aufmachungen oder Präsentationen einer Marke, um eine Differenzierung von bereits bestehenden Produkten zu erreichen, und von denen man sich eine erhöhte Rentabilität verspricht. Der Käufer nimmt den Mehrwert wahr und darüber hinaus besteht kein direkter Preiswettbewerb.

**Produkteinführungspreis** *m* - launch price

▪ Preis, der für ein neues Produkt festgelegt wird. Falls es sich um einen neuen Markt handelt, spricht man vom Markteinführungspreis. Falls er mit einer neuen Gestaltung der Verpackung, des Etiketts, der Produktzusammensetzung oder der Kommunikation einhergeht, spricht man vom Wiedereinführungspreis.

**Produkteinführungstest** *m* - wet test

▪ Verkauf einer begrenzten Auflage eines Produkts vor der Massenfertigung in Abhängigkeit des Erfolgs bei der Vermarktung der Testprodukte.

**Produktentwicklung** *f* - product development

■ Im Marketing, Strategie bestehend aus der Eingabe von Verbesserungen eines Produkts, damit die Anfrage durch den Verbraucher steigt.

**Produktfamilie** *f* - product family

■ Produkte, die eine Gruppe bilden, da sie ähnliche Bedürfnisse befriedigen oder über gemeinsame Produktionsprozesse oder Vertriebswege verfügen. Untereinander unterscheiden sie sich hauptsächlich in der Qualität, auf Grund der verwendeten Rohstoffe und durch den Hersteller. Die Gruppeneinteilung wird hauptsächlich von den Vertreibern verwendet, um die Rentabilität leichter bestimmen zu können, die Aufstellung im Laden zu vereinfachen, Fehlmengen leichter auszugleichen und um den Vergleich zwischen Handelszentren zu ermöglichen. Nicht mit der Produktpalette zu verwechseln.

**Produktimage** *n* - product image

■ Eindruck und Bild, das ein Produkt für sich genommen vermittelt, auch wenn es oft stark vom Markenimage beeinflusst wird.

**Produktionsgut** *n* - production good

■ Gleichbedeutend mit Investitionsgut. Güter, die zur Herstellung von Konsumgütern oder anderen Investitionsgütern verwendet werden.

**Produktionskapazität** *f* - productive capacity

■ Produktionsumfang, den ein Unternehmen erreichen kann, wenn es alle ihm zur Verfügung stehenden Mittel einsetzt oder seine Produktionslinien und Maschinen mit voller Auslastung betreibt, unter Abzug der Stillstände für Wartungsarbeiten und möglicher Störungen.

**produktionsorientiert** - production-oriented

■ Einstellung eines Unternehmens, das sich nicht an der Befriedigung der Bedürfnisse der Kunden orientiert, sondern den Schwerpunkt auf die Einführung neuer Produkte legt, die von den Technikern des Unternehmens entwickelt werden, weil sie leichter herzustellen sind oder sich besser an die Anlagenkapazität anpassen.

**Produktionsorientierung** *f* - product orientation

■ Marketingfokus, bei dem ein Unternehmen seine Aktivität auf die Produktpolitik konzentriert und eher die Produktionskosten analysiert als die Marktanforderungen. Diese Orientierung hat besonders in Sektoren Erfolg, in denen die Produkte selten sind und die Anfrage die Produktivitätsanforderungen überschreitet, wodurch bei der Produktausgabe an den Markt keine Probleme auftreten. In sehr wettbewerbsfähigen Sektoren mit hohem Angebotsniveau eignet sich daher eher die Marktorientierung.

**Produktkategorie** *f* - product class

■ Gruppe aus Ersatzprodukten, die in einem bestimmten Maß die Kohäsion und Gleichartigkeit beibehält, da sie die gleichen Ansprüche befriedigen. Am einfachsten versetzt man sich in die Lage des Verbrauchers und analysiert von seinem Standpunkt aus die die Austauschbarkeit der Produkte, um diese der gleichen Kategorie zuzuordnen.

**Produktlebenszyklus** *m* **(PLC)** - product life cycle (PLC)

■ In der Regel wird der Lebenszyklus eines Produkts zur Vereinfachung in vier Phasen unterteilt: Einführung, Wachstum, Reife und Rückgang. Die Verkaufszahlen steigen in den ersten drei Phasen an und fallen in der letzten Phase. Ähnlich verhält es sich bei den Gewinnen, obwohl es möglich ist, dass während der Einführungsphase Verluste realisiert werden.

**Produktlinie** *f* - product line

■ Gesamtheit gleichartiger Produkte, die ähnliche Bedürfnisse befriedigen und dem Verbraucher unter dem selben Markennamen und mit einer verbundenen Kommunikationspolitik angeboten werden. Handelt es sich um eine vollständige Produktlinie, spricht man von einem Produktfächer. Jedes Produkt kann verschiedene Varianten umfassen, und diese wiederum verschiedene Referenznummern, die man als Artikelpalette bezeichnet.

**Produktlinienharmonisierung** *f* - product range balancing

■ Handlung, mit der die verschiedenen Merkmale (zum Beispiel Ästhetik, Größe, Preise, Sicherheitsvorschriften) einer Produktlinie aufeinander abgestimmt werden, damit sie besser den Bedürfnissen und Wünschen der Verbraucher entsprechen.

**Produktmarke** *f* - product brand

■ Marke, die mit einem Produkt in Verbindung gebracht wird und sich von den anderen Produkte der gleichen Firma abhebt.

**Produkt-Markt-Verhältnis** *n* - product market

■ Konzept, das sich auf die Merkmale des auf dem Markt angebotenen Produkts, die Technik zu dessen Herstellung, die Verbrauchergruppe, an die es sich richtet, oder die zu befriedigende Anforderung in Bezug auf den Verbraucher richtet. Wird auch Geschäftsstrategie genannt, obwohl diese oftmals mehr als das Produkt-Markt-Verhältnis umfasst und daher ein breiter gefasstes Konzept ist.

**Produktpalette** *f* - product range

■ Im engeren Sinn versteht man darunter alle Artikel eines Produkts, die sich durch die Farbe oder andere Zusätze unterscheiden. Die Unterscheidung nach Größen führt zu mehreren Referenzen des selben Artikels. Weiter gefasst, versteht man darunter das Sortiment oder die Produktlinie.

**Produktreihe** *f* - product mix

■ Zusammenstellung von Produkten eines einzigen Herstellers, die untereinander gruppiert werden, um sich gegenseitig zu verstärken. Die Kombination von Produkten ist eine der meist benutzten Marketing-Maßnahmen, um Produkte auf dem Markt einzuführen, die eine niedrige Gewinnspanne hätten. In einigen Fällen werden diese unter der gleichen Marke gruppiert, bzw. jedes Produkt hat eine andere Marke.

**Produkttest** *m* - product trial

■ Test, bei der die Benutzung des Produkts während der Marktforschung von Verbrauchern durchgeführt wird, damit sie das Produkt kennen lernen und danach ihre Meinung darüber weitergeben können.

**Produktwerbung** *f* - product advertising

■ Werbeaktivität, die ein bestimmtes Produkt bei einer Zielgruppe bekannt macht und dessen Ziel die Überzeugung der Zielperson zum Kauf oder zur Nutzung des Produkts ist.

**progressives Marketing** *n* - rollout marketing

■ Technik zur Einführung eines neuen Produkts, die vor allem in den USA verwendet wird und darin besteht, das Produkt in einen Teil des landesweiten Marktes einzuführen, um später die Nachfrage im Rest des Landes zu decken. Es wird in sehr großen und komplexen Märkten verwendet, wenn die Konkurrenten auch nicht vorpreschen und das Produkt landesweit einführen können.

**Prominenten-Werbespot** *m* - cast commercial

■ Fernsehspot, in dem die Schauspieler aus einem TV-Film auftreten. Der Spot kann zwischen zwei Werbeblöcken eingeschoben oder zu einem anderen beliebigen Zeitpunkt ausgestrahlt werden. In einigen Ländern ist diese Praktik verboten, um Unklarheiten bzw. Verwechslungen zwischen Werbung und dem eigentlichen Programm zu vermeiden. Manchmal werden auch Nachrichtensprecher eingesetzt, die zusätzlich zu ihrem Bekanntheitsgrad, Glaubwürdigkeit vermitteln.

**Prototyp** *m* - prototype

■ Originalmodell, mit dem die Endprüfungen durchgeführt werden, bevor es in Serienfertigung geht.

**Prototyp-Markt** *m* - prototype market

▪ Marktumgebung, in der die Zielaktivität der Franchise erfolgreich geprüft und entwickelt wurde, entweder über Piloteinrichtungen oder herkömmliche Verkaufsstellen oder in eigenen Einrichtungen. Die Parameter und Variablen werden geprüft und detailliert in anderen Marktpunkten geprüft, um neue Franchises auszugeben. Die Marktbesonderheiten stellen einen Schlüsselfaktor in jedem Planungsvorgang der Franchise-Expansion dar.

**Prüfer** *m* - watchdog

▪ Person, die damit beauftragt ist, für die Einhaltung des Statuten, Reglementierungen und Abkommen zu sorgen.

**psychografische Analyse** *f* - psychographic analysis

▪ In der Forschung, Studium der Bevölkerung hinsichtlich ihrer Interessen, Meinungen und Einstellungen.

**psychologischer Preis** *m* - psychological price

▪ Preis, der mit einer ungeraden Zahl endet, z. B. 5 oder 9, und unterhalb der runden höheren Zahl liegt, wodurch dem Verbraucher eine Ersparnis suggeriert wird (z. B. Produktpreis von 995 oder 999 Euro statt 1000 Euro).

**Public Relations** *pl* **(PR)** - public relations

▪ Öffentlichkeitsarbeit oder auch Public Relations (PR) bezeichnet: einen weit gefassten Begriff für die Gestaltung der öffentlichen Kommunikation von Organisationen, Unternehmen, Ideen oder Einzelpersonen ein in einem Prozess der zunehmenden Professionalisierung begriffenes Berufsfeld und Forschungsfeld ein soziales Phänomen, das Gegenstand einer Wissenschaft ist, die sich im Spannungsfeld von Kommunikations- und Wirtschaftswissenschaft sowie Psychologie und Soziologie ausdifferenziert alle Maßnahmen zur Pflege der Beziehung zur Öffentlichkeit PR ist die Gestaltung guter, positiver und fruchtbarer Beziehungen einer Unternehmung zur Öffentlichkeit. Diese Arbeit schließt die sachliche Aufklärung und Unterrichtung 'in eigener Sache' mit ein

**Public Relations Society of America (PRSA)** - Public Relations Society of America (PRSA)

▪ US-amerikanische Organisation für Public Relations, die 1947 mit dem Ziel der Entwicklung des Sektors gegründet wurde und deren Mitarbeiter über Ausbildungsprogramme, Foren und Informationsaustausche Projekte lokaler und nationaler Forschung unterstützen.

**Public Relations-Agentur** *f* - public relations agency

▪ Unternehmen, das sich verpflichtet ein günstiges Image seines Kunden innerhalb seines Zielpublikums und der Kommunikationsmedien zu entwickeln.

**Public Relations-Strategieplan** *m* - public relations plan

▪ Projekt der Schritte eines Unternehmens in Bezug auf sein Publikum zum Erreichen der Ziele (Annahme und Unterstützung) oder gegenseitigem Verständnis. Besteht aus vier Phasen: Forschung, Programmierung, Ausführung und Bewertung.

**Publicity** *f* - publicity

▪ Unpersönliche Form zur Anregung der Nachfrage oder Beeinflussung der Meinung oder Einstellung einer Gruppe gegenüber dem Unternehmen durch eine Kommunikation in Massenmedien, die nicht von dem Unternehmen oder der Organisation bezahlt wird, die von ihr profitieren. Manchmal kann diese Information nicht vollständig kontrolliert werden, insbesondere hinsichtlich des Zeitpunkts, zu dem sie erscheint.

**Publikum** *n* – public, audience

▪ Gesamtheit von Personen, die sich durch ein gemeinsames Merkmal auszeichnet. Im Allgemeinen eine unbestimmte Personengruppe, an die ein Produkt, eine künstlerische Darbietung, Dienstleistung oder Botschaft gerichtet ist.

**Publikumsanalyse** *f* - audience analysis

▪ Untersuchung der Personen, die von den verschiedenen Massenmedien in einem bestimmten Zeitraum erreicht werden in Bezug auf ihre demographischen und sozioökonomischen Merkmale und ihren Lebensstil.

**Publikumsprofil** *n* - audience profile

■ Demografische, sozioprofessionelle, sozioökonomische und psychologische Merkmale eines Publikums eines Programms. Es soll festgestellt werden, ob das Profil mit dem der Zielgruppe übereinstimmt und ob es sich deshalb lohnt, Werbezeit in diesem Programm zu kaufen.

**Pulldown-Fenster** *n* - shutter

■ Werbefenster, das sich im Zentrum der Seite einer Website herunterklappt. Es erscheint beim Laden der Seite und klappt sich nach etwa zehn Sekunden wieder zusammen, wobei ein kleines Icon zurückbleibt, das es dem Benutzer ermöglicht, es erneut herunterzuklappen.

# Q

**qualitativ** - qualitative

■ Berücksichtigung der Qualitäten oder Eigenschaften einer Sache. All die Dinge, die nicht an Hand von Zahlen bestimmbar oder messbar sind.

**qualitative Analyse** *f* - qualitative analysis

■ Untersuchung aller Faktoren, die für eine bestimmte Entscheidung relevant sind und nicht quantifiziert werden konnten.

**Qualitätskontrolle** *f* - quality control

■ Normen und Tätigkeiten, um sicherzustellen, dass das Ergebnis eines Prozesses den zuvor erstellten Kriterien entspricht. Sie wird in erster Linie vom Arbeiter selbst und seiner Arbeitsgruppe durchgeführt. Anschließend kann noch eine Qualitätsprüfung durchgeführt werden.

**Qualitätskontrollplan** *m* - quality control plan

■ Programm, das die Ziele der Qualitätskontrolle genau festlegt, die Kontrollmethode festlegt (Fehleranzahl, Eigenschaften oder Messabweichung), das Stichprobenverfahren bestimmt (in welcher Phase, von welchen Personen, Stichprobenumfang) und die Entscheidung trifft, die sich aus dem Ergebnis der Qualitätsprüfung ergibt (Akzeptanz oder Ablehnung des Loses, Überprüfung des Prozesses oder im Zweifelsfall eine Erhöhung des Stichprobenumfanges). Der Plan ist notwendig für die Beziehungen zwischen den einzelnen Abteilungen im Unternehmen selbst sowie für die Beziehungen mit Lieferanten und Kunden.

**Qualitätszertifikat** *n* - quality certificate

■ Eine vom Unternehmen gegebene Garantie darüber, dass das verkaufte Produkt auch über die kennzeichnenden Eigenschaften verfügt, wegen denen man es kauft. Das Qualitätszertifikat beinhaltet meist auch eine Garantie für den Fall, dass das Produkt frühzeitig kaputt geht. In diesem Fall verpflichtet sich das Unternehmen zu einem Umtausch oder einer kostenlosen Schadensregulierung. Das Qualitätszertifikat steht im Zusammenhang mit einer betriebseigenen Qualitätskontrolle.

**quantitativ** - quantitative

■ Mit Rücksicht auf die Menge.

**Querschnitt** *m* - cross section

■ In der Datenbankwerbung versteht man hierunter einen Auszug aus einer willkürlich zusammengestellten Liste, wobei das Auswahlkriterium darin besteht, 1 von n Namen solange auszuwählen, bis man die gesamte Liste durchlaufen hat und dabei die notwendigen Register gewählt hat, so dass der Auszug repräsentativ ist.

**Querschnittsuntersuchung** *f* - cross-sectional study

■ Untersuchung, die sich auf eine bestimmte, im Vorfeld innerhalb einer Bevölkerung oder eines Umfelds abgegrenzte Gruppe konzentriert.

**Quick Response** *f* - quick response

■ Leitsystem basierend auf Verbrauchsprognosemodellen, das den Markt zum

Motor der Produktionsvorgänge und Bestandswartung macht. Mit dem Modell können die Kosten zur Bestandsverwaltung und Produktübergabe zu den mit dem Kunden räumlichen und zeitlichen Bedingungen ausgeführt werden.

**Quotenauswahl** *f* - quota sampling

■ Nicht zufällige Stichprobe, der willkürlichen Auswahl dahingehend ähnlich, dass es keine Bestimmung der enthaltenen Elemente gibt. Sie ist jedoch in soweit korrigiert, als dass bestimmte Merkmale proportional zur Gesamtbevölkerung eingehalten werden (zum Beispiel , dass 51% Frauen in der Stichprobe enthalten sind). Dies sichert weder, dass die für die Fragestellung relevanten Merkmale berücksichtigt werden, noch dass die Stichprobe jeder Quote repräsentativ ist, noch dass sie zufällig ausgewählt ist. Es ist schwierig letztendlich alle Quoten zu erfüllen. Nicht mit der geschichteten Auswahl zu verwechseln.

# R

**Rabatt** *m* - price discount

■ Preisnachlass für Waren oder Dienstleistungen.

**Rabatt** *m* **zur Absatzförderung** - promotional allowance

■ Preisabzug vom Listenpreis aufgrund konjunktureller Gegebenheiten, aufgrund einer Produkteinführung, aufgrund des verstärkten Absatzes in einem bestimmten Gebiet oder aufgrund der Unterstützung eines bestimmten Kunden. Der Rabatt kann auf jedes gekaufte Produkt einzeln gewährt werden, oder aber pauschal (z. B. Kosten für die Kopfposition bei einem Regal oder Anzeige in einer Zeitung oder Preisverzeichnis).

**Radiowerbung** *f* - radio commercial, radio advertising

■ Werbemitteilung, die mit Sprachressourcen und Tonressourcen entworfen (Stimmen, Spezialeffekte, Musik, usw.) und die mithilfe der Audiotechnik hergestellt wurde.

**randlos** - bleed

■ Präsentation einer Anzeige oder eines Textes, der die ganze Seite abdeckt, ohne dass ein Rand bleibt. Gegenteil von randlos mit Abreißstreifen, wo die von der Anzeige bedeckte Fläche kleiner als die Seite ist.

**Ratenkauf** *m* - hire purchase

■ Kauf eines Gegenstandes, den man sofort nutzen kann, aber erst nach und nach bezahlt. Die Bezahlung erfolgt in bereits vor dem Kauf feststehenden Zeitabständen, zusammen mit einem entsprechenden Zins.

**Ratenverkauf** *m* - instalment sale

■ Kreditverkauf, bei dem Teilzahlungen in regelmäßigen Abständen festgelegt werden. Normalerweise sind dies Monats- oder Vierteljahreszeiträume. Die Beträge sind in der Regel konstant und beinhalten die Zinszahlungen und die Tilgung des Kredites (Annuitätenmethode).

**Rationierung** *f* - rationing

■ Verteilung knapper Waren auf die Verbraucher in direkter Form, zu den von den Behörden festgelegten Preisen, Mengen und Bedingungen. Da die Gesetze von Angebot und Nachfrage nicht gelten, ist das Auftauchen eines Schwarzmarktes vorhersehbar.

**Raubkopie** *f* - piracy

■ Illegale Vervielfältigung von Computerprogrammen oder von bekannten Markenprodukten.

**räumlicher Wettbewerb** *m* - spatial competition

■ Rivalität zwischen Unternehmen, die sich auf ein bestimmtes geografisches Gebiet konzentriert.

**räumlicher Zusammenschluss** *m* - spatial association

■ Zusammenschluss von Einzelhändlern an dem gleichen geografischen Ort oder Gebiet, um eine höhere Verbraucherzahl in dieses Gebiet anzuziehen.

**Räumungsverkauf** *m* - liquidation sale

■ Ausverkauf der letzten Bestände vor Aufgabe, Umzug oder Übergabe eines Geschäftes.

**Räumungsverkaufspreis** *m* - knock out price

■ Stark herabgesetzter Ausverkaufspreis mit dem Ziel, die Lagerbestände eines Produktes wegen der Einführung eines anderen Produktes oder wegen Geschäftswechsel oder -aufgabe zu räumen.

**Reaktionsschwelle** *f* - advertising threshold

■ Moment, in dem die erste Reaktion des Verbrauchers auf eine Werbekampagne registriert wird.

**realer Markt** *m* - real market

■ Tatsächliche und verwirklichte Nachfrage nach einer Ware oder Dienstleistung in einem bestimmten Moment. Der Nachfrager kauft von uns oder von unseren Wettbewerbern. Man spricht auch vom bestehenden Markt, und manchmal einfach vom Markt. Kleiner als der potentielle und der theoretische Markt.

**Redimensionierung** *f* - resizing

■ Anpassungsprozeß einer Organisation an die Marktumstände, gewöhnlich verbunden mit einer Herabsetzung des Budgets, Kosteneinsparungen und einer Reduzierung der festangestellten Belegschaft, wobei man auch von Verschlankung sprechen kann.

**Referenzmarke** *f* - gold standard brand

■ Marke, deren Produkt den entsprechenden Markt treffend wiedergibt und für die restlichen Produkte als Bezug dient, z. B. Coca-Cola auf dem Erfrischungsgetränkemarkt und Nescafé bei löslichem Kaffee. Die Referenzmarke hat unter ihren Mitstreitern das höhere Ansehen, weist eine höhere Preisspanne auf und verkauft sich besser.

**Referenzpreis** *m* - reference price

■ Preis mit dem die Verbraucher ein bestimmtes Produkt vergleichen. Die Wichtigkeit besteht in der Tatsache, dass die Verbraucher die Preise vergleichen und nicht den Preis als Absolutum sehen. Ob ein Preis teuer oder billig ist, wird das Produkt mit anderen verglichen und das Resultat bestimmt die persönliche Entscheidung des Käufers.

**Regalfläche** *f* - shelf-space

■ Gesamtheit der Fläche der Vorderansicht, die ein Artikel in einem Verkaufsregal in einem Ladengeschäft einnimmt. Die Größe ist in der Regel proportional zu seiner Rentabilität oder seinem Umsatz, wobei die dem Handelsunternehmen eigenen Marken bevorzugt platziert werden.

**Regalgroßhändler** *m* - rack jobber

■ Zulieferer, der sich exklusiv um die Führung, die Auswahl der Referenzen verschiedener Lieferanten und die Belieferung einer Abteilung eines Kaufhauses kümmert, ohne dass dies für den Verbraucher offensichtlich wäre. Wird bei Produkten mit einer Vielzahl von Varianten und vielen Neuheiten verwendet, z.B. Bücher und Musik. Normalerweise garantiert der Regalgroßhändler dem Geschäftseigentümer einen bestimmten Umsatz und/oder eine Spanne und berechnet eine Provision, wenngleich er in manchen Fällen die Abteilung zu einem festen Preis mietet und den Grenzgewinn oder -verlust alleine übernimmt. Unterscheidet sich von einem Konzessionär, z.B. einem Parfümeriestand, da es hier für den Verbraucher offensichtlich ist, dass die Fläche einem anderen Unternehmen gehört.

**Regalposition** *f* - facings

■ Gesamtzahl der sichtbaren Packungen in einem Geschäftsregal. Diese Zahl wird zum Berechnen der Linearmeter verwendet, die der Kunde unter Vertrag nimmt, um seine Produkte in einem Regal aufzustellen.

**regional gestärkte Kampagne** *f* - market weighting campaign

■ Kampagne, in der der öffentliche Druck in einer Region überproportional zum

Verkauf erhöht wird. Ganz unterschiedlich motiviert u. a. dadurch, dass in dieser Verkaufsregion ein höheres Verkaufspotential ist, mehr wirksame Werbeträger zur Verfügung stehen oder eine zeitweise Schwächung der Konkurrenz festgestellt wurde. Meist werden lokale Medien zur Stärkung eingesetzt, die die nationalen Medien in dieser Region vertreten.

**regionaler Vertrieb** *m* - regional distribution centre

■ Lager mit einem vorbestimmten Vertriebsbereich, in dem die Waren eines Unternehmens zur Weitersendung an die Endverkaufsstellen der entsprechenden Region befindlich sind.

**registrierte Marke** *f* - registered trademark

■ Handelsmarke, die ordnungsgemäß im Markenregister eingetragen wurde. Damit wird dem Eigentümer das Recht der exklusiven Benutzung der Marke und die Ablehnung der Registrierung ähnlicher Marken garantiert. Das Register ist in verschiedene Klassen entsprechend den verschiedenen Wirtschaftszweigen unterteilt, und deckt nur die Rechtslage eines Landes ab, obwohl man eine Ausdehnung oder Eintragung der Marke in anderen Ländern beantragen kann. In manchen Ländern (z.B. USA) ist zur Registrierung einer Marke der reale Verkauf eines Produkts mit der besagten Marke notwendig.

**registriertes Design** *n* - registered design

■ Design oder Logo einer Firma (einschließlich Farben, Form und anderer Merkmale), das ordnungsgemäß eingetragen wurde, sodass seine Nutzung dieser Firma vorbehalten ist.

**reiche Anzeige** *f* - rich ad

■ Internetanzeige mit großer Aussagekraft bezüglich der verwandten Instrumente, einschließlich Animation, Ton, Video und Interaktivität, derzeit meist erstellt mit Flash oder als Streaming und mit Programmiersprachen wie Java oder Javascript.

**Reichweite** *f* - reach

■ In der Internetwerbung, die Zahl der Personen, die durch eine Werbeanzeige oder einen Banner kontaktiert wurden.

**Reifephase** *f* **des Marktes** - market maturity

■ Dritte Phase des Produktlebens- oder Marktlebenszyklus, die sich durch stagnierende Verkäufe und Gewinne auszeichnet. Die Mehrheit der Produkte befindet sich in dieser Phase. Die häufigsten Marketingaktivitäten sind: Neusegmentierung, Neupositionierung der Marke, Förderung der Konsumerhöhung pro Kunden, Verbesserung der Qualität oder der Produktpräsentation, Nutzung massiverer Vertriebskanäle, Verteidigungs- oder Angriffsstrategien in Preiskriegen.

**Reilly-Modell** *n* - Reilly model

■ Mathematisches Modell, laut dem der relative kommerzielle Anreiz zwischen zwei Städten in Bezug auf eine Dritte direkt proportional zu ihrer Bevölkerung ist und antiproportional hoch 2 zum Abstand der Dritten von den beiden ersten ist.

**Reinzeichnung** *f* - finished art

■ Eine Reinzeichnung ist eine reproduktionsfähige Vorlage für den Druck. Sie enthält alle zu druckenden Elemente oder zumindest Platzhalter, in die andere Druckvorlagen montiert werden können.

**relativer Marktanteil** *m* - relative market share

■ Der relative Marktanteil ist das Ergebnis der Division des eigenen Marktanteils durch den Marktanteil des größten Wettbewerbers (derjenige, der über den größten Marktanteil auf diesem Markt verfügt) oder des Nächstgrößeren (wenn es sich bereits um den Marktteilnehmer mit dem größten Marktanteil handelt). Dieser Index zur Bestimmung der Position am Markt dient dazu, die Ziele in einem Preiskrieg zu bestimmen und vor allem zur Bestimmung des Handlungsspielraums und der relativen Kosten die jeder Wettbewerber hat.

**Reorganisation** *f* - reorganisation

■ Anpassung einer bestehenden Organisation an neue Umstände.

**Repertoire** *n* - repertoire

■ Innerhalb einer Produktart, Marken, die ein Verbraucher ab und zu kauft und bereit ist zu kaufen, wenn seine Marke gerade nicht zur Verfügung steht.

**Repräsentativerhebung** *f* - sample survey

■ Studie, die Aussagen über die Gesamtheit ermittelt, indem sie eine repräsentative Teilmenge untersucht.

**Retention Marketing** *n* - retention marketing

■ Ansatz des strategischen Marketing mit dem Ziel, bereits bestehende Kundenbeziehungen zu intensivieren. Ist eine der Unternehmensphilosophien zur Lenkung der Kundenbeziehungen.

**RFM-Methode** *f* - RFM (recency, frequency and money)

■ Kundendaten eines Unternehmens (z. B. Versandhandel) werden unterteilt in: Recency - letztes Kaufdatum, Frequency - Kaufhäufigkeit, Monetary Value - Umsatz.

**richtigstellende Werbung** *f* - corrective advertising

■ Werbeanzeige, die in erster Linie eine vorherige unwahre oder missverständliche Botschaft korrigieren soll. Sie kann aus eigenem Antrieb oder auf Verlangen eines Mitbewerbers oder einer Verbraucherschutzorganisation erfolgen.

**rote Ware** *f* - red good

■ Güter, die sehr schnell abnutzen und neu eingesetzt werden, z. B. Lebensmittel.

**Rückgabe** *f* - return

■ Rückgabe eines erst kürzlich erworbenen Gutes an den Verkäufer, durch den Käufer, innerhalb der Garantiezeit oder auf Grund gravierender Defekte der Ware. Die Rückerstattung schließt die Geldrückgabe an den Käufer durch den Verkäufer mit ein.

**Rückgabepolitik** *f* - policy on returned goods

■ Beschluss zwischen dem Lieferanten und dem Empfänger der Ware zur Bestimmung, in welchem Maß die beiden Beteiligten die Rückgabekosten des Produktes übernehmen, falls der Kunde aus irgendeinem Grund das Produkt zurückgeben möchte.

**Rückwärtsintegration** *f* - backward integration

■ Aufkauf eines Zulieferunternehmens oder Unterzeichnung eines besonderen Zusammenarbeitsvertrages, um die Versorgung mit einem Schlüsselrohstoff sicherzustellen. Form der vertikalen Integration.

**Rückzahlung** *f* - refund

■ Im Allgemeinen, Rückzahlung des gezahlten Preises für eine Ware. Kann teilweise oder gesamt gezahlt werden und vom Verkäufer ausgehen (z. B. bei Nichtleistung eines Dienstes) oder auf Anfrage durch den Käufer.

**Run-Of-Network** *n* - run-of-network

■ Kaufoption für Internetwerbung, bei der die Anzeige auf jeder Seite erscheinen kann, die im Werbenetz enthalten ist.

**Run-Of-Press** *f* - run-of-press

■ Presseanzeige, die ohne vorgegebenen Standort eingefügt wird. Die Anzeige hat keine Einschränkungen hinsichtlich der Seite oder der Thematik auf der Seite. Im Allgemeinen führt die Vorgabe eines festen Standortes zu einem Sonderpreis bzw. Rabatt.

# S

**Saison** *f* - season

■ Zeitraum, der hinsichtlich einer bestimmten Tätigkeit gesondert betrachtet wird, da er spezielle Merkmale aufweist. Kann mehrere Tage, Monate oder sogar Jahre umfassen; während dieser Zeit vervielfacht sich der Verkauf von Saisonartikeln (z. B. Sonnencreme im Sommer). Am Saisonende wird in der Regel eine Preissenkung, ein Aus- oder Schlussverkauf durchgeführt.

**Saisonabhängigkeit** *f* - seasonality

■ Schwankungen in den Verkaufszahlen, die sich jedes Jahr zur gleichen Zeit wiederholen. Dies ist auf die Jahreszeit, die Gewohnheiten und Feiertage zurückzuführen. Es sind jedoch lediglich Saisonprodukte, deren saisonale Absatzschwankungen tatsächlich unmittelbar mit den Jahreszeiten in Verbindung stehen (z. B. Weihnachtgebäck, Badekleidung usw.).

**saisonbedingte Fluktuation** *f* - seasonal fluctuation

▪ Preis- und Umsatzschwankungen eines Produkts in einer bestimmten Jahreszeit. Die saisonbedingten Preisschwankungen übertragen sich auf die zyklischen Schwankungen und auf die langfristigen Tendenzen.

**Saisongeschäft** *n* - seasonal business

▪ Käufe und Verkäufe, die ausschließlich während einer bestimmten Jahreszeit erfolgen. In der Regel sind Saisongeschäfte von Ernten, vom Klima oder von den Gebräuchen jeder Saison abhängig. Häufig fällt das Geschäftsjahr nicht mit dem Kalenderjahr zusammen, sondern endet mit Beginn der nächsten Saison.

**Saisonverkauf** *m* - seasonal sale

▪ Verkauf, der in Abhängigkeit von der Jahreszeit schwankt (Lebkuchen, Regenschirme usw.). Die Unternehmen vervollständigen ihre Produktpalette mit Produkten, die für andere Jahreszeiten typisch sind, versuchen den Konsum ihrer Produkte während des gesamten Jahres zu fördern oder arbeiten nur einige Monate.

**Sammelumfrage** *f* - omnibus survey

▪ Befragung, die ein spezialisiertes Unternehmen für mehrere Kunden durchführt, wobei jeder Kunde eine begrenzte Anzahl von Fragen, die ihn speziell interessieren, einbringen kann. Diese Art der Befragung erlaubt eine gewisse Arbeitsersparnis, da sie die maßgebenden Variablen nicht zu wiederholen braucht (demographische und solche, welche die sozioökonomische Situation betreffen). Außerdem handelt es sich dabei um eine objektivere Form der Befragung.

**Sättigung** *f* - saturation

▪ Maximaler Grad der Nutzung eines Faktors oder der Abdeckung eines Marktes. Die Überschreitung dieser Schwelle führt zu negativen Ergebnissen (z. B. übermäßige Werbung, die eine Ablehnung hervorruft, oder exzessiver Vertrieb eines Produktes, der das Interesse der Geschäfte, dieses anzubieten, verringert).

**Sättigungsschwelle** *f* - saturation point

▪ Niveau, bei dem die Nachfrage nach einer Ware oder Dienstleistung vollständig befriedigt ist, so dass sich der Anstieg der Verkäufe auf Ersatzbeschaffungen und die Abdeckung eines möglichen Bevölkerungswachstums beschränkt.

**Säuberung** *f* - purge

▪ Im Datenbank-Marketing die Löschung von Daten aus einer Liste, die als unnütz angesehen werden.

**Schaufenster** *n* - shop-window

▪ Der Teil eines Ladens, der von außen einzusehen ist und in dem die Artikel ausgestellt und die Nachrichten ausgehängt sind, damit sie vom Publikum gesehen werden können.

**Schaufenstergestaltung** *f* - window dressing

▪ Es handelt sich dabei um die gesamten Techniken, durch die eine klarere und optisch ansprechendere Übermittlung einer Nachricht durch die Gestaltung eines Schaufensters ermöglicht wird. Der Schaufensterdekorateur kennt die Merkmale des Produkts und die der Zielgruppe, die man ansprechen möchte, deren Interesse man wecken möchte, die man über das Produkt informieren möchte und die verstärkt ins Geschäft gelockt werden soll.

**Schaufenstervereinbarung** *f* - advertising showcase agreement

▪ Vereinbarung zwischen einer Verkaufsstelle und einem Werbetreibenden, um im Schaufenster, der Ladengondel oder einer ähnlichen Vorrichtung dessen Produkte oder Werbung auszustellen. Die

Gegenleistung kann in einem fixen Geldbetrag bestehen, einer Verminderung der Einkaufspreise, der kostenlosen Überlassung von Waren, der Zurverfügungstellung von Waren für eine Verlosung oder Tombola oder in ähnlichem. Manchmal veranstaltet der Werbetreibende einen Wettbewerb mit interessanten Preisen um das schönste Schaufenster.

**Schaukorb** *m* - display basket

▪ Großer Korb in einem Geschäft, in dem Sonderangebotsprodukte angeboten werden.

**Schautafel** *f* - display panel

▪ Mittelgroßes Plakat, das Informationen über ein Produkt, eine Versammlung oder ein Ereignis bietet.

**Scheinadresse** *f* - decoy

▪ In ein Archiv eingegebene Daten über eine echte oder erfundene Person, um über jeglichen Gebrauch des Ordners oder der Datei informiert zu sein (autorisiert oder nicht). Wird häufig von Listeninhabern angewendet.

**Schlagwort** *n* - keyword

▪ Im Internet, die Zeichenkombination, die ein Benutzer in eine Suchmaschine oder in eine Site eingibt, um Informationen zu suchen. Eine Werbetechnik besteht darin, dass die Verknüpfung des Werbeträgers angezeigt wird, sobald der Benutzer eine Suche mit einem bestimmten Schlagwort durchführt.

**Schlagwort-Marketing** *n* - keyword marketing

▪ Im Internet, Marketing-Aktivität, deren Ziel der Verkauf von Schlagwörtern in den Suchmaschinen ist.

**Schleichwerbung** *f* - masked advertising

▪ Form der getarnten Werbung mit dem Zweck, Werbebotschaften zu vermitteln, deren werblicher Charakter vom Zuschauer oder Leser entweder nicht auf Anhieb oder überhaupt nicht als solcher zu erkennen sind. Schleichwerbung ist grundsätzlich unzulässig.

**Schlussverkaufspreis** *m* - sales price

▪ Stark herabgesetzter Preis im Schlussverkauf, um die Lagerbestände eines Produktes am Saisonende zu räumen.

**Schnäppchen** *n* - bargain

▪ Produkt, das in einem Räumungsverkauf oder Saisonschlussverkauf billig angeboten wird. Bei langlebigen Konsumgütern bezieht sich der Begriff oft auf den Gebrauchtkauf.

**Schnelldreher** *m/pl* - fast moving consumer products (FMCP)

▪ Darunter fallen vor allem Konsumgüter des täglichen Bedarfs wie Nahrungsmittel, Körperpflegeprodukte, Reinigungsmittel etc., die Konsumenten häufig, spontan, in der Regel routiniert und ohne lange zu überlegen einkaufen, oft in Kaufhäusern mit Selbstbedienung.

**Schockwerbung** *f* - shock advertising

▪ Werbekampagne, im Allgemeinen mit sozialem Charakter, deren Inhalt verbal und/oder visuell ausgedrückt wird, wobei er aufgrund der Härte oder Fremdartigkeit einen “Schock” für den Empfänger bedeutet. Ziel dieser Art Werbung ist es, einen erhöhten Bekanntheitsgrad in Bezug auf Thema oder Problematik zu erreichen. Zum Beispiel in einem britischen Werbespot, in dem sich ein Baby selbst eine Spritze setzt.

**Schwarzmarkt** *m* - black market

▪ Heimlicher Handel von Waren. Tritt bei Rationierung, Konsumverbot oder Preiskontrolle auf. Der Preis ergibt sich durch das Gesetz von Angebot und Nachfrage und ist höher als der gesetzlich festgelegte (falls ein solcher existiert). Typische Beispiele sind Devisen (wenn Beschränkungen bestehen) und Drogen.

**Schwarz-Weiß-Anzeige** *f* **(S/W)** - black and white (B&W)

▪ Anzeige, die nur eine Farbe, normalerweise Schwarz auf weißem Papier, verwendet. Sie ist kostengünstiger herzustellen und billiger für den Werbetreibenden, aber in der Regel weniger attraktiv und aufmerksamkeitsträchtig als eine Farbanzeige.

**Schwellenmarkt** *m* - emerging market

▪ Bezeichnung, für einen Markt mit sehr starkem Wachstum.

**Segment** *n* - segment

■ Teil des Gesamtmarktes, der aus einer Gruppe von Käufern eines Produktes oder einer Dienstleistung besteht, die ausreichend charakterisiert und identifiziert sind, und an einer konkreten Variante dieses Produktes oder dieser Dienstleistung interessiert sind. Das Unternehmen spezialisiert sich in Abhängigkeit von seinen Möglichkeiten und Zielen auf eines oder auf mehrere Segmente, die sehr weit gefasst und allgemein oder Marktnischen sein können.

**Segmentation** *f* **nach Einkommen** - income segmentation

■ Einteilung der Verbraucher in Gruppen nach ihren Einkünften pro Person oder pro Haushalt.

**segmentieren** *v* - segment *v*

■ Eine Gruppe gemäß ihren Gemeinsamkeiten in unterschiedliche Teile aufteilen.

**Segmentierung** *f* - segmentation

■ Tätigkeit, bei der man in sich homogene Käufergruppen zu identifizieren sucht, um die Herstellung, den Vertrieb oder die Kommunikation für eine bestimmte Variante eines Produktes oder einer Dienstleistung spezialisieren zu können. Wenn das Unternehmen eine Segmentierungsuntersuchung durchführt, entdeckt es neue Gelegenheiten, um die Bedürfnisse der Kunden besser zu befriedigen, und ändert seine Produkte, seine Werbung usw.

**Segmentierung nach Geschlecht** *f* - sex segmentation

■ Marketingstrategie, die auf der Differenzierung von Produkten nach dem Geschlecht der potentiellen Käufer(innen) basiert, zum Beispiel bei Babywindeln für Mädchen und für Jungen.

**Segmentierungsbarriere** *f* - segmentation fence

■ Im Marketing die Voraussetzung, die die Verbraucher erfüllen müssen, um vorteilhafte Kaufbedingungen wie einen Preisnachlass zu erhalten. Zum Beispiel wird je nach Produkt gewöhnlich jungen oder älteren Menschen ein Preisnachlass angeboten.

**sektorales Marketing** *n* - sectorial marketing

■ Marketingmethode, die in jedem einzelnen der verschiedenen wirtschaftlichen oder sozialen Tätigkeitsbereiche angewendet wird. So kann unter anderem zwischen Finanzmarketing, Sozialmarketing, touristischem Marketing usw. unterschieden werden.

**sekundärer Werbetreibender** *m* - secondary advertiser

■ Inserent, der die Werbezeit oder Werbefläche des eigentlichen Auftraggebers nutzt, die ihm von diesem überlassen wurde.

**Sekundärforschung** *f* - desk research

■ Untersuchung, die auf dem Studium bereits veröffentlichter Daten (Presse, Jahresberichte usw.) und gelegentlich auch auf telefonischen Auskünften beruht. Die Primärforschung beinhaltet dagegen auch Feldforschung. Die Vorteile der Sekundärforschung liegen darin, dass sie schnell durchführbar und recht kostengünstig ist, und dass eventuelle spätere Felduntersuchungen durch sie zielgerichteter durchgeführt werden können.

**Sekundärpublikum** *n* - pass-along audience

■ Leser einer regelmäßigen Veröffentlichung, die das Exemplar nicht gekauft haben und auch nicht zu den normalen Käufern gehören. Sie lesen diese sehr selten, für kurze Zeit und wahrscheinlich mit weniger Aufmerksamkeit, wodurch sie einen geringeren Wert für die Werbung haben. Werden bei der Berechnung der Audienz miteinbezogen und können in einigen Medien sehr zahlreich sein, z.B. Herz-Schmerz-Zeitschriften, die in Friseursalons gelesen werden. Auch Gelegenheitspublikum genannt.

**Selbstbedienung** *f* - self-service

■ Ladentyp, in dem sich der Kunde die meisten Produkte, die in Regalen angeordnet sind, selbst nehmen kann. Das

Gegenteil dazu stellt der traditionelle Verkauf über den Ladentisch dar. Die Selbstbedienung schließt die Selbstbedienung in Supermärkten und Verbrauchergroßmärkten mit ein.

**Selbstbedienungswerbung** *f* - self-serve advertising

■ Im Internet die Werbung, die direkt auf der Site des Inserenten ohne Mittler, Vertreter oder Verkäufer erworben wird.

**selbstdeckende Werbeprämie** *f* - self-liquidating premium

■ Verkaufsförderung, bei der eine Prämie zu einem reduzierten Preis angeboten wird, welcher die Kosten deckt, aber für den Konsumenten ein sehr attraktives Angebot darstellt. Den niedrigen Preis erhält man dadurch, dass man in großen Mengen einkauft oder einen extra Produktionsauftrag vergibt.

**Selbstkostenpreis** *m* - cost price

■ Im Falle eines vom Unternehmen selbst hergestellten Produkts ist das der Preis, der alle dafür aufgewandten Größen einschließt (Roh- und Hilfsstoffe, Arbeit, Energieverbrauch, Verpackung und Aufteilung der Gemeinkosten, immer unter Ausschluss der Gewinne). Wenn es sich um ein käuflich erworbenes Gut handelt, schließt der Selbstkostenpreis zusätzlich zum Kaufpreis die Steuern, Transportkosten und Versicherungen ein.

**Selbstregulierung** *f* - self-regulation

■ Normen, die ein Unternehmen oder ein Verband (zum Beispiel Werbeagenturen) sich selbst auferlegen, damit ihre Waren oder Dienstleistungen bestimmte Minimalanforderungen erfüllen bezüglich Qualität, Sicherheit, Unparteilichkeit, Objektivität oder dem Ausschluss von Angriffen auf Wettbewerber oder öffentliche Personen.

**Selbstverkaufssystem** *n* - self-selling sale

■ Verkauf, bei dem der Auslieferer auch Verkäufer ist, da er die Regale auffüllt, neue Artikel zu verkaufen versucht, die Ware liefert, in Rechnung stellt und kassiert (z. B. bei Milchprodukten, Erfrischungsgetränken und Tiefkühlprodukten). Unterscheidet sich vom Wandergewerbehandel dadurch, dass das Selbstverkaufssystem von Auslieferern durchgeführt wird, die Angestellte eines Unternehmens sind, das eine wichtige Fabrik oder Vertriebslager hat.

**Selektivauswahl** *f* - judgement sampling

■ Nicht zufällige Stichprobe, in der subjektiv als geeignet ausgewählte Personen befragt werden (zum Beispiel, weil sie Experten sind oder bei früheren Gelegenheiten gute Prognostiken geliefert haben). Sie ist geeignet für Tiefenanalysen und um im Wesentlichen qualitative Schlussfolgerungen zu gewinnen.

**selektive Erinnerung** *f* - selective recall

■ Vorgang, aufgrund dessen das Publikum nur einen Bruchteil der ausgesandten Botschaft behält, normalerweise das, was betont wurde. Manchmal wird allerdings eher das behalten, was neuartig ist oder den erzeugten Erwartungen widerspricht.

**selektive Verzerrung** *f* - selective distortion

■ Vorgang, aufgrund dessen ein Konsument den Inhalt einer Werbebotschaft anders versteht oder auffasst als ein anderer Konsument, da die Informationen durch seine vorhandenen Kenntnisse und Erfahrungen gefiltert werden. Das Verstehen ist die Zwischenphase zwischen Wahrnehmung und Behalten.

**selektive Werbung** *f* - selective advertising

■ Werbung, die an eine sehr eingeschränkte Bevölkerungsgruppe gerichtet ist.

**selektiver Preiskrieg** *m* - selective price war

■ Marktzustand, bei dem der angreifende Markteilnehmer die Teile des Marktes für den Preiskrieg auswählt, in denen sein relativer Marktanteil gering ist. Er bestimmt das Produkt, die Verpackung, die Kundschaft oder das Gebiet, wo er relativ schwach vertreten ist und deshalb weniger zu verlieren hat, falls ein allgemeiner Preiskrieg auf diesem Markt beginnt.

**selektiver Vertrieb** *m* - selective distribution

■ Vertriebsstrategie, die zwischen dem exklusiven Vertrieb und dem intensiven Vertrieb anzusiedeln ist. Es existiert mehr als eine Verkaufsstelle pro Gebiet, aber der Fabrikant kontrolliert und unterstützt die Geschäftsstellen, die seine Marke führen, direkt.

**Self-Mailer** *m* - self-mailer

■ Werbeschriftstück zur Direktwerbung, das per Post ohne Umschlag an einen Adressaten versendet werden kann, da es selbst die Form eines geschlossenen Umschlags annimmt.

**sequentielles Stichprobenverfahren** *n* - sequential sampling

■ Stichprobe, deren Umfang von der Information abhängt, die erhoben werden soll (variabel im Zeitablauf im Gegensatz zur festen Stichprobe). In jeder Phase gibt es ein Entscheidungskriterium dafür, ob die erhobenen Daten ausreichend sind, um zu einer Schlussfolgerung zu gelangen oder ob zusätzliche Daten erhoben werden müssen. Es wird zur Kontrolle von Produktionsserien benutzt.

**Serienwerbung** *f* - range advertising

■ Werbehandlung, die von einer Firma durchgeführt wird und die das Publikum auf die Existenz verschiedener Produktvarietäten der Firma aufmerksam machen soll.

**Servicegrad** *m* - grade of service

■ Im Allgemeinen der Prozentsatz der Aufträge, die vollständig innerhalb der vereinbarten Frist ausgeführt werden. Im Mobilfunkdienst wäre dies beispielsweise die Anzahl der Wählversuche, bei denen eine Gesprächsverbindung zustande kommt; ein hoher Servicegrad ist Voraussetzung für einen qualitativ hochwertigen Dienst und zufriedene Nutzer.

**Servicequalität** *f* - quality of service

■ Subjektive Bewertung eines Dienstes durch seine Nutzer. Sie wird durch objektive Messungen der Faktoren geschätzt, die den größten Einfluss auf die Kundenzufriedenheit haben.

**sexistische Werbung** *f* - sexist advertising

■ Werbung, die die Unterschiede zwischen Männern und Frauen hervorhebt und dabei eine Klischeeversion beider Gesellschaftsgruppen gibt und so die Bildung von Vorurteilen fördert.

**sieben Rs** *n/pl* - seven R's

■ Schema zur Analyse von Gruppenarbeit. Entspricht den Anfangsbuchstaben der englischen Begriffe „reason of being" (Daseinsberechtigung), „rules" (Regeln), „roles" (Rollen), „relations" (Beziehungen), „rituals" (Rituale), „rewards" (Belohnungen) und „results" (Ergebnisse).

**signifikante Stichprobe** *f* - adequate sample

■ Stichprobe, die durch ihre Größe und durch die Art der Auswahl ein getreues Abbild der Gesamtheit darstellt, und bei der das Fehlerrisiko in Bezug auf zufällige Antworten auf eine Umfrage oder auf eine Beobachtungsreihe begrenzt wird. Entspricht einer repräsentativen Stichprobe.

**Skalenerträge** *m/pl* - economies of scale

■ Reduktion der Produktionsstückkosten für ein Gut, die dadurch erreicht wird, dass die Kapazität und die Jahresproduktion dieses Gutes erhöht werden. Die Skalenerträge kommen aus mehreren Gründen zustande: geringere Auswirkung der allgemeinen Kosten auf die Stückkosten, Synergieeffekte bei Einkäufen, Vertrieb und Absatzförderung; Auswirkungen gemäß der Erfahrungswertekurve, stärkere Spezialisierung und effizientere Nutzung des Kapitalvermögens.

**Slogan** *m* - slogan

■ Einprägsamer, kurzer Spruch am Ende einer Werbeanzeige. Dient der Festigung der Positionierung einer Marke oder eines Produkts und auch der Kontinuität einer Multimedia-Werbekampagne, die aus einer Vielzahl von Anzeigen in verschiedenen Medien besteht.

**Soft-Selling** *n* - soft selling

■ Zurückhaltende Verkaufstechnik, basierend auf indirekten Nachrichten, so dass die Kaufentscheidung eine Entscheidung des Kunden ist und nicht auf vom Verkäufer angebotenen Argumenten beruht. Bezeichnet auch den Werbetyp, der auf diesen Grundlagen gegründet ist.

**Sonderangebotspreis** *m* - discount price

▪ Während eines bestimmten Zeitraums zu Promotionszwecken herabgesetzter Preis. Weniger aggressiv als der Schlussverkaufs- oder Räumungspreis. Synonym zu herabgesetzter Preis oder Rabattpreis.

**Sonderkonditionen** *f/pl* - special conditions

▪ Spezielle Kaufkonditionen zu einem niedrigen Kaufpreis, die einem Kunden von einem Verkäufer angeboten werden. Im Vertrieb nutzt der Vertreiber Preisnachlässe von Lieferanten oder Herstellern oft aus verschiedenen Gründen, zum Beispiel frühzeitige Zahlung, saisonbedingte Preisnachlässe, Vergünstigungen usw.

**Sonderverkauf** *m* - promotional sale

▪ Ist dem Ausverkauf ähnlich, setzt aber den Schwerpunkt auf wenige Produkte und Abteilungen. Das Ziel besteht darin, neue Artikel einzuführen und den Kundenverkehr im Geschäft zu erhöhen. Der vorübergehende Nachlass zieht Kunden an und erleichtert ihre Kaufentscheidung.

**Sortiment** *n* - assortment

▪ Gesamtheit der Artikel, die in einem Katalog oder Geschäft angeboten werden. Beinhaltet mehrere Abteilungen, Produktfamilien und Produkte, die jeweils über ihre eigene Produktpalette verfügen. Typisch für ein Sortiment ist seine Vielfalt. Die Analyse des Sortiments ist eine der Hauptaufgaben des Geschäftsführers.

**Sortimentsanalyse** *f* - product range analysis

▪ Untersuchung und Bestimmung der Artikel, die zu jedem Zeitpunkt angeboten werden sollen. Unter den vielen Variablen, die einen Einfluss haben, sind die Festlegung des Geschäftslokales, das Verhalten der Konkurrenz und der Zulieferer, die Vorschläge der Verbraucher, die physischen Möglichkeiten der Lagerhaltung und Ausstellung in den Verkaufsräumen sowie die Bruttospanne und der Umschlag pro Artikel, Produktfamilie und Abteilung.

**Sortimentsbreite** *f* - product range breadth

▪ Durchschnittliche Anzahl von Produkten, die von jeder Abteilung angeboten werden. Die Breite kann von Abteilung zu Abteilung sehr verschieden sein, so dass Vergleiche sich in der Regel auf die gleiche Abteilung in verschiedenen Geschäften beziehen. Ein breites Sortiment mit geringer Tiefe hat das Ziel, die größtmögliche Zahl von Grundbedürfnissen in wiederholter Form zu decken, was einen hohen Warenumschlag sichert und den Verlust von außergewöhnlichen Käufen oder sehr wählerischen Kunden in Kauf nimmt.

**Sortimentspräsentation** *f* **einer Marke** - pack shot

▪ Schluss-Szene eines Werbefilms, in dem die Produkte gesammelt und mit einer klaren Identifikation der Marke gezeigt werden. Diese können zusammen mit Rohstoffen oder Endprodukten präsentiert werden. In der Regel erscheint das Logo des Fabrikanten.

**Sortimentstiefe** *f* - product range depth

▪ Durchschnittliche Anzahl von Artikeln oder Varianten, die von jedem Produkt angeboten werden. Eine große Tiefe besteht dann, wenn der Kunde zwischen vielen Möglichkeiten in Bezug auf Größe, Farben und Zubehör wählen kann. Ist typisch für Fachgeschäfte. Vermindert den Umschlag jedes Artikels, zieht aber wählerische Kundschaft an und kann zur Erhöhung der durchschnittlichen Bruttospanne führen.

**Sortimentstrategie** *f* - assortment strategy

▪ Strategie zur Festlegung der Produktpalette, die ein Groß- oder Einzelhändler auf dem Markt anbieten möchte. Hierzu gehören Breite, Tiefe und Vielfalt des Angebots.

**soziale Mobilität** *f* - social mobility

▪ Bereitschaft, das soziale Umfeld zu wechseln. Kann in horizontale (Wechsel des Wohnorts) und in vertikale (soziale Schicht) soziale Mobilität zerlegt werden.

**soziale Unterstützung** *f* - community support

▪ Hilfe des Staates oder privater Institutionen für Einzelpersonen oder Bevölkerungsgruppen, um diese bei der Lösung finanzieller oder emotionaler Probleme zu unterstützen.

**soziale Verantwortung** *f* **von Unternehmen** - corporate social responsibility

▪ Gesamtheit der sozialen Verpflichtungen, die eine Person, Gruppe, Organisation oder Institution hinsichtlich des sozialen und umweltbezogenen Umfelds, in dem sie ihre geschäftlichen Aktivitäten betreibt, eingehen kann.

**soziale Werbung** *f* - social advertising

▪ Werbeaktivität, in der das Produkt oder die Dienstleistung und deren Nutzen Träger wird für eine soziale Thematik, die der Werbende ansprechen oder „denunzieren" möchte. Ein Werbeträger wird zum Schauplatz der „denunzierten" Sache und die Polemik über dieses Thema ist fast sicher, woraus die Marke Nutzen zieht. Die italienische Modefirma Benetton war in den 90er Jahren eine der erfolgreichsten Werbefirmen auf diesem Gebiet.

**soziales Marketing** *n* - social marketing

▪ Marketing, das Handlungen fördern soll, die positive Auswirkungen auf die Gesellschaft als Ganzes haben. Die Verantwortlichen für soziales Marketing sehen sich einer Konkurrenz ausgesetzt, die das kommerzielle Marketing in der Regel nicht kennt: der freundschaftliche Wettstreit mit anderen sozialen Organisationen, die für die gleiche Sache kämpfen. Diese Wettbewerber können den in sozialen Marketing Tätigen in vielfältiger Weise helfen; die Situation kann aber auch zur Zersplitterung der Kräfte, Problemen mit der Basis und anderen Schwierigkeiten führen.

**soziokultureller Code** *m* - social and cultural codes

▪ Systeme von Bedeutungen und Handlungsvorgaben, die in der Werbung wiedergegeben werden. Zum Beispiel Verhaltensvorgaben, Vorurteile, Klischees oder Modeerscheinungen.

**sozioökonomische Segmentierung** *f* - socio-economic segmentation

▪ Einteilung einer Bevölkerung in Personengruppen gemäß einer oder mehrerer sozioökonomischer Variablen, wie etwa Schulbildung, Beruf, Einkommen oder Religion. Dies wird in der Regel kombiniert mit demographischen Kriterien, um eine größere Genauigkeit bei der Einteilung der Verbraucher in homogene Gruppen zu erreichen, die sich von den anderen Gruppen in diesen Variablen und in ihrem Verhalten hinsichtlich eines bestimmten Produktes oder einer bestimmten Marke unterscheiden.

**Spielraum** *m* **der Preisannahme** - latitude of price acceptance

▪ Bandbreite, die sich zwischen dem Höchstpreis, den der Verbraucher für ein Produkt zahlen würde und dem niedrigsten Preis, ab dem der Verbraucher die Qualität des Produkts in Frage stellt, bewegt.

**Spitzenlasttarif** *m* - peak-load pricing

▪ Preisstrategie, bei der die Nachfrage nach dem Produkt zu schwachen Zeiten mit einer Preispromotion angeregt wird, die von den höheren Preisen zu Hochzeiten getragen wird. Im Telefonsektor ist dise Strategie sehr beliebt.

**Spitzenmontage** *f* - online editing

▪ Digitale Edition höchster Qualität auf der das definitive Bild aufgebaut wird, das Teil der Werbung oder des audiovisuellen Materials sein wird, wobei das Bild nicht komprimiert wird. Wird in speziellen Montageräumen ausgehend von der Basismontage durchgeführt, die bei der Edition geringerer Qualität erhalten wurde, wobei die erforderlichen Effekte und Übergänge durchgeführt werden und in die Plakate und Überdrucke eingeführt werden, die das Endprodukt enthält. Auch Online-Montage.

**Spitzennachfrage** *f* - peak demand

■ Höchste Nachfrage. Zeitraum, in dem eine erhöhte Nachfrage besteht.

**Sponsorenwerbung** *f* - hitchhike ad

■ Bei gesponserten Programmen die Produktanzeige des Sponsors, die unmittelbar nach dem Programm ausgestrahlt wird, um sich die erzeugte Stimmung und die Assoziierung mit der Marke zunutze zu machen, z. B. Krombacher-Werbung bei einem Fußballspiel.

**Sponsoring** *n* - sponsorship

■ Im Internet der wirtschaftliche Beitrag, der zwischen der Eigentümerfirma der Website und einer Sponsorenfirma vereinbart wird, wobei im Allgemeinen im Gegenzug die Unternehmens- und Werbepräsenz des Sponsors auf der Site hervorgehoben wird.

**Sponsoring** *n* - sponsorship

■ Zahlung von Firmen oder Institutionen an Organisatoren von sozialen Projekten oder Aktionen, um das Image der Marke, der Firma oder Organisation zu stärken. Der Unterschied zum Mäzenatentum liegt darin, dass sich dieses auf spielerische, sportliche und informative Aktivitäten konzentriert; und meist punktuell ist für einen Akt oder eine Aktivität während eines oder zwei Jahren.

**spontane Erinnerung** *f* - spontaneous recall

■ Prozentsatz des Publikums, der eine Marke nennt, wenn er dazu aufgefordert wird, sich an die in einem bestimmten Zeitraum beworbenen Marken oder einen sonstigen allgemeinen Reiz zu erinnern. Wird unterhalb der gestützten und der suggerierten Erinnerung eingestuft.

**Sportmarketing** *n* - sports marketing

■ Marketingzweig, der Sportler und Sportclubs als Marken betrachtet, deren Image zu potenzieren und popularisieren ist, wobei das Image einer Firma oder Gesellschaft überlassen wird. Ein Beispiel ist die Firma Real Madrid Marketing Japan, die der spanische Club Anfang 2004 mit verschiedenen japanischen Firmen gegründet hat, um in Japan die Werbenutzung seiner Marke zu kanalisieren.

**Stadtmarketing** *n* - city marketing

■ Marketingbereich, in dem eine Stadt wie eine Marke behandelt wird und ein eigenes Markenzeichen erhält, das je nach Zielsetzung gepflegt und an Veränderungen angepasst werden muss. Ziel ist es, die Attraktivität der Stadt zu entwickeln und Negativpunkte zu beseitigen. Dies läuft im Rahmen einer wettbewerbsfähigen Strategie ab, mit der die Stadt einen unverwechselbaren Stempel erhält, und mit der das Interesse von Besuchern und Investoren geweckt werden soll.

**Stadtmöblierung** *f* **für Werbezwecke** - adshel

■ Installation, die gleichzeitig z. B. als Bushaltestelle und Werbeträger dient. Die Idee, Bushaltestellen durch Werbung zu finanzieren, geht auf J.C. Decaux in den 60er Jahren zurück.

**Standardprodukt** *n* - standardised product

■ Produkttyp, bei dem die Marke für den Kunden nicht sehr wichtig ist, da der Unterschied zwischen den einzelnen Produkten unwesentlich ist. Zu dieser Situation kann es durch die sehr allgemeinen Eigenschaften des Produktes kommen, dass sich daher nur schwer differenzieren lässt (z. B. einige Grundnahrungsmittel), durch eine unzureichende Werbung und durch die Angebotspolitik, wie sie von den Verbrauchergroßmärkten betrieben wird und die dafür sorgt, dass der Kunde seine Kaufentscheidungen im Wesentlichen über den Preis trifft.

**Standortstrategie** *f* - location strategy

■ Kriterien, Parameter und Verfahren, die ein Unternehmen benutzt, um zu entscheiden, wo seine Verkaufsstellen (Geschäfte, Bankfilialen oder Schnellrestaurants) eingerichtet werden sollen. Um das Absatzpotential zu analysieren, untersucht man die Bevölkerung, die angezogen werden kann, ihre Kaufkraft und die Lage anderer Verkaufseinrichtungen des eigenen Unternehmens oder der Konkurrenz, und stellt die Alternativen bei bestehenden Verkaufslokalen hinsichtlich Fläche, Preis und Vertragsarten für Kauf oder Miete gegenüber.

**Standortzuweisung** *f* - space allocation

▪ Optimale Anordnung der Produkte in einem Geschäft, um die Verkäufe zu maximieren. Während gewöhnlich nur die Verkäufe jedes Artikels berücksichtigt und ihm ein dazu proportionaler Raum zugewiesen wird, berücksichtigt die moderne Raumzuweisung auch die potentiellen Verkäufe dieses Produkts und der mit ihm in Beziehung stehenden Artikel sowie die Bruttospannen und die direkten Kosten, die je nach Produkt unterschiedlich hoch sein können.

**Star** *m* - star

▪ In einer Matrix, in der das Wachstum und der Marktanteil abgetragen werden, wird das Unternehmen als „Stern" bezeichnet, das in einem Segment führend ist, das hohe Wachstumsraten verspricht. Es handelt sich dabei um eine ideale Situation, auch wenn dabei genauso viel finanzielle Mittel verbraucht wie erzeugt werden. Dieser Typ von Unternehmen bedarf einer innovatorischen Geschäftsführung.

**statische Werbung** *f* - perimeter advertising

▪ Werbung ohne Bewegung. Wenngleich die Werbung in den Printmedien über die gleiche Eigenschaft verfügt, wird der Name im Allgemeinen auf die Außenwerbung in Straßen oder Sportstadien angewendet, die bei der Übertragung von Sportveranstaltungen oft im Fernsehen übertragen wird.

**statisches Franchisesymbol** *n* - static firm

▪ Symbol oder Kennzeichen, das eine ausreichende Marktentwicklung erzielt hat und folglich die Aufnahme neuer Franchisenehmer verhindert oder einschränkt. Bezieht sich auch auf noch freie Märkte, auf denen es keine neue Marktöffnung erreicht und konstant ist.

**Statussymbol** *n* - status symbol

▪ Produkt, das seinem Benutzer ein Prestige vermittelt und großteils gekauft wird, um als Zeichen der gesellschaftlichen Bedeutung innerhalb des Zielsegments der Bevölkerung zu dienen. Wenn ein Produkt dieses Image erlangt, kann es zu einem höheren Preis verkauft werden, was wiederum die vermittelte Exklusivität und das Prestige steigert. Ein Statussymbol kann allerdings auch Ablehnung bei Personen hervorrufen, die nicht dieses Image vermitteln wollen.

**Stereotyp** *n* - stereotype

▪ Gemeinplatz, allgemein anerkanntes festes Konzept, das keinen wirklichen und durchdachten Überlegungen entspricht. Im weitesten Sinne, beschreibt es eine Idealvorstellung, die man von einer Sache hat.

**stichprobenartige Auswahl** *f* - random sampling

▪ Eine aus einer Gesamtheit gezogene Stichprobe. Die Stichprobe wurde so gezogen, dass jede andere Stichprobe der gleichen Größe mit der gleichen Wahrscheinlichkeit hätte gezogen werden können. Es besteht keinerlei Methode, um die Stichprobe vorherzubestimmen oder zu schichten.

**Stichprobenentnahme** *f* - sampling

▪ Tätigkeit des Auswählens eines Musters (Stichprobe), nachdem der Auswahlprozess zuvor festgelegt worden ist. Die Stichprobe kann zufällig oder nicht zufällig ausgewählt sein, bei Zeitreihenuntersuchungen kann sie fest sein oder jedes Mal neu ausgewählt werden.

**Stichprobenfehler** *m* - sampling error

▪ In der Forschung, ein Fehler aufgrund der Tatsache dass nur eine Teilmenge oder ein Muster und nicht die Gesamtmenge geprüft wurde. Es handelt sich hierbei um die Differenz zwischen den beobachteten Werten und dem Durchschnitt dieser Werte bei wiederholten Messungen.

**Stickiness** *f* - stickiness

▪ Effektivität einer Website in Bezug auf ihre Fähigkeit, Benutzer anzuziehen und zu halten. Vom Marketingstandpunkt ist der Erfolg einer neuen Seite nicht durch die Anzahl von Besuchen zu messen, sondern durch die Qualität sowie die Zeit, die ein Benutzer auf der Seite bleibt, und die Art und Weise, wie er mit den Verantwortlichen der Site in Kontakt tritt.

**Stifter** *m* - donor

■ Beim Direktmarketing die Person, die ein Kaufangebot für ein Produkt oder eine Dienstleistung wahrnimmt und diese im Namen des Käufers an einen Dritten weiterschenkt. Diese Art von Werbung ist vor allem bei den Abonnements sehr häufig.

**stille Klausel** *f* - assumptive clause

■ Bedingung, die zwischen einem Käufer und einem Verkäufer nicht ausdrücklich vereinbart wurde, die sich aber durch die Gewohnheiten der Branche oder aus der Initiative einer der beiden Seiten ergibt. Wenn der Käufer z. B. bestimmte abweichende Verpackungs- und Transportkonditionen verlangt, wird davon ausgegangen, dass er Zusatzkosten dafür übernimmt.

**Stimmung** *f* - atmosphere

■ Im Marketing das Ambiente, durch das der Verbraucher zum Kauf oder Konsum angeregt werden soll.

**Stimulationsmarketing** *n* - stimulational marketing

■ Marketingtyp, bei dem die Zielgruppe am Produkt oder an der Dienstleistung nicht interessiert ist und diesen gleichgültig gegenübersteht. Die Aufgabe dieses Marketingtyps ist es, auf Grund einer Analyse der Bedürfnisse der Verbraucher durch das Anbieten von Produkten mit nützlichen und geschätzten Attributen einen Markt zu schaffen.

**Stoßzeit** *f* - peak time

■ Stunde bzw. Zeitdauer höchster Aktivität (Verkehr, Zuschauer- oder Zuhörerzahl eines Massenmediums, Kunden in einer Einrichtung usw.).

**strategische Allianz** *f* - strategic alliance

■ Vereinigung von Unternehmen mit strategischem Charakter zur Erreichung eines langfristigen Ziels. Werden oft zwischen Unternehmen gegründet, die auf verwandten, jedoch nicht rivalisierenden Märkten tätig sind.

**strategische Forschung** *f* - strategic research

■ Marktforschung, die die notwendige Information sammelt, aufgrund derer ein Programm für die Öffentlichkeitsarbeit entwickelt werden kann.

**strategisches Marketing** *n* - strategic marketing

■ Marketingzweig, der die Gefahren und Möglichkeiten der Umgebung sowie die internen Ressourcen und Kapazitäten eines Unternehmens analysiert, um die angemessenen Maßnahmen zur Erreichung von Organisationszielen mittelfristig und langfristig zu planen.

**Strichcode** *m* - bar code

■ Symbol, das sich aus schwarzen Strichen oder Balken verschiedener Breite mit weißen Abständen dazwischen zusammensetzt. Dank dieses Kodierungsstandards für Konsumgüter kann jeder einzelne Artikel mit einem eigenen Kode gekennzeichnet werden, der jedoch zukünftig durch Radiofrequenz-Etiketten ersetzt werden soll.

**Strichcodelesegerät** *n* - scanner bar-code reader

■ Lesegerät, das sich an der Ausgangskasse eines Geschäfts befindet, das den Strichcode liest, automatisch den Kassenzettel ausdruckt und die Ware vom Bestand abbucht. Durch das Lesegerät wird der Arbeitsaufwand und die Fehlerquote bei der Preisauszeichnung der Ware und der Preiseingabe an der Kasse verringert. Es erlaubt außerdem eine höhere Warenumschlagshäufigkeit, da der Bestand jedes Produktes bekannt ist, was Vorteile im Bestellwesen mit sich bringt.

**strukturierter Fragebogen** *m* - structured questionnaire

■ In der quantitativen Forschung ein Fragebogen, in dem die Fragen und die möglichen Antworten auf jede Frage vorbestimmt sind. Der Interviewer hat die Fragen in der angegebenen Reihenfolge zu stellen und den Text wörtlich wiederzugeben. Er darf keine Antworten notieren, die nicht im Fragebogen stehen. Die Strukturierung eines Fragebogens ermöglicht eine Graduierung je nach Inhalt.

**Stückkosten** *pl* - unit cost
▪ Kosten, die jede produzierte Einheit verursacht. Gleichbedeutend mit Durchschnittskosten.

**Submarke** *f* - sub-brand
▪ Zusätzliche Marke einer Markenfamilie, die ein bestimmtes Produkt bzw. eine Produktvariation kennzeichnet. Unterscheidet sich von der Hauptmarke oder Masterbrand, die alle Produkte eines Herstellers umfasst.

**Subskriptionsverkauf** *m* - sale by subscription
▪ Verkauf, bei dem sich der Käufer einschreibt und verpflichtet, während sich der Verkäufer das Recht vorbehält, den Verkauf nicht vollständig durchzuführen, wenn es nicht genügend Subskriptionen gibt. Der Vorteil für den Käufer besteht in einem niedrigeren Einführungspreis. Wird im Immobilien- und Verlagsbereich praktiziert.

**Substitutionseffekt** *m* - substitution effect
▪ Veränderung in der Nachfragemenge eines Gutes, auf Grund einer Preisänderung bei einem Substitutionsgut, wobei das Einkommen konstant bleibt.

**Substitutionsgüter** *n/pl* - substitute goods
▪ Wirtschaftsgüter, die das selbe Bedürfnis befriedigen. Jede Preiserhöhung bei einem dieser Güter führt zu einer Nachfragesteigerung des anderen Gutes. Es handelt sich dabei um das Gegenstück zu Komplementärgütern.

**subversive Werbung** *f* - subvertising
▪ Aktivität von Einzelpersonen oder Systemgegnern, um eine veröffentlichte Anzeige oder Kampagne oder auch eine Marke oder ein Unternehmen zu kritisieren, wobei das gleiche Werbewerkzeug benutzt wird: z.B. aufgrund einer sozialen Polemik bezüglich einer Produktart (z.B. Alkohol oder Zigaretten), der verwendeten Sprache oder Werbestrategie (z.B. Calvin Klein) oder zur Anprangerung der Unternehmenspolitik von multinationalen Unternehmen (wie McDonald's oder Nike).

**Suchbanner** *n* - search-related banner
▪ Von den Suchmaschinen gebotene Möglichkeit, damit eine spezifische Anzeige erscheint, wenn ein Benutzer ein bestimmtes Schlagwort eingibt.

**suggerierte Erinnerung** *f* - suggested recall
▪ Prozentsatz des Publikums, das sich an eine Marke erinnert, wenn sie ihm genannt wird. Misst den Grad der gesamten Markenwiedererkennung.

**Suggestivfrage** *f* - leading question
▪ Frage, die die Antwort impliziert. Muss vermieden werden, um keine Fehler bei der Informationssammlung zu riskieren.

**Surround-Session** *f* - surround session
▪ Onlinewerbeform der New York Times Digital, dem Onlinebereich der New York Times. Einem Besucher wird nur Werbung von einem einzigen Werbetreibenden gezeigt, egal auf welche Seite er geht.

**SWOT-Analyse** *f* - SWOT analysis
▪ Schema für die Situationsanalyse einer Unternehmung, deren Augenmerk auf den Schwächen, den Bedrohungen, den Stärken und den Möglichkeiten der Unternehmung beruht. Bei der Abkürzung handelt es sich um die englischen Begriffe: strengths, weaknesses, opportunities und threats.

**systematische Stichprobenentnahme** *f* - systematic sampling
▪ Gebündelte Zufallsauswahl, in der sich die Stichprobe aus jedem n-ten Element einer geordneten Liste, nach einer zufälligen Anfangsauswahl, zusammensetzt. Es ist eine einstufige, gebündelte Stichprobenentnahme, da sie die gesamte Bevölkerung der ausgewählten Gruppe mittels arithmetischer Progression

einschließt. Sie kann noch effektiver sein, indem man auch Elemente mit extremen Ausprägungen berücksichtigt (zum Beispiel Ladengeschäfte mit extrem kleiner oder großer Oberfläche). Man muss aufpassen, dass keine periodischen Wiederholungen vorliegen.

# T

**Tachistoskop** *n* - tachistoscope

■ Gerät, das sehr kurze Darbietungen von visuellen Reizen, z.B. Bildern oder Symbolen erlaubt. Wird bei Proben (Pretest) von Werbespots benutzt, um zu erfahren, welche Elemente bei einem Zuschauer das größte Interesse wecken.

**Tagebuchmethode** *f* - diary method

■ Erhebungsmethode unter Verwendung systematischer Aufzeichnungen von Zeitspannen, Beobachtungen und Aufmerksamkeitsgegenständen von Schriftstellern, Wissenschaftlern oder z. B. Projektmitarbeitern von Medienforschungsunternehmen. Nicht mit den sporadischen, nach Lust und Laune erfolgenden (oder unterbleibenden) Notizen von privaten Tagebuchschreibern zu verwechselt. Auch Tagebuchverfahren.

**take or pay** - take or pay

■ Klausel, durch die sich der Käufer verpflichtet, eine Ware in einer bestimmten Menge und in einem bestimmten Zeitraum zu kaufen und zu bezahlen. Wenn er die vereinbarten Bedingungen nicht einhält, ist er dazu verpflichtet, eine Entschädigung zu bezahlen, die bis zum vollen vorgesehenen Warenwert reichen kann. Diese Vertragsform ist typisch für langfristige Zulieferverträge, um den Verkäufer zu schützen, z. B. Energiesektor.

**tätiger Teilhaber** *m* **ohne Kapitaleinlage** - industrial partner

■ Person, die in eine offene Handelsgesellschaft anstelle von Kapital Dienstleistungen und berufliche oder technische Kenntnisse einbringt. Ihr wird eine bestimmte Beteiligung an den Gewinnen und am Liquidationswert der Gesellschaft zuerkannt, obwohl sie kein Kapital eingebracht hat. Sie bringt Arbeitsleistung ein, ist aber nicht unbedingt Geschäftsführer der Gesellschaft; dieser ist in der Regel ein Kapitalgesell-schafter.

**technischer Verkauf** *m* - technical sales

■ Industrieverkauf technisch sehr komplexer Produkte, für den Verkäufer mit einer guten Ausbildung und Fachkenntnissen sowie der Fähigkeit, enge persönliche Beziehungen zu den Kunden aufzubauen und zu pflegen, erforderlich sind. Wichtig ist auch ein guter technischer Kundendienst für Wartung und Reparaturen.

**telefonische Befragung** *f* - telephone interview

■ In Markstudien eine Befragung, die per Telefon durchgeführt wird. Viele telefonischen Befragungen werden mit Hilfe eines Computers durchgeführt, um die Nummern zu wählen und die Antworten unmittelbar aufzuzeichnen.

**Telefonverkauf** *m* - phone selling

■ Verkauf durch direkten Anruf des möglichen Käufers.

**Telemarketing** *n* - telemarketing

■ Kommunikationstechnik, die das Telefon als Emissionskanal oder Antwortmedium benutzt, um Produkte oder Dienstleistungen zu fördern, zu verkaufen oder Meinungsumfragen und Marktstudien auszuführen.

**Telepromotion** *f* - telepromotion

■ Fernsehwerbung für ein Produkt unter Mitwirkung von Sendungen und Moderatoren eines Senders. Die Werbung dauert ungefähr 60 Sekunden, in denen die Moderatoren oder Figuren aus einer Sendung oder Schauspieler eine Situation um das Produkt darstellen.

**Teleshop** *m* - shopping channel

■ Bezeichnet eine Verkaufsform, bei der dem Endverbraucher Produkte oder Dienstleistungen über das Fernsehen präsentiert werden, die er dann direkt telefonisch bestellen kann. Es gibt Kabelfernsehsender, die unverschlüsselt sind und sich ausschließlich dem Teleshop widmen, meist zu Uhrzeiten mit wenig Publikum.

**Televerkauf** *m* - telesales

▪ Verkauf, bei dem der Käufer in keinen direkten Kontakt mit dem Produkt tritt, sondern dies über ein Zwischenmedium erwirbt, z.B. Katalog, Telefon, Fernsehen, Webseite, E-Mail, usw. Auch Fernverkauf.

**Tendenzberater** *m* - coolhunter

▪ Professioneller Analytiker von Geschmacksrichtungen und Modetendenzen, der Agenturen und Berufstätige im Kreativbereich berät. Er sucht das Andere, was möglicher Meinungsführer anzieht, analysiert Lebensstiländerungen, vor allem bei der Jugend und Neuheiten in den Bereichen, die sektorübergreifend sein könnten, weil sie für bestimmte Gruppen anziehend sind und klassifiziert und ordnet die Informationen so, dass sie für Designer und Angestellte des Kreativbereichs nützlich sind.

**Testgeschäft** *n* - pilot store

▪ Prototyp eines Ladens, der als Modell für andere eigene oder im Franchisesystem betriebene Geschäfte verwendet wird, zur Schulung des Personals, oder auch zur Erprobung eines neuen Konzeptes im Bereich der visuellen Gestaltung, des Sortiments, der Preise oder jeder anderen Variablen.

**Testimonial** *n* - celebrity endorsement

▪ Werbebotschaft, die von einer in der Öffentlichkeit bekannten Persönlichkeit übermittelt wird, diese bestätigt Vorzüge und Nutzen des Produkts, von dem sie angibt, es regelmäßig zu verwenden.

**Testimonial-Werbung** *f* - testimonial

▪ Werbeformat, in dem eine Person ihre direkte Erfahrung mit einem Produkt beschreibt. Meistens ein positiver Erfahrungsbericht, durch den das Produkt der Zielgruppe empfohlen wird; kann verschiedene Formen annehmen, vom berühmten Schauspieler bis zum zufriedenen Käufer, der als Vorbild der Zielgruppe dienen soll.

**Testkäufer** *m* - ghost shopper, mystery shopper

▪ Scheinkäufer, der die Qualität der Dienstleistungen eines Unternehmens überprüft und vergleicht, wobei er als normaler Kunde auftritt.

**Testkonzept** *n* - as it falls concept

▪ System, mit dem garantiert wird, dass ein nationaler Medienplan, der sich an einem Stichprobenmarkt orientiert, einen lokalen Medienplan auf Landesebene reproduziert.

**Testmarkt** *m* - test market

▪ Örtliches Gebiet, in dem ein neues Produkt eingeführt wird, um seinen Erfolg zu schätzen. In der Regel werden mehrere für den Gesamtmarkt repräsentative Städte ausgewählt und verschiedenen Marketingplänen unterworfen (z. B. Werbeintensität, Gratisproben, Einführungsangebote oder Coupons in einem anderen Produkt). Man berechnet das Ausmaß der Markenkenntnis, der Probe- und Wiederholungskäufe. Dieses Verfahren ist zwar wirkungsvoll, verzögert aber die Markteinführung, alarmiert die Konkurrenz, und eine Extrapolation ist fragwürdig.

**Textlink** *m* - text link

▪ Werbelinks, die auf einer Webseite erscheinen, E-Mails, Webportale oder jeder beliebige andere Träger, der im Internet in Textform benutzt wird. Können als Teil einer Nachricht, in einer Liste eines Verzeichnisses, in einem Index, als empfohlener Link u. a. erscheinen.

**Textlinkaustausch** *m* - text link exchange

▪ Vereinbarung zwischen zwei Websites, dass jede einen Werbetext auf der Web der anderen veröffentlicht.

**theoretischer Markt** *m* - theoretical market

▪ Theoretische Nachfrage nach einem Gut oder einer Dienstleistung, das heißt, die Personen, die ein Bedürfnis haben, das durch dieses Gut oder Dienstleistung befriedigt werden kann, unabhängig davon, ob diese Personen über die nötigen Mittel verfügen (potentieller Markt) oder tatsächliche Verbraucher sind (gegenwärtiger Markt).

**Titelzeile** *f* - headline

■ Anfangsphrase einer Druckanzeige mit hervorgehobenem Schriftbild, im Allgemeinen in größerer Schrift als der Text, deren Ziel die Aufmerksamkeitserhaschung beim Leser und die Aufforderung zum Lesen des übrigen Textes ist. In den Titelzeilen werden alle möglichen rhetorischen Kniffe verwendet, um die Aufmerksamkeit zu erregen.

**Top-of-mind-Marke** *f* - top-of-mind brand

■ Marke (oder Werbekampagne), die eine führende und außerordentliche Stellung bei den Konsumenten hat, wenn sie dazu befragt werden. Ziel der Werbung ist es, zu erreichen, dass die Marke besser im Gedächtnis bleibt und sich besser an das gewünschte Image anpasst.

**Tortendiagramm** *n* - pie chart

■ Grafische Darstellung der Ergebnisse in einem in Sektoren unterteilten Kreis, bei dem jeder Sektor die Werte der entsprechenden Variablen wiedergibt, sowie deren Anteil am Gesamten.

**Tourismusmarketing** *n* - tourism marketing

■ Marketingform, die spezifisch in der Tourismusbranche Anwendung findet.

**Tourismuswerbung** *f* - tourism advertising

■ Werbetätigkeit, um die Eigenschaften und Besonderheiten von touristischem Interesse eines bestimmten Ortes, einer bestimmten Gegend oder eines Landes bekannt zu machen und als Urlaubsziel zu begünstigen.

**traditionelle Geschäfte** *n/pl* - bricks and mortar

■ Ausdruck aus dem englisch-amerikanischen Sprachgebrauch, mit denen diejenigen Unternehmen bezeichnet werden, deren geschäftliche Aktivitäten nicht auf das Internet konzentriert sind. Der Begriff wird verwendet, um sie von den Unternehmen zu unterscheiden, die ihre Geschäfte im Internet abwickeln. Es wird auch oft der englische Ausdruck verwendet.

**Transaktionsmarketing** *n* - transaction marketing

■ Marketingtyp, der sich auf die Potenzierung punktueller Kontakte zwischen Verkäufer und Kunden und auf den Abschluss von kurzfristigen Transaktionen konzentriert unabhängig von den Folgen für die langfristige Beziehung.

**transnationale Werbeagentur** *f* - transnational advertising agency

■ Werbeunternehmen, das neben seinem Hauptsitz in einem bestimmten Land (USA, Großbritannien, Frankreich, Japan) in anderen Ländern Zweigstellen eröffnet oder Werbeagenturen aufkauft, um international tätig zu sein.

**Transportmittelwerbung** *f* - transport advertising

■ Werbung in einem Verkehrsmittel oder in Verbindung mit ihm, zum Beispiel Plakate in Autobussen.

**Trendsetter** *m* - trendsetter

■ Person, die eine neue Mode oder Trend ins Leben ruft. In der Marktforschung sind Trendsetter ein wichtiger Faktor, der in beim Marketing für Zielpublikum unter 30 und insbesondere Teenager in Betracht gezogen werden muss.

**Treue** *f* - loyalty

■ Loyalität gegenüber einer Marke, einem Produkt oder einer Idee. Ist die Markenloyalität sehr stark ausgeprägt, kauft die entsprechende Person nur oder verstärkt eine bestimmte Marke, auch wenn sie nicht in dem Geschäft erhältlich ist, in dem sie gewöhnlich einkauft, der Preis schwankt oder Substitutionsprodukte auf den Markt kommen. Die Identifizierung der typischen Eigenschaften der Stammkunden dient dazu, das Zielpublikum genauer zu bestimmen.

**Trockengüter** *n/pl* - dry goods

■ Im Deutschen kaum gebräuchliche Bezeichnung, die alle nicht flüssigen oder nicht gasförmigen Waren umfassen würde. In den USA wird der Begriff hauptsächlich für Textilien und Kleidung verwendet.

**typografische Anzeige** *f* - letterpress ad

■ Anzeige, deren Text von der Zeitung, in der sie erscheint, selbst zusammengesetzt wird. Nicht geläufig bei Anzeigen im Großformat, die vollständig von der Agentur zusammengestellt sind, bei Kleinanzeigen sehr häufig.

# U

**über dem Knick** - above the fold

■ Der Teil einer Webseite, der sichtbar ist, ohne nach unten scrollen oder blättern zu müssen.

**überarbeitender Werbetexter** *m* - copywriter adapter

■ Werbetexter, der die notwendigen Veränderungen an einem Text für ein anderes Zielpublikum oder für den Einsatz in einem anderen Land vornimmt.

**überbewertet** - overvalued

■ Merkmal eines Gutes, dessen Preis höher als sein tatsächlicher Wert ist.

**Überproduktion** *f* - overproduction

■ Herstellung einer größeren Menge eines Produkts, als ein Markt zum Verkaufspreis aufnehmen kann. Ein vorübergehender Überschuss kann im Lager gehalten werden (mit den entsprechenden finanziellen Aufwendungen), aber langfristig muss der Produktionsrhythmus reduziert oder es müssen neue Absatzmärkte gefunden werden.

**Übertragung** *f* - broadcast

■ Technik, bei der dieselbe Information gleichzeitig und mithilfe eines Kommunikationsnetzes, einem E-Mail-System, Radio- oder Fernsehsendern oder über Satellit an verschiedene Empfänger gesendet wird.

**überzeugende Kommunikation** *f* - persuasive communication

■ Soziale Interaktion über Mitteilungen, die von der Quelle oder dem Sender mit der Absicht geplant wurden, den Empfänger zum Wechseln von Image, Einstellung, Absicht, Verhalten oder Sitten in Bezug auf ein psychologisch festgelegten Gegenstand, der real oder irreal sein kann, zu bewegen.

**überzeugendes Ziel** *n* - persuasive objective

■ Ziel oder beabsichtigte Wirkung des Senders der überzeugenden Kommunikation, nur dass diese von anderen Kommunikationsarten ausgelöst wird. Hier wird die Suche nach der Etablierung, Änderung oder Verstärkung von Image, Einstellung, Absicht, Verhalten oder Sitten angestrebt, die der Öffentlichkeit als Referenzgegenstand dienen.

**Überzeugung** *f* - persuasion

■ Veranlassung einer Person zu einer Änderung ihrer Einstellungen oder ihres Verhaltens durch die Darlegung von Gründen und Argumenten. Wenn stattdessen die Gefühle angesprochen werden, spricht man von Überredung.

**Umfrage** *f* - survey

■ Vorgehensweise, um Information zu erhalten. Dies kann durch systematische und strukturierte Befragung oder Beobachtung einer Gruppe erfolgen. Ist die Gesamtheit, die man untersuchen möchte recht groß, zieht man eine Stichprobe, die man dann untersucht. Die Untersuchung kann durch Beobachtung erfolgen, obwohl eine Untersuchungen an Hand von Umfragen üblicher ist.

**Umfrage** *f* **durch Subskription** - survey by subscription

■ Feste und einzigartige Befragung, die von einem Spezialunternehmen durchgeführt wird, das die Ergebnisse der Befragung entweder vor oder nach der Befragung an mehrere Kunden mit ähnlichen Bedürfnissen verkauft. Dabei erhalten alle die gleichen Ergebnisse. Diese Art der Befragung darf nicht mit der Omnibusbefragung verwechselt werden.

**Umfragebasis** *f* - sample

■ In der Statistik, Menge ausgewählter Elemente, die repräsentativ für eine Bevölkerung sind. Ihr Umfang und der Prozess der Stichprobenentnahme muss nach wissenschaftlichen Kriterien bestimmt werden, um gültige Schlussfolgerungen ziehen zu können.

**Umfrageführer** *m* - guide to the interview

▪ In der Qualitativforschung, Auflistung der Themen für eine Umfrage. Die Reihenfolge der Themenabhandlung und die Formulierung der Fragen liegen im Ermessen des Umfrageführers.

**Umgehungsangriff** *m* - bypass attack

▪ Angriff auf einen Markt, der für den Hauptkonkurrenten von nebensächlicher Bedeutung ist. Man geht davon aus, dass der Konkurrent an diesem Markt wenig Interesse hat oder ihn nicht gut verteidigen kann. Ziel ist es, Positionen und Marktanteile vor einem späteren direkteren Angriff zu festigen. Zum Beispiel kann man mit einem Exportmarkt beginnen, um sich später auf den inländischen Markt zu konzentrieren.

**Umsatz** *m* - turnover

▪ Gesamtheit der während einer Periode verkauften Produkteinheiten, und insbesondere das Geschäftsvolumen in Geldeinheiten.

**Umstrukturierung** *f* - re-engineering

▪ Neue Untersuchung der Organisation, der Arbeitsabläufe und der in einem Vorgang oder einem Unternehmen gebundenen Ressourcen zum Erreichen von Qualitätsverbesserungen, Kosteneinsparungen, flexibleren Reaktionszeiten und einer Erhöhung der Zufriedenheit der eigenen Mitarbeiter und der Kunden. Ziel ist es, alle Prozesse zu eliminieren, die nicht zur Wertschöpfung für den Kunden beitragen.

**Umweltmarketing** *n* - ecological marketing

▪ Marketingart zur Förderung des Umweltschutzes. Dazu werden Produkte und Verpackungen beworben, die zu einem akzeptablen Preis recycelt werden können, geht einher mit Werbung, die den Verbraucher auf die Nichtverschmutzung der Umwelt aufmerksam macht. Auch grünes Marketing.

**Umweltwerbung** *f* - ecological advertising

▪ Werbeaktivität mit gesellschaftlichem Wert, die sich speziell auf die Erziehung, Bewusstmachung, Vorbeugung oder Handlungen zu Schutz und Aufrechterhaltung der Umwelt bezieht. Im Allgemeinen bezeichnet "umweltfreundlich" eine positive Produkteigenschaft, wie z. B. Eco-Waschmaschine.

**umwerben** *v* - canvass *v*

▪ Befragen einer Person oder einer Gruppe von Personen mit der Absicht, ihre Meinung kennenzulernen, eine bestimmte Diskussion anzuregen und gleichzeitig eine Idee, ein Produkt oder eine Dienstleistung zu verkaufen.

**unabhängiger Handelsbetrieb** *m* - independent trader

▪ Verkaufseinrichtung, die keiner Handelsgruppe angehört. Der unabhängige Händler kann eigenständig bleiben, ohne sich an einen Lieferanten oder eine Organisation, die ihm bei der Vermarktung behilflich ist, zu binden. Er kann sich aber auch einer freiwilligen Handelskette oder einem Franchisesystem anschließen oder sich darin integrieren.

**unbeabsichtigte Aufmerksamkeit** *f* - involuntary attention

▪ Aufmerksamkeit, die dem Hauptteil der Werbung zuteil wird. Trotz Interessenmangels hat die Werbung eine Wirkung, entweder langfristig oder durch Wiederholung.

**undifferenziertes Marketing** *n* - undifferentiated marketing

▪ Marketing, bei dem für alle Kunden die gleiche Kombination aus Preis, Produkt, Werbung und Vertriebskanal eingesetzt wird, da man nicht davon ausgeht, dass so verschiedenartige Segmente existieren, dass ein unterschiedlicher Marketingansatz gerechtfertigt wäre.

**unerwünschte Werbung** *f* - junk mail

▪ Werbesendung, die eine geringe Qualität oder Attraktivität aufweist, nicht adressiert oder schlecht gestaltet ist. Oft wandert sie ungelesen in den Papierkorb. Die Antwortquote kann bei einer schlecht geplanten Werbeaussendung unter einem Promille liegen. Es wird auch oft der englische Ausdruck verwendet.

**unfairer Wettbewerb** *m* - unfair competition

■ Handlungsstil oder Handlungsform, wobei die gesetzlichen Regeln oder das Gewohnheitsrecht, das zwischen den Wettbewerbern am Markt gilt, übertreten wird (zum Beispiel im Bezug auf die Produktqualität, Qualifikation und Bezahlung der Angestellten usw.).

**unfreiwilliges Publikum** *n* - captive audience

■ Publikum, das wegen eines bestimmten Umstandes (z. B. der Teilnahme an einem Seminar), das Empfangen einer bestimmten Werbebotschaft nicht vermeiden kann.

**ungerade Seite** *f* - odd page

■ Die rechte Seite von Druckerzeugnissen. Gelegentlich sind Anzeigen auf der rechten Seite teurer, da sie stärker wahrgenommen werden.

**Ungewissheit** *f* - uncertainty

■ Zweifel, Verlegenheit oder fehlende Sicherheit über ein zukünftiges Ergebnis. Die wirtschaftliche Tätigkeit eines Unternehmens beinhaltet die Übernahme von Risiko und das Handeln unter Ungewissheit.

**unidirektionale Kommunikation** *f* - one-way communication

■ Übertragung von Nachrichten in eine Richtung, vom Sender zum Empfänger ohne Inbetrachtziehung einer Antwort. Tritt bei Nichtvorhandensein der Motivationsforschung der Audienz zutage und bei der Wirkungsforschung, die diese Nachrichten auf das Publikum haben.

**unstrukturiertes Interview** *n* - unstructured interview

■ Befragungsgespräch, das keinem festen Muster oder vorgegebenen Fragen folgt. Es wird in der Anfangsphase einer Untersuchung eingesetzt, um besser sämtliche möglichen Facetten eines Themas zu erkennen und neue Anregungen zu erhalten.

**Unternehmensdesign** *n* - corporate design

■ Disziplin, die sich mit der Entwicklung und Schaffung grafischer Elemente für die visuelle Identität von Unternehmen sowie mit der Anwendung dieser Elemente auf Vordrucke, Briefpapier und Werbematerial des Unternehmens befasst.

**Unternehmensevent** *n* - corporate event

■ Firmenereignis von gewisser Bedeutung und öffentlichem Interesse, z. B. die Eröffnung einer neuen Abteilung oder ein Firmenjubiläum. Beeinflusst das Image des Unternehmens und wird in aller Regel von Fachleuten geplant.

**Unternehmensfarbe** *f* - corporate colour

■ Farbe oder Farben, die ein Unternehmen, eine Organisation oder Institution zu Identifikationszwecken wählt mit dem Ziel, die Wahrnehmung der grundlegenden Elemente visueller Identität (Symbol und Logo) sowie anderweitiger Identitätsträger (Beschriftung, Beschilderung und Architektur) zu verstärken.

**Unternehmensgruppe** *f* - corporate group

■ Einzelne Unternehmen, die durch gemeinsamen Besitz untereinander verbunden sind. Normalerweise besteht eine Dachgesellschaft, die entweder direkt oder über Filialen mehr als 50% des Kapitals der restlichen Unternehmen hält. Man benutzt den Begriff auch, wenn man sich auf einen oder mehrere Einzelaktionäre bezieht, die Besitzer unterschiedlicher Firmen sind, die in konformer Art und Weise geführt werden.

**Unternehmensimage** *n* - corporate image

■ Positive oder negative Meinung, die die Öffentlichkeit von einem Unternehmen, einer Organisation oder Institution hat und die sich auf deren Vorgehensweise, ihre Handlungen und Mitteilungen, ihre Überzeugungen und Werte, ihre Firmenpolitik und anderweitigen Aktivitäten und Ausdrucksformen begründet.

**Unternehmenskommunikation** *f* - corporate communications

■ Interne und externe Verbreitung von Firmeninformation über die jeweils angemessenen Medien und Informationskanäle, die Unternehmen,

Organisationen oder Institutionen für ihre Kunden betreiben.

**Unternehmenskultur** *f* - corporate culture

■ Gesamtheit von Überzeugungen und Verhaltensweisen, die die Philosophie und Eigenart eines Unternehmens, einer Organisation oder Institution widerspiegeln und die in erheblichem Maß die Identität des Unternehmens beeinflussen.

**Unternehmensnetzwerk** *n* - corporate network

■ Ausgedehntes Netz, das aus der Verbindung aller internen Netze eines Unternehmens zusammengesetzt ist, einschließlich der lokalen Netze, der privaten Telefonnetze sowie der Netze zur Übertragung von Sprache, Daten und Videos. Umfasst ebenso die permanent zugeordneten Telekommunikationslinien. Ein typisches Beispiel eines Unternehmensnetzes ist das Intranet.

**Unternehmensplan** *m* **für soziale Verantwortung** - corporate social responsibility plan

■ Investmentprojekt, das ein Unternehmen innerhalb eines bestimmten Zeitraums zur Befriedigung sozialer Interessen umzusetzen versucht. Vorschau der strategisch geplanten Umsetzung einer Reihe von sozialen Aktivitäten für die Öffentlichkeit, um die im PR-Plan des Unternehmens definierten Ziele zu erlangen.

**Unternehmensportal** *n* - corporate portal

■ Offizielle Webseite eines Unternehmens oder einer Organisation. Zusätzlich zu den herkömmlichen Informationen bietet das Unternehmensportal eine andere Art von Zugmitteln oder Funktionalität.

**Unternehmensselbstverständnis** *n* - corporate identity

■ Art und Weise, in der sich ein Unternehmen jeweils unterschiedlichem Publikum vorstellt, mit dem es Beziehungen aufnimmt. Es wird auch der englische Begriff verwendet.

**Unternehmenswerbung** *f* - corporate advertising

■ Werbung, die darauf abzielt, das Image des Unternehmens zu fördern durch Schaffung eines erhöhten Bewusstseins in der Öffentlichkeit oder den Ruf des Unternehmens zu verbessern und weniger konkrete Produkte zu bewerben. Wird auch als institutionelle Werbung bezeichnet.

**Unternehmensziel** *n* - corporate objective

■ Vorsätze oder Ziele, die sich ein Unternehmen in Bezug auf die Zukunft setzt, z. B. dass die Kunden das Unternehmen als Ranglistenersten der Automobilhersteller ansehen.

**unterschwellige Werbung** *f* - subliminal advertising

■ Public-Relations-Aktion, die sich an die Massenmedien richtet und aus einem Dokument mit Informationen über die Organisation besteht, das journalistisch geschrieben ist und das Unternehmen vorstellen soll. Enthält normalerweise Pressemitteilungen. Auch Pressedossier genannt. Werbung, die mittels Reizen der Sinne nah an der Wahrnehmungsschwelle auf das Zielpublikum wirken kann, ohne dass dieses sich dessen bewusst ist. Mit anderen Worten wirkt die unterschwellige Werbung auf das Unterbewusstsein der Verbraucher mittels nicht wahrnehmbarer Reize und regt es so zum Konsum von Werbeprodukten an. Trotz des Mythos der unterschwelligen Werbung ist ihre Wirksamkeit nicht nachgewiesen.

**untreuer Verbraucher** *m* - switcher consumer

■ Verbraucher, der einer Marke für eine Warenkategorie nicht treu ist sondern seinen Konsum zwischen zwei oder mehr Marken abwechselt.

**unverkäuflich** - unsaleable

■ Produkt, das man nicht verkaufen kann oder das nicht zum Verkauf kommen darf. In der Regel ist dies durch Qualitätsmängel bedingt oder auf neue gesetzliche Verfügungen zurückzuführen.

**unverkauft** - unsold

■ Produkt, das nach Ablauf einer Periode noch nicht verkauft wurde. Dies betrifft in der Regel Produkte, die den Modeschwankungen unterworfen sind, auf bestimmte Zeiträume bezogene Kataloge, Saisonprodukte, technisch veraltete Produkte oder solche, bei denen ein besseres Produkt auf den Markt gebracht wurde.

**unvollkommener Wettbewerb** *m* - imperfect competition

■ Marktsituation, in der nicht alle oder keine der notwendigen Voraussetzungen für eine vollkommene Konkurrenz erfüllt sind.

**Upselling** *n* - upselling

■ Verkauf von mehr oder besseren Dienstleistungen als denen, die vom Kunden ursprünglich verlangt wurden.

# V

**Validität** *f* - validity

■ In der Forschungstechnik die Fähigkeit eines Messinstruments zu gewährleisten, dass die beobachteten Unterschiede realen Unterschieden entsprechen und nicht konstanten oder zufälligen Fehlern.

**VALS (values, attitudes and lifestyles)** - VALS (values, attitudes and lifestyles)

■ Klassisches psychografisches Verfahren, das Verbraucher gemäß ihren Lebenswerten und ihrem Lebensstil in vier Hauptkategorien einstuft: geleitet von der Notwendigkeit, von der Außenwelt, vom Inneren und, als Viertes, integriert, wobei diese letzte Kategorie das Beste der beiden vorgenannten kombiniert.

**Varianzanalyse** *f* **(ANOVA)** - analysis of variance (ANOVA)

■ Studie zum Vergleich der statistischen Bedeutung der erhaltenen Unterschiede zwischen verschiedenen Stichproben, wenn diese von unterschiedlichen Zielgruppen stammen.

**Veralterung** *f* - planned psychological obsolescence

■ Ein Produkt wird nicht mehr gewünscht, weil es an Popularität verloren hat und „out" geworden ist. Dies geschieht oft durch Modetrends, aber auch durch technische Entwicklungen. Das Produkt an sich ist aber noch uneingeschränkt nutzbar. In seltenen Fällen wird nur die Verpackung oder Marke des Produkts geändert. Teil der geplanten bzw. künstlichen Obsoleszenz.

**veraltet** - outdated

■ Mangelnde Anpassung oder Angleichung an bestimmte herrschende Umstände, zum Beispiel die Anpassung an eine neue Technologie.

**verbaler Code** *m* - verbal code

■ Gesamtheit von Elementen verbalen Charakters, die in der Werbung benutzt werden können, unter anderem: Überschrift, Einleitung, Textkörper und Endsatz.

**Verbrauch** *m* **des Privatsektors** - private consumption

■ Gesamtverbrauch an Gütern und Dienstleistungen des privatwirtschaftlichen Sektors (Unternehmen, Verbraucher usw.) auf gesamtwirtschaftlicher Ebene.

**Verbraucher** *m* - consumer

■ Person, die ein Gut oder ein Produkt konsumiert, aber nicht zwingend der Käufer desselben sein muss.

**Verbraucherforschung** *f* - consumer research

■ Sammlung und Analyse von Informationen über die typischen Merkmale der Konsumenten bezüglich eines Bedürfnisses oder eines Produktes. Dabei werden die Kauf- und Verbrauchsgewohnheiten, Erinnerungs- und Bekanntheitsgrad einer Marke, zueinander in Verbindung stehende Produkte, jahreszeitliche Schwankungen, tatsächlich befriedigte Bedürfnisse und Kaufabsichten untersucht. Der qualitative Aspekt wird durch detaillierte Interviews und Gruppendiskussionen berücksichtigt;

der quantitative Aspekt durch Umfragen und Konsumentenpanels. Die Verbraucherforschung ergänzt sich mit der Marktforschung.

**Verbraucherorganisation** *f* - consumer association

■ Gruppe von Konsumenten oder Personen, die eine Dienstleistung in Anspruch nehmen oder Güter konsumieren, und die sich vereinigen, um ihre Rechte besser wahrnehmen zu können. Sie verbreitet Information, führt Qualitätskontrollen durch, berät bei Reklamationen und wickelt diese ab. Wird auch als Verbraucherschutzgruppe bezeichnet.

**Verbraucherorientierung** *f* - market-orientation

■ Philosophie, die die Handlungsweise der im Bereich des Marketing fortschrittlichsten Unternehmen prägt. Sie versuchen ständig, die Bedürfnisse der Verbraucher aufzugreifen oder sogar zu antizipieren. Im Gegensatz dazu stehen die Unternehmen, die darauf konzentriert sind, Produkte zu verkaufen, die sie selbst entwerfen oder die der technische Fortschritt hervorbringt.

**Verbraucherpreisindex** *m* **(KPI)** - consumer price index (CPI)

■ Gemäß dem Konsum einer Durchschnittsfamilie gewichteter Index, der das allgemeine Preisniveau dieses Durchschnittskonsums zu einem bestimmten Augenblick misst und ins Verhältnis zu einer früheren Periode setzt. Der Konsumentenpreisindex wird am häufigsten zur Inflationsmessung verwendet.

**Verbraucherschutzverband** *m* - consumers' association

■ Gruppe von Konsumenten oder Personen, die eine Dienstleistung in Anspruch nehmen oder Güter konsumieren, und die sich vereinigen, um ihre Rechte besser wahrnehmen zu können. Sie verbreitet Informationen, führt Qualitätskontrollen durch, berät bei Reklamationen und wickelt diese ab.

**Verbraucherwerbung** *f* - consumer advertising

■ Übermittlung einer Werbebotschaft, die sich direkt an Einzelpersonen oder private Haushalte richtet, im Gegensatz zur Spezial- oder Industriewerbung. Dabei werden Werbeträger mit großer Reichweite, wie Fernsehen, Radio, Zeitschriften, Plakatwände usw. eingesetzt.

**Verbreitung** *f* - circulation

■ Durchschnittliche Anzahl der Exemplare einer Zeitschrift, die vertrieben werden (Abonnements, einzeln verkaufte Exemplare und Gratisexemplare). Multipliziert mit der durchschnittlichen Anzahl von Lesern pro Exemplar, erhält man die Leserschaft pro Ausgabe. Kann auch berechnet werden als gedruckte Auflage abzüglich der nicht vertriebenen Exemplare und der von den Verkaufsstellen zurückgeschickten Exemplare.

**Verbundaktion** *f* - tie-in

■ Marketingaktion, an der in koordinierter Weise verschiedene Körperschaften teilnehmen: Hersteller, Vertreiber, Verkäufer usw. In der Werbung Werbeanzeigen, die von Herstellern und Vertreibern gemeinsam umgesetzt werden.

**Verbundmailing** *n* - co-op mailing

■ In der Direktwerbung versteht man hierunter die Gesamtheit der Werbebotschaften und Aktionen für die Verkaufsförderung verschiedener Produkte, die nicht im Wettbewerb zueinander stehen, aber dasselbe Zielpublikum haben. Wird auch als Gemeinschaftsmailing bezeichnet.

**Verbundvereinbarung** *f* - tie-in agreement

■ Vereinbarung von zwei Unternehmen einer Branche zu gemeinsamen Werbeaktivitäten unter Zusammenschluss ihrer Marken.

**Verbundverkauf** *m* - tie-in sales

■ Verkauf eines Produkts unter der Voraussetzung, dass sich der Käufer gleichzeitig zum sofortigen oder späteren Kauf eines anderen Produkts des Unternehmens verpflichtet. Diese Praxis wird von den Wettbewerbsbehörden verfolgt.

**Verbundvorteil** *m* - economies of scope

■ Kostenreduzierung oder Wirksamkeitssteigerung, die eine Firma erreicht, wenn sie zusätzlich verschiedene verwandte oder ähnliche Produkte anbietet, die dann einen gemeinsamen Kostenpunkt aufweisen. Auch Verbundeffekt.

**Verbundwerbung** *f* - tie-in advertisement

■ Anzeige, die mehr als ein Produkt oder eine Dienstleistung des Werbetreibenden oder einer anderen Firma umfasst,. Ein Sonderfall ist die gemeinschaftliche Werbung, die im Allgemeinen vom Hersteller eines Produkts zusammen mit seinem Vertreiber durchgeführt wird.

**verderbliche Güter** *n/pl* - perishable good

■ Produkte, die dazu bestimmt sind, während einer begrenzten und vorherbestimmten Zeit benutzt oder verbraucht zu werden, da sie danach einen Qualitätsverlust erleiden und unbrauchbar oder ungenießbar (bei Lebensmitteln) sind.

**Verdrängungseffekt** *m* - crowding-out

■ Staatliche Aktivitäten, die zum Ausscheiden der schwächsten Marktteilnehmer und derjenigen, die zum gültigen Marktpreis nicht länger anbieten oder nachfragen wollen, aus einem Markt führt. Der Begriff wird besonders für den Rückgang der privaten Kreditnachfrage verwendet, wenn eine Erhöhung des öffentlichen Finanzbedarfs zu einem Steigen der Zinssätze führt. Man benutzt auch den englischen Ausdruck Crowding-Out.

**Vergessensrate** *f* - rate of forgetfulness

■ Indikator, der misst, wie schnell die Verbraucher eine Marke oder Werbebotschaft vergessen.

**vergeudete Rundsendungen** *f* - waste circulation

■ Exemplare einer Veröffentlichung, die im Hinblick auf eine konkrete Werbekampagne als wertlos betrachtet werden, da sie an Personen außerhalb der Zielgruppe gesendet wurden.

**vergleichende Werbung** *f* - comparative advertising

■ Werbung, bei der der Werbetreibende sein Unternehmen, seine Produkte oder Dienstleistungen denen eines oder mehrerer Konkurrenten gegenüberstellt, um auf diese Weise die Überlegenheit und Vorzüge seines Unternehmens, seiner Produkte oder Dienstleistungen darzustellen. Diese besagen, dass die verglichenen Güter und Dienstleistungen denselben Zweck oder dieselben Bedürfnisse erfüllen müssen, wobei der Vergleich objektiv zwischen einer oder mehr grundlegenden, dazugehörigen, überprüfbaren und repräsentativen Eigenschaften der Güter oder Dienstleistungen, einschließlich des Preises, dargestellt werden muss. In Deutschland ist vergleichende Werbung gemäß § 6 UWG grundsätzlich zulässig, sofern sie nicht unlauter bzw. irreführend ist und den Mitbewerber nicht herabsetzt.

**Vergleichsanalyse** *f* - comparative analysis

■ Bewertung zweier oder mehrerer Alternativen oder Produkte, um Unterschiede oder Ähnlichkeiten zwischen ihnen herauszufinden, Beziehungen zwischen ihnen abzuschätzen und ihre Kosten, ihren Erfolgsbeitrag und ihre relativen Ergebnisse zu messen. Es werden Fakten und Zahlen verwendet, um zu messen, wie wichtig jedes Attribut für die Zielgruppe ist.

**Vergleichstest** *m* - comparison test

■ Bewertung zweier oder mehrerer miteinander konkurrierender Produkte oder Dienstleistungen, durchgeführt von einem Unternehmen oder einem unabhängigen Organ, das eine unvoreingenommene Stellungnahme veröffentlicht, Verbraucherzeitschriften realisieren und veröffentlichen gewöhnlich diese Art von Untersuchungen.

**verhaltensmäßige Segmentierung** *f* - behaviouristic segmentation

■ Einteilung einer Bevölkerung in Gruppen gemäß einer oder mehrerer Variablen, die im Zusammenhang mit dem Verhalten des Verbrauchers und weniger mit seinen demografischen, psychologischen und sozioökonomischen Merkmalen stehen. Diese Variablen beinhalten z. B. die Hauptbedürfnisse, die es zu befriedigen gilt, die Häufigkeit und Umgebung des Einkaufs und die Markentreue.

**Verhaltensuntersuchung** *f* **-**
behaviour scan
■ Untersuchungswerkzeug, das von der Firma IRI (Information Resources Inc.) entwickelt wurde, um das Kaufverhalten in bestimmten Haushalten zu untersuchen. Hierzu werden die Kodes der getätigten Käufe gescannt und mit dem Fernsehkonsum der Familienmitglieder, und folglich mit den so empfangenen Werbebotschaften verglichen.

**Verkauf** *m* **als Sammelwerk -**
serialized sales
■ Verkauf, bei dem der Käufer seine Sammlung regelmäßig ergänzt, ohne sich zum Kauf zu verpflichten, und jede Fortsetzungslieferung zum Zeitpunkt des Erwerbes bezahlt. Die Lieferungen sind in der Regel wöchentlich, können aber auch zweiwöchentlich oder monatlich sein. Nur ein geringer Teil der Personen, welche die Sammlung beginnen, beendet sie auch vollständig. Dieses Verkaufssystem ist typisch im Verlagswesen mit Kioskvertrieb.

**Verkauf** *m* **an Wiederverkäufer -**
trade sale
■ Verkauf, der auf Zwischenhändler eines bestimmten Sektors beschränkt ist und bei dem in der Regel Sondernachlässe eingeräumt werden.

**Verkauf** *m* **aus Verkaufsautomaten -**
vending-machine sales
■ Gleichbedeutend mit Automatenverkauf. Verkauf aus Vertriebsgeräten, in die der Käufer Münzen einwirft oder eine Kreditkarte oder ähnliche Karte einführt, um das Produkt (Zigaretten, Erfrischungsgetränke, Geld bei Bankautomaten usw.) zu erhalten. Diese Automaten werden an Orten mit viel Publikumsverkehr aufgestellt und ermöglichen den Personalabbau. Manchmal mieten spezialisierte Unternehmen den Raum vom Eigentümer des Lokales.

**Verkauf** *m* **durch die Hintertür -**
back-door selling
■ Angebot einer Ware oder Dienstleistung unmittelbar an den Entscheidungsträger oder den Chef des Unternehmens, ohne die entsprechenden Verwaltungsabteilungen zu durchlaufen, die den Vorgang bremsen könnten.

**Verkauf** *m* **im Pyramidensystem -**
pyramid selling
■ Wird auch als Verkauf im Ketten- oder Schneeballsystem bezeichnet. Wenngleich er zahlreiche Varianten hat, besteht der wesentliche Punkt in der Verpflichtung, etwas in der Hoffnung zu kaufen, in der Zukunft viel mehr verkaufen zu können (z. B. Parfümerieartikel, Abonnements oder Schuldscheine). Normalerweise handelt es sich um ein betrügerisches System.

**Verkauf** *m* **mit Inzahlungnahme -**
trade-in sale
■ Verkauf, bei dem zur Zahlung eines Teils des Preises eines neuen Produktes ein ähnliches altes Produkt angenommen wird, wobei dieses von der gleichen oder einer anderen Marke und in funktionsfähigem oder defektem Zustand sein kann. In Wirklichkeit handelt es sich um einen festen Preisnachlass, der eine Diskriminierung zugunsten der bisherigen Benutzer des Produktes darstellt und es vermeidet, den Nachlass auch anderen möglichen Verbrauchern zu gewähren. Dieses Verfahren wird zum Beispiel beim Neuwagenkauf verwendet.

**Verkauf** *m* **nach Muster -** sale by sample
■ Verkauf, bei dem der Käufer sich beim Kauf des Produktes auf die Eigenschaften eines Musters stützt, das ihm der Verkäufer übersandt hat, und berechtigt ist, das Endprodukt zurückzuweisen, wenn es nicht dem Muster entspricht.

**Verkäufermarkt** *m* **-** sellers' market
■ Markt, in dem die Anbieter im Vorteil sind, weil die Nachfrage das Angebot übersteigt.

**Verkaufsanreiz** *m* - sales appeal

■ Fähigkeit einer Verkaufsstelle, eine mehr oder minder wichtige Zahl möglicher Kunden aufgrund der geografischen Lage, und in einem Einkaufszentrum aufgrund des Außen- und Innendesigns anzulocken. So reizt H&M mehr Kunden aufgrund seiner Verkaufslage an, die meist an den privilegierten Stellen einer Stadt ist, als durch Werbeausgaben.

**Verkaufsargument** *n* - selling point

■ Jeder der starken Punkte eines Produktes oder einer Dienstleistung, der benutzt wird, um einen Verkauf zu erreichen.

**Verkaufschef** *m* - sales manager

■ Person, die den Verkäufern und Vertretern eines Unternehmens in einem Gebiet vorsteht. Sie ist hauptverantwortlich für die Aufstellung und Durchführung von Verkaufsplänen.

**Verkaufseinheit** *f* - selling unit

■ Kleinste Einheit eines Produktes, das im Einzelhandel verkauft wird.

**Verkaufsförderung** *f* - sales promotion

■ Teil des Marketing, der die kommerziellen Maßnahmen (Platzierung am Ende einer Regalreihe, Ausstellung, Preisnachlässe) umfasst, die die Einführung und den Verkauf eines Produktes anregen. Wird sporadisch eingesetzt und hat unmittelbare Ziele, im Unterschied zur Werbekommunikation. Entspricht einer Push-Strategie.

**Verkaufsgebiet** *n* - sales region

■ Bereich, den ein Verkäufer oder eine Gruppe von Verkäufern mit Basis in einer Zweigstelle oder einem regionalen Vertriebszentrum abdeckt. Innerhalb jedes Gebietes werden verschiedene Routen festgelegt. Die Aufteilung eines Landes in Gebiete erfolgt nach geographischen Kriterien, auf Grund der Unternehmensgeschichte, der Art von Kunden und Vertrieb, und gelegentlich, um die Übereinstimmung mit den Kriterien von Marktforschungsunternehmen zu erreichen.

**Verkaufsinsel** *f* - store island

■ Mengenmäßig umfangreiche und abgesonderte Aufstellung eines Produktes durch einfache Aufeinanderstapelung oder in einer speziellen Verkaufsvorrichtung, um die Aufmerksamkeit des Publikums in einem Geschäft zu wecken. Die Verkaufsinsel unterscheidet sich von der Positionierung am Regalbeginn oder Regalende dadurch, dass sie abgesondert, für sich allein in der Mitte eines Ganges steht.

**Verkaufskatalog** *m* - sales catalogue

■ Druckmaterial für den Vertreter oder Handelsvertreter einer Firma zur Information der Einzelhändler über die Produktpalette und zur Erregung des Interesses an dessen Verkauf. Wird oft bei der Neukundensuche benutzt, um die Firma in einem guten Licht darzustellen.

**Verkaufskosten** *pl* - selling cost, sales expenses

■ Kosten bezüglich aller Aktivitäten, die notwendig sind, um einem Kunden ein Produkt anzubieten.

**Verkaufskurve** *f* - sales chart

■ Graphische und chronologische Darstellung der Verkaufszahlen, die dazu dient Produkte oder Verkäufer untereinander zu vergleichen, Veränderungen zu früheren Verkaufszahlen festzustellen oder Abweichungen vom Budget zu ermitteln.

**Verkaufslawine** *f* - selling off

■ Panikartiger Verkauf einer Ware oder eines Wertpapiers, deren Preis stark fällt, um einem weiteren Preisverfall zuvorzukommen.

**Verkaufsmarketing** *n* - promotional marketing

■ Begriff, mit dem die Werbeaktionen vom strategischen Gesichtspunkt beurteilt werden. Gegenstück sind die Werbetechniken, die tatsächlich für jeden Fall zutreffen.

**Verkaufsmasche** *f* - sales pitch

■ Leitfaden, den ein Verkäufer für seine berufliche Aktivität benutzt, um einen Käufer dazu bewegen, ein bestimmtes

Produkt zu kaufen. Zusätzlich zu den rationalen Argumenten beinhaltet diese emotionale und affektive Bezeichnungen, die der Verkäufer kombinieren muss, je nach Erfahrung und Geschick.

**Verkaufsmethode** *f* - sales method

▪ Methode zur Festlegung des Werbekostenvoranschlags basierend auf der Verkaufsbeziehung: entweder durch Zuweisung eines Festbetrages in Funktion der einzelnen verkauften oder zu verkaufenden Einheiten oder ein Anteil an den vergangenen und künftigen Verkäufen. Weitere Methoden sind nach Ziel, nach Konkurrenz, Verfügbarkeit und Zufallsmethode.

**Verkaufsorientierung** *f* - sales orientation

▪ Marketing-Fokus für die das Unternehmen eine intensive und aggressive Werbeaktivität mit dem Zweck, über alle Medien den Verbraucher zum Kauf des Produkts zu überzeugen.

**Verkaufspersonal** *n* - sales force

▪ Die Angestellten eines Unternehmens, deren Aufgabe es ist, die Produkte eines Unternehmens durch Kundenbesuche direkt zu verkaufen und die Anpassung der Produkte an die Bedürfnisse der Kunden in ihrem Verkaufsgebiet zu planen und durchzuführen. Dieses zweite Aufgabengebiet setzt Marketingkenntnisse voraus, und es ist notwendig, die langfristigen und qualitativen Ziele festzulegen. Bei den Angestellten handelt es sich um Verkäufer, Beauftragte sowie Niederlassungs- oder Gebietsleiter. Ihr Angestelltenstatus unterscheidet sie von den Kommissionären oder Verkaufsvertretern, obwohl ihr Verdienst in der Regel zu einem großen Teil von erzielten Verkäufen abhängt.

**Verkaufsplan** *m* - sales plan

▪ Grundlegender Teil der Planung in einem Unternehmen, der die zu verkaufenden Produktmengen nach Gebieten, Kunden und Zeiträumen enthält. Er beinhaltet die vorgesehenen Preise und Spannen sowie die Kosten der vorzunehmenden Aktivitäten im Bereich der Absatzpolitik, wie Verkaufsförderung und Werbung. Der Verkaufsplan berücksichtigt Veränderungen der Verkaufsmannschaft, Markteinführung und Vommarktnahme von Produkten, und saisonale Schwankungen, sowie die Handlungen der Konkurrenz und die Entwicklung des gesamten Marktes und der Marktsegmente.

**Verkaufspreis** *m* - selling price

▪ Preis, zu dem ein Produkt verkauft wird. Der zunächst geforderte Preis kann später herabgesetzt werden. Kann mit dem Listenpreis übereinstimmen.

**Verkaufsprognose** *f* - sales forecast

▪ Schätzung der Verkäufe, die ein Unternehmen in einem bestimmten zukünftigen Zeitraum voraussichtlich umsetzen kann. Grundlage sind die Verkaufsergebnisse vergangener Perioden, die voraussichtlichen Marktbedingungen und die durchzuführenden Marketingmaßnahmen.

**Verkaufsprospekt** *m* - sales folder

▪ Gedruckter, illustrierter Prospekt aus hochwertigem Material, den der Handelsvertreter einer Firma zur Förderung eines neuen Produkts an Zwischenhändler benutzt. Didaktische Planung und zur Erreichung eines guten Eindrucks durch den Vertreter, die dann auf die Klientel übergehen kann.

**Verkaufsquote** *f* - sales quota

▪ Vorgesehene Verkaufszahl, die einem Verkäufer, einem Unternehmen oder einer Produktlinie zugewiesen werden. Die Erfüllung der Verkaufszahlen ist mit einem Anreiz oder einer Prämie verbunden. Die Verkaufsquote liegt in der Regel etwas über dem Planwert, der die Grundlage für Investitions- und Produktionsentscheidungen darstellt.

**Verkaufsroute** *f* - sales route

▪ Weg, dem ein Verkäufer folgen muss, um in optimaler Form seine Kunden zu besuchen. Das Routenbuch fasst die zu nehmenden Routen zusammen. Jede Route wird alle 7, 14 oder 28 Tage wiederholt, in Abhängigkeit von der Wichtigkeit der Kunden. Um eine Route zu optimieren, werden gelegentlich Kunden geringer Bedeutung beibehalten, die zur Verringerung der Fixkosten beitragen. Die Auslieferungsroute kann mit der Verkaufsroute übereinstimmen oder nicht, in Abhängigkeit von den erreichten Bestellungen.

**Verkaufsstelle** *f* - point of sale

■ Geschäft oder jede Abteilung des Geschäftes, das eine bestimmte Produktklasse verkauft.

**verkaufsunterstützende Aktivitäten** *f/pl* - sales force support activity

■ Aktivität im Marketing (vor allem in der Werbung oder in der Verkaufsförderung), wird unternommen, um die Arbeit der Verkäufer zu unterstützen (zum Beispiel mit einem Preisausschreiben für die Direktabnehmer oder mit in den Schaufenstern ausliegenden Preisen).

**Verkehr** *m* - traffic

■ In Marktstudien die Gesamtheit der Fahrzeuge oder Personen, die einen bestimmten Punkt passieren, sei es im Äußeren oder im Inneren einer Einrichtung.

**Verkehrsmittelwerbung** *f* - mobile outdoor advertising

■ Eine besondere Form der Außenwerbung, bei der die Werbung an Verkehrsmitteln angebracht wird. Am weitesten verbreitet ist hierbei die Anbringung an öffentlichen Nahverkehrsmitteln, insbesondere Omnibussen, Straßenbahnen oder Taxis.

**verkehrsseitig** - facing traffic

■ In der Außenwerbung, Ausrichtung eines Plakats in Richtung des Verkehrsflusses von Autos.

**Vermarktung** *f* - commercialisation

■ Gesamtheit an Aktivitäten, die darauf gerichtet sind, den Verkauf eines bereits entworfenen Produkts oder einer Dienstleistung zu stärken. Obwohl der Begriff weniger gebräuchlich ist als der des Marketing, beinhaltet er doch viele Marketingaktivitäten, wie etwa Marktforschung, Verkaufsförderung, Verkauf, Verkaufsabwicklung und Vertrieb.

**Verpacken** *n* - packaging

■ Vorbereitung der Ware für die Lagerung oder Beförderung, indem die Ware in geeignete Kisten oder Behälter gepackt wird. Dies schließt auch die Erstellung attraktiver Schmuckverpackungen ein, die im Verkaufslokal zur Vermarktung der Produkte verwendet werden können.

**Verpackung** *f* - package

■ Behälter oder Verpackung, um Produkte darin zu verpacken. Aus absatzfördernder Sichtweise unterscheidet man mehrere Verpackungstypen. Die Geschenkpackung, die man später wiederverwenden kann (z. B. Kaffee). Die Großpackung, die mehr Inhalt hat als die Normalverpackung. Die Sortimentspackung bietet das Produkt zusammen mit anderen, mehr oder weniger komplementären Produkten an, und die Verpackung im Pack enthält mehrere Einheiten des gleichen Produktes. Man spricht von Mehrwegverpackung, wenn die Verpackung zurückgegeben werden kann, wofür man ein Pfand erhält, bzw. wenn sie auf irgendeine andere Art in den Materialkreislauf zurückgeführt werden kann. Die Einwegverpackung oder verlorene Verpackung ist nicht rückführbar und kann nur ein einziges Mal verwendet werden.

**Verpackung** *f* - packaging

■ Verpackungs-, Hüllen-, Etiketten- und Packungsdesign, sowie andere äußerliche Elemente der anzupreisenden Produkte, einschließlich der Auswahl von Materialien und gesetzliche, ästhetische und wirtschaftliche Anforderungen, die zum Vertrieb des Produkts zu beachten sind.

**Verpackungsfirma** *f* - packaging studio

■ Unternehmen, das sich auf den Entwurf der Verpackung, die Präsentation und die Verpackung von Produkten spezialisiert hat.

**verrechnete Gemeinkosten** *pl* - absorbed costs

■ Herstellkosten, die in der Kalkulation indirekt im Rahmen der Gemeinkosten an den Kunden weitergegeben werden, z. B. Versicherungsbeiträge des Unternehmens.

**Versandhandel** *m* - mail-order selling

▪ Verkauf, bei dem der Kaufinteressent in seinem Haushalt oder durch die Presse eine schriftliche Mitteilung erhält, die ihn zum Kauf eines Produktes oder einer Dienstleistung einlädt. Wird in der Regel von spezialisierten Unternehmen durchgeführt; die Adressen werden zufällig ausgewählt oder stammen von früheren Käufern, Mitgliedern eines Vereins oder Berufsverbandes oder Kreditkartenbesitzern. Die Bestellung wird per Post vorgenommen und die Ware auf diesem Wege geliefert, oft gegen Nachnahme.

**Versandkosten** *pl* - postage and handling

▪ Ausgaben, um die Waren vom Herstellungs- oder Kaufort bis zum Verkaufsort oder dem Ort, wo sie gebraucht werden zu transportieren. Zum Beispiel die Transportkosten, Zölle und Versicherungen.

**Versandwerbung** *f* - mail-order advertising

▪ Anzeigen, deren Ziel die Förderung von Produkten ist, die über jede Art von Fernverkauf kommerzialisiert werden. Die Werbung enthält meist ein Bestellformular oder eine Telefonnummer oder E-Mail-Adresse. Die Übergabe des erworbenen Produkts geschieht durch die Post oder einen Kurier.

**Version** *f* - release

▪ Jede der Auflagen oder Veröffentlichungen eines Computerprogramms oder Systems, eines Handbuchs usw. Es handelt sich um Anpassungen mit kleinen Verbesserung einer Basisfassung. Sie werden fortlaufend oder mit dem Ausgabedatum nummeriert.

**Versorgungsmarkt** *m* - provision market

▪ Zentraler Markt oder Ort, an dem die Großhändler die Einzelhändler mit Waren (vor allem verderblichen Produkten) versorgen. Die Großhändler gruppieren sich nach Produktarten, wodurch ein Preisvergleich leicht möglich ist. Gelegentlich gebraucht man diesen Begriff auch dazu um den Ort zu beschreiben, an dem die spezialisierten Einzelhändler ihre Verkaufsstände haben und an die Hausfrauen verkaufen.

**verstärken** *v* – reinforce *v*

▪ Häufigkeit und Gewicht einer Kampagne durch eine höhere Investition ausbreiten.

**versteckte Werbung** *f* - hidden publicity

▪ Diese Werbung führt den Verbraucher über die Klasse, den Ursprung und den Wert der Werbung in Irrglauben, auch wenn der Inhalt der Wahrheit entspricht. Das Publikum erkennt die Klasse oder Natur der Werbefeststellung nicht und glaubt nicht, dass es sich um Werbung handelt. Dadurch bekommt die Werbung eine höhere Glaubwürdigkeit, da sie nicht als solche wahrgenommen wird.

**Versteigerung** *f* - auction

▪ Verkaufssystem, das auf dem direkten und im Allgemeinen öffentlichen Wettbewerb der Käufer um die Abgabe eines besseren Angebotes basiert. Das versteigerte Gut wird dem Käufer zugeteilt, der am meisten Geld dafür geboten hat. Wird auch von der Verwaltung bei der Vergabe von Werk- oder Dienstleistungsverträgen an Einzelne verwendet (in diesem Fall spricht man von Ausschreibung). Außerdem gibt es gerichtliche Zwangsversteigerungen zur Bedienung der Forderungen von Gläubigern. Bei manchen Versteigerungen werden die Gebote in geschlossenen Umschlägen abgegeben, wobei das beste Gebot den Zuschlag erhält, ohne dass nach Bekanntwerden nachgebessert werden kann.

**Versteigerungsverkauf** *m* - sale by auction

▪ Verkauf, bei dem mehrere Bieter untereinander im Wettbewerb um die Zuteilung eines Produktes oder einer Dienstleistung stehen, die derjenige erhält, der das beste Gebot abgegeben hat, wenn dieses den Mindestabgabepreis erreicht oder überschreitet. Die Gebote können im verschossenen Umschlag oder unmittelbar mündlich abgegeben werden, wobei die Kaufinteressenten in letzterem Falle die anderen Gebote erfahren. Es gibt auch die Abwärtsversteigerung, bei welcher der erste Käufer, der den Preis akzeptiert, den Zuschlag erhält; wenn niemand den Preis akzeptiert, senkt ihn der Auktionator weiter (holländische Versteigerung).

**Versuch** *m* - trial

■ Handlung und die daraus resultierenden Auswirkung, die zu beobachten sind, wenn eine Sache ausprobiert wird, bevor sie endgültig zum Einsatz kommt.

**vertikale Diversifikation** f - vertical diversification

■ Diversifizierung der Aktivitäten einer Unternehmung, indem vor- bzw. nachgelagerte Prozesse in den eigenen Betriebsablauf integriert werden. Man kann in der Mehrzahl der Fälle von vertikaler Integration sprechen.

**vertikales Abkommen** *n* - vertical agreement

■ Vereinbarung zwischen Unternehmen, die sich in Bezug auf die Produktions- oder Vertriebskette eines Produkts auf unterschiedlichen Ebenen befinden.

**vertragliche Herstellung** *f* - contract manufacturing

■ Vereinbarung, aufgrund derer ein Unternehmen ein von ihm entwickeltes und vermarktetes Produkt von einem anderen Unternehmen fertigen lässt, manchmal in einem Land mit niedrigeren Produktionskosten.

**Vertrauensniveau** *n* - confidence level

■ Zuverlässigkeit der anhand einer Umfrage erhaltenen statistischen Daten. Sicherheitsgrad, dass der Fehler bei der Umfrage einen bestimmten Wert nicht überschreitet. Hängt vom Umfang der Umfrage und der Art und Weise der Befragung ab. Umfrageninstitute müssen das Vertrauensniveau der ermittelten Daten und die Fehlerspanne der gelieferten Information bekannt geben.

**Vertrieb** *m* - distribution

■ Vorgang, durch den ein Produkt durch die verschiedenen Vertriebskanäle zum Einzelhandel gebracht wird, um an den Endverbraucher verkauft zu werden. Immer häufiger organisieren große Ladenketten den Vertrieb, so dass der Anteil der Wertschöpfung, der von den Herstellern von Massenkonsumartikeln kontrolliert wird, sinkt.

**Vertriebshandbuch** *n* - sales-arguments book

■ Handbuch, das die Stärken und Vorteile eines Produktes oder einer Dienstleistung zusammenfasst, die vom Verkäufer für die Anbahnung eines Geschäfts mit einem möglichen Kunden, verwendet werden können. Es enthält darüber hinaus auch die besten Antworten auf mögliche Einwände.

**Vertriebskanal** *m* - distribution channel

■ Gesamtheit der Unternehmen, die daran beteiligt sind, die Ware vom Produzenten zum Kunden zu bringen. Der Vertriebskanal kann je nach Produkt länger oder kürzer sein. Auch ein und derselbe Hersteller kann unterschiedliche Vertriebskanäle für seine Produkte wählen. Normalerweise umfasst der Vertriebskanal Großhändler und Einzelhändler, aber der Absatz kann auch direkt erfolgen (Direkt- oder Eigenvertrieb) oder eine Importgesellschaft mit einschließen. Der Vertrieb kann auch über einen Kommissionär, einen Verteiler, eine Vertretung oder eine eigene Niederlassung und über den Selbstbedienungsgroßhandel erfolgen.

**Vertriebsnetz** *n* - distribution network

■ Alle Zwischenhändler für den Vertrieb, die die Vermarktung des Guts oder der Ware ermöglichen. Kann im Zusammenhang mit Handel (außer Exklusivhandel), Kauf und Verkauf benutzt werden, kann sich aber auch nur auf den logistischen Aspekt des physischen Versands und der Verteilung beziehen.

**Vertriebsplattform** *f* - distribution platform

■ Vertriebszentrum einer großen Super- oder Hypermarktkette, von dem aus die Verteilung der Produkte an die einzelnen Stationen koordiniert wird.

**Vertriebspolitik** *f* - promotion

■ Im weitesten Sinne ist die Förderung eines der Elemente des Marketing-Mix, bestehend aus dem Zusammenspiel der Aktivitäten zum Erreichen des Verkaufs eines Produkts oder einer Dienstleistung. Die Werbung ist die offensichtlichste dieser Aktivitäten, aber nicht die einzige. Teil der Vertriebspolitik sind ferner Sonderangebote oder Sponsorprodukte.

**Vertriebstext** *m* - dealer copy

■ In einer übergreifenden Anzeige ein Werbetext, den der Vertrieb oder einzelne Händler in den dafür vorgesehenen Raum einsetzen.

**vertriebsunterstützende Aktivitäten** *f/pl* - distribution support activity

■ Aktivität im Marketing, vor allem in der Werbung und in der Verkaufsförderung, die unternommen wird, um die Verkaufsanstrengungen Dritter für das Produkt eines Unternehmens zu unterstützen. Zum Beispiel, eine Anzeige, die ein Werbegeschenk verspricht, falls man ein Automodell beim Vertragshändler zur Probe fährt.

**Vertriebszentrum** *n* - distribution centre

■ Organisation, die Waren an eigene Verkaufsstellen oder an kleine Läden in regelmäßiger Form (maximal wöchentlich) liefert und dabei eine komplette Betreuung anbietet. So können die nötigen Lagerbestände in jeder der Verkaufsstellen verringert, und die Auslieferung der Bestellungen durch die Lieferanten erleichtert werden.

**verunglimpfende Werbung** *f* - denigratory advertising

■ Werbung, die aufgrund ihres Inhalts, ihrer Darstellungsform oder Verbreitung die direkte oder indirekte Verachtung oder Verleumdung einer Person, eines Unternehmens oder seiner Produkte, Dienstleistungen oder Aktivitäten erreicht. Im strengen Sinn wird als verunglimpfende Werbung nur die Werbenachricht betrachtet, die die Produkte, Dienstleistungen oder Aktivitäten eines Unternehmens verleumdet, egal ob dieses Konkurrenz ist oder nicht.

**Verweildauer** *f* - stickiness

■ Effektivität einer Website in Bezug auf ihre Fähigkeit, Benutzer anzuziehen und zu halten. Vom Marketingstandpunkt ist der Erfolg einer neuen Seite nicht durch die Anzahl von Besuchen zu messen, sondern durch die Qualität sowie die Zeit, die ein Benutzer auf der Seite bleibt, und die Art und Weise, wie er mit den Verantwortlichen der Site in Kontakt tritt.

**Verzerrung** *f* - bias

■ In der Statistik versteht man hierunter einen systematischen Fehler, der in den Ergebnissen einer Studie auftritt, da man eine nicht repräsentative Stichprobe der Zielgruppe gewählt hat, eine ablenkende Frage gestellt hat, man notwendige Fragen vergessen oder ähnliche Fehler begangen hat.

**vier Säulen** *f/pl* - four P's of marketing

■ Die vier Säulen des Marketing-Mix sind: Produkt, Preis, Position (Vertrieb) und Promotion.

**Virales Marketing** *n* - viral marketing

■ Sonderform des Marketings, bei der versucht wird, dass die gewonnenen Konsumenten ihrerseits anderen potenziellen Konsumenten den Kauf des Produkts empfehlen. Oftmals ist es nötig, eine Entlohnung und einen Anreiz anzubieten, die die Schaffung eines ausreichend attraktiven Kundennetzes fördern.

**visuelle Corporate Identity** *f* - visual corporate identity

■ Gesamtheit grafischer Elemente, die ein Unternehmen, eine Organisation oder Institution repräsentieren und identifizieren und von allen anderen unterscheiden: Logos, Symbole und unternehmenskennzeichnende Farben.

**Vitrine** *f* - display case

■ Einrichtungsgegenstand, der von einer Glasscheibe geschützt wird und in dem Produkte ausgestellt werden. Der Verbraucher kann das ausgestellte Produkt (z. B. Tiefkühlprodukte) entnehmen, sich dieses von einem Verkäufer aushändigen lassen, oder das angezeigte Geschäft aufsuchen (z. B. wenn sich die Vitrine in einem Flughafen befindet). Der Begriff Schaufenster wird benutzt, wenn die Ausstellung an der Fassade eines Geschäftes angeordnet ist.

**Volkszählung** *f* - census

▪ Registrierung oder Auflistung der Bevölkerung, die von der Verwaltung erstellt wird und eine große Anzahl statistischer Informationen enthält (Alter, Studium, Beruf usw.).

**vollständiger Wettbewerb** *m* - perfect competition

▪ Idealisierte Form des Wettbewerbs, bei der eine große Anzahl an Käufern und Verkäufern gegeben ist, komplette Zugangsfreiheit zum Markt besteht, vollkommene und schnelle Information aller Marktteilnehmer gewährleistet ist und die Transaktions- oder Transportkosten gegenüber dem Preis der Ware vernachlässigbar sind.

**vorcodierter Fragebogen** *m* - pre-coded questionnaire

▪ Fragebogen der vor seiner Verwendung einen Code erhält (meist eine Nummer), um die mögliche Antwort leichter zu digitalisieren und tabellieren.

**vorgegebene Antwort** *f* - prompted reply

▪ In der Marktforschung Antwort des Befragten aus einer Reihe von vorgegebenen möglichen Antwort, die er zum Ausdruck seiner Meinung angeben kann.

**Vorher-Nachher-Vergleich** *m* - before-and-after demonstration

▪ Werbeformat, bei dem die Wirksamkeit des angebotenen Produkts erläutert wird, indem ein visueller Vergleich zwischen dem Umstand vor und der eingetretenen Veränderung nach Gebrauch des Produkts angestellt wird. Dieses Format, das heute kaum noch gebräuchlich ist, verlangte ein hohes Maß an Glaubwürdigkeit hinsichtlich des wundersamen Effekts bestimmter Produkte (wie Haarwuchsmittel und Schlankheitspillen) sowie hoher rhetorischer Freiheit, derer sich die Werbung bediente.

**Vorratskammertest** *m* - pantry check

▪ Feststellung der gekauften Marke in einem visuellen Test durch den Befrager. Der Nachweis wird bei einigen Umfragen direkt in den Haushalten und mithilfe von Verbraucherpanels durchgeführt.

**Vorschlagsbriefkasten** *m* - suggestions box

▪ Kasten, der in einem Verkaufsgeschäft oder am Arbeitsplatz angebracht ist und in den die Kunden oder Angestellten Briefe oder Zettel mit ihren Meinungen, Ratschlägen oder Beschwerden einwerfen können.

**Vortest** *m* - pre-test

▪ Test, der vor dem Treffen einer endgültigen Entscheidung (z. B. Produktion der Werbeoriginals, einer neuen Verpackung oder der Verpflichtung einer Person) durchgeführt wird. Um größere Investitionen zu vermeiden, wird im Test häufig mit Entwürfen gearbeitet. Gleichbedeutend mit Voruntersuchung.

**Voruntersuchung** *f* - pre-survey

▪ Studie vor der Aussendung einer Werbebotschaft, um die mögliche Reaktion zu bestimmen. Dabei kann ein Modellentwurf benutzt werden; besser (allerdings auch teurer) ist es jedoch, den fertig gedrehten Film einzusetzen. Ist in der Regel qualitativ, wobei Gruppentechniken wie die Diskussion mit für das Zielpublikum repräsentativen Personen angewandt werden. Wird auch eingesetzt, um einen Fragebogen vor einer Massenumfrage zu überprüfen, so dass Fehler korrigiert werden können.

**vorverpackt** - pre-pack

▪ Ausstellungssystem einer Versandeinheit (mit Produkt), das gleichzeitig Packung und nach Öffnen Aussteller ist. Generischer Name, mit der die Tischausstellung bezeichnet wird, die mit dem Produkt zusammen verpackt wird und als Einzelteil an die Verkaufsstelle gesendet wird. Diese Art Packung wird meist für Produkte mit hohem Umlauf verwendet, da sie leicht nachgefüllt werden können. Typisches Beispiel dafür sind Automaten.

**Vorwärtsintegration** *f* - forward integration

▪ Aufkauf eines Kundenunternehmens oder Abschluss eines besonderen Zusammenarbeitsvertrages, um die Absatzmöglichkeiten in einem Schlüsselsegment des Marktes sicherzustellen. Form der vertikalen Integration.

**VPI** - CPI

▪ Abkürzung für Verbraucherpreisindex, ein auf dem Konsum einer Durchschnittsfamilie gewichteter Index, der das allgemeine Preisniveau dieses Durchschnittskonsums zu einem bestimmten Augenblick misst und ins Verhältnis zu einer früheren Periode setzt.

# W

**Wahrnehmung** *f* - **Probekauf** *m* - **Wiederholungskauf** *m* - awareness-trial-repeat

▪ Verschiedene Phasen, durch die ein potenzieller Kunde zu einem regelmäßigen Kunden wird. Zuerst erfolgt die Wahrnehmung eines Produkts oder einer Marke, dann ein Probekauf, und wenn der Kunde zufrieden ist, wird er durch Wiederholungskäufe zum regelmäßigen Kunden.

**Wahrscheinlichkeit** *f* - probability

▪ Maß für die Gewissheit oder Möglichkeit, dass ein Ereignis auftreten wird. Die statistische Wahrscheinlichkeit ist, gemäß dem Gesetz der großen Zahlen, der Wert, dem sich die relative Häufigkeit langfristig (d. h. wenn sehr viele Zufallsexperimente durchgeführt werden) annähert. Die Wahrscheinlichkeit ist ein Wert zwischen 0 und 1, der oft auch als Prozentsatz ausgedrückt wird.

**Wahrscheinlichkeitsauswahl** *f* - probability sampling

▪ Stichprobe, in der jedes Element der Bevölkerung eine bekannte, von null verschiedene Wahrscheinlichkeit dafür besitzt, dass es in der Stichprobe enthalten ist. Fast immer ist sie repräsentativer als die nicht zufällige Auswahl, außerdem erlaubt sie, den Stichprobenfehler abzuschätzen. Es gibt im Wesentlichen drei Arten: einfache, geschichtete und gebündelte Wahrscheinlichkeitsauswahl. Sie können in aufeinander folgenden Phasen auch kombiniert benutzt werden.

**Wanderanzeige** *f* - itinerant display

▪ Werbeplakat, das auf einem mobilen Träger angebracht ist und einem festgelegten Standortwechsel folgt. Im Allgemeinen ist die Werbung beidseitig.

**Wandergewerbe** *n* - itinerant sale

▪ Verkauf, der außerhalb eines festen Verkaufslokales durchgeführt wird, normalerweise unter Benutzung von Lastkraftwagen oder Kleintransportern. Insbesondere in ländlichen Gebieten. Oft ohne Beantragung der nötigen Genehmigungen betrieben.

**Wandwerbung** *f* - painted wall

▪ Anzeige, die Wände ohne Fenster nutzt, im Allgemeinen an Seitenwänden von Gebäuden. Die Werbung wird direkt auf die Wand gemalt und ist meist von langer Dauer.

**Ware** *f* - merchandise

▪ Jedes zum Konsum bestimmte Produkt, über das ein individuelles oder gemeinschaftliches Eigentumsrecht bestehen kann. Kann ein Bedürfnis des Menschen befriedigen und ver- und gekauft werden. Gleichbedeutend mit (Konsum-) Gut.

**warmer Punkt** *m* - warm point

▪ Ort eines Verkaufslokals, der für die Verkäufe sehr vorteilhaft ist. Von Natur aus bewirken Orte am Eingang und Ausgang und in der Nähe von Artikeln häufigen Konsums eine stärkere Ausstellung der Produkte. Künstlich können warme Punkte durch die Dekoration, insbesondere die Beleuchtung geschaffen werden. Kalte Punkte sind diejenigen, die nicht zwischen zwei warmen Punkten liegen und daher kaum Kundenverkehr aufweisen.

**Warum** *n* - reason why

▪ Begründung, die besonders auf Druckmedien verwendet wird, über die Aspekte des Produkts, die dem Verbraucher nützen und so eine Argumentation liefern, warum der Verbraucher dieses kauft.

**Wechselkosten** *pl* - switching cost

▪ Bezeichnet diejenigen Transaktionskosten, die einem Käufer durch den Wechsel des Verkäufers entstehen. Summe aus den Integrationskosten des neuen Verkäufers, dem Beginn neuer Preisverhandlungen und der Anpassung bestimmter Standards an die Eigenschaften des Verkäufers.

**wechselseitige Anzeige** *f* - bartered ad

▪ In einem Medium veröffentlichte Anzeige im Gegenzug zu einer Anzeige dieses Mediums in einem anderen Medium oder aufgrund einer anderen Art von Gegengeschäft.

**weiße Ware** *f* - white goods

▪ Haushaltsgeräte wie Kühlschränke, Waschmaschinen und Kühltruhen. Der Name rührt daher, dass die ersten Geräte fast immer weiß waren.

**Welle** *f* - flight

▪ Zeitraum, in dem die Anzeigen einer Kampagne konzentriert auftreten, wobei vorher und nachher keine Aktivität stattfindet. Der Zweck einer derartigen Planung ist die Konzentration der Werbung auf die für den Verkauf besten Zeiten, statt ihrer Ausdehnung auf relativ inaktive Zeiten, in denen die Werbung als Ressourcenverschwendung angesehen werden könnte.

**weltweite Werbung** *f* - global advertising

▪ Werbeaktion, die von einem Unternehmen oder einer Abteilung durchgeführt wird, und internationalen Charakter besitzt, um die gleiche Nachricht in verschiedenen Ländern zu übermitteln.

**Werbeabdeckung** *f* - coverage

▪ Prozentsatz des Zielpublikums, das einer bestimmten Werbekampagne ausgesetzt ist. Gelegentlich versteht man darunter auch die absolute Anzahl oder den Prozentsatz des erreichten Zielpublikums innerhalb einer bestimmten Mediennutzergruppe.

**Werbeagentur** *f* - advertising agency

▪ Unternehmen, das einen Inserenten berät, mit ihm zusammen die Werbestrategie festlegt, die Werbebotschaft erstellt, die Durchführung der Werbekampagne überwacht und gewöhnlich auch die Werbeschaltungen bucht. Werbeagenturen verfügen über zwei Hauptabteilungen, die Kreativabteilung, die für den künstlerischen Teil zuständig ist, und die Kundenabteilung, die den Kontakt zu den Kunden aufrecht erhält und die Projekte leitet. Eine Agentur kann auch über Fachbereiche wie Marktforschung, Produktion und Werbeplanung verfügen.

**Werbeakquisiteur** *m* - advertising agent

▪ Person, die sich beruflich mit der Vermittlung zwischen Inserent und Agentur beschäftigt. Sie kann die Werbeaktion planen, leiten, erarbeiten und/oder durchführen.

**Werbeanzeige** *f* - advertisement

▪ Veröffentlichte Mitteilung, die vom Inserenten bezahlt wird, um seiner Zielgruppe eine Nachricht zu übermitteln. Hierfür kann jedes Kommunikationsmittel verwendet werden.

**Werbeaufruf** *m* - ad impression

▪ Werbedatei, die ein Internetnutzer von einem Werbeserver abruft. Wird in CPM (Tausend-Kontakt-Preis) verrechnet, einer der häufigsten Vorgehensweisen zur Errechnung des Werbepreises im Netz.

**Werbeausgaben** *f/pl* - advertising expense

▪ Betrag, der für Werbung in einem bestimmten Zeitraum ausgegeben wird. Häufig wird fälschlicherweise der Begriff Werbeinvestitionen verwendet, wodurch der Anschein erweckt wird, dass es sich dabei um eine genau geplante Ausgabe handelt, die einen konstanten Wert erwirtschaftet. Tatsächlich handelt es sich um eine regelmäßige Ausgabe, die nur an der Erreichung bestimmter Kommunikationsziele gemessen werden kann.

**Werbebeilage** *f* - bill insert

▪ Werbebotschaft, die in einer personalisierten Sendung enthalten ist und sich auf ein Produkt oder eine Dienstleistung bezieht, mit der die eigentliche Sendung nichts gemein hat. Der Zweck dieser Praktik ist die Reduzierung von Kosten.

**Werbeberater** *m* - advertising consultant

▪ Freiberufler, der den Inserenten bei seinen Werbeaktionen berät.

**Werbeblocker** *m* - ad blocking

▪ Programm, das Werbeanzeigen von einer Webseite löscht. Es erleichtert das Surfen, da keine Werbeinhalte heruntergeladen werden.

**Werbebombardement** *n* - burst

▪ Aktion, bei der eine Anzeige in einem begrenzten Zeitraum wiederholt verbreitet wird, um sicherzustellen, dass man sich daran erinnert. Diese Strategie kann zu Sättigung des Publikums führen, ist aber angebracht, um Bekanntheit zu fördern, die Lanzierung eines neuen Produkts oder die Eröffnung eines neuen Verkaufspunktes zu unterstützen, wenn für den Erfolg das anfängliche Ambiente besonders wichtig ist.

**Werbebotschaft** *f* - advertising theme

▪ Wesentlicher Inhalt der Nachricht, die zur Stärkung der Marktposition übermittelt werden soll. Das Werbekonzept darf nicht verändert werden, obwohl auf lange Sicht gesehen die Werbung in Bezug auf Technik oder Stil leicht geändert werden kann.

**Werbebrief** *m* - sales letter

▪ Brief an potentielle Kunden, um diese dazu zu bewegen, ein Produkt zu kaufen oder an einer Präsentation teilzunehmen.

**Werbebudget** *n* - advertising budget

▪ Ausgaben für bestimmte Marken und Zeiträume. Wird in Abhängigkeit von den zu erreichenden Werbe- und Kommunikationszielen, den verfügbaren Mitteln des Unternehmens, den früheren Ausgaben und den geschätzten Ausgaben der Konkurrenz festgelegt.

**Werbeclaim** *m* - claim

▪ Werbeidee, die die Aufmerksamkeit des Empfängers erregt und ihn somit veranlasst, sich für das Produkt oder die Dienstleistung zu interessieren. In aller Regel ein Wort oder ein Satz, wird auch als Slogan bezeichnet.

**Werbecluster** *n* - cluster

▪ Neue Art und Weise, in der Unternehmen ihre internationalen Werbeaktivitäten handhaben. Dabei werden die Mittel nach Ländergruppen eingeteilt, die um einen Marktführer gruppiert sind. Beispielsweise hat Coca Cola Spanien an die Spitze einer seiner Europa-Gruppen gesetzt, zu der auch Italien und Portugal zählen.

**Werbeeffizienz** *f* - advertising efficiency

▪ Verhältnis zwischen der Wirkung von Werbung in absoluten Werten und den getätigten Werbeausgaben. Die Effizienz der Werbung wird gemessen durch Kosten pro 1000 potentielle Käufer, die durch die verschiedenen Medien erreicht worden sind, Erinnerungswert der Werbebotschaft oder die Wirkung gemessen an spezifischen Antworten auf die Werbung.

**Werbeeinlage** *f* - stuffer

▪ Werbung, die in ein bereits vorhandenes Schreiben eingefügt wird, zum Beispiel Werbung in den Rechnungen von Telefongesellschaften, Elektrizitätsgesellschaften, Banken usw.

**Werbefläche** *f* - ad space

▪ In der Internetwerbung, Bildschirmbereich, der zur Einfügung von Reklame oder Werbung vorbehalten ist. Im Allgemeinen befinden sich diese Flächen im oberen oder seitlichen Bildschirmbereich.

**Werbeflyer** *m* - flyer

▪ Kostengünstige Werbeblätter, die manuell auf der Straße, in Briefkästen, auf Parkplätzen an U-Bahnstationen u. ä. Orten verteilt werden.

**Werbemanager** *m* - advertising manager

▪ Person, die unmittelbar für die Werbung eines Unternehmens verantwortlich ist und dem Marketingchef untersteht. Wenngleich die Organisation nach Produktmanagern, die alle Aspekte eines Produkts einschließlich der Werbung koordinieren, gebräuchlicher ist, haben große Unternehmen, wie etwa Kaufhäuser, einen Manager, der die Werbung koordiniert, die interne Werbeabteilung (falls vorhanden) leitet, die Abstimmung mit den Werbeagenturen durchführt und den Budgetplan für die Kommunikation erstellt und kontrolliert.

**Werbematerial** *n* **für die Verkaufsstelle** - point of sale material

▪ Kommunikationsmittel, welche die Werbebotschaft des Herstellers im Moment des Kaufabschlusses durch den Verbraucher stützen. Kann sehr unterschiedliche Formen haben: Anschläge, Plakate, Aufkleber, Ausstellvorrichtungen, Werbejingle usw.

**Werbeplakat** *n* - poster billboard

▪ Träger für Außenwerbung bestehend aus einem Rahmen mit flacher Fläche, auf dem das mit der Werbung bedruckte Papier geklebt wird. Sehr weit verbreitete Werbemöglichkeit.

**Werbeplan** *m* - advertising plan

▪ Plan mit Werbezielen und den einzusetzenden Mitteln, der eigentlich Teil des übergeordneten Kommunikationsplans ist, aber auf Grund seiner Bedeutung separat erstellt wird. Enthält die Werbestrategie, die Werbeziele, das gewünschte Markenimage, das Zielpublikum, die Werbebotschaft und die Werbemittel.

**Werbeplaner** *m* - account planner

▪ Werbefachmann, der für die Kommunikationsstrategie einer Kampagne zuständig ist. Der Werbeplaner definiert Kommunikationsziele und schlägt die Leitlinien für die Kommunikation während der gesamten Kampagne vor.

**Werbepositionierung** *f* - ad position

▪ Stelle, an der eine Anzeige erscheint (in Printmedien, Radio und Fernsehen). Die Platzierung der Werbebotschaft hängt vom Zielpublikum, dem Markt und dem verfügbaren Budget ab.

**Werbeprämie** *f* - referral premium

▪ Prämie, die der Werbende dem Kunden aufgrund einer Weiterempfehlung und des Verkaufs seiner Produkte oder Dienstleistungen an ein Familienmitglied oder Freunde gewährt.

**Werberegal** *n* - promotion shelf

▪ Regal, das wegen seiner Über- oder Spezialgröße mehr Aufmerksamkeit der Kunden erregt und deshalb dazu bestimmt ist, die Sonderangebots- oder Aktionsprodukte besser sichtbar zu machen.

**Werbeserver** *m* - ad server

▪ Kontrollsystem für Werbeeinschübe im Internet. Diese Programme dienen zur Platzierung unterschiedlicher Kampagnen durch Rotation nach den folgenden Kriterien: Abfolge, Zufall, Klickzahl und Marktsegmentierung. Zunächst werden z. B. die interaktiven Banner oder Poster angezeigt, welche die höchste Weiterleitungszahl aufweisen, sie folgen einer Vorgabe in Bezug auf die Wirksamkeit der Kampagne. Die Werbeserver sammeln Informationen über entstandene Kontakte und die erzeugten Absender.

**Werbespot** *m* - commercial

▪ Audiovisuelle Werbebotschaft, die mithilfe der Film- oder Videotechnik geschaffen und in speziellen Werberäumen und -zeiten in Fernsehmedien verbreitet wird. Kann von verschiedener Länge sein, wobei sie in aller Regel zwischen 20 und 30 Sekunden dauert. Wird auch als Werbefilm bezeichnet.

**Werbesynergie** *f* - advertising synergy

▪ Gemeinsame Aktion mit zwei Werbeprodukten oder -botschaften zur Erzielung einer größeren Wirkung als bei zwei unabhängig voneinander durchgeführten Aktionen mit demselben Budget.

**Werbetexter** *m* - copywriter

▪ Autor von Werbetexten und -botschaften. Arbeitet normalerweise für eine Werbeagentur nach den Anweisungen des Art-Direktors.

**Werbeticker** *m* - ad ticker

▪ Werbeformat im Internet, das über eine Anzeige auf einer Seite (Banner, Skyscraper, gesponserte Werbebox)

eingefügt wird und dem Benutzer in Echtzeit Informationen zu interessanten Themen (z. B. Nachrichten oder Sport) liefert. Hierdurch wird ebenfalls sein Interesse für die Anzeige gesteigert.

**Werbeträger** *m* - ad vehicle, advertising vehicle

■ In einem Medium, jede Fläche auf der Werbung erscheint. Bei Druckmedien jede Ausgabe oder auch jede Seite oder jeder Seitenbereich. Bei audiovisuellen Medien jeder Tag, jede Uhrzeit, jeder Block, jeder Sender. Bei externen Medien jede Struktur, auf der eine Werbung angebracht werden kann. Im Internet jede Seite, jeder Banner.

**Werbewellen** *f/pl* - flighting

■ Einsatz von Anzeigen in einem Medienplan, bei dem die Einfügungen in kurzen Zeiträumen konzentriert werden, auf die Zeiten der Inaktivität folgen.

**Werbewirksamkeit** *f* - advertising effectiveness

■ Fähigkeit einer Werbekampagne, einerseits eine bestimmte Botschaft zu übermitteln (gemessen durch Tests vor und Umfragen nach der Verbreitung der Werbung) und andererseits das erwartete Verhalten zu bewirken (gemessen durch die erreichten Verkäufe).

**Werbewirksamkeitsstudie** *f* - post-test

■ Quantitative Untersuchung, mit Stichprobe aus der Zielgruppe, zur Bestimmung der Reaktion auf eine ausgesendete Werbebotschaft. In einer Erhebung innerhalb von 24 Stunden nach Schaltung werden Erinnerung und erste Reaktionen gemessen, und in einer Umfrage nach Abschluss einer Werbekampagne wird eine tiefer greifende Studie erhoben.

**Werbewirkungsforschung** *f* - publimetry

■ Teilgebiet des Marketing, dessen Aufgabe die Messung der Ergebnisse einer Werbekampagne durch die Analyse der Verbraucher ist.

**Werbezeit** *f* - commercial time

■ Zeit, die innerhalb eines Programmblocks für Werbesports zur Verfügung steht. Die Höchstgrenze kann durch Gesetz, die Selbstkontrolle des Sektors oder eine interne Regelung des Senders festgelegt werden und kann von der Tageszeit und der Art des ausgestrahlten Programms abhängen.

**Werbezeitraum** *m* - promotion validity period

■ Zeit, in der eine Werbekampagne durchgeführt wird. Es kann sich um eine allgemeine vom Franchise-Geber durchgeführte Kampagne für alle Einheiten seines Netzes handelnder Teil des geplanten Werbeprogramms für die Kette sein. Es kann aber auch eine lokale Kampagne für eine bestimmte lokale Einheit der Kette sein, um die Verkaufszahlen zu steigern.

**Werbeziel** *n* - advertising goal

■ Innerhalb eines Marketingplans die konkrete Zielsetzung einer Werbekampagne, einschließlich dessen, was das Zielpublikum sich merken und wie es sich verhalten soll. Wesentlicher Teil der Werbestrategie, deren Erfolg hieran gemessen wird.

**Werbung** *f* - advertising

■ Marketingmaßnahme, mit der einem bestimmten Publikum eine Botschaft übermittelt wird. Die Botschaft ist im Wesentlichen informativ und motivierend und dient gewöhnlich dazu, den Verkauf eines Produkts oder einer Dienstleistung zu fördern. Hierfür kann jedes Kommunikationsmittel benutzt werden.

**Werbung** *f* **aus dem Hinterhalt** - ambush ad

■ Anzeige, die an ungewöhnlicher Stelle oder in ungewöhnlichen Situationen auftaucht und ihren Nutzen aus dem Überraschungseffekt zieht, die sie bei den Empfängern hervorruft. Beispiele hierfür sind Produktstandorte, Umweltwerbung oder die immer häufiger werdende Mischung aus Werbung und Unterhaltung (Advertainment).

**Werbung** *f* **für die Öffentlichkeit** - public service announcement

■ Anzeige, die kostenlos durchgeführt und verbreitet wird, um das soziale

Wohlergehen zu fördern. Die Sender sind meist private oder öffentliche Firmen, die ihre Dienste, Programme oder Aktivitäten vorstellen möchten oder den Empfänger erziehen oder auf etwas aufmerksam machen möchten.

**Werbung** *f* **im Geschäft** - in-store merchandising

■ Entwurf, Organisation und Durchführung von Aktivitäten in einer Handelseinrichtung zur Steigerung der Attraktivität des Produkts für einen Käufer und des Verkaufs, insbesondere bei rentablen Gütern.

**Werbung** *f* **zum Anfassen** - tactile ad

■ Grafische Werbemitteilung, die ein Papier-, Stoff- oder Plastikelement aufweist, das angefasst werden kann, so dass der potentielle Käufer eine bestimmte Eigenschaft eines Produkts „ertasten" kann.

**werbungsfreies Programm** *n* - ad-free programme

■ Fernsehprogramm, das ohne Werbeunterbrechungen ausgestrahlt wird. Im Allgemeinen handelt es sich um ein von einem Inserenten gesponsertes Programm, dessen Werbung nur vor und nach dem Programm läuft. In Sonderfällen wird der Sponsor während des Programms erwähnt.

**Werbungssättigung** *f* - ad saturation

■ Level, den die Werbung in einem Medium in Bezug auf den Gesamtinhalt erreicht. Bei den meisten Medien kann die optimale Sättigung nach eigenem Ermessen bestimmt werden. Im Fernsehen gibt die Europäische Union Richtlinien vor, die besagen, dass Werbung 15% der Sendezeit und 12 Minuten pro Stunde nicht überschreiten darf.

**Werbungstausch** *m* - ad exchange

■ Im Internet die Vereinbarung zweier Webseiten, gegenseitig Werbeanzeigen, Banner, Schaltflächen oder Links einzubauen, die jeweils auf die andere Webseite führen.

**Werbungstreibender** *m* - advertiser

■ Die Person oder Institution, die für die Werbekommunikation bei kommerziellen, politischen oder gesellschaftlichen Anliegen zuständig ist.

**Wert** *m* - value

■ Nutzen eines Gutes, der es ermöglicht, dafür einen bestimmten Geldbetrag als Gegenleistung zu erhalten. Ist etwas Subjektives, das sich nur zum Zeitpunkt des Kaufes bzw. Verkaufes zahlenmäßig ausdrückt.

**Wertanalyse** *f* - value analysis

■ Systematische Vorgehensweise bei der Marktforschung, um jeden Kostenpunkt eines Produktes zu bewerten. Dies geschieht unter Berücksichtigung des Wertes oder des Nutzens, den das Produkt für den Kunden hat. Sie erlaubt ein Hinzufügen oder Entfernen von Merkmalen und Funktionen aufgrund der Vorteile, die der Kunde dadurch erhält, und nicht nur aus rein technischen Gründen.

**wertbezogene Preisfestlegung** *f* - value-based pricing

■ Marktorientiertes Verfahren zur Bestimmung des Preises. Das Hauptaugenmerk liegt dabei auf dem Verbraucher, dem ein bestimmter Wert angeboten wird, der im Gegenzug mit einem Preis verbunden ist, wobei versucht wird, bei der Einführung eines neuen Produkts so kosteneffizient wie möglich zu sein, um das gemachte Angebot rentabel zu machen.

**Wertermittlung** *f* - valuation

■ Gutachterliche Schätzung des Marktwertes eines Vermögensgegenstandes.

**Wertschöpfung** *f* - value added

■ Erhöhung des Preises, die in jeder Phase des Produktionsprozesses erreicht wird. Die Wertschöpfung berechnet sich, indem man vom Preis des Endproduktes die Kosten aller extern bezogenen Materialien und Dienstleistungen abzieht, die benötigt wurden.

**wettbewerbsfähig** - competitive

■ In der Lage, im Wettbewerb durch einen relativen Vorteil zu bestehen, zum

Beispiel durch einen niedrigeren Preis, bessere Qualität oder besseres Ansehen.

**Wettbewerbsvorteil** *m* - competitive advantage

■ Lage oder Umstand, die einem Land oder einem Unternehmen in einer konkreten wirtschaftlichen Aktivität einen Vorteil gegenüber der Konkurrenz verschafft. Der Vorteil kann auf einer überlegenen Technologie, geringeren Kosten bei einem speziellen Produktionsfaktor, bevorzugtem Zugang zu einem Markt, einem größeren Bekanntheitsgrad der Marke usw. beruhen.

**Wettbewerbsvorteile** *m/pl* - competitive claims

■ Eigenschaften und Vorteile eines Produktes gegenüber seinen Wettbewerbern, mit denen der Inserent oder Hersteller wirbt.

**wie gesehen** - as is

■ Produkt, das so verkauft wird, wie es der Kunde sieht. Hierbei besteht kein Anspruch auf Garantie oder Ersatz. Wird bei Sonder- oder Schlussverkäufen eingesetzt.

**Wiedereinführung** *f* - re-launching

■ Kampagne, um einer Aktivität (z. B. Wirtschaft einer Region, Marke, Werbebotschaft usw.) einen neuen Anstoß zu geben. Wird begleitet von oberflächlichen oder Imageverbesserungen, so dass man nicht von der Einführung einer Neuigkeit sprechen kann. Gelegentlich wird auch der englische Begriff Relaunching verwendet.

**Wiedererkennung** *f* - recognition

■ System der Publikumsstudie von Druckmedien, die in der Vorstellung einer Veröffentlichungsreihe mit den entsprechenden Logos besteht, damit die befragte Person diejenigen identifiziert, die sie schon einmal gesehen hat oder sich daran erinnert. Wird auch zur Messung der Wiedererkennung von Anzeigen benutzt.

**Wiederholung** *f* - repetition

■ Anzahl der Male, die eine Werbung auf einem Medium oder Träger innerhalb einer Werbekampagne wiederholt wird. Manchmal zeigt die Wiederholung die Kontaktzahl einer Person mit der Werbung an. Dann ist der Begriff mit Frequenz gleichzusetzen.

**Wiederverkauf** *m* - resale

■ Erneuter Verkauf dessen, was kurz zuvor gekauft wurde, im Allgemeinen zu einem höheren Preis.

**wiederverwertbar** - recyclable

■ Eigenschaft eines Produkts, das aus Materialien hergestellt ist, die für die selbe oder eine neue Verwendung genutzt werden können.

**wiederverwertbare Verpackung** *f* - recyclable container

■ Verpackung, die aus Materialien besteht, die dem Recycling zugeführt und erneut zur Herstellung neuer Verpackungen oder anderer Produkte verwendet werden können, wie zum Beispiel Aluminiumdosen. Im Gegensatz zu einer Pfandverpackung kann sie nicht unmittelbar wieder als Verpackung benutzt werden, sondern das Material der Verpackung muss aufbereitet werden.

**willkürliche Auswahl** *f* - convenience sampling

■ Stichprobe, bei der man Personen befragt, die zufällig zu einer bestimmten Zeit an einem bestimmten Ort sind, oder die ein bestimmtes Radioprogramm hören. Sie besitzt keine wissenschaftliche Gültigkeit, da die Proben oft nicht repräsentativ sind.

**Wirkgrad** *m* - degree of exposure

■ Verbreitung einer Anzeige oder Kampagne in der Anzahl der Zielpersonengruppen, die Zugang haben mit Einbeziehung der Häufigkeit des Zugangs. Je nach Definition handelt es sich um die Zielgruppe oder die Anzahl der Eingaben.

**Wirkung** *f* - impact

■ Reaktion der Öffentlichkeitsmeinung, die aufgrund eines Ereignisses oder einer Werbebotschaft eintritt.

**wissenschaftliches Überzeugungsmodell** *n* - scientific persuasion model

■ Bidirektionales, asymmetrisches Modell der Public Relations. Vereinfachte Darstellung der seitens der Unternehmensführung geplanten Strategie, die sich gründet auf die wissenschaftliche Erforschung der Haltung der Öffentlichkeit, und die deren Beeinflussung anstrebt in Bezug auf Aufbau, Intensivierung oder Verbesserung des öffentlichen Ansehens des Unternehmens, seiner Akzeptanz und der Haltung der Öffentlichkeit ihm gegenüber.

**Wortassoziation** *f* - word association

■ Forschungstechnik, bei der dem Befragten mehrere Schlüsselwörter genannt werden, die dieser durch andere Wörter ersetzen soll, die ihm spontan einfallen oder ihm zur Auswahl vorgelegt werden. Wird zur Erkennung positiver oder negativer Konnotationen benutzt, die gewisse Themen auslösen können.

# Z

**Zapping** *n* - flipping

■ Handlung eines Fernsehzuschauers, die im Umschalten von Kanälen per Fernbedienung besteht, sobald in einem Kanal ein Werbeblock ausgestrahlt wird. Das Werbezapping hat durch das Auftreten der neuen Geräte zur digitalen Aufzeichnung (TiV bzw. Replay TV) eine neue Dimension erreicht, da diese Geräte das Überspringen der Werbung ermöglichen. Das Zapping ist einer der Gründe, warum neue Fernsehwerbung die Werbung in die audiovisuellen Inhalte einfügt.

**zeitliche Präferenz** *f* - time preference

■ Vorliebe des Verbrauchers, die sich in seiner Wahl zwischen Gegenwarts- und Zukunftskonsum (der gleichbedeutend ist mit Sparen in der Gegenwart) ausdrückt.

**zentraler Einkauf** *m* - centralised purchasing

■ Zentralisierung der Einkäufe einer Gruppe von Unternehmenseinheiten, die in einem bestimmten räumlichen Gebiet tätig sind.

**zentrales Transportsystem** *n* - hub transport system

■ Transportverfahren für Waren, bei dem der Transport der Produkte in die verschiedenen Zielorte von einem Referenzstandort aus durchgeführt wird, wobei das Transportfahrzeug nach Ablieferung der Waren an diesen zurückkehrt.

**Zentrallager** *n* - central warehouse

■ Hauptlager eines Unternehmens, das den größten Teil der hergestellten Produkte vereint und von dem aus die Lieferungen zu Satellitenlagern und Verkaufsstellen organisiert wird.

**Zielgruppe** *f* - target group

■ Konkreter Bevölkerungssektor, an den ein Produkt oder eine Botschaft gerichtet ist. Dabei kann zwischen Trendsetter oder Meinungsführer, Käufer und Verbraucher des Produktes unterschieden werden. Das Zielpublikum wird durch demographische, geographische oder sozioökonomische Merkmale und den Lebensstil abgegrenzt.

**Zielgruppenabdeckung** *f* - target reach

■ Bei einer Werbekampagne der Wirkungsbereich einer Zielgruppe, die ein Medium oder Werbeträger erreichen möchte.

**Zielgruppenquote** *f* - audience share

■ Eigentlich Reichweitenquote. Prozentsatz der Zielgruppe, die mit einer bestimmten Werbekampagne erreicht wird. Wird manchmal auch auf den Prozentsatz der erreichten Zielgruppe innerhalb eines bestimmten Publikums angewendet.

**Zielgruppenverhalten** *n* - target group behaviour

■ Verhalten einer Zielgruppe in der Internetwerbung, das ermöglicht, die Reaktion auf die Werbung und somit das Benutzerprofil in Echtzeit zu erfassen.

**Zielpreise** *m/pl* - standard price

■ Einkaufs- oder Selbstkostenpreise und Verkaufspreise, die sich die Unternehmung zum Ziel setzt und bei der Planung festlegt. Werden auch als Plan- , Normal- oder Standardpreise bezeichnet. Unter Berücksichtigung der Geschichte, der Strategie und der Mittel werden Maßnahmen im Bereich der Produktion und des Absatzes geplant, die diese Zielpreise bestimmen. Diese werden mit den tatsächlichen Preisen im Laufe der Periode verglichen, um die Abweichungen zu berechnen.

**Zielpublikum** *n* - useful audience

■ Teil des Publikums, das der Zielgruppe angehört. Es sind die Personen, bei denen davon ausgegangen wird, dass sie das beworbene Produkt kaufen könnten, die charakteristischsten Personen dienen den Werbetreibenden für die Ausarbeitung der Kampagne.

**zollfreier Bereich** *m* - duty-free zone

■ Gebiet oder Orte, die sich zwar im Inland befinden, aber zollrechtlich als Ausland behandelt werden. Auf die dort gelagerten Waren sind keine Einfuhrabgaben zu zahlen, und die Güter können problemlos zurückbefördert werden.

**Zugänglichkeit** *f* - accessibility

■ Merkmale einer Webseite, die die Nutzung durch behinderte Personen ermöglichen.

**Zugangsbarriere** *f* - entry barrier

■ Bestehende Schwierigkeit oder Verbot, mit dem sich ein Unternehmen, das in einem neuen Sektor, Produktbereich oder einem neuen geographischen Gebiet tätig werden möchte, auseinanderzusetzen hat. Z. B. große Kapitalinvestitionen, Patente, rechtliche Voraussetzungen, Kauf von Regalplatz usw.

**Zuhausepublikum** *n* - in-home audience

■ Personengruppe, die sich dem Medium zu Hause aussetzen. Hierbei kann es sich um audiovisuelle und gedruckte Medien handeln. In einigen Fällen ist das Zuhausepublikum qualitativ wichtiger als das Publikum an anderen Orten.

**Zuneigung** *f* - inclination

■ Hang, Neigung oder Liebe zu einer Sache. Psychische, natürliche Tendenz, mehr oder weniger unwiderstehlich.

**Zusatzleistung** *f* - accessory service

■ Leistung, die ein Unternehmen als Ergänzung zu einer Hauptleistung bietet. Kann eine höhere Rentabilität als letztere aufweisen.

**Zusatzverkauf** *m* - upsell

■ Marketingtechnik per Telefon , mit dem Ziel, mehr als eine Einheit eines Produkts zu verkaufen. Erfolgt im Allgemeinen durch Kauf einer zusätzlichen Einheit zu einem günstigeren Preis , sei es als Geschenk oder zur Lagerung.

**Zuschaueranteil** *m* - viewers share

■ Anteil jeden Fernsehsenders an der gesamten Zuschauerschaft zu einem gegebenen Zeitpunkt. Wird in Prozentanteilen ausgedrückt und variiert als Folge der Abwanderung (z. B. Zapping) von einem Programm zum anderen stetig.

**Zuschauerpanel** *n* - viewers' panel

■ Gleichbleibende und repräsentative Stichprobe aus den Fernsehzuschauern einer Region, die zur Schätzung der Zuschauerzahlen jedes Senders und Programms dient.

**Zusendung** *f* **unverlangter Ware** - inertia selling

■ Der Verkauf geschieht automatisch, es sei denn, der Kunde gibt ausdrücklich an, dass er die Ware nicht wünscht. Klassische Verkaufsmethode von Buchclubs wie z. B. Bertelsmann.

**zweckgebundene Werbung** *f* - cause-related promotion

■ Form der Unternehmensförderung, die eine Steigerung der Verkaufszahlen und des Rufs des Unternehmens anstrebt, durch abgesprochene Zusammenarbeit mit einer nicht auf Gewinn ausgerichteten Körperschaft. Kann beispielsweise darin bestehen, einen Teil des Verkaufs oder des daraus gezogenen Gewinns einer bestimmten Nichtregierungsorganisation (NRO) zuzuwenden.

**zwei zum Preis von einem** - BOGOF (buy one, get one free)

▪ System der Verkaufsförderung, bei dem der Kunde zwei gleiche Produkte zum Preis von einem erhält. Aufgrund der gewöhnlichen durchschnittlichen Gewinnspanne der Produkte wird aber vorzugsweise das System drei zum Preis von zwei verwendet, auch wenn diese Option das Interesse des Kunden weniger weckt. Auch nimm 2, zahl 1.

**Zweikomponentenpreis** *m* - two-part price

▪ Im Dienstleistungssektor der Preis, der aus einem festen Geldbetrag für eine vertraglich festgelegte Mindestdienstleistung und einem variablen Betrag je nach Nutzung dieser Dienstleistung besteht. Wird oft von Telefon- und Elektrizitätsgesellschaften und Wasserwerken angewendet.

**Zwei-Stufen-Programm** *n* - two-step programme

▪ Direkte Marketingaktion, die in zwei Stufen ausgeführt wird. In der ersten Stufe wird meistens eine Werbemitteilung unter Angabe einer Hotline-Nummer versendet oder ausgestrahlt, so dass sich die Interessenten telefonisch identifizieren. In der zweiten Stufe wird mit dem Interessent meist telefonisch, per Post oder durch einen persönlichen Besuch Kontakt aufgenommen, um das fragliche Produkt direkt zu verkaufen.

**Zweitlieferant** *m* - second source

▪ Hersteller eines Produkts, der über die Lizenz des Unternehmens verfügt, das das Produkt ursprünglich entwickelt hat, und die Patent- und Gebrauchsrechte besitzt.

**Zweitmarke** *f* - endorsed brand

▪ Durch andere Marke als Garantie unterstützte Marke, z. B. Cornflakes von Kellogg's.

**Zwischenanzeige** *f* - interstitial ad

▪ In der Internetwerbung, Anzeige, die zwischen zwei Inhaltsseiten angezeigt wird. Wenn ein Benutzer die Verknüpfung zu einer anderen Seite anklickt wird die Zwischenanzeige vor der Verbindung mit der folgenden Seite angezeigt. Diese wird in Leerzeiten oder durch Anklicken des Symbols angezeigt.

**Zwischenhändlerauflösung** *f* - disintermediation

▪ Beseitigung von Zwischenhändlern in der Lieferkette.

# Anhang

## Inhalt / Content

## 1. Marketing und Internet Abkürzungen - Deutsch

| | |
|---|---|
| A2C | Administration-to-Customer |
| ANOVA | Varianzanalyse |
| B2A | Business-to-Administration-Geschäft |
| B2B | Business-to-Business-Geschäft |
| B2C | Business-to-Consumer-Geschäft |
| B2E | Business-to-Employees-Geschäft |
| B2G | Business-to-Government-Geschäft |
| C2A | Consumer-to-Administration-Geschäft |
| C2B | Consumer-to-Business-Geschäft |
| C2C | Consumer-to-Consumer-Geschäft |
| CD | Corporate Design |
| CI | Corporate Identity |
| CPC | Klickkosten |
| CPI | Kosten pro Anfrage |
| CPO | Kosten pro Auftrag |
| EVA | einzigartiges Verkaufsargument |
| FuE | Forschung und Entwicklung |
| GIS | Geoinformationssystem |
| KB | Kundenbetreuer |
| KBM | Kundenbeziehungsmanagement |
| KITI | kennwortintegrierte Texteingabe |
| KPI | Konsumentenpreisindex |
| MARKOR | Marktorientierung |
| PLC | Produktlebenszyklus |
| PPC | Bezahlung per Klick |
| PPL | Bezahlung per Aktion |
| PPS | Bezahlung per Kauf |
| PR | Public Relations |
| S/W | Schwarz/Weiß |
| VPI | Verbraucherpreisindex |

## 1. Marketing & Internet Related Abbreviations - English

| | |
|---|---|
| A2C | Administration to Consumer |
| AE | Account Executive |
| ANOVA | Analysis of Variance |
| ASP | Application Service Provider |
| B&W | Black and White |
| B2A | Business to Administration |
| B2B | Business to Business |
| B2C | Business to Consumer |
| B2E | Business to Employees |
| B2G | Business to Government |
| C2A | Citizen to Administration |
| C2B | Consumer to Business |
| C2C | Consumer to Consumer |
| CPA | Cost Per Action |
| CPC | Cost Per Click |
| CPI | Cost Per Inquiry |
| CPI | Consumer Price Index |
| CPM | Cost Per Thousand |
| CPO | Cost Per Order |
| CPS | Cost Per Sale |
| CTR | Click-Through Rate |
| DH | Direct Hit |
| FFA | Free-For-All Link List |
| FMCP | Fast Moving Consumer Products |
| IM | Instant Messaging |
| KITI | Keyword Integrated Text Insertion |

| | |
|---|---|
| KPI | Key Performance Indicator |
| LTF | Life Time Value |
| M2B | Mobile to Business |
| MGM | Member Get Member |
| MLM | Multi-Level Marketing |
| MSN | Microsoft Network |
| OTS | Opportunity to See |
| PFI | Pay For Inclusión |
| PFP | Pay For Performance |
| PLC | Product Life Cycle |
| PPC | Pay Per Click |
| PPCSE | Pay Per Click Search Engine |
| PPL | Pay Per Lead |
| PPS | Pay Per Sale |
| PV | Page View |
| R&D | Research and Development |
| RFM | Recency, Frequency and Money |
| RON | Run Of Network |
| ROS | Run Of Site |
| SEO | Search Engine Optimization |
| SEP | Search Engine Positioning |
| USP | Unique Selling Proposition |
| UV | Unique Visitor |
| VALS | Values and Lifestyles |
| WWW | World Wide Web |

## 2. Organisationen in den Bereichen Marketing, Werbung und Öffentlichkeitsarbeit

2. Marketing, advertising and public relations organisations

| **Deutsche Organisationen** - German Organisations | | |
|---|---|---|
| **DDV** | Deutscher Dialogmarketing Verband e.V. (DDV) | www.ddv.de |
| **DMV** | Deutscher Marketing-Verband (DMV) | www.marketingverband.de |
| **DPRG** | Deutsche Public Relations Gesellschaft e.V. (DPRG) | www.dprg.de |
| **GWA** | Gesamtverband Kommunikationsagenturen e.V. (GWA) | www.gwa.de |
| **ZAW** | Zentralverband der deutschen Werbewirtschaft (ZAW) | www.zaw.de |

| **Britische Organisationen** - British Organisations | | |
|---|---|---|
| **AA** | Advertising Association | www.adassoc.org.uk |
| **ASA** | Advertising Standards Authority (ASA) | www.asa.org.uk |
| **DMA** | Direct Marketing Association (DMA) | www.dma.org.uk |

| **Europäische Organisationen** - European Organisations | | |
|---|---|---|
| **CERP** | European Public Relations Confederation (CERP) | www.cerp.org |
| **EACA** | European Association of Communications Agencies (EACA) | www.eaca.be |
| **EASA** | European Advertising Standards Alliance (EASA) | www.easa-alliance.org |
| **EMC** | European Marketing Confederation (EMC) | www.emc.be |
| **ESOMAR** | European Society for Opinion and Marketing Research (ESOMAR) | www.esomar.org |
| **EURADA** | Association of European Advertising Agencies (EURADA) | www.eurada.net |
| **FEDMA** | Federation of European Direct and Interactive Marketing (FEDMA) | www.fedma.org |

| **Amerikanische Organisationen** - American Organisations | | |
|---|---|---|
| **AAAA** | American Association of Advertising Agencies (AAAA) | www.aaaa.org |
| **AAF** | American Advertising Federation (AAF) | www.aaf.org |
| **AMA** | American Marketing Association (AMA) | www.marketingpower.com |
| **PRSA** | Public Relations Society of America (PRSA) | www.prsa.org |
| **PRSSA** | Public Relations Students Society of America (PRSSA) | www.prssa.org |

| **Internationale Organisationen** - International Organisations | | |
|---|---|---|
| **IAA** | International Advertising Association (IAA) | www.iaaglobal.org |
| | Global Alliance for Public Relations and Communication Management | www.globalpr.org |
| **IAB** | Interactive Advertising Bureau (IAB) | www.iab.net |
| **IABC** | International Association of Business Communicators (IABC) | www.iabc.com |
| **ICCA** | International Congress and Convention Association (ICCA) | www.iccaworld.com |
| **ICCO** | International Communications Consultancy Organisation (ICCO) | www.iccopr.com |
| **ICOGRADA** | International Council of Graphic Design Associations (ICOGRADA) | www.icograda.com |
| **IMSA** | International Mystery Shopping Alliance (IMSA) | www.theimsa.com |
| **IPRA** | International Public Relations Association (IPRA) | www.ipra.org |
| **WFA** | World Federation of Advertisers (WFA) | www.wfanet.org |
| **WFDSA** | World Federation of Direct Selling Associations (WFDSA) | www.wfdsa.org |

| **Weitere nützliche Internet-Links** - Further useful Internet Links | |
|---|---|
| European Patent Office (EPO) | www.european-patent-office.org |
| Markenregister des Deutschen Patent- und Markenamts | https://dpinfo.dpma.de/protect/mar.html |
| Meeting Professionals International (MPI) | www.mpiweb.org |
| The Association for Progressive Communications (APC) | www.apc.org |
| World Intellectual Property Organization (WIPO) | www.wipo.int |

## 3. Marketing-Mix Strategie

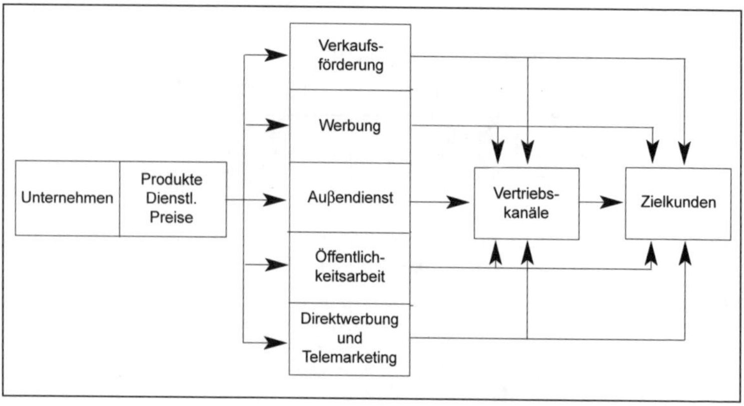


## 3. Marketing Mix Strategy

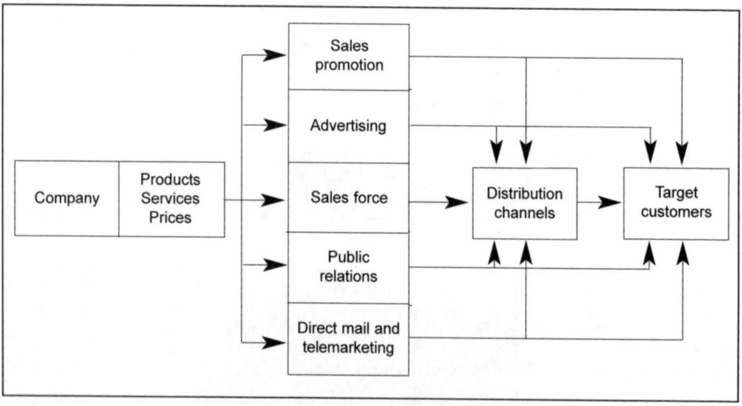

## 4. BCG* Marktwachstums-Matrix

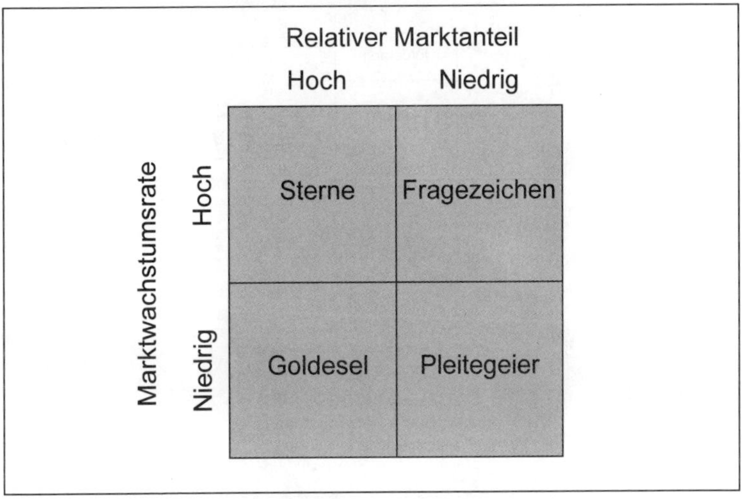


* BCG = Boston Consulting Group.

## 4. BCG* Growth-Share Matrix

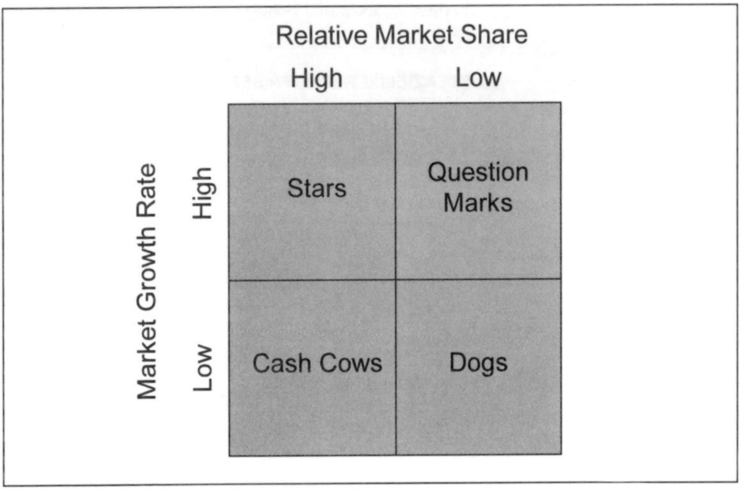


* BCG = Boston Consulting Group.

## 5. Maslow'sche Bedürfnispyramide

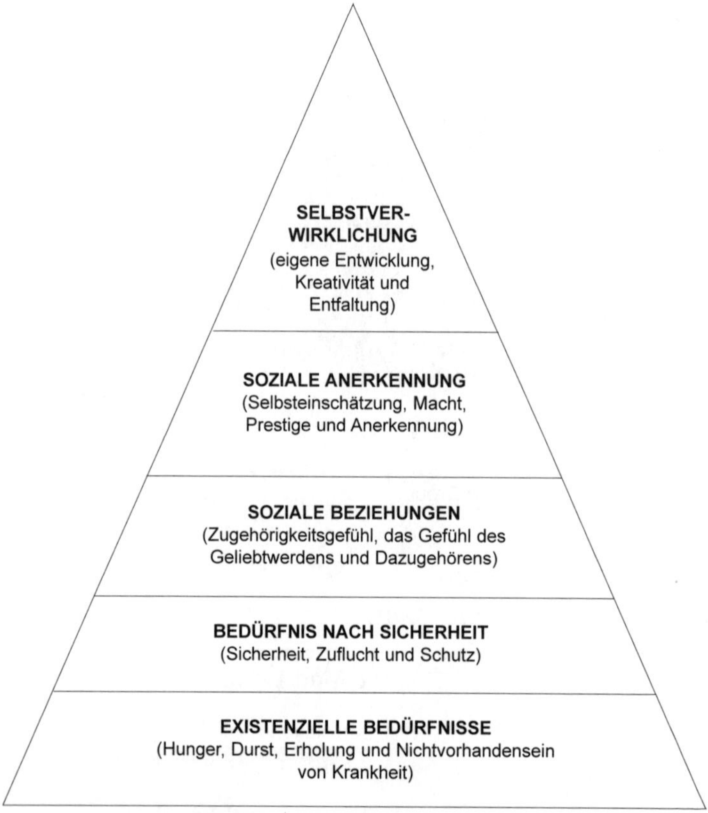

## 5. Maslow's Hierarchy of Needs

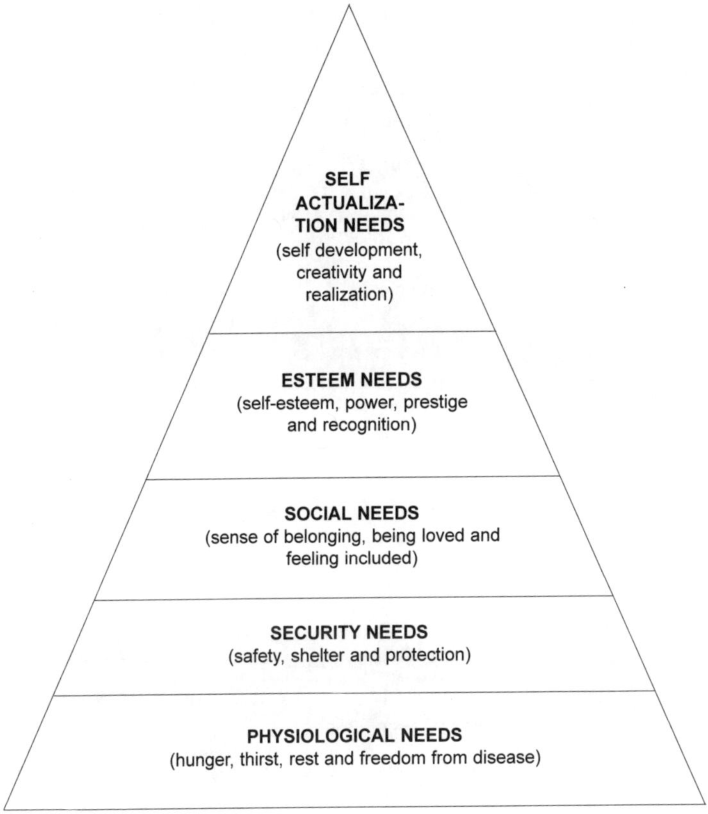

## 6. Einheitsgewicht von Einzelblättern nach Format und Flächengewicht

6. Weight per leaflet depending on format and gramage

| **Größe in DIN**<br>DIN size | **Flächengewicht Papier**<br>Paper grammage | | | | | | | |
|---|---|---|---|---|---|---|---|---|
| | *80* | *90* | *100* | *125* | *135* | *150* | *170* | *200* |
| A6 | 1,24 | 1,40 | 1,55 | 1,94 | 2,10 | 2,33 | 2,64 | 3,11 |
| A5 | 2,49 | 2,80 | 3,11 | 3,89 | 4,20 | 4,66 | 5,28 | 6,22 |
| A4 | 4,99 | 5,61 | 6,24 | 7,80 | 8,42 | 9,36 | 10,60 | 12,47 |
| A3 | 9,98 | 11,23 | 12,47 | 15,59 | 16,84 | 18,71 | 21,21 | 24,95 |
| 630 x 297 mm (Tripthychon A4 / 3-page leaflet) | 14,97 | 16,84 | 18,71 | 23,39 | 25,26 | 28,07 | 31,81 | 37,42 |
| 840 x 297 mm (Quadripthychon A4 / 4-page leaflet) | 19,96 | 22,45 | 24,95 | 31,19 | 33,68 | 37,42 | 42,41 | 49,90 |
| **Formel: Einheitsgewicht = Breite des Blattes in m x Höhe des Blattes in m x Gramm pro Quadratmeter.**<br>Formula: unit weight = width of the page in m. X height of the page in m. X grams per square metre. | | | | | | | | |

**Quelle** / Source: TECNOGRAF.

## 7. Papiermaße

7. Paper measurements

| **Größe in DIN**<br>DIN size | **Millimeter**<br>Milimetres | | | **Zoll bzw. Inch**<br>Inches | | |
|---|---|---|---|---|---|---|
| AO | 841 | x | 1.169 | 33,11 | x | 46,81 |
| A1 | 594 | x | 841 | 23,39 | x | 33,11 |
| A2 | 420 | x | 594 | 16,54 | x | 23,39 |
| A3 | 297 | x | 420 | 11,69 | x | 16,54 |
| A4 | 210 | x | 297 | 8,27 | x | 11,69 |
| A5 | 148 | x | 210 | 5,83 | x | 8,27 |
| A6 | 105 | x | 148 | 4,13 | x | 5,83 |
| A7 | 74 | x | 105 | 2,91 | x | 4,13 |
| A8 | 52 | x | 74 | 2,05 | x | 2,91 |
| A9 | 37 | x | 52 | 1,46 | x | 20,50 |

**Hinweis: AO hat eine Oberfläche von 1 m$^2$. Jede Blattgröße ist jeweils die Hälfte der vorangehenden.**

Note: The size A0 has an area of 1m$^2$. Each size is half the previous size, with the short side becoming the long side.